INDIAN PHILOSOPHY: A CRITICAL SURVEY

UNIVERSITY PAPERBACKS

ABOUT THE AUTHOR

Dr. Chandradhar Sharma, formerly Reader in Philosophy at Banaras Hindu University, is now Professor and Head of the Department of Post-Graduate Studies and Research in Philosophy at the University of Jabalpur. His book, *Indian Philosophy*, was first issued in India in 1952; the British edition appeared in 1960. Dr. Sharma has written seven other major books, among them *Dialectic in Buddhism and Vedanta*.

UNIVERSITY PAPERBACKS

INDIAN PHILOSOPHY:
A CRITICAL SURVEY

CHANDRADHAR SHARMA

M.A., D. Phil., D. Litt., LL.B., Sāhityāchārya, Sāhityaratna, Shāstrī

BARNES & NOBLE, INC.

PUBLISHERS • BOOKSELLERS • SINCE 1873

TO MY REVERED FATHER

who has made me what I am

AMERICAN EDITION published 1962
BY BARNES & NOBLE, INC.

L. C. Catalogue Card Number: 62—18222

Manufactured in the U.S.A.

Published in Great Britain by Rider & Company
(178–202 Great Portland Street, London, W.1)
An imprint of the Hutchinson Group

NOTE ON PRONUNCIATION

VOWELS:

a as *u* in *cut*	ā as *a* in *father*
i as *i* in *pit*	ī as *i* in *machine*
u as *u* in *put*	ū as *u* in *rule*
e as *a* in *made*	ai as *i* in *rite*
o as *o* in *code*	au as *ow* in *how*
ṛ as *ri* in *writ*	ṁ nasalizes the preceding vowel

CONSONANTS:

k, t, p as the unaspirated *k* and *p* in *skin* and *spin*.
kh, th, ph as the aspirated *k* and *p* in *kin* and *pin*.
t and d as soft *t* and *d* as pronounced in French and Italian.
th as *th* in *thumb* or the aspirated *t* in French and Italian.
dh as *dh* or the aspirated *d* as pronounced in French and Italian.
ch as the *ch* in *chunk*.
chh as the same, aspirated.
ṅ as the *ng* in *song*.
ñ as the *n* in Spanish *señor*.
g as the *g* in *gun*.
gh and bh can be heard as the *gh* and *bh* in *doghouse* and *clubhouse*, when pronounced quickly.
ṭ, ṭh, ḍ, ḍh, ṇ as *t, th, d, dh*, and *n* pronounced with the tip of the tongue near the roof of the mouth.
sh as the *sh* in *sheet*.
ṣ as the same, pronounced with the tongue near the roof of the mouth.

ACCENT:

On the next to final syllable if that is long, otherwise on the nearest long syllable before it, and on the first syllable if none are long. A long syllable is one which consists of a long vowel (ā, ī, ū, e, o), a diphthong (ai, au), or a short vowel (a, i, u, ṛ) followed by more than one consonant (except h as in kh, bh, etc.).

NOTE:

In other books, the consonants here represented by ch, chh, and sh will often be found as c, ch, and ś.

CHRONOLOGICAL SUMMARY

I	The Vedic Age: ?–500 B.C.	*Ṛg Veda*	?–1000 B.C.
		Brāhmaṇas	1000– ?
		Early *Upanisads*	1000–750
		Mahāvīra	d. 525 (?)
		Gotama	d. 485 (?)
II	The Great Heterodoxies and the Epic Period: 500 B.C.–0	The formulation of the Jain and Buddist literature and traditions.	
		Bhagavadgītā	
		The Early Mahāyāna Sūtras	
III	Formulation of the Great Traditions: Hinduism, Jainism, Buddhism: 0–500 A.D.	A. The Rise of Mahāyāna	
		Ashvaghoṣa	100– A.D.
		Nāgārjuna	100–200 A.D.
		Asaṅga	300–400 A.D.
		Vasubandhu	300–400 A.D.
		B. The Classical Hindu Systems	300–500
		Sāṅkhya Kārikā, Īshvarakṛṣṇa	
		Yogasūtra, Patanjali	
		Vaisheṣikasūtra, Kanada	
		Nyāyasūtra, Gotama	
		Pūrvamīmāṁsāsūtra, Jaimini	
		Brahmasūtra, Badarayana	
IV	System-building and Commentarial Period: 500–1000 A.D.	Gauḍapada	500–600
		Diṇnāga	
		Chandrakīrti	600
		Shāntideva	600
		Dharmakirti	600
		Shāntarakṣita	700
		Shankara	d. 820 (?)
V	Medieval Philosophers, Rise of Bhakti and Shaiva-Shākta cults: 1000–1500 A.D.	Rāmānuja	d. 1137
		Madhva	d. 1276–8
		Vallabha	d. 1531
		Chaitanya	d. 1533

N.B. All dates, especially the early ones, are approximations.

CONTENTS

PUBLISHER'S NOTE

The new material for the American edition of *Indian Philosophy* was prepared with the assistance of Dr. Robert F. Olson and Dr. Royal Weiler of Columbia University and Mrs. Mary F. Johnson of the Barnes & Noble Editorial Staff.

NOTE ON REFERENCES

The works cited in the footnotes of this book are listed in Part II of the Bibliography, pp. 390ff.

PREFACE

My main aim in this work has been to give a clear, comprehensive and critical account of the various systems of Indian philosophy. It is hoped that the book will be found useful by all those who want a clear and accurate exposition of the development of Indian philosophical thought in one volume which is neither too small nor too big. I shall feel amply rewarded if it arouses a genuine interest in Indian philosophy.

The work is based on my study of the original sources and on my lectures to the post-graduate classes in the Banaras Hindu University for a number of years and I must accept responsibility for the interpretations. On almost all fundamental points I have either quoted from the original texts or referred to them to enable the interested reader to compare the interpretations with the texts. Throughout the exposition of the different systems which involves criticism and evaluation, I have tried to be fair and impartial to them and to present many difficult and obscure points in as clear and correct a manner as I could. Ignorance of Indian philosophy, specially of Buddhism and Vedānta, is still profound and has given rise to un-informed or ill-informed accounts and misleading criticisms. It has been my aim to remove such misconceptions. Honest difference of opinion in interpretation is legitimate in philosophy, but it does not entitle us to impose our own preconceived notions on a system which are repelled by its original texts. The work is only an outline of a vast subject and has no pretensions to completeness.

In the chapters dealing with Mahāyāna Buddhism and Advaita Vedānta, I have incorporated substantial material from my thesis on 'Dialectic in Buddhism and Vedānta' approved for the degree of Doctor of Philosophy by the University of Allahabad. I have also incorporated some relevant material here and there from my thesis on 'The Reign of Dialectic in Philosophy—Indian and Western' approved for the degree of Doctor of Letters by the University of Allahabad.

It is a pleasure to acknowledge my obligations to the eminent scholars who or whose works have been a source of help and inspiration to me. I have derived much help from the works on Indian philosophy by Dr. S. N. Dasgupta, Prof. M. Hiriyanna and Dr. S. Radhakrishnan.

I am deeply obliged to Prof. A. C. Mukerji (retired Professor of Philosophy, Allahabad University) for his kind help and affectionate encouragement. I record my profound obligations to Prof. R. D.

Ranade, Prof. H. D. Bhattacharyya and Dr. Amaranatha Jha who are no more with us now.

This work was first published in India in 1952 under the title *Indian Philosophy*. Its revised British edition was published by Messrs. Rider & Co. of the Hutchinson Publishing Group, London, in 1960 under the title *A Critical Survey of Indian Philosophy*. It is a pleasure to know that an American edition of this book is called for and I thank my publishers, Barnes & Noble, Inc., New York, for bringing it out.

CHANDRADHAR SHARMA

Chapter One

THE VEDAS AND THE UPANIṢADS

I

INTRODUCTION

THE etymological meaning of the word 'philosophy' is 'love of learning'. It signifies a natural and a necessary urge in human beings to know themselves and the world in which they 'live and move and have their being'. It is impossible for man to live without a philosophy. The choice, as Aldous Huxley puts it, is not 'between metaphysic and no metaphysic; it is always between a good metaphysic and a bad metaphysic'.

Western Philosophy has remained more or less true to the etymological meaning of 'philosophy', in being essentially an intellectual quest for truth. Indian Philosophy has been, however, intensely spiritual and has always emphasized the need of practical realization of truth. The word 'darshana' means 'vision' and also the 'instrument of vision'. It stands for the direct, immediate and intuitive vision of Reality, the actual perception of Truth, and also includes the means which lead to this realization. 'See the Self' (ātmā vā are draṣṭavyaḥ) is the keynote of all schools of Indian Philosophy. And this is the reason why most of the schools of Indian Philosophy are also religious sects. Annihilation of the three kinds of pains—ādhyātmika (physical and mental sufferings produced by natural and intra-organic causes), ādhibhautika (physical and mental sufferings produced by natural and extra-organic causes), and ādhidaivika (physical and mental sufferings produced by supernatural and extra-organic causes)—and realization of supreme happiness is the end, and shravaṇa (hearing the truth), manana (intellectual conviction after critical analysis) and nididhyāsana (practical realization) are the means—in almost all the schools of Indian Philosophy.

The Vedas are the oldest extant literary monument of the Āryan mind. The origin of Indian Philosophy may be easily traced in the Vedas. Indian Philosophy, as an autonomous system, has developed practically unaffected by external influences. Unfortunately our knowledge of the Vedic period is, even to this day, too meagre and imperfect. The absence of chronological data, the complete indifference of the ancient Indians towards personal histories, the archaic character of the

Vedic Sanskrit, the break in tradition, and the biased orthodox colouring of interpretation, which instead of a help often proves a hinderance, are some of the main reasons due to which our knowledge about this period remains mostly shrouded in mystery and vagueness.

The name 'Veda' (knowledge) stands for the Mantras and the Brāhmaṇas (mantra-brāhmaṇayor veda-nāmadheyam). Mantra means a hymn addressed to some god or goddess. The collection of the Mantras is called 'Samhitā'. There are four Samhitās—Ṛk, Sāma, Yajuḥ and Atharva. These are said to be compiled for the smooth performance of the Vedic sacrifices. A Vedic sacrifice needs four main priests—Hotā, who addresses hymns in praise of the gods to invoke their presence and participation in the sacrifice; Udgātā, who sings the hymns in sweet musical tones to entertain and please the gods; Adhvaryu, who performs the sacrifice according to the strict ritualistic code and gives offerings to the gods; and Brahmā, who is the general supervisor well-versed in all the Vedas. The four Samhitās are said to be compiled to fulfil the needs of these four main priests—Ṛk for the Hotā, Sāma for the Udgātā, Yajuḥ for the Adhvaryu and Atharva for the Brahmā. Sometimes the Vedas are referred to only as 'Trayī,' omitting the Atharva. Ṛk means a verse, Sāma means a song; Yajuḥ means a prose passage. Thus we see that the Samhitā-bhāga or the Mantra-portion of the Veda is the Hymnology addressed to the various gods and goddesses. Ṛk-Samhitā is regarded as the oldest and also the most important. The Ṛṣis of the Vedas are not the authors, but only the 'seers' of the Mantras (ṛṣayo mantra-draṣṭāraḥ). The Brāhmaṇas, unlike the Mantras, are written in prose. They are the elaboration of the complicated ritualism of the Vedas. They deal with the rules and regulations laid down for the performance of the rites and the sacrifices. Their name 'Brāhmaṇa' is derived from the word 'Brahman' which originally means a prayer. There is little philosophy in these, though some philosophical ideas flash here and there in the course of some speculative digressions. The appendages to these Brāhmaṇas are called Āraṇyakas mainly because they were composed in the calmness of the forests. The Āraṇyakas mark the transition from the ritualistic to the philosophic thought. We find here a mystic interpretation of the Vedic sacrifices. The concluding portions of the Āraṇyakas are called the Upaniṣads. These are intensely philosophical and spiritual and may be rightly regarded as the cream of the Vedic philosophy. The Mantras and the Brāhmaṇas are called the Karma-Kāṇḍa or the portion dealing with the sacrificial actions, and the Āraṇyakas and the Upaniṣads are called the Jñanā-Kāṇḍa or the portion dealing with knowledge. Some people include the Āraṇyakas in the Karma-Kāṇḍa. Really speaking, they represent a transition from the Karma-Kāṇḍa to the Jñanā-Kāṇḍa. The Upaniṣads are also known as 'Vedānta' or 'the end of the Veda', firstly because they are literally the concluding portion, the end, of the Vedas, and secondly because they are the essence, the cream, the height, of the Vedic philosophy.

II

THE VEDAS

WE are concerned here only with the philosophical thought of the Vedic period. As we have already remarked, we find little philosophy in the pre-Upaniṣadic thought. But the seeds of the important philosophical trends might be easily traced there. Moreover, there has been a gradual development of the philosophical thought from the Mantras and the Brāhmaṇas through the Āraṇyakas to the Upaniṣads. It is said that we can notice a transition from the naturalistic and anthropomorphic polytheism through transcendent monotheism to immanent monism in the pre-Upaniṣadic philosophy. The personified forces of nature first changed into real gods and these later on, became mere forms of one personal and transcendental God, the 'Custodian of the Cosmic and Moral Order', who Himself, later on, passed into the immanent Puruṣa. The Upaniṣads developed this Puruṣa into Brahman or Ātman which is both immanent and transcendent. The Mantra portion has been called the religion of Nature, of the poets; the Brāhmaṇa ritualism, the religion of Law, of the priests; the Upaniṣadic portion the religion of Spirit, of the philosophers.

The above-mentioned conception of the development of pre-Upaniṣadic thought is to be taken in a very reserved sense. The western scholars and some of the Indian scholars, inspired by and even obsessed with the western interpretation, are apt to believe that when the early Vedic Āryans, who were primitive, if not semi-civilized and semi-barbarous, settled down and began to wonder at the charming and the tempting and to fear the terrible and the destructive aspects of nature, they personified them in an anthropomorphic fashion and called them gods and goddesses and began to worship them. This was the stage of naturalistic and anthropomorphic polytheism. Then gradually polytheism yielded place to monotheism and the latter to monism. Max Müller introduces 'henotheism' as a transitional stage from polytheism to monotheism. Henotheism means 'belief in *one only* God', because the Vedic Āryans regarded any god they were praising as the most supreme and the only God. If this western interpretation is taken literally and in its entirety, we have no hesitation in saying that it is based on an ignorance of the Vedic literature. Neither polytheism nor henotheism nor even monotheism can be taken as the key-note of the early Vedic philosophy. The root-fallacy in the western interpretation lies in the mistaken belief that the Vedic seers were simply inspired by primitive wonder and awe towards the forces of nature. On the other extreme is the orthodox view that the Vedas are authorless and eternal, which too cannot be philosophically sustained. The correct position seems to us to be that the Vedic sages were greatly intellectual and intensely spiritual personages who in their mystic moments came face to face with Reality and this mystic experience, this direct intuitive spiritual insight overflew in literature as the Vedic hymns. The key-note of the Vedic hymns is the same spiritual monism, the same immanent conception of the identity-in-difference which ultimately transcends even itself, the same indescribable absolutism which holds both monism and pluralism within its bosom and which ultimately transcends both, which we find so beautifully and poetically developed in the Upaniṣads. To read anthropomorphic polytheism and then henotheism and monotheism in the Vedas is, to borrow a phrase from Gauḍapāda, to see the foot-prints of birds in the air. If there were polytheism in the Vedas, how is it that the binding principle of this world, the Supreme Soul of this Universe, the Guardian of this Cosmos, is so much emphasized and repeated? Again, in the ordinary course when polytheism leads to monotheism, the most powerful god among the hierarchy of gods is enthroned as the ruler of this universe. But this is conspicuous by its absence in the Vedas. Instead of taking the trouble of coining the word 'henotheism', Max Müller could have simply said that the gods are regarded as mere manifestation of the Supreme God so that when any god was praised he was not praised in his individual capacity, but merely as the manifestation of the Supreme God. The gods are praised; yet not the gods, but God is praised through them. So there is no question of crude monotheism also in the Vedas. Hence there is no development from polytheism through monotheism to monism, but only of monism from the first Mantra portion to the last Upaniṣadic portion.

Let us take some illustrations. 'The One Real, the wise declare as many'.[1] 'Puruṣa is all this, all that was, and all that shall be'.[2] 'The real essence of the gods is one'.[3] 'The same Real is worshipped as Uktha in the Ṛk, as Agni in the Yajuḥ and as Mahāvrata in the Sāma'.[4] 'Aditi, the Boundless, is the sky, the air, the mother, the father, the son, all the gods and all the men, all that is, all that was and all that shall be'.[5] 'He is the Custodian of the Ṛta (Truth), the binding Soul of the universe, the unity-in-difference in the cosmic and the moral order'.[6] The gods also are the guardians of the Truth (ṛtasya gopā); even the rivers flow in this Ṛta (ṛtamarpanti sindhavaḥ)'. 'Only the wise, the wide awake, the mindful, know the ultimate Abode of the Lord'.[7] 'We make sacrifices to the ultimate Lord of the universe, who runs through every particle

[1] ekam sad viprā bahudhā vadanti.—Ṛgveda, I. 164. 46. [2] Puruṣa evedam sarvam yad bhūtam yachcha bhāvyam.—Ibid, X. 90. [3] Ibid, III. 55. [4] Aitareya Āraṇyaka, III. 2. 3. 12. [5] Ṛgveda, I. 89. 10. [6] Ibid, X. 190. 1. [7] Viṣnoryat paramam padam.—Ibid, I. 22. 21.

of this universe, the whole existence, and who is Blissful and Indescribable'.[1] 'Desireless, self-possessed, immortal, self-proved, ever full of Bliss, inferior to none, ever-young and everlasting is He, the Soul of this universe; through His knowledge alone can one spurn death'.[2] 'There was neither Being nor non-Being, neither air nor sky, neither death nor immortality, neither night nor day; That One breathed calmly, self-sustained; nought else beyond it lay.'[3] 'The Indescribable is the ground of all names and forms, the support of all the creation'.[4] 'All the gods form the body of this World-Soul'.[5] 'He is immanent in all this creation and yet He transcends it.'[6]

III

THE UPANIṢADS

WE now come to the Upaniṣads which are the concluding portion as well as the cream of the Veda and are therefore rightly called 'Vedānta'. The word 'Upaniṣad' is derived from the root 'sad' which means (i) to sit down, (ii) to destroy and (iii) to loosen. 'Upa' means 'near by' and 'ni' means 'devotedly'. The word therefore means the sitting down of the disciple near his teacher in a devoted manner to receive instruction about the highest Reality which loosens all doubts and destroys all ignorance of the disciple. Gradually the word came to signify any secret teaching about Reality and it is used by the Upaniṣads in this sense (rahasya or guhya vidyā). The Muktikopaniṣad gives the number of the Upaniṣads as 108. But ten or eleven Upaniṣads are regarded as important and authentic, on which Shaṅkarāchārya has commented. These are: Īsha, Kena, Kaṭha, Prashna, Muṇḍaka, Māṇḍūkya, Taittirīya, Aitareya, Chhāndogya and Bṛhadāraṇyaka. The teaching, being the highest, was imparted at private sittings only to the qualified disciples. Heraclitus has also said that if men care for gold, they must dig for it or be content with straw. If one wants pearls, one has to dive deep into the ocean or be content with pebbles on the shore.

The traditional view holds that the Upaniṣads as Revealed Texts teach the same doctrine. But there has been extremely wide difference in their interpretation. The problems discussed in them as well as their unique style make them liable to many interpretations. All their teachings are not equally prominent. Some are mere flashes of thought; some are only hinted at; some are slightly developed; some are mentioned by the way; while some are often repeated, emphasized and

[1] kasmai Devāya haviṣā vidhema.—Ibid, X. 121. 1. [2] tameva vidvān na bibhāya mṛtyor ātmānam dhīram ajaram yuvānam.—Atharvaveda, X. 8. 44. tameva viditvā 'timṛtyumeti nānyaḥ panthā vidyate ayanāya.—Yajurveda. [3] nāsadāsīt no sadāsīt tadānīm.—Ṛgveda, X. 129. [4] Atharvaveda, XI. 9. 1. [5] Nirukta, VII. 4. 9. [6] pādo'sya vishvā bhūtāni tripādasyā'mṛtam divi.—Ṛgveda, X. 90. 3

thoroughly dealt with. There is an essential unity of purpose in them. They emphasize the same fundamental doctrine which may be called monistic idealism or idealistic monism. These poetic-philosophic works are full of grand imagery, extremely charming and lucid expression abounding in crystal clarity (prasāda guṇa). To the mind, they bring sound philosophical doctrines and to the heart, peace and freedom. They are full of Ānanda or Supreme Joy out of which all things arise, by which they live and into which they return again. Passionate yearning for knowledge, restless striving after truth, and a ceaseless search for Reality have found a most touching expression in them. Deussen says that the Upaniṣadic seers have thrown, 'if not the most scientific, yet still the most intimate and immediate light upon the last secret of existence,' and that there are in them 'philosophical conceptions unequalled in India or perhaps anywhere else in the world'. Prof. Winternitz writes that these old thinkers 'wrestle so earnestly for the truth and in their philosophical poems the eternally unsatisfied human yearning for knowledge has been expressed so fervently' that these works are invaluable for mankind. Some of them match the Platonic Dialogues. Impressed by them the great German philosopher Schopenhauer declared: 'In the whole world there is no study so beneficial and so elevating. It has been the solace of my life and it will be the solace of my death'. Such masterly works have always been 'the ridicule of fools and the endless meditation of sages'.

The Upaniṣads develop the monistic ideas scattered in the Samhitās. During the Brāhmaṇa period, these scattered philosophical ideas were almost overlooked and emphasis was laid on merely the rigorous ritualistic sacrifices. The Āraṇyakas mark the shifting of the emphasis from the ritualistic to the philosophical thought which work was completed by the Upaniṣads. The Upaniṣads tell us that the Vedas—the storehouse of knowledge—have been breathed forth from Him;[1] but they regard the Karma-Kāṇḍa as secondary, being only a help to purify the mind by which purification one is made fit to receive the real teaching about Brahman. Thus we find the sage Nārada telling Sanatkumāra: 'I know the Ṛgveda, sir, the Yajuḥ, the Sāma, with all these I know only the Mantras and the sacred books, I do not know the Self . . . I have heard from persons like you that only he who knows the Self goes beyond sorrow'.[2] The Muṇḍaka tells us: 'Two kinds of knowledge must be known, the higher and the lower. The lower knowledge is that which the Ṛk, Sāma, Atharva, Ceremonial, Grammar give . . . but the higher knowledge is that by which the immortal Brahman is known'.[3] In the Gītā also the Lord asks Arjuna to rise above the three Guṇas, telling him that the Vedas deal with the three Guṇas and that he who has known Brahman has little to do with the Vedas.[4] Sometimes the Mantras

[1] Bṛh. 2. 4. 10. [2] Chhān. 7. 2. [3] Muṇḍaka I. 1. 4-5. [4] Gītā 2. 45-46.

are interpreted as subjective symbolism or pyschological spiritualism concealed in a concrete and material way to hide the truth from the profane and reveal it only to the qualified and the initiated. Thus Sūrya signifies intelligence, Agni will, Soma feeling; Ashvamedha means meditation where the whole universe is offered as the horse and desires are sacrificed and true spiritual autonomy (svārājya) is attained. The Brāhmaṇa ceremonialism is often contrasted with spiritual meditation. There is a satirical passage in the Chhāndogya where dogs are described as marching in a procession like the priests saying: 'Aum! Let us eat, Aum! Let us drink etc.'[1] Thus the complicated and rigorous ritualism and ceremonialism of the Brāhmaṇas was fortunately arrested in the Upaniṣads. But it is important to note that the criticisms are directed against ritualism and ceremonialism only and not against the lofty philosophical conceptions found in the Mantras, which are faithfully acknowledged and developed.

IV

ĀTMAN

THE individual self stands self-proved and is always immediately felt and known. One is absolutely certain about the existence of one's own self and there can be neither doubt nor denial regarding its existence. The individual self is the highest thing we know and it is the nearest approach to the Absolute, though it is not itself the Absolute. In fact the individual self is a mixture of the real and the unreal, a knot of the existent and the non-existent, a coupling of the true and the false. It is a product of Ignorance. But its essence is the light of the Absolute. Its real nature is pure consciousness, self-shining and self-proved and always the same. It is called the ultimate witness or the Sākṣī and as such is one with the Absolute. The senses, the mind, the intellect, feeling and will, the internal organ are all products of Avidyā and they invariably surround the individual self and constitute its 'individuality'. But the self really is above them, being the Absolute.

The word 'Ātman' originally meant life-breath and then gradually acquired the meanings of feeling, mind, soul and spirit. Shaṅkarāchārya quotes an old verse giving the different connotations of the word 'Ātman'. The verse says that 'Ātman' means that which pervades all; which is the subject and which knows, experiences and illuminates the objects; and which remains immortal and always the same.[2]

The true self has been the main topic of investigation in the Upaniṣads. Socrates of ancient Greece has also persistently advocated the supreme

[1] Chhāndogya I. 12. 4-5. [2] yadāpnoti yadādatte yachchātti viṣayāniha. yachchāsya santato bhāvas tasmād ātmeti kīrtyate.—Shaṅkara's Com. on Kaṭha 2. 1. 1.

necessity of 'Know Thyself'. We may select three Upaniṣads—the Chhāndogya, the Māṇḍūkya and the Kaṭha, for our present purpose. In a dialogue between Prajāpati and Indra, narrated in the Chhāndogya,[1] we find a development of the concept of the self from the waking or the bodily self through the dreaming or the empirical self and the self in deep dreamless sleep to the Absolute Self. The gods and the demons, the dialogue tells us, sent Indra and Virochana respectively, to Prajāpati, to learn the teaching about the self. The teacher asked them to undergo penance for thirty-two years to qualify themselves to receive the teaching. After fulfilling the prescribed condition, both come to Prajāpati who teaches them that the self is that which is seen when one looks into another's eye or into water or a mirror. Virochana was satisfied and went away. But Indra began to think thus: How can the self be the reflection of the body? Or, how can it be identified with the body itself? If the body is well adorned and well dressed this self also is well adorned and well dressed. If the body is beautiful, this self also is beautiful; if the body is blind or lame or crippled, this self also is blind or lame or crippled; in fact if the body perishes, this self also should perish together with it. There is no good in this. Being dissatisfied, Indra approaches Prajāpati again and tells him his doubts and difficulties. Prajāpati now tells him that he who is seen in dreams roaming freely, i.e., the dreaming subject, is the self. Indra, again doubts thus: Though this self is not vitiated with the defects and faults of the body, though it cannot be said to be perishing along with the body, yet it appears as if this self feels afraid and terrified, as if it is being chased and struck, it appears to be conscious of pain and to be weeping. There is no good in this also. Indra again returns to Prajāpati and tells him his doubts. This time Prajāpati teaches him that the enjoyer of deep dreamless sleep is the self. But Indra feels his difficulties. The self, he thinks, in deep sleep reduces itself to mere abstraction. There are no objects to be felt, to be known, to be enjoyed. This self appears to be absolutely unconscious—knowing nothing, feeling nothing, willing nothing. It is a zero, a cipher. There is no good in this too. And again he approaches Prājapati and tells him his doubts. The teacher is now very much pleased with the ability of the disciple. And now follows the real teaching: Dear Indra! The body is not the self, though it exists for the self. The dream-experiences are not the self, though they have a meaning only for the self. The self is not an abstract formal principle of deep sleep too. The eye, the body, the mental states, the presentation continuum, the stream of consciousness—are all mere instruments and objects of the self. The self is the ground of waking, dream and sleep states and yet it transcends them all. The self is universal, immanent as well as transcendent. The whole universe lives and moves and breathes

[1] VIII. 3-12.

in it. It is immortal, self-luminous, self-proved and beyond doubts and denials, as the very principle which makes all doubts, denials and thoughts possible. It is the ultimate subject which can never become an object and which is to be necessarily presupposed by all knowledge.

This dialogue brings out the essential nature of the self and has very important implications. The empiricism of Locke and Berkeley and the scepticism of Hume, the flux of Heraclitus, William James and Bergson, the Copernican revolution of Kant and the abiding contribution of Hegel, the positions of Green, Bradley and McTaggart—all have been long before anticipated in this dialogue. The self, surely, cannot be identified with the body, senses or the internal organ, nor can it be regarded as a mere by-product of matter. The bodily self or the waking self identifies itself with its contents—body, senses, mind, wife, son, daughter, sister, father, mother, brother, relation, friend. It stretches itself and identifies itself with the objects and feels as if they constitute its being, as if it is incomplete, nay, no more, without them. But in fact that which can be known as an object can never itself be the subject. It cannot be a mere bundle of the qualities. It cannot be the empirical self. Dreams have been selected by Prajāpati because here the objects have to be framed by the mind independently of the body or the senses. In the waking life, the objects are there apart from and outside of the mind which are only known and not created by it. Here the mind is helped by the senses which take the fleeting and scattered manifold of sense-impressions caused by external objects to the mind which arranges them into order and gives meaning and unity to them. But in the dreams, the mind has to function alone and fabricate imaginary objects for itself. It is the state, therefore, of perception without sensation. The self in the waking as well as in the dream state is ever changing and therefore cannot be the real self. The self must persist throughout the changes as their knower. The ego, limited by space and time, by birth and death, is a miserable creature. Indra, not being able to find the self in the waking and dreaming states, anticipates Heraclitus, Locke, Berkeley, Hume, William James and Bergson, and also some of the Buddhists. There is only change and you can never bathe twice in the same river, says Heraclitus. Locke regards the mind as a *tabula rasa*, a blank tablet, by itself as good as nothing, on which experience writes with the fingers of sensation and perception. Therefore 'in sleep and trances the mind exists not' declares Berkeley. 'Every drowsy nod explodes the self theory' says Locke. 'I can never catch my *self*' says Hume, 'whenever I try, I always stumble at some sense-impression or idea.' 'The so-called "self" is only a stream of thought;' declares William James, 'the passing thought itself is the thinker.' These empiricists, sceptics and pragmatists take the self as a mere bundle of ideas. Indra also came to the same conclusion. The self in waking and in dreams is ever changing, tortured, chased, vanishing. There is no good in this. What we get here is only a fleeting mass of qualities, the scattered manifold of sense-impressions or ideas, and no permanent self. The same conclusion is arrived at by Bradley also. Indra rightly thinks that in the deep sleep the self becomes a mere abstraction as there are no contents at all. A contentless self in the empirical life is an impossibility. The self, as subject, must oppose itself to an object. But in deep sleep there are no objects at all, neither real nor imaginary. Hence in the absence of the objects the self also ceases to exist. The Copernican revolution of Kant is the celebrated doctrine which he introduced into European Philosophy that knowledge requires both sensation and thought, that 'concepts without percepts are empty and percepts without concepts are blind', and that every knowledge situation necessarily presupposes the self, the 'transcendental unity of pure apperception' which is not a category of unity, but the fundamental postulate of all knowledge which makes possible the play of categories. The abiding contribution of Hegel has been the persistent insistence that the self should not be taken as a substance but as a subject and that this subject does not mean the empirical ego but the transcendental and yet immanent Absolute Idea running though the categories which are the various stages of the development of thought. Green, McTaggart and others have emphasized the same point. In fact, the foundation of this true Idealism was already laid down, many centuries before Kant and Hegel, in the Upaniṣads. Prajāpati's emphasis on the fact that the true self is the ultimate subject, the fundamental postulate of all knowledge, the transcendental background of the empirical trinity of knowledge, knower and known, the self-luminous and the self-proved pure consciousness which manifests itself as the subject and the object, as the self and the not-self, and which at once overreaches that division;[1] Yājñavalkya's declaration in the Bṛhadāraṇyaka that the self, the ultimate knower, can never be known as an object because it knows all objects, and yet it does not reduce itself to an abstraction because never is the knowledge of the knower destroyed, never is the sight of the seer destroyed; that when the sun has set, when the moon has set, and when the fire is extinguished, the self alone shines in its light;[2] the thundering assertion in the Kaṭha that 'Not there the sun shines, nor the moon or the stars, not these lightnings either. Where then could this fire be? Everything shines only after the shining spirit; through its light all this shines;'[3] and in the Mūṇḍaka 'The fire is its head, the moon and the sun are its eyes, the four quarters of the sky its ears, the Vedas are its speech, the wind is its breath, the universe is its heart, for verily it is the immanent self of all beings;'[4] are sufficient to prove our assertion. Prajāpati teaches Indra that the real self illumines consciousness but

[1] Chhāndogya VIII. 12. [2] Bṛh. IV. 3. 6. [3] Kaṭha II. 2. 15. [4] Muṇḍaka II. 1. 4.

itself is not in consciousness. The Ātman is the transcendental background of both self and not-self, and none can doubt its reality.

In the Māṇḍūkya Upaniṣad also we find a similar analysis of consciousness. We are told that the self in the waking state enjoys gross objects, it has the consciousness of the external world and is called 'Vishva'. In the dreaming state it enjoys subtle objects, it has the consciousness of the internal world and creates its own imaginary objects and is called 'Taijasa'. In the state of sound sleep there is no object, neither gross nor subtle, and hence no subject; the subject-object duality is transcended and here the self is called 'Prājña'. In sleep we have absence of pain. We have neither desires nor dreams. We have the shadow of the supreme bliss. It is called shadow because we do not enjoy positive bliss. Ignorance persists in its negative aspect of concealment in this state, although its power of projection is arrested. Ignorance and unconsciousness remain in this state and therefore a higher positive state is necessary. This is the fourth state of the self, a state of pure consciousness where, like the deep sleep, there is no subject-object duality, but unlike it there is enjoyment of positive bliss. All ignorance vanishes here. The self shines in its own light as the ultimate subject without reducing itself to a mere abstraction. This is the true self, the foundation of all existence and the presupposition of all knowledge. It cannot be fully described for descriptions are possible only in the empirical state of subject-object duality. It can be realized directly and intuitively. It is called 'Turīya', the Fourth, or 'Amātra', the Measureless. It is calm, non-dual, blissful and all-consciousness where all plurality is merged. Aumkāra with its parts A-U-M, the waking, dreaming and sleeping states, is its symbol. This self is the common ground of all these states. It manifests itself in these three states and yet in its own nature it transcends them all.

In the Kaṭha Upaniṣad, the Ātman is said to be the ultimate reality. The objects are the roads, the body is the chariot, the senses are the horses, the mind is the reins, the intellect is the charioteer, the ego is the enjoyer and the Ātman is the Lord sitting in the chariot.[1] The senses are further compared to good and bad horses. Plato in his Phaedrus has also compared them to the white and the black horses. The Kaṭha further states that the senses are higher than the objects, the mind is higher than the senses, the intellect is higher than the mind, the subtle reason (mahat) is higher than the intellect, the Unmanifest (avyakta) is higher than the subtle reason, and the Puruṣa (ātman) is higher than the Unmanifest, and there is nothing higher than the Puruṣa which is the ultimate end, the highest reality.[2] Objects, senses, mind, intellect, reason—all exist for the self and serve its purpose. It is the self that is immanent in them and gives them life and meaning. But these cannot be identified with the self, for it transcends them all.

[1] Kaṭha 2. 3-4. [2] Ibid.

This is the crux of the teaching imparted to Nachiketā by Yama. The self is immortal, self-proved and self-luminous and can only be directly realized by transcending the empirical subject-object duality.

V

BRAHMAN

FROM the objective side this ultimate reality is called Brahman. The word is derived from the root 'Bṛh' which means to grow or to evolve. In the beginning it meant sacrifice, then prayer and then it acquired its present meaning of ultimate reality which evolves itself as this world. Brahman is that which spontaneously bursts forth as nature and soul. It is the ultimate cause of this universe. In the Chhāndogya, it is cryptically described as 'Tajjalān'[1]—as that (tat) from which the world arises (ja), into which it returns (la), and by which it is supported and it lives (an). In the Taittirīya, Brahman is defined as that from which all these beings are born, by which they live, and into which they are reabsorbed.[2] The evolution of the elements is given in this order: From Brahman arises ether, from ether air, from air fire, from fire water and from water earth. But the real theory of evolution is given in the doctrine of the five sheaths (koshas) in the Taittirīya.[3] The lowest level is that of matter (annamaya). Matter is unconscious and dead and cannot account for life. It is purely on the physical plane. Brahman cannot rest content with matter. The purpose of matter is fulfilled only when life is evolved. The highest state of matter is therefore life. Though matter cannot account for life, yet there can be no life without matter. The inorganic matter must be transformed into organic life. Hence the second state of evolution is life (prāṇamaya). Now we are on the biological plane. The vegetable life (oṣadhayaḥ) emerges first. But the vegetable life must lead to the animal life. The vegetable products must be transformed into living animal cells. Life pervades the universe and binds man with the rest of creation. But the destiny of life is fulfilled only when consciousness is evolved. Hence the third state of evolution is mind or perceptual Consciousness (manomaya). Here we are on the mental or psychological plane. This state is shared by lower animals with men. Mind or consciousness remains in the lower animal life at the level of instinct and reflex action. Human beings have also got instincts and reflex actions and these play an important part in determining the human life. But brute instinct is mute and rebels against itself. It wants to express itself. It is on the level of infra-relational undifferentiated feeling. The subject-object duality is absent here because it has not yet been evolved. The

[1] III. 14. [2] III. 1. [3] II. 1-5.

end of this instinctive consciousness will be fulfilled only when a higher principle has been evolved where consciousness becomes self-conscious or rational. Hence the fourth state of evolution is self-conscious reason (vijñānamaya). Here we are on the metaphysical plane. This state is the sole monopoly of human beings. Reason becomes self-conscious only at this state and this fact distinguishes human beings from lower animals. Arts, sciences, aesthetics, morals, poetry, philosophy, religion, all become possible only at this state. The empirical trinity of knower, knowledge and known has been evolved. But even this will not suffice. There is a higher experience of which we get a negative glimpse in the empirical life and which cannot be accounted for by mere intellect. The relational and analytical, the discursive and dichotomous intellect points to something higher as its end in which it wants to merge itself. The subject-object duality wants to transcend itself; not that it wants to fall back on the instinctive undifferentiated feeling which it has left far behind, but it wants to fulfil its destiny by merging itself in the Absolute, the Abode of Bliss, where there is no trace of duality and plurality. The fifth and the highest state of evolution, therefore, is the non-dual bliss (ānandamaya). Here we are on the mystic plane. The empirical trinity of knower, known and knowledge has been fused into a transcendental unity. Here philosophy terminates. This Brahman, the supreme Reality, transcends all, yet it underlies all as their background. The lower is not lost or annihilated; it is simply transformed in the higher. Matter is not lost in life; life is not lost in mind; mind is not lost in reason; reason is not lost in bliss. Brahman pervades them all. It is the immanent inner controller of all (antaryāmin) and the self of all (sarva-bhūtāntarātmā). As all spokes are contained in the axle and the wheel, so all beings, all gods, all worlds, all organs are contained in the Universal Self, the Brahman.[1] This is the Brahman, the self-luminous, the immortal, the support of all the worlds, the highest and leaving nothing beyond it.[2] Matter is its body, it is its soul; the individual souls are its body, it is their soul. It holds the self and the not-self together which are equally its own manifestations and yet in its own nature it transcends both.

VI

BRAHMAN AND ĀTMAN

WE have seen that the same reality is called from the subjective side as 'Ātman' and from the objective side as 'Brahman'. The two terms are used as synonyms. The Absolute of the Upaniṣads manifests itself as the subject as well as the object and transcends them both.

[1] Bṛh 2. 5. 15. [2] Kaṭha 2. 6. 1.

The Absolute is as certain as the Ātman and also as infinite as the Brahman. This blending of the subject and the object in a transcendental principle, this synthesis of the self and the not-self in the Absolute, this dialectical march of pure self-consciousness from the subject through the object to its own synthetic nature was arrived at by the Upaniṣadic sages centuries before Hegel, and many many years before Plato was born. To quote Deussen: 'It was here that for the first time the original thinkers of the Upaniṣads, to their immortal honour, found it when they recognized our Ātman, our inmost individual being, as the Brahman, the inmost being of universal nature and of all her phenomena'.[1] 'That thou art' (tat tvam asi) is the great saying (mahāvākya) of the Upaniṣads. 'I am Brahman.' 'Ātman is Brahman.' 'I am that.' 'I am the non-dual Bliss.' The subject lacked infinitude and the object lacked certitude. The Absolute has both infinitude and certitude. The self and the not-self are equally manifestations of the Absolute and are at bottom one. The individual self is, in fact, no longer individual, but universal. The microcosm and the macrocosm are blended together. In microcosm we find the three states of waking, dreaming and sound sleep and we find the self as the Fourth, the immanent yet transcendent reality. In macrocosm waking (jāgrat) corresponds to Virāṭ, dreaming (svapna) to Hiraṇyagarbha, deep sleep (suṣupti) to Īshvara, and the Fourth (turīya) to Brahman. In macrocosm, body corresponds to Virāṭ, life and mind correspond to Hiraṇyagarbha, self-consciousness corresponds to Īshvara and bliss corresponds to Brahman. The Absolute is Pure Existence, Pure Knowledge, and Pure Bliss—all in one. It is called Sachhidānanda. It is Satyam (Truth), Jñānam (Knowledge) and Anantam (Infinite). It is Truth, Goodness and Beauty—Satyam-Shivam-Sundaram. By knowing it the unseen becomes the seen, the unknown becomes the known, the unthought of becomes the thought of.

All this is beautifully described in the Chhāndogya in a dialogue between Uddālaka and Shvetaketu.[2] The father teaches his son Shvetaketu thus: 'In the beginning Sat alone was, without a second. It thought "May I be many".' Then it evolved itself into this manifold world. Thou, O Shvetaketu! art that—'Tat tvam asi Shvetaketo!'. This teaching blends the subject with the object, the indubitable with the infinite, the microcosm with the macrocosm, the self with the not-self. None of them can be taken as independent and separate. Both are relative terms and like the two sides of the same coin, both are manifestations of the same Sat. The Sat runs through them (tadevānuprāvishat) and constitutes their being. Yet the Sat cannot be confined to them. In its own nature it transcends them both. The individual self of Shvetaketu of which he is immediately conscious and absolutely certain is identified with the

[1] Philosophy of the Upaniṣads, p. 40. [2] Chhāndogya. 6,

infinite objective reality which is the cause of this universe including the individual selves and the world of matter. But how can a portion of the effect be identified with the whole cause? How can the self of Shvetaketu which is itself an effect along with others (i.e., other selves and matter) be one with the cause, the Brahman? How can the private and the limited self of Shvetaketu be the cause of this entire universe? The answer is that both the self and the not-self are mere manifestations of the Absolute. The Absolute is immanent in them all and constitutes their being. The self of Shvetaketu is one with the Universal Self which is immanent in it. 'I live, yet not I, but God liveth in me.'

This Brahman is described in two ways in the Upaniṣads. It is called cosmic, all-comprehensive, full of all good qualities—Saprapañcha, Saguṇa and Savisheṣa. And it is also called acosmic, qualityless, indeterminate, indescribable—Niṣprapañcha, Nirguṇa, Nirvisheṣa and Anirvachanīya. This distinction is the root of the celebrated distinction made by Shaṅkarāchārya between God and the Absolute. The former is called lower Brahman (apara Brahma) or Ishvara, and the latter higher Brahman (para Brahma) or the Absolute. God is the personal aspect of the Absolute and the Absolute is the impersonal aspect of God. Matter, self and God are only manifestations of the Absolute. But Rāmānujāchārya has challenged this distinction. To him, the Absolute is the personal and the immanent God, and matter and selves alike form His real body, He, being the soul of nature and the soul of souls. Rāmānuja interprets the Upaniṣads in the sense of Brahma-pariṇāma-vāda; Brahman really transforms Himself as the world of matter and of souls. Shaṅkara interprets them in the sense of Brahma-vivarta-vāda; Brahman unreally appears, through Ignorance, as the world of matter and of souls. Shaṅkara does not deny the existence of a personal God. He is the highest appearance admitted by Advaitism.

The cosmic Brahman is regarded as the cause of production, maintenance and destruction of this universe. All beings arise from Him, live in Him and are absorbed in Him.[1] The Māṇḍūkya calls Him 'the lord of all, the knower of all, the inner controller of all, the *fons et origo* of all, the final haven of all'. Like sparks arising from fire, like earthen-ware arising out of earth, like gold ornaments being made out of gold, like cob-web coming out of a spider, like hair coming out of the body, like the lustre shooting out of a pearl, like the musical sound coming out of a lute, the entire creation arises out of Brahman. Just as when clay is known, everything made out of clay becomes known, for it is only 'name and form', the reality being only clay, similarly when Brahman, the cause is known, everything, being a mere effect, becomes known, for the effects are only names and forms, the reality is Brahman alone. In the Bṛhadāraṇyaka we are told that nature is the body of God Who is

[1] Chh. 3. 14. 1.; Taitt. 3. 1.

its soul. Earth, water, fire, air, ether, the sun, the moon, the stars, the sky, the quarters, the rivers, the mountains, in fact, all beings, all creatures, all life, all senses, all speech, all minds are the body of God. God is immanent in them all and controls them from within and holds them together. He knows them all, but they do not know Him, for how can the body know the soul? He who knows this Antaryāmin, knows the Ātman, knows the Brahman, knows the Vedas, knows all the worlds, in fact, he knows all.[1] God is not only the soul of nature, He is also the soul of souls. The souls are His body; He is their soul. The souls are souls in relation to the bodies, but in relation to God, they become His body and He becomes their soul. Just as the spokes are held together in the axle and the wheel, so all the souls are held together in the Supreme Soul.[2] Just as sparks emanate from fire, so all the souls emanate from the Supreme Soul.[3]

The acosmic Brahman is the transcendental Absolute, the Turīya or the Fourth, the Amātra or the Measureless, the Anirvachanīya or the Indescribable. It is the foundational consciousness, the fundamental postulate of all knowledge. It holds the subjective and the objective world in a transcendental unity. It is the background of the empirical trinity of knowledge, knower and known. It is the indubitable ultimate knower which is presupposed by all affirmations and negations, all positions and doubts and denials. It is self-luminous and self-proved. The discursive intellect cannot know it for the ultimate subject cannot be made an object of knowledge. As Kant says: 'What I must presuppose in order to know an object, I cannot know as an object.' How can he be known by whom all this is known? How, O dear, can the knower be known?[4] All speech together with the mind turns away unable to reach it.[5] The eye does not go there, nor does speech, nor does mind. We cannot know it. We cannot teach it.[6] The Absolute can be best described only in a negative way, though it is not itself negated by it. Yājñavalkya describes it thus: 'This is the imperishable, O Gārgī, which wise people adore—not gross, not subtle, not short, not long, without shadow, without darkness, without air, without space, without attachment, without taste, without smell, without sight, without ears, without speech, without mind, without light, without breath, without mouth, and without either inside or outside. It does not eat anything nor can anything eat it.'[7] Lest this description should be mistaken as mere solipsism and pure nonsense, Yājñavalkya is cautious enough to add immediately that 'never is the sight of the seer destroyed; never is the knowledge of the knower destroyed,' that when it is said that the Absolute does not see what is really meant is that it sees and yet does not see. There is nothing outside it which it may see. The Eternal knower, the

[1] Bṛh. III. 7. [2] Bṛh 2. 5. 15. [3] Ibid 2. 1. 20. [4] Bṛh. 2. 4. 13. [5] Taitt. 2. 4. [6] Kena 2. 3.; Muṇḍaka, 2. 1.; Kaṭha 1, 3, 10. [7] Bṛh 3. 8. 8.

self-luminous Real shines forth by itself.[1] Silence is the ultimate philosophy and Yājñavalkya has to tell Gārgī: Gārgī! ask not too much, ask not too much, otherwise thy head will fall.[2] In the Kena we are told: That which cannot be spoken by the speech, but by which speech is made possible; that which cannot be thought by the mind, but by which, they say, the mind thinks; that which cannot be seen by the eye, but by which the eye is made to see; that which cannot be heard by the ear, but by which the ear is made to hear; that which does not breathe, but by which breath is made possible, know that alone to be the Brahman, not this which they worship outside.[3] Brahman is known to him who says he does not know it and it is unknown to him who says he knows it.[4] The meaning is that he who knows the Brahman as the Indescribable really knows its nature and he who thinks that Brahman can be adequately described by the finite mind misses its nature. The empirical and negative description of the Absolute by means of *neti neti* (not this, not this) or 'the neither-nor' necessarily presupposes the affirmation of the Absolute as all-Comprehensive and culminates in the transcendental Absolute which goes beyond both negation and affirmation. The *neti neti* negates all descriptions about the Brahman, but not the Brahman itself. In fact, the Absolute is the Existence of all existences, the Truth of all truths, the Reality of all realities.[5] Realizing this, a wise person should remain merged in it and transcending all categories of the intellect, should acquire child-like innocence.[6] There is no plurality here. Those who are engrossed in plurality go on revolving in the cycle of birth and death. Fear proceeds from diversity. Unity is fearlessness. Grief and delusion are gone for him who realizes this unity.[7] All joys fade into insignificance before the supreme Joy of Brahman.[8] Just as rivers, leaving their names and forms, merge in the ocean, so a wise man, arising above name and form, becomes one with the Absolute.[9] He who knows Brahman becomes Brahman. This is the secret teaching. Only by knowing it can one cross the ocean of birth-and-death; there is no other way for liberation.[10]

VII

MĀYĀ OR AVIDYĀ

SOMETIMES it is said that the doctrine of Māyā or Avidyā is either borrowed by Shaṅkara from Buddhism or it is a fabrication of the fertile brain of Shaṅkara. Both these views are wrong. The fact is that the theory of Māyā is present in the Upaniṣads and Shaṅkara has elaborated it like a true thinker. Prof. R. D. Ranade, in his great work,

[1] Ibid 4. 3. 23. [2] Ibid 3. 6. 1. [3] Kena 1, 4-8. [4] Ibid 2, 3. [5] Bṛh 2. 3. 6. [6] Ibid 3. 5. 1. [7] Īsha 7; Taitt. 2. 7. 1. [8] Taitt. 2, 8, 1-4. [9] Muṇḍaka, 3, 2, 8. [10] Shvetāshvatara 6, 15.

'A Constructive Survey of Upaniṣadic Philosophy', has rightly pointed out the origin of this doctrine in the Upaniṣads. He gives the following points:

"(1) Īsha tells us that the veil that covers the truth is golden, so rich, gaudy and dazzling that it takes away the mind of the observer from the inner contents. (Īsha, 15.)

(2) Kaṭha says how people live in ignorance and thinking themselves wise, move about wandering, like blind men following the blind. (1, 2, 4-5.)

(3) Muṇḍaka compares ignorance to a knot which a man has to untie before he gets possession of the self in the recess of his own heart. (II, 1, 10.)

(4) Chhāndogya tells us that knowledge is power and ignorance is impotence. (I, 1, 10.)

(5) Bṛhadāraṇyaka compares Unreality to Not-being, to Darkness and to Death. (I, 3, 28.)

(6) Prashna tells us that we cannot reach the world of Brahman unless we have shaken off the crookedness in us, the falsehood, the illusion. (I, 16.)

(7) Bṛhadāraṇyaka tells us 'as if there were a duality' implying thereby that there is really no duality. Māyā is a semblance, an as-it-were, an appearance. (II, 4, 14.)

(8) Chhāndogya tells us that Ātman is the only Reality, everything else is merely a word, a mode and a name. (VI, 1, 4.)

(9) Shvetāshvatara describes God as a Māyin who creates this world by His power. (IV, 9.)"

VIII

UPANIṢADS, THE SOURCE OF INDIAN PHILOSOPHY

THE Upaniṣads are rightly regarded as the fountain-head of all Indian philosophy. Bloomfield remarks: 'There is no important form of Hindu thought, heterodox Buddhism included, which is not rooted in the Upaniṣads.' Dr. S. Radhakrishnan says: 'Later systems of philosophy display an almost pathetic anxiety to accomodate their doctrines to the views of the Upaniṣads, even if they cannot father them all on them.' Prof. R. D. Ranade says: 'The Upaniṣads constitute that lofty eminence of philosophy, which from its various sides gives birth to rivulets of thought, which, as they progress onwards towards the sea of life, gather strength by the inflow of innumerable tributaries of speculation which intermittently join these rivulets, so as to make a huge expanse of waters at the place where they meet the ocean of life.'

The Bramha-sūtra claims to be an aphoristic summary of the

Upaniṣads. The Gītā is the milk milked out of the Upaniṣad-cows and is particularly influenced by the Kaṭha and the Īsha. The various Āchāryas of Vedānta—Shaṅkara, Rāmānuja, Nimbārka, Madhva and Vallabha—have always regarded the Upaniṣads as the sacred texts and have interpreted them so as to make them suit their theories. The heterodox Jainism has taken its idealism and its doctrine of Karma from the Upaniṣads. The heterodox Buddhism derives its idealism, monism, absolutism, the theory of momentariness of all worldly things, the theory of Karma, the distinction between the empirical and the absolute standpoints, and the theory that Ignorance is the root-cause of this cycle of birth-and-death and that Nirvāṇa can be attained by right knowledge alone, from the Upaniṣads. Sāṅkhya derives from them the doctrine of Prakṛti (from Shvetāshvatara), the theory of the three Guṇas (from the three colours in the Chhāndogya), the doctrine of Puruṣa, the relation of mind, intellect and soul (from Kaṭha), the doctrine of Liṅga-sharīra (from Prashna). Yoga is rooted in Shvetāshvatara. Kaṭha speaks of Dhāraṇā and Muṇḍaka speaks of the soul as a mere onlooker. Īsha preaches the combination of Karma and Jñāna; Mīmāmsā takes up Karma; Vedānta takes up Jñāna; and some writers take up the combination itself.[1]

[1] For a detailed study of this the reader is referred to Prof. R. D. Ranade's 'A Constructive Survey of Upaniṣadic Philosophy'.

Chapter Two

BHAGAVADGĪTĀ

I

INTRODUCTION

BHAGAVADGĪTĀ literally means 'The Lord's Song', i.e., the philosophical discourse of Lord Kṛṣṇa to persuade the reluctant Arjuna to fight. It is the most popular and sacred book of the Hindus and is contained in the Bhīṣma-Parva of the Mahābhārata, the greatest Sanskrit epic.

Various are the praises showered on this work both by Indian and European scholars. Lokamānya Tilak calls it 'a most luminous and priceless gem which gives peace to afflicted souls and makes us masters of spiritual wisdom'. Mahāmanā Mālavīyaji sees a unique synthesis of 'the highest knowledge, the purest love and the most luminous action' in it. Mahātmā Gāndhī calls it 'the universal mother whose door is wide open to anyone who knocks,' and further says that 'a true votary of the Gītā does not know what disappointment is. He ever dwells in perennial joy and peace that passeth understanding'. The Gītā deals with metaphysics, religion and ethics, and has been rightly called the 'Gospel of Humanity'.

The central teaching of the Gītā can be beautifully summarized in this sentence of Annie Besant: 'It is meant to lift the aspirant from the lower levels of renunciation, where objects are renounced, to the loftier heights where desires are dead, and where the Yogī dwells in calm and ceaseless contemplation, while his body and mind are actively employed in discharging the duties that fall to his lot in life.' The Gītā tries to build up a philosophy of Karma based on Jñāna and supported by Bhakti in a beautiful manner.

In the beginning we find Arjuna horrified at the thought that he has to fight with his relatives and friends and he says to Kṛṣṇa that he can foresee no advantage in killing relatives and he flatly refuses to fight—'I would not like to kill these, even though I may be killed by them'.[1] Kṛṣṇa, then, proceeds to instruct him that it is his duty as a prince, as a warrior, as a righteous man to fight against evil and restore peace and

[1] I, 35.

order. Some people have tried to read in the Gītā a 'cult of murder'. But this simply shows to what extent a noble work can be misinterpreted. To fight against evil is the duty of man. To make the situation poignant relatives and beloved friends and revered elders stand on both sides and Arjuna has to vindicate his claim, he has to follow his Svabhāva and Svadharma. It is a significant fact that though Lord Kṛṣṇa in the beginning repeatedly asks Arjuna to fight, in the end when the teaching has been imparted to him, the Lord simply says—'Do as you please.'

II

BEING

THE fundamental metaphysical teaching of the Gītā is that 'of the unreal there is no being, and of the real there is no non-being'.[1] The soul is indestructible (avināshi), eternal (nitya), unborn (aja), undiminishing (avyaya), all-pervasive (sarva-gata), immovable (achala), ancient (sanātana), unmanifest (avyakta), unthinkable (achintya) and immutable (avikārya). Only bodies are destroyed, not the soul. It is neither born nor does it die. It is immortal and everlasting. Not being subject to birth and death, it cannot perish along with the body. Just as a person casts off worn-out garments and puts on the new ones, so does the soul cast off worn-out bodies and enters into others that are new.[2] The infinite underlies and animates all finite existences, and the soul being essentially one with it, is not affected by birth and death, by growth and decay, by finitude or change, 'even though our body be "dust returning unto dust" '. He who sees the Ultimate Reality seated equally in all beings and unperishing within the perishing, sees truly.[3]

III

YOGA

THE Gītā represents a unique synthesis of Action, Devotion and Knowledge. Man is a complex of intellect, will and emotion; he is a being who thinks, wills and feels. Intellect has given rise to the philosophy of Knowledge; will to the philosophy of Action; and emotion to the philosophy of Devotion. Modern Psychology teaches us that these three aspects of mind are distinguishable only in thought and not divisible in reality. There is no watertight division separating one from the rest. The teaching of the Gītā is in keeping with this view. To quote Dr. S. Radhakrishnan: 'The Absolute reveals itself to those seeking for knowledge as the Eternal Light, clear and radiant as the sun at noon-day;

[1] II, 16. nāsato vidyate bhāvo nābhāvo vidyate sataḥ. [2] II, 22. [3] VI, 29.

to those struggling for virtue as the Eternal Righteousness, steadfast and impartial; and to those emotionally inclined as Eternal Love and Beauty of Holiness.' Different people attain the same goal of salvation by these three different paths of knowledge, action and devotion.

All these three ultimately stand synthesised. This synthesis is called 'Yoga'. The literal meaning of the word is union, i.e., of the individual with the Absolute. It means equanimity or balance of mind (samatva). It means the higher perspective of action which comes through detachment (karmasu kaushalam). The Yogi is the ideal ascetic who curbs his passions and maintains calmness in cold and heat, in joy and sorrow, in honour and dishonour.[1] 'As a lamp flickers not in a windless place, that is the simile for the Yogī who curbs his thoughts and yields himself entirely to absorption.'[2] We find the following beautiful description of Yoga: 'Where seeing the self by the self, one is satisfied in oneself; where one experiences the absolute bliss, known only to higher reason, but ever beyond the senses, and standing where one swerves not from the truth; where no other gain is considered greater, and where one is not moved by the greatest pain—that state free from misery is Yoga.'[3] A Yogī is a Sthita-prajña—one firmly rooted in higher reason and unmoved by the pairs of opposites. He attains to the highest state of Brahman (Brāhmī-sthiti), where he is never bewildered (naināṃ prāpya vimuhyati) and from which he never falls down (yad gatvā na nivartante).

IV

JÑANA

THIS Yoga is essentially and predominantly the path of knowledge. The Yogī's ideal is self-realization which cannot be attained without knowledge. Even the devotees are granted knowledge by the Lord so that they may realize the goal.[4] Yoga, bereft of knowledge, is an impossibility. We may weaken the power of the senses by fasting and abstaining from necessities, but unless we rise above the relish and the desire, the psychological attachment to the sense-objects, we are not true Yogīs. And this relish can go away only with the rise of true knowledge.[5] How high the Gītā places knowledge can be seen from the following: 'Even the most sinful man can cross over the ocean of Samsāra by means of the boat of knowledge alone. As a fire well-kindled reduces fuel to ashes, so the fire of knowledge reduces all actions to ashes. The culmination of action is in knowledge. Having obtained knowledge, one soon embraces peace. There is nothing purer than knowledge'.[6] The knower is identified by the Lord with His own self.[7]

[1] VI, 7, 8; XIV, 24, 25. [2] VI, 19. [3] VI, 20, 23. [4] dadāmi buddhiyogam tam yena māmupayānti te. X, 10. [5] II, 59. [6] nahi jñānena sadṛsham pavitramiha vidyate, IV, 38. [7] jñānītvātmaiva me matam, VII, 18.

V

KARMA

KARMAYOGA is not opposed to Jñānayoga. In fact, the former is possible only when the latter is attained. No embodied being can completely renounce actions.[1] The constituent Guṇas of Prakṛti, Sattva, Rajas and Tamas, necessarily give rise to actions. As Wordsworth says:

'The eye cannot choose but see,
We cannot bid the ear be still,
Our bodies feel where'er they be
Against or with our will.'

The universe itself depends on actions.[2] Inertia is not liberty, but death. Work keeps up the cycle of the universe and it is the duty of every individual to help it. He who does not do so and finds pleasure in the senses is sinful and lives in vain.[3] The ideal of the Gītā is not negativism, asceticism or escapism. It is not negation of actions, but performance of actions in a detached spirit. It is not Naiṣkarmya, but Niṣkāma Karma. The giving up is not of action itself, but of interest, desire, fruit, attachment regarding action. Desire binds a man; he should therefore act in such a way when action does not bind. The Gītā synthesises both Pravṛtti and Nivṛtti. As Prof. M. Hiriyanna says: 'The Gītā-teaching stands not for renunciation *of* action, but for renunciation *in* action.' It is emphatically stated that Saṁnyāsa does not mean the renunciation of action, but of interest, desire and attachment; it means the giving up of the fruit of all work.[4] Actions are our sphere; fruits are not our concern. We should never be attached to the fruits of actions and at the same time we should never be inactive.[5] And without knowledge, renunciation of desire and attachment is not possible. So only a true jñānī can perform niṣkāma karma. Therefore the Gītā says: Only fools and not wise people speak of jñāna and karma as different and opposed; really they are one.[6]

Here arises an apparent contradiction in the Gītā where it is also remarked that for him who has realized the self, who is enjoying the bliss of the self, and who remains ever satisfied in the supreme peace of the self, *for him* there remains nothing to be done.[7] This verse emphasises the word 'tasya' ('for him'). The perfect man has no axe of his own to grind. He simply acts for the good of the people. The Lord Himself,

[1] nahi dehabhṛtā shakyam tyaktum karmāṇyasheṣataḥ, XVIII, 11. [2] loko'yam karmabhandhanaḥ, III, 9. [3] III, 16. [4] kāmyānām karmaṇām nyāsam sannyāsam kavayo viduḥ, XVIII, 2. [5] II, 47. [6] sāṅkhyayogau pṛthag bālāḥ pravadanti na paṇḍitāḥ, V, 4. [7] tasya kāryam na vidyate, III, 17.

though He has nothing to accomplish for Himself, acts for the benefit of humanity. The perfect man also has to work for the benefit of humanity (loka-saṅgraha) in the spirit of perfect detachment, disinterest, selflessness, with no desire to reap the fruit. He alone is capable of doing so. The liberated 'cave-dweller' in Plato goes again into the cave to free others. He who performs actions in a detached manner, thinking himself to be a mere instrument of God, is not contaminated by sin like the lotus-leaf, though living in water, yet not being contaminated by it.[1] But the Gītā definitely recognizes a supra-social state for the liberated sage. He cannot be forced to work. He may not be living in society, yet his very presence in the world confers benefits upon humanity, like the presence of the sun.

An objection is raised here that absolutely disinterested action is a psychological impossibility. But it is not valid. Firstly, the liberated sage has risen much above the psychological plane. He is on the transcendental mystic plane and empirical injunctions and prohibitions, ordinary rules of practice, and psychological rules do not apply to him. Intellect cannot grasp this state; it can only point towards it. Secondly, for the aspirant, we may say that the Gītā recommends, not the annihilation of all desires, but the merging of all desires in one supreme desire—the desire for the development of spiritual life. All actions, therefore, should be inspired by this supreme desire. The betterment of our spiritual life is the single motive and the only end prescribed for all our actions.

VI

BHAKTI

BHAKTI or devotion is defined as disinterested service to God. So it is a form of Karma. And disinterested action, as we have seen, is not possible without knowledge. Hence Bhakti too, like Niṣkāma Karma, can be performed only by a true jñānī. Only he can completely resign himself to the Lord. The devotee is confident of the guarantee given by the Lord—'Never does My devotee perish'[2] and 'The doer of good never comes to grief'.[3] The Lord says: 'Even if a very ill-conducted man worships me, not worshipping any one else, he must certainly be deemed to be good, for he has well resolved. He soon becomes devout of heart and obtains lasting tranquillity. O Arjuna, know firmly that My devotee is never ruined. He who does My work, who yields himself upto Me, who is devoted to Me, void of attachment, without hatred to anyone, O Arjuna, comes to Me.'[4]

[1] lipyate na sa pāpena padmapatram ivāmbhasā, V, 10. [2] na me bhaktaḥ praṇashyati, IX, 31. [3] VI, 40. [4] IX, 30, 31, 34.

The object of devotion is the personal God, the Puruṣottama on Whose mercy the devotee has to throw himself utterly. Absolute dependence and utter faith are very necessary. The Lord says: 'Merge thy mind in Me, be My devotee, prostrate thyself before Me, thou shalt come upto Me. I pledge thee My Word; thou art dear to Me. Abandoning all *dharmas* come unto Me alone for shelter; sorrow not, I will liberate thee from all sins'.[1] The Lord Himself lifts up His devotees from the ocean of birth-and-death.[2] The love of God is the supreme Love and every other form of it is an imperfect manifestation of this supreme Love. Out of the four kinds of devotees—the suffering (ārta), the seeker for truth (jijñāsu), the self-interested (arthārthī), and the wise (jñānī), the last one is the best. He alone knows that the Lord pervades the entire universe (vāsudevaḥ sarvam). He sees the Lord in everything and everything in the Lord.[3] He knows that all is strung on God, like pearls on a string,[4] that God is the immanent inner controller of all. 'When devotion is perfect, then the individual and his God become suffused into one spiritual ecstasy, and reveal themselves as aspects of one life. Absolute monism is therefore the completion of the dualism with which the devotional consciousness starts.'

VII

GĪTA AND UPANIṢADS

THUS we see that Jñāna is the most important thing, being the very essence of Reality. Karma and Bhakti, understood in their proper senses, are only manifestations of jñāna. Without jñāna, liberation is impossible and so is detachment or renunciation in action and so is disinterested devotion to God. The Lord has to give knowledge to his devotees so that they may reach Him. There is nothing purer than knowledge.

There is undoubedly a great influence of the Upaniṣads on the Gītā. Tradition also supports this view when it makes Shrī Kṛṣṇa a cow-herd milking the celestial milk of Gītā from the Upaniṣads pictured as cows, Arjuna acting as a calf, for the sake of the wise.[5] In the Gītā the absolutism of the Upaniṣads is tinged with theism. Lord Kṛṣṇa is a personal God; He is the Creator, eternal and imperishable, and yet He takes birth in the world to preserve Dharma when it is going down.[6] But ultimately, theism culminates in absolutism which is the highest note. Reality is transcendent as well as immanent.

[1] XVIII, 65, 66. [2] teṣāmaham samuddhartā mṛtyusaṁsārasāgarāt, XII, 7. [3] VII, 16, 17, 19. [4] mayi sarvamidam protam sūtre maṇigaṇā iva, VII, 7. [5] sarvopaniṣado gāvo dogdhā Gopālanandanaḥ. Pārtho vatsaḥ sudhīr bhoktā dugdham Gītāmṛtam mahat. [6] IV, 7, 8.

VIII

GĪTA AND SĀṄKHYA

SOME scholars see the influence of Sāṅkhya on the Gītā. Certainly there are some striking similarities between them, but there are differences also. For example, let us compare Kaṭha and Gītā here with Sāṅkhya. In the Kaṭha we find that the senses are higher than the objects; the mind is higher than the senses; the intellect is higher than the mind; the Mahat is higher than the intellect; the Avyakta is higher than the Mahat; and the Puruṣa is higher than the Avyakta; and there is nothing higher than the Puruṣa which is the Limit, the Ultimate End.[1] In the Gītā we find: the senses are higher than the objects; the mind is higher than the senses; the intellect is higher than the mind; and He that is higher than the intellect is the Ultimate End.[2] The Gītā also uses the words: 'the three qualities of Sattva, Rajas and Tamas', 'Prakṛti', 'Puruṣa', 'Avyakta' etc. Some scholars opine that this suggests the influence of Sāṅkhya on the Gītā. Moreover, the Gītā uses the words 'Sāṅkhya' and 'Yoga' also. But we may explain, following Shaṅkarāchāṛya, that Sāṅkhya means 'knowledge' and Yoga means 'action' in the Gītā. And it is precisely in this sense that these words are used here. The words 'Avyakta' and 'Prakṛti' mean the unmanifest power of God. We may explain them as due to the influence of the Upaniṣads, e.g. Kaṭha cited above, unless we are prepared to believe that Kaṭha itself is influenced by Sāṅkhya which is a very controversial point. Further, the important differences between the Gītā and the Sāṅkhya might be noted. The Prakṛti of the Gītā is not an independent entity, but only the power of God. The Puruṣa here means the Jiva who is regarded as a part of God.[3] God is immanent in all and He is the Puruṣottama, the supreme Soul. The plurality of souls is, therefore, out of question. The ideal of the Gītā is the positive and blissful union with the Absolute, and not the negative Kaivalya of the Sāṅkhya.

IX

GENERAL

SOME of the contradictions, though they are only apparent and superficial to us, in the Gītā have led scholars to different opinions. Some explain them as due to the fact that the Gītā is not a systematic philosophical work, but a mystic poem. On the other hand, some scholars try to explain them by saying that there are certain interpolations in it.

[1] Kaṭha, II, 3, 4. [2] III, 42. [3] XV, 7; XVIII, 61.

Some say that the Gītā was originally pantheistic, but later on, was made theistic by the devotees of Viṣṇu. This is absurd because Lord Kṛṣṇa is essentially a personal God and theism is quite dominant in the Gītā. Accepting this position, Garbe made an attempt to reconstruct the original Gītā by pointing out the interpolations in it which, he thought, were made by the Vedāntic philosophers. Prof. Winternitz agreed with Garbe, but some repeated studies of the Gītā afterwards made him admit that it taught 'theism tinged with pantheism'. He, therefore, did not regard those passages where Kṛṣṇa speaks of Himself as immanent in the world as interpolated; but he still believed with Garbe, that the passages which suddenly describe Brahman without reference to Kṛṣṇa (II, 72; V, 6-7-10 etc.) as well as those which glorify rituals and sacrifices (III, 9-18 etc.) were interpolated. Perhaps, some more revisions of the Gītā would have made Prof. Winternitz allow some more concessions. Dr. Belvelkar has tried to show that there are no interpolations in the Gītā. We are also tempted to agree with Dr. Belvelkar. In our view, the root-fallacy lies in believing that theism and pantheism, that qualified monism and unqualified monism are opposed to each other. At least they are not so in Indian Philosophy. The unqualified monists are absolutists and they never quarrel with qualified monists; on the other hand, they admit qualified monism as the highest appearance which we have. They only say that it is not final, that there is one step more to be taken when similarity merges in transcendental unity and all qualifications merge in the Absolute. In our view this is amply illustrated by the teachings of the Gītā.

Chapter Three

MATERIALISM

I

INTRODUCTION

THE school of Materialism in India seems to be very old. References are found to it in the epics and in the early Buddhistic literature. Garbe says: 'Several vestiges show that even in the pre-Buddhistic India proclaimers of purely materialistic doctrines appeared.'[1] It must have arisen as a protest against the excessive monkdom of the Brāhmaṇa priests. The externals of ritualism which ignored the substance and emphasized the shadow, the idealism of the Upaniṣads unsuited to the commoners, the political and the social crises rampant in that age, the exploitation of the masses by the petty rulers, monks and the wealthy class, the lust and greed and petty dissensions in an unstable society paved the way for the rise of Materialism in India in the post-Upaniṣadic and pre-Buddhistic age. But Materialism in Indian Philosophy has never been a force. Born in discontent, it soon died in serious thought. Though the materialistic way of life, the way of enjoying the pleasures of the senses and the flesh is as old as humanity itself and will surely last as long as humanity lasts, yet Materialism as metaphysics has never found favour with the Indian philosophers. Jainism and Buddhism arose immediately and supplied the ethical and spiritual background which ejected Materialism.

Bṛhaspati, a heretical teacher, is regarded as the traditional founder of this school. His Sūtra, which we have no reason to doubt, has unfortunately perished. Sometimes this Bṛhaspati is equated with the teacher of the gods who propagated materialism among the Asuras so that they might be ruined. Chārvāka, after whose name this school is so called, is said to be the chief disciple of Bṛhaspati. According to another view, Chārvāka is the name of the founder of this school. According to still another view, the word 'Chārvāka' is not a proper name, but a common name given to a materialist, and it signifies a person who believes in '*eat*, drink and be merry' (the root 'charv' means to eat), or a person who eats up his own words, or who eats up all moral and ethical considerations,[2] or a person who is 'sweet-tongued' (chāruvāk) and

[1] The Philosophy of Ancient India, p. 25. [2] charvante puṇyapāpādikam vastujātam iti Chārvākāḥ.

therefore whose doctrine is superficially attractive. Another synonym of Chārvāka is Lokāyata which means a commoner and therefore, by implication, a man of low and unrefined taste. Nāstika-Shiromaṇi or an 'arch-heretic' is another name for a materialist. In Rāmāyaṇa, they are called 'fools who think themselves to be wise and who are experts in leading people to doom and ruin'.[1] References to them are also found in Mahābhārata and Manusaṁhitā.[2] In Majjhima Nikāya, i, we find a reference to Ajitakeshakambalin, a materialist, probably so called because he must be having a blanket of hair with him, who believed only in perception and in four elements. Shāntarakṣita also refers to him as Kambalāshvatara (the man with a blanket and a mule).[3]

No original work of this school is extant with the single exception of a much later work, Tattvopaplavasiṁha of Jayarāshi Bhaṭṭa, published by the Oriental Institute of Baroda in 1940. It is therefore very difficult to have a correct idea of it. Our chief sources of information are given in the works of the other schools. But this is done only to refute materialism. Thus we find the tenets of materialism often misrepresented. The weak points in this school are exaggerated and the strong points are omitted. So we get only a faint caricature and not a true picture. The Sarva-darshana-saṅgraha gives a summary of this school, but that too seems to be based on such accounts. It is indeed very difficult to believe that Materialism which is allowed the status of an independent school of Indian Philosophy should really be so crude and degenerate as it is painted. But in the absence of the original works, we have to remain satisfied with these meagre and one-sided accounts.

II

SOURCES

IN the second Act of the allegorical play called Prabodhachandrodaya, Kṛṣṇapati Mishra sums up the teachings of Materialism thus: 'Lokāyata is the only Shāstra; perception is the only authority; earth, water, fire and air are the only elements; enjoyment is the only end of human existence; mind is only a product of matter. There is no other world: death means liberation.' Some of the important Sūtras of Bṛhaspati which are quoted in the various philosophical writings may be gleaned as follows:

(1) Earth, water, fire and air are the elements.[4]
(2) Bodies, senses and objects are the results of the different combinations of elements.[5]

[1] Rāmāyaṇa, Ayodyākāṇḍa, 100, 38. [2] Shāntiparva 1414, 1430-42; Manu III, 150, 161; IV, 30, 61, 163. [3] Tattvasaṅgraha, 1864. [4] pṛthivyaptejovāyuriti tattvāni. [5] tatsamudāye sharīrendriyaviṣayasaṁjñā.

(3) Consciousness arises from matter like the intoxicating quality of wine arising from fermented yeast.[1]
(4) The soul is nothing but the conscious body.[2]
(5) Enjoyment is the only end of human life.[3]
(6) Death alone is liberation.[4]

The Sarva-darshana-saṅgraha[5] gives the following summary of the Chārvāka position:

'There is no heaven, no final liberation, nor any soul in another world; nor do the actions of the four castes, orders etc. produce any real effect. The Agnihotra, the three Vedas, the ascetic's three staves and smearing one's self with ashes, were made by Nature as the livelihood of those destitute of knowledge and manliness. If a beast slain in the Jyotiṣṭoma rite will itself go to heaven, why then does not the sacrificer forthwith offer his own father? . . . If beings in heaven are gratified by our offering the Shrāddha here, then why not give the food down below to those who are standing on the house top? While life remains let a man live happily, let him feed on ghee (clarified butter) even though he runs in debt; when once the body becomes ashes, how can it ever return here? . . . (All the ceremonies are) a means of livelihood (for) Brāhmaṇas. The three authors of the Vedas were buffoons, knaves and demons.'

III

EPISTEMOLOGY

THE epistemological doctrine of the Chārvāka school is that perception (pratyakṣa) is the only means of valid knowledge. The validity even of inference is rejected. Inference is said to be a mere leap in the dark. We proceed here from the known to the unknown and there is no certainty in this, though some inferences may turn out to be accidentally true. A general proposition may be true in perceived cases, but there is no guarantee that it will hold true even in unperceived cases. Deductive inference is vitiated by the fallacy of *petitio principii*. It is merely an argument in a circle since the conclusion is already contained in the major premise the validity of which is not proved. Inductive inference undertakes to prove the validity of the major premise of deductive inference. But induction too is uncertain because it proceeds unwarrentedly from the known to the unknown. In order to distinguish true induction from simple enumeration, it is pointed out that the former, unlike the latter, is based on a causal relationship which means invariable

[1] kiṇvādibhyo madashaktivad vijñānam. [2] chaitanyavishiṣṭaḥ kāyaḥ puruṣaḥ. [3] kāma evaikaḥ puruṣārthaḥ. [4] maraṇamevā'pavargaḥ. [5] Chapter I.

association or vyāpti. Vyāpti therefore is the nerve of all inference. But the Chārvāka challenges this universal and invariable relationship of concomitance and regards it a mere guess-work. Perception does not prove this vyāpti. Nor can it be proved by inference, for inference itself is said to presuppose its validity. Testimony too cannot prove it, for, firstly, testimony itself is not a valid means of knowledge and secondly, if testimony proves vyāpti, inference would become dependent on testimony and then none would be able to infer anything by himself. Hence inference cannot be regarded as a valid source of knowledge. Induction is uncertain and deduction is argument in a circle. The logicians, therefore, find themselves stuck up in the mud of inference.[1]

It is interesting here to note that Shūnyavāda Buddhism and Advaita Vedānta also have rejected the ultimate validity of inference. There has been a long controversy between Udayana, the logician and Shrīharṣa, the Vedāntin regarding the validity of inference and Shīharṣa has denounced all attempts to prove the validity of inference. But there is a radical difference between the Chārvāka view on the one hand, and the Shūnyavāda and the Vedānta view on the other. The Chārvāka accepts the validity of *perception* and thereby upholds the truth of the means of valid knowledge, though he rejects all other means of knowledge as invalid. But the Shūnyavādin and the Advaitin reject the ultimate validity of *all means* of knowledge as such including perception, though they insist on the empirical validity of all means of knowledge. The distinction between ultimate and empirical knowledge is unknown to the Chārvāka. To accept the validity of perception and, at the same time and from the same standpoint, to reject the validity of inference is a thoughtless self-contradiction.

The crude Chārvāka position has been vehemently criticized by all systems of Indian Philosophy all of which have maintained the validity of at least perception and inference. To refuse the validity of inference from the empirical standpoint is to refuse to think and discuss. All thoughts, all discussions, all doctrines, all affirmations and denials, all proofs and disproofs are made possible by inference. The Chārvāka view that perception is valid and inference is invalid is itself a result of inference. The Chārvāka can understand others only through inference and make others understand him only through inference. Thoughts and ideas, not being material objects, cannot be perceived; they can only be inferred. Hence the self-refuted Charvāka position is called sheer nonsense and no system of philosophy. Perception itself which is regarded as valid by the Chārvāka is often found untrue. We perceive the earth as flat but it is almost round. We perceive the earth as static

[1] visheṣe'nugamābhāvāt sāmānye siddhasādhanāt. anumābhaṅgapaṅke'smin nimagnā vādidantinaḥ.

but it is moving round the sun. We perceive the disc of the sun as of a small size, but it is much bigger than the size of the earth. Such perceptual knowledge is contradicted by inference. Moreover, pure perception in the sense of mere sensation cannot be regarded as a means of knowledge unless conception or thought has arranged into order and has given meaning and significance to the loose threads of sense-data. The Chārvāka cannot support his views without giving reasons which presuppose the validity of inference.[1]

IV

METAPHYSICS

THE Chārvāka admits the existence of four elements—earth, water, fire and air—only and he rejects the fifth, the ether, because it is not perceived but inferred. Similarly, soul and God and the Hereafter are rejected. Everything which exists, including the mind, is due to a particular combination of these four elements. The elements are eternal, but their combinations undergo production and dissolution. Consciousness is regarded as a mere product of matter. It is produced when the elements combine in a certain proportion. It is found always associated with the body and vanishes when the body disintegrates. Just as the combination of betel, areca nut and lime produces the red colour,[2] or just as fermented yeast produces the intoxicating quality in the wine,[3] though the ingredients separately do not possess either the red colour or the intoxicating quality, similarly a particular combination of the elements produces consciousness, though the elements separately do not possess it. Consciousness is the result of an emergent and dialectical evolution. It is an epi-phenomenon, a by-product of matter. Given the four elements and their particular combination, consciousness manifests itself in the living body. 'Matter secretes mind as liver secretes bile.' The so-called soul is simply the conscious living body. God is not necessary to account for the world and the values are a foolish aberration. Sadānanda in his Vedāntasāra mentions four different materialistic schools. One identifies the soul with the gross body (sthūla sharīra); another with the senses (indriya); another with vital breaths (prāṇa) and the last with the mental organ (manas).[4] All the schools agree in regarding the soul as a product of matter. Shāntarakṣita says that the materialist Kambalāshvatara maintains the view that consciousness arises out of the material body associated with vital breaths.[5]

[1] Tattvasaṅgraha, K. 1456. [2] Sarvasiddhāntasaṅgraha, 27. [3] Sarvadarshanasaṅgraha, ch. I. [4] Vedāntasāra, p 26-27. [5] Tattvasaṅgraha, K. 1864.

Severe and contemptuous criticism has been levelled against this doctrine by all schools of Indian Philosophy. If consciousness means self-consciousness as it means in the human beings, then it cannot be identified with the living body. The animals also possess the living body, but not rational consciousness. The Chārvāka replies that it is a particular combination of the elements which obtains only in the human body that produces consciousness and that therefore living human body and consciousness are always associated together and nobody has seen consciousness apart from the living human body. But the argument is wrong. If consciousness is an essential property of the human body, it should be inseparable from it as the Chārvāka claims. But it is not. In swoons, fits, epilepsy, dreamless sleep etc. the living body is seen without consciousness. And on the other hand, in dreams, consciousness is seen without the living body. When a dreamer awakes, he disowns the dream-body but owns the dream-consciousness. The dream-objects are sublated in the waking life, but the dream-consciousness is not contradicted even in the waking life. When a person gets up after seeing a tiger in a dream, he realizes that the tiger is unreal, being only a dream-tiger, but the fact that he saw a tiger in a dream remains a fact even in the waking life. This proves that consciousness persists through the three stages of waking life, dream life and deep sleep life and is much superior to material body which is its instrument and not its cause. Moreover, the subject, the knower cannot be reduced to the object, the known, since all objects presuppose the existence of the subject. Again, the subject is the enjoyer and the object is the enjoyed and the two cannot be identified. Again, the mere fact that consciousness is not experienced without the material body, is no argument to prove that it is a mere product of matter. The eye, e.g., cannot see in darkness. Sight is not possible without light, yet light cannot be regarded as the cause of sight. Mere co-existence is not causation. The two horns of a bull which are always found together cannot be regarded as causally related. The body is a mere instrument for the manifestation of consciousness and cannot be regarded as its cause. Moreover, if consciousness is a property of the body, it must be perceived like other material properties, But it is neither smelt nor tasted nor seen nor touched nor heard. Again. if consciousness is a property of the body, then there should be no consciousness of the body, for why should the body, qualified to produce consciousness, itself stand in need of being manifested by consciousness? Further, if it is a property of matter, then like other material properties it should be known by all in the same manner and should not be private. But we find that consciousness is intimately private and consciousness of an individual cannot be shared by others. Again, if the existence of the soul surviving death cannot be *demonstrated*, its non-existence too cannot be so demonstrated.

V

ETHICS

IN Ethics the Chārvāka regards sensual pleasure as the *summum bonum* of life. Eat, drink and be merry, for once the body is reduced to ashes, there is no hope of coming back here again. There is no other world. There is no soul surviving death. Religion is the means of livelihood of the priests. All values are mere phantoms created by a diseased mind. The Ethics of the Chārvāka is a crude individual hedonism; pleasure of the senses in this life and that too of the individual is the sole end. Out of the four human values—Dharma, Artha, Kāma and Mokṣa—only Kāma or sensual pleasure is regarded as the end and Artha or wealth is regarded as the means to realize that end, while Dharma and Mokṣa are altogether rejected. Pleasure is regarded as mixed up with pain, but that is no reason why it should not be acquired. 'Nobody casts away the grain because of the husk.'[1] Should nobody cook because of beggars? Should nobody sow seeds because of animals?[2]

Rejection of the authority of the Veda and the denouncement of the Brāhmaṇa priests must have considerably helped the downfall of the Chārvākas. But it is not the sole cause, since the Jainas and the Buddhists also have been equally contemptuous towards them. Rejection of God also is not so much responsible for their downfall, because the Jainas, the Buddhists, the Sāṅkhyas and the Mīmāmsakas too do not believe in the existence of God. The denial of the soul is shared along with Materialism by some schools of Buddhism also. The assertion of the reality of matter is shared with Materialism by all schools of realistic pluralism. The theoretical reduction of the mind to the matter also cannot be regarded as the main cause to merit universal contempt that has fallen to the lot of the Chārvāka. The individual hedonism also has an appeal to the animal in man and pleasure, in fact, is desired by all. The main cause, therefore, should be sought for in the Chārvāka's denial of all human values which make life worth living. Life without values is the animal life, not the human life. Sensual pleasure is a very faint shadow of the supreme pleasure. There is a qualitative difference in pleasure. The pleasure of the pig is certainly not the same as the pleasure of the philosopher. It was for this reason that, later on, distinction was made between Crude and Refined Materialists. The celebrated work Kāmasūtra of Vātsyāyana, recommending the desirability of pleasure including sensual pleasure, yet regards Dharma or the moral values as the supreme end of life and says that acquision of pleasure should be in conformitv with Dharma. Vātsyāyana recommends a harmonious cultivation of all

[1] Sarvadarshanasaṅgraha, p. 4. [2] Kāmasūtra, I, 2, 48.

the three values of life—Dharma, Artha and Kāma. No value should be rejected, suppressed or even looked down.[1] As man after all is also a biological animal, satisfaction of the senses is as natural as the satisfaction of hunger or thirst. But because man is not merely a biological animal, but also a psychological and a moral creature, a rational and a self-conscious person capable of realizing the values, he should, therefore, instead of falling down to the level of the beast, transform the animal pleasure into human pleasure by means of urbanity, self-control, education, culture and spiritual discipline.

[1] parasparasyānupaghātakam trivargam seveta, Kāmasūtra, Ch. 2.

Chapter Four

JAINISM

I

INTRODUCTION

THE word Jainism is derived from 'Jina' which means 'conqueror' —one who has conquered his passions and desires. It is applied to the liberated souls who have conquered passions and desires and karmas and obtained emancipation. The Jainas believe in 24 Tīrthaṅkaras or 'Founders of the Faith' through whom their faith has come down from fabulous antiquity. Of these, the first was Ṛṣabhadeva and the last, Mahāvīra, the great spiritual hero, whose name was Vardhamāna. Mahāvīra, the last of the prophets, cannot be regarded as the founder of Jainism, because even before him, Jaina teachings were existent. But Mahāvīra gave a new orientation to that faith and for all practical purposes, modern Jainism may be rightly regarded as a result of his teachings. He flourished in the sixth century B.C. and was a contemporary of the Buddha. His predecessor, the 23rd Tīrthaṅkara, Pārshvanātha is also a historical personage who lived in the eighth or ninth century B.C.

II

KNOWLEDGE

THE Jainas classify knowledge into immediate (aparokṣa) and mediate (parokṣa). Immediate knowledge is further divided into Avadhi, Manaḥparyāya and Kevala; and mediate knowledge into Mati and Shruta. Perceptual knowledge which is ordinarily called immediate, is admitted to be relatively so by Jainism and therefore included in mediate and not immediate knowledge. It is included under Mati. Pure perception in the sense of mere sensation cannot rank the title of knowledge. It must be given meaning and arranged into order by conception or thought. Perceptual knowledge therefore is regarded as mediate since it presupposes the activity of thought. Mati includes both perceptual and inferential knowledge. Shruta means knowledge derived from authority. Thus Mati and Shruta which are the two kinds of mediate knowledge have as their instruments perception, inference and authority, the three Pramāṇas admitted by Jainism. Avadhi-jñāna, Manaḥ-paryāya-jñāna and Kevala-jñāna, are the three kinds of immediate knowledge which may be called extra-ordinary and extra-sensory perceptions. Avadhi is clairvoyance; Manaḥparyāya is telepathy; and Kevala is omniscience. Avadhi is direct knowledge of things even at a distance of space or time. It is called Avadhi or 'limited' because it functions within a particular area and up to a particular time. It cannot go beyond spatial and temporal limits. Manaḥ-paryāya is direct knowledge of the thoughts of others. This too is limited by spatial and temporal conditions. In both Avadhi and Manaḥparyāya, the soul has direct knowledge unaided by the senses or the mind. Hence they are called immediate, though limited. Kevala-jñāna is unlimited and absolute knowledge. It can be acquired only by the liberated souls. It is not limited by space, time or object. Besides these five kinds of right knowledge, we have three kinds of wrong knowledge—Saṁshaya or doubt, Viparyaya or mistake and Anadhyavasāya or wrong knowledge through indifference.

III

PRAMĀṆA AND NAYA

KNOWLEDGE may again be divided into two kinds—Pramāṇa or knowledge of a thing as it is, and Naya or knowledge of a thing in its relation. Naya means a standpoint of thought from which we make a statement about a thing.[1] All truth is relative to our standpoints. Partial knowledge of one of the innumerable aspects of a thing is called 'naya'.[2] Judgment based on this partial knowledge is also included in 'naya'.

There are seven 'nayas' of which the first four are called 'Artha-naya' because they relate to objects or meanings, and the last three are called 'Shabda-naya' because they relate to words. When taken as absolute, a 'naya' becomes a fallacy—'nayābhāsa'.

The first is the 'Naigama-naya'. From this standpoint we look at a thing as having both universal and particular qualities and we do not distinguish between them. It becomes fallacious when both universals and particulars are regarded as separately real and absolute, as is done by Nyāya-Vaisheṣika. The second is the 'Saṅgraha-naya'. Here we emphasize the universal qualities and ignore the particulars where they are manifested. It becomes fallacious when universals alone are treated as absolutely real and particulars are rejected as unreal, as is done by Sāṅkhya and Advaita Vedānta. The third is the 'Vyavahāra-naya' which is the conventional point of view based on empirical knowledge. Here things are taken as concrete particulars and their specific features are

[1] ekadeshavishiṣṭo'rtho nayasya viṣayo mataḥ, Nyāyāvatāra, 29. [2] nīyate gamyate arthaikadesho'neneti nayaḥ, Syādvādaratnākara, p. 8. Also Āptamīmāṁsā, X, 106.

emphasized. It becomes fallacious when particulars alone are viewed as real and universals are rejected as unreal, as is done by Materialism and Buddhist realistic pluralism. The fourth is called 'Ṛjusūtra-naya'. Here the real is identified with the momentary. The particulars are reduced to a series of moments and any given moment is regarded as real. When this partial truth is mistaken to be the whole truth, it becomes fallacious, as in some schools of Buddhism. Among the nayas which refer to words, the first is called 'Shabda-naya'. It means that a word is necessarily related to the meaning which it signifies. Every word refers either to a thing or quality or relation or action. The second is 'Samabhirūḍa-naya' which distinguishes terms according to their roots. For example, the word 'Paṅkaja' literally means 'born of mud' and signifies any creature or plant born of mud, but its meaning has been conventionally restricted to 'lotus' only. Similarly the word 'gauḥ' means 'any thing which moves', but has conventionally become restricted to signify only a 'cow'. The third is called 'Evambhūta-naya' which is a specialized form of the second. According to it, a name should be applied to an object only when its meaning is fulfilled. For example, a cow should be called 'gauḥ' only when it moves and not when it is lying down.

Each naya or point of view represents only one of the innumerable aspects possessed by a thing from which we may attempt to know or describe it. When any such partial viewpoint is mistaken for the whole truth, we have a 'nayābhāsa' or a fallacy. The 'nayas' are also distinguished as 'Dravyārthika' or from the point of view of substance which takes into account the permanent nature and unity of things, and as 'Paryāyāthika' or from the point of view of modes which takes into account the passing modifications and the diversity of things. When a thing is taken to be either as permanent only or as momentary only, either as one only or as many only, fallacies arise.

IV

ANEKĀNTAVĀDA

THE Jaina metaphysics is a realistic and relativistic pluralism. It is called Anekāntavāda or the doctrine of the manyness of reality. Matter (pudgala) and spirit (jīva) are regarded as separate and independent realities. There are innumerable material atoms and innumerable individual souls which are all separately and independently real. And each atom and each soul possesses innumerable aspects of its own. A thing has got an infinite number of characteristics of its own.[1] Every object possesses innumerable positive and negative characters. It is not possible for us, ordinary people, to know all the qualities of a thing. We can know

[1] anantadharmakam vastu. anantadharmātmakameva tattvam—Anyayoga, p. 22.

only some qualities of some things. To know all the aspects of a thing is to become omniscient. Therefore the Jainas say that he who knows all the qualities of one thing, knows all the qualities of all things, and he who knows all the qualities of all things, knows all the qualities of one thing.[1] Human knowledge is necessarily relative and limited and so are all our judgments. This epistemological and logical theory of the Jainas is called 'Syādvāda'. As a matter of fact, both Anekāntavāda and Syādvāda are the two aspects of the same teaching—realistic and relativistic pluralism. They are like the two sides of the same coin. The metaphysical side that reality has innumerable characters is called Anekāntavāda, while the epistemological and logical side that we can know only some aspects of reality and that therefore all our judgments are necessarily relative, is called Syādvāda.

A thing has many characters and it exists independently. It is called substance (dravya). It persists in and through all attributes and modes. Substance is defined as that which possesses qualities and modes.[2] Out of these innumerable qualities of a substance, some are permanent and essential, while others are changing and accidental. The former are called attributes (guṇa) and the latter modes (paryāya). Substance and attributes are inseparable because the latter are the permanent essence of the substance and cannot remain without it. Modes or modifications are changing and accidental. Reality is a unity-and-difference or difference-and-unity. Viewed from the point of view of substance, a thing is one and permanent and real; viewed from the point of view of modes, it is many and momentary and unreal. Jainism here becomes a 'theological mean, between Brahmanism and Early Buddhism'. Brahmanism emphasizes the one, the permanent, the real; Early Buddhism emphasizes the many, the changing, the unreal; Jainism points out that both are the two sides of the same thing. Substance, therefore, is also defined as that which possesses the three characteristics of production, destruction and permanence.[3] Substance has its unchanging essence and therefore is permanent. But it also has its changing modes and therefore is subject to origination and decay. To mistake any one-sided and partial view as the whole truth is to commit the fallacy of Ekāntavāda. As Jainism takes into account all these partial views, it is called Anekāntavāda.

V

SYĀDVĀDA

SYĀDVĀDA which is also called Sapta-bhaṅgī-naya is the theory of relativity of knowledge. Sapta-bhaṅgī-naya means 'dialectic of the seven

[1] eko bhāvaḥ sarvathā yena dṛṣṭaḥ sarve bhāvāḥ sarvathā tena dṛṣṭāḥ. [2] guṇa-paryāyavad dravyam.—Tattvārthasūtra, V, 37. [3] utpādavyayadhrauvyasaṁyuktam sat.—Ibid, V, 29.

steps' or 'the theory of seven-fold judgment'. The word 'syāt' literally means probable, perhaps, may be. And Syādvāda is sometimes translated as the theory of probability or the doctrine of the may-be. But it is not in the literal sense of probability that the word syāt is used here. Probability suggests scepticism and Jainism is not scepticism. Sometimes the word 'syāt' is translated as 'somehow'. But this too smacks of agnosticism and Jainism, again, is not agnosticism. The word 'syāt' is used here in the sense of the relative and the correct translation of Syādvāda is the theory of Relativity of knowledge. Reality has infinite aspects which are all relative and we can know only some of these aspects. All our judgments, therefore, are necessarily relative, conditional and limited. 'Syāt' or 'Relatively speaking' or 'Viewed from a particular view-point which is necessarily related to other view-points' must precede all our judgments. Absolute affirmation and absolute negation both are wrong. All judgments are conditional. This is not a self-contradictory position because the very nature of reality is indeterminate and infinitely complex and because affirmation and negation both are not made from the same standpoint. The difficulty of predication is solved by maintaining that the subject and the predicate are identical from the point of view of substance and different from the point of view of modes. Hence categorical or absolute predication is ruled out as erroneous. All judgments are double-edged. Affirmation presupposes negation as much as negation presupposes affirmation. The infinitely complex reality (ananta-dharmakam vastu) admits of all opposite predicates from different standpoints. It is real as well as unreal (sadasadātmakam). It is universal as well as particular (vyāvṛty-anugamātmakam). It is permanent as well as momentary (nityānityas-varūpam). It is one as well as many (anekamekātmakam).[1] Viewed from the point of view of substance, it is real, universal, permanent and one; viewed from the point of view of modes, it is unreal, particular, momentary and many.[2] The Jainas are fond of quoting the old story of the six blind men and the elephant. The blind men put their hands on the different parts of the elephant and each tried to describe the whole animal from the part touched by him. Thus the man who caught the ear said the elephant was like a country-made fan; the person touching the leg said the elephant was like a pillar; the holder of the trunk said it was like a python; the feeler of the tail said it was like a rope; the person who touched the side said the animal was like a wall; and the man who touched the forehead said the elephant was like the breast. And all the six quarrelled among themselves, each one asserting that his description alone was correct. But he who can see the whole elephant can easily know that each blind man feels only a part of the elephant which he mistakes to be the whole animal. Almost all philosophical,

[1] Anyayogavyavachchedikā, 25. [2] Ibid, 23.

ideological and religious differences and disputes are mainly due to mistaking a partial truth for the whole truth. Our judgments represent different aspects of the manysided reality and can claim only partial truth. This view makes Jainism catholic, broad-minded and tolerant. It teaches respect for others' points of view.

We can know an object in three ways through durnīti, naya and pramāṇa. Mistaking a partial truth for the whole and the absolute truth is called 'durnīti' or 'bad judgment', e.g., the insistence that an object is absolutely real (sadeva). A mere statement of a relative truth without calling it either absolute or relative is called 'naya' or 'judgment', e.g., the statement that an object is real (sat). A statement of a partial truth knowing that it is only partial, relative and conditional and has possibility of being differently interpreted from different points of view is called 'pramāṇa' or 'valid judgment' (syāt sat).[1] Every naya in order to become pramāṇa must be qualified by syāt. Syāt is said to be the symbol of truth.[2] It is relative and successive knowledge.[3] It removes all contradictions among different points of view.[4] To reject 'syāt' is to embrace unwarranted absolutism which is directly contradicted by experience.[5]

Everything exists from the point of view of its own substance, space, time and form and it does not exist from the point of view of other's substance, space, time and form. When we say 'This table exists', we cannot mean that this table exists absolutely and unconditionally. Our knowledge of the table is necessarily relative. The table has got innumerable characteristics out of which we can know only some. The table exists in itself as an absolutely real and infinitely complex reality; only our knowledge of it is relative. For us the table must exist in its own matter as made of wood, in its own form as having a particular shape, length, breadth and height, at a particular space and at a particular time. It does not exist in other matter, other form and at other space and time. So a table is both existent and non-existent viewed from different standpoints and there is no contradiction in it.

The Jaina logic distinguishes seven forms of judgment. Each judgment, being relative, is preceded by the word 'syāt'. This is Syādvāda or Sapta-bhaṅgī-naya. The seven steps are as follows:—

(1) Syādasti: Relatively, a thing is real.
(2) Syānnāsti: Relatively, a thing is unreal.
(3) Syādasti nāsti: Relatively, a thing is both real and unreal.
(4) Syādavaktavyam: Relatively, a thing is indescribable.
(5) Syādasti cha avaktavyam: Relatively, a thing is real and is indescribable.

[1] sadeva sat syāt sad iti tridhārtho mīyeta durnīti-naya-pramāṇaiḥ, Ibid, 28. [2] syātkāraḥ satyalāñchhanaḥ.—Āptamīmāṁsā, X, 112. [3] kramabhāvi cha yajjñānam syādvādanayasaṁskṛtam, X, 101. [4] Ibid, I, 20. [5] Ibid, I, 7.

(6) Syānnāsti cha avaktavyam: Relatively, a thing is unreal and is indescribable.

(7) Syādasti cha nāsti cha avaktavyam: Relatively, a thing is real, unreal and indescribable.

From the point of view of one's own substance, everything is, while from the point of view of other's substance, everything is not. As we have just remarked that we can know a thing in relation to its own matter, form, space and time as a positive reality, while in relation to other's matter, form, space and time it becomes a negative entity. When we affirm the two different stand-points *successively* we get the third judgment—a thing is both real and unreal (of course in two different senses). If we affirm or deny both existence and non-existence *simultaneously* to any thing, if we assert or negate the two different aspects of being and non-being together, the thing baffles all description. It becomes indescribable, i.e., either both real and unreal simultaneously or neither real nor unreal. This is the fourth judgment. The remaining three are the combinations of the fourth with the first, second and third respectively.

VI

CRITICISM OF SYĀDVĀDA

THE Buddhists and the Vedāntins have criticized Syādvāda as a self-contradictory doctrine. Taking the word 'syāt' in its popular sense of probability, they have found it easy to condemn this theory. Contradictory attributes like existence and non-existence cannot belong to the same thing in the same sense. Like light and darkness they cannot remain together. Dharmakīrti says: These shameless and naked Jainas make contradictory statements like a mad man.[1] Shāntarakṣita says that Syādvāda which combines the real and the unreal, the existent and the non-existent, the one and the many, the identity and the difference, the universal and the particular, is like a mad man's cry.[2] Similarly, Shaṅkarāchārya also says that Syādvāda appears like the words of a lunatic. You cannot blow hot and cold in the same breath. Unity and plurality, permanence and momentariness, reality and unreality cannot remain at the same time and in the same thing, like light and darkness.[3] Rāmānuja also says that contradictory attributes such as existence and non-existence, like light and darkness, can never be combined.

But these criticisms are off the mark. Jainism never says that contradictory attributes belong to the same thing at the same time and in the same sense. Anekāntavāda asserts that the real has infinite attributes

[1] Pramāṇa-Vārtika, I, 182-185. [2] Tattva-Saṅgraha, 311-327. [3] Shārīraka-Bhāṣya, II, 2, 33.

because it is an identity-and-difference and that though, from the standpoint of substance, it is a unity, permanent and real, yet from the standpoint of modes, it is a plurality, changing and unreal. A thing is regarded as real from the view-point of its own matter, form, space and time; and it is regarded as unreal, not from the same standpoint, but from the view-point of other's matter, form, space and time. There is no room for contradiction here.[1] The very nature of reality is infinitely complex and it, being an identity-and-difference, admits of contradictory attributes from different points of view which are all partial and relative. Existence, non-existence, both existence and non-existence successively, and indescribability are attributed to a thing from different view-points. Not understanding this and fearing imaginary contradictions and mistaking partial and relative views as absolute, fools fall from the right position.[2]

The Vedāntin levels another charge against Syādvāda. He says that no theory can be sustained by mere probability. If everything is probable, then Syādvāda, by its own assertion, becomes only probable. The Jainas might retort that Syādvāda does not mean the theory of probability, that it is not self-condemned scepticism, but it means the theory of relativity of knowledge. All judgments are relative and conditional and all truth is partial. But even now, the objection of Shaṅkarāchārya stands with full force. Relativity itself cannot be sustained without the Absolute. If all truth is partial, then Syādvāda itself is only partially true and therefore partially false. Relativity itself is related to the Absolute and presupposes its existence. The fact that all our judgments are relative requires us to presuppose an Absolute in which all the relatives fall and through which they are manifested.

When we examine the seven steps in the Syādvāda, we find that the last three are superflous and redundant. They are merely the combination of the fourth with the first, second and third respectively. If we take to combinations, we may have as many steps as we like. The retort of Kumārila that thus instead of seven steps you may have hundred steps[3] seems to be quite right to us. Hence only the first four steps are real. These are not the inventions of the Jainas. They are borrowed from the famous 'Chatuṣkoṭis' or the four categories of thought accepted by Buddhism and Vedānta. It is significant to note in this connection that the doctrine of Syādvāda in its fully developed form of seven steps is found perhaps for the first time in Kundakunda's Panchāstikāya and Pravachanasāra.[4] Two passages have been traced in the Jaina canon which contain a reference to the Syādvāda. They are in the Bhagavatīsūtra

[1] svarūpa-dravya-kṣetra-kāla-bhāvaiḥ sattvam, pararūpa-dravya-kṣetra-kāla-bhāvais tvasattvam. tadā kva virodhā-vakāshaḥ?—Syādvādamañjarī, p. 176-7. [2] Anyayoga, 24. [3] saptabhaṅgīprasādena shatabhaṅgyapi jāyate. [4] siya atthi ṇatthi uhayam avvattavvam puṇo ya tattidayam. davvam khu sattabhaṅgam ādesavaseṇa saṁbhavadi, Panchāstikāyasāra, 14.

and are quoted by Mallavādi in his Naya-chakra. One reference runs thus—'Relatively, the soul is knowledge; relatively, the soul is ignorance';[1] and the other—'Relatively, the soul exists; relatively, the soul does not exist; relatively, the soul is indescribable'.[2] Here at the most only three steps are mentioned. In the Buddhist 'Dīgha-nikāya' and 'Majjhima-nikāya' we find references to the four categories of thought—'is', 'is not', 'both is and is not', and 'neither is nor is not'.[3] In our opinion, therefore, Syādvāda is definitely influenced by the Anirvachanīyatā-vāda of Shūnyavāda Buddhism and Advaita Vedānta.

Jainism rightly points out that all our knowledge is necessarily relative, conditional and partial. All human knowledge is empirical and therefore relative. The Buddhist doctrine of Dependent Origination (pratītyasamutpāda) also tells us that all things have dependent and conditional origination and are therefore relative. Shūnyavāda, Vijñānavāda and Advaita Vedānta have always maintained the necessarily relative character of our empirical knowledge. But while they have made a distinction between the empirical and the absolute, the phenomenal and the noumenal, the conditional and the unconditional, the Samvṛti and the Paramārtha or the Paratantra and the Parinișpanna or the Vyavahāra and the Paramārtha, Jainism has bluntly refused to make any such distinction. It refuses to rise higher than the relative. It has a bias against absolutism and in favour of common sense realistic pluralism. Being wedded to common sense realism and having pinned its faith to seeming pluralism, Jainism has conveniently forgotten the implications of its own logic and has refused to rise above the relative.

Syādvāda gives us only seven scattered forms of judgments and makes no attempt to synthesize them. These seven forms of judgment are like scattered pearls or beads or flowers. They cannot be woven into a philosophical garland in the absence of the Absolute which alone can act as the thread. The relatives are bound together in the Absolute. It is the Absolute which gives life, meaning and significance to the relatives. If you throw away the Absolute, you cannot have even the relatives. If you reject the noumenal, you cannot retain even the phenomenal. Syādvāda itself becomes relative and partial. The Jainas do not give us a real identity-*in*-difference. What they give is merely identity *plus* difference. But reality is not a mathematical sum total of partial viewpoints. The Absolute is not all the relatives put together. The Jainas forget that organic synthesis and not arithmetical addition is the secret of reality. They forget their prejudice against absolutism when they *absolutely* assert that their teaching alone represents the whole truth, while all other systems give partial truths. Some schools teach Being, Permanence, Identity and Universality, while others teach Non-being,

[1] āyā siya ṇāṇe siya aṇṇāṇe. [2] siya āyā, siya no āyā, siya avattavvam āyā. [3] See, e.g., 'Sāmaññaphalasutta', Brahmajālasutta.

Momentariness, Plurality and Particularly. The Jainas have combined both, thinking that a mere combination of partial truths will give them the whole truth. But this is not the way of reaching truth. The Jainas make a distinction between sakalādesha and vikalādesha. The scattered partial truths are called vikalādesha. But when they are put together they become the whole truth which is called sakalādesha. Like the Shūnyavādins and the Vedāntins, the Jainas also have criticized one view by advancing the arguments of its opposite view and the latter by means of the arguments given by the former. Thus they criticize permanence through the arguments in favour of momentariness and the latter through the arguments supporting the former. They criticize satkāryavāda through asatkāryavāda and vice versa. And so on. But while the Shūnyavādins and the Vedāntins synthesize the two partial views into a higher reality, the Jainas simply put them together and think they have reached the whole truth thus impartially. All other views are partial and defective; but if they are put down together, they become the Jaina view and Lo! by the magic lamp of Aladin all their defects vanish overnight and they represent the whole truth! Thus Yashovijaya says that the Jaina view is evidently the best because it has woven together all the nayas in it.[1] But the difficulty is that the nayas have not been woven together; they have been simply put together. The Absolute is the only thread which can weave them together and it has been wantonly thrown away by Jainism. He further says that Anekāntavāda is impartial and treats all the nayas equally like one's own children.[2] This impartiality is rather dangerous as it goes against the qualitative differences in the nayas. Hemachandra also says that other systems are relative and partial and fight against one another, while Jainism alone is impartial because it puts all the nayas together.[3] It is forgotten that a mere pooling together of the nayas by no means removes their contradictions. For this a proper synthesis is required which will unify all the nayas, preserve their merits and remove their defects. In the absence of the Absolute, this synthesis is an impossibility for Jainism. Again, to say that other systems, being relative and partial, are like fire-flies giving only broken light, while Jainism alone, being the complete truth, is like the luminous sun, is to make a half-hearted confession of Absolutism, for by a mere addition of the light of innumerable fire-flies you cannot have the light of the sun.[4] So far as other systems are concerned, they are repeatedly accused by the Jainas of committing the fallacy of mistaking a relative truth to be the absolute truth. They are called Ekāntavāda. Jainism alone is said to be really relative—Anekāntavāda, and relativity is proclaimed to be the only truth. Thus, by its own assertion Jainism becomes partially false. And in practice this relativity is often forgotten. Jainism is often

[1] sarvair nayair gumphitā.—Adhyātmasāra. [2] Ibid, p. 61. [3] Anyayoga, 30. [4] Ayogavyavachchedikā, 8.

made an exception and absolute validity is claimed for it. While all other teachings are *relatively real*, the Jaina teaching is held to be *absolutely real*. This goes against the Jaina doctrine itself. If relativity is the only truth, how can the Jaina teaching be absolutely true? How can a mere bundle of the relatives become itself Absolute? Hemachandra, for example, commits this fallacy when in his religious zeal he proclaims in a loud and solemn voice before his opponents that Vītarāga is the *only* God and that Anekānta is the *only* philosophy.[1] Is it not a confession of Absolutism? Akalaṅka, Vidyānanda, Siddhasena, Samantabhadra, Haribhadra, Vādideva, Hemachandra, Malliṣeṇa and others have criticized and refuted the views of other systems. It is interesting to note that their objections are almost the same as those which are used by the Buddhist and the Vedāntin dialecticians, so far as other systems are concerned. For example, the Jainas say: If the effect pre-exists in its cause, it is already an existent fact and needs no repeated birth; if the effect does not pre-exist in its cause, it is like a sky-flower and cannot be produced. If reality is eternal and permanent, change becomes impossible, for how can the eternal change? If reality is momentary and fleeting, change becomes impossible, for what is that which changes? And so on. The whole offshoot of these dialectics is that without Anekānta we cannot explain reality; without Anekānta, pain and pleasure, actions and fruits, bondage and liberation, good and evil, existence and non-existence, one and many, permanence and change, universal and particular—all become impossible. Hence the opponents are out to destroy the world which is to be preserved only by the Jainas.[2] The Buddhists and the Vedāntins also claim the same thing for themselves.[3] They say that all objects of thought are necessarily relative and so if reality is to be experienced, it can be realized only by transcending the categories of thought and merging them in the Absolute. The Absolute is immanent in all the categories and gives life and meaning to them. Everything throbs with its presence. The whole world is the manifestation of the Absolute. Hence if the reality of the world is to be preserved, it can be done only by transcending the world, otherwise even the empirical will be lost to us. The relatives are preserved only because they are synthesized in the Absolute. The Jainas, on the other hand, want to preserve the relatives by throwing away the Absolute and by combining the relatives together. The Jainas, the Buddhists and the Vedāntins all join in saying that the world is not absolutely real and that it is not absolutely unreal also. But whereas the Buddhists and the Vedāntins say that because the world is *neither real nor unreal*, it is indescribable and false, and ultimately it is non-different

[1] na Vītarāgāt paramasti daivatam na chāpyanekāntamṛte nayasthitiḥ, Ibid, 2.8
[2] Anyayoga, 27. Āptamīmāṁsā, III, 40. [3] Mādhyamika-Kārikā, XXIV, 36. Chandrakīrti's Com. on MK., p. 67. Brahma-siddhi, p. 9.

from the Absolute where it is transcended, the Jainas say that because the world is neither absolutely real nor absolutely unreal, it is *both real and unreal* from different points of view, They refuse to go higher. But putting together different standpoints does not solve the contradictions of the world. The Jainas criticize the conception of the indescribable as self-contradictory.[1] They have forgotten that they themselves have made a place for the indescribable in the fourth step of the sapta-bhaṅgī. The avaktavya is also the anirvachanīya which is neither real nor unreal. Moreover, the Buddhists and the Vedāntins also agree that the indescribable world is self-contradictory and if you want to remove the contradiction, you have to transcend the world. If you throw away the Absolute in your zeal to preserve the relative, you lose not only the Absolute but also the relative. And this is exactly what the Jainas have done.

The conception of Kevala-jñāna or absolute knowledge is a half-hearted confession of Absolutism made by Jainism in spite of its Syādvāda. The highest kind of knowledge is called Kevala-jñāna which is pure, full, perfect, direct, immediate and intuitive omniscience. It constitutes the essence of the soul in its pure and undefiled condition. As it is held to be perfect and intuitive omniscience, it is supra-empirical, absolute and transcendental. This is certainly an admission of Absolutism. Though the Jainas have always explicitly rejected the distinction between the empirical and the transcendental, yet they have by implication always admitted it. Ousted from the front-door, it has crept in through the back-door. The distinction is vital and has always been maintained in some form or the other by all great philosophers of the world. The *Kato* and *Ano* of Heraclitus; the opinion and truth of Parmenides; the world and the form of Socrates; the sense and the idea of Plato; the matter and the mover of Aristotle; the modes and the substance of Spinoza; the phenomenal and the noumenal of Kant; the illusion and the absolute of Hegel; the appearance and reality of Bradley; the Preyas and the Shreyas; the Aparā Vidyā and Parā Vidyā of the Upaniṣads; the Samvṛti and Paramārtha of Shūnyavāda; the Parikalpita and Pariniṣpanna of Vijñānavāda; the Vyavahāra and Paramārtha of Vedānta are some instances in point. In Jainism this distinction appears as the distinction between the indirect (parokṣa) and the direct (aparokṣa) knowledge (perceptual knowledge which is ordinarily regarded as direct, is here called indirect); between Syādvāda, the relative knowledge and Kevalajñāna, the absolute knowledge; between Naya (the relative view point) and Pramāṇa (knowledge of the thing-in-itself); between Vyavahāra or Samvyavahāra or Vyavaharaṇa and Paramārtha; between Abhūtārtha and Bhūtārtha; between Paryāya and Dravya.

[1] Āptamīmāṁsā, III, 49-50.

The fundamental fallacy of Jainism that the whole truth means only a mathematical sum total of relative truths vitiates their Kevala-jñāna also. The absolute knowledge is viewed as a hodge-podge bundle of the relative tit-bits. The strong bias in favour of pluralistic realism and against absolutism prevents Jainism to realize the implications of its own logic. They remain content with common sense pluralism and feel no need for any synthesis. Yet Absolutism and synthetical philosophy raise their heads here and there in Jainism. Dr. S. Radhākrishnan rightly remarks: 'In our opinion the Jaina logic leads us to a monistic idealism, and so far as the Jainas shrink from it they are untrue to their own logic. . . . The theory of relativity cannot be logically sustained without the hypothesis of an absolute. . . . If Jaina logic does not recognize the need for this principle . . . it is because it takes a partial view for the whole truth. . . . The Jainas cannot logically support a theory of pluralism.'[1] Prof. Hiriyanna also says: 'The half-hearted character of the Jaina inquiry is reflected in the seven-fold mode of predication (saptabhaṅgī), which stops at giving us the several partial views together, without attempting to overcome the opposition in them by a proper synthesis. . . . The reason for it, if it is not prejudice against Absolutism, is the desire to keep close to common beliefs.'[2]

We have already pointed out that the distinction between Parokṣa and Aparokṣa, between Syādvāda and Kevala-jñāna, between Naya and Pramāṇa, between Paryāya and Dravya, between Abhūtārtha and Bhūtartha, between Vyavahāra and Paramārtha is a half-hearted confession of Absolutism made by Jainism. But as outwardly, the Jainas undermine the distinction between the phenomenal and the noumenal, what they give us as the absolute knowledge is in fact not really absolute, but a crude caricature of the absolute, being merely a sum total of the relatives. Thus Samantabhadra says that Syādvāda and Kevala-jñana both illuminate all reality; the only difference between them is that Syādvāda does so in a relative and indirect manner, while Kevala-jñāna does it in the absolute and direct manner.[3] Kevala-jñāna illuminates all things simultaneously and intuitively, while Syādvāda does so successively and partially.[4] Hemachandra says that other systems, being relative and partial, fight against each other and destroy each other, while Jainism which gives the whole truth remains undefeated.[5] This reminds us of Gauḍapāda's remark that it is only the dualists who fight against one another in order to prove their respective theses, while Advaita quarrels with none.[6] Vardhamāna Mahāvīra takes the place of the Absolute and is identified with Pure Self. He is beyond senses, speech

[1] Indian Philosophy, p. 305, 306, 308. [2] Outlines of Indian Philosophy, p. 172, 173. [3] syādvādakevalajñāne sarvatattvaprakāshane. bhedaḥ sakṣādasākṣāchcha hyavastvanyatamam bhavet, Āptamīmāṁsā, X, 105. [4] tattvajñānam pramāṇam te yugapat sarvabhāsanam. kramabhāvi cha yajjñānam syādvādanayasaṁskṛtam. [5] Anyayoga, 26. [6] Māṇḍūkya-Kārikā, III, 17.

and thought and is the indescribable pure consciousness undefiled by any impurity.[1] Just as all water comes from the ocean through the clouds, flows into the form of rivers and ultimately merges through the rivers into the ocean, similarly all relative view-points arise from the Absolute and ultimately merge themselves in the Absolute. Just as the ocean is implicit in the rivers but not explicitly visible, though the rivers explicitly merge in the ocean, similarly the Absolute is implicit in the relative view-points which explicitly merge in the Absolute.[2] Here the Absolute asserts itself in Jainism and Siddhasena has given vent to it. Nobody would like to deny Anekāntavāda and Syādvāda provided they are legitimately restricted to the phenomenal only.[3] No doubt, the phenomenal world cannot be rightly explained without them, but they themselves cannot be rightly explained without the Absolute. Kundakunda often approaches Absolutism. He clearly states the distinction between the empirical and the absolute view-points. Vyavahāra is empirically true and ultimately false; it is only the Shuddha-naya, the Paramārtha which is ultimately true.[4] Kundakunda goes to the extent of frankly saying that even Knowledge, Conduct and Faith, the three Jewels of Jainism, which are regarded by Umāsvāmī as the Path of Liberation,[5] are true only from the empirical standpoint; from the absolute standpoint, there is neither Knowledge nor Conduct nor Faith, because the ultimate knower is the Pure Self.[6] The importance of the empirical standpoint lies in the fact that it is the only means available to us. We can go to the higher only through the lower. Without vyavahāra, Paramārtha cannot be taught, just as a Mlechha cannot be talked to except through his language.[7] The commentator Amṛtachandra explains that vyavahāra should be valued as the only means to reach Paramārtha, but it should not be treated as the end, for Paramārtha should not be degraded to vyavahāra.[8] Nāgārjuna and Āryadeva, the Shūnyavādins, also say exactly the same thing.[9] Amṛtachandra further says that just as a baby who has not yet learnt to walk requires the helping hand of an adult, but when he has grown up and has learnt to walk, no longer requires the helping hand, similarly a person, who remains on the empirical plane, needs the empirical standpoint, but when he has arisen higher to the Absolute, he sees everything as a

[1] Anyayoga, 1; Ayoga, 1. [2] udadhāviva sarvasindhavaḥ samudīrṇāstvayi nātha dṛṣṭayaḥ. na cha tāsu bhavān pradṛshyate pravibhaktāsu saritsvivodadhiḥ, Siddhasena. Cf. rūchīnām vaichitryād etc. in Mahimna-stotra; Muṇḍaka, II, 8; Gītā, XI, 28; Raghuvaṁsha, X, 2. [3] jena vinā logassa vivahāro savvahā na nivvaḍai, Siddhasena. [4] vavahāro'bhūyattho bhūyattho desido du suddhaṇao.—Samayasāra. [5] samyag-darshana-jñāna-chāritrāṇi mokṣamārgaḥ.—Tattvārthasūtra. [6] vavahāreṇu vadissai ṇāṇissa charitta dassaṇam ṇāṇam. navi ṇāṇam na charittam na dassaṇam jāṇago suddho.—Samayasāra, 7. [7] jaha ṇavi sakkamaṇajjo aṇajjabhāsam vinā ugāheum. taha vavahāreṇa vinā paramatthu vayesaṇamasakkam.—Ibid, 8. [8] Ibid, p. 20. [9] vyavahāramanāshritya paramārtho na deshyate—MK., XXIV, 10. nānyayā bhāṣayā mlechchaḥ shakyo grāhayitum yathā. na laukikamṛte lokaḥ shakyo grāhayitum tathā.—Chatuḥshataka, K, 194.

manifestation of Consciousness and realizes that nothing except Pure Consciousness is.[1] The Nayas do not arise; the Pramāṇas are set at rest; the Nikṣepachakra fades into nothingness; what else can we say? When this self-luminous Absolute which transcends all is directly realized through intuition, *all duality* vanishes.[2] He who knows the self as neither bound nor defiled, neither one nor many, knows the whole teaching of the Jina.[3] The essence of the self lies in the fact that it transcends all relative view-points.[4] Those who have left the partiality of the relative view-points far behind, who ever dwell in the essential nature of the self, who have acquired mental peace by transcending the meshes of the categories of finite thought, they alone really drink nectar, they alone really enjoy immortality.[5] He who has realized the truth and has arisen above the relative view-points of the intellect, always sees the eternal consciousness and *nothing but consciousness*.[6] Ignorance is the cause of bondage and pure knowledge of the self which transcends all difference is the cause of liberation.[7] He who sleeps over Vyavahāra awakes in Paramārtha, and he who is awake in Vyavahāra sleeps over Paramārtha.[8] Is this not Absolutism?

VII

CATEGORIES

WE have seen that substance, according to Jainism, has infinite characters and is subject to production, destruction and permanence. The whole universe is brought under the two everlasting, uncreated, eternal and co-existing categories which are called Jiva and Ajiva. Jiva means the conscious spirit and Ajīva means the unconscious non-spirit. Ajīva includes not only matter which is called 'Pudgala', but also space, motion, rest and time. Spirit, matter, motion, rest and space (respectively called jīva, pudgala, dharma, adharma and ākāsha) are described as asti-kāyâ dravyas or substances which possess constituent parts extending in space; while time (kāla) is the only anasti-kāya dravya which has no extension in space.

Jiva is generally the same as the Ātman or the Puruṣa in other pluralistic schools with this important difference that it is identified with life of which consciousness is said to be the essence. Like the monads of

[1] tadapi paramamartham chichchamatkāramātram paravirahitamantaḥpashyatām naiṣa kiñchit—Com. on Samayasāra, p. 29. [2] kimaparamabhidadhmo dhāmni sarvaṅkaṣe'smin anubhavamupayāte bhāti na dvaitameva—Ibid, p. 35. [3] jo passadi appāṇam abaddhaputṭham aṇaṇṇamavisesam apadesasuttamajjham passadi jiṇasāsaṇam savvam.—Samayasāra, 15. [4] pakkhātikkanto puṇa bhaṇṇdi jo so samayasāro.—Ibid, 142. [5] vikalpajālachyutashāntachittās ta eva sākṣād amṛtam pibanti—Com. on Samayasāra, p. 202. [6] yastattvavedī chyutapakṣapātas tasyāsti nityam khalu chichchideva. [7] ajñānameva bandhahetuḥ, jñānameva mokṣahetuḥ—Ibid, p. 223. tato nirastasa-mastabhedam ātmasvabhāvabhūtam jñānamevaikam ālambyam—Ibid, 291. [8] Mok-ṣaprābhṛta, 31. Cf. Gītā, II, 69.

Leibnitz, the Jīvas of Jainism are qualitatively alike and only quantitatively different and the whole universe is literally filled with them. The jīvas are divided first into those who are liberated (mukta) and those who are bound (baddha). The bound souls are further divided into mobile (trasa) and immobile (sthāvara). The latter live in the atoms of earth, water, fire and air and in the vegetable kingdom and have only one sense—that of touch. The mobile souls are again classified as those who have two senses (e.g. worms), three senses (e.g. ants), four senses (e.g. wasps, bees etc.) and five senses (e.g. higher animals and men).

Consciousness is regarded as the essence of the soul (chetanālakṣaṇo jīvaḥ). Every soul from the lowest to the highest possesses consciousness. The degrees of consciousness may vary according to the obstacles of karma. The lowest souls which inhabit material atoms appear to be lifeless and unconscious, but in fact life and consciousness are present in them though in a dormant form. Purest consciousness is found in the emancipated souls where there is no shred of karma. All souls are really alike. The degrees of consciousness are due merely to the karma-obstacles. The soul in its intrinsic nature possesses Infinite Faith, Infinite Knowledge, Infinite Bliss and Infinite Power.[1] In the case of the bound souls these characteristics are obscured by karma. A jīva is a real knower (jñātā), a real agent (kartā) and a real experient (bhoktā). It is included in the astikāya dravyas because its constituents possess extension in space. But it does not extend in space like matter. It is like the light. Just as the light fills the space where it is burning and just as many lights may remain in the same place without coming into conflict with one another, similarly the soul fills the space and many souls may remain together without any conflict. Though itself formless, it takes the form of the body which it illuminates. The soul of an ant is as big as the body of it and the soul of an elephant is as big as the elephant itself. The soul is coextensive with the body. Though we find souls in this world as embodied and as possessing the senses and the manas which help the souls to know, yet really the body, the senses and the manas are obstructions placed by karma and hinder the souls in their direct knowledge. Knowledge is not a property of the soul; it is its very essence. Every soul, therefore, can directly and immediately know everything if it is not obstructed by matter. Freedom from matter means omniscience and emancipation.

The category of Ajīva is divided into matter (pudgala), space (ākāsha), motion (dharma), rest (adharma) and time (kāla). They are all without life and consciousness. Time is anastikāya because it does not extend in space. It is infinite. It is not perceived, but inferred from its charac-

[1] ananta darshana, ananta jñāna, ananta sukha and ananta vīrya are called ananta-chatuṣṭaya.

teristics which make possible continuity (vartanā), modification (pariṇāma), activity (kriyā), 'now' or 'new' (paratva), and 'then' or 'old' (aparatva). It is one and indivisible. Some Jaina writers have distinguished between real (pāramarthika) and empirical (vyāvahārika) time. The former makes continuity or duration possible and is infinite, one and indivisible. The latter can be divided into moments, hours, days, months and years and makes other changes, except duration, possible.

Like time, space is also infinite, eternal and imperceptible. It is inferred as the condition of extension. All substances except time have extension and extension is afforded only by space. Space itself is not extension; it is the locus of extension. Two kinds of space are distinguished. In one, motion is possible and it is called Lokākāsha or filled space; in the other, motion is not possible and it is called Alokākāsha or empty space. The former contains all the worlds where life and movement are; the latter stretches itself infinitely beyond the former. At the summit of Lokākāsha is Siddhashilā, the Abode of the Liberated Souls.

Dharma and Adharma are used here not in their popular sense of merit and demerit, but in the technical sense of the conditions of movement and rest. Like space and time, these also are eternal and imperceptible. They are inferred as the conditions which help motion and rest respectively. They are formless and passive. Dharma cannot generate motion nor can Adharma arrest it. They only help or favour motion or rest, like water helping the motion of a fish or like earth supporting things which rest on it.

Matter is called Pudgala which means that which is liable to integration and disintegration (pūrayanti galanti cha). This word is used in Buddhism in the sense of a soul, while in Jainism it is used for matter. An atom (aṇu) is supposed to be the smallest part of matter which cannot be further divided. Compound objects (saṅghāta or skandha) of the material world including senses, mind (manas) and breath are the combinations of atoms. Matter possesses the four qualities of colour, taste, smell and touch. Sound is regarded not as a quality, as other systems have done, but only as a modification (pariṇāma) of matter. These atoms are supposed to house the souls. Like the ancient Greek atomists Democritus and Leucippus and unlike the Nyāya-Vaisheṣika thinkers, the Jainas do not maintain any qualitative difference in the atoms. All atoms are qualitatively alike and indistinguishable. They become differentiated by developing the qualities of colour, taste, smell and touch. Hence the distinction of the elements of earth, water, fire and air is secondary and transmutation of elements is quite possible. Matter in its subtle form constitutes karma which infiltrates into the souls and binds them to samsāra.

VIII

BONDAGE AND LIBERATION

KARMA is the link which unites the soul to the body. Ignorance of truth and four passions—anger (krodha), greed (lobha), pride (māna) and delusion (māyā) which are called kaṣāya or sticky substances where karmic particles stick, attract the flow of karmic matter towards the soul. The state when karmic particles actually begin to flow towards the soul to bind it is called Āsrava or flow. The state when these particles actually infiltrate into the soul and bind it is called Bandha or bondage. The ideal bondage (bhāva-bandha) of the soul takes place as soon as it has bad disposition and the material bondage (dravya-bandha) takes place when there is actual influx of karma into the soul. In bondage, the karmic matter unites with the soul by intimate interpenetration, just as water unites with milk or fire unites with the red-hot iron ball. It is for this reason that we find life and consciousness in every part of the body. By the possession and practice of right faith, knowledge and conduct, the influx of fresh karma is stopped. This state is called samvara or stoppage. Then, the already existing karma must be exhausted. This state is called Nirjarā or wearing out. When the last particle of karma has been exhausted 'the partnership between soul and matter is dissolved', and the soul shines in its intrinsic nature of infinite faith, knowledge, bliss and power. This state is called Mokṣa or liberation. Here kevala-jñāna or omniscience is attained. The liberated soul transcends samsāra and goes straight to siddha-shilā at the top of the world and dwells there in eternal knowledge and bliss. Bondage, therefore, means union of the soul with matter and consequently liberation means separation of matter from the soul. We, conscious living souls, find ourselves bound to karmic matter and the end of our life is to remove this karmic dross and regain our intrinsic nature. Hence Jainism is primarily an ethical teaching and its aim is the perfection of the soul. Āsrava or the flow of matter towards the soul is the cause of bondage and samvara or the stoppage of this flow is the cause of liberation. Everything else in Jainism is said to be the elaboration of this fundamental teaching. These five states together with the Jīva and the Ajīva make the seven principles of Jainism. Sometimes virtue (puṇya) and vice (pāpa) are added to these seven to make up the nine categories of Jainism.

Passions attract the flow of karmic matter into the souls. And passions are due to ignorance. So ignorance is the real cause of bondage. Here Jainism agrees with Sānkhya, Buddhism and Vedānta. Now, ignorance can be removed only by knowledge. So right knowledge is the cause of liberation. This right knowledge is produced by faith in the teachings of the omniscient Tīrthankaras. Hence faith is necessary. And it is right conduct which perfects knowledge since theory without practice is empty and practice without theory is blind. Right knowledge dawns when all the karmas are destroyed by right conduct. Hence right faith, right conduct and right knowledge all the three together form the path of liberation which is the joint effect of these three. Right faith (samyak darshana), knowledge (jñāna) and conduct (chāritra) are the three Jewels (tri-ratna) of Jainism. They are inseparably bound up and perfection of one goes with the perfection of the other two.

IX

ETHICS AND RELIGION

THE Jaina Saṅgha or community contains monks and nuns, and lay-brothers and lay-sisters. In Buddhism the clergy and the laity were not organically connected and the former were emphasized at the expense of the latter. In Jainism the two are organically related and the difference between them is only one of degree and not of kind. Laymen are afforded opportunities to rise to the spiritual height of the monks by easy steps. There is only one fundamental five-fold spiritual discipline in Jainism. In the case of monkdom it is extremely strict, rigid and puritanic, while in the case of lay life it is modified. The five vows of the clergy are called 'Great Vows' (mahā-vrata), while those of the laity are called 'Small Vows' (aṇu-vrata). These five vows are: (1) Ahimsā or non-injury in thought, word and deed, including negative abstention from inflicting positive injury to any being, as well as positive help to any suffering creature; (2) Satya or truth in thought, word and deed; (3) Asteya or not to steal, i.e., not to take by thought, word or action, anything to which one is not entitled; (4) Brahmacharya or abstention from self-indulgence by thought, speech or action; and (5) Aparigraha or renunciation by thought, word and deed. In the case of the monks, these are to be followed very rigorously. But in the case of the laymen, they are modified and diluted. For example, Brahmacharya is restricted to chastity and Aparigraha to contentment.

Jainism like Buddhism is a religion without God. The Jainas are sometimes called 'nāstikas' or heretics. If nāstika means one who denies the spirit, the ethical conduct and the life beyond, the Chārvāka is the only system in Indian Philosophy which can be called nāstika. Jainism, like Buddhism and in a sense even more than Buddhism, is intensely spiritual and ethical. The Jainas, therefore, are not atheistic in this sense. Denial of God does not necessarily mean atheism in Indian Philosophy. Otherwise, the Sāṅkhya and the Mīmāṁsā which do not believe in the existence of God, would not have been called orthodox. The word 'nāstika', therefore, is used for him who denies the authority of the Veda. In this sense Jainism like Buddhism is nāstika. Moreover, though Jainism denies God, it does not deny godhead. Every liberated soul is a god. The Tīrthaṅkaras who were mortal beings like us, but obtained liberation through personal efforts, are always there to inspire us. We are all potential Jinas, for what man has done man can do. Jainism is a religion of self-help. There is no necessity of bringing in God to explain creation, for the world was never created. Production, destruction and permanence characterize all substances. Things have creation and dissolution because of their modes. Strictly speaking, there is no room for devotion in Jainism. The fire of asceticism must burn all emotions and desires to ashes. But the common Jaina due to the weakness of man has not been able to rise to this strict logic and has, under the influence of Brāhmaṇism, deified the Tīrthaṅkaras, has built temples for them, has worshipped their idols, and has shown the same devotion to them as other Hindu orthodox people have shown to their gods.

X

GENERAL ESTIMATE

WHILE criticising the doctrines of Syādvāda and Anekāntavāda, we have pointed out in detail that the doctrine of relativism cannot be logically sustained without Absolutism and that Absolutism remains implied in Jainism as the necessary implication of its logic in spite of its superficial protests. The same bias against Absolutism is responsible for the pluralism of souls and material elements. Though the Jīvas are intrinsically all alike and all possess infinite faith, knowledge, bliss and power, yet they must exist separately. All the material elements are reduced to one category of Pudgala and all of them and even their atoms are all declared to be qualitative alike. When Jainism has rejected all qualitative differences in souls as well as in atoms, why should it inconsistently stick to numerical differences which are only nominal and not real? No attempt is made to synthesize Jīva and Pudgala, spirit and matter, subject and object, into a higher unity. It is very important here to remember that while Sāṅkhya maintains absolute distinction between Prakṛti and Puruṣa which never really come into contact, Jainism does not take this distinction as absolute. Spirit and matter are really united. Jīva and Pudgala imply each other. They are always found together. But the problem before Jainism is: How can spirit and matter really unite? Spirit is regarded as possessing pure consciousness, pure bliss, pure power, pure faith. Matter is regarded as unconscious, lifeless and a dangerous obstruction. Karma is supposed to be the link which binds the soul to matter. Karma is due to passions. Passions are due to ignorance. Now the question is: How can the soul which is pure consciousness and power be really tinged with ignorance, passions and karma? If ignorance and karma are inseparable from the soul, liberation is impossible; if ignorance and karma are external to the soul, bondage is impossible. The Jainas have no real answer to this question. No realistic pluralism can give a satisfactory answer to this question. Jainism says that experience tells us that we never find spirit and matter as separate entities. They are always presented to us as mixed up and inter-acting. So the union of spirit and matter is to be regarded as beginningless. But if spirit is really tied to a real and beginningless matter, the Jainas should give up all hopes of liberation, for that which is beginningless and real, cannot be removed. Why not frankly admit that all this show is due to beginningless Avidyā? Why not regard spirit and matter as the two aspects of the same reality which ultimately transcends them both? Nobody denies relativity and plurality in this empirical world. The only thing is that this relativity and plurality is not the final truth. It may be actual but not real. If kevala-jñana is a reality, if the inherent nature of the spirit is pure consciousness and pure bliss, if ignorance is the root-cause of bondage, if the union of the soul with matter is beginningless, if relativity and plurality are the necessities of empirical life, then Jainism has necessarily to accept the Absolute in order to avoid the contradictions which its bias in favour of common-sense realism and relativistic pluralism has made it subject to.

XI

SECTS OF JAINISM

JAINISM is divided into two sects called Shvetāmbara or 'white-clad' and Digambara or 'sky-clad' or nude. Both follow the teachings of the Jina. The differences between them do not affect the fundamental philosophical doctrines. The differences are only in some minor details of faith and practice. The Digambaras are more rigorous and puritanic, while the Shvetāmbaras are more accommodating. The rule of being white-clad or nude is, it is important to remember, only for the highest monks and not for the laymen nor for the inferior monks. According to the Shvetāmbaras, the highest monks should wear white robes, while according to the Digambaras, they should give up even clothes. The Digambaras maintain that the perfect saint (Kevalī) needs no food and that women cannot obtain liberation (without being born as men in next life), and that the original canon of Mahāvīra's teachings is lost, while the Shvetāmbaras reject these views.

Chapter Five

EARLY BUDDHISM

I

INTRODUCTION

IT was in the sixth century B.C. that the world saw the Light of Asia, that perfect embodiment of knowledge, courage, love and sacrifice whose heart overflowed with purest emotion on seeing that human life was essentially fraught with misery and pain, that a shallow optimism was rooted in a deep pessimism, that behind the superficial momentary glow of sensual pleasure there lay the misery of old age, sickness and death; who, moved by that spectacle to seek a remedy for men's ills, at the age of twenty-nine, boldly left not only the material luxuries of the Shākya kingdom but also his beloved wife, whose exquisite beauty and lovely nature were renowned far and wide, and still more beloved new-born son, who had cemented the tie of love between his parents; who in short, kicked away gold, women and fame, the three universal fetters for man; and who, after six years' rigorous religious austerities, at last found enlightenment as he lay emaciated under a tree near Gaya, dispelling the dark clouds of ignorance and conquering Māra, the Prince of Evil; who then preached the truth he had discovered, without distinction of caste, creed or colour. Thus Buddha taught. And Buddhism was embraced by the rich and the poor, the high and the low, the intellectual and the dull alike. It spread like wild fire far and wide from the lofty Himalayas to Cape Camorin and ranged beyond the frontiers of its homeland to Ceylon, Burma, Siam, Malaya, Java, Sumatra and then again to Nepal, Tibet, Mongolia, Korea, China and Japan. It became a world-religion and a great cultural force at least in Asia.

Prince Siddhārtha has gone, but the Buddha remains. The Four Noble Truths and the Noble Eightfold Path have a meaning for us even today. The Enlightenment which dawned upon the mortal Siddhārtha and transformed him into the immortal Buddha, serves us even today. The Dharma-chakra, the Wheel of the Law, first turned by the Buddha at the deer park in Sarnath still revolves. The Great Decease of the Buddha at Kushīnārā (modern Kasaya, District Gorakhpur) at the ripe old age of eighty-two, so vividly described in the Mahāparinirvāṇasūtra, proves it beyond doubt that every one of us is a potential Buddha.

II

LITERATURE

BUDDHISM is divided into many philosophical schools and has a vast literature. It is very difficult to say what exactly are the teachings of Buddha himself and what are the interpretations, amplifications and elaborations put upon them by the disciples. The teachings of Buddha were oral and were recorded much later by his disciples. Buddha was primarily an ethical teacher and a social reformer than a theoretical philosopher. He referred to a number of metaphysical views prevalent in his times and condemned them as futile. Whenever metaphysical questions were put to him, he avoided them saying that they were neither profitable nor conducive to the highest good. 'Philosophy purifies none, peace alone does.' He is reported to have said in one of the Suttas: 'Surely do I know much more than what I have told you. And wherefore, my disciples, have I not told you that? Because, my disciples, it bring you no profit, it does not conduce to progress in holiness, because it does not lead to the turning from the earthly, to the subjection of all desire, to the cessation of the transitory, to peace, to knowledge, to illumination, to Nirvāṇa.'[1] He repeatedly told his disciples: 'Two things only, my disciples, do I teach—misery and the cessation of misery.' Human existence is full of misery and pain. Our immediate duty, therefore, is to get rid of this misery and pain. If instead we bother about barren metaphysical speculations, we behave like that foolish man whose heart is pierced by a poisonous arrow and who, instead of taking it out whiles away his time on idle speculation about the origin, the size, the metal, the maker and the shooter of the arrow.[2]

A few weeks after Buddha's death (*circa* 483 B.C.) the first Buddhist Council was held at Rāja-gṛha to establish the canon of the Vinaya, the Discipline of the Order. After about a century, there arose a violent controversy on certain points of the Vinaya, which led to a schism and divided the Buddhists into Sthaviravādins and Mahāsāṅghikas. The Second Buddhist Council was held at Vaishālī to do away with the ten controversial points of the Vinaya. The Third Buddhist Council was summoned by Ashoka, the Great, at Pāṭaliputra (*circa* 249 B.C.) in which about one thousand monks participated. Its object was to compile a canon of the Doctrine of the Elders (Sthaviravāda). The present Pāli Canon was probably compiled by this Council. Gradually Sthaviravāda was divided into eleven and the other into nine schools, thus making the twenty schools of Hīnayāna mentioned by Vasumitra. The most important school of Hīnayāna was Sarvāstivāda. The Fourth Buddhist

[1] Oldenberg: Buddha, p. 204. [2] Majjhimanikāya, 63.

Council was held in the first or second century A.D. under King Kaniṣka to reconsider and compile the tenets of the Sarvāstivāda school.

The Pāli Canon is called 'Tipiṭaka' or the Three Baskets. The first Basket is the Vinaya-Piṭaka which deals with the discipline of the Order. The second is the Sutta-Piṭaka which is said to be a compilation of the utterances of the Master himself and consists of five collections called Nikāyas— Dīgha, Majjhima, Anguttara, Samyutta and Khuddaka. The third is called Abhidhamma-Piṭaka which deals with philosophical discussions. Besides these, there is a vast non-canonical Pāli literature including Milinda-Pañho, Dīpavamsa, Mahāvamsa, Visuddhi-magga and a rich commentary literature on the Tipiṭaka.

The above is the literature of the Hīnayāna sect which is compiled long after the death of Buddha. Some Buddhists who felt that it did not present the real teachings of the Master and contained many horrible misinterpretations of Buddha's teachings, called themselves Mahāyānīs, dubbing the others as Hīnayānīs and had a separate literature in Sanskrit.

III

TEACHINGS OF THE BUDDHA

UNDER these circumstances, it is difficult to say what exactly are the teachings of the Buddha who was mainly an ethical teacher and a mystic rather than a metaphysician and who preached only orally. Yet, a fairly good account of his teachings can be gleaned. It may be said to be threefold—The Four Noble Truths, the Noble Eightfold Path and the Doctrine of Dependent Origination.

The Four Noble Truths (ārya satya) are:—

(1) There is suffering (duḥkha): Life is full of misery and pain. Even the so-called pleasures are really fraught with pain. There is always fear lest we may lose the so-called pleasures and their loss involves pain. Indulgence also results in pain. That there is suffering in this world is a fact of common experience. Poverty, disease, old age, death, selfishness, meanness, greed, anger, hatred, quarrels, bickerings, conflicts, exploitation are rampant in this world. That life is full of suffering none can deny.

(2) There is a cause of suffering (duḥkha-samudaya): Everything has a cause. Nothing comes out of nothing—*ex nihilo nihil fit*. The existence of every event depends upon its causes and conditions. Everything in this world is conditional, relative, limited. Suffering being a fact, it must have a cause. It must depend on some conditions. 'This being, that arises',

'the cause being present, the effect arises', is the causal law of Dependent Origination.

(3) There is a cessation of suffering (duḥkha-nirodha): Because everything arises depending on some causes and conditions, therefore if these causes and conditions are removed the effect must also cease. The cause being removed, the effect ceases to exist. Everything being conditional and relative is necessarily momentary and what is momentary must perish. That which is born must die. Production implies destruction.

(4) There is a way leading to this cessation of suffering (duḥkha-nirodha-gāminī pratipat): There is an ethical and spiritual path by following which misery may be removed and liberation attained. This is the Noble Eight-fold Path.

The Noble Eight-fold Path consists of eight steps which are: (1) Right faith (samyag dṛṣṭi), (2) right resolve (saṅkalpa), (3) right speech (vāk), (4) right action (karmānta), (5) right living (ājīva), (6) right effort (vyāyāma), (7) right thought (smṛti) and (8) right concentration (samādhi). This is open to the clergy and the laity alike.

In the old books we also find mention of a triple path consisting of Shīla or right conduct, Samādhi or right concentration and Prajñā or right knowledge. They roughly correspond to Darshana, Jñāna and Chāritra of Jainism. Shīla and Samādhi lead to Prajñā which is the direct cause of liberation.

Buddha's ethical 'middle path' is like the 'golden mean' of Aristotle. Self-indulgence and self-mortification are equally ruled out. In his very first Sermon at Sāranātha he said: 'There are two extremes, O monks, from which he who leads a religious life must abstain. One is a life of pleasure, devoted to desire and enjoyment: that is base, ignoble, unspiritual, unworthy, unreal. The other is a life of mortification: it is gloomy, unworthy, unreal. The Perfect One, O monks, is removed from both these extremes and has discovered the way which lies between them, the middle way which enlightens the eyes, enlightens the mind, which leads to rest, to knowledge, to enlightenment, to Nirvāna.'[1]

This is the Noble Eight-fold Path contained in the Fourth Noble Truths.

IV

PRATĪTYASAMUTPĀDA

THE doctrine of Pratītyasamutpāda or Dependent Origination is the foundation of all the teachings of the Buddha. It is contained in the Second Noble Truth which gives us the cause of suffering, and in the Third Noble Truth which shows the cessation of suffering. Suffering

[1] Oldenberg: Buddha, p. 127.

is Samsāra; cessation of suffering is Nirvāṇa. Both are only aspects of the same Reality. Pratītyasamutpāda, viewed from the point of view of relativity is Samsāra; while viewed from the point of view of reality, it is Nirvāṇa.[1] It is relativity and dependent causation as well as the Absolute, for it is the Absolute itself which appears as relative and acts as the binding thread giving them unity and meaning. Pratītyasamutpāda tells us that in the empirical world dominated by the intellect everything is relative, conditional, dependent, subject to birth and death and therefore impermanent. The causal formula is: 'This being, that arises,'[2] i.e., 'Depending on the cause, the effect arises.' Thus every object of thought is necessarily relative. And because it is relative, it is neither absolutely real (for it is subject to death) nor absolutely unreal (for it appears to arise). All phenomenal things hang between reality and nothingness, avoiding both the extremes. They are like the appearances of the Vedāntic Avidyā or Māyā. It is in this sense that Buddha calls the doctrine the Middle Path, *Madhyamā Pratipat*, which avoids both eternalism and nihilism. Buddha identifies it with the Bodhi, the Enlightenment which dawned upon him under the shade of the bo tree in Gaya and which transformed the mortal Siddhārtha into the immortal Buddha. He also identifies it with the Dharma, the Law: 'He who sees the Pratītyasamutpāda sees the Dharma, and he who sees the Dharma sees the Pratītyasamutpāda.' Failure to grasp it is the cause of misery. Its knowledge leads to the cessation of misery. Nāgārjuna salutes Buddha as the best among the teachers, who taught the blessed doctrine of Pratītyasamutpāda which leads to the cessation of plurality and to bliss.[3] Shāntarakṣita also does the same.[4]

Troubled by the sight of disease, old age and death, Buddha left his home to find a solution of the misery of earthly life. Pratītyasamutpāda is the solution which he found. Why do we suffer misery and pain? Why do we suffer old age and death? Because we are born. Why are we born? Because there is a will to be born. Why should there be this will to become? Because we cling to the objects of the world. Why do we have this clinging? Because we crave to enjoy the objects of this world. Why do we have this craving, this thirst for enjoyment? Because of sense-experience. Why do we have this sense-experience? Because of sense-object-contact. Why do we have this contact? Because of the six sense-organs (the sixth sense being the mind). Why do we have the six sense-organs? Because of the psycho-physical organism. Why do we have this organism? Because of the initial consciousness of the embryo. Why do we have this consciousness? Because of our predispositions or impressions of Karma. Why do we have these impressions? Because of Ignorance. Hence Ignorance is the root-cause of all suffering.

[1] Mādhyamika-Kārika, 25, 9. [2] asmin sati, idam bhavati. [3] Mādhyamika-Kārika Opening Verse. [4] Tattvasaṅgraha, Opening Verse.

Thus we get the twelve links of the Causal Wheel of Dependent Origination:

(1) Ignorance (avidyā).
(2) Impressions of karmic forces (samskāra).
(3) Initial consciousness of the embryo (vijñāna).
(4) Psycho-physical organism (nāma-rūpa).
(5) Six sense-organs including mind (ṣaḍāyatana).
(6) Sense-object-contact (sparsha).
(7) Sense-experience (vedanā).
(8) Thirst for sense-enjoyment (tṛṣṇā).
(9) Clinging to this enjoyment (upādāna).
(10) Will to be born (bhava).
(11) Birth or rebirth (jāti).
(12) Old age and death (jarā-maraṇa).

Out of these twelve links the first two are related to past life, the last two to future life and the rest to present life. This is the cycle of birth-and-death. This is the twelve-spoked wheel of Dependent Origination. This is the vicious circle of causation. It does not end with death. Death is only a beginning of a new life. It is called Bhava-chakra, Saṁsāra-chakra, Janma-maraṇa-chakra, Dharma-chakra, Pratityasamutpāda-chakra etc. It can be destroyed only when its root-cause, Ignorance, is destroyed. Otherwise, Ignorance being present, impressions arise; impressions being present, initial consciousness arises and so on. And Ignorance can be destroyed only by Knowledge. So Knowledge is the sole means of liberation. Ignorance is bondage; Knowledge is liberation. An analysis of these twelve links shows their psychological significance. It is important here to note that life is not regarded by Buddha as a product of the blind play of mechanical nature, but as due to the internal urge, the life-force, the *e'lan vital*, the will to be born.

The doctrine of Dependent Origination is the central teaching of the Buddha and his other teachings can be easily deduced from it as corollaries. The theory of Karma is based on this, being an implication of the law of causation. Our present life is due to the impressions of the Karmas of the past life and it will shape our future life. Ignorance and Karma go on determining each other in a vicious circle. Again, the theory of Momentariness (kṣaṇa-bhaṅga-vāda) is also a corollary of Dependent Origination. Because things depend on their causes and conditions, because things are relative, dependent, conditional and finite, they must be momentary. To say that a thing arises depending on its cause is to admit that it is momentary, for when the cause is removed the thing will cease to be. That which arises, that which is born, that which is produced, must necessarily be subject to death and destruction. And that which is subject to death and destruction is not permanent. And that which is not permanent is momentary. The theory of No-Ego (nairātmyavāda), the theory that the individual ego is ultimately false is also based on this doctrine. When everything is momentary, the ego is also momentary and therefore relative and false. The theory that the so-called matter is unreal, that there is no material substance (saṅghātavāda) is also derived from this doctrine. Matter, being momentary, is relative and therefore ultimately unreal. The theory of causal efficiency (artha-kriyā-kāritva) is also based on it, because each preceding link is causally efficient to produce the succeeding link and thus the capacity to produce an effect becomes the criterion of existence.

V

HĪNAYĀNA AND MAHĀYANA

THE above account represents the teachings of the Buddha himself. They have been variously interpreted and developed by his disciples and this accounts for the different schools of Buddhism. Religiously Buddhism is divided into two important sects—Hīnayāna and Mahāyāna. Hīnayāna, like Jainism, is a religion without God, Karma taking the place of God. Relying on the words of Buddha: 'Be a light unto thyself' (ātmadīpo bhava), and his last words: 'And now, brethren, I take my leave of you: all the constituents of being are transitory; work out your salvation with diligence,'[1] Hīnayāna emphasises liberation for and by the individual himself. It is the difficult path of self-help. Its goal is Arhathood or the state of the ideal saint who obtains personal salvation, Nibbāna, which is regarded as the extinction of all misery. Mahāyāna, the Great Vehicle, the Big Ship, which can accommodate a much larger number of people and can safely and securely take them to the shore of Nirvāṇa from the troubled waters of the ocean of Samsāra, dubs earlier Buddhism as Hīnayāna, the small vehicle. The idea of liberation in Hīnayāna is said to be negative and egoistic. Mahāyāna believes that Nirvāṇa is not a negative cessation of misery but a positive state of bliss. Its ideal saint is Bodhisattva who defers his own salvation in order to work for the salvation of others. Buddha is here transformed into God and worshipped as such. He is identified with transcendental reality and is said to possess the power of reincarnation. The Buddha is the Absolute Self running through all the so-called individual selves. He is the Noumenon behind all phenomena. The Bodhisattva is he who attains perfect wisdom, ever dwells in it, and inspired by the love of all beings, ceaselessly works for their salvation which is to be obtained here in this world. He is ready to suffer gladly so that he may liberate others. He is guided by the spirit of the Buddha who said: 'Let all the

[1] Mahāparinirvāṇa Sūtra, VI, 1,

sins and miseries of the world fall upon my shoulders, so that all the beings may be liberated from them.'[1] Dry asceticism of the Hīnayāna is replaced by an enlightened and loving interest in this world. The negative and individual conception of Nirvāṇa is replaced by the positively blissful and universal conception of it. The denial of God is replaced with the Buddha's Divinity. The explosion of matter and mind by reducing them to the series of momentary atoms and momentary ideas respectively, is replaced by the admission of the relative reality of both, the transcendental reality being the Absolute, the Luminous Body of the Buddha. The greatness of the Mahāyāna lies in its spirit of selfless service of humanity, its accommodating spirit and its missionary zeal. The Mahāyānists are reasonably proud of their faith as a progressive and dynamic religion which throbs with vitality because it has the capacity to adapt itself with the changing environmental conditions, preserving its essentials intact.

The oldest school of Hīnayāna Buddhism is the Sthaviravāda (Theravāda in Pāli) or the 'Doctrine of the Elders'. The present Pāli Canon is the canon of this school. Its Sanskrit counterpart which is more philosophical is known as Sarvāstivāda or the doctrine which maintains the existence of all things, physical as well as mental. Gradually, from Sarvāstivāda or Vaibhāsika branched off another school called Sautrāntika which was more critical in outlook.

The Sarvāstivāda school cannot be said to be the real teaching of the Buddha. It has ignored some important implications in the teachings of the Master and has misinterpreted many. Some of the main doctrines of the Buddha have been taken to their *reductio ad absurdum* pitch. As a matter of fact, there was nothing in the teachings of the Buddha which would seriously militate against the Upaniṣads. The Lamp of Dharma bequeathed by the Buddha to his disciples was borrowed from the Upaniṣads. But the Hīnayāna made the constant and the luminous light of this Lamp flickering and faint.[2] 'The Śākyan mission', says Mrs. Rhys Davids, 'was out "not to destroy, but to fulfil", to enlarge and enhance the accepted faith-in-God of their day, not by asseverating or denying, but by making it more vital. It were Brahmans who became the leading disciples.'[3] The Hīnayāna, therefore, represents not the real teaching of the Buddha, but, as Mrs. Rhys Davids says, 'the verbal superstructures, the formulas often being held up as what he (Buddha) taught.'[4] Mahāyāna also says that Hīnayāna philosophy is either due to the adjustment in the teaching by the Buddha to suit the needs of the less qualified disciples (upāya-kaushalya) or due to their lack of understanding the real significance of the teachings of the Master.

[1] kalikaluṣakṛtāni yāni loke mayi tāni patantu vimuchyatām hi lokaḥ. [2] See my Dialectic in Buddhism and Vedānta. [3] A Manual of Buddhism, p. 194. [4] Ibid, preface, IX.

VI

METAPHYSICS OF HĪNAYĀNA

LET us give the main tenets of the Sarvāstivāda or the Vaibhāṣika school which the Sautrāntikas also admit. Sarvāstivāda denies outright the existence of God whose place is taken by the Buddha and the theory of Karma. The so-called soul is reduced to a series of fleeting ideas. The so-called matter is nothing more than a series of momentary atoms of earth, water, fire and air. Everything is momentary. Change is the rule of the universe. Liberation is the extinction of all desires and passions.

The most important doctrine of this school is Kṣaṇabhangavāda, i.e., the theory of Momentariness. Sometimes it is also called Santānavāda or the theory of Flux or Ceaseless Flow. It is applicable to mind and matter alike for both are momentary. Sometimes it is also referred to as Saṅghātavāda or the theory of Aggregates which means that the so-called 'soul' is only an aggregate of the five fleeting Skandhas, and the so-called 'matter' is only an aggregate of the momentary atoms. The denial of an eternal substance, spiritual as well as material, is called Pudgala-nairātmya.

Everything is momentary. Nothing is permanent. Body, sensation, perception, disposition, consciousness, all these are impermanent and sorrowful. There is neither being nor not-being, but only becoming. Reality is a stream of becoming. Life is a series of manifestations of becoming. There is no 'thing' which changes; only ceaseless change goes on. Everything is merely a link in the chain, a spoke in the wheel, a transitory phase in the series. Everything is conditional, dependent, relative, pratītyasamutpanna. Everything is subject to birth and death, to production and destruction, to creation and decay. There is nothing, human or divine, that is permanent. To quote the excellent words of Shelley:

> 'Worlds on worlds are rolling ever,
> From creation to decay,
> Like the bubbles on a river,
> Sparkling, bursting, borne away.'

'Everything is sorrow (sarvam duḥkham); everything is devoid of self (sarvam anātma); everything is momentary (sarvam kṣaṇikam)' is said to be the roaring of the Sugata-Lion (saugata siṁhanāda). Two classical similes are given to illustrate the doctrine of universal momentariness, that of the stream of a river and that of the flame of a lamp. Heraclitus said: 'You cannot bathe twice into the same river.' Hume said: 'I never can catch "*myself*". Whenever I try, I stumble on this or that perception.' William James said: 'The passing thought itself is the thinker.' Bergson said: 'Everything is a manifestation of the flow of *É'lan Vital.*' A river is not the same river the next moment. The water in which you have once taken your dip has flown away and has been replaced by another water. A river is only a continuous flow of different waters. Similarly a flame is not one and the same flame. It is a series of different flames. One volume of water or one flame continually succeeds another volume of water or another flame. The rapidity of succession preserves continuity which is not broken. Similarity is mistaken as identity or sameness. The so-called 'same flame' is only a succession of so many similar flames, each flame lasting for a moment. The fact that a flame is a series of so many similar flames can be easily noticed when in a hurricane lantern, due to some defect, the succession of flames is obstructed and one flame succeeds another after a slight interval. Identity, therefore, is nothing but continuity of becoming. The seed becomes the tree through different stages. The child becomes the old man through different stages. Rapidity of succession gives rise to the illusion of unity or identity or permanence. 'Just as a chariot wheel in rolling rolls only at one point of the tyre, and in resting rests only at one point; in exactly the same way the life of a living being lasts only for the period of one thought. As soon as that thought has ceased the living being is said to have ceased.'[1] 'The wheel of the cosmic order goes on without maker, without beginning.'[2]

Buddha avoided the extremes of eternalism and nihilism. He denied the ultimate reality of the empirical self, though he asserted its empirical reality. He is reported to have said: 'If I, Ānanda, when the wandering monk Vachchhagotta asked me: "Is there the ego?" had answered: "The ego is," then that Ānanda, would have confirmed the doctrine of the Samaṇas and Brāhmaṇas who believe in permanence. If I, Ānanda, when the wandering monk Vachchhagotta asked me: "Is there the ego?" had answered: "The ego is not," then that, Ānanda, would have confirmed the doctrine of the Samaṇas and the Brāhmaṇas, who believe in annihilation.' Buddha said: 'O, ye monks, I am going to point out to you the burden as well as the carrier of the burden: the five states are the burden and the pudgala is the carrier of the burden; he who holds that there is no ego is a man with false notions.' And he also said: 'O, ye monks, the body is not the eternal ego. Nor do feeling, perception, disposition and consciousness together constitute the eternal ego; he who holds that there is an eternal ego is a man with false notions.' The Hīnayāna interprets this wrongly as an outright denial of the ego and reduces it to the five states. The soul is a bundle of the five Skandhas—rūpa or matter, vedanā or feeling, sāmjña or perception, samskāra or

[1] Buddhaghoṣa: Visuddhimagga, viii. [2] Ibid, xvii.

disposition and vijñāna or consciousness. The first skandha is material. It is the physical organism with which the other four psychical skandhas are invariably associated in empirical life. The soul or the psycho-physical organism is an aggregate of these five factors. The body may be more lasting, but the soul is ever restless. There is no underlying unity. These five skandhas are also found as the links in the Wheel of Dependent Origination. Samjñā is mentioned there as nāma and the entire psycho-physical organism is taken together in the fourth link as nāmarūpa. Vedanā is the seventh, samskāra is the second and vijñāna is the third link. Only these five states of consciousness (including the material frame) are real; the mind or the ego or the soul is unreal. The soul is an aggregate of the body, the sensations and the ideas. All this is beautifully illustrated in the 'Questions of King Milinda' (Milinda-pañho), a dialogue between King Milinda (perhaps the Greek King Menander) and a Buddhist sage Nāgasena. Some extracts from this dialogue may be profitably quoted here:

> 'And Milinda began by asking, "How is your Reverence known, and what, sir, is your name?"
>
> "I am known as Nāgasena, O King, and it is by that name that my brethren in the faith address me, yet this is only a generally understood term, a designation in common use. For there is no permanent individuality (no soul) involved in the matter."
>
> Then Milanda said: "If there be no permanent soul involved in the matter, who is it, pray, that enjoys robes, food and lodging? Who is it that lives a life of righteousness? Who is it who devotes himself to meditation? Who is it who attains Nirvāṇa? . . . There is neither merit nor demerit; there is neither doer nor causer of good or evil deeds; there is neither fruit nor result of good or evil Karma. If, most reverend Nāgasena, we are to think that were a man to kill you there would be no murder, then it follows that there are no real masters or teachers in your Order, and that your ordinations are void. . . . Do you mean to say that the hair on the body is Nāgasena?"
>
> "I don't say that, great king."
>
> "Or is it the nails, the teeth, the skin, the flesh, the nerves, or the brain, or any or all of these, that is Nāgasena?"
>
> And to each of these he answered no.
>
> "Is it the skandha of rūpa, or vedanā, or samjñā, or samskāra, or vijñāna, that is Nāgasena?"
>
> And to each of these he answered no.
>
> "Then is it all these skandhas combined that are Nāgasena?"
>
> "No, great king."
>
> "But is there anything outside the five skandhas that is Nāgasena?"
>
> And still he answered no.

And then the venerable Nāgasena asked king Milinda: "Great King hast thou come on foot, or in a chariot?"

"I came in a chariot, sire."

"Then define the chariot. Is the pole the chariot? Is the axle the chariot? Are the wheels or the spokes, or the framework or the yoke or the goad that is the chariot?"

And to each of these he answered no.

"Then is it all these parts put together that are the chariot?"

"No, sir."

"But is there anything outside them that is the chariot?"

And still he answered no.

And then the venerable Nāgasena said: "Just as the 'chariot' on account of its having all these things—the pole, the axle, the wheels, the spokes, the framework, the yoke and the goad—comes under the generally understood symbol, the designation in common use, of 'chariot', similarly 'soul' or 'individuality' or 'being' or 'personality' is only a generally understood symbol, the designation in common use, for the five skandhas. There is no permanent soul involved in the matter." '[1]

It is important to remember that both mind and matter, 'soul' and 'chariot' alike, are reduced to mere conventional symbols for the aggregate of ideas or of atoms. The soul is a stream of ideas. The matter is a stream of atoms of the four elements—earth, water, fire, and air.

Hīnayānism admits action without an agent, transmigration without a transmigrating soul. It is the 'character' which transmigrates, not the 'soul'. Karma is an impersonal law which works by itself. Unlike the orthodox Hindu 'Karma', the Bauddha 'Karma' does not depend on any divine power. And also unlike the Jaina 'Karma', the Bauddha 'Karma' is not subtle matter pulling down the soul from its spiritual height. The theory of Karma is an impersonal law and it works by itself without needing any agent or soul.

In upholding all these doctrines, the Vaibhāṣika and the Sautrāntika are in agreement. They differ in the following:

(1) The Vaibhāṣika attaches supreme importance to the commentaries called Mahāvibhāṣā and Vibhāṣā on an Abhidharma treatise called Abhidharma-jñāna-prasthāna, while the Sautrāntika attaches supreme importance to the Sūtrāntas or Sūtras of the Sūtrapiṭaka. Hence their names.

(2) The Vaibhāṣika, like Descartes and some modern neo-realists, believes in direct realism and may be called a presentationist, while the Sautrāntika, like Locke and some

[1] Milindapañho, ii, 1, 1.

modern critical realists, believes in the 'copy theory of ideas' and may be called a representationist. According to the Vaibhāṣika, external objects are directly known in perception. He believes in Bāhya-pratyakṣa-vāda. The Sautrāntika, on the other hand, believes in Bāhyānumeyavāda because, according to him, external objects are not directly perceived, but only indirectly inferred. We do not know the thing-in-itself or the svalakṣaṇa. We know only ideas which are copies or mental pictures of reality and from these copies we infer the existence of the originals. The criticism of the Vaibhāṣika against this view is that if we do not know the originals, we cannot even say that our ideas are the copies of the things-in-themselves.

(3) The Vaibhāṣika accepts seventy-five dharmas, the ultimate momentary elements of existence; the Sautrāntika cuts their number down to forty-three and treats the rest as a result of mental construction.

(4) The Sautrāntika is more critical and like Kant emphasizes the *a priori* element of thought-construction (kalpanā or vikalpa) in knowledge and paves the way for Vijñānavāda.

VII

NIRVĀṆA

THE ideal saint of both the schools of Hīnayāna is the Arhat who has simply 'blown' himself out of existence by annihilating all desires and passions. The ideal is said to be negative, individual and selfish. Nibbāna is said to be a negative cessation of all earthly miseries. It is given in the third Noble Truth about the cessation of suffering. It is often compared with the extinction of the flame of a lamp.[1] Just as a lamp when it becomes extinguished goes neither hither nor thither, neither to the earth nor to the sky, neither to this direction nor to that, it has been utterly blown out on account of the oil being consumed; similarly a sage obtains Nirvāṇa when the desires and the passions have been consumed; he goes neither this way nor that, but obtains utter peace.[2] The very word 'Nirvāṇa' means 'blowing out'. It is the dissolution of the five skandhas. It is the cessation of all activities (chittavṛttinirodha) and of all becoming (bhavanirodha). But there are many verses and passages in the Pāli Canon which emphatically reject this negative conception of Nirvāṇa. Here the real nature of Buddha's teachings bursts forth breaking the outward covering of the Hīnayāna. Nirvāṇa is identified with positive bliss. It is said to be the highest and the

[1] nibbanti dhīrā yathāyam padipo—Suttanipāta, Ratansutta. [2] Saundarananda.

indestructible state.[1] It is the fearless goal.[2] It gives happiness here and hereafter.[3] It is the highest bliss.[4] We are even told that to mistake Nirvāṇa as annihilation is 'a wicked heresy'.[5] This repudiates the views of Rhys Davids, Oldenberg and Paul Dahlke and the earlier view of Mrs. Rhys Davids that Nirvāṇa is only negative extinction. Unfortunately, the Pāli Canon gives both the negative and the positive descriptions of Nirvāṇa and Hīnayāna inclines towards the former.

VIII

GENERAL ESTIMATE

IF Nirvāṇa is to be taken as positive bliss, the theory of momentariness would be relegated to the sphere of the empirical alone. Momentariness is inconsistent with ethical life and with spiritual experience. If it is given universal application, it contradicts even the empirical life. To negate the distinction between the empirical and the absolute and to grant mistaken absolute application to momentariness is not only to lose the Absolute which is wantonly thrown away, but to lose even the empirical. The essential objection of King Milinda that if the soul is a flux of momentary ideas, then who is it that preforms acts and who is it that reaps their fruits? remains unanswered. To maintain action without an agent is to have a marriage without a bride, an 'alehouse without a customer', a drama without an actor. The charge of vicarious liability asserts itself. The momentaıy idea which performs an action vanishes without reaping its fruit (kṛtapraṇāsha), and another momentary idea reaps the fruit of an action it never performed (akṛtābhyāgama). The ethical theory of Karma is thus thrown overboard. Bondage and liberation both become impossible. One momentary idea is bound and another is liberated. Suffering itself is momentary. So why should a person at all try to overcome suffering when he himself together with the suffering will vanish in the next moment? Thus the first noble truth and the other three which presuppose it become useless. The noble eightfold path too becomes uninspiring. The very aim of the Buddha becomes defeated. Hīnayāna answers these charges by saying that the preceding link does not perish before transmitting its content to the succeeding link and so the continuity is never broken. The successor bears all the burden of the predecessor. The law of Karma, being an impersonal force, makes action possible without an agent and transmigration without a transmigrating soul. Bondage means the flow of an impure series beginning with Ignorance, while liberation means the

[1] nibbānam padam achchutam.—Suttanipāta, Vijanasutta. [2] nibbānam akutobhayam.—Itivuttaka, 112. [3] iha nandati pechcha nandati.—Dhammapada, 18. [4] nibbānam paramam sukham.—Ibid, 203. [5] Saṁyuttanikāya, III, 109.

transformation of this flow into that of a pure series beginning with Knowledge. But all these answers are unavailing. Knowledge itself becomes impossible without a synthesizing subject. Perception, conception, memory and recognition all become impossible without such a subject. One perception cannot perceive another. The momentary idea cannot ideate itself. Without the self, the 'transcendental unity of pure apperception', the foundational consciousness, the synthesizing subject, perceptions remain at the level of scattered sense-data and cannot become knowledge. He who experiences the flux is, for that very reason, above the flux. Identity of the subject cannot be explained away by similarity, for, firstly, similarity cannot account for identity, and secondly, similarity itself presupposes identity. There must be a self which is not itself momentary to recognize and compare two things as similar. The different pieces of empirical consciousness must be connected in one self-consciousness. It is the permanent self which unites all the scattered ideas and weaves them into knowledge. This is the essence of the classic criticism offered by Shaṅkarāchārya against the theory of Momentariness. Hemachandra, a great Jaina writer, also says that the theory of Momentariness makes the law of Karma, bondage, liberation, empirical life, recognition and memory impossible.[1] The theory of Momentariness, therefore, cannot be upheld without a permanent self.

Thus the Sarvāstivāda school of Hīnayānism which is a radical pluralism based on the doctrine of Universal Momentariness is a bundle of contradictions. Though outwardly it says it believes in the reality of all, yet in fact it has undermined the reality of all. It has reduced mind to momentary ideas, matter to momentary atoms and God to the relics of the Buddha's body.

[1] kṛtapraṇāshākṛtakarmabhogabhavapramokṣasmṛtibhaṇgadoṣān. upekṣya sākṣāt kṣaṇabhaṇgamichchhannaho mahāsāhasikaḥ paraste.—Anyayoga, 18.

Chapter Six

SHŪNYAVĀDA

I

ASHVAGHOṢA, THE FIRST SYSTEMATIC EXPOUNDER OF MAHĀYĀNA

THE great philosophical work of Ashvaghoṣa, the *Mahāyāna-shraddhotpāda-shāstra* or the 'Awakening of Faith in the Mahāyāna' which entitles him to the rank of the first systematic expounder of Mahāyāna is not available in original Sanskrit.[1] It has been translated into English from the Chinese translation of Paramārtha by D. T. Suzuki and also by T. Richard. Our study of Ashvaghoṣa is mainly based on these two translations.

Ashvaghoṣa tells us that after Buddha's Nirvāṇa, there were very few persons who could understand the real implication of the many-sided teachings of Buddha, and that therefore the object of his Shāstra is to unfold the fundamental teaching of the Tathāgata as against the errors of the laymen (pṛthag-jana) and of the Hīnayānists—the Shrāvakas and the Pratyekabuddhas.[2]

Reality is Tathatā. As the ultimate Existence, it is called Bhūtatathatā; as Pure Spirit it is called Bodhi or Prajñā or Ālayavijñāna; as a Harmonious Whole, it is called Dharmakāya or Dharmadhātu; and as Bliss having infinite merits, it is called Tathāgatagarbha. Viewed from the empirical standpoint, it is saṁsāra or the cycle of birth and death; viewed from the ultimate standpoint, it is Nirvāṇa or the realization of positive bliss. It is essentially Indescribable because intellect cannot compass it. It is beyond the four categories of the understanding. It is neither existence nor non-existence nor both nor neither; it is neither unity nor plurality nor both nor neithei; it is neither affirmation nor negation nor both nor neither.[3] When it is said that all worldly things are unreal what is meant is that they are only phenomenally real. The Absolute is the ultimate Reality. All phenomena are found to be merely relative. Relativity (pratītyasamutpāda) is the work of Ignorance.

[1] Profs. Takakusu and Winternitz maintain that Ashvaghoṣa is not the author of this work. But we think Prof. Suzuki has given strong arguments to prove and support the Chinese tradition that Ashvaghoṣa is the author of this work. [2] The Awakening of Faith in the Mahāyāna: Suzuki, p. 47. Richard, p. 1. [3] Ibid, Suzuki, p. 59.

Ignorance has no existence of its own, yet it is not entirely unreal as it produces the objective world. 'It is wrong to take the work of Ignorance as ultimate and to forget the foundation on which it stands.'[1]

Relational intellect cannot give us Reality. 'When one can apprehend that which is behind (discursive) thought, one is on the way to Buddhist Wisdom' says Ashvaghoṣa.[2] 'The reason why the Tathāgata nevertheless endeavours to instruct by means of words and definitions is through his good and excellent skilfulness. He only provisionally makes use of words and definitions to lead all beings, while his real object is to make them abandon symbolism and directly enter into Reality.'[3] But intellect all the same is not to be annihilated. Ashvaghoṣa emphatically asserts that 'If we dispense with finite enlightenment, we cannot conceive of true enlightenment'.[4] It is Reason itself which appears as intellect. The Absolute itself through Ignorance appears as this manifold world of phenomena. Just as, says Ashvaghoṣa, calm water of the ocean, on account of wind, appears as waves, similarly consciousness, on account of ignorance, appears as finite intellects.[5] Just as clay is transformed into various kinds of pottery, similarly One Consciousness manifests itself as so many finite intellects.[6] Absolute Suchness, ultimately speaking, transcends everything. But tainted with Ignorance it manifests itself as Conditional Suchness. And our phenomenal world, subjective as well as objective, is the result of the sport of this Conditional Suchness. When true knowledge dawns we realize that we are no more finite beings but Absolute Suchness itself. This is the self-existent immortal Reality, Calm and Blissful, which must be realized.[7] Buddha, the Shining Sun of Enlightenment, kindly rises in this world to destroy the darkness of Ignorance. A Bodhisattva, though he has realized what is to be realized and though for him nothing remains to be done, yet, following the example of Buddha, he has, out of compassion, to defer his own Nirvāṇa in order to liberate those who are still entangled in the meshes of suffering.[8]

There is hardly any important doctrine in any school of Mahāyāna which cannot be traced back to Ashvaghoṣa. The point that Reality is Indescribable and beyond all the categories of intellect and that therefore it can be called neither Shūnya nor Ashūnya nor both nor neither, was developed by Shūnyavāda, and the point that Reality is Consciousness was developed by Vijñānavāda.

[1] Outlines of Mahāyāna Buddhism: Suzuki, p. 124. [2] The Awakening of Faith in the Mahāyāna: Richard, p. 7. [3] Ibid, Suzuki, p. 112. [4] Ibid, Richard, p. 10. [5] See Richard, p. 8. [6] See Richard, p. 11. [7] shāntam shivam sākṣikuruṣva dharmam. kṣeman padam naiṣṭhikam achyutam tat. Saundarananda, XVI, 26 and 27. [8] Saundarananda, XVIII, 54.

II

SHŪNYAVĀDA

SHŪNYAVĀDA is one of the most important schools of Buddhism. Nāgārjuna cannot be called its founder because it was present before him in the Mahāyāna Sūtras, some of which are prior even to Ashvaghoṣa, and in Ashvaghoṣa. Nāgārjuna is only the first systematic expounder of Shūnyavāda. However it is to the glory of Nāgārjuna that he seized these threads and wove them into unity; it is to the greatness of Nāgārjuna that he developed these more or less scattered ideas almost to perfection in a thoroughly consistent manner.

Shūnyavādins call themselves Mādhyamikas or the followers of the Middle Path realized by Buddha during his Enlightenment, which Path, avoiding the errors of existence and non-existence, affirmation and negation, eternalism and nihilism, also at once transcends both the extremes. It is a great irony of fate that the followers of such a path are condemned by some as nihilists.

Unfortunately the word 'Shūnya' has been gravely misunderstood. The literal meaning of the word which is negation or void has been the cause of much misunderstanding. The word is used by the Mādhyamikas in a different philosophical sense. Ignoring the real philosophical meaning of the word 'Shūnya' and taking it only in its literal sense, many thinkers, eastern and western, ancient, medieval and modern have unfortunately committed that horrible blunder which has led them to thoroughly misunderstand Shūnyavāda and to condemn it as a hopeless scepticism and a self-condemned nihilism. Shūnya, according to the Mādhyamika, we emphatically maintain, does not mean a 'nothing' or an 'empty void' or a 'negative abyss'. Shūnya essentially means Indescribable (avāchya or anabhilāpya) as it is beyond the four categories of intellect (chatuṣkoṭi-vinirmukta). It is Reality which ultimately transcends existence, non-existence, both and neither. It is neither affirmation nor negation nor both nor neither. Empirically it means Relativity (pratītya-samutpāda) which is phenomena (saṁsāra); absolutely it means Reality (tattva) which is release from plurality (nirvāṇa). The world is Indescribable because it is neither existent nor non-existent; the Absolute is Indescribable because it is transcendental and no category of intellect can adequately describe it. Everything is Shūnya: appearances are *Svabhāva-shūnya* or devoid of ultimate reality and Reality is *Prapañcha-shūnya* or devoid of plurality. Thus Shūnya is used in a double sense. It means the relative as well as the Absolute. It means Relativity as well as Reality. It means Saṁsāra as well as Nirvāṇa. That which is phenomenal, that which is dependent and conditional and therefore relative cannot be called ultimately real, even as borrowed wealth cannot be called real capital. All appearances (dharmas) being relative (pratītyasamutpanna), have no real origination (paramārthato 'nutpanna) and are therefore devoid of ultimate reality (svabhāva-shūnya or nissvabhāva or anātman). But they are not absolutely unreal. They must belong to Reality. It is the Real itself which appears. And this Real is the Absolute, the Non-dual Harmonious Whole in which all plurality is merged (prapañchashūnya or niṣprapañcha or advaya tattva). Shūnya therefore does not mean 'void'; it means, on the other hand, 'devoid', so far as appearances are concerned 'of ultimate reality', and so far as Reality is concerned, 'of plurality'. It is clearly wrong to translate the word 'Shūnya' as 'nothing or void'; and even to translate it as 'Relativity' as Prof. Stcherbatsky has done, is but to represent only one aspect of it.

Ashvaghoṣa said that Tathatā is neither Shūnya nor Ashūnya nor both nor neither because it transcends all categories of the intellect. 'All things in the world from beginning are neither matter nor mind (empirical ego), nor consciousness (momentary and individual), nor non-being, nor being; they are after all, inexplicable.'[1] But this does not mean that there is no reality because it is the Real itself which appears. 'The divine nature of the Absolute Reality is not unreal.' [2]

The Shūnyavādins take 'existence', 'is', 'affirmation', 'being' in the sense of absolute existence or ultimate reality; it means Eternalism. Those who maintain that the world exists are committing a great error because when we penetrate deep we find that this entire world with all its manifold phenomena is essentially relative and therefore ultimately unreal. And those who advocate non-existence or non-being are also committing a great error because they are denying even the phenomenal reality of the world. They are condemned by the Shūnyavādins as nihilists (nāstikas). Eternalism and Nihilism are both false. Intellect which is essentially discursive, analytic and relational involves itself in contradictions. All that can be grasped by it is essentially relative. It gives us four categories—existence, non-existence, both and neither—and involves itself in sixty-two antinomies.[3] It cannot give us Reality. Reality transcends all the categories and reconciles all the antinomies of intellect. It is to be directly realized through spiritual experience. It is the Non-dual Absolute in which all plurality is merged. We must rise above the subject-object duality of the intellect and the plurality of the phenomena.

[1] The Awakening of Faith in the Mahāyāna: Suzuki, p. 111-12. [2] Ibid: Richard, p. 26. [3] Dīghanikāya, 1, Saddharmapuṇḍarīka, p. 48.

III

MAHĀYĀNA-SŪTRAS: DESTRUCTIVE DIALECTIC

THE *Saddharma-puṇḍarīka-Sūtra* says: Not knowing that in the reign of intellect, Relativity holds the sway, not knowing that everything phenomenal is dependent, not knowing that 'this being, that arises' is the empirical law called Dependent Origination, people, like blind-born men, go on revolving in the wheel of Birth-and-Death that is Saṁsāra.[1] He who knows that all empirical *dharmas* are Shūnya or devoid of self-reality, knows the supreme wisdom of the Buddhas.[2] He who knows that all worldly objects are like illusion and dreams, essenceless like a plantain trunk, only echoes of Reality, that there is neither bondage nor release, that all dharmas are absolutely equal, that in fact difference does not exist, knows the truth and attains to the immortal blissful Nirvāṇa.[3]

It is declared again and again in the *Aṣṭasāsharikā Prajñāpāramitā* that no object of thought can resist ultimate scrutiny, that every phenomenal object, when taken to be ultimately real, will be found self-contradictory or shūnya; the mere fact that it is an object of finite intellect proves that it has only conditional relative existence. The five skandhas are an illusion. There is no 'person' that can be liberated nor is there any doctrine by which he may be liberated; there is no 'person' that can be bound nor is there anything by which he may be bound. The 'thinghood' of a thing is an illusion. Nothing has an origination. There is no element, no person, no dharma. Mahāyāna is a self-contradiction. Nirvāṇa is an illusion. Even if there is anything greater than Nirvāṇa, that too will be only an illusion.[4] A Bodhisattva is a mere dream. Even the Buddha is only a name. Even the Perfect Wisdom itself is a mere name. Dreams, echoes, reflections, images, mirage, illusion, magic, void—such are all objects of intellect.[5] The *Shatasāhasrikā Prajñāpāramitā* also condemns all dharmas as illusory. They have neither origination nor decay, they neither increase nor decrease, they are neither suffering nor its cessation, they are neither affirmation nor negation, neither eternal nor momentary, neither shūnya nor ashūnya.[6] They are mere names and forms. They are Māyā. And Māyā is declared to be an inconsistent category which cannot resist dialectical scrutiny and which is ultimately found to be neither existent nor non-existent.[7] All phenomena are mere names; they are only a convention, a usage, a practical

[1] Saddharmapuṇḍarīka. p. 139. [2] Ibid, p. 138. [3] Saddharmapuṇḍarīka, p. 142-3. [4] nirvaṇamapi māyopamam svapnopamam. Astasāhasrika, p. 40. [5] Ibid, p. 25, 39, 196, 198, 200, 205, 279, 483, 484. [6] Shatasāhasrikā, p. 119, 120, 185, 262. [7] namarūpameva māyā māyaiva nāmarūpam Ibid, p. 898. māyāyāḥ padam na vidyate, Ibid, p. 1209.

compromise.[1] The *Laṅkāvatāra* also condemns them to be like an illusion, a dream, a mirage, a hare's horn, a barren woman's son, a magic city, the double moon, a moving fire-brand presenting an appearance of a circle, a hair seen floating in the atmosphere by defective vision, an empty space, a sky-flower, a mere echo, a reflection, a painting, a puppet-like mechanism, which can be called neither existent nor non-existent.[2] The *Lalitavistara*,[3] the *Samādhirāja*,[4] and the *Suvarṇaprabhāsa*[5] also join in such descriptions.

The *Laṅkāvatāra* tells us that intellect gives us discrimination (vikalpa) and dualism (dvaita), not Reality. The entire phenomenal practices of the world depend on the four categories of the intellect.[6] Entangled in these categories, people do not try to realize Reality through mystic vision. Consciousness (jñāna) has got two aspects: the first is called intellect (tarka) which proceeds with the subject-object duality; the second is spiritual experience (prajñā) which enables us to realize the Formless and Unqualified Absolute.[7] Those who are entangled in the meshes of intellect are worse than dogs and they can never know the Real.[8] Just as elephants are stuck in deep mud, so are these fools entangled in language, in letters, words and names.[9] 'Everything has a cause' and 'nothing has a cause'; 'everything is eternal' and 'everything is momentary'; everything is unity' and 'everything is plurality'; 'everything is expressible' and 'everything is inexpressible'; 'soul exists' and 'soul does not exist': 'matter exists' and 'matter does not exist'; 'the other world exists' and 'the other world does not exist'; 'there is liberation' and 'there is no liberation'— all this is gross and crude philosophy (lokāyata). In real philosophy we have to transcend the categories of intellect.[10]

Thus it becomes clear that the change from Hīnayāna to Mahāyāna was a revolution from a radical pluralism (dharmavāda) to a radical Absolutism (advayavāda), from dogmatism (dṛṣṭivāda) to criticism (shūnyavāda), from the plurality of the momentary elements (dharma-vāda) to the essential unity underlying them (dharmatāvāda), from the unreality of an eternal substance (pudgala-nairātmya) to the unreality of all elements (dharmanairātmya).

IV

SHŪNYAVĀDA: DESTRUCTIVE DIALECTIC

BEFORE the mighty strokes of the destructive dialectic of *Nāgārjuna* and his commentator *Chandrakīrti* the entire structure of phenomenal

[1] yachcha prajñaptidharmam tasya notpādo na nirodho'nyatra saṁjñāsaṁketa-mātreṇa vyavahriyate, Ibid. p. 325. [2] Lankāvatāra, p. 22, 51, 62, 84, 85, 90, 95, 105. [3] See pages 164, 165, and 169. [4] See pages 15 and 17. [5] See pages 19, 20, and 32. [6] Chātuṣkoṭikam cha Mahāmate! lokavyavahāraḥ.—Laṅkāvatāra, p. 88. [7] Ibid, p. 130. [8] Ibid, p. 167. [9] Ibid, p. 113. [10] Ibid, p. 176, 177.

objects crumbles down like a house of cards or a palace on sand. The external objects and the individual subject, matter, motion, causality, time, space, thinghood, qualities, relation, attributes, substance, soul, God, religion, morality, the four Noble Truths, Nirvāṇa and the Buddha are all found to be hypostatised relations. But from the empirical viewpoint they are all quite real, though ultimately they are all merged in the bosom of the Absolute.

In the very first stanza of his Mādhyamika-Kārikā, Nāgārjuna gives his famous eight 'No'-es and in the next salutes Buddha, the perfectly Enlightened and the greatest of all teachers, who has taught Pratītyasamutpāda which, viewed from the absolute standpoint is blissful Nirvāṇa itself wherein all plurality is merged. From the absolute standpoint there is neither destruction nor production, neither nihilism nor eternalism, neither unity nor plurality, neither coming in nor going out.[1]

Nāgārjuna opens his work by boldly proclaiming the doctrine of No-origination. Never and nowhere can anything be produced. A thing can originate neither out of itself nor out of a not-self nor out of both nor out of neither.[2] A thing cannot arise out of itself. If the effect is already existent in its cause, it is already an existing fact requiring no further production; if the effect does not exist in its cause, nothing can produce it for nothing can produce a hare's horn or a barren woman's son. And if a thing cannot arise out of itself, how can it arise out of a not-self? Again, to say that a thing can arise out of both itself and not-self is to maintain that light and darkness can remain together. And certainly nothing can arise at random and uncaused. Chandrakīrti also gives similar arguments.[3]

Nāgārjuna then examines the four conditions (pratyaya) of the Hīnayāna. A producing cause (hetu) is an impossibility because if a cause has no essence it is like a hare's horn, and how can a cause have any essence when neither an existent thing nor a non-existent thing nor a thing which is both, can be produced. So is the case with an object (ālambana). If in the beginning, a subject arises independently of an object, how can that subject afterwards depend on its objective counterpart? Again, when things do not exist, how can they disappear? Therefore there can be no immediately preceding moment (samanantara). Moreover, if an immediately preceding moment disappears, how can it be a cause? If a seed is destroyed, then what is that which will be called the cause of a sprout? Again, if things are relative they cannot have an independent existence or ultimate reality. And a thing which is not

[1] anirodham anutpādam anuchchhedam ashāshvatam. anekārtham anānārtham anāgamam anirgamam. yaḥ pratītyasamutpādam prapañchopashamam shivam. deshayāmāsa Saṁbuddhas tam vande vadatām varam.—Mādhyamika Kārikā, p. 11.
[2] na svato nāpi parato na dvābhyām nāpyahetutah. utpannā jātu vidyante bhāvāḥ kvachana kechana. Ibid, I, 1. [3] See his Madhyamakāvatāra as quoted in his Mādhyamikavṛtti on pages 13, 36 and 38.

real can be neither produced nor destroyed. So the decisive factor (adhipati) or the formula 'this being, that arises' (asmin sati idam bhavati) becomes nonsense. Hence in none of these four pratyayas, neither singly nor jointly, can we find the so-called 'effect'. And if it does not exist in them, how can it be produced out of them? If the effect pre-exists in the cause, then milk should be called curd and threads should be called cloth. And if the effect does not pre-exist in the cause, then curd should be produced out of water and cloth should be produced out of reeds. In the former case, the effect is already an existent fact and its repeated birth is nonsense; in the latter case, the effect is like a hare's horn and cannot be produced. So production in all cases is an impossibility. Both cause and effect are relative and therefore causality is only an appearance, not reality.[1]

Motion is impossible. We cannot travel a path which has already been travelled, nor can we travel a path which is not yet travelled. And a path which has neither been travelled nor yet to be travelled, is also not being travelled. The mover does not move; the non-mover of course does not move. What is that third, then, which is neither a mover nor a non-mover, which can move? Hence motion, mover and destination are all unreal. Similarly, the seer, the seen and the sight are also unreal.[2]

The five skandhas are also unreal. For example, matter (rūpa) does not exist. If matter exists then it can have no cause because it is already existent; and if it does not exist then too it can have no cause because then it is a non-entity like a hare's horn; and uncaused matter is impossible. So matter is unreal. Similarly feeling (vedanā), conception (saṁjñā), forces (saṁskāra), and even individual consciousness (vijñāna) are all unreal.[3] The elements of earth, water, fire and air and space are all unreal.[4]

We know only the attributes or qualities, we do not know the substance or the thing. Without attributes we cannot know a substance and without a substance attributes cannot exist. But attributes exist neither in the substance nor outside it. Where, then, can they exist? Substance and attributes are neither the same nor different. Both are therefore relative and unreal. Moreover, production, continuance and destruction can characterize a composite substance (saṁskṛta) neither singly nor jointly. Production is impossible because nothing can originate. And if there is no production, how can there be continuance and destruction? They are like an illusion, a dream, a magic city of the Gandharvas. And when they are unreal, a composite substance is also unreal.[5]

The individual self is also unreal. It is neither identical with nor different from the five skandhas. Buddha's teaching is Dependent Origination which is relativity. It is neither eternalism nor nihilism. Therefore neither those who uphold the identity of the individual self

[1] Ibid: I, 7-14. [2] Ibid: II and III. [3] Ibid, IV. [4] Ibid, V. [5] Ibid, VII.

and the skandhas nor those who advocate their difference, know the real teaching of the Buddha.[1] If the Ego be the same as the skandhas, then it too, like them, will be subject to birth and death; and if the Ego be different from the skandhas, it cannot be known.[2] When the 'I' and the 'mine' cease to function the entire structure of the universe—subjective as well as objective—crumbles to the ground. The skandhas no more operate. The cycle of birth and death comes to a stand-still.[3]

Buddha said that the universe is beginningless and endless. And it is an accepted canon of logic, urges Nāgārjuna, that if a thing does not exist in the beginning and in the end, it cannot exist in the middle also.[4] Hence beginning, middle and end; birth, persistence and death are all unreal. Not only the universe in beginningless but all objects of intellect are equally beginningless and hence middleless and endless [5]

Change too is impossible. If the changeless does not exist, then what is it that changes? And if a thing is changeless, how can it change? If Reality does not exist, then what is that which appears? And if it is Reality, how can it be an appearance?[6]

The subject, the object and the subject-object relation are unreal.[7] Action and its result are also unreal. If action really exists, it will be eternal and actionless. Then all phenomenal practices will collapse. Suffering, actions, bodies, doers, results are all unreal. They are like an illusion, a magic city, a dream, a mirage.[8] Time is also unreal because past, present and future are all relative.[9]

Even the Buddha, the Tathāgata is only an illusion. He is neither identical with nor different from the skandhas. He is really Shūnya. We cannot say whether he exists or does not exist or does both or neither, either after Nirvāṇa or even during lifetime. He transcends all categories of finite thought.[10]

Intellect gives rise to the famous fourteen antinomies which Buddha answered by silence. We cannot say whether the world is finite (antavān) or not or both or neither (1-4). We cannot say whether the world is permanent (shāshvata) or not or both or neither (5-8). We cannot say whether the Tathāgata, after Nirvāṇa is existent or not or both or neither (9-12). We cannot say whether matter and mind are identical or not (13-14). These antinomies, says Nāgārjuna, are insoluble by intellect. They are all relative and therefore mere appearances.[11]

The Four Noble Truths are also unreal. There is neither suffering nor its cause nor its cessation nor the way towards its cessation. The three Jewels are also unreal. There is neither the Order, nor the Religion, nor the Buddha.[12]

[1] Ibid, X, 16. [2] Ibid, XVIII, 1. [3] Ibid, XVIII, 4. [4] naivāgram nāvaram yasya tasya madhyam kuto bhavet? Ibid, XI, 2. [5] Ibid, XI, 8. [6] kasya syādanyathābhāvaḥ svabhāvashchenna vidyate, kasya syādanyathābhāvaḥ svabhāvo yadi vidyate? Ibid, XIII, 4. [7] Ibid, XIV, 3. [8] Ibid, XVII, 33. [9] Ibid, XIX. [10] Ibid, XXII. [11] Ibid, XXV, 21-23. [12] Ibid, XXIV.

Nirvāṇa itself is an illusion. Bondage and release are relative and therefore unreal. Neither the forces nor the ego can be either bound or liberated. Neither that which is the skandhas nor that which is not the skandhas can be either bound or liberated. Neither that which is bound nor that which is unbound nor that which is both nor that which is neither can be either bound or liberated.[1] He who thinks like this: 'Transcending the five skandhas, I shall obtain liberation', is still entangled in the terrible clutches of the skandhas themselves.[2] There is no bondage and consequently no liberation. Both are relative and hence unreal. When neither Samsāra is destroyed nor Nirvāṇa is attained, why should Samsāra and Nirvāṇa be at all imagined.[3]

Again, Nirvāṇa cannot be existence because then, like other existing things, it will be subject to birth and death. And then it will have a cause also and will be based on the Skandhas like all other Samskṛta dharmas. Nirvāṇa cannot be non-existence too for then it will not be independent as non-existence necessarily depends upon existence. Nirvāṇa cannot be both existence and non-existence together for the very conception is absurd and self-contradictory. Existence and non-existence are absolutely opposed like light and darkness. How can they exist simultaneously in one place? Again, Nirvāṇa cannot be neither existence nor non-existence for then it will not be conceived at all. Hence if Nirvāṇa is neither existence nor non-existence nor both nor neither, it is only an appearance, not reality.[4]

Āryadeva, *Chandrakīrti* and *Shāntideva* also condemn all world-objects to be mere illusions and appearances. But as their arguments are essentially similar to those of Nāgārjuna, it is not desirable to repeat them.

V

MAHĀYĀNA-SŪTRAS: CONSTRUCTIVE DIALECTIC

THE Shūnyavādin is neither a thorough-going sceptic nor a cheap nihilist who doubts and denies the existence of everything for its own sake or who relishes in shouting that he does not exist. His object is simply to show that all world-objects when taken to be ultimately real, will be found self-contradictory and relative and hence mere appearances. True, he indulges in condemning all phenomena to be like illusion, dream, mirage, sky-flower, son of a barren woman, magic etc. etc. which suggest that they are something absolutely unreal. But this is not his real object. He indulges in such descriptions simply to emphasize the ultimate unreality of all phenomena. He emphatically asserts again and again that he is not a nihilist who advocates absolute negation, that he, on the other hand, maintains the empirical reality of all phenomena.

[1] Ibid, XVI, 4-8. [2] Ibid, XVI, 9. [3] Ibid, XVI, 10. [4] Ibid, XXV, 4-16.

He knows that absolute negation is impossible because it necessarily presupposes affirmation. He only denies the ultimate reality of both affirmation and negation. He condemns intellect from the ultimate standpoint only for he knows that its authority is unquestionable in the empirical world. He wants that we should rise above the categories and the contradictions of the intellect and embrace Reality. He asserts that it is the Real itself which appears. He maintains that Reality is immanent in appearances and yet it transcends them all, that Reality is the Non-dual Absolute, Blissful and beyond intellect, where all plurality is merged. This is the constructive side of the dialectic in Shūnyavāda which we propose to consider now. Here intellect is transformed into Pure Experience.

The *Saddharma-puṇḍarīka* tells us that as long as we are entangled in the categories of the intellect we are like blind-born men completely in the dark; when we reach the limit where finite thought confesses its weakness and points towards Reality our blindness is cured but our vision is still blurred; it is only when we embrace Pure Knowledge of the Buddha that we gain true vision. This is Reality which is Calm and Deep and Pure Knowledge of the Buddha, which transcends intellect and which is to be directly realized through pure knowledge. It is the Most Excellent and the Final Enlightenment (uttama agra bodhi) by which we become one with the Buddha.[1]

There are six Perfections (pāramitās) of which the last and the highest is the Supreme or Perfect Knowledge (prajñā-pāramitā). The *Aṣṭasāhasrikā Prajñā-pāramitā* declares it to be clear and transparent like the sky, to be devoid of plurality, to be beyond finite thought, Indescribable, Divine Mother, One with the Buddha just as moonlight is one with the moon, terrible to the fools but most affectionate to the wise, the Seal of the Law, the Light of Existence, the Trumpet of Religion, the Vision of the Doctrine, the Body of Bliss, and the only Path towards Liberation.[2] It is Reality itself. It is Indescribable and Unthinkable in the sense that intellect fails to describe it adequately. Here the cries of intellect are satisfied and its contradictions reconciled.[3] It is subtler than the subtle, and profounder than the profound.[4] Here all desires and all doubts are set at rest.[5] There are two standpoints—the empirical and the absolute. The former deals with the categories of intellect (koṭi), with name and form (nāma-rūpa), with dependence (nimitta), with relativity (vikalpa or saṅga), with practical compromises (nāma-mātra), with phenomena or appearances (vyavahāra or saṁvṛti); the latter transcends the former and deals with Perfect Knowledge (prajñā-parāmitā) which is Non-dual (advaya), Independent (animitta), Real (sāra) and Absolute (paramārtha).[6] Ultimately it is the Real which appears. The

[1] Saddharma-puṇḍarīka, p. 134, 29, 39, 116. [2] *Astasāhasrikā Prajñā-pāramitā*, pp. 1-3 and 529. [3] Ibid, pp. 52-53, 192. [4] Ibid, p. 38. [5] Ibid, p. 176. [6] Ibid, pp. 177, 191, 192, 274, 356, 444.

Real is at once immanent and transcendent. The suchness of all dharmas is the suchness of Reality. The phenomenal is the noumenal and the noumenal is the phenomenal. Appearances *are* Reality. They are grounded in the Real, the Brahman which at once transcends the duality of the relative and the absolute. They are not two reals set against each other. They are not diverse, they do not form a duality.[1] It is only from the absolute standpoint that we realize the true nature of the world. But the phenomenal is not to be utterly condemned; intellect need not commit suicide because it is from the phenomenal that we can go to the noumenal, it is from the lower that we can go to the higher. From the empirical viewpoint, the Buddha, the Bodhisattvas, Religion, Morality, Doctrine, Truth, Nirvāṇa, nay all the dharmas do exist.[2] We shall rise to the Absolute, not by denying the relative, but by transcending it with its own help. If a ship capsizes in the sea, those among the crew who catch hold of some small canoe or a piece of wood or a log or even a corpse will reach the shore. But those who will not are sure to be drowned. Similarly those who will take the help of the True Doctrine, of Rational Faith, of the Six Perfections, however phenomenal they may ultimately be, will reach the Absolute, the safe, the immortal and the blissful shore of Nirvāṇa. But those who deny the phenomenal will be surely drowned in it.[3] Just as an old man too weak to stand alone can be taken to the destination by his friends, similarly we who cannot realize the Truth with the help of the intellect alone, may be helped by our true friends, the Six Perfections.[4] In an unbaked earthen pot we cannot fetch water. If we do so we shall spoil both the pot and the water. The pot will become a lump of mud and the water will become muddy. In order to have clear water we shall have to use a fully baked pot.[5] To transcend the phenomenal we shall have to take the help of the fully mature phenomenal intellect itself. Those who deny it will be themselves destroyed and will destroy others.[6]

The *Laṅkāvatāra* also declares Reality to be Spiritual Experience which is beyond the categories of the intellect, beyond discrimination (vikalpa) and dualism (dvaita), and which can be directly realized by the Pure Knowledge of the Buddha. Buddhas become Enlightened by transcending the dualism of the intellect, by realizing the ultimate unreality of all objects (dharma-nairātmya) and of empirical subjects (pudgala-nairātmya), by removing the screen of suffering (kleshāvaraṇa) and of ignorance in the form of objects covering the Real (jñeyāvaraṇa). Reality is Silence. From that night when Buddha became Enlightened up to that night when he attained Nirvāṇa, not a single word was uttered by him. The teaching of Buddha is truly beyond language. He who teaches with

[1] na Subhūte! Tathatāvinirmukto'nyaḥ kashchid dharma upalabhyate. (p. 453) . . . sarvadharmā nāgachchhanti na gachchhanti na rajyante na virajyante asaktāḥ saṅgāsaṅgavigatāḥ Brahmabhūtāḥ. (pp. 476-477). [2] Ibid, p. 23. [3] Ibid, p. 236. [4] Ibid, pp. 290-291, 396-397. [5] Ibid, pp. 287-288. [6] Ibid, p. 181.

words merely babbles for Reality is beyond language and intellect.[1] The Buddha is beyond all plurality. And that which is beyond plurality is Reality for it is beyond intellect.[2] A finger is needed to point at the moon, but the finger itself should not be mistaken for the moon. Similarly the Absolute is preached through the phenomenal, but the phenomenal should not be mistaken for the Absolute.[3] Ultimately even this distinction is transcended. Appearances *are* Reality. Like Saṁsāra and Nirvāṇa, all things are non-dual.[4] Reality is not to be sought for apart from phenomena. Shūnyavāda is not nihilism. True, the Aṣṭasāhasrikā says that even if the Buddha, the Perfectly Enlightened shouts at the top of his voice for aeons and aeons innumerable like the sand-particles of the Gaṅgā that 'a thing exists', 'a thing exists', there certainly can be no 'thing' that has had or has or will have an origination nor can there be a 'thing' that has had or has or will have a cessation.[5] But this should not be understood in the sense of utter negation. It only means, as the Laṅkāvatāra says,[6] that all things are unoriginated and are indescribable because they can be described neither as existent nor as non-existent nor as both. They are merely relative and so ultimately unreal. Shūnya, therefore, is not merely negative. It is far better to entertain, from the empirical standpoint, an idea of Existence or Affirmation, as big in magnitude as the Sumeru mountain, than to understand by 'Shūnyatā' a 'mere nothing'. One who maintains in a self-contradictory manner the existence of a 'mere nothing' is a self-condemned nihilist.[7] Of the seven kinds of Shūnyata, mere negation is the worst (sarvajaghanyā). The best is the *Paramārthāryajñānamahā-shūnyatā* which is the Absolute itself that can be realized by Pure Experience which follows the knowledge that all things are essentially inexpressible (sarvadharmanirabhilāpya-shūnyatā).[8] Existence and non-existence, purity and impurity, etc. etc., says the *Samādhirāja Sūtra*, are the cries of intellect. The 'Middle Path' avoids the errors of both these extremes and at once transcends the extremes as well as the middle'.[9]

The practical way by which the intellect may be transformed into Spiritual Experience is indicated by four Meditations (dhyāna), three Samādhis, and ten stages of Bodhisattvahood. In the first *Meditation*, there is the working of intellect (savitarka, savichāra) and there is pleasure (prīti, sukha). In the second, intellect is in the process of giving place to Vision (avitarka, avichāra) and pleasure to higher happiness (samādhijaprīti-sukha, ātma-samprasāda). In the third, intellect ceases (avicharā) and pleasure ends (niṣprītika) and there is only higher happiness

[1] avachanam Buddhavachanam . . . yo'kṣarapatitam dharmam deshayati sa pralapati nirakṣaratvād dharmasya. Laṅkāvatāra pp. 142-143, 194. [2] yat sarvaprapañchātītam sa Tathāgataḥ, Ibid, p. 190. [3] Ibid, pp. 223-224. [4] Ibid, p. 76. [5] Aṣṭasāhasrikā, p. 47. [6] buddhyā vivichyamānānām svabhāvo nāvadhāryate. tasmādanabhilapyāste niḥsvabhāvāshcha deshitāḥ, Laṅkāvatāra p. 116 [7] Ibid, p. 146. [8] Ibid, p. 74. [9] tasmādubhe anta vivarjayitvā madhye'pi sthānam na karoti paṇḍitaḥ, Samādhirāja, p. 30.

(sukhavihāra). In the fourth, intellect becomes one with Experience; pain and pleasure are transcended (aduḥkhāsukha) and this yields a sort of unique bliss (vihāra).[1] In the first *Samādhi* (shūnyatā-samādhi) we know that the phenomenal is devoid of ultimate reality (svabhāva-shūnya) and that Reality is devoid of plurality (prapañcha-shūnya). In the second (ānimitta-samādhi) we know the real cause of everything, we know that it is the Real itself which through Ignorance appears as the world of plurality. In the third (apraṇihita-samādhi) we directly embrace Reality which transcends the categories of the intellect.[2] In the first *Stage* (pramuditā) a Bodhisattva, realizing the inability of intellect, begins, with great pleasure, his quest for true knowledge. In the second (vimalā) he acquires the ten noble deeds. In the third (prābhākarī) he knows the subject-object duality and the categories of intellect to be unreal. In the fourth (archiṣmatī) all doubts and cries of intellect are set at rest. In the fifth (sudurjayā) he understands the empirical and the absolute points of view. In the sixth (abhimukhī) the Ego is conquered and Dependent Origination is fully understood. In the seventh (dūraṅgamā) shūnyatā in its double aspects is fully realized. In the eighth (achalā) absolute non-duality of appearances and Reality is realized. In the ninth (sādhumatī) constant contact with Reality is attained. And in the tenth (dharma-meghā) he becomes one with the Real, the Absolute and like an heir-apparent is consecrated with 'Pure Knowledge'.[3] He then defers his Nirvāṇa in order to liberate others. He carries the suffering humanity in the Great Ship of the True Doctrine from the stormy sea of birth-and-death to the eternal and blissful shore of Nirvāṇa.[4] He makes the people burning with suffering cool by the showers of knowledge.[5] He blows the Trumpet of the True Law and the Conch of the True Doctrine; he lights the Torch of the Divine Truth and rains the showers of the Sacred Religion.[6] If one does not understand the truth, it is his fault, not the fault of the teacher, nor of the doctrine, just as if a patient does not take the medicine, it is his fault, not the fault of the doctor nor of the medicine.[7]

VI

SHŪNYAVĀDA: CONSTRUCTIVE DIALECTIC

NĀGĀRJUNA defines Reality (tattva) as that which can only be directly realized, that which is Calm and Blissful, that where all plurality is merged, that where all cries of intellect are satisfied, that which is the Non-dual Absolute.[8] Buddha's teaching relates to two aspects of

[1] Shatasāhasrikā, p. 1443; Lalitavistara, pp. 129 and 343. [2] Shatasāhasrikā, pp. 1439-1440. [3] Dashabhūmikasūtra, pp. 25-86. [4] Lalitavistara, p. 216. Rāṣṭrapāla-paripṛchhā, p. 14. [5] Ibid, p. 45. [6] Suvarṇaprabhāsa, p. 33. [7] Samādhirāja, p. 31. [8] aparapratyayam shāntam prapañchairaprapañchitam. nirvikalpam anānārtham etat tattvasya lakṣaṇam, Mādhyamika-Kārikā, XVIII, 9.

Truth—the empirical and the absolute. The first is *Saṁvṛti* or *Vyavahāra*; the second is *Paramārtha*. Those who do not know these two standpoints cannot understand the teaching of the Buddha.[1] Samvṛti is a sort of covering. It hides the real truth. It is a workable reality, a practical makeshift, a necessary compromise. In the end it is no truth at all. But this can be realized from the absolute standpoint only. Though this distinction is a distinction within and by finite thought itself, yet it has got to be transcended. Intellect must be transformed into Spiritual Experience. But this distinction is quite valid in the phenomenal sphere. The empirical cannot be condemned by its own logic. A dreamer, while he is dreaming, cannot condemn his own dream. Pure negation is an impossibility. It necessarily pre-supposes affirmation. Even an illusion, a mirage, a dream, a reflection, as such *exists*. Appearances are not to be utterly condemned because it is only through the lower that we can go to the higher.

Nāgārjuna explains the meaning of Shūnyatā. It has a double aspect. In the realm of the phenomenal it means Svabhāva-shūnyatā or Nissvabhāvatā. It means that appearances are devoid of ultimate reality It is Pratītya-samutpāda or Relativity. It means that everything that can be grasped by the intellect is necessarily relative. It is the Madhyama-mārga or the Middle Path between affirmation and negation—a Path which ultimately transcends both.[2] The twelve-linked Wheel of Causation beginning with Ignorance and ending with Decay-and-Death will go on revolving unless and until its root-cause, Ignorance, is destroyed. And this can be destroyed by knowledge alone.[3] This knowledge is the knowledge of Reality. Shūnyatā, in its second aspect, is therefore Reality itself wherein all plurality is merged, all categories of intellect are transcended.[4] Absolutely speaking, Reality is neither Shūnya nor Ashūnya nor both nor neither. It is called Shūnya only from the empirical standpoint.[5] In the phenomenal, Relativity reigns supreme. What is not relative is for intellect as good as nothing. But it does not mean that we should take Relativity itself as the final truth. To do so is to refuse to rise above the phenomenal. Relativity itself is relative. It is related to the Absolute without which it loses all meaning. The Buddhas have preached Shūnyatā in order to enable us to rise above all the entangling categories of the intellect. Those who take Shūnyatā in the sense of a category of intellect, in the sense of affirmation or negation or both or neither are incorrigible and hopeless and are destined to doom.[6] Chandrakīrti quotes Ratnakūṭa-Sūtra to the effect: A doctor administers

[1] dve satye samupāshritya Buddhānām dharmadeshanā. lokasamvṛtisatyañcha satyañcha paramārthataḥ. ye'nayor na vijānanti vibhāgam satyayor dvayoḥ. te tattvam na vijānanti gambhīram Buddhashāsane. Ibid, XXIV, 8-9. [2] yaḥ pratītyasamutpādaḥ shūnyatām tām prachakṣmahe. sā prajñaptir upādāya pratipat saiva madhyamā, Ibid, XXIV, 18. [3] Ibid, XXVI, 11. [4] Ibid, XVIII, 5. [5] Ibid, XXII, 11. [6] shūnyatā sarvadṛṣṭīnām proktā niḥsaraṇam Jinaiḥ yeṣām tu shūnyatādṛṣṭis tān asādhyān babhāṣire, Ibid, XIII, 8.

a very strong purgative to a patient of constipation. Now, that purgative, after throwing all impurities out of the abdomen, should itself also come out. If that strong purgative does not itself come out but remains in the abdomen, do you think, O Kāshyapa, that that person is cured?[1] Shūnyatā, if wrongly understood in the sense of any category of intellect, will surely sound the philosophical death-knell of the person who misunderstands it, just as a snake, if carelessly caught, will bite the person who catches it and will kill him by its poison or just as wrong knowledge may create havoc or tantra, if wrongly practised, will destroy the person who practises it.[2] Knowing that Shūnyatā cannot be easily grasped, the Buddha just after his Enlightenment, became silent and uninclined towards teaching.[3] But if rightly understood Shūnyatā itself is Nirvāṇa.

People, says Nāgārjuna, not understanding the meaning of Shūnya, accuse us of nihilism. Taking Shūnya in the sense of mere negation they urge that we have negated all phenomena, that we have utterly denied the Four Noble Truths, the Bondage and Liberation, the Order, the Religion and even the Buddha, and that we have logically no room even for practical compromises.[4] We reply: These people do not understand even the meaning of Shūnyatā much less its real significance. Misunderstanding Shūnyatā in the sense of mere negation, they wrongly criticize it and charge us with defects which our doctrine does not possess.[5] Shūnyatā is the negation of all views and is itself not a view. It is the realization by thought, at a higher level of dialectical self-consciousness, of its relative self-contradictory nature and of its inability to reveal the Real and an attempt to rise above and merge in spiritual experience.

If everything is Ashūnya, then it must exist independently and must be absolutely real. Then there should be no dependent origination and hence no production, no destruction, no bondage, no liberation, no Noble Truths, no Order, no Religion and no Buddha. Everything, being real, should be eternal and motionless. Then there should be no change, no motion, no world. Thus those who maintain the absolute reality of world-objects undermine the distinction between the relative and the absolute with the result that they lose even the phenomenal. They deny Dependent Origination and by denying Relativity they negate all phenomena and all worldly practices.[6] On the other hand, if everything is Shūnya in the sense of absolute negation, then the world cannot be called even an appearance. Verily the hare's horn does not even appear. Absolute negation is an impossibility. It must logically pre-suppose affirmation. Again, if everything is Shūnya in the sense of

[1] Mādhyamika-Vṛtti, p. 248. [2] Mādhyamika-Kārikā, XXIV, 11. [3] Ibid, XXIV, 12. [4] Ibid, XXIV, 1-6. [5] Ibid, XXIV, 7 and 13. [6] sarvasamvyavahārānshcha laukikān pratibādhase. yat pratītyasamutpādashūnyatām pratibādhase, Ibid, XXIV, 36.

being relative then too there is no production, no destruction, no bondage and no liberation.[1] This view is also one-sided because Relativity itself is relative; it is related to the Absolute without which it becomes meaningless.

We, the Shūnyavādins, take Shūnyatā in its double aspect. We know that phenomena are essentially relative and therefore ultimately unreal, and we also know that Reality is the Non-dual Absolute where all plurality is merged. Therefore we alone, and not our opponents, can truly understand and explain the reality and the worth of all appearances together with their intellectual, ethical and religious implications. It is we, who know that Relativity reigns supreme in the phenomenal world, who can realize the true significance of Dependent Origination and of the four Noble Truths.[2]

In his *Vigraha-Vyāvarttanī*, Nāgārjuna gives the anticipated objections of the opponents against Shūnyatā and then refutes all of them. The arguments of the opponents are:

(1) *Shūnyatā* which denies the existence of all *dharmas* is not true:

(*a*) Because the arguments used for the *existence* of Shūnyatā are also unreal;

(*b*) And if they are not unreal, they undermine the Shūnyavādin's premises for then he at least maintains the *reality* of his arguments;

(*c*) And Shūnyavāda has no *pramāṇa* to establish itself.

Nāgārjuna replies:

(1) Shūnyatā which denies the ultimate reality of all dharmas is true:

(*a*) Because the ultimate unreality of words and arguments does not render Shūnyatā unreal. By Shūnyatā we do not mean mere negation; by it we mean Dependent Origination or Relativity.[3]

(*b*) Our arguments do not undermine our premises. We do not say: This particular argument of ours is true while all others are false. We say: All arguments are ultimately unreal.[4] Absolutely speaking, we have no thesis to prove and hence no words and no arguments. How can we be charged with defects then? But from the empirical standpoint we admit the reality of arguments because the phenomenal cannot be condemned by its own logic.[5]

[1] Ibid, XXV, 1. [2] Ibid, XXIV, 40. [3] Vigrahavyāvarttanī, Kārikā, 22, 67.
[4] yadi hi vayam brūmaḥ idam vachanam ashūnyam sheṣāḥ sarvabhāvāḥ shūnyā iti tato vaiṣamikatvam syāt. na chaitadevam—Ibid, p. 12. [5] Ibid, p. 14.

(*c*) The validity of pramāṇas themselves cannot be established. A means of cognition (pramāṇa), like fire, cannot prove itself. If fire can enkindle itself, it will also burn itself. If fire can enkindle itself and other subjects, then surely darkness too will cover itself and other objects. A pramāṇa cannot be established by another pramāṇa for it will lead to infinite regress. A pramāṇa cannot be proved by an object of cognition (prameya). The opponent admits that a prameya is to be proved by pramāṇas. If he now admits that pramāṇas, in their turn, are to be proved by prameyas, his argument amounts to this laughable position: a father begets a son; now that son in his turn, should beget his own father. And of course a pramāṇa cannot be proved at random. The validity of pramāṇas, therefore, can be established neither by themselves nor by other pramāṇas nor by prameyas nor by accident.[1]

Reality is above refutation and non-refutation. We do not negate anything. There is nothing which can be negated. Even the charge that the Shūnyavādin negates everything is made by our opponent. We, however, go beyond affirmation and negation.[2]

In his *Ratnāvalī*, Nāgārjuna says that just as a learned grammarian may teach even the alphabets, similarly Buddha taught according to the capacity of his disciples. To the ordinary people he taught affirmation so that they may avoid all evil deeds. To the mediocres he taught negation so that they may realize the unreality of the ego. Both these are based on duality. To the best he taught the blissful Shūnya, the deeper truth, terrible to the fools but kind to the wise.[4] Nāgārjuna condemns nihilism (nāstikya) by saying that negation leads to hell; affirmation leads to heaven; and non-dual truth which transcends affirmation and negation leads to liberation.[5] This Pure Knowledge where affirmation and negation, good and evil, heaven and hell are merged, is called Liberation by the wise.[6] From the absolute standpoint we have no thesis, no morality, no intellect, because they are all grounded in Pure Knowledge (bodhi), the Reality. How can we be condemned as nihilists then?[7] Negation is possible only as a destruction or as an antithesis of affirmation. But when there is no affirmation, how can there be any negation?[8] Synthesis alone is real. Both thesis and antithesis are appearances. The universe therefore is neither real nor unreal, and hence only an appearance.[9] Please ask the Sāṅkhyas, the Vaisheṣikas, the Jainas, the Soul-upholders and the Skandhavādins whether they declare the world as 'neither existent nor

[1] Ibid, K. 32-52. [2] Ibid, K. 64. [3] Ratnāvalī, IV, 94. [4] Ibid, IV, 95-96. [5] Ibid, I, 57. [6] Ibid, I, 45. [7] Ibid, I, 60. [8] Ibid, I, 72. [9] iti satyānṛtātīto loko'yam paramārthataḥ, Ibid, II, 4-5.

non-existent.'[1] The Real transcends all categories of intellect and the phenomenal is the relative as it is 'neither real nor unreal'—this is the noble Present of our Religion, the Deep Truth, the Nectar of the Teaching of the Buddha.[2]

What is called the phenomenal world or the cycle of birth-and-death from the empirical standpoint, viewed through the glasses of Causation and Relativity, that very world is called Nirvāṇa or the Absolute, from the ultimate standpoint, viewed without Causation and Relativity.[3] Bondage, viewed *sub specie aeternitatis*, is Liberation. The Absolute *is* its appearances. There is not the slightest difference between Saṁsāra and Nirvāṇa.[4] Those who want to bring the non-dual Buddha within the four categories of the intellect cannot realize the Tathāgata, entangled as they are in the meshes of plurality.[5] The essential nature of all objects, like Nirvāṇa, is beyond production and destruction. When this truth is realized, the subject-object duality is transcended and the cries of intellect are satisfied. Intellect is transformed into realization. Philosophy is equated with silence.[6] From the absolute standpoint, to no person, at no place, no doctrine was ever taught by the Buddha.[7] He, out of compassion for all beings, descended to the phenomenal level and preached the truth in order to enable us to rise above all the categories of the intellect, to shake off all plurality and to directly realize Reality.[8] Reality cannot be realized by negating appearances. We can rise to the higher only through the lower. We cannot give even an idea of the Absolute without the help of the phenomenal. And if we know nothing about the Absolute, how can we try to realize it?[9] Thus it is that he who has realized the truth of Shūnyatā, realizes the meaning and significance of everything and can explain everything. On the other hand he who has not realized the truth of Shūnyatā, fails to realize the meaning and significance of anything and can explain nothing.[10]

Āryadeva says that the world is like a moving fire-brand, a magical creation, a dream, an illusion, a reflection, an echo, a mirage, a passing cloud.[11] But he also preserves the empirical reality of all phenomena. Egoism, he says, is far better than nihilism. Our doctrine is not nihilism. Nihilism trembles with fear even at the very name of our doctrine.[12] It is true Nairātmya as it transcends the empirical ego. It is terrible to the false notions. It is non-dual and blissful. It can be realized only by the Buddhas.[13] However, it can be preached only from the phenomenal

Ibid, I, 61. [2] Ibid, I, 62. [3] ya ājavañjavībhāva upādāya pratītya vā. so'pratītyānupādāya nirvāṇamupadishyate, Mādhyamika-Kārikā, XXV, 9. [4] Ibid, XXV, 20. [5] Ibid, XXII, 15. [6] Ibid XVIII, 7. [7] sarvopalambhopashamaḥ prapañchopashamaḥ shivaḥ. na kvachit kasyachit kashchid dharmo Buddhena deshitaḥ, Ibid, XXV, 24. [8] sarvadṛṣṭiprahāṇāya yaḥ saddharmam adeshayat, Ibid, XXVII, 30. [9] vyavahāramanāshritya paramārtho na deshyate. paramārtham anāgamya nirvāṇam nādhigamyate, Ibid, XXIV, 10. [10] sarvañcha yujyate tasya shūnyatā yasya yujyate. sarvam na yujyate tasya shūnyam yasya na yujyate. Ibid, XXIV, 14; Vigrahavyāvarttanī, K. 71. [11] Chatuḥshataka, Verse, 325. [12] Ibid, 287, 289. [13] Ibid, 288.

standpoint. One can explain a thing to a *Mlechchha* only when one speaks his language. Similarly one can explain Reality only when one descends to the level of thought and language.[1] Reality transcends intellect and he who seeks to prove neither existence nor non-existence nor both can never be refuted.[2]

Reality, according to Āryadeva is the Pure Self (chitta). In its real nature, it is above discrimination, is absolutely pure, unoriginated, uncontaminated, and self-luminous. On account of ignorance it appears as intellect, even as a white marble appears as coloured on account of a coloured object placed near it. The Jewel of Self appears to be fouled with the mud of Ignorance. A wise person should at once busy himself with clearing away this mud instead of increasing it.[3] Ignorance (avidyā) is error (bhrānti). Just as when 'shell' is known the 'shell-silver' vanishes, when 'rope' is known the 'rope-snake' vanishes, similarly when knōwledge dawns ignorance vanishes.[4]

Chandrakīrti fully supports and explains Nāgārjuna. The Prāsāṅgika-Mādhyamika school of Buddhapālita which condemns logic is upheld by Chandrakīrti against the Svatantra-Mādhyamika School of Bhāvaviveka which wants to support Shūnyavāda by independent reasoning.[5] Chandrakīrti says that for him who accepts the ultimate validity of logic the Mādhyamika system is a hindrance rather than a help.[6] Logic has only a negative value for us. We only refute the theory of our opponent without, however, accepting the converse view. Our words are not policemen. They cannot arrest us. They simply enable us to express something.[7] Ultimately every argument is either unreal (asiddha) or self-contradictory (viruddha). But then, urges the opponent, is not this very argument, being an argument, ultimately unreal or self-contradictory? Chandrakīrti replies: this objection is valid only against those who give an independent status to reasoning. For us logic has only phenomenal validity. We simply repudiate the arguments of our opponents. We have no thesis of our own to prove. We are not positively proving that every argument is either unreal or self-contradictory for the simple reason that we cannot do so. We accept the empirical reality of logic, but it is a reality which ultimately undermines itself. From the absolute point of view Reality is silence. But we descend to the phenomenal and point out to our opponent that his thesis cannot be supported even by his own logic. We have no thesis of our own. We only demonstrate negatively that every argument is ultimately unreal because self-contradictory.[8] Criticism of all views is itself not a view; rejection of all theories is itself not a theory.

[1] Ibid, 194. [2] sadasatsadasachcheti yasya pakṣo na vidyate. upālambhash chireṇāpi tasya vaktum na shakyate, Ibid, 400. [3] Chittavishuddhi-prakaraṇa, [4] Ibid, 66-88. [5] Mādhyamika-Vṛtti, pp. 24-25. [6] Ibid, p. 25. [7] Ibid, p. 24. [8] na vayam svatantram anumānam prayuñjmahe, parapratijñāniṣedhaphalatvād asmad anumānānām. Ibid, p. 34.

The objection of our opponent is based on a confusion between the two standpoints we have repeatedly advocated. From the absolute standpoint we have no thesis to prove, no belief to uphold, no assertion to maintain, simply because Reality is beyond all duality, beyond all theses and anti-theses, beyond all belief and doubt, beyond all assertion and denial. We do not maintain any belief for the simple reason that we do not have any doubt. Belief and doubt are correlatives. One is the thesis; the other is antithesis. One is impossible without the other. And because we do not have any doubt, we cannot have any belief. What should we then try to support by arguments? Why should we inquire into the number, definition, and object of Pramāṇas? We transcend all cries of finite thought.[1] From the absolute standpoint we cannot say whether we believe or do not believe in arguments. How can we utter even a word? Ultimately silence is the highest philosophy. Reality cannot tolerate any plurality or duality.[2] When saints preach Reality, they do not put forward their own arguments. They simply resort to intellect as a practical necessity and make others understand by common arguments and methods that Reality is beyond all the categories of intellect.[3]

Chandrakīrti vehemently criticizes the Svatantra-Vijñānavāda School of Diṅnāga. He says that the efforts of the Buddhist logicians to improve on the Naiyāyikas are futile. Logic has, after all, only phenomenal reality. If the cognition of objects depends upon the means of cognition (pramāṇa), then upon what do these pramāṇas themselves depend? Nāgārjuna has made it clear in his Vigrahavyāvarttanī that a pramāṇa can be established neither by itself nor by any other pramāṇa nor by prameya nor at random.[4]

Diṅnāga maintains that knowledge is the result of constructive thought and pure sensation. Words are relational and so they can give us only the universal (sāmānya), not the Real which is a unique momentary particular or a thing-in-itself (svalakṣaṇa) which can be realized by self-consciousness (svasaṁvitti). It is the indescribable Real. Chandrakīrti points out that the Svalakṣaṇa cannot be self-conscious. He quotes a passage from the Ratnachūḍa-paripṛchchā to the effect that consciousness cannot apprehend itself just as the edge of a sword cannot cut itself or the tip of a finger cannot touch itself.[5] Both subject and object are relative and therefore ultimately unreal. If fire can enkindle itself it will equally burn itself. Again, the Svalakṣaṇa cannot be called indescribable (avāchya). It is not like our Shūnya. For us Reality is indescribable because no category of intellect can adequately describe it. Intellect always proceeds with dichotomy and is forced to land in antinomies. Ultimately both the thesis and the antithesis are unreal. Diṅnāga wants that both should be viewed as indescribable and this is

[1] Ibid, pp. 53-57. [2] paramārtho hyāryāṇām tūṣṇīmbhāvaḥ, Ibid, p. 57. [3] Ibid, p. 57. [4] Ibid, p. 59. [5] Ibid, p. 62.

impossible.[1] Moreover, the Svalakṣaṇa cannot be regarded as an absolute reality because of the momentariness and the plurality of these so-called reals. It is as relative as any universal. In fact, it involves a double relation, that of sense and thought, and that of 'in-itself' and 'not in-itself'. A 'thing-in-itself' loses all meaning unless it is contrasted with a thing which is 'not in-itself'. Both Svalakṣaṇa and Sāmānyalakṣaṇa are correlatives. And what is relative is only an appearance, not Reality.[2] Although Diṅnāga apparently accepts the distinction between the phenomenal and the absolute by admitting the absolute reality of the Svalakṣaṇa, yet really he is undermining this distinction by his transcendental logic. His Svalakṣaṇa is not absolute but only relative and hence Dinnāga does not have even the phenomenal reality because without an Absolute, the phenomenal itself ceases to be phenomenal. This distinction is fundamental and it must be maintained otherwise we lose even the phenomenal.[3]

From the absolute standpoint we declare the phenomenal to be a mere appearance but by doing so we do not undermine its empirical reality. Even the Buddha has preached his doctrine from the phenomenal point of view according to our common logic.[4] Ultimately there is neither Saṁsāra nor Nirvāṇa. When there is no Saṁsāra how can it be destroyed? The non-existent 'snake' wrongly superimposed on a rope in darkness is not 'destroyed' when in light we recognize the thing to be only a rope.[5] Shūnyatā is taught to enable us to rise above all categories. If someone wrongly understands Shūnyatā in the sense of a category his case is hopeless. If a seller says to a buyer: 'I shall sell nothing to you', and that buyer replies: 'Please sell to me this "nothing",' how can that foolish buyer be convinced about that 'nothing'?[6]

We are not nihilists, says Chandrakīrti, because our doctrine transcends both affirmation and negation. We show the non-dual path which leads to the blissful city of Nirvāṇa. We do not deny empirical reality to phenomena; we simply say that they are ultimately unreal.[7] Suppose a person has committed theft. Now a man, not knowing this, gives evidence, simply prompted by the enemies of the thief, before a court that that person is the thief. Another man who caught the thief *flagrante delicto* also gives evidence to the same effect. The evidence in both cases is the same. But the former man is a liar even though he has unintentionally spoken the truth, while the latter man is truthful because he knows and has intentionally told the truth. The difference between the nihilist and the Mādhyamika is the difference between the former and the latter.[8] Moreover, the nihilist, in a self-contradictory manner,

[1] Ibid, p. 64. [2] Ibid, pp. 66-88. [3] Ibid, pp. 67-69. [4] laukika eva darshane sthitvā Buddhānām bhagavatām dharmadeshanā, Ibid, p. 75. [5] vastukachintāyām tu saṁsāra eva nāsti. tat kuto'sya parikṣayaḥ pradīpāvasthāyām rajjūragaparikṣayavat, Ibid, p. 220. [6] Ibid, pp. 247-248. [7] na vayam nāstikāḥ, Ibid, p. 329. [8] Ibid, p. 368.

denies everything, while the Mādhyamika admits the empirical reality of everything.[1] It is only from the absolute standpoint that he declares the phenomenal to be unreal. Thus his doctrine transcends affirmation as well as negation. Shūnyatā, from this standpoint, because it is devoid of all plurality, is Nirvāṇa itself.[2]

Reality is non-dual, blissful, beyond plurality and finite thought. It can only be directly realized. But it cannot be realized by denying the phenomenal which must be accepted as a practical necessity. Just as a person who desires to fetch water must have some vessel, similarly he who wants to rise to Nirvāṇa must accept the phenomenal as relatively real.[3] Ultimately there are no degrees of truth and Reality. But phenomenally they exist. Chandrakīrti compares phenomena to a staircase in which each step is higher—through which we reach the Palace of Reality.[4]

Samvṛti is 'covering'. It hides the real nature of all things. It also means dependent origination (paraspara-sambhavana) or relativity. It is a practical reality (saṁketa).[5] It is ignorance (avidyā) or delusion (moha) which covers Reality and gives a false view.[6] The true aspect is Reality; the false is appearance. A man of defective vision sees hair floating in the atmosphere. But his experience cannot contradict the true experience of persons of good vision who see no hair. Similarly phenomenal intellect cannot contradict Pure Knowledge.[7] The empirical truth is only a means (upāya); the absolute truth is the end (upeya).[8] Chandrakīrti further distinguishes two aspects in the phenomenal reality itself—that which is phenomenally true (tathyasaṁvṛti) and that which is phenomenally false (mithyāsaṁvṛti). When people with rightly functioning sense-organs, recognize things as real, those things are phenomenally true, and those things which are perceived when the sense-organs are not properly functioning, e.g., things in a dream, a mirage, hair in the atmosphere, double-moon etc., are phenomenally false.[9] Thus Chandrakīrti recognizes the Pratibhāsa and the Vyavahāra of Vedānta by splitting Saṁvṛti into two. Ultimately however, everything phenomenal, because relative, is unreal. From this standpoint Reality is equated with silence. But because the distinction between the phenomenal and the absolute is itself not absolute, Reality from the phenomenal standpoint is heard and preached.[10]

In the much-inspired verses of his *Bodhicharyāvatāra*, *Shāntideva*,

[1] Ibid, p. 368. [2] shūnyataiva sarvaprapañchanivṛttilakṣaṇatvān nirvāṇam ityuchyate, Ibid, p. 351. [3] Ibid, p. 494. [4] Chatuḥshataka-Vṛtti, p. 8. [5] samantād varaṇam samvṛtiḥ ajñānam hi samvṛtir iti uchyate. parasparasambhavanam vā samvṛtir anyonyasamāshrayeṇa. athavā samvṛtiḥ saṁketo lokavyavahāraḥ, M. K. Vṛtti, p. 492. [6] Mādhyamakāvatāra as quoted in Bodhicharyāvatārapañjikā, 353. [7] Ibid, p. 369. [8] upāyabhūtam vyavahārasatyam upeyabhūtam paramārthasatyam, Ibid, p. 372. [9] Ibid, p. 353. [10] anakṣarasya dharmasya shrutiḥ kā deschanā cha kā? shruyate deshyate chāpi samāropād anakṣaraḥ. Quoted in the Mādhyamika-Vṛtti, p. 264.

the last great philosopher of Shūnyavāda, praises the *Bodhi-chitta* or the True Self which is Pure Consciousness. He who wants to overcome the manifold miseries of this world, who wants to remove the innumerable sufferings of all beings, and who wants to enjoy immeasurable happiness, should never cease to direct his thought towards Supreme Enlightenment.[1] The realization of the True Self which is Pure Knowledge can at once turn an impure mortal into the Pure Buddha.[2] We should translate into practice what we read. Mere reading is insufficient. A patient will not be cured if he does not take the medicine but simply reads the prescription.[3] When all other beings, like myself, like happiness and hate fear and pain, then what is the difference between my 'ego' and their 'ego' that I should protect myself and not others.[4] We must defer our Nirvāṇa for the sake of the liberation of other beings. If we are ready to sacrifice everything for the benefit of humanity, if we earnestly work for the salvation of all beings, then oceans of bliss will be for us which will far excel the so-called pleasure of selfish and individual liberation.[5]

Truth has got two aspects—the conditional and the absolute. The Absolute is the transcendent which is beyond finite intellect and the conditional is the finite intellect itself.[6] The conditional is contradicted by the absolute, but not vice versa. Even among the philosopher-saints there are degrees. The higher sublate the lower. These degrees represent different stages in the development from intellect to spiritual realization.[7]

We deny only the ultimate reality, not the relative existence, of phenomena. But we do not stop here. Afterwards we transcend even Relativity itself. By transcending Relativity we transcend intellect itself. When there is neither affirmation nor negation, then intellect, finding no categories for its support, merges in the Absolute.[8] Buddha has taught his doctrine to enable us to overcome all suffering and thus to become real *Bhikṣus* (bhinnaklesho bhikṣuḥ) and obtain Nirvāṇa. But as long as the duality of the subject and the object is not transcended, neither Bhikṣutā nor Nirvāṇa can be realized.[9] Ignorance is of two kinds: Ignorance due to suffering (kleshāvaraṇa), and Ignorance in the form of objects covering the Real (jñeyāvaraṇa). Shūnyatā is the antithesis of Ignorance of both kinds. It is Pure Knowledge. Why should one fear Shūnyatā which really removes all fears?[10]

[1] Bodhicharyāvatāra, I, 8. [2] Ibid, I, 10. [3] Ibid, V, 109. [4] Ibid, VIII, 95-96. [5] Ibid, VIII, 108. [6] buddheragocharas tattvam buddhiḥ samvṛtiruchyate, Ibid, IX, 2. [7] Ibid, IX, 3-4. [8] Ibid, IX, 33, 35. [9] Ibid, 45. [10] kleshajñeyāvṛtitamaḥ-pratipakṣo hi shūnyatā. shūnyatā duḥkhashamanī tataḥ kim jāyate bhayam? Ibid, IX, 55-56.

Chapter Seven

VIJÑĀNAVĀDA

I

INTRODUCTION

JUST as the followers of Shūnyavāda were called Shūnyavādins and were also known as the Mādhyamikas because they adhered to the Middle Path, similarly the followers of Vijñānavadā were called Vijñānavādins and were also known as the Yogāchāras because they emphasized the importance of Yoga for the realization of Pure Knowledge (bodhi) in order to become Buddha by going through all the ten stages (bhūmi) of Bodhisattvahood.

It is generally believed that Asaṅga is the founder of this School. MM. Pt. Hara Prasad Shastri has pointed out that Maitreyanātha, the teacher of Asaṅga, and not Asaṅga, is the real founder of this School.[1] But even Maitreyanātha cannot be taken as its founder because, as we have seen, Vijñānavāda was already present in the Laṅkāvatarā and in Ashvaghoṣa. Maitreyanātha is its first systematic expounder. His fame was overshadowed by his able disciple Asaṅga. Vijñānavāda reached its zenith in Asaṅga's younger brother Vasubandhu who alone has the signal honour of being called 'the Second Buddha'.[2]

Asaṅga in his *Mahāyānābhidharmasaṅgīti-shāstra* gives the following seven major features of Mahāyāna:[3]

(1) Mahāyāna is comprehensive.
(2) It shows universal love for all beings.
(3) It displays wide intellectual outlook by denying the ultimate reality of the object as well as of the subject and by admitting the reality of Consciousness only.
(4) Its ideal saint is the Bodhisattva who has wonderful spiritual energy to work for the salvation of all beings.
(5) It maintains that Buddha, by his Excellent Skilfulness (upāya-kaushalya) preached according to the grasp and disposition of different people.
(6) Its final aim is Buddhahood which can be attained by undergoing the ten stages of Bodhisattvahood.
(7) A Buddha can satisfy the spiritul needs of all beings.

[1] *Indian Historical Quarterly I*, 1925, pp. 465f. [2] *Buddhist Logic*, Vol. I, Stcherbatsky, p. 32. [3] See *Outlines of Mahāyāna Buddhism*, Suzuki, pp. 62-65.

Asaṅga in his *Mahāyānasaṁparigraha-Shāstra* gives the following ten essential features of the Yogāchāra School:[1]

(1) The Ālayavijñāna is immanent in all beings.
(2) There are three kinds of knowledge—illusory, relative and absolute.
(3) The objective world and the subjective ego are only manifestations of the Universal Consciousness (Ālaya).
(4) Six Perfections are emphasized.
(5) In order to realize Buddhahood we have to pass through the ten stages of Bodhisattvahood.
(6) Mahāyāna is far superior to Hīnayāna which is individualistic, selfish and narrow, and which has misunderstood the teaching of Buddha.
(7) The goal is to become one, through Bodhi, with the Dharmakāya or Buddha's Body of Pure Existence.
(8) The subject-object duality is to be transcended and unity with Pure Consciousness is to be attained.
(9) From the ultimate standpoint there is absolutely no difference between Samsāra and Nirvāṇa; and Nirvāṇa is to be realized here and now by embracing 'Sameness' (samatva) and by discarding 'Plurality' (nānātva).
(10) Reality is Dharmakāya or Buddha's Body of Pure Existence which is at once Pure Consciousness and which manifests itself from the point of view of Samsāra, as Nirmāṇakāya or the Body of Becoming, and from the point of view of Nirvāṇa, as Sambhogakāya or the Body of Bliss.

II

LAṄKĀVATĀRASŪTRA

WE have seen that *Ashvaghoṣa* identified Tathatā with Bodhi or Ālayavijñāna and the latter with Tathāgatagarbha. The Laṅkāvatāra also did the same.

The Laṅkāvatāra declares that all dharmas, except Consciousness, are unreal. *Consciousness-only* is the established truth preached by the Buddha. All the three worlds (kāma, rūpa and arūpa, i.e. of Matter, Form and No-form) are the result of discrimination (vikalpa) or thought-relations. No external object exists in reality. All that is, is Consciousness.[2]

Though sometimes the Laṅkāvatāra appears to support the doctrine of crude Subjectivism, yet really it is pregnant with deeper expressions

[1] Ibid, pp. 65-74. [2] Laṅkāvatāra, pp. 186, 158.

which forbid us to draw such a conclusion. The external world is the creation, not of the individual consciousness or mind (manas, chitta or vijñāna), but of the Absolute Consciousness (Ālaya or Tathāgatagarbha). The confusion arises on account of the loose use of the words 'Manas', 'Chitta' and 'Vijñāna' by the Laṅkāvatāra.

Consciousness is first divided into individual consciousness (pravṛtti-vijñāna) and Absolute Consciousness (Ālaya-vijñāna). The former is further divided into seven vijñānas. The six vijñānas of the Sarvāstivādins (chakṣu, ghrāṇa, shrotra, jivhā and kāya-vijñānas representing the five sense-cognitions and Manovijñāna or normal consciousness) are recognized and a seventh Manovijñāna (kliṣṭa-manovijñāna) representing Continuous Consciousness is added to them. This is a sort of intermediary between the sixth Manovijñāna and the Ālaya. By the first five vijñānas, an object is imagined or rather *sensed*; by vijñāna (manovijñāna) it is *thought*; by Manas (kliṣṭa-manovijñāna) it is *perceived*; and at the background of these all is the 'synthetic unity of apperception' called Chitta (Ālaya).[1]

It is generally believed that Ālayavijñāna is an ever-changing stream of consciousness. But in the Laṅkāvatāra it is said to be a *permanent, immortal and never-changing store-house of Consciousness* which underlies the apparent subject-object duality. It is declared to be one which transcends the subject-object duality (grāhya-grāhakavisaṁyukta), which is beyond production, existence and destruction (utpāda-sthiti-bhaṅgavarjya), and beyond all the plurality of imagination (vikalpa-prapañcha-rahita), and which is to be directly realized by Pure Knowledge (nirābhāsa-prajñā-gochara).[2] The force behind creation is the beginningless tendency inspired by Ignorance in the Ālaya to manifest itself as subject and as object. The locus (āshraya) and the object (viṣaya) of this tendency is the Ālaya itself. Creation, therefore, is the result of this beginningless tendency inspired by Ignorance which leads to plurality (anādikāla-prapañcha-dauṣṭhulyavāsanā).[3] Individual Pravṛtti-vijñānas are manifestation of the Ālaya. They are neither identical with nor different from the Ālaya. Just as a lump of earth is neither identical with nor different from the atoms of earth or a gold ornament from gold. If they were identical with the Ālaya then their cessation would also mean the cessation of the Ālaya; and if they were different from the Ālaya, then they would not arise out of it.[4] Ālaya is the ocean; Pravṛtti-vijñānas are the waves. Just as the waves stirred by the wind dance on the ocean, similarly the manifold individual vijñānas stirred by the wind of objects which are the creation of Ignorance, dance on the Ālaya.[5] The waves are neither identical with nor different from the ocean, similarly the seven Pravṛtti-vijñānas are neither identical with nor different from the Absolute Chitta or the Ālaya. The plurality

[1] Ibid, p. 46. [2] Ibid, pp. 42-43. [3] Ibid, p. 38. [4] Ibid, p. 38. [5] Ibid, p. 46.

of the waves is the manifestation of the ocean; the manifold vijñānas are the manifestation of the Ālaya. Ultimately there is not the slightest difference between the individual vijñānas and the Ālaya. It is only by the discursive intellect that the Ālaya is compared to the ocean and the vijñānas to the waves. Ultimately the Ālaya is Indescribable and transcends all categories of the intellect.[1]

The Ālaya is also called the Tathāgata-garbha or the Womb of the Tathāgata, pregnant with all possibilities and throbbing with seeds of all vijñānas. Noticing that the Ālaya comes very near the Brahman or the Ātman of the Upaniṣads, the Laṅkāvatāra itself takes pains to distinguish it from the Ātman of the Non-Buddhists (Tīrthika): Mahāmati asks Bhagavān—Tathāgatagarbha is declared by you, O Lord, to be intrinsically shining or self-luminous (prakṛti-prabhāsvara), to be absolutely pure (ādi-vishuddha), to be immanent in all beings (sarva-sattva-dehāntar-gata), to be immortal (nitya) and permanent (dhruva) and eternal (shāshvata) and blissful (shiva). Then how, O Lord, is it not similar to the Ātman of the Non-Buddhists? . . . Bhagavān replied: No, Mahāmati, the Tathāgatagarbha is not similar to the Ātman because it transcends all categories of finite thought (nirvikalpa), because it is neither affirmation nor negation nor both nor neither, and because it is to be directly realized by Spiritual Experience (nirābhāsa-gochra); while the Ātman leads to Eternalism because it clings to affirmation.[2]

We may however remark that Bhagavān of the Laṅkāvatāra clearly forgets or poses to forget that the Ātman of the Upaniṣads from which is derived the Tathāgatagarbha is also Nirvikalpa and Nirābhāsaprajñā-gochara.

III

ASAṄGA

IN his *Mahāyāna-Sūtrālaṅkāra-Shāstra*,[3] Asaṅga clearly declares that Mahāyāna cannot be realized by relational intellect. Intellect (tarka) is based on Religious Texts (āgama-nishrita). It is only provisional, not final, because what is held true today may be found untrue tomorrow and what is held true by some may be found untrue by others (niyata). It is partial, not all-pervasive or omniscient, because it cannot know everything (avyāpi). It is phenomenal, not real (sāmvṛta). It leads to dissatisfaction, woeful discussions, insoluble antinomies and misery—'Knowledge increaseth sorrow' (khedavān). Only unwise persons cling to it (bālāshraya). It cannot give us Reality.[4]

[1] Ibid, pp. 47-48. [2] Ibid, pp. 77-79. [3] Prof. H. Ui and Prof. Winternitz suggest that this Shāstra in all probability, is the work of Maitreyanātha. Prof. Ui also suggests that the commentary is written by Vasubandhu. Prof. S. Levi regards the Kāriksā and the Commentary as the work of Asaṅga. We agree with Prof. Levi.
[4] Mahāyānasūtrālaṅkāra, I, 12.

Asaṅga tries to prove that every phenomenal thing, being relative, is momentary. Everything which arises out of causes and conditions is necessarily momentary. If it is not momentary then it will not come into existence at all. The preceding moment is the cause of the succeeding moment. If a thing were permanent, then how could it afterwards cease to exist? The scriptures also tell that the Yogis realize that Saṁskāras come into existence and cease every moment. Again, if a thing which is produced, afterwards becomes permanent, then does it become so by itself or by any other cause? It cannot become permanent by itself because afterwards it ceases to exist. And if it is not permanent by itself, how can it be made permanent by anything else? Change is the law of this universe. External objects do not exist outside of thought. The empirical ego is also unreal. The water of a river is always flowing. Fresh waters are coming in every moment. In a lamp one flame is continually succeeding another. There is nothing in the world which is not momentary.[1]

It is important to remember that it is only the phenomenal which is declared to be momentary by Asaṅga and Vasubandhu. Momentariness does not even touch Reality which is above all categories.

The Vijñānavādins deny the ultimate reality of the empirical self or the ego. All miseries and sufferings come out of the false notion of the 'I' and the 'Mine'. When the self does not exist really, how can it be taken as a seer or a knower or a doer or an enjoyer? When Buddha preached the existence of the self it was only to attract the simple-minded and to encourage them to perform good deeds and to refrain from evil ones. In reality there is no ego. If an ego really existed, then there would be either liberation without any effort or no liberation at all. The notion of the ego is due to beginningless Ignorance which must be overcome.[2]

It is important to remember that it is only the empirical self or the ego which is declared to be unreal by Asaṅga and Vasubandhu. Pure Consciousness or the Universal Self is not only admitted but is declared to be the only Reality. By its very nature it is Self-luminous; all impurities are adventitious.[3]

The Real, says Asaṅga, is essentially Non-dual. It is neither existence nor non-existence, neither affirmation nor negation, neither identity nor difference, neither one nor many, neither increasing nor decreasing, neither pure nor impure, neither production nor destruction. It is beyond Ignorance and beyond intellect.[4]

The ego is neither real nor unreal nor both real and unreal. It is only an illusion (bhrama). Liberation, therefore, is only the destruc-

[1] Mahāyānasūtrālaṅkāra, pp. 149-154. [2] Ibid, 154-159. [3] matañcha chittam prakṛtiprabhāsvaram sadā tadāgantukadoṣadūṣitam, Ibid, XIII, 19. [4] Ibid, VI, 1. Also se: IX, 22, 24, 26.

tion of illusion or ignorance.[1] How unfortunate it is that people directly perceiving the truth of Dependent Origination forget it and take recourse to a so-called independent ego! How deep-rooted is this Ignorance which makes a complete fool of a man and tosses him like a shuttlecock from affirmation to negation and from negation to affirmation! What sort of Ignorance is this which obscures the truth and makes a man fall upon either existence or non-existence?[2] Truly speaking, there is absolutely no difference between Bondage and Liberation. Still, from the phenomenal point of view, we say that by good deeds and true knowledge, the cycle of birth and death is stopped and liberation is achieved.[3] A Bodhisattva first realizes that external objects are only imaginary and that mind alone exists. Then he realizes that individual mind too is as much an imagination as any external object. Thus shaking off all duality, he directly perceives the Absolute which is the unity underlying phenomena (dharmadhātu).[4]

The Supreme Reality wherein all categories merge removes all the defects of the intellect just as a strong medicine removes the effect of poison.[5] By becoming one with the Reality, a Bodhisattva realizes the Last Meditation (chaturtha-dhyāna; like turīya) and ever dwells in the Blissful *Brahman*.[6] He becomes fully qualified to work for the real emancipation of humanity just as a bird, when it has developed full wings, becomes able to soar high.[7]

When a vessel containing water is broken, reflection of the moon is not visible in it. Similarly in impure persons the reflection of the Buddha is not visible.[8] But knowing the ultimate unreality of the ego and of the dharmas and realizing that Reality is essentially non-dual, a wise man will embrace it recognizing it to be Pure Consciousness. After that even this recognition will be transcended and that indescribable state is called Liberation where all the cries of intellect are satisfied and all its categories are merged.[9] Buddha has never taught the Doctrine by speech because it is to be directly realized by Pure Consciousness.[10] Every phenomenon is merged in the harmonious bosom of Reality. 'No appearance is so low that the Absolute does not embrace it'.[11] Knowing this world to be merely a composite of Forces (samskāras), knowing that the ego and the objects do not exist, and knowing further that all this is merely suffering, a wise man will leave far behind the baneful existence of the empirical ego and will embrace the Universal Soul (mahātman).[12] Setting on the right path, understanding the true doctrine of Nairātmya, and clearly grasping the real meaning of Shūnyatā, the Enlightened

[1] tatashcha mokṣo bhramamātrasaṅkṣayaḥ, Ibid, VI, 2. [2] Ibid, VI, 4. [3] na chāntaram kiñchana vidyate'nayoḥ sadarthavṛtyā shamajanmanoriha, Ibid, VI, 5. [4] Ibid, VI, 7. [5] Ibid, VI, 9. [6] brāhmair vihārair viharatyudāraiḥ, Ibid, VII, 3. [7] Ibid, VII, 8. [8] Ibid, IX, 16. [9] Ibid, XI, 47. [10] Ibid, XII, 2. [11] Dharmadhātur vinirmukto yasmād dharmo na vidyate, Ibid, XIII, 12. [12] vihāya yo'narthamayātmadṛṣṭim mahātmadṛṣṭim shrayate mahārthām, Ibid, XIV, 37.

Ones transcend the individual existence and realize the Pure Soul (shuddhātman) and thus become one with that Universal Soul.[1] This is the Pure Existence of the Buddha and is called the Highest Soul (paramātman).[2] Rivers after rivers pour themselves into the Ocean, but the Ocean is neither satisfied nor does it increase; Buddhas after Buddhas pour themselves into Reality, but the Absolute is neither satisfied nor does it increase. How wonderful it is![3] Different rivers with different waters flowing through different places are called only 'rivers'; when they merge in the ocean, they become one with it. No more are they called 'rivers'; they are 'the ocean'. Similarly, different persons holding different views are called 'finite intellects'. But when they merge in the Buddha, the Absolute, they become one with it; they are the Absolute.[4]

The Yogāchāras stress the importance of different Vihāras and Bhūmis which purify a Bodhisattva just as fire purifies gold[5] and by which discursive intellect is transformed into Spiritual Experience.

IV

VASUBANDHU: ABSOLUTISM OF PURE CONSCIOUSNESS

VASUBANDHU formerly belonged to the Sautrāntika School though he wrote his Kosha following the Kāshmīra-Vaibhāṣika branch of the Sarvāstivāda School of Hīnayāna.[6] He was later on converted to Vijñanavāda by his elder brother Asaṅga. Even in his earlier work, the Abhidharmakosha, the influence of Mahāyāna is visible. Here the word 'Abhidharma' is identified with Pure Knowledge together with its means. It is declared that the phenomenal is like 'water in a jar', while the Absolute is like the vast ocean.[7] The intellect is transcended in the last Meditation in which the meditator becomes one with the Real.[8] This Pure Knowledge is called Shrāmaṇya as well as Brāhmaṇya.[9]

In his *Vijñapti-Mātratā-Siddhi: Vimshatikā*, with his own commentary on it, Vasubandhu proves that Reality is Pure Consciousness and that external objects do not exist outside of thought, by refuting the objections of the opponents. And in his *Vijñapti-Mātratā-Siddhi: Trimshikā*, Vasubandhu develops his theory to fullness.

In Mahāyāna, the *Vimshatikā* tells us, all the three worlds do not exist outside of thought. Mind, thought, consciousness, knowledge are synonyms.[10] External objects depend on thought like the hair seen

Buddhāḥ shuddhātmalābhatvād gatā ātmamahātmatām, Ibid, IX, 23. [2] anena Buddhānām anāsrave dhātau paramātmā vyavasthāpyate, Ibid, pp. 37-38. The Mahāparinirvāṇasūtra of the Sanskrit Canon identifies the Mahātman with the Tathāgatagarbha just as the Laṅkāvatāra identifies the Ālaya with the Tathāgatagarbha. See Systems of Buddhistic Thought: Yamakami Sogen, p. 25. [3] Ibid, IX, 55. [4] Ibid, IX, 82-85. [5] Bodhisattvabhūmi, given as an Appendix to the Dashabhūmika-Sūtra edited by Rahder, p. 10. [6] Kāshmīra-Vibhāṣikanītisiddhaḥ prāyo mayā'yam kathito'bhidharmaḥ, Abhidharmakosha, VIII, 40. [7] Ibid, VI, 4. [8] mahābrahmatvam tatphalam, Ibid, VIII, 23. [9] shrāmaṇyam amalo mārgaḥ, Ibid, VI, 51 and brāhmaṇyameva tat, Ibid, VI, 54. [10] Viṁshatikā-Vṛtti on Kārikā, 1.

floating in the atmosphere or like the perception of the double-moon.[1] The opponent urges that if external objects do not exist then we cannot account for their spatial determination (desha-niyama), their temporal determination (kāla-niyama), the indetermination of the perceiving stream of consciousness (santānāniyama) and the fruitful activity which follows their knowledge (kṛtya-kriyā).[2] If representations arise without there being any external sense-objects, then how is it that an object is seen in a particular place and a particular time? And how is it that all persons, and not one person only, present at that particular place and time perceive that particular object? And how is it that fruitful activity is possible? If things like food, water, cloth, poison, weapons etc. seen in a dream are purely imaginary and devoid of activity, it does not mean that real food and real water also cannot satisfy hunger and thirst. External objects therefore must exist.[3]

Vasubandhu replies: These four things mentioned by the opponent do not justify independent existence of external objects because they are found even in dreams and in hell where there are no external objects. Even in a dream things like a city, a garden, a woman, a man etc. are seen in a particular place and at a particular time and not in all places and at all times. Fruitful activity too results from unreal dream-objects, for the roaring of a dream-tiger causes real fear and disturbs sleep and an erotic dream is followed by consequences which are physically real. Again, all those persons, and not one of them only, who, on account of their bad deeds, go to hell, see the same river of pus etc. Thus there is indetermination of the stream of consciousness. So in dreams and in hell all these four things are present though there are no external objects. The infernal guards cannot be real because they themselves do not suffer the agony of hell. The opponent admits that infernal guards are produced by the force of the deeds of those persons who go to hell. But the force or the impression (vāsanā) of the deed is in consciousness, while its result is wrongly imagined by the opponent to be outside consciousness. How can it be possible? The impression as well as the result of the deed must be in consciousness itself. Hence consciousness is the only reality.[4]

Consciousness manifests itself into subject as well as into object. It arises out of its own seed and then it manifests itself as an external object. Therefore Buddha said that there are two bases of cognition—internal and external. By knowing this, one realizes that there is no personal ego and that there are no external objects, as both are only manifestations of consciousness.[5]

The Indescribable Pure Consciousness which is to be directly realized by the Buddhas can never be denied. It cannot be conceived by

[1] Viṁshatikā, K. 1. [2] yadi vijñaptir anarthā niyamo deshakālayoḥ. santānasyāniyamashcha yuktā kṛtyakriyā na cha, Ibid. K. 2. [3] Viṁshatikā-Vṛtti on K. 2. [4] Viṁshatikā, K. 6-7. [5] Ibid, K. 9-10.

intellect. The idea of Pure Consciousnessas conceived by finite thought with the help of its category of 'existence' is also unreal. For, if it were real, the conceptions of intellect would be real and this would undermine the doctrine that Pure Consciousness alone exists. Pure Consciousness cannot be grasped by intellect as an object. But this does not mean that Pure Consciousness in itself does not exist. It can be directly realized by Spiritual Experience which transcends the subject-object duality.[1]

Vasubandhu refutes other arguments of the opponent. Perception, he says, cannot guarantee the existence of external objects because the awareness is the same even in dreams and in the perception of the double-moon. Memory too does not imply the perception of an external object but only its consciousness. The opponent urges that if there is no difference between dreaming and waking states then we should know even when we are fully awake that external objects do not exist in the manner in which we know that the dream-objects are unreal. To this objection Vasubandhu's answer is that before we are fully awake we cannot know that dream-objects are unreal. Things seen in a dream are as real to the dreamer as any object is to us. It is only when we are awake that we realize the unreality of dream-objects. Similarly, the worldly people are slumbering in ignorance. They do not realize, as long as they are under the infatuation of ignorance, that this world does not really exist. It is only when true knowledge dawns that the fact that Reality is Pure Consciousness can be realized.[2] Intellect inevitably involves itself in dualism. And unless the subject-object duality is transcended, we cannot realize Reality.[3] Vasubandhu concludes his Vimshatikā by pointing out that he has, according to the best of his ability, proved that Reality is Pure Consciousness. But as this Reality is beyond discursive intellect it cannot be fully grasped by it. It can be only realized by transcending the subject-object duality, by going beyond all the categories of intellect and by embracing Pure Consciousness, in short, by becoming a Buddha.[4]

V

THE ABSOLUTE AND ITS APPEARANCES

STHIRAMATI in his Commentary on the Trimshikā tells us that the aim of Vasubandhu in writing this treatise is to show the real meaning of the ultimate unreality of the subject (pudgala-nairātmya) and of the object (dharma-nairātmya). There are two kinds of Ignorance. The first

[1] yo bālair dharmāṇām svabhāvo grāhya-grāhakādiḥ parikalpitas tena kalpitena ātmana teṣām nairātmyam na tvanabhilapyena ātmanā yo Buddhānām viṣaya iti, Vimshatikā-Vṛtti on K. 10. [2] svapne dṛgviṣayābhāvam nāprabuddho'vagachchhati, Vimshatikā, K. 17. [3] Ibid on K. 21. [4] Vijñaptimātratāsiddhiḥ svashaktisadṛshī mayā. kṛteyam sarvathā sā tu na chintyā Buddhagocharaḥ, Ibid, K. 22.

is Kleshāvaraṇa, which leads to all sorts of suffering and is due to the false notion of the reality of the individual subject. The second is Jñeyāvaraṇa which screens the real nature of the objects and is due to the false notion of the reality of external objects. To destroy these two kinds of Ignorance is the aim of Trimshikā. Some philosophers maintain that even external objects, like consciousness, are absolutely real; while others declare that even consciousness, like external objects, is only relative and therefore unreal. To demolish these two extreme views (ekāntavāda) is also the aim of this treatise.

Some scholars maintain that Shūnyavāda declares even consciousness to be unreal. But in the last chapter we have shown that this is not the case. It is very important to remember that it is only the individual subject which is declared to be unreal by Shūnyavāda. Vijñānavāda also agrees here. Shūnyavāda criticizes self-consciousness if it means consciousness of consciousness. Fire cannot burn itself. The edge of a sword cannot cut itself. The tip of a finger cannot touch itself. Consciousness of consciousness leads to infinite regress. But Shūnyavāda maintains the reality of Pure Consciousness. Nāgārjuna himself identifies his Pranpañcha-Shūnya Tattva with Bodhi or Prajñā. If the Bodhi of Nāgārjuna, the Chitta of Āryadeva and the Bodhi-Chitta of Shāntideva are not Pure Consciousness or the Self-luminous Self which is the Absolute, what else can they be?

Reality, says the Trimshikā, is Pure Consciousness. This Reality (Vijñaptimātra) on account of its inherent power (shakti) suffers threefold modification. First of all it manifests itself as Ālayavijñāna or Vipāka which is a Store-house Consciousness where the seeds of all phenomena are present. Then this Universal Consciousness further manifests itself in two forms. Firstly it takes the form of an individual subject or ego (manana or kliṣṭa manovijñāna), and secondly it manifests itself in the form of the various mental states and of the so-called external objects (viṣaya-vijñapti). Behind these three modifications is the permanent background of eternal and unchanging Pure Consciousness (Vijñāna or Vijñaptimātra).[1]

It is important to note the difference between the Ālaya of the Laṅkāvatāra and the Ālaya of Vasubandhu. The Ālayavijñāna of the Laṅkāvatāra which is identified with Tathāgatagarbha or the Pure Chitta is identical with the Vijñaptimātra of Vasubandhu. Both are Pure Consciousness which is the permanent background of all phenomena, subjective as well as objective, and which ultimately transcends the subject-object duality. The Ālayavijñāna of Vasubandhu is only a phenomenal manifestation of this Pure Consciousness. It contains the seeds of all phenomena, subjective as well as objective (Sarva-bījakam,

[1] ātmadharmopachāro hi vividho yaḥ pravartate. vijñānapariṇāme'sau pariṇāmaḥ sa cha tridhā. vipāko mananākhyashcha vijñaptir viṣayasya cha, Trimshikā, K. 1-2

Kārikā 2). It is a continually changing stream of consciousness like a stream of water (vartate srotasaughavat, K. 4). When Buddhahood is realized, its flow at once comes to an end (tasya vyavṛtirarhatve, K. 5).

The individual self (kliṣṭa manovijñāna) depends on the Ālaya and is accompanied by four kinds of suffering—self-notion, self-delusion, self-pride and self-love.[1] It ceases to function when the false notion of the ego is destroyed and when the categories of intellect are transcended.[2]

The third modification, the form of the objects, the mental states (manovijñāna) and the so-called external objects (viṣaya-vijñāna), which appears as the six Vijñānas (ṣaḍvidha) is of two kinds—pure (kushala) and impure (akushala) and is accompanied by various sufferings (klesha) and sub-sufferings (upaklesha).[3] These Vijñānas stand in the same relation to the Ālaya as waves stand to water (taraṅgāṇām yathā jale, K. 15).

Thus we see that the subject as well as the object are only modifications of the Ālaya which itself is only a modification of Pure Consciousness. Hence it is established that Pure Consciousness is the only Reality.[4]

VI

TRISVABHĀVA

THE Paramārtha of Shūnyavāda is also called Pariniṣpanna by Vijñānavāda, and the Samvṛti of Shūnyavāda is further divided into Paratantra and Parikalpita by Vijñānavāda. The former is the relative while the latter is the imaginary. The Laṅkāvatāra says that the Parikalpita is the purely imaginary like a hare's horn or a barren woman's child or a sky-flower or a dream or a mirage or the perception of double-moon etc.; the Paratantra is the relative which depends on causes and conditions, which is based on discursive intellect, and which comes under the realm of the phenomenal; the Pariniṣpanna is the Paramārtha, the absolutely real which is based on spiritual experience which transcends the subject-object duality of the intellect and the plurality of the phenomena, and which is variously called as Tathatā or Tathāgata-garbha or Ālayavijñāna or Āryajñāna or Samyagjñāna or Prajñā.[5] Maitreyanātha also says that the Parikalpita is the purely imaginary or absolutely unreal (atyanta-shūnya); the Paratantra is the relative based on intellect (laukikagochara); and the Pariniṣpanna is the absolutely real based on direct realization (avikalpa-jñāna-gochara).[6] Asaṅga says that the imaginary is a mere name (nāma or jalpa); the relative is also like an error (bhrānti); it is an appearance (tasmin na tadbhāvaḥ), t is conditional or phenomenal (samvṛti), it is infected with

[1] Ibid, K. 6. [2] Ibid, K. 7. [3] Ibid, K. 8-9. [4] Ibid, K. 17. [5] Laṅkāvatāra, pp. 56, 67, 68, 222, 229. [6] Madhyāntavibhāga, p. 19.

the subject-object duality of the intellect (grāhyagrāhaka-lakṣaṇa). Both the imaginary and the relative are indescribable because they can be described neither as existent nor as non-existent. They are not existent because they do not exist in fact; they are not non-existent because they exist as an illusion or as an appearance. The Absolute, which also is indescribable, being beyond intellect, is the only reality.[1] Vasubandhu also observes that the imaginary is purely imagined by the intellect; the relative arises out of causes and conditions; and the absolute exists independently in itself and by itself.[2] All these three aspects are Nissvabhāva in three different senses. The imaginary is devoid of existence (nissvabhāva) because it is absolutely unreal (though it exists as a name or as an illusion); the relative is devoid of independent existence (nissvabhāva) because it does not ultimately exist (though it exists as an appearance); the absolute is devoid of thought-constructions (nissvabhāva) because it cannot be grasped by any category of the intellect (though it exists independently and by itself and can be directly realized through spiritual experience.[3])

VII

ABHŪTAPARIKALPA

THE Vijñānavādin also, like the Shūnyavādin, warns us against a nihilistic misconception of shūnyatā. Shūnyatā is not absolute negation, but negation *of* something *in* something. The superimposed alone can be negated. That which is negated is unreal; but that which is the supporting ground of superimposition is real. Pure Consciousness, as the transcendental background of all phenomena, is the only Reality; the superimposed phenomena are all unreal. The only difference between the Vijñānavādin and the Shūnyavādin here is one of degree. The former has given a clear and a detailed account of that which the latter has allowed to remain more or less implicit. Herein lies one of the chief merits of Vijñānavāda inasmuch as it has cleared the misunderstandings and has left no scope for possible misconceptions about shūnyatā. The Vijñānavādin has done this by his conception of the *abhūtaparikalpa* which, like shūnyatā, applies to both phenomena and noumenon. We have explained in the foregoing chapter that shūnyatā, when applied to the Absolute, means prapañcha-shūnyatā or 'the self-proved Absolute devoid of all plurality of thought-constructions', and, when applied to phenomena, means svabhava-shūnyatā or 'the relative phenomenal world devoid of independent existence'. Similarly, abhūtaparikalpa, when applied to the Absolute, means 'the Real Transcendent Ground

[1] Mahāyānasūtrālaṅkāra, XI. [2] Trimshikā, K. 20-21. [3] Ibid, K. 23. Also Madhyāntavibhāga, I, 6.

of all superimposed phenomena' (abhūtasya parikalpo yasmin saḥ) and when applied to phenomena, means 'the phenomenal world of subject-object duality manifested by the self-creative energy of the Ālaya, the Constructive Consciousness' (abhūtasya parikalpo yasmāt saḥ). The term 'abhūtaparikalpa' is usually used for Ālayavijñāna (Constructive Consciousness), also known as the āshraya or the immanent supporting ground of all phenomena. It is the dynamic stream of Constructive Consciousness which manifests itself, through its own power of beginningless and transcendental Ignorance, as the phenomenal world of subject-object duality. It is also called vikalpa (thought-constructing energy) and paratantra (conditioned by causation; relative). Identified with its contents, it is relative; viewed in its own essence, it is the Absolute. The Absolute is at once immanent in phenomena as well as transcendent to them. The abhūtaparikalpa, as Ālaya, is relative; it is the connecting link between the Real and the unreal—its essence is the Real and its contents are unreal. The word abhūtaparikalpa is also used for all the three svabhāvas or levels of existence in three different senses. The Absolute (pariniṣpanna) is abhūtaparikalpa in the sense of being the Transcendental Non-dual Ground-Reality which is totally free of all duality, not involving itself in superimposition, but allowing itself to be indirectly superimposed upon (abhūtasya parikalpo yasmin saḥ). The Relative (paratantra) is abhūtaparikalpa in the sense of Constructive Consciousness which acts as the immanent ground constructing the phenomenal world of subject-object duality through its own power (abhūtasya parikalpo yasmāt saḥ). The Imaginary (parikalpita) is abhūtaparikalpa in the sense of unreal subject-object duality which is superimposed (abhūtash chāsau parikalpitaḥ). All the individual subjects as well as the objects in all the three worlds are declared to be imaginary (parikalpita).[1] Their support, the immanent Ālaya, is said to be the relative reality (paratantra).[2] The Transcendental Ground-Reality, where the Ālaya is shorn of all its adventitious characters and thus transcended (āshrayaparāvṛtti), is the absolute Reality (pariniṣpanna).[3]

When the unreality of the external objects is realized, says Vasubandhu, the individual subject also becomes unreal because subject and object being correlative, one cannot exist without the other. When the subject-object duality is transcended, one dwells in the harmonious bosom of the Absolute.[4] As long as the individual consciousness does not realize its essential unity with Pure Consciousness, so long will the intellect go on giving rise to the subject-object duality.[5] Ultimately even the sentence—'Reality is Pure Consciousness' is also unreal because it is an expression of the intellect itself. Intellect cannot grasp Reality by

[1] abhūtaparikalpastu chitta-chaittās tridhātukāḥ, Madhyāntavibhāga, I, 9. [2] abhūtaparikalpo'sti dvayam tatra na vidyate, Ibid, I, 2. [3] shūnyatā vidyate tvatra tasyāmapi sa vidyate, Ibid. [4] Trisvabhāvanirdesha, K. 36-37. [5] yāvad Vijñaptimātratve vijñānam nāvatiṣṭhate grāhadvayasyānushayas tāvan na vinivartate. Trimshikā, K. 26.

its category of existence. But this should not mean that Reality in itself does not exist because it can be directly realized through Experience which transcends the subject-object duality. Intellect wants to catch the Absolute as an object and this it cannot do.[1] This Pure Consciousness transcends the intellect and all its categories as well as the plurality of the phenomenal world. It is Pure and Undefiled Existence (anāsravo dhātuḥ); it is beyond finite thought (achintyaḥ); it is the Good (kushalaḥ); it is the Eternal (dhruvaḥ); it is Blissful (sukhaḥ); it is Liberation (vimukti); it is Buddha's Body of Pure Existence (dharmakāya).[2]

VIII

GENERAL ESTIMATE

IT is generally believed that Vijñānavāda is a crude subjectivism which denies the reality of the external objects and takes them as the projections of the momentary Vijñānas, that it denies the existence of the Self and maintains that it is nothing over and above the momentary ideas, that it maintains the doctrine of constant flux, and that Reality, according to it, is only the individual momentary Vijñāna. Our exposition of Vijñānavāda, we are sure, deals a death-blow to all such and allied false notions. In no standard work of the Vijñānavāda do we find any of these doctrines. It is a great irony of fate that Shūnyavāda should be condemned as Nihilism and that Vijñānavāda which is Absolute Idealism should be condemned as subjectivism advocating the doctrine of Universal Flux.

We have clearly shown that the application of the theory of Momentariness is restricted by Vijñānavāda to phenomena only. It is only the phenomenal which is momentary. And in this sphere momentariness is emphasized. But momentariness does not even touch Reality. Reality, truly speaking, transcends all the categories of the intellect. It is neither momentary nor permanent. But from the phenomenal point of view it must be described as the eternal, immortal and permanent background of all momentary phenomena. We have also shown that it is only the empirical self or the individual subject or the Ego that is declared to be unreal by Vijñānavāda. The reality of Pure Consciousness alone, variously called as Ālayavijñāna (of the Laṅkāvatāra), Tathāgatagarbha, Chittamātra, Vijñaptimātra, is emphatically maintained. The Pure Consciousness transcends the dualism of the subject and the object as well as the plurality of phenomena. It is the same as the Self-luminous Self.

[1] Vijñaptimātramevedam ityapi hyupalambhataḥ, Ibid, K. 27. [2] achitto'nupalambho'sau jñānam lokottarañcha tat, Ibid, K. 29. sa evānāsravo dhātur achintyaḥ kushalo dhruvaḥ. sukho vimuktikāyo'sau dharmākhyo'yam Mahāmuneḥ, Ibid, K. 30.

Vijñānavāda cannot be called subjectivism. It is not the individual consciousness (kliṣṭa manovijñāna) as associated with other momentary functional ideas (pravṛttivijñāna) that creates the external world. The external world is declared to be a manifestation or modification of Absolute Consciousness. When the external world is declared to be unreal what is meant is that it does not exist independently and outside of Consciousness. True, the dream state and the waking state are placed on a par. But it should not be forgotten that the Parikalpita is distinguished from the Paratantra. Both agree in being ultimately unreal and in existing inside Consciousness. They cannot break the adamantine circle of Consciousness. The subject and the object dance within this circle which they cannot overstep. The *objectivity* of the external world is not denied. The objects appear *as objects* to the subject which perceives them. Only their objectivity does not fall outside of Consciousness because the distinction of the subject and the object is within Consciousness itself which ultimately transcends the subject-object duality. Consciousness is immanent in all phenomena and it is also the permanent transcendental background of all phenomena.

MM. Pt. Vidhushekhara Bhattacharya has raised an interesting point. He says that the Pure Consciousness of Vasubandhu is not absolutely permanent (kūṭastha-nitya) but only relatively so (āpekṣika-nitya). Pt. Bhattacharya distinguishes between 'absolutely permanent' and 'relatively permanent'. He calls the former as 'Nitya' and the latter as 'Dhruva'. He says that Vasubandhu (in his Triṁshikā, Kārika 30) uses the word 'Dhruva' and not 'Nitya' for his Vijñaptimātra. It is therefore only relatively permanent or 'enduring' like a stream or a flame. It may be called 'Pravāhanitya' or 'Santatinitya'.[1]

Pt. Bhattacharya is perfectly right in saying that the Ālayavijñāna is relatively permanent. Vasubandhu himself has made it clear that the Ālaya is only a phenomenal manifestation of Pure Consciousness and is like a stream (srotasaughavat). It may be rightly called 'Santati-nitya'. But perhaps Pt. Bhattacharya fails to distinguish the Ālayavijñāna of Vasubandhu from his Vijñaptimātra. Pt. Bhattacharya is certainly wrong in saying that the Vijñaptimātra is also relatively permanent. His distinction between Nitya and Dhruva is not absolute because these words are often used as synonyms by Buddhism as well as by Vedānta. The words 'Dhruva', 'Nitya', 'Ajara', 'Amara', 'Shāshvata', 'Kūṭastha' etc. are often used as synonyms. Vasubandhu uses the word 'Dhruva' here in the sense of the absolutely permanent. The Vijñaptimātra or the Pure Consciousness which is the only Reality is not 'enduring' but 'absolutely permanent'. Sthiramati, the commentator on Vasubandhu, while explaining the Kārikā in which Vijñaptimātra is declared to be 'Dhruva', clearly points out that the word 'Dhruva' means 'Nitya'. This is sufficient

[1] The Āgamashāstra of Gauḍapāda, Introduction, p. CXLII.

to prove the falsity of Pt. Bhattacharya's contention. Sthiramati openly says that Vijñaptimātra is eternal and permanent; that it is blissful because it is permanent for what is permanent is bliss and what is momentary is misery.[1]

Vasubandhu's system, therefore, is Absolute Idealism. In fact we can say that in the Advaita Vedānta, Vijñaptimātra gives place to Brahman or Ātman, Ālayavijñāna to Īshvara, Kliṣṭa Manovijñāna to Jīva, Viṣayavijñapti to Jagat, and Pariṇāma to Vivarta.

[1] dhruvo nityatvād akṣayatayā, sukho nityatvād eva. yadanityam tad duḥkham ayañcha nityaḥ ityasmāt sukhaḥ, Trimshikā-Bhāsya, p. 44.

Chapter Eight

SVATANTRA-VIJÑĀNAVĀDA

I

INTRODUCTION

THIS school is called Svatantra-Vijñānavāda or Svatantra-Yogāchāra or Sautrāntika-Yogāchāra School of Buddhism. It accepts the metaphysical truth of Vijñānavāda that Reality is Pure Consciousness and wants to support it with independent logical arguments. It wants to combine the metaphysical Idealism of Vijñānavāda with the logical and epistemological Critical Realism of the Sautrāntika School. We may call it the Logical School of Buddhism.

Vasubandhu's disciple Diṅnāga who founded this school is also the founder of Medieval Indian Logic, just as Gotama is the founder of the Ancient and Gaṅgesha of the Modern Indian Logic. Founded by Diṅnāga, fully elaborated and explained by Dharmakīrti, developed almost to perfection by Shāntarakṣita, this school culminated in Kamalashīla, the last great teacher of Buddhism in India.[1]

Buddhist logic is at once logic, epistemology and metaphysics combined. It is logic because it deals with syllogism (parārthānumāna), inference (svārthānumāna) and import of Words (apoha). It is epistemology because it undertakes a thorough investigation of sense-perception (pratyakṣa), of the validity of knowledge (prāmāṇya), and of the Means of Cognition (pramāṇa). It is metaphysics because it discusses the real nature of sensation and of thought and admits that Reality is supra-logical.

Nāgārjuna wrote Vigrahavyāvarttanī, a logical treatise. Asaṅga introduced the Nyāya syllogism into Buddhism. Vasubandhu wrote two logical treatises—Vādavidhi and Vādavidhāna. We are surprised to find Diṅnāga telling us that Vādavidhi is not the work of Vasubandhu.[2] But our curiosity is satisfied by the commentator, Jinendrabuddhi who

These Buddhists are generally regarded as Vijñānavādins and no distinction is made between earlier Vijñānavāda and this later form of Vijñānavāda advocated by these writers. According to us this confusion between the original Vijñānavāda of Laṅkāvatāra, Asaṅga and Vasubandhu and this later development of it by these writers treated in this chapter has begot many worse confusions and has been mainly responsible for giving rise to many misunderstandings. It is, therefore, very necessary to treat these writers as belonging to a separate school which may be called Svatantra-Vijñānavāda. [2] Pramāṇa-Samuchchaya, i, 14.

points out that it 'is not what Vasubandhu would have said in his ripe years; that it was composed while he was yet a Vaibhāṣika. . . . In his Vādavidhāna, Vasubandhu is supposed to have corrected his formulations'.[1] Diṅnāga undertook to complete the logical teachings of his master Vasubandhu and founded the Logical School.

It is very important to remember that though the Logical School accepts the fundamental doctrine of Vijñānavāda that Reality is Pure Consciousness, it rejects the permanence of Consciousness. Vijñānavāda restricts the application of the theory of Momentariness to phenomena only and openly declares Reality to be permanent Consciousness. Svatantra-Vijñānavāda accepts that Reality is Pure Consciousness but it universalizes the theory of Momentariness and openly declares even this Pure Consciousness to be only momentary. Confessing that he agreed with Vasubandhu in metaphysics, Diṅnāga consented to remain on the logical plane and under the disguise of supporting Absolute Idealism with independent logical arguments, he really tried to revive the theory of Momentariness in a subtle manner and actually busied himself with logical revival in order to modify the Absolute Idealism of Vasubandhu by trying to fuse it somehow with Critical Realism. Although the Svatantra-Vijñānavādins, Diṅnāga, Dharmakīrti, Shāntarakṣita and all, pay lip-homage to Vasubandhu by confessing that so far as ultimate reality is concerned they are following in the footsteps of Vasubandhu, yet what they actually do is to undermine the whole metaphysics of Vasubandhu by degrading his permanent Consciousness to the level of a momentary Vijñāna or a unique momentary Particular which they call Svalakṣaṇa. The Ālayavijñāna and the Vijñaptimātra are completely ignored by them.

Unfortunately the *magnum opus* of Diṅnāga, the Pramāna-Samuchchaya, is not available in original Sanskrit. Only its first chapter has been reconstructed into Sanskrit from its Tibetan Version by Mr. H. R. Rangaswamy Iyenger. The Pramāṇa-Vārtika of Dharmakīrti and the Tattva-Saṅgraha of Shāntarakṣita are fortunately available in original.

The Naiyāyika and the Mīmāṁsaka were the two major opponents of Buddhism at that time. Diṅnāga had ruthlessly criticized the Nyāya-Sūtras of Gotama and the Nyāya-Bhāṣya of Vātsyāyana. Uddyotakara in his Nyāya-Vārtika refuted the charges of Diṅnāga and defended the Nyāya position. Dharmakīrti in his Pramāṇa-Vārtika demolished all the arguments of Uddyotakara in such a merciless manner that the eminent Advaitin, Vāchaspati Mishra, at a much later date, had to comment on Uddyotakara in his Nyāya-Vārtika-Tātparya-Tīkā in order to 'rescue the old argument-cows of Uddyotakara which were entangled in the mud of Buddhistic criticism'. Dharmakīrti's attack on Mīmāṁsā also was so damaging that it provoked Kumārila to write his voluminous Sholka-

[1] Buddhist Logic, Vol. I, Stcherbatsky, p. 30.

Vārtika to refute Buddhism and defend Mīmāṁsā. The attacks of the Naiyāyikas and of the Mīmāmsakās, in their turn, gave rise to the writings of Shāntarakṣita and Kamalashīla. Shāntarakṣita in his Tattvasaṅgraha and Kamalashīla in his Pañjikā on it, refute extensively all the charges of the Naiyāyikas, especially of Uddyotakara, and of the Mīmāṁsakas, especially of Kumarila, and criticize all other schools prevalent in their time. But ultimately Buddhism could not resist the onslaught of Brahmanism and was being rapidly ousted from the land of its birth. Shāntarakṣita himself was forced to retire to Tibet where he called his disciple Kamalashīla also. Kamalashīla was the last great scholar of Buddhism in India, though even after him up to a much later date, a Buddhist scholar here and a Buddhist scholar there continued to write. Thus it is that the Svatantra-Vijñānavāda school, after producing an enormously rich philosophical literature by way of approval and by way of criticism, came to an end and with it virtually ended Buddhist philosophy in India.

Now, keeping this background in mind, we proceed to deal with this school. Here we are concerned more with its metaphysical side than with its logical side.

II

THE REVIVAL OF THE DOCTRINE OF MOMENTARINESS

THE Logical School maintains that sensation and thought are the two radically different sources of knowledge. Sensation reflects the unique, momentary, existent, ultimate reality (svalakṣaṇa). Thought conceives a chain of moments by constructing relations and images (sāmānyalakṣaṇa). Accordingly there are two sources of knowledge—perception (pratyakṣa) and inference (anumāna). Perception gives us direct, vivid and concrete reflection of the object. Inference gives us only indirect, vague and abstract thought-constructions.

Right knowledge is successful or efficacious knowledge. Momentariness is equated with motion or change and efficiency is equated with existence. The real is the causally efficient; the unreal is the inefficient. The ultimately existent, says Dharmakīrti, is the efficient.[1] The inefficient is the unreal and we have nothing to do with its existence or non-existence just as a prospective bride has nothing to do with the beauty or ugliness of a eunuch.[2] A real fire is that which burns and cooks and sheds light. A fire which neither burns nor cooks nor sheds light is unreal. The ultimately existent is the momentary particular 'thing-in-itself'. It is the 'this', the 'here', the 'now', the 'present moment of efficiency'. It is indescribable and unutterable because it is shorn of all objectivized

[1] arthakriyāsāmarthyalakṣaṇam paramārthasat, Nyāyabindu, I, 15. [2] Pramāṇa-Vārtika, I, 212.

images. Everything else has only indirect, borrowed or second-rate reality. All thought-relations are fictitious. They are a figment of the imagination.

Existence is efficiency and efficiency is change. The changeless is the inefficient and the inefficient is the unreal. Reality is motion or change. It is instantaneous and kinetic. Only ceaseless change exists. Motion is nothing but the moving thing itself; efficiency is the efficient thing itself; existence is the unique momentary particular itself. Motion, change, efficiency, existence are only names for the momentary thing-in-itself. Similarly, non-existence also is only a name for the thing annihilated. Existence and non-existence are thus two different sides of the same reality.

We are told that reality is motion and we are also told that motion is impossible. Motion is an illusion because things being momentary have no time to move. Motion is only a series of immobilities. Flashes of energy follow one another giving rise to an illusion of motion. In a stream fresh waters are coming in every moment. In a lamp a series of different flames presents an illusion of one flame. The apparent contradiction is solved by the fact that motion is not something over and above the moving things. Things themselves are motion.

Causality is not real production. It is only functional interdependence. The cause does not produce the effect. It has not time to do so. The cause merely preceeds the effect and the effect merely follows the cause. Existence is efficiency and efficiency itself is the cause. Things arise neither out of self nor out of not-self nor out of both nor out of neither. They are not produced at all. The effects are merely functionally dependent upon their causes.[1] All dharmas, therefore, are inactive and forceless (nirvyāpārāḥ akiñchit-karāḥ sarvadharmāḥ). The seeming contradiction that Reality is efficiency and that all elements are inactive is solved by the fact that there is no efficiency over and above existence, that existence itself is causal efficiency (sattaiva vyāpṛtiḥ).

Dharmakīrti says that everything is momentary. Whatever is produced must be destroyed. That which comes into existence and afterwards ceases to exist is called momentary. Reality is annihilation. Change exists by itself and always. Reality is such that it is momentary. Annihilation or destruction, therefore, does not require any cause. Because annihilation is uncaused, it automatically follows everything. Annihilation does not mean destruction of a positive entity. Hence the view that a positive entity is destroyed should be rejected. So when we say that a thing is destroyed what we really mean is that a thing is momentary.[2]

Similarly Shāntarakṣita also observes that all produced things are

[1] na svato nāpi parato na dvābhyām nāpyahetutaḥ. pratītya yat samutpannam notpannam tat svabhāvataḥ. [2] Pramāṇa-vartika, I, 280.

necessarily momentary because they do not depend for their destruction on any cause. They are always and everywhere independent of any cause in regard to their destruction. The so-called causes of destruction are entirely inefficacious and forceless.[1] All entities, being produced, are destroyed. Destruction, therefore, does not depend on any cause except on the fact of being produced.

Shāntarakṣita and Kamalashīla maintain that destruction is neither an entity nor a non-entity. Destruction is of two kinds. Firstly it means the 'momentary character of a thing' (kṣaṇa-sthiti-dharma-rūpa-vināsha). This is transcendental impermanence. Secondly it means 'disruption' (dhvaṁsa-rūpa-nāsha). This is empirical annihilation. An entity itself, because it exists for a moment only, is called 'destruction'. This destruction has a cause. It is only disruption which is causeless. When we admit that transcendental impermanence has a cause what we mean is simply this that an entity is itself the cause of its destruction because the very fact that a momentary entity is produced implies that it is destroyed. There can be no other cause of its destruction.[2] 'The character of coming immediately after the thing' (vastvanantarabhāvitva) does not belong to this destruction because this destruction is born along with the production of the momentary thing itself.[3] Again, disruption too can have no cause. When we say that there is empirical annihilation of a thing what we mean is simply that the thing is not there. This destruction does not convey the affirmation of anything.

That thing which exists for a moment only is called momentary. Kṣaṇa is not a time-moment. It is the character of being destroyed immediately after being produced. The very nature of a thing to disappear after existing for one moment only is called 'Kṣaṇa'. That thing which has this nature is called 'Kṣaṇika'. As a matter of fact there is absolutely no difference between the momentary character and the thing which is supposed to possess this momentary character. The momentary character itself is the momentary thing. The distinction is entirely a product of intellect. It is the creation of language. Though ultimately unreal this distinction is justified in the empirical world because the use of words depends on the pure whim of the speaker.[4]

Only a momentary thing can exist because it alone can be efficient. A permanent entity is inefficient and hence unreal. A permanent entity should produce all its effects simultaneously because the efficient cause being present there is no reason why its effects should be delayed. If it is urged that a permanent entity can produce successive effects because of its association with successive accessories (kramiṇaḥ sahkārinaḥ),

[1] Tattva-saṅgraha, K. 357. [2] yo hi bhāvaḥ kṣaṇasthāyi vināsha iti gīyate, Ibid, K. 375. [3] chalabhāvasvarūpasya bhāvenaiva sahodayāt, Ibid, K. 376. [4] utpādāntarā'sthāyi svarūpam yachcha vastunaḥ. taduchyate kṣaṇah so'sti yasya tat kṣaṇikam matam, Ibid, K. 388-389.

then the question arises whether the accessories work by producing a peculiar modification (atishaya) in the permanent cause or they work independently. In the former case, is the peculiar modification identical with or different from the permanent cause? If it is identical, then it is this peculiar modification, not the permanent entity, which is the cause; if it is different, then how can it be related to the permanent entity? In the latter case, how can a permanent cause tolerate the independent functioning of the accessories? Again, the relation between the permanent cause and its accessories cannot be of the nature of identity (tādātmya) or of productivity (tadutpatti) because the accessories are different from the permanent cause. Nor can it be of the nature of inherence (samavāya) because it is only of the nature of assistance (upakāra). Again, if the nature of the permanent cause together with its accessories is the same as without them, then either the accessories are also permanent and then should give rise to simultaneous creation, or they are useless.[1]

The Naiyāyika and the Mīmāṁsaka object that if things are momentary, then the theory of Karma is thrown overboard. An action is done by one while its result befalls another. Moreover, how can recognition be explained since there is no perceiver who can compare the present with the past? How can a momentary cause which does not abide till the production of the effect, produce it? How can bondage or liberation belong to a momentary entity? Are not all efforts for liberation futile?

Shāntarakṣita and Kamalashīla reply: Identity means only similarity. Recognition is due to memory and memory is due to false imagination. If an entity perceived now is the same as perceived previously, then the difficulty is that how can a cognition of the past apprehend a cognition of the present? The mistake is due to intellect. We know that a 'flame' is nothing but a series of different flames appearing and disappearing every moment. Still we call it the 'same flame'. It is only conventional. Again, the notion of the 'doer' or 'enjoyer' becomes possible in reference to the supposed 'unity of the chain or the series'. This unity is only a creation of the intellect. It is not real.[2] The formula of causation is 'this being produced, that is produced'. The preceding states produce the subsequent states. The cause perishes after it has produced the effect, not before. It perishes in the second moment. The causal efficiency ceases immediately after the production of the effect. The effect is thus produced by the causal efficiency of the first moment. And before the production of the effect that efficiency does not cease. The Vaibhāṣikas maintain that the effect is produced at the third moment. In their view, of course, an effect is produced when the causal efficiency has ceased. But in our view the cause comes into existence in the first moment and produces the effect in the second moment and immediately after producing

[1] Ibid, K. 397-424. [2] Ibid, K. 504.

it the cause ceases to exist.[1] Cause and effect cannot be simultaneous because the cause comes into existence in the first moment before the effect is produced. The cause does not produce the effect holding it, as it were, in a pair of tongs, nor does the effect arise clinging firmly to the cause, as it were, like a lover passionately clinging to his beloved, by reason of which cause and effect may be regarded as simultaneous.[2] There is no causal operation separate from the cause. Causality itself is efficiency. Causality means invariable antecedence (ānantaryaniyama). Existence means efficiency (sattaiva vyāpṛtiḥ). The mere existence of the cause is the efficient causal operation. Cause being present, effect necessarily follows. Causality is the determination of the succeeding states by the preceding states.[2] In fact, there is neither a doer nor an enjoyer. There is none who recognizes or remembers. What exists is only a series of changing mental states; the 'unity' of the series is an illusion. Every Kṣaṇa is a unique momentary existent. Persons engrossed in false notions of the 'Soul' etc. do not perceive this truth. But those who have fully realized this ultimate truth know very well that everything is in a perpetual flux, that the preceding moments invariably go on determining the succeeding moments and knowing this they perform good deeds.[3] Bondage, therefore, means only the series of painful states produced by ignorance and the rest, and liberation means the cessation of this series and the consequent purity of mental states produced by right knowledge.[4]

Indeed, the theory of Momentariness repudiates at one stroke all metaphysical permanent entities like Primordial Matter, Self, God etc. etc.[5]

III

THE PRAMĀṆĀS

CONFORMING to the two kinds of Prameyas or objects of cognition —the direct unique Particular given in pure sensation or pure consciousness and the indirect vague Universal given in thought-construction, there are only two valid Pramāṇas or means of cognition—Perception (pratyakṣa) and Inference (anumāna).

Exposition of Perception:

According to Nyāya, perception is that non-illusive cognition which is produced by the contact of the senses with external objects. For the Svatantra-Vijñānavādin external objects do not exist outside of thought.

[1] tasmādanaṣṭāt taddhetoḥ prathamakṣaṇabhnāvinaḥ. kāryamutpadyate shaktād dvitīyakṣaṇa eva tu., Ibid, K. 512. [2] sattaiva vyāpṛtistasyām satyām kāryodayo yataḥ. ya ānantaryaniyamaḥ saivāpekṣa'bhidhīyate, Ibid, K. 520-521. [3] Ibid, K. 542. [4] kāryakāraṇabhūtāshcha tatrā'vidyādayo matāḥ. bandhas tad vigamādiṣṭā muktir nirmalatā dhiyaḥ, Ibid, K. 544. [5] Ibid, K. 350.

Diṇnāga therefore defines perception as devoid of all thought-determinations, names, universals etc.[1] The adjective 'Non-illusive'(abhrānta) used by Asaṅga is dropped by Diṅnāga as merely superfluous meaning only 'Non-constructive' which idea is already conveyed by the adjective 'devoid of all thought-determinations' (kalpanāpoḍha). The Vaisheṣika maintains that an object qualified by five real predicables—generality, particularity, relation, quality and action—is given in perception which has two moments, the first moment consisting of pure sensation (ālochana-mātra) and the second moment consisting of determination. The Naiyayika develops this into his indeterminate (nirvikalpa) and determinate (savikalpa) perception. Diṅnāga condemns these five predicables to be mere fictions of the intellect. The only object of perception is the unique momentary thing-in-itself shorn of all relations. Dharmakīrti reintroduces the adjective 'non-illusive' in the definition of perception because he thinks it necessary to exclude the sense-illusions like the perception of the double-moon as distinguished from the illusions of thought. He therefore defines perception as devoid of all thought-determinations and illusions.[2] Shāntarakṣita and Kamalashīla agree with Dharmakīrti and define perception as devoid of illusion and determination which is the conceptual content.[3]

Exposition of Inference:

Inseparable connection or Vyāpti is the nerve of inference. In inference an object is cognized through its 'mark' or a valid 'middle term' which has three characteristics—(1) it is present in the *probandum* (anumeya), (2) it is also present in that which is like the *probandum*, and (3) it is absent in that which is not like the *probandum*. Inference for another is a syllogism. The Nyaya syllogism has five members: (1) Thesis, (2) Reason, (3) Example with inseparable connection, (4) Application, and (5) Conclusion. Diṅnāga and his followers reject Thesis, Reason, and Conclusion and retain only two—(1) Example with Inseparable Connection or the General Rule, and (2) Application which includes Reason and Conclusion.

Prof. Dhruva has shown that Diṅnāga cannot be credited with the invention of Vyāpti as 'the doctrine was held by Nyāya and Vaisheṣika writers long before the time of Diṅnāga.[4]'

It is important to note that for Diṅnāga and his followers the validity of inference is only on the phenomenal plane. Inference has no reference to ultimate reality which is indescribable and beyond all thought-determinations. 'This whole business of *probans* and *probandum*,'

[1] pratyakṣam kalpanāpoḍham nāmajātyādyasamyutam, Pramāṇa-Samuchchaya, I, 3. Also Randle's Fragments from Diṅnāga, Fragment 'A'. [2] pratyakṣam kalpanāpoḍham abhrāntam, Nyāyabindu, i, 3. Pramāṇa-Vartika, iii, 123. [3] abhilāpinī pratītiḥ kalpanā, Tattva-Saṅgraha, K. 1214. [4] Nyāya-Pravesha: Prof. Dhruva; Introduction, p. XXXI.

observes Diṅnāga, 'depends on the relation of quality and possessor of quality, a relation which is imposed by thought; and it has no reference to an external existence and non-existence.'[1] 'Vāchaspati Mishra quotes a Buddhist who remarks that these relations considered as objective realities are unfair dealers, who buy goods without ever paying any equivalent.'[2]

Inference is the work of intellect. Although ultimately it has no reference to Reality, yet in the phenomenal world its authority is unquestionable. Refuting the charge of Bhartṛhari that inference may be invalidated on account of the difference in condition, place and time and that an inference which is held true by some may be found false by others of more developed intellect, Shāntarakṣita remarks that a true inference can never be invalidated by any body.[3] Similarly, Dharmakīrti also remarks that fire shall always be inferred from smoke.[4] Shāntarakṣita says that those who deny the validity of inference involve themselves in self-contradiction because by their denial they pre-suppose the validity of inference as they desire that their intention should be inferred from their words.[5]

Criticism of other Pramāṇas:—The Svatantra-Vijñānavādins maintain the validity of perception and inference only. All other Pramāṇas can be either reduced to these two or they are no Pramāṇas at all. Verbal Testimony (shabda) is valid only if it can be tested at the touch-stone of reason. Analogy (upamāna) is a combination of perception and memory. Implication (arthāpatti) can be easily reduced to Inference. For example, we can say:

All fat persons who do not eat during day, eat during night. (Major Premise).

Devadatta is a fat person who does not eat during day. (Minor Premise).

Therefore fat Devadatta eats during night. (Conclusion).

Negation (abhāva) is either a non-entity or it is included in Perception. Other Pramāṇas are no Pramāṇas at all.

Criticism of the Veda:—The Mīmāṁsaka maintains that the Veda is eternal. Words, meanings and their relationship are all eternal. The injunctions and the prohibitions of the Veda are all that we need. The Veda has neither a before nor an after; therefore it is authorless and eternal. Dharmakīrti, Shāntarakṣita and Kamalashīla bitterly criticize this view: The Mīmaṁsaka says that ignorance, jealousy, hatred, etc., which are the causes of the unreliability of words are found in persons; words of persons, therefore, are unreliable. The Buddhist retorts that

[1] sarvo'yam anumānānumeyabhāvo budhyārūḍhena dharmadharmibhāvena na bahiḥ sadasattvam apekṣate. Fragment 'O'. [2] Buddhist Logic; Stcherbatsky, p. 247. [3] Tattvasaṅgraha; K. 1477. [4] Pramāṇa-Vārtika IV 53. [5] Tattvasaṅgraha, K. 1456.

knowledge, non-jealousy non-hatred etc. which are the causes of the reliability of words are found in persons; words of persons, therefore, are reliable.[1] It is only a person who can speak or write or understand words. The Veda itself cannot reveal its meaning. It is indeed a wonder that there are people who can uphold such a clearly absurd view that because we do not remember the authors of the Veda, therefore the Veda is not the creation of persons! Fie on the pitched darkness of ignorance which pervades this world! This view can be valid only for the blind followers who are ignorant of logic.[2] By this logic many other works also whose authors are not known will have to be regarded as authorless. And absolute reliability shall have to be attached to those words of heterodox outsiders, the origin of which cannot be traced, and to those horrible customs of the Mlechchhas or the Pārasīkas, like marrying one's own mother or daughter, the origin of which is not remembered.[3] Again, if the Mīmāṁsaka thinks it his right to give peculiar meanings to such ordinary words like 'Svarga', 'Urvashī', etc. which occur in the Veda, then who can reasonably check us if we proclaim that this sentence of the Veda—'One who desires heaven should perform sacrifice', means that 'One should eat the flesh of a dog' or that 'Buddha is omniscient'?[4] The argument that because some sentences of the Veda are true, therefore the entire Veda is true is clearly wrong because some sentences, even of a trustworthy person, may be wrong while some sentences, even of an untrustworthy person, may be right. It is only the true words of trustworthy persons which do not contradict our experience that should be recognized as the Āgama.[5] If the Mīmāṁsaka is really eager to establish the authority of the Veda, he should try to prove that the Veda is the work of some faultless author of supra-normal vision who has risen above all ignorance. Indeed, right words embodying truth and goodness, and emanating from persons highly intelligent and merciful do claim validity.[6]

The authority of inference is unquestionable in this world. An inference firmly rooted in facts cannot be set aside by the so-called 'Revealed Word'.[7] The words of the Shāstra, the truth of which is proved by reasoning and the true words of any other trustworthy person including oneself, are of equal validity.[8] Dharmakīrti says: in respect to those things the truth of which can be proved by perception or inference, even if we ignore the Shāstra there is absolutely no harm. And in respect to those things, the truth of which cannot be verified by perception or inference, the Shāstra too is impotent.[9] Who has made it a rule that for everything one should take recourse to the Shāstra and

[1] Pramāṇa-Vārtika, I, 227. [2] Pramāṇa-Vārtika, I, 247. Tattva-Saṅgraha, K. 1509. [3] Pramāṇa-Vārtika, I, 247; Svavṛtti, p. 456. Tattva-Saṅgraha, K. 2447. [4] Pramāṇa-Vārtika, I, 320, 322; Tattva-Saṅgraha, K. 3527. [5] Pramāṇa-Vārtika, I, 317. [6] Tattva-Saṅgraha, K. 2400, 3123, 2402. [7] Ibid, K. 2439. [8] Pramāṇa-Vārtika, IV, 93. [9] Ibid, IV, 106.

that without the authority of the Shāstra one should not infer fire from smoke? By whom are the simple-minded innocent persons, unable to know the truth or falsehood by themselves, deluded to the belief that for everything they should fall back on the Shāstra? By whom, alas! are these terrible fetters of the Shāstra imposed upon the innocent folk?[1] A husband with his own eyes saw his wife in an undesirable position with another person. When he rebuked her, she cried addressing her friends—'Oh friends, see the utter folly of my husband. He relies on his bubble-like eyes and refuses to believe the words of his faithful wife'! To have blind faith in every word of the Shāstra even at the expense of perception and inference is like believing a corrupt woman at the cost of one's own eyes.[2]

IV

CRITICISM OF THE CATEGORIES OF NYĀYA-VAISHESIKA

A SUBSTANCE (dravya) is neither the same as nor different from its qualities (guṇa). When we perceive anything, say a cloth, we see only the qualities like colour, length, breadth, thickness, smoothness etc., we do not see any material substance.[3] There are also no 'wholes' or 'composite objects' apart from parts. Only parts are real because we perceive only parts, attributes, qualities. Without seeing the dewlap, horns, hoofs etc, we do not see 'the cow'. If ten pieces of gold are heated into a lump, there is no difference in the weight. If the 'whole' has anything besides the parts, the weight of the lump should have increased. And if the 'whole' is nothing over and above the parts, then the ten different pieces of gold should be called a lump.[4]

Again, if there are eternal atoms, then because they always remain the same, all things should be produced from them either now or never, either all at once or not at all. The laymen imagine a 'mass', a 'composite object' a 'whole'; and people who do not understand the real nature of reality, on the basis of this 'mass' assume atoms. In fact the word 'substance' and the word 'atom' are only conventional; we may give the name 'Lord' to a beggar![5]

The six categories and their properties cannot be related. The relation between them can be neither of conjunction which is restricted to substance, nor of inherence.[6] When 'substance' does not exist, then qualities etc. which depend on it also do not exist. The relation of inherence too by which the qualities are supposed to be related to the substance is a myth.

The category of action (karma) is also unreal because things being

[1] Ibid, IV, 53-54. [2] Pramāṇa-Vārtika-Svavṛtti, p. 613. [3] Pramāṇa-Vārtika, III, 202, 335; Tattva-Saṅgraha, K. 565. [4] Pramāṇa-Vārtika, IV, 154-158. [5] Tattva-Saṅgraha, K. 552, 603, 604. [6] Ibid, K. 574-575.

momentary have no time to move. And if things are permanent, they cannot move. If motion is the essence of mover, rest is impossible; if motion is the essence of non-mover, motion is impossible. If a thing moves at one time and does not move at another, then it will be two different things. Thus whether things are momentary or permanent, says Shāntarakṣita, motion is in both cases an impossibility.[1]

Because there are no 'substances' there can be no specific particulars (visheṣa). They are mere moments.

Inherence (samavāya) is supposed to be the relation between the parts and the whole and it is held to be eternal because its cause is not known. But parts do not exist apart from the whole and there is no whole over and above its parts. If cloth is different from threads then it should appear in potsherds also; and if cloth is not different from threads the latter should be called cloth. Again, if inherence is eternal, then all things should become eternal.[2]

The refutation of the categories of substance, qualities and motion implies the refutation of the category of 'Universal' (sāmānya) which is supposed to reside in the above three categories. The Universal is a mere figment of the imagination. Diṅnāga says: 'It is great dexterity that what (the universal) resides in one place should, without moving from that place, reside in what comes to exist in a place other than that place. It is joined with this thing (which is now coming into existence) in the place where the thing in question is; and yet it does not fail to pervade the thing which is in *that* place. Is not this very wonderful? It does not *go* there—and it was not there before; and yet it is there afterwards—although it is not manifold, and does not quit its former receptacle. What a series of difficulties!'[3] Words, says Dharmakīrti, depend on mere usage. Reality is the individual cow; 'the universal cow' is a figment of the imagination. The reality of the absolutely dissimilar individuals is covered by the imagined universal. The universal therefore is the result of the 'covering' (saṁvṛti) of the intellect.[4] It is only a practical necessity. If every individual was to be named, names would have enormously increased. This work would have been impossible too. Moreover, it would have been fruitless. Therefore in order to differentiate similar individuals of a so-called community from individuals of other communities, the wise persons resorted to conventional names and coined the Universal.[4] Similarly Shāntarakṣita also says that the universal is a mere convention. People use the term 'cow' (go) in respect of an object which serves the purpose of yielding milk etc. Thus a convention in regard to that term is established. It is a mere name.[6]

[1] Ibid, K. 692-707. [2] Ibid, K. 835, 836, 854. [3] Randle: Fragments from Diṅnāga, Frg. Q.; Translation Randle's. na yāti na cha tatrāsīd asti pashchān na chānshavat. jahāti pūrvam nādhāram aho! vyasanasantatiḥ, Ibid, I, 70. [4] Pramāṇa-Vārtika, 69-71. Pramāṇa-Vārtika, I, 139. [5] Tattva-Saṅgraha, K. 727-728.

Reality is the unique and absolutely dissimilar particular thing-in-itself. Intellect, words, names, concepts cannot even touch it. The whole business of the *probandum* and the *probans*, of substance and qualities, of unity and difference, belongs to the empirical reality, not to the absolute momentary thing-in-itself. Reality neither gets united nor does it differ. It cannot be the object of discursive intellect. Reality is one particular thing-in-itself; how can intellect which is diversity grasp it?[1] It cannot be grasped by names and concepts for it transcends language and intellect.[2] No object of finite thought will resist ultimate scrutiny. It is because the intellect cannot even touch Reality, that the wise persons have declared that the more an object of intellect is dialectically examined the more will it give way.[3]

V

EXPOSITION OF THE DOCTRINE OF APOHA

DIṄNĀGA says that all words, all names, all concepts are necessarily relative and so unreal. A word can be described only negatively. It can express its meaning only by rejecting the opposite meaning. A 'cow' means a 'not non-cow'. Names give us universals which are purely imaginary. Names, therefore, are illusory and negative. They do not touch Reality which is real and affirmative though ultimately it transcends both affirmation and negation, nay, all categories of the intellect. Dharmakīrti too has repeatedly stressed that the thing-in-itself is beyond language and intellect and that names and concepts are pure imagination. They express themselves only through negation. Shāntarākṣita also observes that conceptual notions and verbal expressions have no real basis. Their only basis is the purely subjective imagination.[4] The very essence of unique existents is that the object of a word is never apprehended. Neither the thing-in-itself, nor the universal, nor the relation to the universal, nor something which possesses the universal, nor the form of the cognition of the object can really be called the import of words. The thing-in-itself cannot be denoted by words for it is beyond all convention, language and intellect. And others are only a figment of the imagination.[5]

The Naiyāyikas and the Mīmāṁsakas say that the Buddhists in maintaining that the word 'cow' denotes the universal 'negation of the non-cow' admit, by this very expression, the reality of the universal 'cow' as an entity. In fact, non-existence implies existence and negation

[1] Pramāṇa-Vārtika, I, 80, 85, 86, 87, 88, 90, 93, 129, 136; IV, 183-184. [2] nābhidhānavikalpānām vṛttirasti svalakṣaṇe. savram vāggocharātītamūrtir yena svalakṣaṇam, Tattva-Saṅgraha, K. 734. [3] idam vastubalāyātam yad vadanti vipashchitah. yathā yathārthāsh chintyante vishīryante tathā tathā, Pramāṇa-Vārtika, III, 209. [4] Tattva-Saṅgraha, K. 869; Pramāṇa-Vārtika, I, 73. [5] Tattva-Saṅgraha, K. 870-872.

necessarily pre-supposes affirmation. The cognition of the meaning of words is always positive; it is never of the nature of Apoha. If the negation of a negation is different from it then it is a positive thing; if not, then cow becomes the same as the non-cow.

Shāntarakṣita and Kamalashīla in refuting these objections remark: Negation is of two kinds; (1) Relative negation or exclusion (paryudāsa), and (2) Absolute negation or denial (niṣedha). Relative negation too is of two kinds; (a) due to difference of idea (buddhyātma), and (b) due to difference of object (arthātma).[1] In fact, things are absolutely dissimilar, yet on account of certain well-defined potencies (niyata-shakti) some of them become the basis of the conception of similarity. On account of this basis there arises a *reflection* (pratibimbaka) in cognition which is wrongly grasped as '*an object*'. Apoha is the conception of this reflection. The denotative function of the word consists only in the production of this reflection. When this reflection is cognized, the 'exclusion of other objects' follows by implication (sāmarthya). The notion of 'other objects' is not a part of the reflection. Thus only the relative negation is directly cognized while the absolute negation is indirectly cognized by implication. Thus we see that there is no affirmation without negation.[2]

Apoha is the denotation of the word; the positive universal is a false creation of the intellect. Truly speaking, words are neither synonymous nor not-synonymous because they denote neither unity nor plurality. In fact unity and plurality belong to real things only. Exclusions are cognized by conceptual contents which are the result of conventional ignorance. And these conceptual contents only, not things, differ among themselves. Things-in-themselves are neither unified nor diversified; it is only the conceptual content that appears as diverse.[3] The object 'cow' and the object 'non-cow' both are separate realities. Their reality is well-established. It is only the word which is unreal because it depends on the pure whim of the person using it. Words do not cognize external objects. They cognize only their own reflections. And on account of the force of ignorance words mistake their own internal reflections to be external objects. This is all that they can do. Words cannot even touch the object. No object can be denoted as qualified by Apoha.[4] Words can reflect individuals only and so the individuals may be denoted by words. But words cannot reflect universals. So universals can be neither denoted nor excluded by words. And even if they are excluded they cannot become real. When a thing excludes another, it is called its Apoha. But by this, neither the thing becomes negative nor does the Apoha really become positive.[5] Thus the 'cow' which is a

[1] Tattva-Saṅgraha, K. 1004. [2] Ibid, K. 1005-1006, 1011-1021. [3] Ibid, K. 1047, 1049. Also Pramāṇa-Vārtika, I, 88. [4] Ibid, K. 1066-1067. Also Pramāṇa-Vārtika, I, 80, 136. [5] Ibid, K. 1082.

'negation of the non-cow' is a positive entity and is different from the non-cow. But from the phenomenal standpoint, Apohas are recognized as positive and so they cannot be taken to be mere nonentities. From the ultimate standpoint however there can be no object which may be denoted by Apoha for there is neither that which denotes nor that which is denoted. Things being momentary, all this business is impossible.[1]

VI

CRITICISM OF THE PRIMORDIAL MATTER (PRAKṚTI) OF SĀṄKHYA

THE Sāṅkhya maintains the existence of an eternal Prakṛti, Pradhāna or Avyakta, because all individual things are limited and finite, because they imply a common cause, because one eternal Matter transforms itself into various evolutes, because there is a distinction between cause and effect and because the unity of the universe points to a single cause. The effect, therefore, must pre-exist in the cause. Five reasons are adduced for the doctrine of Satkāryavāda: (1) the nonexistent, like the sky-lotus, cannot be produced; (2) the cause is always implied; (3) everything cannot be produced by everything; (4) the efficient alone can produce that for which it is efficient; and (5) the effect is the essence of the cause.

Shāntarakṣita and Kamalashīla criticize this doctrine as follows: The arguments adduced by Sāṅkhya against Asat-kāryavāda can be urged with equal force against its Satkāryavāda. We can say that the effect does not pre-exist in the cause because (1) the existent cannot be produced as its production will be a vain repetition; if curd pre-exists in milk then milk should taste like curd; (2) because there is nothing to be produced, there can be no implication of the cause and so (3) no specific cause; (4) no efficient cause; and (5) no essence or operation of the cause.[2]

To us Asat-kāryavāda too is a misnomer. We do not advocate the production of a non-entity. What is produced is a thing itself which, before its production, was non-existent. Reality itself is efficient causation. Production means 'becoming a thing'. This production has no connection with existence or non-existence. It is related only to a non-existent concept. The seed of this conception is the fact that a thing which exists for one moment only was non-existent in the preceding moment. Production is the 'own essence' of a thing which exists for one moment only, irrespective of all connection with the past and the future. In fact there is no non-existent entity which can be produced; the view that the non-existent is produced is therefore purely imaginary.[3]

Again, even if the three qualities are admitted, the existence of an

[1] Ibid, K. 1089. [2] Ibid, K. 16-21. [3] Ibid, K. 32-33; Pañjikā, pp. 32-33.

eternal Prakṛti is not proved. An eternal is inefficient and can never be a cause. Then creation should be simultaneous. If accessories are admitted, then either they, and not the eternal Matter, are the causes or they are useless.[1] Again, it is highly absurd that Prakṛti knows only to perform and not to enjoy. Again, according to our view everything cannot be produced out of everything because the potency in the causes varies. So without taking recourse to Prakṛti, we can explain the diversity in effects and causes by diversity in the potencies.[2]

VII

CRITICISM OF GOD (ĪSHVARA)

DHARMAKĪRTI says that an eternal God cannot be regarded as the cause of this world. To Chaitra, a weapon causes a wound and a medicine heals that up. Both the weapon and the medicine are regarded as causes because they are momentary and capable of successful activity. God is neither momentary nor is He efficient. If the opponent is so fond of taking an inactive and inefficient entity like God to be the cause of this world, he should better hold a dry trunk of a tree as the cause of this universe. God is eternal and so He cannot change. And unless He changes, He cannot be a cause. Moreover, it is difficult to understand as to why an eternal God should acquire the power to become the cause only at a particular time when He starts the creation. An effect arises from a combination of causes and conditions. Now, if any other thing except that particular combination is wrongly regarded as the cause of that effect, then infinite regress is bound to creep in. We shall have to search for a cause of God Himself and then another cause of that cause and so on *ad infinitum*. The argument of the opponent that creation implies the Creator, just as a pot implies a potter is answered by Dharmakīrti by pointing out that though an effect presupposes a cause, yet all effects do not pre-suppose the same cause, otherwise from fog we shall infer fire and even an ant-hill will be regarded as the work of a potter. The capacity to produce an effect lies in a combination of causes, not in eternal things like God.[3]

Shāntarakṣita and Kamalashīla also point out that when there are no composite objects in this world, how can there be an Intelligent Being who is supposed to produce them? It is like proving that an ant-hill is the creation of a potter. Even objects like houses, stair-cases, gates, towers etc. are made by persons who are many and who have fleeting ideas. If the opponent means only this that all effects presuppose an intelligent cause, we have no quarrel with him because we also

[1] Ibid, K. 19-20; Also Pramāṇa-Vārtika, I, 166-167. [2] Ibid, K. 45. [3] Pramāṇa-Vārtika, II, 12-28.

maintain that this diverse universe is the result of intelligent actions. We only refute his one Intelligent and Eternal Creator. Logically his eternal Creator should have His own cause and this cause should have another cause and so on *ad infinitum*. Again, either God is a nonentity like a sky-lotus and so incapable of producing anything, or the entire creation should be simultaneous. If God depends on accessories, He is not independent; if He does not, then creation should be simultaneous.[1]

Again, why should God create this world at all? If He is determined by someone else, He is not free. If he is prompted by compassion, He should have made this world absolutely happy and not full of misery, poverty, grief and pain. Moreover, before creation there were no objects for whom compassion might have been felt by God. Again, if He is guided in creating and destroying this world by good or bad actions of persons, then He is not free. If He creates the world through sport, then He is not even master of His own amusement as He depends on His playful instincts. If creation is due to His very existence or nature, then there must be simultaneous production. If He has no power to create in the beginning, He cannot acquire it afterwards. If it is said that like a spider gradually producing webs out of its very nature, God also gradually produces this world out of His very nature, it is wrong, because a spider does not, by its very nature, produce webs. What produces them is the saliva which comes out of the mouth of the spider on account of its eager desire to eat insects. If it is said that creation emanates from God unintentionally, then how can God be called intelligent? Even a fisherman thinks twice before he acts.[2]

The arguments which refute Prakṛti and Īshvara, also refute their *joint causality* as admitted by Yoga.

Nor can creation be *at random* without any cause. Even the lotus and its filaments, sharpness of thorns, beauty of peacock-feathers etc. are caused by seeds, earth, water etc.[3]

VIII

CRITICISM OF BRAHMAN

IF it is maintained that Brahman in itself is an undifferentiated unity and appears as diversity only because of Ignorance, then we urge, say Shāntarakṣita and Kamalashīla, that this unity is neither proved by perception nor by inference. Moreover, Brahman cannot even produce a cognition, for consciousness is successive and momentary. Brahman is therefore like the son of a barren woman. Again, if Brahman is always of

[1] Tattva-Saṅgraha, K. 56-87. [2] Ibid, K. 156-169. [3] Ibid, K. 113-115; Also Pramāṇa-Vārtika, II, 180-182.

the nature of Pure Consciousness, then Ignorance and its result bondage are impossible. All persons without the least effort on their part will be emancipated. Again, if Ignorance is regarded as the essential nature of Brahman, then liberation will be impossible. Again, Ignorance cannot be viewed as something apart from and independent of Brahman for then the monism will be destroyed. Further, it is improper to describe Ignorance as 'indescribable', or even as something which can be described 'neither as existent nor as non-existent', because in order to be an entity, Ignorance must be either existent or non-existent. Again, because Brahman is one, so bondage of one means the bondage of all and liberation of one means the liberation of all.

For us, on the other hand, Ignorance is a disposition or force of false attachment. For us bondage means a series of defiled cognitions produced by Ignorance, while liberation means a series of pure cognitions produced by Right Knowledge.[1]

IX

CRITICISM OF THE SELF (ĀTMAN)

(*a*) *Of the Self of the Followers of the Upaniṣads:* The Advaitins who follow the Upaniṣads[2] maintain that one eternal Consciousness is the only reality which illusorily appears as subject and as object. Shāntarakṣita says that this view contains only a very slight error and that error is that this Pure Self which is Pure Consciousness is regarded as *eternal.*[3] We perceive only changing cognitions and so, apart from them there is no eternal cognition. If there were only one eternal consciousness, then how can the diverse cognitions be explained? They too will have to be cognized all at once. If ultimate reality is one eternal consciousness, then all distinction between wrong and right knowledge, between bondage and liberation will be wiped off. And all Yogic practices for right knowledge and consequent liberation will be useless.[4]

(*b*) *Of the Self of Nyāya-Vaisheṣika:* This School maintains that our ideas must have a self which knows them and in which all our desires, feelings and ideas inhere. Shāntarakṣita and Kamalashīla point out that knowledge does not require a knower for its illumination, nor do desires, feelings and ideas require a receptacle like material things, for they are regarded as immobile by the opponents. Consciousness itself when associated with the notion of the Ego is called the Self. It has only phenomenal reality. Ultimately it denotes nothing.[5] Desires, feelings

[1] Ibid, K. 144-151, 544; Also Pañjikā, 74-75; Also Pramāṇa-Vārtika, II, 202-205. [2] advaitadarshanāvalambinashcha aupaniṣadikāḥ, Pañjika, p. 123. [3] teṣām alpāparādhan tu darshanam nityatoktitaḥ, Tattva-Saṅgraha, K. 330. [4] Ibid, K. 328-335. [5] ahaṅkārāshrayatvena chittamātmeti gīyate. samvṛyā, vastuvṛtyā tu viṣayo'sya na vidyate. Ibid, 204.

and ideas are momentary and arise in succession like the material seed, sprout and creeper etc. They do not need any permanent self to inhere.[1]

(*c*) *Of the Self of Mīmāṁsā:*—Kumārila maintains that just as a snake remains a snake, though sometimes it may assume a coiled and sometimes a straight posture, similarly the self is essentially of the nature of eternal and pure Consciousness, though it may pass through many phases of feelings, volitions and thoughts. Self-consciousness proves the existence of the Self and the fact of recognition repudiates the No-soul theory. To this the Buddhists object that if the Self is regarded as one eternal Consciousness, then all cognitions will have to be regarded as one and eternal. Kumārila replies that the diversity of cognitions is due to the diversity of objects. Just as fire which has the nature of burning burns only those combustible objects which are presented to it or just as a mirror or a crystal, though it has the power to reflect, reflects only those objects which are put before it, similarly the Self, though it is of the nature of eternal consciousness, apprehends only those sense-data which are presented to it by sense-organs. The Buddhists retort that if cognitions are influenced by the changing functions of the sense-organs and the sense-objects, they cannot be regarded as one and eternal. Moreover, the diversity of cognitions in dreams and hallucinations where there is no objective counterpart will not be explained. Again, if fire burns all combustible objects, then the whole world will be at once reduced to ashes. Again, a mirror or a crystal which is itself momentary is only an apparatus to produce an illusory image. Again, if the changing feelings, volitions and thoughts etc. are identical with the Self, then the Self will not be permanent; and if they are different from the Self, then how can their change affect the Self? Again, the simile of the snake is also wrong. The snake becomes coiled etc. because it is itself momentary. Had it been permanent like the Self it could have never changed. In fact the Self or the ego-notion is due to beginningless ignorance. There is no apprehender of the notion of the 'I'. Hence there is no knower. Recognition is based on the false notion of memory and it cannot prove the existence of the Self.[2]

(*d*) *Of the Self of Sāṅkhya:*—Sāṅkhya also maintains that the Self is pure and eternal consciousness and is different from buddhi or the faculty of cognition. Against this view it is urged by the Buddhists that if the Self only enjoys what is reflected in buddhi, then are these reflections identical with or different from the Self? If identical, then the Self should also change with the reflections; if not, then the Self cannot enjoy them. Again, if actions belong to buddhi while fruits belong to the Self, then the charge of vicarious suffering stands. Again, if it is said that Prakṛti and Puruṣa work together like the blind and the lame, and that Prakṛti gives fruits to Puruṣa according to his desires, then how

[1] Ibid, K. 191-217. [2] Ibid, K. 241-283.

is it that many times an intense desire for a thing is felt but the desired thing is absent? Again, at the time of enjoyment, if there is modification in the Puruṣa, he is not eternal; and if there is no modification in him, he cannot be the enjoyer and Prakṛti can be of no help to him. Moreover, if Prakṛti brings about this diverse creation in accordance with the Self's 'desire to see', then how can Prakṛti be called Unconscious? To hold that Prakṛti only knows to prepare delicious dishes but does not know to eat them is highly absurd.[1]

Indeed intellect, volition, consciousness, knowledge, sentience are all synonyms. There is no harm if Consciousness is described as the Self. We only object to its being called *eternal.*[2]

(*e*) *Of the Self of the Jainas:*—The Jainas like the Mīmāṁsakas maintain that the Self is Consciousness. But they regard it as an Identity-and-difference. As substance (dravya) it is identity and is inclusive (anugamātmaka); and as 'successive factors' (paryāya), it is diversity and is exclusive (vyāvṛttimat), just as a Man-Lion (Nara-Siṁha), though one, has a double nature. But this view is absurd. Either pure identity alone or pure difference alone can be logically maintained. Both cannot exist side by side in the same entity. Man-Lion too is not of a double nature. He is only an aggregate of fleeting atoms.[3]

The shameless and naked Jainas, says Dharmakīrti, make such non-sensical and contradictory remarks that Reality is both existence and non-existence, unity and plurality, inclusion and exclusion. If it is so then curd is curd as well as a camel. Then, when a person is asked to eat curd, he should run to eat a camel![4]

(*f*) *Of the Self of the Vātsīputrīyas:*—These Hīnayānists, says Shāntarakṣita, even though they call themselves Buddhists (saugataṁmanyāḥ), uphold the Self under the name of the Pudgala and declare it to be neither identical with nor different from the five skandhas, to be neither real nor unreal and hence to be indescribable. They should know that the Pudgala is like a sky-lotus; it is ultimately unreal. In order to be an 'entity' a thing must be either real or unreal. Only a non-entity like a sky-lotus can be called 'indescribable'.[5] Efficiency or successful activity is the definition of existence. Only a momentary thing can be efficient and therefore real. The indescribable cannot be called an existent entity. Great persons like Vasubandhu etc. have successfully explained the seeming contradictions in the scripture by pointing out that the apparently contradictory teachings of the Merciful Buddha are due to his Excellent Skill, that he provisionally taught the existence of the Pudgala only to remove the false notion of non-existence.[6]

[1] Ibid, K. 288-300. [2] chaitanye chātmashabdasya niveshe'pi na naḥ kṣatiḥ. nityatvam tasya duḥsādhyam akṣyādeḥ saphalatvataḥ, Ibid, K. 302, 305. [3] Ibid, K. 311-327. [4] Pramāṇa-Vārtika, I, 182-185. [5] Tattva-Saṅgraha, K. 339. [6] Ibid, K. 348.

X

CRITICISM OF EXTERNAL OBJECTS AND EXPOSITION OF THE DOCTRINE THAT REALITY IS PURE CONSCIOUSNESS

DIṄNĀGA in his Ālambana-parīkṣā criticizes the atoms of the Vaibhāṣikas and of the Vaisheṣikas and the arguments used by him are similar to those used by Vasubandhu in his Viṁshatikā. Consciousness is the only reality. The so-called external objects do not exist independently and outside of consciousness. Consciousness manifests itself as the subject as well as the object. The so-called external object is only the 'knowable-aspect' (grāhya-bhāga) or the 'object-condition' (ālambana-pratyaya) of consciousness. Its *objectivity* is not denied for it is said to appear as *object* to the knowing subject. Only its objectivity does not fall outside of consciousness. The opponent objects that if the object is a part of consciousness and appears simultaneously with it, then how can it be a condition to consciousness itself? Diṅnāga answers this by pointing out that the object, the essence of which is consciousness and which is only the knowable-aspect of consciousness, appears *as if* it is something external and also serves as a condition to consciousness because of its invariable association with consciousness and also because of its transmitting the force in succession. The sense-organ is only the force in consciousness which force acts as an auxiliary cause to enable consciousness to manifest itself. This force is not something opposed to consciousness for it is inside consciousness itself. Thus the object which is only the knowable-aspect of consciousness and the sense-organ which is only the force of consciousness go on determining each other from beginningless time.[1]

Dharmakīrti also asserts that an object is nothing but relative existence and the latter is nothing but dependence on causes and conditions. The form in which consciousness manifests itself under causes and conditions is called an 'external object'.[2] The diversity among intellects is due to the different mental dispositions (saṁskāra) or forces (vāsanā), and not to the so-called plurality of external objects.[3] When it is proved that consciousness itself appears as an object, Dharmakīrti says that he himself does not know through what beginningless ignorance an external object is taken to be real![4] Indeed to those whose vision is blurred by magic, small round potsherds look like coins and pebbles look like diamonds![5] It is only when philosophers, like elephants, close their eyes from the ultimate reality and descend on the phenomenal

[1] yadantarjñeyarūpam hi bahir-vad avabhāsate, Ālambana-Parīkṣā, K. 6-8. [2] Pramāṇa-Vārtika, III, 224. [3] Ibid, III, 336. [4] Ibid, III, 353. [5] Ibid, III, 355.

plane that they take external objects as a practical necessity.[1] Reality is Pure Consciousness. It manifests itself internally as subject and externally as object. But the distinction between internal and external is *within* Consciousness itself. Consciousness is a unity. Its manifestation as subject and object is therefore only an appearance, not reality.[2] The subject-aspect and the object-aspect of Consciousness are mutually relative. One without the other is unreal. Reality which is this non-dual Pure Consciousness ultimately transcends the subject-object duality.[3] Everything which can be defined, which can be brought under the categories of intellect is an appearance and does not fall outside the subject-object duality. Appearances, therefore, are declared to be unreal because they are indefinable.[4] It is only through Ignorance that the non-dual Pure Consciousness appears as the duality of the subject and the object.[5] Like the external object, the internal subject is also unreal. It is the ego-notion and is the root-cause of all suffering.[6] The real Self is self-luminous Consciousness; all impurities are adventitious.[7]

Shāntarakṣita and Kamalashīla call themselves Nirākāra-Vijñānavādins or the upholders of Formless Consciousness. Shāntarakṣita frankly confesses that the fact that Pure Consciousness is the ultimate reality has been clearly established by eminent Āchāryas like Vasubandhu in his Vijñaptimātratā-siddhi and like Diṅnāga in his Ālambanaparīkṣā, and that so far as ultimate reality is concerned he is following the same path.[8] Whether consciousness arises as formless (anirbhāsa) or with form (sanirbhāsa) or with something else (anyanirbhāsa), the fact is that it can never cognize any external object for the simple reason that such object does not really exist.[9] Consciousness needs nothing else for apprehension. Self-consciousness means the necessarily non-unconscious character of consciousness. It means that knowledge is essentially self-luminous. The objection of Kumārila that though cognition is illuminative yet it needs a potent external object for its function of apprehension is answered by pointing out that there is no distinction between cognition and its function, that cognition means apprehension of the object and that therefore it needs neither any other function nor any external object.[10]

Consciousness ultimately transcends the subject-object duality. It is 'without a second' (advaya). It needs neither a knowing subject nor a known object. It is essentially self-luminous.[11] The objection of Bhadanta Shubhagupta that for proving that Consciousness is the ultimate reality

[1] tadupekṣitatattvārthaih kṛtvā gajanimīlanam. kevalam lokabuddhyaiva bāhyachintā pratanyate, Ibid, III, 219. [2] Ibid, III, 212. [3] Ibid, III, 213. [4] Ibid, III, 215. [5] avibhāgo'pi buddhyātmā viparyāsitadarshanaiḥ. grāhyagrāhakasamvittibhedavān iva lakṣyate, Ibid, III, 354. Ibid, II, 196. [7] prabhāsvaram idam chittam prakṛtyā'gantavo malāḥ, Ibid, II, 208. [8] Vijñāptimātratāsiddhir dhīmadbhir vimalīkṛtā. asmābhis tad dishā yātam paramārthavinishchaye, Tattva-Saṅgraha, K. 2084 [9] Ibid, K. 1999. [10] Ibid, K. 2017, 2022. [11] Ibid, K. 2079.

the argument given is that consciousness is essentially consciousness, which is no argument at all, is answered by pointing out that consciousness is essentially self-luminous and no external object can be regarded as self-luminous. External object, therefore, cannot be real. It is only a knowable-aspect of consciousness which on account of ignorance appears *as if* it is something external. Though a part of consciousness, it becomes a condition to consciousness because it is invariably associated with it.[1] Pure Consciousness is self-luminous and by its very nature is the essence of true knowledge. All impurities come from outside. Consciousness, therefore, is essentially self-consciousness because it is self-luminous and free from all impositions.[2] Consciousness really transcends the subject-object duality. Neither the subject nor the object is ultimately real. The Buddhas have therefore declared consciousness to be free from these two aberrations. Who will entertain a wrong notion about consciousness unless he be confused with duality and determination?[3] This pure Consciousness is in fact the Pure Self. True knowledge consists in the realization of this Pure Self (vishuddhātma-darshana) and it arises when it is known that Ultimate Reality is Pure Consciousness which is devoid of all adventitious impurities.[4] This is the highest Truth taught by the Buddha, the Expounder of Truth. It is the cause of all prosperity and ultimate Good. It is the true Dharma for the wise people have declared that to be Dharma from which prosperity and ultimate Good result. It has not been realized by the non-Buddhist Keshava (of the Gītā) and others.[5]

XI

EXPOSITION OF THE BUDDHA

WITH all religious fervour, Dharmakīrti salutes the Buddha whom he declares to be Pure Consciousness transcending all categories of the intellect (vidhūtakalpanājāla); from whom rays of Consciousness burst forth in every direction (samantasphuraṇatviṭ); who is Pure Existence (dharmakāya); who is Deep and Pure Bliss (gambhīrodarā-mūrti, i.e. sambhogakāya); and who is full of compassion on all sides (samantabhadra, i.e. nirmāṇakāya.)[6] But in strict conformity with his acute logic he is forced to say that the Buddha is absolutely reliable, not because he is omniscient, but because he possesses true knowledge, because he knows and prescribes the means to achieve true knowledge to realize what is good and what is bad.[7] Dharmakīrti thus denies omniscience even to the Buddha. The Buddha is reliable because he possesses true

[1] Ibid, K. 2082-2083. [2] Ibid, K. 3435, 3437. [3] Ibid, K. 3536, 3538. [4] etadeva hi tajjñānam yad vishuddhātmadarshanam. āgantukamalāpetachittamātratvavedanāt, Ibid, K. 3535. [5] Ibid, K. 3486, 3540. [6] Pramāṇa-Vārtika, I, 1. [7] Ibid, II, 32.

knowledge (jñānavān), because he is full of compassion (kāruṇikaḥ) and because he is overwhelmingly kind (dayāvān). His words are not false because, having realized true knowledge and the right path, he has prescribed them for all to practise.[1] A reliable person should be neither omniscient nor far-sighted. Omniscience in this world is impossible and if far-sightedness is to be the criterion of truth, then let us all adore the vultures![2]

Shāntarakṣita, however, strongly differs from Dharmakīrti on this point and emphatically declares the Buddha to be Omniscient. The Mīmāṁsaka argues that an omniscient Being is impossible. One cannot know even all the atoms and the hair of one's body, how can one claim to know everything? Of course one may call him 'All-knowing' (sarvavit) who knows the meaning of the word 'All' (sarva)! Moreover, if Buddha is omniscient, why not Kapila? And if both, why the difference between their teachings? It is possible for more intelligent persons to know something more but not everything. By practice one may jump about fifteen feet in the sky; but surely one cannot jump over eight miles, though practice one may for innumerable times. It is said that the Buddha is like the Chintāmaṇi Jewel and when he sits in meditation, even the walls freely proclaim his teachings. Such absurd statements can be believed only by those who have blind faith. We are not blind followers. We want reasons.[3]

The objections of the Mīmāṁsaka are answered by Shāntarakṣita and Kamalahīla thus:

It is wrong to say that because the Omniscient Being is not perceived therefore he does not exist. Mere non-apprehension cannot prove the non-existence of a thing. Even if his existence is not proved there should be *only doubt* about his existence, not certainty about his non-existence.[4] Moreover, we maintain that an omniscient Being exists. He cannot be perceived by ordinary people. How can a person perceive the Omniscient unless he himself becomes Omniscient. Only the saints can directly realize him. Or the Omniscient Being, being Self-luminous, Himself sees Himself.[5]

We do not propound the existence of the Omniscient Being merely on the authority of the scripture. When the inferential mark is present why should recourse be taken to verbal testimony?[6] In fact, omniscience is nothing else than the highest stage of knowledge.[7] The young one of a regal swan cannot even come out of its nest. But through practice it can fly even across the ocean. Similarly a man by acquiring true knowledge through constant yogic practices can become the Buddha. The Buddha for our benefit has proclaimed the doctrine of Nairātmya which

[1] Ibid, II, 145-146. [2] Ibid, II, 33. [3] Tattva-Saṅgraha, K. 3269, 3270, 3311.
[4] Ibid, K. 3276. [5] svayamevātmanātmānam ātmajyotiḥ sa pashyati, Ibid, K. 3290.
[6] Ibid, K. 3510. [7] Pañjikā, p. 908.

is the unique Gateway to Bliss and which frightens the wrong doctrines. One who has realized this truth cannot be tainted with any defect, for defect and truth, like darkness and light, are opposed to each other. And when there is no defect and no attachment, all 'coverings' of ignorance are removed and consequently Omniscience is realized and Oneness with the Buddha is attained.[1] When the truth that Consciousness is the only reality and that ultimately there is no object (dharma-nairātmya) and no subject (pudgala-nairātmya) is realized, the cycle of birth-and-death comes to a standstill. This state is called Apavarga.[2]

The Merciful Buddha who is the true friend of all, has taught the right doctrine to everybody without making any distinction of any kind.[3] The wise Brāhmaṇas pay their respects to the Omniscient Buddha.[4] The real Brāhmaṇas are those who have removed all their sins by practising the teaching of Nairātmya and they are to be found in the religion founded by the Enlightened Sage.[5] The spurious Brāhmaṇas, unable to defend their wrong views by means of sound arguments fall back upon the authority of the Veda. The Great Buddha, on the other hand, confident of his power to expound the right doctrine through reasonable arguments, curbing the arrogance of the maddened elephant-like opponents, fearlessly roars like a lion in the following manner:—'O Bhikṣus, accept my words not out of mere respect for me, but after testing them at the touchstone of reason, just as gold is accepted as true by the wise after heating, cutting and rubbing against the touchstone'.[6]

[1] Tattva-Saṅgraha, K. 3322, 3338-3339. [2] Ibid, K. 3488, 3491, 3539, 3492. [3] Ibid, K. 3569. [4] Ibid, K. 3512. [5] Ibid, K. 3589. [6] 'tāpāch chhedāch cha nikaṣāt suvarṇam iva paṇḍitaiḥ. parīkṣya bhikṣavo! grāhyam mad vacho na tu gauravāt'. Ibid, quoted as K. 3588.

Chapter Nine

SĀṄKHYA

I

INTRODUCTION

SĀṄKHYA is undoubtedly one of the oldest systems of Indian Philosophy. We find references to the Sāṅkhya-Yoga doctrines in some of the Upaniṣads, e.g., in the Chhāndogya,[1] the Prashna,[2] the Kaṭha[3] and particularly in the Shvetāshvatara;[4] in the Mahābhārata;[5] in the Gītā;[6] and in the Smṛtis and the Purāṇas. Bādarāyaṇa, the author of the Vedānta-sūtra, repeatedly refers to the view whether the Sāṅkhya can be regarded as the teaching of the Upaniṣads and rejects it,[7] besides undertaking refutation of the Sāṅkhya in the Tarkapāda on rational grounds. Shaṅkarāchārya regards it as the 'main opponent' (pradhāna-malla) of Vedānta and says that though Sāṅkhya and Yoga are generally accepted by the wise as conducive to the Highest Good, yet these systems advocate dualism and cannot be supported by the Shruti. These words are used in the Shruti and the Smṛti in the sense of knowledge and action respectively and words like Mahat, Avyakta etc. are used in the sense of names and forms.[8] The fact that Bādarāyaṇa and Shaṅkara are keen to reject the view that Sāṅkhya, though accepted by the wise, is not based on the Upaniṣads because it advocates dualism, suggests that there must have been some thinkers belonging to the Sāṅkhya who claimed it to be the teaching of the Upaniṣads. Though nothing can be said with absolute certainty, it seems highly probable that the Sāṅkhya in the beginning was based on the Upaniṣads and had accepted the theistic Absolute, but later on, under the influence of the Jaina and the Buddhist thought, it rejected theistic monism and was content with spiritualistic pluralism and atheistic realism. And it is this Sāṅkhya to which Bādarāyaṇa and Shaṅkara are opposed. This also explains why some of the later Sāṅkhyas, e.g. Vijñānabhikṣu in the sixteenth century, tried to revive the earlier theism in Sāṅkhya.

Tradition regards Kapila as the founder of this system. But Sāṅkhya-pravachana-sūtra which is attributed to him is generally regarded by

[1] VI, 4, 1. [2] VI, 2. [3] I, 3, 10-13. [4] IV, 5, 10, 12, 16; VI, 10, 13, 18. [5] XII, 318; Shāntiparva 303-308. [6] II, 39; III, 42; V, 4-5. [7] I, 1, 5-11; II, 1, 1-3. [8] Shāṅkara-Bhāsya, I, 1, 5-10; I, 4, 1-3 and 28; II, 1, 3.

scholars as a work of the fourteenth century A.D., because it has not been referred to by the earlier writers of the other schools, because it criticizes the rival systems and because it wants to revive theism. So far as theism is concerned, we maintain that the original Sāṅkhya was theistic. But the fact that this work has been ignored and Īshvara-kṛṣṇa's Kārikā has been referred to instead by the other earlier writers, as well as the fact that it criticizes other systems go against this work being regarded as that of Kapila himself. As Īshvarakṛṣṇa himself speaks of Kapila, Āsuri, and Pāñchashikha, it seems probable that these were historical personages whose works have been lost. Kapila certainly flourished before Buddha and he must have composed Sāṅkhya-sūtra which work was unfortunately lost long ago. Īshvarakṛṣna's Sāṅkhya-Kārikā seems to be the earliest available and the most popular work of this system. Besides this we have Gauḍapāda's Sāṅkhya-Kārikā-bhāṣya, Vāchaspati Mishra's Tattva-Kaumudī and Vijñāna-bhikṣu's Sāṅkhya-pravachana-bhāsya.

The word 'Sāṅkhya' is derived from the word 'Saṅkhyā' which means right knowledge as well as number. The Gītā uses this word in the sense of knowledge, so does the Mahābhārata at other places also. Sāṅkhya means the philosophy of right knowledge (samyak khyāti or jñāna). The system is predominantly intellectual and theoretical. Right knowledge is the knowledge of the separation of the Puruṣa from the Prakṛti. Yoga, as the counterpart of Sāṅkhya, means action or practice and tells us how the theoretical metaphysical teachings of Sāṅkhya might be realized in actual practice. Thus Sāṅkhya-Yoga forms one complete system, the former being the theoretical while the latter being the practical aspect of the same teaching. Sāṅkhya is also the philosophy of numbers, because it deals with twenty-five categories. As a philosophy of numbers, it might have influenced the Pythagorean philosophy.

Īshvarakṛṣṇa (fifth century A.D.) is the representative of the classical Sāṅkhya which had divorced itself from the Upaniṣads under the influence of Jainism and Buddhism, yet the Vedāntic teaching of absolutism with which the original Sāṅkhya was associated, asserts itself implicitly in Īshvarakṛṣṇa. We have seen that absolutism is implicit in Jainism and explicit in Mahāyāna Buddhism and we shall see how it is implicit in Īshvarakṛṣṇa also.

Sāṅkhya maintains a clear-cut dualism between Puruṣa and Prakṛti and further maintains the plurality of the Puruṣas, and is silent on God. It is a pluralistic spiritualism and an atheistic realism and an uncompromising dualism.

II

THEORY OF CAUSATION

LET us first consider the Sāṅkhya theory of causation on which its doctrine of Prakṛti is based. The basic question involved in any theory of causation is: Does the effect pre-exist in its material cause? Those who answer this question in the negative are called Asatkāryavādins, while those who answer it in the affirmative are called Satkāryavādins. According to the former, the effect is a new creation, a real beginning. The effect (kārya) does not pre-exist (asat) in its material cause. Otherwise, there would be no sense in saying that it is produced or caused. If the pot already exists in the clay and the cloth in the threads and curd in milk, then why should the potter exert himself in producing the pot out of the clay, and why should not the threads serve the purpose of the cloth and why should not milk taste like curd? Moreover, its production would be its repeated birth which is nonsense. Nyāya, Vaisheṣika, Hīnayāna Buddhism, Materialism and some followers of Mīmāṁsā believe in Asatkāryavāda, which is also known as Ārambhavāda, i.e., the view that production is a new beginning. Materialism believes in Svabhāvavāda; Hīnayāna Buddhism in Anitya-paramāṇuvāda or Kṣaṇabhaṅgavāda and Nyāya-Vaisheṣika and some followers of Mīmāṁsā in Nitya-paramāṇu-kāraṇavāda. The Satkāryavādins, on the other hand, believe that the effect is not a new creation, but only an explicit manifestation of that which was implicitly contained in its material cause. Here, another important question arises: Is the effect a real transformation or an unreal appearance of its cause? Those who believe that the effect is a real transformation of its cause are called Pariṇāmavādins (pariṇāma = real modification); while those who believe that it is an unreal appearance are called Vivartavādins (vivarta = unreal appearance). Sāṅkhya, Yoga and Rāmānuja believe in Pariṇāmavāda. The view of Sāṅkhya-Yoga is called Prakṛti-pariṇāma-vāda, while the view of Rāmānuja is called Brahma-pariṇāmavāda. Shūnyavāda, Vijñānavāda and Shaṅkara believe in Vivartavāda. Their views may be respectively called Shūnyatā-vivarta-vadā, Vijñāna-vivarta-vāda and Brahma-vivarta-vāda. The view of Jainism and of Kumārila may be called Sadasatkāryavāda because according to them the effect is both real as well as unreal before its production—real as identical with the cause and unreal as a modal change thereof, though ultimately both incline towards Pariṇāmavāda.

Sāṅkhya believes in Satkāryavāda. All material effects are the modification (pariṇāma) of Prakṛti. They pre-exist in the eternal bosom of Prakṛti and simply come out of it at the time of creation and return to it at the time of dissolution. There is neither new production nor utter destruction. Production means development or manifestation (āvirbhāva); destruction means envelopment or dissolution (tirobhāva). Production is evolution; destruction is involution. Sāṅkhya gives five arguments in support of Satkāryavāda:

(1) If the effect does not pre-exist in its cause, it becomes a mere nonentity like the hare's horn or the sky-flower and can never be produced (asadakaraṇāt).
(2) The effect is only a manifestation of its material cause, because it is invariably connected with it (upādānagrahaṇat).
(3) Everything cannot be produced out of everything. This suggests that the effect, before its manifestation, is implicit in its material cause (sarvasambhavābhāvāt).
(4) Only an efficient cause can produce that for which it is potent. This again means that the effect, before its manifestation, is potentially contained in its material cause. Production is only an actualization of the potential (shaktasya shakyakaraṇāt). Were it not so, then curd should be produced out of water, and cloth out of reeds, and oil out of sand-particles.
(5) The effect is the essence of its material cause and as such identical with it. When the obstructions in the way of manifestation are removed, the effect naturally flows out of its cause. The cause and the effect are the implicit and the explicit stages of the same process. The cloth is contained in the threads, the oil in the oil-seeds, the curd in the milk. The effect pre-exists in its material cause (karaṇabhāvāt).[1]

III

PRAKṚTI

THE theory that causation means a real transformation of the material cause leads to the concept of Prakṛti as the root-cause of the world of objects. All worldly effects are latent in this uncaused cause, because infinite regress has to be avoided. It is the potentiality of nature, 'the receptacle and nurse of all generation'. As the uncaused root-cause, it is called Prakṛti; as the first principle of this Universe, it is called Pradhāna; as the unmanifested state of all effects, it is known as Avyakta;

[1] asadakaraṇād upādānagrahaṇāt sarvasambhavābhāvāt. shaktasya shakyakaraṇāt karaṇabhāvāchcha satkāryam. Sāṅkhya-Kārikā, 9.

as the extremely subtle and imperceptible thing which is only inferred from its products, it is called Anumāna; as the unintelligent and unconscious principle, it is called Jaḍa; and as the ever-active unlimited power, it is called Ṣhakti. The products are caused, dependent, relative, many and temporary as they are subject to birth and death or to production and destruction; but Prakṛti is uncaused, independent, absolute, one and eternal, being beyond production and destruction. The extreme subtleness of Prakṛti makes it unmanifest and imperceptible; we infer its existence through its products. Motion is inherent in it in the form of Rajas. As the source of the inanimate world, it is unconscious. The entire world of objects is implicit in the bosom of Prakṛti. Evolution is the explicit manifestation of this world of objects, while dissolution is the returning of this world to Prakṛti. Sāṅkhya believes that consciousness cannot be regarded as the source of the inanimate world, as Vedānta and Mahāyāna believe, because an intelligent principle cannot transform itself into the unintelligent world. On the other hand, the material atoms of the physical elements too cannot be regarded as the cause of this world, as Chārvākas, Nyāya and Vaisheṣika, Jainism and Hīnayāna Buddhism, and Mīmāṁsā wrongly believe, because they cannot explain the subtle products of matter like intellect, mind and ego (these are different from pure consciousness which belongs to Puruṣa alone, and are regarded here as internal organs), and further because the unity of the universe points to a single cause while the atoms are scattered and many. Unintelligent, unmanifest, uncaused, ever-active, imperceptible, eternal and one Prakṛti alone is the final source of this world of objects which is implicitly and potentially contained in its bosom.

Sāṅkhya gives five proofs for the existence of Prakṛti which are as follows:

(1) All individual things in this world are limited, dependent, conditional and finite. The finite cannot be the cause of the universe. Logically we have to proceed from the finite to the infinite, from the limited to the unlimited, from the *peros* to the *aperos*, from the temporary to the permanent, from the many to the one. And it is this infinite, unlimited, eternal and all-pervading Prakrti which is the source of this universe (bhedānām parimāṇat).

(2) All worldly things possess certain common characteristics by which they are capable of producing pleasure, pain and indifference. Hence there must be a common source composed of three Guṇas, from which all worldly things arise (samanvayāt).

(3) All effects arise from the activity of the potent cause. Evolution means the manifestation of the hitherto implicit as the

explicit. The activity which generates evolution must be inherent in the world-cause. And this cause is Prakṛti (kāryataḥ pravṛtteścha).

(4) The effect differs from the cause and hence the limited effect cannot be regarded as its own cause. The effect is the explicit and the cause is the implicit state of the same process. The effects, therefore, point to a world-cause where they are potentially contained (kāraṇakāryavibhāgāt).

(5) The unity of the universe points to a single cause. And this cause is Prakṛti. (avibhāgāt vaishvarūpyasya).[1]

Prakṛti is said to be the unity of the three Guṇas held in equilibrium (guṇānām sāmyāvasthā). The three Gunas are Sattva, Rajas and Tamas. They are the constituents of Prakṛti and through it of the worldly objects. Being subtle and imperceptible their existence is inferred from their effects—pleasure, pain and indifference respectively. Although they are called Guṇas, yet they are not ordinary qualities or attributes like the Nyāya-Vaisheṣika Guṇas. They themselves possess qualities like lightness, activity, heaviness etc. They are extremely fine and ever-changing elements. They make up Prakṛti which is nothing apart from them. They are not the qualities which Prakṛti, the substance, possesses; on the other hand they themselves constitute Prakṛti. They are the factors or the constituents or the elements of Prakṛti. They are called Guṇas[2] because they are the elements of Prakṛiti which alone is called substantive; or because they are subservient to the end of the Puruṣa, or because they are intertwined, like three strands, to make up the rope of Prakṛti which binds the Puruṣas.

Sattva literally means real or existent and is responsible for the manifestation of objects in consciousness. It is called goodness and produces pleasure. It is light and bright, buoyant (laghu) and illuminating (prakāshaka). Luminosity of light, power of reflection, upward movement, pleasure, happiness, contentment, bliss are all due to it. Its colour is white. Rajas, which literally means foulness, is the principle of motion. It produces pain. Restless activity, feverish effort and wild stimulation are its results. It is mobile (chala) and stimulating (upaṣṭambhaka). Its colour is red. Tamas, which literally means darkness, is the principle of inertia. It produces apathy and indifference. Ignorance, sloth, confusion, bewilderment, passivity and negativity are its results. It is heavy (guru) and enveloping (varaṇaka) and as such is opposed to Sattva. It is also opposed to Rajas as it arrests activity. Its colour is dark. These three guṇas which constitute Prakṛti are never separate. They

[1] bhedānām parimāṇāt samanvayāt kāryataḥ pravṛtteshcha. kāranakāryavibhāgād avibhāgād vaishvarūpyasya, Sāṅkhya-Kārikā, 15. [2]Guṇa means 'quality', 'secondary' and 'strand of a rope'.

conflict and yet co-operate with one another and are always found intermingled. They are compared to the oil, the wick and the flame of a lamp, which, though opposed, yet co-operate to produce the light of a lamp. They are imperceptible and are inferred from their effects. All things are composed of these three guṇas and their differences are due to the different combinations of these guṇas. The nature of a thing is determined by the preponderance of a particular guṇa. Things are called good, bad or indifferent; intelligent, active or slothful; pure, impure or neutral, on account of the predominance of sattva, rajas or tamas respectively. When these guṇas are held in a state of equilibrium, that state is called Prakṛti. Evolution of worldly objects does not take place at this state. These guṇas are said to be ever-changing. They cannot remain static even for a moment. Change is said to be of two kinds—homogeneous or sarūpa-pariṇāma and heterogeneous or virūpa-pariṇāma. During the state of dissolution (pralaya) of the world, the guṇas change homogeneously, i.e., sattva changes into sattva, rajas into rajas and tamas into tamas. This change does not disturb the equilibrium of the guṇas and unless the equilibrium is disturbed and one predominates over the other two, evolution cannot take place. Evolution starts when there is heterogeneous change in the guṇas and one predominates over the other two and brings about terrific commotion in the bosom of Prakṛti.

The nature of these guṇas is beautifully brought out in a Hindi couplet by Rasalīna. The poet says that the eyes of the beloved are white, red and dark, and are full of nectar, intoxication and poison, with the result that once they pierce the heart of the lover, he experiences the joy of life, the agony of restlessness and the inertia of death. The recollection of the beloved gives him joy and makes life worth living; separation causes acute pain and makes him restless; intensity of love makes him forget everything and become inactive, unconscious and almost dead.[1] Sattva is white and is like nectar and gives joy; rajas is red and is like intoxication and gives pain; tamas is dark and is like poison and produces unconsciousness. 'We bow to Prakṛti,' says Īshvarakṛṣṇa, 'the red-white-dark, the unborn mother and "nurse and receptacle of all generation".'[2] Such is the conception of Prakṛti in Sāṅkhya.

IV

PURUṢA

THE other of the two co-present co-eternal realities of Sāṅkhya is the Puruṣa, the principal of pure Consciousness. Puruṣa is the soul, the self, the spirit, the subject, the knower. It is neither body nor senses nor

[1] amī-halāhala-mada-bhare shveta-shyāma-ratanāra. jiyata, marata, jhuki jhuki parata, jehi chitavata ika bāra. [2] ajāmekām lohita-shukla-kṛṣṇām bahvīḥ prajāḥ sṛjamānām namāmaḥ.

brain nor mind (manas) nor ego (ahaṅkāra) nor intellect (buddhi). It is not a substance which possesses the quality of Consciousness. Consciousness is its essence. It is itself pure and transcendental Consciousness. It is the ultimate knower which is the foundation of all knowledge. It is the pure subject and as such can never become an object of knowledge. It is the silent witness, the emancipated alone, the neutral seer, the peaceful eternal. It is beyond time and space, beyond change and activity. It is self-luminous and self-proved. It is uncaused, eternal and all-pervading. It is the indubitable real, the postulate of knowledge, and all doubts and denials pre-suppose its existence. It is called nistraiguṇya, udāsīnā, akartā, kevala, madhyastha, sāksī, draṣṭā, sadāprakāshasvarūpa, and jñāta.[1]

Sāṅkhya gives the following five proofs for the existence of the Puruṣa:

(1) All compound objects exist for the sake of the Puruṣa. The body, the senses, the mind and the intellect are all means to realize the end of the Puruṣa. The three guṇas, the Prakṛti, the subtle body—all are said to serve the purpose of the self. Evolution is teleological or purposive. Prakṛti evolves itself in order to serve the Puruṣa's end. This proof is teleological (saṅghātaparārthatvāt).

(2) All objects are composed of the three guṇas and therefore logically presuppose the existence of the Puruṣa who is the witness of these guṇas and is himself beyond them. The three guṇas imply the conception of a nistraiguṇya—that which is beyond them. This proof is logical (triguṇādiviparyayāt).

(3) There must be a transcendental synthetic unity of pure Consciousness to co-ordinate all experiences. All knowledge necessarily presupposes the existence of the self. The self is the foundation (adhiṣṭhāna), the fundamental postulate of all empirical knowledge. All affirmations and all negations equally presuppose it. Without it, experience would not become experience. This proof is ontological (adhiṣṭhānāt).

(4) Non-intelligent Prakṛti cannot experience its products. So there must be an intelligent principle to experience the worldly products of Prakṛti. Prakṛti is the enjoyed (bhogyā) and so there must be an enjoyer (bhoktā). All objects of the world have the characteristics of producing pleasure, pain and bewilderment. But pleasure, pain and bewilderment have meaning only when there is a conscious principle to

[1] tasmāchcha viparyāsāt siddham sākṣitvamasya puruṣasya. kaivalyam mādhyastham dṛṣṭṛtvam akartṛbhāvashcha, Sāṅkhya-Kārikā, 19.

experience them. Hence Puruṣa must exist. This argument is ethical (bhoktṛbhāvāt).

(5) There are persons who try to attain release from the sufferings of the world. The desire for liberation and emancipation implies the existence of a person who can try for and obtain liberation. Aspiration presupposes the aspirant. This proof is mystical or religious (kaivalyārtham pravṛtteḥ).

Unlike Advaita Vedānta and like Jainism and Mīmāmsā, Sāṅkhya believes in the plurality of the Puruṣas. Like the Jīvas of the Jainas, the souls of Rāmānuja and the monads of Leibnitz, the Sāṅkhya Puruṣas are subject to qualitative monism and quantitative pluralism. The selves are all essentially alike; only numerically are they different. Their essence is consciousness. Bliss is regarded as different from consciousness and is the product of the sattvaguṇa. Sāṅkhya gives the following three arguments for proving the plurality of the Puruṣas:

(1) The souls have different sensory and motor organs and undergo separate births and deaths. Had there been only one Puruṣa, the birth or death of one should have meant the birth or death of all and any particular experience of pleasure, pain or indifference by one should have been equally shared by all. Hence the souls must be many.

(2) If the self were one, bondange of one should have meant bondage of all and liberation of one should have meant liberation of all. The activity of one should have made all persons active and the sleep of one should have lulled into sleep all other persons.

(3) Though the emancipated souls are all alike and differ only in number as they are all beyond the three guṇas, yet the bound souls relatively differ in qualities also, since in some sattva predominates, while in others rajas, and in still others tamas.[2] Hence their difference.

V

EVOLUTION

WE have seen that Prakṛti is regarded as essentially dynamic. If motion were not inherent in Prakṛti, it could not be given to it by any outside agency; and if motion once ceased in Prakṛti, it could not reappear. Hence Prakṛti is always changing.[3] Even in dissolution, there is

[1] saṅghātaparārthatvāt triguṇādiviparyayād adhiṣṭhānāt. puruṣo'sti bhoktṛbhāvāt kaivalyārtham pravṛtteshcha, Ibid, 17. [2] jananamaraṇakaraṇānām pratiniyamād ayugapat pravṛtteshcha. puruṣabahutvam siddham traigunyaviparyayāchchaiva.
[3] pratikṣṇapariṇāmino hi sarvabhāvā ṛte chitishakteḥ.

homogeneous change (sarūpa or sajātīya parināma) in Prakṛti when all the three guṇas are in the state of equilibrium. It is only when heterogeneous change takes place and rajas vibrates and makes sattva and tamas vibrate that the equilibrium is disturbed and evolution takes place. Sattva, the principle of manifestation and rajas, the principle of activity were formerly held in check by tamas, the principle of non-manifestation and non-activity. But when rajas, the principle of activity vibrates and makes the other two vibrate, the process of creation begins. And creation is not the new creation of the worldly objects, but only their manifestation. It is only making explicit of that which was formerly implicit. Evolution is regarded as cyclic and not linear. There is no continuous progress in one direction, but alternating periods of evolution (sarga) and dissolution (pralaya) in a cyclic order. Evolution is again said to be teleological and not mechanical or blind. Evolution takes place for serving the purpose of the Puruṣa. Prakṛti, the guṇas, the senses, the mind, the ego, the intellect, the subtle body—all are constantly serving the end of the Puruṣa. This end is either worldly experience (bhoga) or liberation (apavarga). Puruṣa needs Prakṛti for enjoyment as well as for liberation, for saṁsāra as well as for Kaivalya. Evolution supplies objects to be enjoyed to the Puruṣa and also works for his liberation by enabling him to discriminate between himself and Prakṛti

Now the question is: How does evolution take place? Evidently when heterogeneous motion arises and rajas disturbs the equilibrium of the guṇas. But how is the equilibrium disturbed? Sāṅkhya fails to answer this question satisfactorily. The fundamental blunder of Sāṅkhya has been to separate Prakṛti and Puruṣa as absolute and independent entities. As a matter of fact, the subject and the object are two aspects of the same reality which holds them together and yet transcends them. All realistic pluralism, of whatever brand it may be, has failed to answer this question satisfactorily. If Prakṛti and Puruṣa are absolutely separate and independent entities, then they can never unite together, nor can there be any *tertium quid* to unite them. And if they cannot unite evolution cannot take place. Sāṅkhya says that the disturbance of the equilibrium of the guṇas which starts evolution is made possible by the contact of Puruṣa and Prakṛti. Puruṣa without Prakṛti is lame and Prakṛti without Puruṣa is blind. 'Theory without practice is empty and practice without theory is blind.' 'Concepts without percepts are empty and percepts without concepts are blind.' Prakṛti needs Puruṣa in order to be known, to be seen, to be enjoyed (darshanārtham); and Puruṣa needs Prakṛti in order to enjoy (bhoga) and also in order to obtain liberation (apavarga), in order to discriminate between himself and Prakṛti and thereby obtain emancipation (kaivalyārtham). If Prakṛti and Puruṣa remain separate, there is dissolution. For creation they must unite. Just as a lame man and a blind man can co-operate and the lame may sit on the shoulders of the blind and point to him the way, while the blind may walk and thus both can reach the destination, though neither of them could have done that separately, similarly the inactive Puruṣa and the non-intelligent Prakṛti co-operate to serve the end, and this union disturbs the equilibrium of the guṇas and leads to evolution.[1] But how can the two opposed and independent entities really come into contact? Sāṇkhya realizes this difficulty and in order to avoid it says that there is no real contact between Puruṣa and Prakṛti and that only the proximity of the Puruṣa, only the fact that Puruṣa is near to Prakṛti (puruṣa-sannidhi-mātra), is sufficient to disturb the equilibrium of the guṇas and thus lead to evolution. But here Sāṅkhya falls into another difficulty. The Puruṣa being always near to Prakṛti (for the inactive Puruṣa cannot move), evolution should never stop and dissolution would become impossible. Evolution, then, would be beginningless and the very conception of Prakṛti as the state of equilibrium of the three guṇas would be impossible. Sāṅkhya finds itself between these two horns of a dilemma—either no contact and hence no evolution or else no equilibrium and hence no Prakṛti and no dissolution. In order to avoid these difficulties, Sāṅkhya now posits the theory of the semblance of a contact (samyogābhāsa). Of course, there is no real contact (samyoga) between Puruṣa and Prakṛti; there is the semblance of a contact and it is this semblance which leads to evolution. Puruṣa is reflected in the intellect (buddhi) and wrongly identifies himself with his own reflection in the buddhi. It is this reflection of the Puruṣa which comes into contact with Prakṛti and not the Puruṣa himself. But buddhi or mahat is regarded as the first evolute of Prakṛti and how can it arise before evolution to receive the reflection of the Puruṣa? To avoid this difficulty it is said that the Puruṣa is reflected in the Prakṛti itself. If so, then liberation and dissolution would become impossible because Prakṛti being always there and it being the essential nature of the Puruṣa to identify himself with his reflection in the Prakṛti, he would never get liberation and the very purpose for which evolution starts would get defeated. Moreover, the reflection being always there, there would be no dissolution and so no equilibrium of the guṇas and hence no Prakṛti. Again, if semblance of a contact is sufficient to disturb the equilibrium, then evolution itself becomes a semblance of evolution, an appearance only (vivarta) and no real transformation (pariṇāma) of Prakṛti. Thus we see that in order to defend the initial blunder of regarding Puruṣa and Prakṛti as absolute and independent entities, Sāṅkhya commits blunders after blunders.

[1] puruṣasya darshanārtham kaivalyārtham tathā pradhānasya. paṅgvandhavad ubhayor api saṁyogas tatkṛtaḥ sargaḥ, Ibid, 21.

VI

THE EVOLUTES

THE first product of the evolution is called Mahat, the Great. It is the germ of this vast world of objects including intellect, ego and mind. It is cosmic in its nature. But it has a psychological aspect also in which it is called buddhi or intellect. Buddhi is distinguished from consciousness. Puruṣa alone is pure consciousness. Buddhi or intellect, being the evolute of Pṛakṛti, is material. It is made of finest matter and is thus capable of reflecting clearly the consciousness of the Puruṣa, like a wireless set capable of receiving the aerial waves. On account of the reflection of the Puruṣa in it, it becomes apparently conscious and intelligent. The senses, the mind and the ego function for buddhi or intellect which functions directly for the Puruṣa. Its functions are said to be ascertainment and decision. It arises when sattva predominates. Its original attributes are virtue (dharma), knowledge (jñāna), detachment (vairāgya) and power (aishvarya). When it gets vitiated by tamas, these attributes are replaced by their opposites. Memories and recollections are stored in buddhi.

Mahat produces Ahaṅkāra. It is the principle of individuation. Its function is to generate self-sense (abhimāna). It produces the notion of the 'I' and the 'mine'. It is the individual ego-sense. Puruṣa wrongly identifies himself with this ego and knows himself as the agent of actions, desirer of desires and striver for ends, and possessor and enjoyer of ideas, emotions and volitions and also of material objects. Ahaṅkāra is said to be of three kinds:

(1) Vaikārika or sāttvika, when sattva predominates. Viewed as cosmic, it produces manas and five sensory organs and five motor organs. Viewed as psychological, it produces good deeds.
(2) Bhūtādi or tāmasa, when tamas predominates. Viewed as cosmic, it produces the five subtle elements (tan-mātras). Viewed as psychological, it leads to indifferent acts or to idleness and sloth.
(3) Taijasa or rājasa, when rajas predominates. Viewed as cosmic, it supplies the energy by which the Sāttvika and the Tāmasa produce their respective evolutes. Viewed as psychological, it produces evil deeds.

Manas or mind which arises from the Sāttvika Ahaṅkāra is the subtle and central sense-organ. It can come into contact with the several sense-organs at the same time. According to the Nyāya-Vaisheṣika

School, manas is eternal and atomic and cannot come into contact with several senses simultaneously. According to Sāṅkhya, it is neither eternal nor atomic. It is made up of parts and so can come into contact with the different senses simultaneously. Sāṅkhya assigns to manas the important function of synthesizing the sense-data into determinate perceptions, passing them on to the ego, and carrying out the orders of the ego through the motor organs.

The Sāttvika Ahaṅkāra produces, besides manas, the five sensory and the five motor organs. The five sensory organs (jñānendriya) are the functions of sight, smell, taste, touch and sound. According to the Nyāya-Vaisheṣika, the five sensory organs are derived from the five gross physical elements. But according to the Sāṅkhya, the five senses are the functions of the mind and are derived from Ahaṅkāra. The five motor organs (karmendriya) are the functions of speech, prehension, movement, excretion and reproduction.

Buddhi, ahaṅkāra and manas represent the three psychological aspects of knowing, willing and feeling or cognition, conation and affection respectively. Sāṅkhya calls them material and derives them from Prakṛti. They shine through the light of the Puruṣa and are apparently conscious. All the three are called the internal organs or antaḥkaraṇa and vital breaths (prāṇas) are said to be their modifications. The five sensory and the five motor organs together are called the ten external organs or bāhyakaraṇa. These are the thirteen karaṇas or organs of the Sāṅkhya.

From the Tāmasa Ahaṅkāra arise the five subtle essences which are called Tanmātras or 'things-in-themselves'. These are the essences of sight, smell, taste, touch and sound. Unlike the Nyāya-Vaisheṣika ones, they are not derived from the gross elements. Rather the gross elements themselves arise out of these. They are neither the qualities nor the differentia of the gross elements nor the functions which are the sensory organs, but the subtle essences which produce the gross elements as well as their qualities. From the essence of sound (shabdatanmātrā) arises the element of ether (ākāsha) together with the quality of sound. From the essence of touch combined with the essence of sound, arises the element of air together with the qualities of sound and touch. From the subtle essence of colour or sight combined with those of sound and touch, arises the element of fire or light together with the qualities of sound, touch and colour. From the essence of taste combined with those of sound, touch and colour, arises the element of water together with the qualities of sound, touch, colour and taste. And lastly, from the essence of smell combined with those of sound, touch, colour and taste, arises the element of earth together with the qualities of sound, touch, colour, taste and smell.

Evolution is the play of these twenty-four principles which, together with the Puruṣa who is a mere spectator and outside the play of evolution, are the twenty-five categories of Sāṅkhya. Out of these twenty-five principles, the Puruṣa is neither a cause nor an effect; Prakṛti is only the cause and not the effect; Mahat, Ahaṅkāra and the five subtle essences are both causes and effects; while the five sensory and the five motor organs and the five gross elements and manas are effects only.[1] This may be depicted by the following table:

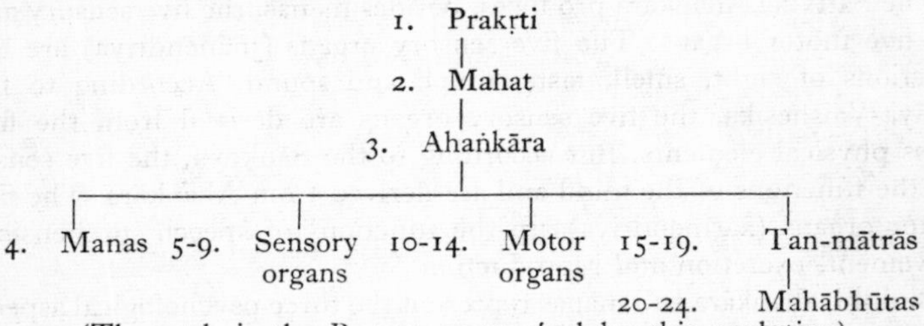
1. Prakṛti
2. Mahat
3. Ahaṅkāra
4. Manas
5-9. Sensory organs
10-14. Motor organs
15-19. Tan-mātrās
20-24. Mahābhūtas

(The 25th is the Puruṣa, untouched by this evolution)

The evolution is teleological. Everything works to serve the purpose of the Puruṣa though unconciously. Just as non-intelligent trees grow fruits, or water flows on account of the declivity of the soil, or iron-filings are attracted towards a magnet, or milk flows through the udders of the cow in order to nourish the calf, similarly everything unconsciously tends to serve the purpose of the Puruṣa, whether it is enjoyment or liberation.[2] Prakṛti is the benefactress of Puruṣa. Though Puruṣa is inactive and indifferent and devoid of qualities, yet the virtuous and the generous Prakṛti which is full of qualities and goodness ceaselessly works through various means in a spirit of detachment for the realization of the Puruṣa, without any benefit to herself.[3] Prakṛti works to liberate the Puruṣa.[4] There is immanent teleology in Prakṛti. Though Puruṣa is neither a cause nor an effect, yet relatively it is he who should be regarded as the efficient cause as well as the final cause of evolution though Sāṅkhya regards Prakṛti as both the material and the efficient cause. He is like Aristotle's God, the unmoved mover who is beyond evolution. God, the pure intelligence, like the Puruṣa, does not actively participate in evolution. He is the end towards which the creation moves. And the creation moves by His mere presence. The guṇas, which mutually differ and yet always co-operate, work like the oil, wick and flame of a lamp and illuminate the entire purpose of the Puruṣa and present it to the buddhi or the intellect.[5] All the organs work for the realization of the Puruṣa's end and for no other end.[6] The subtle body too works for the sake of the Puruṣa's end.[7] Thus the whole creation unconsciously tends

[1] mūlaprakṛtir avikṛtir mahadādyāḥ prakṛtivikṛtayaḥ sapta. ṣoḍashakas tu vikāro na prakṛtir na vikṛtiḥ puruṣaḥ, Ibid, 3. [2] Ibid, 57. [3] Ibid, 60. [4] Ibid, 58. [5] Ibid, 36. [6] Ibid, 31. [7] Ibid, 42.

towards the realization of the purpose of the Puruṣa. And creation will continue till all the Puruṣas are liberated. The entire evolution of Prakṛti, therefore, right from the first evolute, the Mahat, up to the last evolutes, the gross elements, is for the purpose of liberating each individual Puruṣa.[1]

VII

BONDAGE AND LIBERATION

THE earthly life is full of three kinds of pain. The first kind, called ādhyātmika, is due to intra-organic psychophysical causes and includes all mental and bodily sufferings. The second, ādhibhautika, is due to extra-organic natural causes like men, beasts, birds, thorns etc. The third, ādhidaivika, is due to supernatural causes like the planets, elemental agencies, ghosts, demons etc. Wherever there are guṇas there are pains. Even the so-called pleasures lead to pain. Even the life in heaven is subject to the guṇas. The end of man is to get rid of these three kinds of pain and sufferings. Liberation means complete cessation of all sufferings which is the *summum bonum*, the highest end of life (Apavarga or Puruṣārtha).

Puruṣa is free and pure consciousness. It is inactive, indifferent and possesses no attributes. Really speaking, it is above time and space, merit and demerit, bondage and liberation. It is only when it mistakes its reflection in the buddhi for itself and identifies itself wrongly with the internal organ—the intellect, the ego and the mind, that it is said to be bound. It is the ego, and not the Puruṣa, which is bound. When the Puruṣa realizes its own pure nature, it gets liberated which in fact it always was. Hence bondage is due to ignorance or non-discrimination between the self and the not-self and liberation is due to right knowledge or discrimination between the self and the not-self. Liberation cannot be obtained by means of actions. Karma, good or bad or indifferent, is the function of the guṇas and leads to bondage and not to liberation. Good actions may lead to heaven and bad actions to hell but heaven and hell alike, like this wordly life, are subject to pain. It is only knowledge which leads to liberation because bondage is due to ignorance and ignorance can be removed only by knowledge.[2] The Jīva has to realize itself as the pure Puruṣa through discrimination between Puruṣa and Prakṛti. Actions and fruits, merits and demerits, pleasure and pain all belong to the not-self. The knowledge that 'I am not (the not-self)', that 'nothing is mine', that 'ego is unreal', when constantly meditated upon, becomes pure, incontrovertible and absolute and leads to liberation.[3] Sāṅkhya

[1] Ibid, 56. [2] jñānena chāpavargo viparyayād iṣyate bandhaḥ, Ibid, 44. [3] evam tattvābhyāsān nāsmi na me nāham ityaparisheṣam. aviparyayād vishuddham kevalam utpadyate jñānam, Ibid, 64.

admits both Jīvanmukti and Videhamukti. The moment right knowledge dawns, the person becomes liberated here and now, even though he may be embodied due to prārabdha karma. On account of the momentum of past deeds, the body continues to exist for some time, just as the wheel of a potter goes on revolving for some time due to previous momentum even though the potter has withdrawn his hand from it. As the liberated saint, though embodied, feels no association with the body, no new karma gets accumulated as all karma loses causal energy.[1] The final and the absolute emancipation, the complete disembodied isolation automatically results after death.[2] Sāṅkhya liberation is a state of complete isolation, freedom from all pain, a return of the Puruṣa to its pure nature as consciousness. There is no pleasure or happiness or bliss here, for pleasure presupposes pain and is relative to it. Pleasure is the result of sattva guṇa and liberation transcends all guṇas.

Sāṅkhya believes that bondage and liberation alike are only phenomenal. The bondage of the Puruṣa is a fiction. It is only the ego, the product of Prakṛti, which is bound. And consequently it is only the ego which is liberated. Puruṣa, in its complete isolation, is untouched by bondage and liberation. If Puruṣa were really bound, it could not have obtained liberation even after hundred births, for real bondage can never be destroyed. It is Prakṛti which is bound and Prakṛti which is liberated. Īshvarakṛṣṇa frankly says: Puruṣa, therefore, is really neither bound nor is it liberated nor does it transmigrate; bondage, liberation and transmigration belong to Prakṛti in its manifold forms.[3] Prakṛti binds itself with its seven forms.[4] There is nothing finer and subtler than Prakṛti; she is so shy that she never reappears before that Puruṣa who has once 'seen' her in her true colours.[5] Just as a dancing girl retires from the stage after entertaining the audience, similarly Prakṛti also retires after exhibiting herself to the Puruṣa.[6]

VIII

GOD

THE original Sāṇkyha was monistic and theistic. But the classical Sāṅkhya, perhaps under the influence of Materialism, Jainism and Early Buddhism, became atheistic. It is orthodox because it believes in the authority of the Veda. It does not establish the non-existence of God. It only shows that Prakṛti and Puruṣas are sufficient to explain this universe and therefore there is no reason for postulating a hypothesis of God. But some commentators have tried to repudiate the existence of

[1] Ibid, 67. [2] Ibid, 68. [3] tasmān na badhyate'ddhā na muchyate nāpi saṁsarati kashchid. saṁsarati badhyate muchyate cha nānāshrayā prakṛtiḥ, Ibid, 62. [4] Ibid, 63. [5] Prakṛteḥ sukumārataram na kinchidastīti me matir bhavati. yā dṛṣṭāsmīti punar na darṣhanam upaiti puruṣasya, Ibid, 61. [6] Ibid, 59.

God, while the later Sāṅkhya writers like Vijñānabhikṣu have tried to revive the necessity for admitting God. Those who repudiate the existence of God give the following arguments: if God is affected by selfish motives, He is not free; if He is free, He will not create this world of pain and misery. Either God is unjust and cruel or He is not free and all-powerful. If He is determined by the law of Karma, He is not free; if not, He is a tyrant. Again, God being pure knowledge, this material world cannot spring from Him. The effects are implicitly contained in their cause and the material world which is subject to change requires an unintelligent and ever-changing cause and not a spiritual and immutable God. Again, the eternal existence of the Puruṣas is inconsistent with God. If they are the parts of God, they must have some divine power. If they are created by God, they are subject to destruction. Hence there is no God.

IX

GENERAL ESTIMATE

LET us now proceed to give a critical estimate of the Sāṅkhya system. The logic of the Sāṅkhya system, like that of Jainism, impels it to embrace idealistic monism or absolutism but it clings, like Jainism, to spiritualistic pluralism and dualistic realism. The fundamental blunder of Sāṅkhya is to treat Prakṛti and Puruṣa as absolutely separate and independent realities. The Prakṛti and Puruṣa of Sāṅkhya thus become mere abstractions torn away from the context of concrete experience. The object and the subject are relative and not independent and absolute. Experience always unfolds them together. Like the two sides of the same coin, they are the two aspects of the same reality. To dig a chasm between them is to undermine them both. And that is what Sāṅkhya has done. The logic of Sāṅkhya requires it to maintain the ultimate reality of the transcendental Puruṣa alone and to regard Prakṛti as its inseparable power. When this Puruṣa is reflected in its own power Prakṛti, it becomes the empirical ego, the Jīva, the phenomenal. Plurality belongs to this Jīva, not to the transcendental Puruṣa. The subject and the object, the Jīva and the Prakṛti, are the two aspects of the Puruṣa which is their transcendental background. It is the Puruṣa which sustains the empirical dualism between Prakṛti and Jīva and which finally transcends it. Every Jīva is the potential Puruṣa and liberation consists in the actualization of this potentiality. This is the philosophy to which the Sāṅkhya logic points and which is throughout implicit in Sāṅkhya, but which is explicitly rejected by Sāṅkhya with the inevitable and unfortunate result that Sāṅkhya has reduced itself to a bundle of contradictions.

If Prakṛti and Puruṣa are absolute and independent, they can never come into contact and hence there can be no evolution at all. As

Shaṅkara has pointed out, Prakṛti being unintelligent and Puruṣa being indifferent and there being no third principle, no *tertium quid*, there can be no connection of the two. Neither real contact (saṁyoga) nor semblance of contact (saṁyogābhāsa) nor mere presence of Puruṣa (sānnidhya-mātra), as we have noticed above, can explain evolution. Sāṅkhya realizes the mistake, but in order to defend the initial blunder it commits blunders after blunders.[1]

The Sāṅkhya account of Prakṛti makes it a mere abstraction, an emptiness of pure object. The original state of Prakṛti is not a harmony, but only a tension of the three guṇas. The guṇas point to a state beyond them. It is this state which gives harmony to the guṇas and transcends them. Prakṛti does not do that. Hence it is not real. Reality is the Puruṣa alone. Again, Prakṛti is unconscious and unintelligent. How can it then explain the teleology which is immanent in creation? If Prakṛti is unconscious and blind, evolution must be mechanical and blind and there can be no freedom of the will. And if Prakṛti and all its evolutes from Mahat to the Mahābhūtas tend to serve the purpose of the Puruṣa, it can be neither unconscious nor independent. Again, if Prakṛti is blind and non-intelligent, it cannot evolve this world which is full of harmony, order, design and purpose. Stones, bricks and mortar cannot account for the design of a building. Mere clay cannot fashion itself into a pot. How can Prakṛti explain the original impetus, the first push, the *élan vital* which disturbs the equilibrium of the guṇas? The argument that Prakṛti works unconsciously for the emancipation of the Puruṣa just as unintelligent milk flows for the nourishment of the calf is untenable because milk flows as there is a living cow and there is the motherly love in the cow for the calf. Nor can the modification of Prakṛti be compared to that of grass which turns into milk. Grass becomes milk only when it is eaten by a milch cow, and not when it lies uneaten or is eaten by a bull. The simile of the blind and the lame is also misleading since the blind and the lame are both intelligent and active beings who can devise plans to realize a common purpose, while Prakṛti is unconscious and Puruṣa is indifferent and there is no common purpose. The simile of magnet and iron is also misleading because the proximity of the Puruṣa being permanent, there would be no dissolution and hence no liberation and the very state of Prakṛti as the equilibrium of the guṇas would be impossible since the presence of the Puruṣa would never permit the state of equilibrium. Moreover, activity is said to belong to Prakṛti and enjoyment to Puruṣa. This overthrows the moral law of Karma and brings in the charge of vicarious liability. Poor Puruṣa suffers for no fault of its own. Prakṛti performs actions and Puruṣa has to reap their fruits, good or bad. And Prakṛti knows how to make delicious dishes, but not to enjoy them!

Though Prakṛti is called absolute and independent yet there is a note

[1] Supra, pp. 158-9.

of relativism in the conception of Prakṛti. As a triad of the guṇas it points towards the nistraiguṇya Puruṣa as the transcendental reality. At every step, it shows its dependence on Puruṣa. It cannot evolve this world by itself without being influenced by the Puruṣa—whether that influence is due to real contact or semblance of contact or mere presence. How can Prakṛti be absolute then? An absolute Prakṛti is a contradiction-in-terms. If it is absolute why should it care to serve the purpose of the Puruṣa? Does it not make it subservient to the Puruṣa? And if it is unconscious and blind, how can it serve this purpose? Though Sāṅkhya calls Prakṛti as impersonal, yet its descriptions of Prakṛti are full of personal notes. Prakṛti is called a dancing girl; she is feminine, she is virtuous and generous; she is the benefactress of the Puruṣa; she serves Puruṣa's purpose in a spirit of perfect detachment for no gain to herself; and yet she is blind; she is extremely delicate and shy and cannot stand the eye of the Puruṣa; she is seven-rainbow-coloured and wants to attract the Puruṣa. How can such Prakṛti be absolute and impersonal? Puruṣa is untouched by bondage, liberation and transmigration. It is Prakṛti who binds herself and liberates herself and transmigrates. Prakṛti is said to vanish for that Puruṣa who has 'seen' her, though she continues to exist for others. Does this not make Prakṛti relative? If she 'vanishes', how can she be absolute and eternal? Why not frankly equate Prakṛti with Avidyā? Either maintain a plurality of Prakṛtis or equate it with Avidyā. These descriptions of Prakṛti clearly show that Vedānta is *implicit* in Sāṅkhya.

Sāṅkhya throughout makes a confusion between the Puruṣa, the transcendental subject and the Jīva, the empirical ego, the product of the reflection of Puruṣa in Buddhi or Mahat. Sāṅkhya rightly emphasizes that the Puruṣa is pure consciousness and that it is the foundation of all knowledge and that it is beyond bondage, liberation and transmigration. Puruṣa has really nothing to do with the play of Prakṛti. It is a mere spectator and is not among the *dramatis personae*. It is not contaminated by action. It is self-proved and self-shining. It is the transcendental subject which appears as the phenomenal ego. We cannot derive consciousness from Prakṛti or matter, nor can we regard consciousness as a quality. The self is not a substance but a subject. It is the Alone, the unseen seer, the transcendental Absolute. But Sāṅkhya soon forgets its own position and reduces the ultimate Puruṣa to the level of the phenomenal ego. Some of the proofs advanced in support of the existence of Puruṣa, are proofs only for the phenomenal ego. Puruṣa is called enjoyer and Prakṛti enjoyed. But if Puruṣa is the transcendental subject, how can it be an enjoyer? If it is passive, indifferent and inactive, how can it enjoy? Again, how can the transcendental reality be split into the many reals? How can there be a plurality of the transcendental subjects, the Puruṣas? Of course, no one denies the plurality of the empirical egos, the Jīvas. But the manyness of the egos, the empirical souls, does not lead us to the manyness of the transcendental selves, the Puruṣas. In fact, all the arguments advanced by Sāṅkhya to prove the plurality of the Puruṣas turn out to be arguments to prove the plurality of the Jīvas which none has ever denied. Sāṅkhya proves the plurality of the Puruṣas by such flimsy arguments that if there were only one Puruṣa, the birth or death or bondage or liberation or experience of pleasure or pain or indifference of one should lead to the same result in the case of all, forgetting its own doctrine that the Puruṣa is not subject to birth or death or bondage liberation or any action. Realizing this grave defect, the commentators like Vāchaspati, Gauḍapāda and Vījñānabhikṣu have maintained the reality of one Puruṣa only. If Sāṅkhya can reduce all objects to one Prakṛti, why can it not reduce all the empirical souls to one Puruṣa by the same logic? And why can Prakṛti and the empirical Puruṣa be not reduced to the Absolute Puruṣa by the same logic? Again, if all the Puruṣas are essentially similar, if the essence of all is pure consciousness, how can they be really many? Differences and distinctions constitute individuality. If all the Puruṣas are essentially the same, there is no meaning in proclaiming their quantitative plurality. Numerical pluralism is sheer nonsense.

Another grave defect in Sāṅkhya is in its conception of liberation. Liberation is regarded as a negative cessation of the three kinds of pain and not as a state of positive bliss. Sāṅkhya feels that bliss is a product of Sattva guṇa and cannot remain in liberation which is the state beyond the guṇas. But Sāṅkhya forgets that the bliss in liberation is not empirical happiness produced by sattva. This bliss is also transcendental in character. It is beyond both pain and pleasure. What is related to pain is empirical pleasure and not transcendental bliss. The negative Kaivalya suggests an influence of the Hīnayāna Nirvāṇa. Will the liberated Puruṣas, the eternally isolated units not represent 'a vast array of sad personalities'? If liberation is an annihilation (nāsmi, nāham) of human personality and not its perfection, the ideal of liberation is most uninspiring. It must be substituted by an ideal of positively blissful eternal existence in the bosom of the Absolute.

Sāṅkhya, therefore, should let its Prakṛti glide into Avidyā, the inseparable power of the Puruṣa; its Prakṛti-pariṇāma-vāda into Puruṣa-vivarta-vāda; its so-called empirical Puruṣa into phenomenal Jīva; its negative Kaivalya into positively blissful Mokṣa, and should, instead of maintaining the plurality of Puruṣas and creating an unbridgable chasm between the subject and the object, recognize the Absolute Puruṣa, the transcendental subject which gives life and meaning to the empirical subject and object and holds them together and ultimately transcends them both.

Chapter Ten

YOGA

I

INTRODUCTION

PATAÑJALI is the traditional founder of the Yoga system. The word 'Yoga' literally means 'union', i.e., spiritual union of the individual soul with the Universal Soul and is used in this sense in the Vedānta. The Gītā defines Yoga as that state than which there is nothing higher or worth realizing and firmly rooted in which a person is never shaken even by the greatest pain; that state free from all pain and misery is Yoga. According to Patañjali, Yoga does not mean union but spiritual effort to attain perfection through the control of the body, senses and mind, and through right discrimination between Puruṣa and Prakṛti.

Yoga is intimately allied to Sāṅkhya. The Gītā calls them one. Yoga means spiritual action and Sāṅkhya means knowledge. Sāṅkhya is theory; Yoga is practice. For all practical purposes, Sāṅkhya and Yoga may be treated as the theoretical and the practical sides of the same system. Yoga mostly accepts the metaphysics and the epistemology of Sāṅkhya. It shows the practical path by following which one may attain Viveka-jñāna which alone leads to liberation. Yoga accepts the three pramāṇas—perception, inference and testimony of Sāṅkhya and also the twenty-five metaphysical principles. Yoga believes in God as the highest Self distinct from other selves. Hence it is sometimes called 'Seshvara Sāṅkhya' or 'theistic Sāṅkhya' as distinct from classical Sāṅkhya which is nirīshvara or atheistic.

The Yoga-sūtra is divided into four parts. The first is called Samādhipāda which deals with the nature and aim of concentration. The second, Sādhanapāda, explains the means to realize this end. The third, Vibhūtipāda, deals with the supra-normal powers which can be acquired through Yoga. The fourth, Kaivalyapāda, describes the nature of liberation and the reality of the transcendental self.

II

CHITTA AND ITS VṚTTIS

PĀTAÑJALA YOGA is also known as Rāja Yoga. Yoga is defined as the cessation of the modifications of chitta.[1] This cessation is through meditation or concentration which is also called Yoga (yogaḥ samādhiḥ). Chitta means the three internal organs of Sāṅkhya—buddhi or intellect, ahaṅkāra or ego and manas or mind. Chitta is the same as antaḥkaraṇa. It is mahat or buddhi which includes ahaṅkāra and manas. Chitta is the first evolute of Prakṛti and has the predominance of Sattva. It is in itself unconscious. But being finest and nearest to Puruṣa, it has the power to reflect the Puruṣa and therefore appears as if it is conscious. When it gets related to any object, it assumes the 'form' of that object. This form is called Vṛtti or modification. The light of consciousness which comes from the Puruṣa and illuminates this 'form' is called 'jñāna'. Puruṣa is essentially pure consciousness and is free from the limitations of Prakṛti. But it wrongly identifies itself with its reflection in the Chitta and appears to be undergoing change and modification. Chitta, therefore, is the physical medium for the manifestation of the spirit. Just as in a red-hot iron ball, formless fire appears spherical and cold iron appears hot, similarly on account of its reflection in the Chitta, Puruṣa appears changing and Chitta appears conscious. Just as the moon appears as moving when seen reflected in the moving waves, and waves appear as luminous, similarly Puruṣa appears as undergoing modifications and Chitta appears as conscious due to Puruṣa's reflection in it. When the Puruṣa realizes that it is completely isolated and is only a passive spectator, beyond the play of Prakṛti, it ceases to identify itself with its reflection in the Chitta with the result that the light is withdrawn and the modifications of the Chitta fall to the ground. This cessation of the modifications of the Chitta through meditation is called 'Yoga'. It is the return of the Puruṣa to its original perfection.

The modifications of the Chitta are of five kinds: (1) right cognition (pramāṇa), (2) wrong cognition (viparyaya), (3) verbal cognition or imagination (vikalpa), (4) absence of cognition or sleep (nidrā), and (5) memory (smṛti). Right cognition is of three kinds: (*a*) perception (pratyakṣa), when the Chitta, through the sense-organs, comes into contact with the external object and assumes its form, or comes into contact with the internal mental state, (*b*) inference (anumāna), when the Chitta cognizes the generic nature of things, and (*c*) verbal testimony (shabda). Viparyaya is positively wrong knowledge like that of a rope-snake. Vikalpa is mere verbal cognition like that of a hare's horn. Nidrā

[1] yogashchittavṛttinirodhaḥ.

is called absence of cognition, yet it is a mental modification because after sleep a person says 'I slept sound and knew nothing' and therefore there must be some mental modification to support this absence of knowledge. Smṛti is the recollection of past experience through the impressions left behind.

In fact the Puruṣa is the eternally pure and transcendental consciousness. It is the Chitta with the reflection of the Puruṣa in it or the Puruṣa as reflected in the Chitta, which is the phenomenal ego or Jīva, which is subject to birth and death and transmigration and to all painful or pleasurable experiences, and which imagines itself as the agent and the enjoyer. There are five kinds of sufferings (klesha) to which it is subject. These are: (1) ignorance (avidyā), (2) egoism (asmitā), (3) attachment (rāga), (4) aversion (dveṣa), and (5) clinging to life and instinctive fear of death (abhinivesha). The bondage of the self is due to its wrong identification with the mental modifications and liberation, therefore, means the end of this wrong identification through proper discrimination between Puruṣa and Prakṛti and the consequent cessation of the mental modifications. It is the aim of Yoga to bring about this result.

There are five levels of mental life (chittabhūmi). The differences in the levels are due to the predominance of the different guṇas. The lowest level is called Kṣipta or restless, because the mind here is restless due to the excess of rajas and is tossed about like a shuttlecock between different sense-objects. The second is called Mūḍha or torpid. The mind here has the predominance of tamas and tends towards ignorance, sleep and lethargy. The third is called Vikṣipta or distracted. Here sattva predominates, but rajas also asserts itself at times.[1] The fourth is called Ekāgra or concentrated. The mind here is entirely dominated by sattva, and rajas and tamas are subdued. The mind becomes concentrated on the object of meditation. The fifth and the highest level is called Niruddha or restricted. Here the mental modifications are arrested, though their latent impressions remain. The first three levels are not at all conducive to Yogic life. Only the last two are.

III

AṢṬĀṄGA YOGA

YOGA advocates control over the body, the senses and the mind. It does not want to kill the body; on the other hand, it recommends its perfection. A sound mind needs a sound body. Sensual attachment and

[1] Vikṣipta here does not mean 'extremely restless' (visheṣeṇa kṣiptaḥ) as its name suggests, but 'better than kṣipta' (kṣiptād vishiṣṭaḥ), because in kṣipta rajas predominates while in vikṣipta sattva predominates.

passions distract the body as well as the mind. They must be conquered. To overcome them, Yoga gives us the Eightfold Path of Discipline (Aṣṭāṅga Yoga):

(1) Yama: It means abstention and includes the five vows of Jainism. It is abstention from injury through thought, word or deed (ahimsā), from falsehood (satya), from stealing (asteya), from passions and lust (brahmacharya), and from avarice (aparigraha).
(2) Niyama: It is self-culture and includes external and internal purification (shaucha), contentment (santoṣa), austerity (tapas), study (svādhyāya) and devotion to God (Īshvara-praṇidhāna).
(3) Āsana: It means steady and comfortable posture. There are various kinds of postures which are a physical help to meditation. This is the discipline of the body.
(4) Prāṇāyāma: It means control of breath and deals with regulation of inhalation, retention and exhalation of breath. It is beneficial to health and is highly conducive to the concentration of the mind. But it must be performed under expert guidance otherwise it may have bad after-effects.
(5) Pratyāhāra: It is control of the senses and consists in withdrawing the senses from their objects. Our senses have a natural tendency to go to outward objects. They must be checked and directed towards the internal goal. It is the process of introversion.

These five are called external aids to Yoga (bahiraṅga sādhana), while the remaining three which follow are called internal aids (antaraṅga sādhana).

(6) Dhāraṇā: It is fixing the mind on the object of meditation like the tip of the nose or the mid-point of the eyebrows or the lotus of the heart or the image of the deity. The mind must be steadfast like the unflickering flame of a lamp.
(7) Dhyāna: It means meditation and consists in the undisturbed flow of thought round the object of meditation (pratyayaikatānatā). It is the steadfast contemplation without any break.
(8) Samādhi: It means concentration. This is the final step in Yoga. Here the mind is completely absorbed in the object of meditation. In dhyāna the act of meditation and the object of meditation remain separate. But here they become one. It is the highest means to realize the cessation of mental modifications which is the end. It is the ecstatic state in which the connection with the external world is broken and through which one has to pass before obtaining liberation.

Samādhi is of two kinds: Conscious or saṁprajñāta and supra-conscious or asaṁprajñāta. In the former consciousness of the object of meditation persists, in the latter it is transcended. The former is Ekāgra, the latter is Niruddha. In the former the mind remains concentrated on the object of meditation. The meditator and the object of meditation are fused together, yet the consciousness of the object of meditation persists. This state is said to be of four kinds:

(*a*) Savitarka: When the Chitta is concentrated on a gross object of meditation like the tip of the nose or the mid-point of the eyebrows or the image of the deity.
(*b*) Savichāra: When the Chitta is concentrated on a subtler object of meditation like the tanmātrās.
(*c*) Sānanda: When the Chitta is concentrated on a still subtler object of meditation which produces joy, like the senses.
(*d*) Sāsmitā: When the Chitta is concentrated on the ego-substance with which the self is generally identified. Here we have conscious ecstasy where individuality persists.

Asaṁprajñāta Samādhi is that supra-conscious concentration where the meditator and the object of meditation are completely fused together and there is not even consciousness of the object of meditation. Here no new mental modifications arise. They are checked (niruddha), though the latent impressions may continue. If fire is restricted to a particular fuel, it burns that fuel alone; but when that fuel has been completely burnt, the fire also dies down. Similarly in conscious concentration, the mind is fixed on the object of meditation alone and modification arises only in respect of this object of meditation; but in supra-conscious concentration, even this modification ceases. It is the highest form of Yoga which is divine madness, perfect mystic ecstasy difficult to describe and more difficult to attain. Even those who attain it cannot retain it longer. Immediately or after very short time, the body breaks and they obtain complete liberation.

Yoga generates certain supra-normal powers. But they should be avoided and attention should be fixed only on liberation which is the end of human life. The ideal is Kaivalya, the absolute independence and eternal and free life of the Puruṣa, free from Prakṛti.

IV

GOD

YOGA accepts the existence of God. The interest of Patañjali himself in God seems to be practical, but the later Yogins have taken also a theoretical interest in Him and have tried to prove His existence as a necessary philosophical speculation. Patañjali defines God as a special kind of Puruṣa who is always free from pains, actions, effects and impressions.[1] He is eternally free and was never bound nor has any possibility of being bound. He is above the law of Karma. He is omniscient and omnipotent and omnipresent. He is perfection incarnate. He is purest knowledge. He is the teacher of the ṛṣis (sa pūrveṣāmapi guruḥ) and the teacher of the Veda. 'Aum' is His symbol. Devotion to God is one of the surest means of obtaining concentration. The proofs advanced for His existence are: (*a*) The Veda tell's us that God exists; (*b*) the law of continuity tells us that there must be the highest limit of knowledge and perfection which is God; (*c*) God is responsible for the association and dissociation of Puruṣa and Prakṛti; (*d*) devotion to God is the surest way of obtaining concentration and thereby liberation.

But God of Yoga is not the creator, preserver or destroyer of this world. He is only a special Puruṣa. He does not reward or punish the souls. Innumerable Puruṣas and Prakṛti, all eternals and absolutes, are there to limit Him. He cannot grant liberation. He can only remove the obstacles in the upward progress of the devotees. Directly He has nothing to do with the bondage and the liberation of the Puruṣas. Ignorance binds and discrimination between Prakṛti and Puruṣa liberates. The end of human life is not the union with God, but only the separation of Puruṣa from Prakṛti. Such a conception of God is certainly unsatisfactory.

The Yoga system of Patañjali should not be confused with magic and tantra and self-hypnotization. It is a great system of spiritual discipline and has found favour with all schools of Indian Philosophy except the Chārvāka. It is founded on the metaphysics of Sāṅkhya and gives us a practical path of purification and self-control in order to realize the true nature of man.

[1] kleshakarmavipākāshayair aparāmṛṣṭaḥ puruṣavisheṣa Īshvaraḥ, Yogasūtra, I, 24.

Chapter Eleven

VAISHEṢIKA

I

INTRODUCTION

THE Vaisheṣika system is next to Sāṅkhya in origin and is of greater antiquity than the Nyāya. It may be prior to and is certainly not later than Buddhism and Jainism. The word is derived from 'Visheṣa' which means particularity or distinguishing feature or distinction. The Vaisheṣika philosophy, therefore, is pluralistic realism which emphasizes that diversity is the soul of the universe. The category of Visheṣa or particularity is dealt with at length in this system, and is regarded as the essence of things.

The founder of this system is Kaṇāda who is also known as Kaṇabhuk, Ulūka, and Kāshyapa. This system is also called after him as Kāṇāda or Aulūka darshana. He was called Kaṇāda because he used to live as an ascetic on the grains picked up from the fields. Kaṇa (in addition to meaning 'grain') also means a particle or a particular and the word Kaṇāda suggests one who lives on the philosophy of particularity—visheṣa.

Prashastapāda has written his classical Padārthadharmasaṅgraha which is called a Bhāṣya or Commentary on the Vaisheṣikasūtra of Kaṇāda, but is really a very valuable independent treatise. It has been commented upon by Udayana and Shrīdhara. The Vaisheṣika was, later on, fused together with the Nyāya which accepted the ontology of the former and developed it in the light of its epistemology. Thus Shivāditya, Laugākṣi Bhāskara, Vishvanātha and Annambhatta treat of the two systems together.

II

PADĀRTHA

THE Vaisheṣika system is regarded as conducive to the study of all systems.[1] Its main business is to deal with the categories and to unfold its atomistic pluralism. A category is called padārtha and the entire universe is reduced to six or seven padārthas. Padārtha literally means

[1] Kāṇādam Pāṇinīyañcha sarvashāstropakārakam.

'the meaning of a word' or 'the object signified by a word'. All objects of knowledge or all reals come under padārtha. Padārtha means an object which can be thought (jñeya) and named (abhidheya). The Aristotelean categories are the mere modes of predication and represent a logical classification of predicates. The Kantian categories are the moulds of the understanding under which things have to pass before becoming knowable. The Hegelian categories are the dynamic stages in the development of thought which is identified with reality. The Vaisheṣika categories are different from them all. While the Aristotelean categories are a logical classification of predicates only, the Vaisheṣika categories are a metaphysical classification of all knowable objects or of all reals. They are not, as the Kantian categories are, mere moulds of the understanding. Nor are they, as the Hegelian categories are, dynamic stages in the development of thought. Hegel's is a philosophy of Absolute Idealism, a dynamic and concrete Identity-in-difference. The Vaisheṣika system is a pluralistic realism, a philosophy of identity *and* difference, which emphasizes that the heart of reality consists in difference. It is a mere catalogue of the knowables, an enumeration of the diverse reals without any attempt to synthesize them.

Originally the Vaisheṣika believed in the six categories and the seventh, that of abhāva or negation, was added later on. Though Kaṇāda himself speaks of abhāva, yet he does not give it the status of a category to which it was raised only by the later Vaisheṣikas. The Vaisheṣika divides all existent reals which are all objects of knowledge into two classes—bhāva or being and abhāva or non-being. Six categories come under bhāva and the seventh is abhāva. All knowledge necessarily points to an object beyond and independent of it.[1] All that is real comes under the object of knowledge and is called a padārtha. The seven padārthas are: (1) substance (dravya), (2) quality (guṇa), (3) action (karma), (4) generality (sāmānya), (5) particularity (visheṣa), (6) inherence (samavāya), and (7) non-being (abhāva).

III

DRAVYA

SUBSTANCE or dravya is defined as the substratum where actions and qualities inhere and which is the coexistent material cause of the composite things produced from it.[2] Substance signifies the self-subsistence, the absolute and independent nature of things. The category of substance at once unfolds the pluralistic realism of this system. Substance is the substratum of qualities and actions. Without substance,

[1] na chāviṣayā kāchid upalabdhiḥ. See Vaisheṣika-Sutra, I, 1, 15.

[2] kriyāguṇavat samavāyikāraṇam dravyam.

we cannot have qualities and actions for they cannot hang loose in the air, but must be contained somewhere. Substance is the basis of qualities and actions, actual or potential, present or future. Nor can substance be defined apart from qualities and actions. Ultimate substances are eternal, independent and individual and are either infinite or infinitesimal. All compound substances (avayavidravya) which are made of parts and arise out of the simple ultimate substance are necessarily transient and impermanent and subject to production and destruction. But simple ultimate substances which are the material causes of the compound substances are eternal and not subject to production and destruction. The dravyas are nine and include material as well as spiritual substances. The Vaisheṣika philosophy is pluralistic and realistic but not materialistic since it admits spiritual substances. The nine substances are: (1) earth (pṛthivi), (2) water (Ap), (3) fire (tejas), (4) air (vāyu), (5) ether (ākāsha), (6) time (kāla), (7) space (dik), (8) spirit (ātman) and (9) mind or the internal organ (manas).

Earth, water, fire and air really signify not the compound transient objects made out of them, but the ultimate elements, the suprasensible eternal partless unique atoms which are individual and infinitesimal. Ether is not atomic but infinite and eternal. These five are called elements (bhūta) and are physical. Each of them possesses a peculiar quality which distinguishes it from the rest. The peculiar qualities of earth, water, fire, air and ether are smell, taste, colour, touch and sound respectively which are sensed by the five external senses. The external senses are constituted by the respective elements whose specific qualities are sensed by them—the sense of smell is constituted by the element of earth and so on. The elements are the substrata of these qualities. Time and space, like ether, are one each (eka), eternal (nitya) and all-pervading (vibhu). They are imperceptible and infinite substances and are partless and indivisible. They are conventionally spoken of as having parts and divisions. Time is the cause of our cognitions of past, present and future and of 'younger' and 'older'. Space (dik) is the cause of our cognitions of 'east' and 'west', 'here' and 'there', 'near' and 'far' and is different from ether (ākāsha) which is the substratum of the quality of sound. There are innumerable souls and each is an independent, individual, eternal and all-pervading spiritual substance. It is the substratum of the quality of consciousness. Consciousness is not the essence of the self. It is not even an inseparable quality of the self. It is regarded as an adventitious attribute possessed by the self. It is adventitious because the self does not possess this quality during deep sleep. The quality of consciousness must reside somewhere. It is not the property of the body or the senses or even of mind. It resides in the self. Other important qualities possessed by the self are desire (ichchhā) and volition (yatna). Jñāna, ichchhā and yatna are cognition, affection and conation respectively. The fact that the self is the substance of these qualities is directly known through expressions: 'I know', 'I am happy', 'I want to do this' etc. Mind (manas) is also regarded as a substance. It is the internal sense (antarindriya). It is atomic; but unlike the first four atomic dravyas, it does not give rise to compound objects. It is many and each is eternal and imperceptible. Each self has a mind. It is the organ through which the self comes into contact with the objects. Its existence is inferred from the fact that the self must perceive internal states of cognition, desire and conation through an internal sense, just as it perceives external objects through external senses. Moreover, in the perception of external objects the mind is selective and active. We do not perceive colour, touch, taste, smell and sound simultaneously, even though all the external senses may be in contact with their objects. Perception requires attention and attention is active turning of the mind towards the object of perception. Hence in perception, the self must fix the manas on the object of perception with which the external sense is already in contact. Manas, therefore, is a substance and it is atomic and partless and can come into contact with one sense only at one time. These are the nine substances of the Vaisheṣika. All of them are objective realities. Earth, water, fire, air, and manas are atomic and eternal. The first four produce composite things; manas does not. Earth, water, fire, air and ether are the five gross elements. These and manas are physical. Soul is spiritual. Time and space are objective and not subjective forms of experience. Ether, space, time and soul are all-pervading and eternal. Atoms, minds and souls are infinite in number. Ether, space and time are one each.

IV

GUṆA

THE second category is guṇa or quality. Unlike substance, it cannot exist independently by itself and possesses no quality or action. It inheres in a substance and depends for its existence on the substance and is not a constitutive cause of anything. It is called an independent reality because it can be conceived (prameya), thought (jñeya) and named (abhidheya) independently of a substance where it inheres. The qualities are therefore called objective entities. They are not necessarily eternal. They include both material and mental qualities. They are a static and permanent feature of a substance, while action is a dynamic and transient feature of a substance. A quality, therefore, is different from both substance and action. It is defined by Kaṇāda as 'that which inheres in a substance, which does not possess quality or action, which does not produce any composite thing, and which is not the cause of conjunction and disjunction like an action.'[1]

Kaṇāda mentions seventeen qualities to which seven more are added by Prashastapāda. These twenty-four qualities are recognized by the Nyāya-Vaisheṣika School. It is not necessary to mention them all as their importance is not much philosophical. They include material as well as spiritual properties. Smell is the quality of earth; taste of water; colour of fire; touch of air; and sound of ether. Cognition, pleasure, pain, desire, aversion, volition are the mental qualities which inhere in the self.

V

KARMA

THE third category is Karma or action. Like quality, it belongs to and inheres in a substance and cannot exist separately from it. But while a quality is a static and permanent feature of a substance, an action is a dynamic and transient feature of it. Unlike a quality, an action is the cause of conjunction and disjunction. Action is said to be of five kinds: (1) upward movement (utkṣepaṇa), (2) downward movement (avakṣepaṇa), (3) contraction (ākuñchana), (4) expansion (prasāraṇa), and (5) locomotion (gamana).

VI

SĀMĀNYA

THE fourth category is Sāmānya or generality. It is class-concept, class-essence or universal. It is the common character of the things which fall under the same class. The sāmānya is more like the 'universal' than like the 'genus'. The genus stands for the class and includes the sub-classes or species. The sāmānya stands, not for the class, but for the common characteristic of certain individuals and does not include the sub-classes. It is the universal by the possession of which different individuals are referred to as belonging to one class. It is called eternal, one and residing in many.[2] It is one, though the individuals in which it resides are many. It is eternal, though the individuals in which it inheres are subject to birth and death, production and destruction. It is common to many individuals. There is the class-essence of the universal of man, called 'man-ness' or 'humanity', which inheres in all individual men. Similarly 'cowness' inheres in all individual cows. Kaṇāda calls generality and particularity as relative to thought (buddhyapekṣa). But this does not mean that the universal and the particular are mere subjective concepts in our mind. Both are objective realities. The system is staunchly realistic. The universal has as much objective reality as the

[1] Vaiṣhesikasūtra I, 1, 16. [2] nityam ekam anekānugatam sāmānyam.

particular. It is not a subjective class-concept in our mind, but an objective eternal timeless entity shared by many particulars and corresponding to a general idea or class-concept in our mind. The universals reside in substances, qualities and actions.[1] They are of two kinds, higher and lower. The higher generality is that of 'being' (sattā). It includes everything and itself is not included in anything. Every other generality is lower because it covers a limited number of things and cannot cover all things. A universal cannot subsist in another universal, otherwise an individual may be a man, a cow, and a horse at the same time. Only one universal subsists in all individuals of a class. What subsists in one individual only, like etherness subsisting in ether, is not a universal. Conjunction inheres in many substances it conjoins, but it is not a universal since it is not eternal. Non-being is eternal and belongs to many things, but it is not a universal since it does not inhere in them.

The three views of realism, conceptualism and nominalism with which we are familiar in Western Logic appear in Indian Philosophy in the schools of Nyāya-Vaisheṣika, Jainism and Vedānta, and Buddhism respectively. Buddhistic Apohavāda is nominalism. According to it, the universals are only names and not reals. A cow is called a 'cow', not because it shares the universal 'cowness', but because it is different from all objects which are 'not-cow'. A cow, therefore, means a not non-cow. There is no universal as a real; it is only a name with a negative connotation. Other schools reject this view. Among them Jainism and Vedānta believe in conceptualism. They maintain that the universal is not a mere name. But they, unlike the realists, do not maintain objective and independent reality of the universal over and above the particulars. The universal exists apart from our mind in the particulars, but not over and above them. In point of existence it is identical with the particulars. The Nyāya-Vaisheṣika School is an advocate of realism. It believes that both the particulars and the universals are separately real.

VII

VISHEṢA

THE fifth category is Visheṣa or particularity. It enables us to perceive things as different from one another. Every individual is a particular, a single and a unique thing different from all others. It has got a uniqueness of its own which constitutes its particularity. It is opposed to generality. Generality is inclusive; particularity is exclusive. Generality forms the basis of assimilation; particularity forms the basis of discrimination. It is very important to remember that the compositive objects of this world which we generally call 'particular' objects, are

[1] dravyaguṇakarmavṛtti.

not real 'particulars' according to Nyāya-Vaisheṣika. Compound objects can be easily distinguished from one another by the differences of their parts. Thus no compound object, from the dyad to any gross object, is a particular. It is only in the case of the simple ultimate eternal substances which are otherwise alike that a need arises to postulate the category of Visheṣa in order to distinguish them from one another. Thus for example, one atom is similar to another atom of the same element and one soul is similar to another soul. Now, how to account for their separate reality? Nyāya-Vaisheṣika, being a school of staunch realism, maintains not only quantitative but also qualitative pluralism. One atom differs from another not only in numerical existence but also in qualitative existence. The category of Visheṣa or particularity is invented to defend this position and the Vaisheṣika derives its name from this. Each partless ultimate substance has an original peculiarity of its own, an underived uniqueness of its own which is called 'particularity' or Visheṣa. Visheṣa, therefore, is the differentium (vyāvartaka) of ultimate eternal substances (nityadravyavṛtti) which are otherwise alike. There are innumerable eternal Vishesas. They distinguish the substances where they inhere from other substances and they also distinguish themselves from other particularities. Though they, like qualities and actions, inhere in the substances, yet they are a distinct category. The Vaisheṣika emphasizes realistic pluralism. Atoms, souls, space, time and manas all have their particularities.

VIII

SAMAVĀYA

THE sixth category is Samavāya or inseparable eternal relation called 'inherence'. It is different from conjunction or saṁyoga which is a separable and transient relation and is a quality (guṇa). Samavāya is an independent category (padārtha). Kaṇāda calls it the relation between cause and effect. Prashastapāda defines it as 'the relationship subsisting among things that are inseparable, standing to one another in the relation of the container and the contained, and being the basis of the idea, "this is in that".'[1] The things related by samavāya are inseparably connected (ayutasiddha). It is 'inseparable relationship'. It is eternal because its production would involve infinite regress. It is imperceptible and is inferred from the inseparable relation of two things. The things which are inseparably connected are these: the part and the whole, the quality and the substance, the action and the substance, the particular and the universal, the Visheṣa and the eternal substance.[2] Samavāya is

[1] ayutasiddhānām ādhāryādhārabhūtānām yaḥ sambandha ihapratyayahetuḥ sa samavāyaḥ. [2] yayor dvayor madhye ekam avinashyad aparāshritamevāvatiṣṭhate tāvayutasiddhau—avayavāvayavinau, guṇaguṇinau, kriyākriyāvantau, jātivyaktī, visheṣanityadravye cheti—Tarkasaṅgraha.

found in these. The whole inheres in the parts; a quality inheres in its substance; an action inheres in its substance; the universal inheres in the individual members of the same class; the particularity (visheṣa) inheres in its eternal substance. Samavāya is one and eternal relationship subsisting between two things inseparably connected.

IX

ABHĀVA

THE seventh category is Abhāva or non-existence. Kaṇāda does not mention it as a separate category. It is added afterwards. The first six categories are positive. This is negative. The other categories are regarded as absolute, but this category is relative in its conception. Absolute negation is an impossibility, a pseudo-idea. Negation necessarily presupposes some affirmation. The Vaisheṣika, being a realist, believes that just as knowledge is different from the object known which exists independently of that knowledge and necessarily points to some object, similarly knowledge of negation is different from the thing negated and necessarily points to some object which is negated. Absence of an object and knowledge of its absence are different. Non-existence is of four kinds: (1) antecedent non-existence (prāgabhāva), (2) subsequent non-existence (pradhvaṁsābhāva), (3) mutual non-existence (anyonyābhāva), and (4) absolute non-existence (atyantābhāva). The first is the non-existence of a thing before its production. The second is the non-existence of a thing after its destruction. The third is the non-existence of a thing as another thing which is different from it. The fourth is a pseudo-idea, the absence of a relation between two things in the past, the present and the future. A pot does not exist before its production; nor after its destruction; nor as a cloth; nor is there a 'liquid pot'. Antecedent negation has no beginning, but it has an end. It ends when the thing is produced. Subsequent negation has a beginning, but has no end. It begins when the thing is destroyed and has no end since the same thing cannot be produced again. Mutual negation is exclusion and is opposed to identity. It is both beginningless and endless. Absolute negation is a pseudo-idea. It is both beginningless and endless. Hare's horn, barren woman's child, sky-flower etc. are its classical examples. Mutual negation or anyonyābhāva means non-existence of a thing *as* another thing—'S is not P'. The other three negations—antecedent, subsequent and absolute—are called non-existence of correlation or Saṁsargābhāva which implies the non-existence of something *in* something else—'S is not *in* P'. If antecedent negation is denied, then all things would become beginningless; if subsequent negation is denied, then all things would become eternal; if mutual negation is denied, then all things would become indistinguishable; and if absolute negation is denied, then all things would exist always and everywhere. The view of non-existence is based on this ontological conception of the Vaisheṣika.

X

ATOMISM

LET us now consider the Vaisheṣika theory of Atomism. Unlike the Sāṅkhya-Yoga, the Nyāya-Vaisheṣika believes in the doctrine of Asatkāryavāda which means that the effect does not pre-exist in its cause. The effect is a new beginning, a fresh creation. Of course, it presupposes a cause. But it is not contained implicitly in the cause nor is it identical with the cause. The doctrine is also known as Ārambhavāda or Paramāṇukāraṇavāda. We find that the material objects of the world are composed of parts and are subject to production and destruction. They are divisible into smaller parts and the latter are further divisible into still smaller parts. By this logic we have to accept the minutest particle of matter which may not be further divisible. This indivisible, partless and eternal particle of matter is called an atom (paramāṇu). All physical things are produced by the combinations of atoms. Creation, therefore, means the combination of atoms in different proportions and destruction means the dissolution of such combinations. The material cause of the universe is neither produced nor destroyed. It is the eternal atoms. It is only the atomic combinations which are produced and which are destroyed. These combinations do not form the essential nature of the atoms nor do they pre-exist in them. Hence the Nyāya-Vaisheṣika advocates Asatkāryavāda.

The atoms are said to be of four kinds—of earth, water, fire and air. Ether or ākāsha is not atomic. It is one and all-pervading and affords the medium for the combinations of the atoms. The atoms differ from one another both in quantity and in quality. Each has a particularity of its own and exists as a separate reality. The atoms of earth, water, fire and air differ in qualities also. Their qualities too are eternal. The atoms of air are the finest of all and have the quality of touch. The atoms of fire possess touch and colour. The atoms of water possess touch, colour and taste. The atoms of earth possess touch, colour, taste, and smell. Besides these all atoms have velocity, number, distinctness etc. The qualities of compositive products are due to the qualities of the atoms. The atoms possess the primary as well as the secondary qualities. They are said to be spherical or globular (parimaṇḍala). They are co-eternal with the souls and are the material cause of the world. They are inactive and motionless in themselves. During dissolution, they remain inactive. Motion is imparted to them by the Unseen Power (adṛṣṭa) of merit (dharma) and demerit (adharma) which resides in the individual souls and wants to fructify in the form of enjoyment or suffering. They are supra-sensible. The atoms combine in geometrical progression and not in arithmetical one. They increase by multiplication and not by mere addition. When motion is imparted to them by the Unseen Power, they begin to vibrate (parispanda) and immediately change into dyads. A dyad is produced by the combination of two atoms. The atoms are its inherent cause; conjunction is its non-inherent cause; and the Unseen Power is its efficient cause. An atom is indivisible, spherical and imperceptible. A dyad (dvyaṇuka) is minute (aṇu), short (hrasva) and imperceptible. Three dyads form a triad (tryaṇuka) which is great (mahat), long (dīrgha) and perceptible. And so on by geometrical progression till the gross elements of earth, water, fire and air arise.

The Vaisheṣika Atomism is not materialistic because the Vaisheṣika School admits the reality of the spiritual substances—souls and God—and also admits the Law of Karma. The atoms are the material cause of this world of which God, assisted by the Unseen Power, is the efficient cause. The physical world presupposes the moral order. Evolution is due to the Unseen Power consisting of merits and demerits of the individual souls which want to bear fruits as enjoyments or sufferings to be experienced by the souls.

The Vaisheṣika atomism agrees with the Greek atomism of Leucippus and Democritus in regarding the atoms as the indivisible, partless, imperceptible and ultimate portions of matter which are eternal and are the material cause of this physical universe. But further than this there is hardly any agreement. Leucippus and Democritus maintain only quantitative or numerical differences in the atoms and regard them as qualitatively alike. The Vaisheṣika maintains both quantitative and qualitative differences in the atoms. The atoms of earth, water, fire and air possess different qualities. Secondly, the Greek atomists regarded atoms as devoid of secondary qualities, while the Vaisheṣika regards them as possessing secondary qualities also. Thirdly, the Greek atomists believed that atoms were essentially active and motion was inherent in them, but the Vaisheṣika regards the atoms as essentially inactive and motionless. Motion is imparted to them by the Unseen Power. Fourthly, the Greek view held that atoms constituted even the souls, while the Vaisheṣika distinguishes between the souls and the atoms and regards them as co-eternal distinct entities, each possessing a particularity of its own. Fifthly, the Greek view was materialistic and the evolution was thought of as mechanical, while the Vaisheṣika view is guided by the spiritual and the moral law and the later Vaisheṣikas frankly admit God as the efficient cause.

The Jaina conception of the atom, like that of the Greeks and the Vaisheṣika, regards it as one, eternal and indivisible unit of the material elements. But it differs from the Vaisheṣika view and agrees with the Greek view in that it maintains no qualitative differences among the atoms. The atoms are all homogeneous and become differentiated into heterogeneous elements by different combinations. Moreover, the Jainas do not regard the qualities of the atoms as permanent, while the Vaisheṣika does.

XI

GOD

THE Vaisheṣika believes in the authority of the Veda and in the moral law of Karma. Kaṇāda himself does not openly refer to God. His aphorism—'The authority of the Veda is due to its being His (or their) Word',[1] has been interpreted by the commentators in the sense that the Veda is the Word of God. But the expression 'Tadvachana' may also mean that the Veda is the Word of the seers. But all great writers of the Vaisheṣika and the Nyāya systems, including Prashastapāda, Shrīdhara and Udayana, are openly theistic and some of them, e.g. Udayana, give classical arguments to prove the existence of God. We cannot, therefore, treat the founder of the Vaisheṣika as an atheist. Moreover, Kaṇāda believes in spiritualism and makes the physical universe subservient to the moral order. The Veda is authoritative, but it is neither eternal nor authorless. It is the Word of God and this makes it authoritative. God is omniscient, eternal and perfect. He is the Lord. He is guided by the Law of Karma representing the Unseen Power of merits and demerits. The Unseen Power is unintelligent and needs God as the supervisor and the controller. He is the efficient cause of the world of which the eternal atoms are the material cause. Atoms and souls are co-present and co-eternal with God. He cannot create them. He simply gives motion to the atoms and sets the ball rolling. He is responsible for the first push, the original impetus, and then the atoms go on combining.

XII

BONDAGE AND LIBERATION

THE Vaisheṣika also regards bondage as due to ignorance and liberation as due to knowledge. The soul, due to ignorance, performs actions. Actions lead to merits or demerits. They are due to attachment or aversion and aim at obtaining pleasure or avoiding pain. If actions are in conformity with the Veda's injunctions, they lead to merit; if they are prohibited by the Veda, they lead to demerit. The merits and demerits of the individual souls make up the unseen moral power, the adṛṣṭa.

[1] tadvachanād āmnāyasya prāmāṇyam. I, 1, 3; X, 2, 9.

According to the law of Karma, one has to reap the fruits of actions one has performed whether they are good or bad according to the karmas one performed. This adṛṣṭa, guided by God, imparts motion to the atoms and leads to creation for the sake of enjoyment or suffering of the individual souls. As long as the soul will go on performing actions, it will be bound. To get rid of bondage, the soul must stop actions. Liberation comes through knowledge. When actions stop, new merits and demerits do not get accumulated and old merits and demerits also are gradually worn out. The soul is separated from the fetters of the mind and the body and realizes its own pure nature. That is liberation which is absolute cessation of all pain. The individual soul is treated as a substance and knowledge, bliss etc. are regarded as its accidental qualities which it may acquire when it is embodied. Hence in liberation these qualities cannot exist because the soul here is not connected with the mind (manas) and the body. Liberation is the cessation of all life, all consciousness, all bliss, together with all pain and all qualities. It is the qualityless, indeterminate, pure nature of the individual soul as pure substance devoid of all qualities. The liberated soul retains its own peculiar individuality and particularity and remains as it is—knowing nothing, feeling nothing, doing nothing.

XIII

GENERAL ESTIMATE

WE now proceed to give a critical evaluation of the Vaisheṣika system. The realistic pluralism of the Vaisheṣika is not a synthetic philosophy. It is a mere common-sense explanation and may, at best, be regarded as scientific analysis. The Vaisheṣika gives us a mere catalogue of categories without making any attempt to synthesize them. Jainism, Sāṅkhya-Yoga, Mahāyāna Buddhism and Vedānta mark an advance on Nyāya-Vaisheṣika in this respect. Atomistic pluralism is no final philosophy, but it is an important stage in the development of Indian philosophy. It emphasizes scientific thinking and is an advance on the materialistic standpoint.

The Vaisheṣika gives us seven categories and treats them as ultimate objective existents, the independent reals. But we are told that quality and action cannot exist without a substance and therefore depend on it. How can we, then, raise quality and action to the same status as that of substance? Universality, particularity and inherence, being necessarily related to concepts, depend more on thought and cannot be raised to the level of substance. Non-existence is evidently relative, being related to existence and so cannot be treated as absolute. The only fundamental category, therefore, is that of substance. This substance too cannot be known in the absence of qualities and relations and reduces itself to a mere 'I-know-not-what', a mere nothing. Again, this substance is divided into nine eternal kinds. Of these, ether is imagined only to provide medium for the combination of atoms and to act as a substratum for the quality of sound, while space and time are intuitional and mind is only an internal atomic organ. So there remain only the atoms of earth, water, fire and air, and the souls. It is absurd to maintain qualitative differences in the atoms. Hence the real metaphysical division of the reals should have been the physical atoms and the spiritual souls. Jainism and Sāṅkhya represent an advance on Nyāya-Vaisheṣika by bringing the material entities under one common category of Pudgala and Prakṛti respectively, though they too maintain spiritual pluralism in spite of their logic. The atoms, the eternal material points, must be united under one common category. And the account of the souls in Jainism and Sāṅkhya is much better than that in the Nyāya-Vaisheṣika for which the soul is a mere substance and not a subject and consciousness is not its essence, but only an accidental quality.

The acceptance of negation as a separate category and the recognition of inherence appear as two great advances made by the Vaisheṣika. But the general atomistic and pluralistic and empirical character of the system takes away much of their importance. The problem of negation is a very important problem of modern epistemology and metaphysics. The Vaisheṣika recognizes the important truth that affirmation and negation existence and non-existence, thesis and anti-thesis presuppose each other. But it does not try to reconcile them in a synthesis. It does not feel the necessity of overcoming the conflict. Reality is a system where all contradictions are reconciled and dualism is sublated. The realistic pluralism chains the Vaisheṣika to mere common-sense analysis and does not permit it to rise to the higher truth. The same is the case with inherence. Inherence or the inseparable organic relationship is the pivot of the Vaisheṣika system. The part and the whole, the particular and the universal, the quality and the substance are inseparably related. The Vaisheṣika logic points to the fact that the whole is not a mere aggregate of its parts, but is something over and above it. It is a Concrete Universal, an Identity-in-difference, a synthesis reconciling the thesis and the anti-thesis within its bosom. Inherence, really, is coherence. It is an organic and internal relation. And as such its importance can be realized only by Absolute Idealism. No pluralistic realism can rise to this height. And therefore the Vaisheṣika has failed to treat inherence as an organic and internal relation or as real coherence. In the Vaisheṣika, inherence has remained only partially inseparable and eternal relation and has not become internal, organic and coherent. The Vaisheṣika maintains that though qualities cannot remain without substance, though a composite product cannot remain without the component parts, yet the substance can remain without qualities and the universal can remain without the particulars. In Vaisheṣika inherence, only one term depends upon the other and is inseparable from it, but the other term can remain independent and separable from the first. But as a matter of fact, both the terms should have been regarded as mutually dependent and inseparable and a need should have been felt to reconcile both the terms in a higher unity.

Negation and inherence, being essentially the core of Absolute Idealism, could not be developed by the pluralistic and realistic Vaisheṣika. But it could have developed the conception of ultimate particularity or individuality, from which it derives its name, consistently with its logic. Had it done that, it could have thrown some light on the problem of individuation which is a taxing problem for Philosophy. But here too the Vaisheṣika has not done justice to this conception. It has merely hinted at it. Every atom and every soul has a uniqueness of its own. But what is that which constitutes this uniqueness? The Vaisheṣika does not attempt the answer.

Shaṅkara has pointed out the contradictions in the Vaisheṣika categories. His objections against the Vaisheṣika conception of Samavāya are fundamental and may be noted here. Firstly, the distinction that saṁyoga is a quality and samavāya is a category cannot be justified because both are relations, may be, one is separable and the other inseparable. Again, inherence being different from the two things which it relates, stands in need of another inherence to relate it to them and this second inherence requires a third and so on *ad infinitum*. Again, if samavāya is not different from the terms it relates, then where does it inhere? If it inheres in the first term, it cannot relate it with the second; and if in the second, it cannot relate it with the first; and the same samavāya cannot inhere in both the terms as it cannot be divided. Hence inherence is impossible.

The categories of the Vaisheṣika are mere assumptions and if we proceed with assumptions we may assume any number of categories we like instead of six or seven.

The Atomism of the Vaisheṣika is also highly defective. The qualitative differences in the atoms cannot be upheld. If the atom of earth possesses the greatest qualities and the atom of air the least, there should be difference between their weight and magnitude. Moreover, if the atoms possess qualities like smell, taste, touch, colour etc. how can they be eternal? And if the qualities of the atoms are eternal and cannot be separated from them, then why maintain that the qualities of the souls can be separated from them in liberation, and why maintain that the substance can remain without qualities? Again, if the cause transfers its qualities to its effect, then why does the atom not transfer its spherical nature to the dyad, and why does the dyad not transfer its minuteness and shortness to the triad etc. which are regarded great and long? Again, if the effect does not pre-exist in the cause, then anything can be produced out of anything, or the effect itself may become like the hare's horn for it is non-existent. Moreover, on the Vaisheṣika hypothesis, there can be no creation and no dissolution. Are the atoms essentially active or inactive or both or neither? If active, then creation would become permanent; if inactive, then creation would be impossible; if both, the very conception is contradictory since activity and inactivity, being opposed like light and darkness, cannot be combined; and if neither, then the activity must come from outside agency. Now, is this agency seen or unseen? If seen, it could not be present before creation. And if unseen, then it being always present near the atoms, creation would become permanent, and if the proximity of the Unseen Power to the atoms is denied, then creation would be impossible. In all cases, therefore, there can be no creation from atoms. It is no explanation of this world that it is due to essentially inactive, imperceptible, eternal, abstract material points. It is necessary to synthesize them and reduce them to one common source.

The fate of individual souls is worse still. The individual soul is regarded as a mere substance and consciousness is regarded as its accidental property. The soul is treated just like an object. The object has really devoured the subject. The soul is essentially unconscious and is regarded as a mere substratum to receive consciousness which may occasionally pour itself into it when the soul comes into contact with the body, the senses and the manas. Any atom as well could have easily done that. And like atoms, they are regarded as innumerable, each having a peculiarity of its own. Barring the Chārvāka position which reduces the soul to a product of matter, the conception of the soul in the Vaisheṣika is the most absurd and degrading in the whole field of Indian Philosophy. Even Hīnayāna Buddhism, though it has reduced the soul to a stream of momentary ideas, has retained the throb of consciousness intact.

The fate of God is no better. He is not the creator of this universe. Innumerable atoms and innumerable souls are co-eternal and co-present with Him to limit Him and to distort His glory and greatness. He has been reduced to the status of a supervisor. And even as a supervisor His hands and feet are chained by the shackles of the Law of Karma unfolding itself as the Adṛṣṭa. He has simply to pass on motion from the Unseen Power to the atoms and to withdraw it when the time for dissolution comes. He Himself, without adṛṣṭa, cannot give motion to the atoms. In fact He has nothing vital to do with the souls. It is the Unseen Power of the merits and the demerits of the souls that starts creation. The Vaisheṣika system could have easily done away with a God. The liberated souls do not merge themselves in God, do not even share His knowledge and bliss, do not experience any communion with Him. Bhakti has no place in this system, since God is powerless to help or harm. The Vaisheṣika does not maintain any internal relation at all. The atoms and the souls and God are all externally related to one another. As a matter of fact, though God is regarded as the efficient cause of this world, He is not even that. It is the Unseen Power which is the real efficient cause. If it is said that the Unseen Power being unintelligent requires the guidance of an intelligent person and God is that, we may urge that God is regarded as the highest soul and if the liberated soul is devoid of intelligence, God should also be devoid of intelligence or He should be regarded as eternally bound since it is only in bondage that a soul can possess intelligence.

The Vaisheṣika conception of liberation as the real state of the soul free from all qualities reduces the soul to a mere nothing. The root-fallacy lies in viewing the subject just as an object. To regard the soul as a mere substance is ultimately to explode it. The soul is nothing if it is not a subject and if consciousness is not its essence. True, the essence of the soul is not the empirical and relative and analytical intellect or understanding, nor is bliss in liberation identical with earthly happiness. Discursive intellect presupposes the foundational consciousness, the transcendental subject, and bliss in liberation transcends empirical happiness and pain alike. This truth has been forgotten by the Vaisheṣika and the result has been that we are offered a state of petrification as liberation. A Vaiṣṇava saint has said: It is far better to be born even as a jackal in the lovely forest of Vṛndāvana than to desire the liberation offered by the Vaisheṣika.[1] Shaṅkara calls the Vaisheṣika the 'semi-destroyer' of this world,[2] as opposed to the Hīnayānī Bauddha who is the 'full destroyer'. Shrīharṣa condemns the Vaisheṣika philosophy as the real Aulūka Darshana—owlish philosophy.[3]

[1] varam Vṛndāvane ramye shṛgālatvam vṛṇomyaham. na cha Vaisheṣikīm muktim prārthayāmi kadāchana. [2] ardhavaināshika. [3] Aulūka darshana means the philosophy of Ulūka and Ulūka is another name for Kaṇāda and also means an owl.

Chapter Twelve

NYĀYA

I

INTRODUCTION

THE sage Gotama is the founder of Nyāya School. He is also known as Gautama and as Akṣapāda. Nyāya means argumentation and suggests that the system is predominantly intellectual, analytic, logical and epistemological. It is also called Tarkashāstra or the science of reasoning; Pramāṇashāstra or the science of logic and epistemology; Hetuvidyā or the science of causes; Vādavidyā or the science of debate; and Ānvīkṣikī or the science of critical study.

Gotama's Nyāya-sūtra was commented upon by Vātsyāyana in his Nyāya-bhāṣya. On this Uddyotakara wrote his Vārtika which was commented upon by Vāchaspati in his Tātparya-ṭīkā. Udayana's Nyāya-kusumāñjali and Jayanta's Nyāya-mañjarī are the other important works of this school. The Navya-nyāya or the modern school of Indian logic begins with the epoch-making Tattva-chintāmaṇi of Gaṅgesha. Vāsudeva, Raghunātha, Mathurānātha, Jagadīsha and Gadādhara are the eminent logicians of this school.

II

NYĀYA AND VAISHEṢIKA

NYĀYA is a system of atomistic pluralism and logical realism. It is allied to the Vaisheṣika system which is regarded as 'Samānatantra' or similar philosophy. Vaisheṣika develops metaphysics and ontology; Nyāya develops logic and epistemology. Both agree in viewing the earthly life as full of suffering, as bondage of the soul and in regarding liberation which is absolute cessation of suffering as the supreme end of life. Both agree that bondage is due to ignorance of reality and that liberation is due to right knowledge of reality. Vaisheṣika takes up the exposition of reality and Nyāya takes up the exposition of right knowledge of reality. Nyāya mostly accepts the Vaisheṣika metaphysics. But there are some important points of difference between them which may be noted. Firstly, while the Vaiṣhesika recognizes seven categories and classifies all reals under them, the Nyāya recognizes sixteen categories and includes all the seven categories of the Vaisheṣika in one of them called Prameya or the Knowable, the second in the sixteen. The first category is Pramāṇa or the valid means of knowledge. This clearly brings out the predominantly logical and epistemological character of the Nyāya system. Secondly, while the Vaisheṣika recognizes only two Pramāṇas—perception and inference and reduces comparison and verbal authority to inference, the Nyāya recognizes all the four as separate—perception, inference, comparison and verbal authority.

III

KNOWLEDGE AND PERCEPTION

KNOWLEDGE (jñāna) or cognition (buddhi) is defined as apprehension (upalabdhi) or consciousness (anubhava). Nyāya, being realistic, believes that knowledge reveals both the subject and the object which are quite distinct from itself. All knowledge is a revelation or manifestation of objects (arthaprakāsho buddhiḥ). Just as a lamp manifests physical things placed before it, so knowledge reveals all objects which come before it. Knowledge may be valid or invalid. Valid knowledge (pramā) is defined as the right apprehension of an object (yathārthānubhavaḥ). It is the manifestation of an object as it is. Nyāya maintains the theory of correspondence (parataḥ prāmāṇya). Knowledge, in order to be valid, must correspond to reality. Valid knowledge is produced by the four valid means of knowledge—perception, inference, comparison and testimony. Invalid knowledge includes memory (smṛti), doubt (saṁshaya), error (viparyaya) and hypothetical reasoning (tarka). Memory is not valid because it is not presentative cognition but a representative one. The object remembered is not directly presented to the soul, but only indirectly recalled. Doubt is uncertainty in cognition. Error is misapprehension as it does not correspond to the real object. Hypothetical reasoning is no real knowledge. It is arguing like this—'if there were no fire, there cannot be smoke'. When you see a rope as a rope you have right knowledge. If you are uncertain whether it is a rope or a snake, you have doubt. If you recall the rope you have seen, you have memory. If you mistake the rope for a snake, you have error.

Knowledge is produced in the soul when it comes into contact with the not-soul. It is an adventitious property of the soul which is generated in it by the object. If the generating conditions are sound, knowledge is valid; if they are defective, knowledge is invalid. A man of sound vision sees a conch white, while a man suffering from jaundice sees it yellow. Correspondence with the object is the nature of truth. If knowledge corresponds to its object, it is valid; if it does not, it is invalid. Valid knowledge corresponds to its object (yathārtha and avisamvādi) and leads to successful activity (pravṛttisāmarthya). Invalid knowledge does not correspond to its object (ayathārtha and visamvādi) and leads to failure and disappointment (pravṛttivisamvāda). Fire must burn and cook and shed light. If it does not, it is no fire. Knowledge intrinsically is only a manifestation of objects. The question of its validity or invalidity is a subsequent question and depends upon its correspondence with its object. Truth and falsity are extrinsic characteristics of knowledge. They are apprehended by a subsequent knowledge. They arise and are apprehended only when knowledge has already arisen. They are neither intrinsic nor self-evident. Validity and invalidity of knowledge arise (utpattau paratah prāmāṇyam) after knowledge has arisen, and they are known (jñaptau parataḥ prāmāṇyam) after knowledge has arisen and they have also arisen. Correspondence is the content and successful activity is the test of truth. The Nyāya theory of knowledge, therefore, is realistic and pragmatic; realistic as regards the nature and pragmatic as regards the test of truth.

Perception, inference, comparison or analogy and verbal testimony are the four kinds of valid knowledge. Let us consider them one by one.

Gotama defines perception as 'non-erroneous cognition which is produced by the intercourse of the sense-organs with the objects, which is not associated with a name and which is well-defined'.[1] This definition of perception excludes divine and yogic perception which is not generated by the intercourse of the sense-organs with the objects. Hence Vishvanātha has defined perception as 'direct or immediate cognition which is not derived through the instrumentality of any other cognition'.[2] This definition includes ordinary as well as extra-ordinary perception and excludes inference, comparison and testimony. Perception is a kind of knowledge and is the attribute of the self. Ordinary perception presupposes the sense-organs, the objects, the manas and the self and their mutual contacts. The self comes into contact with the manas, the manas with the sense-organs and the sense-organs with the objects. The contact of the sense-organs with the objects is not possible unless the manas first comes into contact with the sense-organs, and the contact of the manas with the sense-organs is not possible unless the self comes into contact with the manas. Hence sense-object contact necessarily presupposes the manas-sense contact and the self-manas contact. The sense-organs are derived from the elements whose specific qualities of smell, taste, colour, touch and sound are manifested by them. The manas is the mediator between the self and the sense-organs. The external

[1] indriyārthasannikarṣotpannam jñānam avyapadeshyam avyabhichāri vyavasāyātmakam pratyakṣam, Nyāya-Sūtra, I, 1, 4. [2] jñānākaraṇakam jñānam pratyakṣam.

object, through the senses and the manas, makes an impression on the self. The theory, therefore, is realistic.

The Naiyāyika maintains two stages in perception. The first is called indeterminate or nirvikalpa and the second, determinate or savikalpa. They are not two different *kinds* of perception, but only the earlier and the later stages in the same complex process of perception. These two stages are recognized by Gotama in his definition of perception quoted above. Perception is 'unassociated with a name' (avyapadeshya) which means 'indeterminate', and it is 'well-defined' (vyavasāyātmaka) which means 'determinate'. All perception is determinate, but it is necessarily preceded by an earlier stage when it is indeterminate. Nyāya recognizes the fundamental fact about knowledge which is said to be the distinct contribution of Kant to western philosophy that knowledge involves both sensation and conception. 'Percepts without concepts are blind and concepts without percepts are empty.' Perception is a complex process of experience involving both sensation and conception. All perception we have is determinate because it is perceptual knowledge or perceptual judgment. Sensation is the material and conception is the form of knowledge. Bare sensation or simple apprehension is nirvikalpa perception; perceptual judgment or relational apprehension is savikalpa perception. Nyāya avoids the fallacy of the psychical staircase theory that we have first sense-experience, then conception and then judgment. Perception is a complex presentative-representative process in which we cannot really separate direct awareness from relational judgment. Indeterminate perception forms the material out of which determinate perception is shaped, but they can be distinguished only in thought and not divided in reality. Nirvikalpa perception is the immediate apprehension, the bare awareness, the direct sense-experience which is undifferentiated and non-relational and is free from assimilation, discrimination, analysis and syntheis. The consciousness of the 'that' is not yet determined by the consciousness of the 'what'. But as the 'that' cannot be really known as separated from the 'what', the 'substance' cannot be known apart from its 'qualities', we immediately come to savikalpa perception where the mere awareness of the 'that' and the 'what' and their 'inherence' as something undifferentiated, unrelated, dumb and inarticulate, is transformed into differentiated, relational, conceptual and articulate knowledge involving assimilation, discrimination, analysis and synthesis. For example, when we go, from broad daylight, into a dark cinema hall to see a matinée show, we first do not see the seats or the audience clearly, but have only a dim sensation of the objects present there which gradually reveal themselves to us; the dim sense-experience of the objects in the hall is indeterminate perception while the clear perception of them is determinate perception. The mere apprehension of some object as something, as the 'that', is indeterminate perception, while the clear perception of it together with its attributes is determinate perception. We see in dusk a straight something lying on the road and find out by going near it that it is a rope. We see a white moving object at a distance and when it comes near we see it is a white cow. The earlier stage is indeterminate and the later one determinate perception. We are in a hurry to go somewhere and want to finish our bath before starting. We do not know whether the water was cold and the bath refreshing, though we did feel the coolness of water and the refreshing character of bath. We feel water and we feel its coolness but we do not relate the two. Indeterminate perception presents the bare object without any characterization. In determinate perception we relate the substance with its attributes. The feeling of indeterminate perception is psychological, but its knowledge is logical. As bare awareness, as mere apprehension, we *sense* indeterminate perception, we *feel* it, but the moment we try to *know* it even as 'bare awareness' it has passed into conception and has become determinate. Hence all our perception being a cognition is determinate and is a perceptual judgment. We can separate indeterminate from determinate perception only in thought and not in reality. Hence, though we feel indeterminate perception as a psychological state of sense-experience, its knowledge even as indeterminate perception is a result of logical deduction. We do feel it directly but only as an awareness, not as a cognition. Mere apprehension, being infra-relational, cannot be cognized. As cognition it is inferred afterwards when conception has transformed mere sensation into a perceptual judgment.

Vātsyāyana says that if an object is perceived with its name we have determinate perception; if it is perceived without its name, we have indeterminate perception. Jayanta Bhaṭṭa says that indeterminate perception apprehends substance, qualities and actions and universals as separate and indistinct something and is devoid of any association with a name, while determinate perception apprehends all these together with a name. Gaṅgesha Upādhyāya defines indeterminate perception as the non-relational apprehension of an object devoid of all association of name, genus, differentia etc. Annaṁ Bhaṭṭa defines it as the immediate apprehension of an object as well as of its qualities, but without the knowledge of the relation between them. The substance and the qualities, the 'that' and the 'what' are felt separately and it is not apprehended that those qualities inhere in that substance or that the 'what' characterizes the 'that'. Indeterminate perception is 'mere acquaintance' which William James calls 'raw unverbalized experience', while determinate perception is relational apprehension.

Perception, again, may be ordinary (laukika) or extraordinary (alaukika). When the sense-organs come into contact with the objects present to them in the usual way, we have Laukika perception. And if the contact of the sense-organs with the objects is in an unusual way, i.e., if the objects are not ordinarily present to the senses but are conveyed to them through an extraordinary medium, we have Alaukika perception. Ordinary perception is of two kinds—internal (mānasa) and external (bāhya). In internal perception, the mind (manas) which is the internal organ comes into contact with the psychical states and processes like cognition, affection, conation, desire, pain, pleasure, aversion etc. External perception takes place when the five external organs of sense come into contact with the external objects. It is of five kinds—visual, auditory, tactual, gustatory and olfactory, brought about by the sense-organs of sight, sound, touch, taste and smell respectively when they come into contact with the external objects. The external sense-organs are composed of material elements of earth, water, fire, air, and ether and therefore each senses the particular quality of its element. Thus the sense-organ of smell is composed of the atoms of earth and perceives smell which is the specific quality of earth and so on.

Extra-ordinary perception is of three kinds—sāmānyalakṣaṇa, jñānalakṣaṇa and yogaja. Sāmānyalakṣaṇa perception is the perception of the universals. According to Nyāya, the universals are a distinct class of reals. They inhere in the particulars which belong to different classes on account of the different universals inhering in them. An individual belongs to a particular class because the universal of that class inheres in it. Thus a cow becomes a cow because it has the universal cowness inhering in it. Ordinarily we perceive only the particulars and not the universals. We perceive particular cows but we do not perceive a 'universal cow'. Hence the Nyāya maintains that the universals are perceived extraordinarily. Whenever we perceive a particular cow we first perceive the 'universal cowness' inhering in it. The second kind of extraordinary perception is called jñānalakṣaṇa perception. It is the 'complicated' perception through association. Sometimes different sensations become associated and form one integrated perception. Here an object is not directly presented to a sense-organ, but is revived in memory through the past cognition of it and is perceived through representation. For example, I look at a blooming rose from a distance and say 'I *see* a fragrant rose'. But how can fragrance be *seen*? It can only be *smelt*. Fragrance can be perceived by the sense-organ of smell and not by the sense-organ of vision which can perceive only colour. Here the visual perception of the rose revives in memory the idea of fragrance by association, which was perceived in the past through the nose. The perception of the fragrant rose through the eye, therefore, is called jñānalakṣaṇa perception or perception revived in memory through the cognition (jñāna) of the object in the past. Other examples of it are: 'the piece of sandalwood *looks* fragrant', 'ice *looks* cold', 'stone *looks* hard', 'tea *looks* hot', etc. etc. The theory of illusion accepted by Nyāya called 'Anyathākhyāti' is based on this kind of perception. When we mistake a rope for a snake, the idea of snake perceived in the past is imported in memory through this extraordinary jñānalakṣaṇa perception and is confused with the object (i.e., rope) which is directly presented to the sense-organ. When shell is mistaken for silver, the idea of silver perceived in the past in a shop (āpaṇastha) (or anywhere else) is revived in memory through jñānalakṣaṇa perception and is confused with the object (i.e., shell) which is directly presented to the sense-organ. The past impression represents the object to our mind. Error is due to a wrong synthesis of the presented and the represented objects. The represented object is confused with the presented one. The word 'anyathā' means 'elsewise' and 'elsewhere' and both these senses are brought out in an erroneous perception. The presented object is perceived elsewise and the represented object exists elsewhere. The shell and the silver, the rope and the snake are both separately real; only their synthesis is unreal. The shell and the rope are directly presented as the 'this' (when we say: '*this* is silver' or '*this* is a snake'), while the silver and the snake exist elsewhere and are revived in memory through jñānalakṣaṇa perception. The third kind of extraordinary perception is called yogaja perception. This is the intuitive and immediate perception of all objects, past, present and future, possessed by the Yogins through the power of meditation. It is like the Kevalajñāna of the Jainas, the Bodhi of the Buddhists, the Kaivalya of the Sāṅkhya-Yoga and the Aparokṣānubhūti of the Vedāntins. It is intuitive, supra-sensuous and supra-relational.

IV

INFERENCE

THE second kind of knowledge is anumā or inferential or relational and its means is called anumāna or inference. It is defined as that cognition which presupposes some other cognition. It is mediate and indirect and arises through a 'mark', the 'middle term' (liṅga or hetu) which is invariably connected with the 'major term' (sādhya). It is *knowledge* (māna) which arises *after* (anu) other knowledge. Invariable concomitance (vyāpti or avinābhāvaniyama) is the nerve of inference. The presence of the middle term in the minor term is called pakṣadharmatā. The invariable association of the middle term with the major term is called vyāpti. The knowledge of pakṣadharmatā as qualified by vyāpti is called parāmarsha. And inference is defined as knowledge arising through parāmarsha,[1] i.e., the knowledge of the presence of the major

[1] Parāmarshajanyam jñānam anumitiḥ. Vyāptivishiṣṭapakṣadharmatājñānam parāmarshaḥ.

in the minor through the middle which resides in the minor (pakṣa-dharmatā) and is invariably associated with the major (vyāpti). Like the Aristotelian syllogism, the Indian inference has three terms. The major, the minor and the middle are here called sādhya, pakṣa and liṅga or hetu respectively. We know that smoke is invariably associated with fire (vyāpti) and if we see smoke in a hill we conclude that there must be fire in that hill. Hill is the minor term; fire is the major term; smoke is the middle term. From the presence of smoke in the hill as qualified by the knowledge that wherever there is smoke there is fire, we proceed to infer the presence of fire in the hill. This is inference. Indian logic does not separate deduction from induction. Inference is a complex process involving both. Indian logic also rejects the verbalist view of logic. It studies thought as such and not the forms of thought alone. The formal and the material logic are blended here. Verbal form forms no integral part of the inference. This becomes clear from the division of inference into svārtha (for oneself) and parārtha (for others). In the former we do not require the formal statement of the different members of inference. It is a psychological process. The latter, the parārtha which is a syllogism, has to be presented in language and this has to be done only to convince others. There are five members in the Nyāya syllogism. The first is called Pratijñā or proposition. It is the logical statement which is to be proved. The second is Hetu or 'reason' which states the reason for the establishment of the proposition. The third is called Udāharaṇa which gives the universal concomitance together with an example. The fourth is Upanaya or the application of the universal concomitance to the present case. And the fifth is Nigamana or conclusion drawn from the preceding propositions. These five propositions of the Indian syllogism are called 'members' or avayavas. The following is a typical Nyāya syllogism:

(1) This hill has fire (pratijñā).
(2) Because it has smoke (hetu).
(3) Whatever has smoke has fire, e.g., an oven (udāharaṇa).
(4) This hill has smoke which is invariably associated with fire (upanaya).
(5) Therefore this hill has fire (nigamana).

If we compare it with the Aristotelian syllogism which has only three propositions, we will find that this Nyāya syllogism corresponds to the Barbara (AAA) mood of the First Figure which is the strongest mood of the strongest figure. Though the Nyāya syllogism has five and the Aristotelian has three propositions, the terms in both are only three—the sādhya or the major, the pakṣa or the minor and the hetu or the middle. Out of the five propositions, two appear redundant and we may easily leave out either the first two or the last two which are essentially the same. The first coincides with the fifth and the second with the fourth. If we omit the last two, the first three propositions correspond with the conclusion, the minor premise and the major premise respectively. Or, if we omit the first two, the last three propositions correspond to the major premise, the minor premise and the conclusion of the Aristotelian syllogism. Hence if we leave out the first two members of the Nyāya syllogism which are contained in the last two, we find that it resembles the Aristotelian syllogism in the First Figure:

(1) All things which have smoke have fire (Major premise).
(2) This hill has smoke (Minor premise).
(3) Therefore this hill has fire (Conclusion).

And the typical Aristotelian syllogism may be stated in the Nyāya form thus:

(1) Socrates is mortal (pratijñā).
(2) Because he is a man (hetu).
(3) Whoever is a man is a mortal, e.g., Pythagoras (udāharaṇa).
(4) Socrates is a man who is invariably a mortal (upanaya).
(5) Therefore Socrates is mortal (nigamana).

But there are certain real differences between the Nyāya and the Aristotelian syllogism apart from the nominal difference between the number of the propositions in each. The Aristotelian syllogism is only deductive and formal, while the Nyāya syllogism is deductive-inductive and formal-material. The Nyāya rightly regards deduction and induction as inseparably related, as two aspects of the same process—the truth now realized in western logic. Inference, according to Nyāya, is neither from the universal to the particular nor from the particular to the universal, but from the particular to the particular through the universal. The example is a special feature of the Nyāya syllogism and illustrates the truth that the universal major premise is the result of a real induction based on the law of causation and that induction and deduction cannot be really separated. Again, while in the Aristotelian syllogism the major and the minor terms stand apart in the premises though they are connected by the middle term with each other, in the Nyāya syllogism all the three terms stand synthesized in the Upanaya. Again, while the Aristotelian syllogism is verbalistic, the Nyāya recognizes the fact that verbal form is not the essence of inference and is required only to convince others. Some people like Dr. Vidyābhūṣana and Prof. Keith have suggested that the Nyāya syllogism is influenced by Greek thought. But it is absolutely false. We find the development of the Nyāya inference before Aristotle. There are also certain fundamental differences between the two views and the view of Nyāya is accepted as better by the modern western logicians also. The view that vyāpti, the nerve of inference, was introduced by the Buddhist logician Diṅnāga who was influenced by Greek thought is also wrong. Vyāpti was recognized much before Diṅnāga,[1] nor did he 'borrow' his doctrine from Greece. It is more reasonable to explain the similarities between the two as due to a parallel development of thought. Indian logic has been a natural growth.

There are five characteristics of the middle term:

(1) It must be present in the minor term (pakṣadharmatā); e.g., smoke must be present in the hill.
(2) It must be present in all positive instances in which the major term is present; e.g., smoke must be present in the kitchen where fire exists (sapakṣasattva).
(3) It must be absent in all negative instances in which the major term is absent; e.g., smoke must be absent in the lake in which fire does not exist (vipakṣāsattva).
(4) It must be non-incompatible with the minor term; e.g., it must not prove the coolness of fire (abādhita).
(5) It must be qualified by the absence of counteracting reasons which lead to a contradictory conclusion; e.g., 'the fact of being caused' should not be used to prove the 'eternality' of sound (aviruddha).

Inference is generally regarded as of two kinds—Svārtha and Parārtha which we have already discussed. Gotama speaks of three kinds of inference—pūrvavat, sheṣavat and sāmānyatodṛṣṭa. The first two are based on causation and the last one on mere coexistence. A cause is the invariable and unconditional antecedent of an effect and an effect is the invariable and unconditional consequent of a cause. When we infer the unperceived effect from a perceived cause we have pūrvavat inference, e.g., when we infer future rain from dark clouds in the sky. When we infer the unperceived cause from a perceived effect we have sheṣavat inference, e.g., when we infer past rain from the swift muddy flooded water of a river. When inference is based not on causation but on uniformity of co-existence, it is called sāmānyatodṛṣṭa, e.g., when we infer cloven hoofs of an animal by its horns. According to another interpretation, a pūrvavat inference is based on previous experience of universal concomitance between two things, a sheṣavat inference is parisheṣa or inference by elimination, and a sāmānyatodṛṣṭa is inference by analogy.

Another classification of inference gives us the kevalānvayi, kevalavyatireki and anvayavyatireki inferences. It is based on the nature of

[1] See Prof. A. B. Dhruva's Introduction to Nyāya-pravesha of Diṅnāga.

vyāpti and on the different methods of establishing it. The methods of induction by which universal casual relationship is established may be anvaya, vyatireka or both. The first corresponds to Mill's Method of Agreement, the second to his Method of Difference, and the third to his Joint Method of Agreement and Difference or the Method of Double Agreement. We have kevalānvayi inference when the middle term is always positively related to the major term. The terms agree only in presence, there being no negative instance of their agreement in absence, e.g.,

All knowable objects are nameable;
The pot is a knowable object;
∴ The pot is nameable.

We have kevalavyatireki inference when the middle term is the differentium of the minor term and is always negatively related to the major term. The terms agree only in absence, there being no positive instance of their agreement in presence, e.g.,

What is not different-from-other-elements has no smell;
The earth has smell;
∴ The earth is different-from-other-elements.

We have anvayavyatireki inference when the middle term is both positively and negatively related to the major term. The vyāpti between the middle and the major is in respect of both presence and absence. There is Double Agreement between the terms—they agree in presence in the positive instances and they also agree in absence in the negative instances; e.g.,

All things which have smoke have fire;
This hill has smoke;
∴ This hill has fire; and
No non-fiery things have smoke;
This hill has smoke;
∴ This hill is not non-fiery;
i.e., This hill has fire.

In Indian logic a fallacy is called hetvābhāsa. It means that the middle term *appears* to be a reason but is not a valid reason. All fallacies are material fallacies. We have mentioned the five characteristics of a valid middle term. When these are violated, we have fallacies. Five kinds of fallacies are recognized:

(1) Asiddha or Sādhyasama: This is the fallacy of the unproved middle. The middle term must be present in the minor term

(pakṣadharmatā). If it is not, it is unproved. It is of three kinds—

(*a*) āshrayāsiddha: The minor term is the locus of the middle term. If the minor term is unreal, the middle term cannot be present in it; e.g., 'the sky-lotus is fragrant, because it is a lotus, like the lotus of a lake'.

(*b*) svarūpāsiddha: Here the minor term is not unreal. But the middle term cannot by its very nature be present in the minor term; e.g., 'sound is a quality, because it is visible'. Here visibility cannot belong to sound which is audible.

(*c*) vyāpyatvāsiddha: Here vyāpti is conditional (sopādhika). We cannot say, e.g., 'wherever there is fire there is smoke'. Fire smokes only when it is associated with wet fuel. A red-hot iron ball or clear fire does not smoke. Hence 'association with wet fuel' is a condition necessary to the aforesaid vyāpti. Being conditioned, the middle term becomes fallacious if we say: 'The hill has smoke because it has fire'.

(2) Savyabhichāra or Anaikāntika: This is the fallacy of the irregular middle. It is of three kinds:

(*a*) Sādhāraṇa: Here the middle term is too wide. It is present in both the sapakṣa (positive) and the vipakṣa (negative) instances and violates the rule that the middle should not be present in the negative instances (vipakṣāsattva); e.g., 'the hill has fire because it is knowable'. Here 'knowable' is present in fiery as well as non-fiery objects.

(*b*) Asādhāraṇa: Here the middle term is too narrow. It is present only in the pakṣa and neither in the sapakṣa nor in the vipakṣa. It violates the rule that the middle term should be present in the sapakṣa (sapakṣasattva); e.g., 'sound is eternal, because it is audible'. Here audibility belongs to sound only and is present nowhere else.

(*c*) Anupasaṁhāri: Here the middle term is non-exclusive. The minor term is all-inclusive and leaves nothing by way of sapakṣa or vipakṣa; e.g., 'all things are non-eternal, because they are knowable'.

(3) Satpratipakṣa: Here the middle term is contradicted by another middle term. The reason is counter-balanced by another reason. And both are of equal force; e.g., 'sound is eternal, because it is audible' and 'sound is non-eternal, because it is produced'. Here 'audible' is counter-balanced by 'produced' and both are of equal force.

(4) Bādhita: It is the non-inferentially contradicted middle. Here the middle term is contradicted by some other pramāṇa and not by inference. It cannot prove the major term which is disproved by another stronger source of valid knowledge; e.g., 'fire is cold, because it is a substance'. Here the middle term 'substance' becomes contradicted because its major term 'coldness' is directly contradicted by perception.

(5) Viruddha: It is the contradictory middle. The middle term, instead of being pervaded by the presence of the major term, is pervaded by the absence of the major term. Instead of proving the existence of the major term in the minor term, it proves its non-existence therein; e.g., 'sound is eternal, because it is produced'. Here 'produced', instead of proving the eternality of sound, proves its non-eternality. Here the middle term itself disproves the original proposition and proves its contradictory, while in the savyabhichāra the middle term only fails to prove the conclusion, and in the satpratipakṣa the middle term is inferentially contradicted by another middle term both of which are of equal force, and in the bādhita the middle term is non-inferentially contradicted and the major is disproved by a stronger pramāṇa other than inference.

V

COMPARISON

THE third kind of valid cognition is Upamiti and its means is called Upamāna. It is knowledge derived from comparison and roughly corresponds to analogy. It has been defined as the knowledge of the relation between a word and its denotation.[1] It is produced by the knowledge of resemblance or similarity. For example, a man who has never seen a gavaya or a wild cow and does not know what it is, is told by a person that a wild cow is an animal like a cow, subsequently comes across a wild cow in a forest and recognizes it as the wild cow, then his knowledge is due to upamāna. He has heard the word 'gavaya' and has been told that it is like a cow and now he himself sees the object denoted by the word 'gavaya' and recognizes it to be so. Hence upamāna is just the knowledge of the relation between a name and the object denoted by that name. It is produced by the knowledge of similarity because a man recognizes a wild cow as a 'gavaya' when he perceives its similarity to the cow and remembers the description that 'a gavaya is an animal like a cow'.

[1] saṁjñāsaṁjñisambandhajñānam upamitiḥ. tatkaraṇam sādṛshyajñānam.

The Buddhists reduce Upamāna to perception and testimony. The Sāṅkhya and the Vaisheṣika reduce it to inference. The Jainas reduce it to recognition or pratyabhijñā. The Mimāṁsakas recognize it as a separate source of knowledge, but their account of it is different from that of Nyāya, which will be considered in the chapter on Mīmāṁsā.

VI

VERBAL TESTIMONY

THE fourth kind of valid knowledge is Shabda or Āgama or authoritative verbal testimony. Its means is also called Shabda. It is defined as the statement of a trustworthy person (āptavākya) and consists in understanding its meaning. A sentence is defined as a collection of words and a word is defined as that which is potent to convey its meaning.[1] The power in a word to convey its meaning comes, according to ancient Nyāya, from God, and according to later Nyāya, from long established convention. Testimony is always personal. It is based on the words of a trustworthy person, human or divine. Testimony is of two kinds—Vaidika and secular (laukika). The Vaidika testimony is perfect and infallible because the Vedas are spoken by God; secular testimony, being the words of human beings who are liable to error, is not infallible. Only the words of trustworthy persons who always speak the truth are valid; others are not. A word is a potent symbol which signifies an object and a sentence is a collection of words. But a sentence in order to be intelligible must conform to certain conditions. These conditions are four—ākānkṣā, yogyatā, sannidhi and tātparya. The first is mutual implication or expectancy. The words of a sentence are interrelated and stand in need of one another in order to express a complete sense. A mere aggregate of unrelated words will not make a logical sentence. It will be sheer nonsense, e.g., 'cow horse man elephant'. The second condition is that the words should possess fitness to convey the sense and should not contradict the meaning. 'Water the plants with fire' is a contradictory sentence. The third condition is the close proximity of the words to one another. The words must be spoken in quick succession without long intervals. If the words 'bring', 'a', and 'cow' are uttered at long intervals they would not make a logical sentence. The fourth condition is the intention of the speaker if the words are ambiguous. For example, the word 'saindhava' means 'salt' as well as a 'horse'. Now, if a man who is taking his food asks another to bring 'saindhava', the latter should not bring a horse.

The Nyāya admits only these four pramāṇas. Arthāpatti or implication

[1] āptavākyam shabdaḥ. āptastu yathārthavaktā. vākyam padasamūhaḥ. shaktam padam. Īshvara-saṅketaḥ shaktiḥ.

is reduced to inference. For example, when we say: 'Fat Devadatta does not eat during day', the implication is that he must be eating during night otherwise how can he be fat? Mīmāṁsā grants the status of an independent pramāṇa to implication. But Nyāya reduces it to inference thus:

All fat persons who do not eat during day, eat during night;
Devadatta is a fat person who does not eat during day;
∴ Devadatta is a fat person who eats during night.

Abhāva or non-existence which also is regarded as a separate pramāṇa by Bhāṭṭa Mīmāṁsā is reduced here either to perception or to inference. Abhāva is non-existence of a thing and the same sense-organ which perceives a thing, perceives its non-existence also. If the thing is imperceptible and can only be inferred, then, its non-existence too may be equally inferred.

VII

CAUSATION

LET us now consider the Nyāya theory of Causation. A cause is defined as an unconditional and invariable antecedent of an effect and an effect as an unconditional and invariable consequent of a cause. The same cause produces the same effect and the same effect is produced by the same cause. Plurality of causes is ruled out. The first essential characteristic of a cause is its antecedence; the fact that it should precede the effect (Pūrvavṛtti). The second is its invariability; it must invariably precede the effect (Niyatapūrvavṛtti). The third is its unconditionality or necessity; it must unconditionally precede the effect (Ananyathāsiddha). Unconditional antecedence is immediate and direct antecedence and excludes the fallacy of remote cause. Thus we see that the Nyāya definition of a cause is the same as that in Western inductive logic. Hume defines a cause as an invariable antecedent. J. S. Mill defines it as an unconditional and invariable antecedent. Carveth Read points out that unconditionality includes immediacy. A cause, therefore, is an unconditional, immediate and invariable antecedent of an effect.[1] Nyāya recognizes five kinds of accidental (anyathāsiddha) antecedents which are not real causes. Firstly, the qualities of a cause are mere accidental antecedents. The colour of a potter's staff is not the cause of a pot. Secondly, the cause of a cause or a remote cause is not unconditional. The potter's father is not the cause of a pot. Thirdly, the co-effects of a cause are themselves not causally related. The sound produced by the potter's staff is not the cause of a pot, though it may invariably precede

[1] ananyathāsiddhatve sati kāryaniyatapūrvavṛtti kāraṇam.

the pot. Night and day are not causally related. Fourthly, eternal substances like space are not unconditional antecedents. Fifthly, unnecessary things like the potter's ass are not unconditional antecedents; though the potter's ass may be invariably present when the potter is making a pot, yet it is not the cause of the pot. A cause must be an unconditional and necessary antecedent. Nyāya emphasizes the sequence view of causality. Cause and effect are never simultaneous. Plurality of causes is also wrong because causal relation is reciprocal. The same effect cannot be produced by any other cause. Each effect has its distinctive features and has only one specific cause. Further, like Western logic, the Nyāya regards a cause as 'the sum-total of the conditions, positive and negative, taken together'. The cause is an aggregate of the unconditional or necessary and invariable antecedent conditions which are called kāraṇasāmagrī. The absence of negative counteracting conditions is called pratibandhakābhāva.

An effect (kārya) is defined as the 'counter-entity of its own prior non-existence' (prāgabhāvapratiyogi). It is the negation of its own prior-negation. It comes into being and destroys its prior non-existence. It was non-existent before its production. It did not pre-exist in its cause. It is a fresh beginning, a new creation. This Nyāya-Vaisheṣika view of causation is directly opposed to the Sāṅkhya-Yoga and Vedānta view of satkāryavāda. It is called asatkāryavāda or ārambhavāda. The effect (kārya) is non-existent (asat) before its creation and is a new beginning (ārambha), a fresh creation, an epigenesis. It is distinct from its cause and can never be identical with it. It is neither an appearance nor a transformation of the cause. It is newly brought into existence by the operation of the cause.

There are three kinds of causes—samavāyi, asamavāyi and nimitta. The first is the samavāyi or the inherent cause, also called as the upādāna or the material cause. It is the substance out of which the effect is produced. For example, the threads are the inherent cause of the cloth and the clay is the inherent cause of a pot. The effect inheres in its material cause. The cloth inheres in the threads. The effect cannot exist separately from its material cause, though the cause can exist independently of its effect. The material cause is always a substance (dravya). The second kind of cause is asamavāyi or non-inherent. It inheres in the material cause and helps the production of the effect. The conjunction of the threads (tantusaṁyoga) which inheres in the threads is the non-inherent cause of the cloth of which the threads are the material or the inherent cause. The colour of the threads (tanturūpa) is the non-inherent cause of the colour of the cloth. The cloth itself is the inherent cause of its colour. The effect as well as its non-inherent cause both co-inhere in the material cause. The non-inherent cause is always a quality or an action (guṇa or karma). The third kind of cause is nimitta or efficient. It is the power which helps the material cause to produce the effect. The weaver is the efficient cause of the cloth. The efficient cause includes the accessories (sahakāri), e.g., the loom and shuttle of the weaver or the staff and wheel of the potter. The efficient cause may be a substance, a quality or an action.

Sometimes a distinction is made between a general or an ordinary (sādhāraṇa) and a peculiar or an extraordinary (asādhāraṇa) cause. Space, time, God's knowledge, God's will, merit, demerit, prior-non-existence and absence of counteracting factors are the eight general causes. The extraordinary cause is called the karaṇa or the instrumental cause and is included in the efficient cause. It is the motive power which immediately produces the effect, e.g., the staff of the potter. The modern Nyāya regards the efficiency itself which inheres in this cause as the real instrumental cause. The inherent cause, the non-inherent cause, the efficient cause and the purpose correspond to Aristotle's material, formal, efficient and final causes.

VIII

SOUL

THE law of Causation is subservient to the law of Karma. The Nyāya, like the Vaisheṣika, believes in teleological creation. The material cause of this universe are the eternal atoms of earth, water, fire and air and the efficient cause is God. The infinite individual souls are co-eternal with atoms. And God is co-eternal with atoms and souls and is external to both. Nyāya advocates atomism, spiritualism, theism, realism and pluralism. Creation means combinations of atoms and destruction means dissolution of these combinations through the motion supplied to or withdrawn from the atoms by the Unseen Power working under the guidance of God. The innumerable eternal atoms and the innumerable eternal souls are both beyond creation and destruction. God can neither create them nor destroy them. God is not the real creator as He is not the material cause of this universe. And though He is called the ruler of the Universe being regarded as the efficient cause, the real efficiency belongs to the Unseen Power. The view of causation is asatkāryavāda because the different combinations of atoms are regarded as new creations, as real fresh beginnings. It is the doctrine of epigenesis as the new products arise as real creations having the distinctive features of their own and adding new properties to reality. The individual soul is regarded as the substratum of the quality of consciousness which is not its essence but only an accidental property. The soul is a real knower, a real enjoyer and a real active agent and an eternal substance. It is not transcendental consciousness and it is different from God who is the Supreme Soul. Cognitions, affections and conations are the attributes of the soul which is one, partless and all-pervading. Each soul has its manas during its empirical life and is separated from it in liberation. It is distinct from the body, the senses and the mind (manas). Bondage is due to ignorance and Karma. Liberation is due to Knowledge and destruction of Karma. The Vedas are the work of God and therefore claim absolute authority.

IX

GOD

NYĀYA accepts the metaphysics of the Vaisheṣika School and the accounts of matter, soul and God are almost the same as those in the Vaisheṣika. We have discussed the metaphysics of the Vaisheṣika School and so we need not repeat it here. The categories, the doctrine of asatkāryavāda, the account of creation and destruction, the nature of atoms and souls, the account of bondage and liberation, the authority of the Veda, the nature and function of God, the Unseen Power—all these are accepted by Nyāya. The criticisms which we levelled against the Vaisheṣika also apply against the Nyāya position in so far as both are identical. While Kaṇāda himself has not specifically mentioned God, the later Vaisheṣikas and particularly the later Naiyāyikas have given an elaborate account of God and the latter have made God's Grace an essential thing for obtaining true knowledge of the realities which alone leads to liberation. They refer to God as the creator, maintainer and destroyer of this world and introduce the element of devotion. But in our opinion all this can be done only by courtesy. God, as an eternal external reality, is always limited by the co-eternal atoms and souls and has to be guided by the law of karma. Though the later Naiyāyikas are forced to amend the absurd position that eternal consciousness is not the essence of God by raising consciousness from the position of a separable accident to the position of an inseparable attribute in the case of God, yet they have failed to rise to the correct position by not taking consciousness as the essence of God. An atomistic and spiritualistic pluralism can lead only to an external theism where God, souls and atoms all fall apart and the dualism of matter and spirit can never be overcome. God is said to possess all the six perfections in their fullness—majesty, power, glory, beauty, knowledge and freedom. But then why are the liberated souls not allowed to share these qualities? If liberation consists in getting rid of all qualities, then God will be regarded as eternally bound. Again, God is called the moral governor of all beings (prayojaka kartā). But then, either the souls are not free or the law of karma is thrown overboard. If the law of karma represents the self-determination of God and therefore does not bind God, then Karma and God would become identical and external theism would vanish. The Nyāya should reduce its so-called eternal and independent atoms to a single material principle and its so-called innumerable eternal souls to a single spiritual principle and then should reconcile the dualism of matter and spirit in God by making them His aspects. Unless this is done, the contradictions in Nyāya would not be avoided. If it wants to be self-consistent, the Nyāya has to give up its atomistic and spiritualistic pluralism and its external theism. Yet in spite of these defects, the Nyāya theism is a step forward. Udayana's arguments for the existence of God have become classical for theism and may be briefly noted here. He gives the following nine arguments to prove the existence of God:

(1) The world is an effect and hence it must have an efficient cause. This intelligent agent is God. The order, design, co-ordination between different phenomena comes from God (kāryāt).
(2) The atoms being essentially inactive cannot form the different combinations unless God gives motion to them. The Unseen Power, the Adṛṣṭa, requires the intelligence of God. Without God it cannot supply motion to the atoms (āyojanāt).
(3) The world is sustained by God's will. Unintelligent Adṛṣṭa cannot do this. And the world is destroyed by God's will (dhṛtyādeḥ).
(4) A word has a meaning and signifies an object. The power of words to signify their objects comes from God (padāt).
(5) God is the author of the infallible Veda (pratyayataḥ).
(6) The Veda testifies to the existence of God (shruteḥ).
(7) The Vedic sentences deal with moral injunctions and prohibitions. The Vedic commands are the Divine commands. God is the creator and promulgator of the moral laws (vākyāt).
(8) According to Nyāya-Vaisheṣika the magnitude of a dyad is not produced by the infinitesimal magnitude of the two atoms each, but by the *number* of the two atoms. Number 'one' is directly perceived, but other numbers are conceptual creations. Numerical conception is related to the mind of the perceiver. At the time of creation, the souls are unconscious. And the atoms and the Unseen Power and space, time, minds are all unconscious. Hence the numerical conception depends upon the Divine Consciousness. So God must exist (saṅkhyāvisheṣāt).
(9) We reap the fruits of our own actions. Merit and demerit accrue from our actions and the stock of merit and demerit is

called Adṛṣṭa, the Unseen Power. But this Unseen Power, being unintelligent, needs the guidance of a supremely intelligent God (adṛṣṭāt).[1]

But all these proofs are ultimately unavailing. Reason, as Kant points out while criticizing Descartes' arguments for the existence of God, leads to antinomies which are insoluble. The Vedāntins, Shaṅkara, Rāmānuja, Madhva, Nimbārka, Vallabha and all, have rejected the Nyāya arguments and have fallen back on the Shruti alone for the existence of God. Kant in the West and the Vedāntins in India were 'forced to destroy reason in order to make room for faith'.

The chief value of Nyāya lies in its epistemology, logic and methodology which have influenced all schools of Indian philosophy. But its ontology of atomism, pluralism, realism, theism and spiritualism huddled together in one mass is defective. The logic of pluralistic realism is a common-sense view of the world. If liberation means negation of all qualities including consciousness and bliss, the soul liberated is the soul petrified and Gotama by propounding such philosophy, says Shīharṣa, is justifying his name 'Gotama'—an Excellent Bull.[2]

[1] kāryāyojanadhṛtyādeḥ padāt pratyayataḥ shruteḥ. vākyat saṅkhyāvisheṣāchcha sādhyo vishvavidavyayaḥ, Nyāya-Kusumāñjali, V, 1. [2] muktaye yaḥ shilātvāya shāstram ūche sachetasām. Gotamam tamavekṣyaiva yathā vittha tathaiva saḥ. Naiṣadha-Charita XVII, 75.

Chapter Thirteen

PŪRVA-MĪMĀṀSĀ

I

INTRODUCTION

THE word 'Mīmāṁsā' literally means 'revered thought' and was originally applied to the interpretation of the Vedic rituals which commanded highest reverence. The word is now used in the sense of any critical investigation. The school of Mīmāṁsā justifies both these meanings by giving us rules according to which the commandments of the Veda are to be interpreted and by giving a philosophical justification for the Vedic ritualism. Just as Sāṅkhya and Yoga, Vaisheṣika and Nyāya are regarded as allied systems, similarly Mīmāṁsā and Vedānta are also treated as allied systems of thought. Both are based on and both try to interpret the Veda. The earlier portion of the Veda, i.e., the Mantra and the Brāhmaṇa portion, is called Karmakāṇḍa, while the later portion, i.e., the Upaniṣads is called Jñānakāṇḍa, because the former deals with action, with the rituals and the sacrifices, while the latter deals with the knowledge of reality. Mimāṁsā deals with the earlier portion of the Veda and is therefore called Pūrva-Mīmāṁsā and also Karma-Mīmāṁsā, while Vedāntā deals with the later portion of the Veda and is therefore called Uttara-Mīmāṁsā and also Jñāna-Mīmāṁsā. The former deals with Dharma and the latter with Brahma and therefore the former is also called Dharma-Mīmāṁsā, while the latter is also called Brahma-Mīmāṁsā. There has been a long line of pre-Shaṅkarite teachers of Vedānta of whom Maṇḍana Mishra seems to be the last, who have regarded Mīmāṁsā and Vedānta as forming a single system and who have advocated the combination of action and knowledge, known as Karma-Jñāna-samuchchaya-vāda. According to them, the sūtras, beginning with the first sūtra of Jaimini and ending with the last sūtra of Bādarāyaṇa, form one compact shāstra. These teachers held that Karma (action) and Upāsanā (meditation) were absolutely essential to hasten the dawn of true knowledge. Even the great Shaṅkarāchārya who treated action and knowledge as being absolutely opposed like darkness and light and who relegated Karma to the sphere of Avidyā, had to admit that Karma and Upāsanā do purify the soul, though they are not the direct cause of liberation and that therefore the study of Pūrva Mīmāṁsā, though not essential for the study of Vedānta, was a good means for the purification of the soul. In this connection it is also important to remember that it is the great Mīmāṁsaka Kumārila Bhaṭṭa himself who may be rightly regarded as the link between the Pūrva and the Uttara Mīmāṁsā. Rāmānuja and Bhāskara believe that the Pūrva and Uttara Mīmāṁsās together form one science and the study of the former is necessary before undertaking the study of the latter. Madhva and Vallabha, though they make devotion to God as a necessary prerequisite for the study of Vedānta, yet believe that Vedānta is a continuation of Mīmāṁsā.

Pūrva Mīmāṁsā regards the Veda as eternal and authorless and of infallible authority. It is essentially a book of ritual dealing with commandments prescribing injunctions or prohibitions. Greatest importance is attached to the Brāhmaṇa portion of the Veda to which both the Mantras and the Upaniṣads are subordinated. The aim of the Mīmāṁsā is to supply the principles according to which the Vedic texts are to be interpreted and to provide philosophical justification for the views contained therein. The work of finding the principles for the right interpretation of the Vedic texts was undertaken by the Brāhmaṇas themselves and mainly by the Shrauta-sūtras. Mīmāṁsā continues this work. But had it done only that, it would have been, at best, only a commentary on the Vedic ritual. The main thing which entitles it to the rank of a philosophical system is its keen desire to provide philosophical justification for the Vedic views and to replace the earlier ideal of the attainment of heaven (svarga) by the ideal of obtaining liberation (apavarga). It undertakes a thorough investigation into the nature and validity of knowledge and into the various means which produce valid knowledge and also into other metaphysical problems. Curious though it may seem, the Mīmāṁsā has been much influenced by the Nyāya-Vaisheṣika school, many important doctrines of which it has either borrowed or rejected.

II

LITERATURE

THE earliest work of this system is the Mīmāṁsā-sūtra of Jaimini which begins with an inquiry into the nature of Dharma. It is the biggest of all the philosophical sūtras and discusses about one thousand topics. Shabarasvāmin has written his great commentary on this work and his commentary has been explained by Prabhākara and Kumārila Bhaṭṭa who differ from each other in certain important respects and form the two principle schools of Mīmāṁsā named after them. Prabhākara's commentary Bṛhatī has been commented upon by Shālikanātha who has also written another treatise Prakaraṇa-pañchikā. Kumārila's huge work is divided into three parts—Shlokavārtika, Tantravārtika and Ṭupṭīkā, the first of which has been commented upon by Pārthasārathi Mishra who has also written his Shāstradīpikā. Tradition makes Prabhākara a pupil of Kumārila who nicknamed him as 'Guru' on account of his great intellectual powers. But some scholars like Dr. Gangānātha Jha believe that the Prabhākara school is older and seems to be nearer the spirit of the original Mīmāṁsā.

III

VALIDITY OF KNOWLEDGE

LET us first consider the nature of valid knowledge according to Mīmāṁsā. Prabhākara defines valid knowledge as apprehension (anubhūti). All apprehension is direct and immediate and valid *per se*. A cognition which apprehends an object cannot be intrinsically invalid. Memory arises from the impression of a prior cognition and therefore cannot be treated as valid knowledge. Kumārila defines valid knowledge as apprehension of an object which is produced by causes free from defects and which is not contradicted by subsequent knowledge. Pārthasārathi defines it as apprehension of an object which has not been already apprehended, which truly represents the object, which is not produced by defective causes, and which is free from contradiction. A valid cognition therefore must fulfil these four conditions. Firstly, it must not arise from defective causes (kāraṇadoṣarahita). Secondly, it must be free from contradiction. It must be self-consistent and should not be set aside by subsequent knowledge (bādhakajñānarahita). Thirdly, it must apprehend an object which has not already been apprehended. Novelty is an essential feature of knowledge (agṛhītagrāhi). Thus memory is excluded from valid knowledge by Kumārila also. Fourthly, it must truly represent the object (yathārtha).

The Mīmāṁsaka upholds the theory of Svataḥprāmāṇyavāda which may be translated as the theory of self-validity or intrinsic validity of knowledge. All apprehension is intrinsically valid. All knowledge is valid by itself. It is not validated by any other knowledge. Its validity arises from those very causes from which knowledge itself arises. Validity of knowledge arises from the essential nature of the causes of knowledge. It is not due to any extraneous conditions. Prabhākara and Kumārila both uphold the intrinsic validity of knowledge. Prabhākara says: 'All cognitions *as* cognitions are valid; their invalidity is due to their disagreement with the real nature of their objects.' Kumārila also says: 'The validity of knowledge consists in its apprehending an object; it is set aside by such discrepancies as its disagreement with the real nature of the object.' All knowledge, therefore, is presumably valid and our normal life runs smooth on account of this belief. A need for explanation is felt only when knowledge fails to be valid. And its invalidity is inferred either from some defect in the instrument of knowledge or from a subsequent contradicting knowledge. If a person suffering from jaundice sees a conch yellow, the knowledge of the yellow conch is invalidated on account of the defect in the organ of vision, i.e., on account of the presence of the bile in the eye. If a rope is mistaken for a snake, the knowledge of the rope-snake is invalidated by the subsequent knowledge of the rope. Though the invalidity of knowledge is inferred, yet knowledge itself is intrinsically presumed to be valid. Its validity is not subject to inference. Truth is normal; error is abnormal. Belief is natural; disbelief is an exception. The Mīmāṁsaka advocates the self-validity of knowledge both in respect of its origin (uṭpatti) and ascertainment (jñapti). The validity of knowledge arises together with that knowledge and it is also known as soon as that knowledge is known. The very conditions which give rise to knowledge also give rise to its validity as well as to the belief in that validity. Validity of knowledge and knowledge of that validity arise together with that knowledge and from those very conditions which give rise to that knowledge. Neither validity nor belief in that validity is due to any external condition and neither requires any verification by anything else. The theory of self-validity of knowledge is advocated in these two aspects. If the necessary conditions which give rise to knowledge, e.g., absence of defects in the instruments of knowledge and absence of contradiction, are present, knowledge arises and it arises with a belief in its validity. The conditions which give rise to knowledge also give rise to its validity (prāmāṇyam svataḥ utpadyate). And this validity is known as soon as the knowledge has arisen (pramāṇyam svataḥ jñāyate cha).

Mādhavāchārya in his Sarvadarshanasaṅgraha has mentioned four theories of the validity and invalidity of knowledge. According to Sāṅkhya, both the validity (prāmāṇya) and the invalidity (aprāmāṇya) of knowledge are self-evident. According to some schools of Buddhism, knowledge is intrinsically invalid and becomes valid through extraneous conditions. According to Nyāya-Vaisheṣika, both the validity and the invalidity of knowledge are due to extraneous conditions. According to Mīmāṁsā, knowledge is intrinsically valid, though its invalidity is due to extraneous conditions.

The Mīmāṁsaka criticizes the Sāṅkhya view by pointing out that the same knowledge cannot be both intrinsically valid and invalid. It would be clear self-contradiction to maintain that. If it is said that the same knowledge is not regarded as valid and invalid, but what is maintained is only this that valid knowledge reveals its validity and invalid knowledge reveals its invalidity without depending on external conditions, then it would be difficult to distinguish between valid and invalid knowledge, because invalidity cannot be known without external conditions. The Buddhist view is criticized by pointing out that if knowledge is not intrinsically valid it can never be validated afterwards, for the second knowledge which is said to validate the first, being itself knowledge is intrinsically invalid and requires another knowledge to validate itself and so on *ad infinitum*.

The controversy between the Mīmāṁsaka and the Naiyāyika regarding the validity of knowledge has become classic. Nyāya advocates the theory of extrinsic validity of knowledge called Parataḥprāmāṇyavāda.[1] According to it, knowledge is neither valid nor invalid in itself. It is neutral. The question of its validity or invalidity arises only after knowledge has arisen. The nature of knowledge is its correspondence with its object. And the test of truth is fruitful activity (saṁvādipravṛtti). If knowledge leads to fruitful activity, it is valid; if it does not, it is invalid. Validity and invalidity are not intrinsically connected with knowledge. They are the result of a subsequent test. Validity is due to excellence (guṇa) in the causes of knowledge and invalidity is due to defect (doṣa) in the causes of knowledge. Knowledge arises simply as knowledge and afterwards becomes valid or invalid due to extraneous conditions. The Mīmāṁsaka agrees with the Naiyāyika so far as the invalidity of knowledge (aprāmāṇya) is concerned, because both regard it as due to extraneous conditions. But he criticizes the Naiyāyika in regard to the validity (prāmāṇya) of knowledge. All knowledge is intrinsically valid. If the validity of knowledge also, like its invalidity, depends on extraneous conditions, no knowledge would ever become valid. The Naiyāyika contends that knowledge arises simply as knowledge, that it is neutral and that the question of its validity or invalidity arises afterwards and depends on external test. The Mīmāṁsaka points out that the so-called 'neutral' knowledge is an impossibility. We always experience either valid or invalid knowledge. There is no third alternative; we never experience neutral knowledge. To say so is to maintain the absurd position that knowledge when it arises is devoid of all logical value. Hence neutral knowledge is no knowledge at all. All knowledge must be either valid or invalid. We admit that the invalidity of knowledge is due to extraneous conditions, e.g., due to some defect in the causes which produce knowledge or due to some contradiction. But the validity cannot be due to any extraneous condition. Nothing can validate knowledge if knowledge is not self-valid. The presence of any excellence (guṇa) in the causes of knowledge cannot make it valid, for no such excellence is known. There is no necessity of assuming any excellence in the causes of knowledge. Freedom from defect and contradiction is sufficient to account for the rise of valid knowledge. If the validity of knowledge is due to an external condition like some excellence in the

[1] Supra, p. 180.

causes of knowledge or correspondence or fruitful activity, then this second knowledge of excellence or correspondence or fruitful activity would require a third knowledge to validate itself before it can validate the first knowledge and so on *ad infinitum*. The fallacy of infinite regress cannot be avoided since the knowledge of the external condition which is said to validate any knowledge, being itself knowledge, would require another external condition to validate it. Hence all knowledge must be regarded as self-valid. The so-called extraneous conditions like excellence or correspondence or fruitful activity are really neither extraneous nor mere conditions. Excellence means only freedom from defect. Fruitful activity means absence of contradiction. Correspondence means true representation of the object. Now, these things are the necessary conditions which give rise to valid knowledge. These are the essential prerequisites of any valid knowledge. In their absence valid knowledge would not arise at all. They are internally and intimately connected with the causes which produce knowledge. Hence they are neither extraneous nor mere conditions nor tests of the validity of knowledge. They are the essential and necessary causes which produce valid knowledge. These causes being present, knowledge would arise and it would arise together with its validity and the belief in that validity.

The Nyāya theory of Paratahprāmāṇya and the Mīmāṁsā theory of Svataḥprāmāṇya are respectively compared to the theory of Correspondence and the theory of Coherence in Western logic. According to Western realism, the nature and criterion of truth is correspondence with external reality, while according to Western idealism, it is coherence or self-consistency. The theory of Correspondence advocates that truth is a determinate and external relation between two distinct and independent things. It is a one-one relation between ultimately simple elements. Our knowledge in order to be true must correspond to the external reality as it is. The theory is criticized on the ground that a purely external relation is meaningless as well as impossible. If the terms related are conceived as ultimately simple and independent entities, there can be no relation between them. The entities, being independent, the relation cannot inhere in either or in both, and if the relation falls outside them both, then the relation itself becomes a third entity and needs another relation to relate it to the first two and so on *ad infinitum*. Moreover, relation is possible only within a whole and a mere juxtaposition of the so-called atomic or independent entities does not constitute a real whole. Again, the external substance is unknown and unknowable. It is, what Locke has said, a 'I-know-not-what'. Then, how can we compare our knowledge with the unknowable substance? If we do not know the original, how can we even say that our knowledge is a copy of the real? How can we know that it *corresponds* to the real? Again, correspondence itself must exist *for* a mind which actively discovers truth and does not invent it. Thus the so-called correspondence becomes a subsequent experience and when we say that our knowledge *corresponds with* reality what we really mean is that our two experiences are consistent and do not contradict. Hence correspondence glides away in coherence. The Coherence theory is advocated by the idealists who believe that Reality is a concrete Identity-in-difference, a real Whole which is immanent in all its diverse parts which are organically related to it. Reality is the ultimate subject of all our judgments and a judgment is defined as an ideal content referred to reality. Thought is neither an abstract identity nor a mere difference, but a living process, a significant Whole which is an Identity-in-difference. It is self-consistent and coherent. Reality is free from contradictions not because it has annihilated them but because it has overcome their antagonism in its harmonious bosom. And truth is the systematic coherence which is a characteristic of a significant whole. This theory is criticized on the ground that according to it no truth is completely true, because coherence, being in discursive judgments, fails of concrete coherence which is the absolute truth. Coherence may be the test of truth, but if it is regarded as the nature of truth, then no 'truth' can be completely true. Coherence is mediacy and if validity is mediate, then no cognition can be absolutely valid. Prof. Stout remarks: 'In the absence of immediate cognition the principle of coherence would be like a lever without a fulcrum. . . . If mediate cognition could only be mediated by cognitions which are themselves merely mediate, knowledge could never get a start. It is as if one should say that, in building a wall, every brick must be laid on the top of another brick and none directly on the ground.'

The Nyāya theory may be compared to the theory of Correspondence. The Nyāya advocates realistic pluralism and believes like the Western realists that correspondence with external reality is the nature of valid knowledge. But whereas the Western realists make correspondence also the test of truth, the Nyāya realizes the difficulty and falls back on an indirect test, that of consistent (saṁvādi) and fruitful activity or practical efficiency (arthakriyājñāna). Here it accepts pragmatism. The Mīmāṁsa rightly points out that fruitful activity really means freedom from contradiction. It is, as the Nyāya itself half-heartedly admits, self-consistency (saṁvāda). The Mīmāṁsā theory of svataḥ-prāmāṇya bears resemblance with the theory of Coherence, but there are striking differences also. The Coherence theory can be really advocated by idealism alone. The Mīmāṁsā is a system of rank realism and believes, like the Nyāya, that every knowledge points to an external and independent object beyond it. It admits like the Nyāya that valid knowledge should truly represent the external object, that correspondence with the external object is the nature of valid knowledge (yathārtham jñānam pramāṇam). It also agrees with Nyāya in maintaining that invalidity is due to extraneous conditions. It only says that all knowledge is intrinsically valid. The conditions of freedom from defects and non-contradiction being satisfied, all knowledge arises as self-valid. Coherence and self-consistency is the nature of valid knowledge. But this coherence of the Mīmāṁsā is not a real coherence which is a characteristic of a significant whole. Reality is not regarded as a concrete Whole, but only a juxtaposition of the distinct independent atomic entities. The realism of the Mīmāṁsā does not allow it to rise to real coherence and taking all knowledge as intrinsically valid it simply dispenses with the need of finding out any test for it. But by accepting non-contradiction as well as correspondence with the external object as the nature of truth and further by accepting the view that cognition is immediate apprehension, the Mīmāṁsā avoids the criticism levelled against the Coherence theory.

IV

PERCEPTION AND INFERENCE

BOTH Prabhākara and Kumārila regard knowledge itself as pramāṇa or means of knowledge. Jaimini admits three pramāṇas—perception, inference and testimony. Prabhākara adds two more—comparison and implication. Kumārila further adds non-apprehension. Let us consider these one by one.

Both Prabhākara and Kumārila recognize two kinds of knowledge—immediate and mediate. Perception is regarded as immediate knowledge by both and both admit two stages in perception—indeterminate and determinate. Prabhākara defines perception as direct apprehension (sākṣāt pratītiḥ pratyakṣam). Kumārila defines it as direct knowledge produced by the proper contact of the sense-organs with the presented objects, which is free from defects. Mīmāṁsā broadly agrees with Nyāya in its view of perception. The self comes into contact with the mind (manas); the mind comes into contact with the sense-organ; and the sense-organ comes into contact with the external object. We have already dealt with the account of perception in the Nyāya system and need not repeat it here. We may only note the main differences between the Nyāya and the Mīmāṁsā account of perception. The Mīmāṁsaka regards the auditory organ as proceeding from space (dik) while the Naiyāyika regards it as proceeding from ether (ākāsha). Again, according to Nyāya, the indeterminate perception is a stage inferred afterwards as a hypothesis to account for the determinate perception. All perception is determinate and indeterminate perception serves no fruitful purpose; it is inferred as a necessary earlier stage in the complex process of perception. But the Mimāṁsaka regards it as part of normal experience.

It is the vague, indefinite and primitive stage of perception, the awareness of the 'that' without its relation to the 'what', which gains clarity and definiteness afterwards when it becomes determinate. But like the determinate perception, indeterminate perception also serves a fruitful purpose. It is the basis of activity for children and animals and even adults whose mental growth is imperfect. Even normal adults act upon it when they are in a hurry and confusion. In determinate perception, the self apprehends the pure object (shuddha vastu) and though the genuine and the specific characters are given in it, their relation to the object is not perceived. It is the bare awareness (ālochanamātra) which is non-relational and therefore indeterminate.

The Mīmāṁsā account of inference also generally agrees with that of the Nyāya and need not be repeated here. There are certain minor differences also, e.g., the Mīmāṁsaka recognizes only three members of a syllogism, either the first three or the last three, thus bringing the Indian syllogism in conformity with the Aristotelian one.

V

COMPARISON

THE Mīmāṁsā view of comparison or Upamāna differs from the Nyāya view. According to Nyāya, comparison is the knowledge of the relation between a word and the object denoted by that word (saṁjñā-saṁjñisambandhajñāna). It is the knowledge of similarity of an unknown object like a wild cow with a known object like a cow. The knowledge is like this—'the perceived wild cow is like the remembered cow' (gosadṛsho gavayaḥ). The Mīmāṁsaka refutes this account of comparison. He points out that the knowledge of the relation between a word and the object denoted by that word is derived by verbal authority (e.g., by the words of the person who tells that a wild cow is similar to a cow) and not by comparison. It is known through the recollection of what was learnt from the verbal authority of the person. And the knowledge of the wild cow itself is due to perception and not comparison. Hence comparison, according to Mīmāṁsā, apprehends the similarity of the remembered cow to the perceived wild cow. This knowledge is like this: 'the remembered cow is like the perceived wild cow' (gavayasadṛshī gauḥ). It is the cow as possessing similarity with the wild cow that is known by comparison. A person need not be told by anybody that a wild cow is similar to a cow. Any person who has seen a cow and happens to see a wild cow himself remembers the cow as similar to the wild cow he is perceiving. This knowledge of similarity is comparison. It is distinguished from inference because the vyāpti or the invariable concomitance is not needed here.

VI

VERBAL TESTIMONY

SHABDA-PRAMĀṆA has got the greatest importance in Mīmāṁsā. Testimony is verbal authority. It is the knowledge of supra-sensible objects which is produced by the comprehension of the meanings of words. Kumārila divides testimony into personal (pauruṣeya) and impersonal (apauruṣeya). The former is the testimony of the trustworthy persons (āptavākya). The latter is the testimony of the Veda (Vedavākya). It is valid in itself. It has intrinsic validity. But the former is not valid in itself. Its validity is inferred from the trustworthy character of the person. It may be vitiated by doubt and error and may be contradicted afterwards. The Veda is eternal and authorless. It is not the work of any person, human or divine. The sages are only the 'seers' not the authors of the Veda. The Veda is not composed or spoken even by God. The Veda deals with Dharma and the objects denoted by it cannot be known by perception, inference, comparison or any other means of valid knowledge. Hence the Vedic injunctions can never be contradicted by any subsequent knowledge. And there can be no internal contradictions in the Veda itself. Hence the Vedic testimony is valid in itself. Prabhākara admits only Vedic testimony as real testimony and reduces human testimony to inference because its validity is inferred from the trustworthy character of the person. Again, testimony may give us knowledge of the existent objects (siddhārtha vākya) or may command us to do something (vidhāyaka vākya). Kumārila admits the distinction between existential and injunctive propositions and limits the scope of the Veda to the latter (abhihitānvayavāda). The Veda deals with injunctions. Prohibitions are injunctions in disguise. The Veda commands us to do certain things and to refrain from doing certain things. It deals with the supra-sensible dharma or duty. If we follow the Vedic commands we incur merit and if we do not, we incur demerit. Action, therefore, is the final import of the Veda. The Veda is broadly divided into Vidhivāda or injunctions and Arthavāda or explanations. The existential or the assertive propositions of the Veda are merely explanatory passages which explain the injunctions of the Veda which are its final import. Prabhākara takes a strictly pragmatic view of all knowledge. Knowledge leads to successful activity. Action is the only import of knowledge. He, therefore, refuses to accept that knowledge deals with existent things. All propositions must be injunctive. All knowledge, whether Vedic or secular, points to activity. The so-called assertive or explanatory propositions in the Veda are authoritative only when they help persons to perform their duties (anvitābhidhānavāda).

Testimony is verbal cognition and is derived from the meanings of words which compose sentences. To uphold the eternality and the authorlessness of the Veda, the Mīmāṁsaka puts forward the theory that words and meanings as well as their relation are all natural and eternal. A word (shabda) is made of two or more letters (varṇa) and is a mere aggregate of the letters and not a whole (avayavi), though the letters must occur in a particular order. A varṇa is regarded as an articulated sound. It is eternal (nitya), omnipresent (sarva-gata) and integral (niravayava). It is different from its sound (dhvani) if it is spoken and also different from its symbolic form (rūpa) if it is written. The sound and the form are merely its accidental features which reveal it. A varṇa is eternal and immutable, while its dhvani and rūpa are momentary and changing. If many varṇas are spoken, they are manifested through a temporal series of utterances; if they are written, they are manifested through a spatial series of written symbols. The sound and the symbol are only the vehicles of the manifestation of the eternal varṇa. When a varṇa is pronounced or written in ten different ways, there are not ten different varṇas, but only ten different manifestations of the same varṇa. Therefore a word which is an aggregate of two or more eternal varṇas is itself eternal. A word does not signify the particular things which come into existence and pass away, but the eternal universals underlying these particulars. Hence the meanings or the objects denoted by words, being universals, are eternal and unchanging. And the relation between a word and its meaning also, being natural, necessary, inseparable and internal, is eternal and unchanging. This relation is not conventional. It is due neither to God's will nor to convention as the old and the modern schools of Nyāya respectively believe. It is natural and eternal. Language is not a creation of the human or even the divine mind. Philology is a natural science. The conventional element in language is secondary (sahakāri) and helps the manifestation of the eternal words and their meanings, just as light helps the manifestation of sight. The Naiyāyika also believes in the authority of the Veda, but he regards the Veda as the work of God and so challenges the eternality and authorlessness of the Veda. According to him, words are not eternal and language is due to the divine will or to convention. The Mīmāṁsaka refutes this view and points out that only the sounds and the symbols are created and destroyed, while the real words are eternal. Words are manifested through human efforts. The sounds and the symbols are the vehicles of the manifestation of the eternal words.

But even the permanence of the word and its meaning and the relation between the two does not make the Veda eternal. The Veda is a literary work consisting of sounds and symbols. According to the Mīmāṁsā view, all the uttered or written words are really permanent, though the sounds and the symbols through which they are manifested may be evanescent and changing. Then what is the difference between the Veda and any other literary work? The Mīmāṁsaka answers this question by saying that the Veda is authorless, while all other works are the creation of their authors. The order in which the words occur in the literary works is determined by their authors and therefore the works are subject to defects, doubts and errors. But the order in which the words occur in the Veda is self-determined and therefore intrinsically valid. The Veda is not the creation of any author, human or divine. It is self-proved and self-manifesting. The *particular order* in which the words occur in the Veda (ānupūrvī) is self-determined and eternal. It is the permanence of the text of the Veda which is emphasized by the Mīmāṁsaka. The Veda together with its text is eternal and authorless because the words, their meanings and their relation are all eternal and because long-standing tradition is silent on the authorship of the Veda. This view of the Mīmāṁsā cannot be supported by any rational argument and remains more or less a theological dogma.

VII

IMPLICATION

PRABHĀKARA and Kumārila both, unlike the Naiyāyika, admit Arthāpatti as an independent means of valid knowledge. It is presumption or postulation or implication. It is the assumption of an unperceived fact in order to reconcile two apparently inconsistent perceived facts. If Devadatta is alive and he is not in his house, we presume that he is elsewhere. 'Being alive' and 'not being in the house' are two perceived facts which appear to be inconsistent. Their apparent inconsistency is removed when we presume the fact of 'being elsewhere'. If Devadatta is fat and he does not eat during day, we presume that he must be eating during night, otherwise the inconsistency between 'being fat' and 'not eating during day' cannot be explained. The Naiyāyika reduces presumption to inference. The Mīmāṁsaka regards it as an independent pramāṇa. Prabhākara holds that the element of doubt distinguishes presumption from inference. In presumption, there must be a doubt regarding the truth of the two perceived facts which doubt is removed by presumption, while in inference there is no such doubt. Kumārila believes that doubt is not the basis of presumption. This basis is the mutual inconsistency of the two perceived facts. This inconsistency is removed by presumption. In inference there is no such inconsistency. Prabhākara and Kumārila both agree in holding that in presumption there is no middle term at all which is the basis of inference. Neither of the two perceived and apparently inconsistent facts can separately serve as a middle term. Both the facts combined appear to be the middle term. But then this combination already includes the conclusion, while a valid middle term should not include the conclusion. Hence presumption is different from inference. But the Naiyāyika points out that presumption is disjunctive reasoning which might be reduced to categorical form also. If alive Devadatta is not at his house, the fact of his being elsewhere is inferred thus:

> Alive Devadatta is either in his house or elsewhere,
> Alive Devadatta is not in his house,
> Therefore alive Devadatta is elsewhere.

This disjunctive reasoning might also be reduced to a categorical syllogistic form thus:

> All alive persons who are not in their house are elsewhere,
> Devadatta is an alive person who is not in his house,
> Therefore Devadatta is an alive person who is elsewhere.

Similarly, if fat Devadatta does not eat during day, then the fact of his eating during night is inferred thus:

> Fat Devadatta eats either during day or night,
> Fat Devadatta does not eat during day,
> Therefore fat Devadatta eats during night.

This may be reduced to a categorical form thus:

> All fat persons who do not eat during day are persons who eat during night,
> Devadatta is a fat person who does not eat during day,
> Therefore Devadatta is a fat person who eats during night.

VIII

NEGATION

KUMĀRILA admits non-apprehension (anupalabdhi) as the sixth independent pramāṇa. The Naiyāyika and Prabhākara reject it. The Naiyāyika, like Kumārila, admits negation as an independent ontological category, but he, unlike Kumārila, does not believe in non-apprehension as an independent means of knowledge to know negation. According to him negation is known either by perception or by inference according as the correlate (pratiyogi) of negation is a subject of perception or of inference. The same sense-organ which perceives any object perceives its non-existence also, and the same inference which infers the existence of any object infers its non-existence also. Thus according to the

Naiyāyika, though negation is a separate category, non-apprehension as a separate pramāṇa is not required as its means. He reduces non-apprehension either to perception or to inference. Prabhākara does not admit negation itself as an independent category and hence has no need to admit non-apprehension as its means. Prabhākara agrees with theNaiyāyika, against Kumārila, in rejecting non-apprehension as a separate pramāṇa. But he differs from the Naiyāyika inasmuch as he rejects negation itself as a separate category. To him negation can be represented as a positive entity. There is no non-existence over and above existence. Existence may be perceived either in itself or as related to something else. The apprehension of bare existence, of the locus in itself, is wrongly called non-existence. Thus the so-called 'non-existence of the jar on the ground' is nothing but the apprehension of the bare ground itself. The so-called 'non-existence of a jar before its production' is nothing but the clay itself. Kumārila, siding with the Naiyāyika, refutes Prabhākara's view and maintains that non-existence or negation exists as a separate category and is different from bare existence or locus itself. Negation is not mere nothing. When we perceive the bare ground, we perceive neither the jar nor its non-existence. Hence the perception of the bare ground is different from the non-existence and the non-cognition of the jar. Kumārila also refutes the Naiyāyika's view that non-apprehension may be reduced to perception or inference. Negation cannot be perceived, for there is no sense-object-contact. Negation cannot be inferred, for the invariable concomitance is not known here. Negation cannot be known by testimony, for there is no verbal cognition here. Nor can it be known from comparison or presumption. Hence negation which is an independent category is known by an independent pramāṇa called non-apprehension.

IX

NATURE OF KNOWLEDGE

WE have discussed the Mīmāṁsaka's theory of the intrinsic validity of knowledge and also the different means of valid knowledge. Before we come to the problem of error, we may add a few words to explain the nature of knowledge according to Prabhākara and Kumārila. Prabhākara's theory of knowledge is known as tripuṭīpratyakṣavāda. He regards knowledge as self-luminous (svaprakāsha). It manifests itself and needs nothing else for its manifestation. Though self-luminous, it is not eternal. It arises and vanishes. Knowledge reveals itself and as it does so, it also simultaneously reveals its subject and its object. In every knowledge-situation we have this triple revelation. The subject and the object both are manifested by knowledge itself simultaneously with its own manifestation. Cognition is known as cognition. The self is known as the knower and it can never be cognized as an object. An object is known as a known object. The tripuṭī of the jñātā, jñeya and jñāna is simultaneously revealed in every act of cognition. The subject, the object and the knowledge are simultaneously manifested in every act of knowledge which is self-luminous. It does not need any other knowledge for its revelation. The self and the object both depend on knowledge for their manifestation. The self, therefore, is not self-luminous. The self is not cognized in deep sleep because there is no knowledge to manifest it. Every knowledge has a triple manifestation—the cognition of the self as the knower (ahaṁvitti), the cognition of the object as the known (viṣayavitti) and the self-conscious cognition (svasaṁvitti).

Kumārila's theory of knowledge is known as jñātatāvada. He differs from Prabhākara and does not regard knowledge as self-luminous. Knowledge is not perceptible. It cannot be known directly and immediately. Kumārila regards knowledge as a mode of the self and it is essentially an act (kriyā) or a process (vyāpāra). It cannot reveal itself nor can it be revealed by another cognition as the Nyāya-Vaisheṣika believes. It can only be inferred. And it is inferred from the cognizedness (jñātatā) or manifestness or illuminedness (prākaṭya) of its object. It is the means of knowing the object and is inferred as such because without it the object could never have become known by the subject. Cognition relates the self to the object and enables it to know the object. It is the act of the self by which it knows an object and it is inferred by the fact that an object has become 'known' by the self. The cognitive act is inferred from the cognizedness of the object. An act involves four things—an agent (kartā), an object (karma), an instrument (karaṇa) and a result (phala). An action is found in the agent, but its result is found in the object. Let us take an illustration, that of rice being cooked. The cook is the agent. The rice-grain is the object. The fire is the instrument. The cookedness or softness of the rice is the result. The act of cooking is found in the agent, but its result, the 'cookedness' or 'softness' (vikleda) is found in the object cooked. Similarly cognition arises in the self, but its result—'cognizedness'—is seen in the object known. Just as a person who has not seen the rice being cooked can very well infer from the 'cookedness' or 'softness' of the rice that it has been cooked, that the act of cooking must have taken place before softness has arisen in the rice, similarly the act of cognition is inferred to have taken place in the self by the fact that the object has become cognized. Knowledge is the *tertium quid* between the knower and the known. It is a modal change (pariṇāma) in the self and as such it is adventitious (āgantuka) and not essential. It produces a peculiarity, a result (atishaya) in its object. It is inferred from the cognizedness of the object. Cognition manifests the object and is inferred by this fact. It cannot manifest itself nor can be manifested by any other cognition.

X

PRABHĀKARA'S THEORY OF ERROR

WE have seen that according to the theory of intrinsic validity of knowledge, all knowledge is held to be self-valid by the Mīmāṁsaka. Validity is inherent in knowledge, while invalidity is inferred on account of some defect or contradiction in the causes of knowledge. But if all knowledge is self-valid, how can error at all arise? Prabhākara and Kumārila give different answers to this question. Prabhākara's view is known as Akhyāti and Kumārila's as Viparītakhyāti.

Prabhākara, in strict accordance with his view of intrinsic validity of knowledge, does not admit error in the logical sense. All knowledge is valid *per se*. To experience is always to experience validly. Error, therefore, is only partial truth. It is imperfect knowledge. All knowledge, as knowledge, is quite valid, though all knowledge is not necessarily perfect. Imperfect knowledge is commonly called 'error'. But error is true so far as it goes; only it does not go far enough. All knowledge being true, there can be no logical distinction between truth and error. Prabhākara is true to his realistic position in maintaining that knowledge can never misrepresent its object. Error is one of omission only, not of commission. It is only non-apprehension, not mis-apprehension. It is not a *unitary* knowledge, not a single psychosis, but, in fact, it consists of two psychoses, it is a composite of two cognitions which really fall apart unrelated. Error is due to non-discrimination between these two cognitions and their separate objects. It is a mere non-apprehension of the distinction between the two cognitions and their objects. Hence this view of error is called akhyāti or non-apprehension. Error arises when we forget the fact that instead of one cognition there are really two cognitions denoting two separate objects and further forget the fact that these two cognitions as well as their objects are distinct and unrelated. Two factors are involved in error. One is positive and the other is negative. The positive factor consists in the presence of two cognitions which reveal their respective objects only partially. The negative factor consists in overlooking the distinction between these two cognitions and their objects. Both these cognitions may be presentative or both may be representative or one may be presentative and the other representative. If both the cognitions are presentative, error is due to non-discrimination between perception and perception; if both are representative, error is due to non-discrimination between memory and memory; if one is presentative and the other representative, error is due to non-discrimination between perception and memory. In all cases error is due to non-discrimination which means non-apprehension of the distinction between two cognitions and their objects. It is called vivekākhyāti or bhedāgraha or asaṁsargāgraha. Let us take some illustrations. When a person suffering from jaundice sees a white conch yellow, two cognitions arise. There is a cognition of the conch as the 'this' minus its white colour, and there is also a cognition of the yellow colour alone of the bile. Both these cognitions are partial and imperfect, though quite valid as far as they go. The conch is perceived as the 'this' and not as the 'conch'. The bile is perceived as the 'yellowness' and not as the 'bile'. And the distinction between the 'this' of the conch and the 'yellowness' of the bile is not apprehended. Here, there is non-discrimination beween perception and perception, as both the cognitions are presentative in character. Similarly, when a white crystal is perceived as red on account of a red flower placed near it, there is non-apprehension of the distinction between two cognitions which are partial and imperfect—the cognition of the crystal minus its whiteness and the cognition of the redness alone of the flower. Here also, there is non-discrimination between two partial perceptions. Again, if person recollects that he saw yesterday a long snake lying on the road when really he saw only a piece of rope, here also two imperfect cognitions arise—the recollection of the rope as the 'that' minus its ropeness and the recollection of the snake 'robbed of its thatness'. Here, there is non-discrimination between two memory-images. Again, when a person mistakes a shell for a piece of silver and says, 'this is silver', two imperfect cognitions arise. The 'this' of the shell is actually perceived together with certain qualities like whiteness and brightness which the shell shares in common with silver, but minus its shellness. The common qualities revive in memory the impression of silver which the person has perceived previously elsewhere. Silver is imported in memory merely as silver, 'robbed of its thatness' (pramuṣṭatattākasmaraṇa). Silver is represented as a memory-image, though at the time the fact of its being only a memory-image and not perception is forgotten due to certain defect (smṛtipramoṣa). And the discrimination between the perceived 'this' of the shell and the remembered 'silver' without its thatness is not apprehended. Here, there is non-discrimination between perception and memory, between a presented thing and a represented image. There is only non-apprehension of the distinction between these two imperfect cognitions and their partially presented objects. But there is no misapprehension because the 'shell' is not mis-perceived as 'silver', as the shell never enters consciousness. The 'this' is never sublated for when the error is known, the person says: '*this* is shell'.

XI

KUMĀRILA'S THEORY OF ERROR

KUMĀRILA agrees with Prabhākara in maintaining the intrinsic validity of knowledge. But he differs from Prabhākara inasmuch as he maintains the logical distinction between truth and error. He recognizes error as such and regards it as misapprehension and not as mere non-apprehension. He further holds that error is a single psychosis, a *unitary* knowledge and not a composite of two imperfect cognitions. Error is not only of omission, but also of commission. Kumārila agrees with Prabhākara in maintaining that in the erroneous perception of 'this is silver', two things are present. The shell is perceived as the 'this' bereft of its shellness and silver is imported in memory merely as silver bereft of its thatness, on account of the qualities of whiteness and brightness which are common to both shell and silver. But he differs from Prabhākara and maintains that there is a positive wrong synthesis of these two elements—the perceived and the remembered, and that error is not due merely to the non-apprehension of the distinction between them. The two elements are not united in fact. But they appear to be so in error. Error is partial misrepresentation. Error is not akhyāti or non-apprehension but viparīta-khyāti or misapprehension. It is not due to non-discrimination between two imperfect cognitions (vivekākhyāti or bhedāgraha or asaṁsargāgraha), but it is due to a positive wrong synthesis of the two imperfect cognitions which, though in fact unrelated, are welded together as a unitary knowledge in error (saṁsargagraha or viparītagraha). Thus error becomes a single psychosis, a unitary cognition, a positive misapprehension and therefore one of commission. The shell is misperceived as silver. Error is a wrong apprehension of one object as another object which in fact it is not. This misapprehension arises due to some defect in the causes of knowledge and is set aside by a subsequent sublating knowledge. But as long as error is experienced it is valid as a cognition *per se*. Its intrinsic validity is set aside by extraneous conditions like defects in the causes of cognition or a contradicting cognition. Kumārila gives up his realism to the extent he admits the subjective or the ideal element in error. When error is regarded as misapprehension, the subjective element creeps into it. Though the two relata are separately real, yet the relation between them is not so.

XII

NYĀYA THEORY OF ERROR

KUMĀRILA'S Viparīta-khyāti is much similar to Anyathā-khyāti of the Nyāya-Vaisheṣika, though there are certain differences in details. The Nyāya-Vaisheṣika also believes like Kumārila that error is due to a wrong synthesis of the presented and the represented objects. The represented object is confused with the presented one. The word 'anyathā' means 'elsewise' and 'elsewhere' and both these meanings are brought out in error. The presented object is perceived elsewise and the represented object exists elsewhere. The shell and the silver are both separately real; only their synthesis, their relation as 'shell-silver', is unreal. The shell is misperceived as silver which exists elsewhere, e.g., in the market (āpaṇastha). The Nyāya-Vaisheṣika, like Kumārila, recognizes the subjective element in error. Error is due to a wrong synthesis of the presented objects. Vātsyāyana says: 'What is set aside by true knowledge is the wrong apprehension, not the object'. Uddyotakara remarks: 'The object all the while remains what it actually is . . . the error lies in the cognition'. Gaṅgesha observes: 'A real object is mistaken as another real object which exists elsewhere'. The difference between the Naiyāyika and Kumārila is that while Kumārila is boldly prepared to forsake his realism to the extent of maintaining the ideal element in error, the Naiyāyika in order to perserve his realism vainly falls back upon extraordinary perception to explain the revival of 'silver' in memory. He maintains that the revival of 'silver' in memory is due to a 'complicated perception' (jñānalakṣaṇapratyakṣa) which is a variety of extraordinary (alaukika) perception. Thus he wants to make the represented silver as actually perceived, though in an extraordinary way. Kumārila admits no such extraordinary perception. The Naiyāyika further differs from Kumārila in maintaining that knowledge is not intrinsically valid but becomes so on account of extraneous conditions. He regards correspondence as the nature of truth. But realizing the difficulty that correspondence cannot serve as the test of truth, he proposes successful activity (samvādipravṛtti), as the test of truth and accepts pragmatism so far as the criterion of truth is concerned. Kumārila holds non-contradiction to be the nature of truth and regards all knowledge as intrinsically valid. Knowledge becomes invalid when some defects are discovered in the causes of knowledge or when it is set aside by a subsequent sublating knowledge. Thus Kumārila takes a detached and scientific view of truth as well as of error. Prabhākara, rejecting alike the Naiyāyika's theory of extrinsic validity of truth and the Naiyāyika's and Kumārila's account of error as positive misapprehension and maintaining no logical distinction between truth and error, falls back on the Naiyāyika's pragmatic test of truth agreeing with him that truth is that which 'works' and error is that which does not and lacks practical worth.

XIII

RĀMĀNUJA'S THEORY OF ERROR

THE view of error in earlier Sāṅkhya and in Rāmānuja technically called sat-khyāti is similar to the view of Prabhākara's akhyāti. Earlier Sāṅkhya, Prabhākara and Rāmānuja all believe that error is non-apprehension and not misapprehension. Error is only partial truth. Cognition as such is never invalid. Error means imperfect and incomplete truth. The way to remove error is to acquire more perfect and complete knowledge. There is no subjective or ideal element in error. Truth only supplements error and does not cancel it. Rāmānuja adopts Prabhākara's theory with some modification and his theory is called yathārthakhyāti or satkhyāti or akhyāti-saṁvalitasatkhyāti or 'Non-apprehension-cum-apprehension of Reality'. Rāmānuja goes to the extent of saying that the shell appears as silver because there are some particles of silver in it and explains this by his interpretation of triplication or quintuplication (trivṛt-karaṇa or pañchī-karaṇa). All apprehension is real (yathārtam sarvavijñānam). Error is right so far as it goes; only it does not go sufficiently far enough. The distinction between error and truth, therefore, is not logical, but only practical. The difference between Prabhākara and Rāmānuja is that while the former is content with the non-apprehension of the distinction between perceived shell and remembered silver, the latter advocates real perception of the element of silver in the shell, and while the former takes a fully pragmatic view of knowledge, regarding knowledge as only a means to successful activity, Rāmānuja 'values knowledge more for the light it brings than for the fruits it bears'. The later Sāṅkhya, like the Sāṅkhya-sūtra, and Jainism believe in Sadasatkhyāti which agrees mainly with the view of Kumārila and need not be repeated. Error is here regarded as misapprehension and is held as due to a wrong synthesis of two cognitions which are separately real (sat), though the synthesis itself is unreal (asat).

XIV

THEORY OF ERROR IN MAHĀYĀNA AND ADVAITA VEDĀNTA

WE have thus far considered the theories of error in those schools which claim to be realistic in one way or the other. These realistic schools are divided in their view of error and may be broadly classified under two groups according as they regard error as mere non-apprehension or as misapprehension—the fact which divides Prabhākara and Kumārila. The akhyāti of Prabhākara, the satkhyāti of earlier Sāṅkhya and the akhyātisaṁvalitasatkhyāti or the yathārtha-khyāti of Rāmānuja fall under one group which holds error as mere non-apprehension and rejects the subjective element in error altogether. Error is here treated as partial truth. The viparītakhyāti of Kumārila, the anyathākhyāti of Nyāya, and the sadasatkhyāti of later Sāṅkhya and of Jainism fall under the second group which regards error as misapprehension and admits the subjective element in error. Error is here treated as partial misrepresentation. But all these theories fail to account satisfactorily for the fact of error. Error cannot be taken as mere non-apprehension, for there is definitely a subjective element involved in error which is later on contradicted by the sublating cognition. This view ignores the fact that as long as error lasts, it is taken as true and prompts activity though it may result in failure. There is actual presentation of 'silver' to consciousness and not a mere memory-image. If the two cognitions stand apart unrelated and if error is due to mere non-apprehension of their distinction, the natural question which arises is—Do these two cognitions appear in consciousness or not? If they do, then there must be the cognition of their distinction also; if they do not, they are unreal. Again, neither correspondence can be taken to be the nature of truth nor pragmatic activity its test. Again, Prabhākara at least has no right to maintain non-apprehension, when he rejects negation itself as an independent category. The other group which regards error as misapprehension equally fails to explain error. If error is purely subjective, if knowledge can misrepresent its object, then realism stands rejected. How can the shell be misperceived as silver? Silver cannot be perceived because it is not there and there can be no sense-contact with it. It cannot be a mere memory-image, because as long as error lasts, there is actual presentation of silver to consciousness. The extraordinary jñānalakṣaṇa perception admitted by Nyāya is a mere arbitrary assumption. The dilemma before the realist is this: If silver is real, it cannot be contradicted afterwards by the sublating cognition of shell; and if silver is unreal, how can it appear to consciousness during error? Realism cannot give any satisfactory answer to this. This question is answered by the idealist schools of Mahāyāna Buddhism and Advaita Vedānta. Shūnyavāda, Vijñānavāda and Advaita Vedānta advocate the view known as anirvachanīya-khyāti. Orthodox tradition, probably due to the fact that the original works of Shūnyavāda and Vijñānavāda were not available to it, ascribes to Shūnyavāda the view of asatkhyāti which means that the object of cognition is unreal for reality itself is void, and to Vijñānavāda the view of ātmakhyāti which means that error is the superimposition of the form of cognition on the so-called external object which is unreal, for the real is only the momentary cognition. But it is a great blunder to ascribe these views to these schools. Neither Shūnyavāda is nihilism nor is Vijñānavāda subjective idealism. Our account of these schools has clearly proved that they believe in Absolute Idealism and are the forerunners of Advaita Vedānta. They advocate anirvachanīyakhyāti. Of course the school of Svatantra-vijñānavāda may be rightly charged with subjective idealism and may therefore be regarded as an advocate of ātmakhyāti. The theory is clearly absurd for according to it, instead of 'this is silver' we should have the cognition 'I am silver' or at least 'the idea of "this" is the idea of silver'. Let us now consider the true solution of the problem of error given by the above-mentioned three schools of Absolute Idealism. Reality is pure consciousness which is direct, immediate and self-luminous and is the transcendental background of the world of phenomena which is its appearance due to the power of beginningless Ignorance. Affirmation and negation are the phases of the same reality. The distinction between truth and error is relative and empirical. Reality transcends this distinction. Error is of two kinds. One is the transcendental or the universal error and the other is the subjective or the individual error. The former is called by Shūnyavāda as tathya-samvṛti, by Vijñānavāda as paratantra and by Vedānta as vyavahāra. The latter is called by Shūnyavāda as mithyā-samvṛti, by Vijñānavāda as parikalpita and by Vedānta as pratibhāsa. Both are based on contradiction, negativity, limitation and relativity. For convenience we call the former 'appearance' and the latter 'error'. Both baffle all description and are the offspring of the real and the unreal. Both are indescribable for they can be called neither as real nor as unreal. Contradiction is the essence of all appearances, for non-contradiction belongs only to reality which is of the nature of pure knowledge. Knowledge, therefore, removes contradiction and the moment contradiction is removed, error vanishes. When the shell is mistaken for silver, the shell-delimited consciousness is the ground on which silver and its cognition are illusorily imposed by beginningless Ignorance. This 'silver' is not real, because it is contradicted afterwards when the shell is known; and it cannot be unreal, because it appears as silver as long as illusion lasts. It is therefore called anirvachanīya or indescribable either as real or as unreal. Avidyā hides the nature of the shell and makes it look like silver. Negatively it covers shellness (āvaraṇa) and positively it projects (vikṣepa) silver on it. Error is indescribable superimposition which does not really affect the ground and is removed by right knowledge. Error is true as long as it lasts and becomes unreal only when it is contradicted by a higher knowledge. The illusory is sublated by the phenomenal and the latter by the transcendental.

XV

REALISM OF MĪMĀṀSĀ

WE now turn to the metaphysics of the Mīmāṁsā. The Mimāṁsaka is a pluralistic realist. He believes in the reality of the external world and of the individual souls. There are innumerable individual souls, as many as there are living bodies, plus the bodiless liberated souls. There are also innumerable atoms[1] and the other eternal and infinite substances. Mīmāṁsā believes in the Law of Karma, in Unseen Power (apūrva), in heaven and hell, in liberation and in the ultimate authority of the eternal authorless Veda. God is ruled out as an unnecessary hypothesis, though the later Mīmāṁsakas like Āpadeva and Laugākṣi try to bring in God. Mīmāṁsā does not admit the periodic creation and dissolution of this world. The world was never created and never shall it be destroyed. Though individuals come and go, though the finite material products arise and perish, yet the world as such, the universe as a whole goes on for ever, uncreated and imperishable. There never was a time when the universe was different from what it is now.[2]

Prabhākara admits seven categories—substance (dravya), quality (guṇa), action (karma), generality (sāmānya), inherence (paratantratā), force (shakti) and similarity (sādṛshya). Out of these the first five are similar to the categories of the Vaisheṣika, though inherence is here called paratantratā instead of samavāya; and the last two, shakti and sādṛshya, are added; the Vaisheṣika category of particularity is equated with the quality of distinctness (pṛthaktva) and the category of negation is rejected. Kumārila recognizes four positive categories, substance, quality, action and generality, and the fifth category of negation which is of four kinds—prior, posterior, mutual and absolute. He rejects particularity and inherence. Like Prabhākara, he reduces particularity to the quality of distinctness. Inherence is reduced to identity-in-difference. It is tādātmya or bhedābheda. It is identity between two different but inseparable objects. Kumārila, like Shaṅkara, criticizes the reality of inherence and says that in order to avoid infinite regress, inherence must be regarded as identity which is really identity-in-difference. Kumārila rejects force and similarity as independent categories and includes them under substance. Kumārila admits the nine substances of the Vaisheṣika and adds two more—darkness and sound—which are rejected by Prabhākara. The conception of the categories and the substances etc. in Mīmāṁsā is generally the same as in the Nyāya-Vaisheṣika.

[1] Kumārila says that all Mīmāṁsakas do not necessarily believe in atoms: mīmāṁsakaishcha nāvashyam iṣyante paramāṇavaḥ, Shlokavārtika, p. 404. [2] na kadāchid anīdṛsham jagat.

XVI

SELF AND KNOWLEDGE

PRABHĀKARA and Kumārila both admit the plurality of the individual souls and regard the self as an eternal (nitya), omnipresent (sarvagata), ubiquitous (vibhu), infinite (vyāpaka) substance (dravya) which is the substratum (āshraya) of consciousness and which is a real knower (jñātā), enjoyer (bhoktā) and agent (kartā). The self is different from the body, the senses, the mind and the understanding. The self is the enjoyer (bhoktā); the body is the vehicle of enjoyment (bhogāyatana); the senses are the instruments of enjoyment (bhogasādhana); and the internal feelings and the external things are the objects of enjoyment (bhogyaviṣaya). Consciousness is not regarded as the essence of the self. Prabhākara, agreeing with the Nyāya-Vaisheṣika, holds that the self is essentially unconscious (jaḍa) and that consciousness is only an accidental quality which may or may not be possessed by the soul-substance. Cognitions, feelings and volitions are the properties of the self and arise due to merit and demerit. In liberation, which is due to the exhaustion of merit and demerit, the self remains as a pure substance divested of all its qualities including consciousness and bliss. Kumārila, differing from Prabhākara and Nyāya-Vaisheṣika, regards consciousness as a modal change (pariṇāma) in the self. It is a mode, an act, a process of the self by which the self cognizes the objects. It is neither the essence nor an accidental static property of the self. Kumārila, like the Jainas, regards the self as identical as well as different, as changeless as well as changing. As substance, it does not change and always remains the same; as modes, it undergoes change and becomes diverse. The substance remains the same; it is only the modes which appear and disappear. Modal change does not militate against the permanence of the self. The self is not wholly unconscious as Prabhākara and Nyāya-Vaisheṣika believe. It is conscious-unconscious (Jaḍabodhātmaka or chidachidrūpa). As substance, it is unconscious; as modes, it is conscious. The self is characterized by the potency to know. Potential consciousness is the nature of the self (jñānashaktisvabhāva). Kumārila too, like Prabhākara and Nyāya-Vaisheṣika, believes that in liberation the self remains as a pure substance divested of all qualities and modes including consciousness and bliss, though he adds that the self then, as in deep sleep, is characterized by potential consciousness. To the question: how is the self known? Prabhākara, Kumārila and the Naiyāyika give different answers.

Prabhākara advocates the theory of simultaneous revelation of knower, known and knowledge (tripuṭipratyakṣavāda). He believes, like the Naiyāyika, that the self is essentially unconscious, but unlike him, he maintains that knowledge is self-luminous. Self-luminous knowledge, therefore, reveals the self as the subject and the known thing as the object simultaneously with itself. In every knowledge-situation the self is simultaneously revealed as the subject of that knowledge. The self is not self-luminous because it is not revealed in deep sleep. It is unconscious like the object and like it requires knowledge for its manifestation. Knowledge is not eternal, though the self is. Knowledge appears and disappears and as it does so it reveals the self as the subject and the known thing as the object together with itself. The self is necessarily implied in every knowledge as the subject and it can never become an object. It is impossible to know the self as an object. All consciousness is necessarily self-consciousness.

Kumārila advocates the theory of cognizedness of object (jñātatāvāda). He believes, like the Naiyāyika and unlike Prabhākara, that self-consciousness is a later and a higher state of consciousness. But whereas the Naiyāyika believes that both consciousness and self are directly revealed in this higher and later state of self-consciousness through introspection (anuvyavasāya), Kumārila believes that consciousness is only inferred indirectly through the cognizedness (jñātatā or prākaṭya) of the object, though the self is directly revealed as the object of self-consciousness or the I-notion or the Ego-cognition. According to Kumātila, the self is not revealed as the subject by consciousness together with itself. Consciousness can reveal neither itself nor the subject. It can reveal only the object. Consciousness is not self-luminous. It is not known directly. It is inferred through the cognizedness of the object. Consciousness is a dynamic mode of the self and its result is seen only in the object which becomes illumined by it. Hence the self is known as the object of the I-notion. Kumārila takes 'self-consciousness' in its literal sense. The self is of the nature of the 'I' and it is apprehended by itself and by nothing else. It is an object of the I-consciousness. The self is both the subject and the object. There is no contradiction in maintaining this because the self becomes an object only to itself and to nothing else. The knower becomes the known to itself.

It is clear from the above account that Prabhākara and Kumārila both struggle for the correct view of the self, though both of them miss it. Prabhākara is right in maintaining that knowledge is self-luminous, and that the self as the subject is necessarily involved in every knowledge-situation and that the self which is the subject can never be known as an object. But he is wrong in confusing pure knowledge with momentary cognitions and in regarding the self as the unconscious substance and consciousness as its accidental quality. Kumārila is right in saying that consciousness is not an accidental quality of the self and that the self is not explicitly revealed in all knowledge and that self-consciousness is higher than consciousness. But he is wrong in saying that consciousness is a dynamic mode of the self, in confusing the self with the ego, in denying the self-luminosity of knowledge and making it a thing only to be inferred, and in treating the self as the object of the I-notion. The real self is the transcendental knower and, as the ultimate subject, is identical with eternal and foundational consciousness. Prabhākara and Kumārila, influenced by the Nyāya-Vaisheṣika in their pluralistic realism, fail to treat the self as the real subject and cling to the wrong view that it is essentially a substance.

XVII

DHARMA

DHARMA is the subject of inquiry in Mīmāṁsā. Jaimini defines dharma as a command or injunction which impels men to action.[1] It is the supreme duty, the 'ought', the 'categorical imperative'. Artha and Kāma which deal with ordinary common morality are learnt by worldly intercourse. But Dharma and Mokṣa which deal with true spirituality are revealed only by the Veda. Dharma is supra-sensible and consists in the commands of the Veda. Action is the final import of the Veda which commands us to do certain acts and to refrain from doing certain other acts. The authoritativeness of the Veda is supported by social consciousness as well as by individual conscience. Dharma and adharma deal with happiness and pain to be enjoyed or suffered in the life beyond. Actions performed here produce an unseen potency (apūrva) in the soul of the agent which yields fruit when obstructions are removed and time becomes ripe for its fructification. The apūrva is the link between the act and its fruit. It is the causal potency (shakti) in the act which leads to its fructification. Actions are first divided into three kinds—obligatory (which must be performed, for their violation results in sin, though their performance leads to no merit); optional (which may or may not be performed; their performance leads to merit, though their non-performance does not lead to sin); and prohibited (which must not be performed, for their performance leads to sin, though their non-performance does not lead to merit). Obligatory actions are of two kinds—those which must be performed daily (nitya) like daily prayers (sandhyāvandana) etc., and those which must be performed on specified occasions (naimittika). Optional actions are called kāmya and their performance leads to merit, e.g., he who wants to go to heaven should perform certain sacrifices (svargakāmo yajeta). Prohibited actions are called pratiṣiddha and their performance incurs sin and leads to hell. Then, there are expiatory acts (prāyashchitta) which are performed in order to ward off or at least mitigate the evil effect of the performed prohibited

[1] chodanālakṣaṇo'rtho dharmaḥ.

actions. The earlier Mīmāṁsaka believed only in dharma (and not in mokṣa) and their ideal was the attainment of heaven (svarga). But later Mīmāṁsakas believe in mokṣa and substitute the ideal of heaven by that of liberation (apavarga). Prabhākara and Kumārila both believe that the goal of human life is liberation, though both conceive it in a negative manner like the Nyāya-Vaisheṣika. The soul is chained to Saṁsāra on account of its association with the body, the senses, the mind and the understanding. Through this association, the soul becomes a knower, an enjoyer and an agent. This association is due to karma which is the cause of bondage. When the cause is removed, the effect also ceases to exist. So abstention from karma automatically leads to the dissolution of the 'marriage-tie' of the soul with the body, the senses, the mind etc. and consequently to the return of the soul to its pure nature as a substance rid of all qualities and modes including consciousness and bliss also. It is a state of freedom from all pain and desire and consciousness, though Kumārila adds that the soul is here characterized by potential consciousness. Prabhākara and Kumārila both admit that abstention from karma does not mean abstention from all karmas, but abstention from the optional (kāmya) and the prohibited (pratiṣiddha) kinds of karma only. The performance of the former leads to merit and to heaven, while that of the latter to demerit and to hell. The seeker for liberation has to rise above both merit and demerit, above both heaven and hell. But even he should perform the obligatory (nitya and naimittika) actions enjoined by the Veda. Prabhākara believes in 'duty for duty's sake'. Obedience to the Veda is an end in itself and is of ultimate value (puruṣārtha). These actions must be performed in an absolutely detached manner without any consideration of reward simply because they are the commands of the Veda. Kumārila believes in psychological hedonism and makes the performance of these actions a means to realize the ultimate end, i.e., liberation, by overcoming past sin and by avoiding future sin which would otherwise surely result from their neglect. Prabhākara believes in the utter supremacy of action, though he admits knowledge also as a means of liberation. Kumārila believes in jñāna-karma-samuchchayavāda or in a harmonious combination of knowledge and action as a means to liberation and thus paves the way for Advaita Vedānta. He admits that upāsanā or meditation which is a kind of action leads to knowledge which ultimately leads to liberation. Kumārila's view of the self as potential consciousness, his emphasis that action is not an end in itself but only a means to obtain liberation, his acceptance of the view that knowledge of the self born of true meditative act is the immediate cause of liberation, and his implicit theism—all go to make him a veritable link between Prabhākara and Shaṅkara, between the Pūrva and the Uttara Mīmāṁsās. It was Kumārila who was actively engaged in a life-long fight against the Buddhists and if the credit for turning out Buddhism from the land of its birth, apart from the internal weaknesses of Buddhism itself and the changed social, economic and political conditions, goes to a single person, it should go to Kumārila alone. Shaṅkara simply beat the dead horse. Kumārila represents the transitional phase from the Mīmāṁsā to the Vedānta and is responsible for giving rise to a series of Pre-Shaṅkarite Advaitic teachers of Vedānta of whom Maṇḍana Mishra was probably one of the last. Kumārila and the Buddhists, like two lions, fought against each other and the fight led both to bleed to death. Shaṅkara corrected the defects of both and synthesized the merits of both in his Advaitism. This should not mean that Shaṅkara's work was merely eclectic. Shaṅkara like a true genius built his immortal system with an originality of his own by which even the dust that passed into his hands became an enchanted powder. What we mean is that Kumārila paved the way by his voluminous works and his strenuous life-long efforts for the system of Shaṅkara and saved much of the trouble to the latter in carrying out the spade-work. Kumārila himself says that Mīmāṁsā was misinterpreted by some of his predecessors in a thoroughly empirical and materialistic manner (the reference here is probably to Bhartṛmitra and Prabhākara) and that his task was to give its correct (āstika) interpretation.[1] Kumārila accepts the triple spiritual discipline of the Vedānta and points out that Shabara, the great Commentator, has proved the existence of the eternal self by means of rational arguments and that in order to make the knowledge of the self firm one has to take recourse to the triple spiritual discipline of the Vedānta,[2] which Pārthasārathi explains as study (shravaṇa), critical thinking (manana) and realization (nidhidyāsana). Though, according to the interpretation of Pārthasārathi, Kumārila does not regard liberation as a state of bliss, yet it is significant to note that there were some people, for example Nārāyaṇa Bhaṭṭa, the author of the Mānameyodaya, who thought that Kumārila advocated blissful liberation.[3] Kumārila says in his Tantravārtika: This shāstra called the Veda, which is Sound-Brahman, is supported by the one Supreme Spirit.[4] The very first verse of the Shlokavārtika is capable of two interpretations.[5] The word 'somārdhadhāriṇe' in this verse may mean 'sacrifice equipped with the vessels of somarasa', and it may also mean 'Lord Shiva who bears the semi-circular Moon on His forehead'. Pārthasārathi interprets it as referring to sacrifice. But the prayer to Lord Shiva is also unmistakably implied here. All this proves our contention that Kumārila is a link between the Pūrva and the Uttara Mīmāṁsās.

[1] prāyeṇaiva hi mīmāṁsā loke lokāyaītkṛtā. tām āstikapathe kartum ayam yatnaḥ kṛto mayā, Shlokavārtika, I, 10. [2] dṛḍhatvam etadviṣayashcha bodhaḥ prayāti vedāntaniṣevaṇena, Ibid, p. 728. [3] duḥkhātyantasamuchchhede sati prāg ātmavartinaḥ. sukhasya manasā bhuktir muktir uktā Kumārilaiḥ, Mānameyodaya, p. 212. [4] sabdabrahmeti yachchedam shāstram vedākhyam uchyate. tadapyadhiṣṭhitam sarvam ekena paramātmanā, Ibid, p. 719. [5] vishuddhajñānadehāya trivedīdivyachakṣuṣe. shreyaḥprāptinimittāya namaḥ somārdhadhāriṇe.

Chapter Fourteen

PRE-SHAṄKARA VEDĀNTA

I

GAUḌAPĀDA-KĀRIKA

THE Upaniṣads, the Brahma-Sūtra and the Gītā are called 'Prasthāna-traya' or the three basic works of Vedānta on which almost every great Āchārya has commented.

Just as the various schools of Mahāyāna recognize the Mahāyāna-Sūtras as the Āgama which embody the real teachings of the Buddha and just as their teachings were summarized by Ashvaghoṣa, the first systematic expounder of the Mahāyāna, and were developed into a full-fledged school of Shūnyavāda by its first systematic expounder, Nāgārjuna, similarly the Upaniṣads are regarded as the shruti by the Vedāntins and their teachings were summarized by Bādarāyaṇa in his Brahma-Sūtra and were developed into the school of Advaita Vedānta by its first systematic expounder, Gauḍapāda.

The Māṇḍūkya-Kārikā or the Gauḍapāda-Kārikā also known as the Āgama-Shāstra is the first available systematic treatise on Advaita Vedānta. There can be no doubt that Gauḍapāda's philosophy is essentially based on the Upaniṣads, particularly on the Māṇḍūkya, the Bṛhadāraṇyaka, and the Chhāndogya. Probably he has also drawn upon the Brahma-sūtra and the Gītā. There can also be no doubt that Gauḍapāda is much influenced by Mahāyāna Buddhism—by Shūnyavāda and Vijñānavāda. In fact it can be correctly stated that Gauḍapāda represents the best that is in Nāgārjuna and Vasubandhu. Tradition says that Gauḍapāda was the teacher of Govindapāda who was the teacher of Shaṅkarāchārya. Shaṅkara himself most respectfully salutes Gauḍapāda as his 'grand-teacher who is the respected (teacher) of (his) respected (teacher)',[1] and quotes from and refers to him as the 'teacher who knows the tradition of the Vedānta'.[2] Shaṅkara's disciple Sureshvara also refers to him as the 'Revered Gauḍa'.[3]

The long-accepted traditional view that the Kārikās of Gauḍapāda are a commentary on the Māṇḍūkya Upaniṣad is challenged by Mm.

[1] yastam pūjyābhipūjyam paramagurumamum pādapātair nato'smi, Māṇḍūkya-Kārikā-Bhāsya, last verse. [2] atroktam Vedāntasampradāyavidbhir āchāryaiḥ. sampradāyavido vadanti, Shāriraka-Bhāsya, II, 1, 9; I, 4, 14. [3] evam Gauḍair Drāviḍair naḥ pūjyair arthaḥ prabhāṣitaḥ, Naiskarmya-siddhi, IV, 44.

Pt. Vidhushekhara Bhattacharya. His thesis is that '(i) The Kārikās in Book I are not the exposition of the Māṇḍūkya Upaniṣad. (ii) The Māṇḍūkya Upaniṣad is mainly based on the Kārikās, and not *vice versa.* (iii) And as such the Māṇḍūkya Upaniṣad is later than the Kārikās'.[1]

To us all the arguments which Pt. Bhattacharya gives in support of his thesis seem to be entirely unconvincing. His arguments may be summarized thus:

(1) Madhva regards only Book I as Shruti and thinks that the other three Books form a separate work or works which are not commented upon by him.
(2) The Kārikās do not explain many important and difficult words in the Māṇḍūkya.
(3) The Māṇḍūkya has drawn upon other Upaniṣads and upon the Kārikās.
(4) By comparing some prose passages of the Māṇḍūkya with some Kārikās, it becomes clear that the prose passages are later developments.

The first argument can be answered by pointing out that Shaṅkara and Sureshvara who are Advaitins and who flourished long before Madhva who is a Dvaitin, do not regard the Kārikās as Shruti. Pt. Bhattacharya adduces no sound reasons as to why we should believe Madhva against Shaṅkara and Sureshvara.

The second argument can be easily answered by pointing out that the Kārikās are a free commentary, almost an independent work which is based essentially on the Upaniṣad and hence it was not necessary for Gauḍapāda to explain every word occurring in the Māṇḍūkya text.

In answer to the third argument we say that we also admit that the Māṇḍūkya has much similarity with the Bṛhadāraṇyaka and the Chhāndogya, and we add that many passages which occur in these two Upaniṣads also occur in Upaniṣads other than the Māṇḍūkya, and even if we grant that the Māṇḍūkya is later and has drawn upon earlier Upaniṣads, it does not mean that it has drawn upon the Kārikās also.

In answer to the fourth argument we say that by comparing the prose passages of the Māṇḍūkya with the Kārikās we find just the opposite to be the case. The prose passages appear to be earlier ones. Moreover, we may also add that generally scholars have regarded the prose passages of the Upaniṣads to be earlier than the verse portions.

Another contention of Pt. Bhattacharya is that 'these four Books are four independent treatises and are put together in a volume under the

[1] The Āgama-Shāstra of Gauḍapāda: Introduction, p. XLVI.

title of the Āgama-Shāstra'.[1] This contention too is untenable. To support his view Pt. Bhattacharya gives these arguments:—

(1) If Book II is supported by reasoning, is there no reasoning at all in Book I?
(2) Does one find in Book II anything improper, nonsensical, unintelligible or incomplete without assuming its connection with Book I? No.
(3) There is nothing against one's thinking that Book III too is an independent work.
(4) Certain things like Ajātivāda, already indicated in Book I and discussed in Book III, are again discussed in Book IV. Why should the author of Book IV indulge in such a useless action?

In answer to these arguments we say that if Gauḍapāda uses independent arguments in Book II, should he be debarred from using reasoning in Book I? If there is nothing unintelligible in Book II without the help of Book I, how can it necessarily mean that Book II is an absolutely independent work? Even in the works of many modern scholars there are chapters which may be read by themselves. The third argument, being purely negative, is no argument at all. In answer to the fourth argument we urge that repetition is not always useless. An author may consider repetition necessary in order to emphasize some important points. The difficulty with Pt. Bhattacharya seems to be that he expects strictest unity and utmost homogeneity of presentation from Gauḍapāda, the saint, as he may expect from a reputed writer on philosophy. Moreover, we maintain that there is a considerable unity running through the different Books of the Āgama-Shāstra.

The chief merit of Pt. Bhattacharya's work is to point out the similarities between Gauḍapāda and Mahāyāna Buddhism. Though we differ from Pt. Bhattacharya on certain grave points of interpretation, we generally agree with him so far as these similarities are concerned. We agree with him in maintaining that Gauḍapāda was much influenced by Mahāyāna Buddhism, especially by Nāgārjuna and Vasubandhu. Pt. Bhattacharya is perfectly right in remarking: 'It is true that he (Gauḍapāda) advocates the Vijñānavāda, but certainly it is originally adopted by him from the Upaniṣadic source . . . Upaniṣadic seed of idealism being influenced by its elaborate system in Buddhism and the vast literature on it by the Buddhist teachers who flourished before Gauḍapāda, has developed into what we now find in the Āgama-shāstra . . . it must be accepted that it did not first originate with the Buddhists, though it has much developed in their system later on'.[2] But he does not

[1] Ibid: Introduction, p. LVII. [2] The Āgama-Shastra of Gauḍapāda: Introduction p. CXXXII.

develop this point; rather he sometimes seems to forget this. And therefore we differ from him on one important point of emphasis. By pointing out the similarities between Gauḍapāda and Mahāyāna, Pt. Bhattacharya's aim, more or less, has been to prove that Gauḍapāda is a Crypto-Buddhist, while our aim, on the other hand, is to prove that Mahāyāna and Advaita are not two opposed systems of thought but only different stages in the development of the same thought which originates in the Upaniṣads, and that Gauḍapāda's philosophy as well as Mahāyāna so far as Gauḍapāda agrees with it, both are rooted in the Upaniṣads, and that therefore instead of dubbing Gauḍapāda as a Crypto-Buddhist it will be far truer to dub the Mahāyānists as crypto-Vedāntins. We shall pursue this point later on.

II

AJĀTIVĀDA

THE fundamental doctrine of Gauḍapāda is the Doctrine of No-origination (ajātivāda). Negatively, it means that the world, being only an appearance, is in fact never created. Positively, it means that the Absolute, being self-existent, is never created (aja).

Gauḍapāda agrees with Shūnyavāda in maintaining that origination, from the absolute standpoint, is an impossibility. He examines the various theories of creation and rejects them all. Some say that creation is the expansion (vibhūti) of God; others maintain that it is like a dream (svapna) or an illusion (māyā); some believe that it is the will (ichchhā) of God; others declare that it proceeds from Time (kāla); still others say that it is for God's enjoyment (bhoga); while some maintain that it is God's sport (krīḍā). All these views are wrong. What desire can God have who has realized all desires? Essentially therefore creation is but the very nature of God. It is His inherent nature. It flows from Him. It simply emanates from Him.[1] But it only appears to be so; in fact there is no creation at all. If this world of plurality really existed, it would have surely come to an end. Duality is only an appearance; non-duality is the real truth.[2] To those who are well-versed in Vedānta the world appears only as a dream or an illusion or a castle in the sky or a city of the Gandharvas.[3] From the ultimate standpoint there is neither death nor birth, neither disappearance nor appearance, neither destruction or production, neither bondage nor liberation;

[1] Māṇḍūkya-Kārikā, I, 7-9. Devasyaiṣa svabhāvo'yam āptakāmasya kā spṛhā? Ibid, I, 9. [2] māyāmātramidam dvaitam advaitam paramārthataḥ, Ibid, I, 17. [3] svapnamāye yathā dṛṣṭe gandharvanagaram yathā. tathā vishvamidam dṛṣṭam Vedānteṣu vichakṣaṇaih, Ibid, II, 31. Compare Saddharma: p. 142, Aṣṭasāhasrikā pp. 39, 40, 205; Laṅkāvatāra: pp. 90-96, 105; Lalitavistara p. 181; Samādhirāja p. 27; Mādhyamika-Kārikā: XXIII, 8; XVII, 33; VII.

there is none who works for freedom, none who desires salvation, and none who has been liberated; there is neither the aspirant nor the emancipated—this is the highest truth.[1] There is neither unity nor plurality. The world cannot be regarded as manifold by its very nature. It is neither one nor many—thus the wise know it.[2] The imagination of the Ātman as different things and the imagination of different things themselves which in fact do not exist, depend on the Non-dual Absolute or the Pure Ātman, just as the imagination of a snake in the case of a rope-snake depends upon the rope. The Absolute alone, therefore, is blissful.[3]

Reality is No-origination. It always remains the same. It is the complete absence of misery. If we know this we shall at once understand how things which in fact are never born, yet appear as if they are born. The Absolute is Non-dual. There is no difference at all.[4] When sometimes the Upaniṣads declare the creation as distinct from its cause and give the illustrations of earth, iron and sparks etc., they do so only as a means (upāyaḥ so'vatārāya) in order to make us understand the supreme end of No-origination.[5] Jagat is not different from Jīva and Jīva is not different from Ātman and Ātman is not different from Brahman. The non-dual Absolute appears as diverse only on account of illusion. The Unborn can never tolerate any distinction. If it really becomes diverse then the immortal would become mortal. The dualists want to prove the birth of the Unborn. But the Unborn is Immortal and how can the Immortal become mortal? The Immortal can never become mortal and the mortal can never become Immortal. Ultimate nature can never change.[6] The Shruti declares: 'There is no plurality here' (neha nānāsti kiñchana; Br. IV. 4, 19 and Kaṭha II. 1, 11); 'The Lord through His power appears to be many' (Br. II. 5, 19); and 'The Unborn appears to be born as many' (ajāyamāno bahudhā vijāyate). It is to be known, therefore, that the Unborn appears to be born only through illusion. In fact He is never born. By declaring that 'those who are attached to creation or production or origination (sambhūti) go to utter darkness' (Īsha, 12), the Shruti denies creation; and by declaring that 'the Unborn does not take birth again, who, then, can indeed produce Him?' (Br. III, 9, 28), the Shruti denies the cause of creation.[7]

Not only by Shruti, but also by independent reasoning can it be proved that ultimately nothing originates. He who maintains the birth of the existent accepts the absurd position that that which is already existent is being born again. And the non-existent can never be born at all. Verily, the son of a barren woman can be born neither through

[1] na nirodho na chotpattir na baddho na cha sādhakaḥ. na mumukṣur na vai mukta ityeṣā paramārthatā, Ibid, II, 32. Compare Mādhyamika-Kārikā, Opening Verse. [2] Ibid, II, 34. [3] Ibid, II, 33. [4] upāyaḥ so'vatārāya nāsti bhedaḥ kathañchana, Ibid, III, 15. [5] Ibid, III, 15. [6] Ibid, III, 19-21; IV, 6-7. Compare Mādhyamika-Kārikā, XIII, 4. [7] Ibid, III, 24-24.

illusion nor in reality. The doctrine of No-origination, therefore, is the ultimate truth.[1]

Dualists, says Gauḍapāda, quarrel among themselves. Some say that it is the existent which is born, while others say that it is the non-existent which is born. Some say that nothing originates from Being, while others say that nothing originates from Not-being. We do not quarrel with these dualists because these disputants, taken together, proclaim, like the non-dualists, the doctrine of No-origination.[2] These disputants want to prove the birth of the Unborn. But how can the Unborn be born? How can the Immortal become mortal? Ultimate nature cannot change. It is self-proved, self-existent, innate and uncaused. All things by their very nature are free from decay and death. Those who believe in decay and death, fall low on account of this wrong notion.[3]

There are some (i.e. the Shūnyavādins) who uphold non-dualism (advayavāda) and reject both the extreme views of being and not-being, of production and destruction, and thus emphatically proclaim the doctrine of No-origination. We approve, says Gauḍapāda, of the doctrine of No-origination proclaimed by them.[4]

Sāṅkhya maintains that the effect pre-exists in the cause and that causation consists in the manifestation of the permanent cause (avyakta) as the changing effects (vyakta jagat). Gauḍapāda objects that if the cause is produced, how can it be unborn? If it becomes the changing 'many', how can it be changeless and permanent? Again, if the effect is identical with the cause, then the effect too should be immortal or the cause too should be mortal. How can the permanent cause be identical with the changing effect and still be permanent?[5] Verily, adds Shaṅkara in his Commentary, one cannot cook half a portion of a hen and at the same time reserve another half for laying eggs.[6] Again, if the effect does not pre-exist in the cause it is like a hare's horn and cannot be produced. Again, cause and effect cannot be simultaneous, for then the two horns of a bull will have to be regarded as causally related.[7] Again, those who maintain that the cause precedes the effect and the effect also precedes the cause, maintain the absurd position that a son also begets his father.[8] Therefore nothing can be produced.

Nothing can originate because:

(1) there is *lack of energy* in the cause to produce the effect. Cause must have some energy to produce the effect otherwise everything can be produced from everything or nothing can be produced from anything. This energy can belong neither

[1] Ibid, III, 27-28, 48. Compare Mādhyamika-Kārikā, I, 1; I, 7; Mādhyamika-Vṛtti pp. 13, 36, 38. [2] Ibid, IV, 3-4. [3] Ibid, IV, 10. Compare Mādhyamika-Kārikā, XI, 3-8. [4] khyāpyamānām ajātim tair anumodāmahe vayam, Ibid, IV, 5. [5] Ibid, IV, 11-12. [6] Commentary on IV, 12. [7] Kārikās, IV, 16. [8] Ibid, IV, 15.

to that which is existent nor to that which is non-existent nor to that which is both nor to that which is neither;

(2) there is *absence of knowledge* of the beginning and the end. The effect which is neither in the beginning nor in the end must be non-existent in the middle also; and

(3) there is *incompatibility of the order of succession*. Antecedence and consequence are unproved. We cannot say which of the two is prior and is therefore the cause.

Thus, says Gauḍapāda, have *the Buddhas*, the Enlightened, clarified the doctrine of No-origination. Causality is therefore an impossibility.[1] It cannot be proved that Saṁsāra is without a beginning, but has an end, nor can it be proved that Mokṣa has a beginning, but has no end.[2] In truth, because it is the Unborn which appears as if it is born, therefore No-origination is the very nature of the Unborn. That which exists neither in the beginning nor in the end, cannot exist in the middle also; that which is unreal in the past and in the future must be unreal in the present too.[3] Origination is impossible because neither the existent nor the non-existent can be produced either by the existent or by the non-existent.[4]

III

REALITY AS PURE CONSCIOUSNESS

GAUḌAPĀDA also agrees with the Vijñānavādins in maintaining that the world is ultimately unreal, for it cannot exist independently and outside of Consciousness which is the only Reality. Even Shaṅkara says that Gauḍapāda accepts the arguments of the Vijñānavādins to prove the unreality of the external objects.[5]

Ordinary people, says Gauḍapāda, cling to the view that this world exists, because they say that things are perceived and because there is practical utility. They are always afraid of the doctrine of No-origination. It is for such ordinary people that *the Buddhas*, the Enlightened, from the phenomenal standpoint, have proclaimed origination. But from the ultimate standpoint, perception and practical utility are invalid arguments to prove the reality of the world because even in a magical elephant and dream-objects both perception and practical utility may be found.[6]

[1] ashaktir aparijñānam kramakopo' thavā punaḥ. evam hi sarvathā Buddhair ajātiḥ paridīpitā, Ibid, IV, 19. Compare the arguments of Shūnyavādins. See Supra pp., 77-78. [2] Ibid, IV, 30; Compare Mādhyamika-Kārikā: XI, 1; XVI, 10. [3] ādāvante cha yan nāsti vartamane'pi tat tathā, Ibid, II, 6; IV, 31. Compare Mādhyamika-Kārikā, XI, 2. [4] Ibid, IV, 40. Compare Mādhyamika-Kārikā, 1, 7. [5] Vijñānavādino bauddhasya vachanam bāhyārthavādipakṣapratiṣedhaparam āchāryeṇa anumoditam, Commentary on IV, 27. [6] upalambhāt samāchārād astivastutvavādinām. jātis tu deshitā Buddhair ajātes trasatām sadā, Ibid, IV, 42.

The Sarvāstivādins refute the Vijñānavādins and advocate the existence of external objects. They say that cognition must have its objective cause otherwise the distinction between the subject and the object will be impossible. The external objects must exist because cognition and suffering depend (para-tantra) upon them. This is the view of Sarvāstivāda (para-tantra).[1] The Vijñānavādins reply that the upholders of external objects want to prove that cognition must have a cause. But the objective cause which they adduce is no cause at all. The object exists as an object for the knowing subject; but it does not exist outside of consciousness because the distinction of the subject and the object is within consciousness itself. Consciousness is the only reality and it is never related to any external object, neither in the past nor in the present nor in the future.[2]

Gauḍapāda is in complete agreement with the Vijñānavādins here. The external world is unreal because it does not exist always, as Reality must do. It is also unreal because the relations which constitute it are all unreal; because space, time and causality are impossible. It is also unreal because it consists of objects and whatever can be presented as an object is unreal. Reality is the Pure Self which is Pure Consciousness and which is at the background of everything. The waking state and the dreaming state are on a par. Both are real within their own order. The water in a dream can quench the thirst in a dream as much as real water can quench real thirst. And both are alike, though not equally, unreal from the ultimate standpoint.[3] The self-luminous Self through its own power of illusion imagines itself by itself and it is this Self which cognizes the manifold objects. This is the established conclusion of Vedānta.[4] Just as in darkness, a rope is imagined to be a snake, similarly the Self is imagined to be individual subjects, mental states and external objects. And just as when the rope is known, the imagined snake vanishes, similarly when the non-dual Ātman is realized, the subject-object duality vanishes at once.[5] The luminous Self through its own power of illusion becomes itself infatuated.[6] It is Consciousness itself which throbs as the subject and as the object in dream as well as in waking. This whole universe, this entire duality of the subject and the object, is therefore only the imagination of the Self. Neither the individual soul nor the external object is ultimately real. Those who see the creation of the individual self or of the external object see the foot-prints of birds in the sky.[7] The external objects are not the creation of the individual self for both are only manifestations of Consciousness. That which has empirical existence cannot be called ultimately real. Consciousness which is immanent in the subject and in the object, yet transcends them both. It transcends the trinity of knower, known and knowledge.

[1] Ibid, IV, 24. [2] Ibid, IV, 25-27. [3] Ibid, II, 4-10. [4] Ibid, II, 12. [5] Ibid, II, 17-18.
[6] māyaiṣā tasya Devasya yayā sammohitaḥ svayam, Ibid, II, 19. [7] Ibid, IV, 28.

Consciousness is really Asaṅga; it has no attachment or connection or relation with anything else. It is called 'Unborn' (aja) from an empirical standpoint only. From the ultimate standpoint, it cannot be called even 'Unborn' for it is really indescribable by intellect.[1] Realizing the truth of No-origination, one bids good-bye to all sorrow and desire and reaches the fearless goal.[2]

We have seen that Gauḍapāda agrees with Vijñānavāda in maintaining that Reality is Pure Consciousness which manifests itself as, and ultimately transcends, the subject-object duality. We shall see in the next chapter how Shaṅkara bitterly criticizes Vijñānavāda. Much of the criticism of Shaṅkara loses its force against Vijñānavāda since it does not deny the objectivity of the external world, but only its existence outside of consciousness. Shaṅkara himself in a sense admits this. But his view represents a definite advance on Vijñānavāda and also on Gauḍapāda. He emphasizes that the dream-state and the waking-state are not on a par. He wants to prove the unreality of the external world not by saying that it does not fall outside of consciousness, but by saying that it is essentially indescribable as existent or as non-existent (sadasadanirvachanīya). What we want to stress here is that this view is not an altogether new creation of Shaṅkara. It was developed in Shūnyavāda and accepted by Gauḍapāda. Gauḍapāda also says that the world is unreal because it is essentially indescribable or unthinkable either as existent or as non-existent. He says that just as a moving fire-brand appears as straight or curved, similarly consciousness, when it moves, appears as the subject-object duality. And just as an unmoving fire-brand produces no illusion, similarly unflinching knowledge produces no subject-object illusion. The appearances in a moving fire-brand are not produced by anything else; and when the fire-brand does not move, the appearances also do not rest in anything else; nor do they enter into the fire-brand; nor do they go out of it. Similarly the manifold phenomena are not produced by anything other than Consciousness nor do they rest in anything else; nor do they enter into it; nor do they go out of it. They are mere appearances. And they are so because *they are essentially indescribable or unthinkable*, because they can be called *neither real nor unreal*, neither existent nor non-existent.[3] This fact is strengthened by Gauḍapāda's agreement with Shūnyavāda, by his doctrine of No-origination, by his maintaining that the world is neither existent nor non-existent nor both. This doctrine of Avidyā was further developed by Shaṅkara.

[1] ajaḥ kalpitasamvṛtyā paramārthena nāpyajaḥ, Ibid, IV, 74. Compare with Asaṅga and Vasubandhu; see Supra: pp. 112, 115, 116, 120. [2] Ibid, IV, 78. [3] Ibid, IV, 47-52. Ibid, IV, 52.

IV

ASPARSHAYOGA

NOW we proceed to deal with Gauḍapāda's own contribution. It is his doctrine of Vaishāradya or Asparshayoga or Amanībhāva. Even this doctrine was hinted at by the Buddhists.[1] But it is essentially based on the Upaniṣads and its development is Gauḍapāda's own.

Taking his stand on the Bṛhadāraṇyaka, the Chhāndogya and the Māṇḍūkya, Gauḍapāda identifies the Unborn and Non-dual Absolute with the Ātman or Brahman or Amātra or Turīya or Advaita which can be directly realized by Pure Knowledge or Asparshayoga or Vaishāradya or Amanībhāva. This Absolute manifests itself in three forms, in Jāgrat, Svapna, and Suṣupti, as Vishva, Taijasa and Prājña.[2] In reality it transcends all the three forms. It is the Turīya or the Fourth. It is the Measureless or the Amātra. Praṇava or Auṁkāra is its symbol. In fact there is no distinction between the symbol and the symbolized. Praṇava itself is the Brahman, the Fearless Goal. It is the cause as well as the effect. It is phenomenal as well as noumenal, saguṇa as well as nirguṇa, apara as well as para. It is the shining Self or the self-luminous Consciousness.

It is called Vishva (All) when it has the consciousness of outside; it is called Taijasa (Luminous) when it has the consciousness of inside; and it is called Prājña (Intelligent) when it is concentrated consciousness. These correspond to the waking state, dream state and deep sleep state respectively. Vishva enjoys the gross; Taijasa enjoys the subtle; Prājña enjoys the bliss. Vishva and Taijasa are both causes and effects; Prājña is only the cause. Turīya is neither cause nor effect. It is called Īshāna, Prabhu or Deva. It is all-pervading, capable of removing all sufferings, lord of all, changeless, non-dual, luminous, one without a second. Prājña knows no objects and so it cannot be called even the subject. It is a mere abstraction. It knows nothing, neither itself nor others, neither truth nor falsehood. But Turīya being pure and self-luminons Consciousness is All-seeing. Though duality is absent in Prājña and in Turīya, yet Prājña is connected with deep sleep where the seed of ignorance is present, while Turīya knows no sleep. Vishva and Taijasa are connected with dream or false knowledge (anyathāgrahaṇa or vikṣepa) and with sleep or absence of knowledge (agrahaṇa or āvaraṇa or laya); Prājña is connected with sleep. In Turīya there is neither sleep nor dream. In

[1] For example, Āryadeva says: nahyasparshavato nāma yogaḥ sparshavatā saha, Chatuḥshataka, 333. The Vijñānavādins prescribed various yogic rules for Amanībhāva or for the transformation of relational intellect into Pure Consciousness.

[2] bahiṣprajño vibhur vishvo hyantaḥprajñastu taijasaḥ. ghanaprajñas tathā prājña eka eva tridhā smṛtaḥ, Ibid, 1.

dream we know otherwise; in sleep we do not know the truth. The so-called waking life is also a dream. When the negative absence of knowledge which is sleep, and the positive wrong knowledge which is dream and waking, are transcended, the Fourth, the Goal is reached.[1] The fearless light of the self-luminous Self shines all round. When the individual self (jīva), slumbering in beginningless Ignorance, is awakened, then the Unborn, the Dreamless, the Sleepless, the Non-dual Absolute (ātman) is realized.[2] It moves nowhere; there is no going to or coming from it. It is the Lord immanent in the universe abiding in the hearts of all. He alone is a sage (muni) who has embraced this infinite and measureless Auṁkāra which is the cessation of all duality and which is all bliss.[3] All categories of the intellect are merged in it. All plurality of the phenom ena ceases here. It is realized by the sages who have known the essence of the Vedas and who are free from fear, anger and attachment.[4]

Ātman is like space; the individual souls are like space in jars. When the jars are destroyed, their spaces merge into Space. So do the jīvas merge into the Ātman when Ignorance is destroyed by Right Knowledge. Just as, if a particular space in a particular jar is contaminated with dust, smoke etc., all other spaces in all other jars do not become so contaminated, similarly if a particular jīva is contaminated with happiness or misery etc., all jīvas do not become so contaminated. Spaces in jars differ in forms, functions and names, but there is no difference in space, similarly jīvas differ in forms, functions and names, but there is no difference in the Ātman. Just as the space in a jar is neither a transformation nor a modification nor a part of space, similarly a jīva is neither a transformation nor a modification nor a part of the Ātman. Ultimately there are no grades of reality, no degrees of truth. The same immanent Absolute is reflected in all pairs of objects related by sweet Reciprocity (madhuvidyā), in microcosm as well as in macrocosm, just as the same space is immanent in the outside world as well as inside the stomach.[5]

Just as the Mahāyānists say that Buddha, on account of his excellent skill, preached the truth to suit the different needs of the shrāvakas, the pratyeka-buddhas and the bodhisattvas, similarly Gauḍapāda also says that the Merciful Veda prescribes three different spiritual stages (āshramas) for the three kinds of people, of lower, middle and higher intellect. Karma and upāsanā are taught to the lower and the middle, while jñāna is taught to the higher.[6] It is only the dualists that quarrel with one another in order to strengthen their respective views. The Advaitin quarrels with none.[7] For the dualists, there is duality from the empirical as well as from the absolute standpoint. For us non-duality is the ultimate truth. For us there is non-duality (advaita) even between

[1] Ibid, I, 1-15. [2] anādimāyayā supto yadā jīvaḥ prabudhyate. ajam anidram asvapnam advaitam budhyate tadā, Ibid, I, 16. [3] Ibid, I, 29. [4] Ibid, II, 35. [5] Ibid, III, 3-12. [6] Ibid, III, 16. [7] svasiddhāntavyavasthāsu dvaitino nishchitā dṛḍham parasparam virudhyante tair ayam na virudhyate, Ibid III, 17.

unity (advaita) and diversity (dvaita). The neti neti of the Shruti is not solipcism. By negating all plurality and difference, the Shruti manifests the positive Unborn, the Absolute. The fact is that the Absolute cannot be grasped by the intellect and so the best method of describing the Indescribable is by negative terms. But all these negations point to the same ineffable Reality.[1] Duality is the creation of the intellect. When the intellect is transcended (amanībhāva), duality and plurality disappear.[2] This is pure Consciousness, devoid of all thought-determinations and imagination. It is Unborn and is not different from the Knowable. The Knowable (jñeya) is the Brahman. It is calm and eternal Light. It is the fearless and unshakable Meditation (samādhi). It is Asparshayoga or the Uncontaminated Meditation difficult to be realized even by great yogins. They are afraid of it, imagining fear where there is really no fear at all.[3] Verily, the absence of fear, the end of suffering, the perpetual wakefulness and the eternal peace, all depend upon the control of mind.[4] When both laya and vikṣepa are transcended, when the mind does not fall into sleep nor is it distracted again, when it becomes unshakable and free from illusion, it becomes Brahman.[5] The aspirant should be free from attachment, from misery and happiness alike. When the Brahman is realized there is a unique Bliss which transcends misery and happiness and which is called Nirvāṇa. It is indescribable, highest and unshakable. It is Unborn, non-dual and always the same. It can be realized by the Buddhas only.[6] The ignorant perceive only the four-fold 'covering' (āvaraṇa) 'is', 'is not', 'both is and is not', and 'neither is nor is not'. The Absolute appears to be obscured by these four categories (koṭi) of the intellect. In fact it is never touched by them. He who has transcended these categories and embraced Pure Self, realizes the Absolute and becomes omniscient.[7] Omniscience results when the trinity of knowledge, knower and known is transcended. This is Transcendental Knowledge (lokottaram jñānam).[8] He who has realized this Omniscience, this non-dual Brahman, this Goal which befits a true Brāhmaṇa, what else can he desire?[9] All souls by their very nature are always in the state of enlightenment. They are all unborn. All elements of existence, subjective as well as objective, are by their very nature calm from the beginning, Unborn and merged in the Absolute. They are so because they are nothing else than the Brahman itself which is Unborn, Same and Transparent.[10] Those who move in difference can never acquire transcendental purity (vaishā-

[1] Ibid, III, 26. manaso hyamanībhāve dvaitam naivopalabhyate, Ibid, III, 31. [2] asparshayogo vai nāma durdarshaḥ sarvayogibhiḥ. yogino bibhyati hyasmād abhaye bhayadarshinaḥ, Ibid, III, 39. [4] Ibid, III, 40. [5] Ibid, III, 46. [6] Ibid, III, 47. Ibid, IV, 80. [7] koṭyashchatasra etāstu grahair yāsām sadāvṛtaḥ. Bhagavān ābhir asprṛṣṭo yena dṛṣṭaḥ sa sarvadṛk, Ibid, IV, 84. [8] Ibid, IV, 88, 89. [9] Ibid,IV, 85. [10] Ibid, IV, 91-93. ādishāntā hyanutpannāḥ prakṛtyaiva sunirvṛtāḥ. sarve dharmāḥ samābhinnā ajam sāmyam vishāradam, Ibid, IV, 93. Compare Ratna-Megha-Sūtra as quoted in Mādyamika-Vṛttī, p. 225.

radya). Their case is indeed pitiable.[1] We salute that Highest Reality, says Gauḍapāda, which is Unborn, Same, Pure, and Free from all traces of duality and plurality, according to the best of our ability.[2] He who has become the Buddha, the Enlightened, his knowledge (jñānam) is not related to anything (dharmeṣu na kramate), neither to the subject nor to the object, because it is supra-relational, nor is anything (sarve dharmāḥ), neither the subject nor the object, related to his knowledge, because there is nothing outside his knowledge. He has transcended the duality of the subject and the object and the trinity of knowledge, knower and known. He has become one with Pure Consciousness.[3]

V
CONCLUSION

WE have seen how Gauḍapāda agrees with Shunyavāda and Vijñānavāda. In fact he represents the best in Nāgārjuna and Vasubandhu. He has great respect for Buddha. He says: Him, one of the Greatest of Men, who has known the truth that the individual souls (dharmāḥ) are identical with the pure Self (jñeya), I salute.[4] Shaṅkara explains that this Greatest of Men is Puruṣottama or Nārāyaṇa, the sage of Badarikāshrama, the first teacher of the Advaita School.[5] But this may also refer to Buddha.

Gauḍapāda uses many words which were frequently used in the Mahāyāna works. It may be pointed out that these words were not the monopoly of the Mahāyāna. They were the current philosophical coins of the day and Gauḍapāda had every right to use them. They were the heritage of the language. The impartial spirit of Gauḍapāda is to be much admired. His breadth of vision, his large-heartedness, his broad intellectual outlook and his impartial spirit add to his glory and greatness. He has respect for Buddha. He frankly admits that in certain respects he agrees with Shūnyavādins and Vijñānavādins. But this should never mean that Gauḍapāda is a crypto-Buddhist. He is a thorough-going Vedāntin in and out. His mission is to prove that Mahāyāna Buddhism and Advaita Vedānta are not two opposed systems of thought, but only a continuation of the same fundamental thought of the Upaniṣads. He has based his philosophy on the Upaniṣads. When he says in the end 'this truth was not *uttered* by Buddha',[6] what he means is that his own philosophy as well as the philosophy of Buddha and of the Mahāyāna so far as he agrees with it, both are directly rooted in the Upaniṣads, that Buddha preached this Upaniṣadic Truth not by words but by silence, that his (Gauḍapāda's) preaching is the essence of the Vedānta, that it is not an original contribution of Buddha or of Buddhists.

[1] vaisharadyam tu vai nāsti bhede vicharatām sadā, Ibid, 94. [2] Ibid, IV, 100. [3] Ibid, IV, 99. [4] Ibid, IV, 1. [5] Introduction to the Commentary on Chapter IV and Commentary on IV, 1. [6] naitad Buddhena bhāṣitam, Kārikā, IV, 99.

Chapter Fifteen

SHAṄKARA VEDĀNTA

I

METAPHYSICAL VIEWS

To quote Dr. S. Radhakrishnan: 'It is impossible to read Shaṅkara's writings, packed as they are with serious and subtle thinking, without being conscious that one is in contact with a mind of a very fine penetration and profound spirituality. . . . His philosophy stands forth complete, needing neither a before nor an after . . . whether we agree or differ, the penetrating light of his mind never leaves us where we were'.[1]

Ultimate Reality, according to Shaṅkara, is Ātman or Brahman which is Pure Consciousness (jñāna-svarūpa) or Consciousness of the Pure Self (svarūpa-jñāna) which is devoid of all attributes (nirguṇa) and all categories of the intellect (nirvisheṣa). Brahman associated with its potency (shakti) māyā or mūlāvidyā appears as the qualified Brahman (saguṇa or savisheṣa or apara Brahma) or the Lord (Īshvara) who is the creator, preserver and destroyer of this world which is His appearance.

Jīva or the individual self is a subject-object complex. Its subject-element is Pure Consciousness and is called the Sākṣin. Its object-element is the internal organ called the antaḥkaraṇa which is bhautika as it is composed of all the five elements, with the predominance of tejas which makes it always active except in deep sleep or states like swoon or trance. The source of the internal organ is Avidyā which causes individuality. In perception, the internal organ, when a sense-organ comes into contact with an object, assumes the 'form' of that object. It is the vṛtti or the mode of the internal organ. This vṛtti inspired by the Sākṣin takes the form of empirical knowledge. In waking state, the internal organ is aided by the senses; in dream state, it functions by itself; and in deep sleep it is lost in its cause Avidyā. In this state too individuality persists because the Sākṣin is associated with Avidyā. In liberation, Avidyā is destroyed by Jñāna and the Sākṣin is realized as the Brahman which it always is.

Māyā or Avidyā is not pure illusion. It is not only absence of knowledge. It is also positive wrong knowledge. It is a cross of the real and

[1] Indian Philosophy: Dr. S. Radhakrishan, Vol. II, pp. 446-447.

the unreal (satyānṛte mithunī kṛtya). In fact it is indescribable. It is neither existent nor non-existent nor both. It is not existent for the existent is only the Brahman. It is not non-existent for it is responsible for the appearance of the Brahman as the world. It cannot be both existent and non-existent for this conception is self-contradictory. It is called neither real nor unreal (sadasadvilakṣana). It is false or mithyā. But it is not a non-entity like a hare's horn (tuchchha). It is positive (bhāvarūpa). It is potency (shakti). It is also called superimposition (adhyāsa). A shell is mistaken as silver. The shell is the ground on which the silver is superimposed. When right knowledge (pramā) arises, this error (bhrānti or bhrama) vanishes. The relation between the shell and the silver is neither that of identity nor of difference nor of both. It is unique and is known as non-difference (tādātmya). Similarly, Brahman is the ground on which the world appears through Māyā. When right knowledge dawns and the essential unity of the jīva with the Paramātman is realized, Māyā or Avidyā vanishes.

Shaṅkara emphasizes that from the phenomenal point of view the world is quite real. It is not an illusion. It is a practical reality. He distinguishes the dream state from the waking state. Things seen in a dream are quite true as long as the dream lasts; they are sublated only when we are awake. Similarly, the world is quite real so long as true knowledge does not dawn. But dreams are private. They are creations of the jīva (jīvasṛṣṭā). The world is public. It is the creation of Īshvara (Īshvara-sṛṣṭa). Jīva is ignorant of the essential unity and takes only diversity as true and wrongly regards himself as agent and enjoyer. Avidyā conceals the unity (āvaraṇa) and projects names and forms (vikṣepa). Īshvara never misses the unity. Māyā has only its vikṣepa aspect over him. The Highest Brahman (Para-Brahma) is both the locus (āshraya) and the object (viṣaya) of Māyā. When the jīva realizes through knowledge and knowledge alone, karma being subsidiary, this essential unity, liberation is attained here and now (jīvan-mukti) and final release (videha-mukti) is obtained after the death of the body.

This is a short summary of Shaṅkarāchārya's philosophy. He too is considerably influenced by Buddhism. He preserves the best that was in Mahāyāna in his own philosophy. He uses many words, especially in his Upaniṣad-Bhāṣyas, which were commonly used in Mahāyāna literature. But outwardly he is an enemy of Buddhism. Gauḍapāda had love and respect for Mahāyāna. Shaṅkara has nothing but strong and even bitter words for it. It is very important and interesting too to note that Shaṅkara does not at all criticize the two most important schools of Mahāyāna, the Shūnyavāda and the Vijñānavāda. What he criticizes under the name of Vijñānavāda is in fact Svatantra-Vijñānavāda; and he summarily dismisses Shūnyavāda as a self-condemned nihilism which is below criticism. Shaṅkara observes that there are three important schools of Buddhism—the Sarvāstivāda, the Vijñānavāda and the Shūnyavāda. The Sarvāstivāda school of Hīnayāna, which, according to Shaṅkara, includes both the Vaibhāṣika and the Sautrāntika schools, was bitterly criticized by the Mahāyānists themselves. Shaṅkara's criticism against it is not new. It must be admitted that Shaṅkara's exposition of Buddhism is correct and faithful and his criticism of it is perfectly justified. He avoided Shūnyavāda by taking the word Shūnya in its popular sense and easily dismissing Shūnyavāda as nihilism. And he did not at all touch real Vijñānavāda. By Vijñānavadins he means Svatantra-Vijñānavādins who were his immediate predecessors. It was easy for him to criticize their momentary consciousness. No reference do we find to Asaṅga or Vasubandhu or to their doctrines with the solitary exception, however, of the Ālaya-Vijñāna. On the other hand, we find verses quoted from Diṅnāga and Dharmakīrti and their views correctly exposed and criticized. And we also find references to and criticisms of the views of Shāntarakṣita as well as replies to the objections raised by Shāntarakṣita. In regard to those points, however, which Svatantra-Vijñānavāda shares in common with Vijñānavāda, Shaṅkara's criticism applies indirectly to Vijñānavāda also. But here it loses much of its force because Vijñānavāda regards Consciousness as absolute and permanent. Shaṅkara, however, represents a definite advance on Vasubandhu as well as on Gauḍapāda who agrees with Vasubandhu.

II

CRITICISM OF THE PRAKṚTI-PARIṆĀMA-VĀDA OF SĀṄKHYA

WE have given the arguments advanced by Sāṅkhya in favour of its Prakṛti.[1] Shaṅkara agrees with Sāṅkhya in maintaining that the design, harmony or order in the universe must presuppose a single cause which is eternal and unlimited. But he criticizes Sāṅkhya when it says that such a cause is the unintelligent Prakṛti. According to Shaṅkara the Intelligent Brahman only can be such a cause. How can immanent teleology in nature be explained by unintelligent Prakṛti? We do proceed from the finite to the infinite, from the limited to the unlimited, from the *peros* to the *aperos*, from the effect to the cause, from plurality to unity. But only the Conscious Brahman associated with its Māyā Shakti can be the creator, preserver and destroyer of this world. Unintelligent Prakṛti is too poor and too powerless to be its cause.[2] We see that stones, bricks and mortar cannot fashion themselves into a well-designed building without the help of intelligent workmen. How can, then, the unintelligent

[1] See Supra, p. 141. [2] Shārīraka-Bhāṣya, II, 2, 1: Also Chhāndogya-Bhāṣya, VI 2, 3-4.

Pradhāna account for the beauty, symmetry, order and harmony of this great universe—internal and external? Again, how can Pradhāna explain the original impetus, the first push, the *élan* which is supposed to disturb the equilibrium of the three guṇas? Mere clay, without a potter, cannot fashion itself into a pot. Chariots cannot move without horses etc. Why should Sāṅkhya hesitatingly admit that the initial activity comes from the mere presence of the Puruṣa (puruṣa-sannidhimātra)? Why should it not frankly admit that it comes from the Conscious Brahman?[1] Again, the argument of Sāṅkhya that just as unintelligent milk flows for the nourishment of the calf, similarly unintelligent Prakṛti works for the emancipation of the Puruṣa is untenable because milk flows as there is a living cow and a living calf and there is also the motherly love in the cow for the calf. Again, because Prakṛti is regarded as an absolutely independent entity in itself it cannot be related in any way to the indifferent Puruṣa who can neither energize nor restrain it. Then, Prakṛti should sometimes evolve and sometimes should not evolve. Nor can the modification of Prakṛti be compared to that of grass which turns into milk. Grass becomes milk only when it is eaten by a milch cow, not when it lies uneaten or is eaten by a bull.

Again, even if we grant activity to Pradhāna, it cannot explain the teleology which Sāṅkhya takes to be immanent in nature. Unconscious Pradhāna can have no purpose; indifferent neutral Puruṣa too can have no purpose. If Sāṅkhya tries to solve the difficulty by pointing out that Prakṛti and Puruṣa combine like the blind and the lame and then Puruṣa, like the magnet moving the iron, may move Prakṛti to accomplish his goal, it is mistaken, for the blind and the lame persons are both intelligent and active beings, while Prakṛti is unconscious and Puruṣa is indifferent. The simile of the magnet and the iron is also wrong. If the mere presence of the Puruṣa is sufficient to move the Pradhāna, then Puruṣa being always co-present, there should be perpetual movement. Thus creation should have no beginning and no end. The liberation of Puruṣa will also become impossible. Again, Prakṛti and Puruṣa can never be related. Prakṛti is unconscious; Puruṣa is indifferent; and there is no third principle, no *tertium quid*, to relate them. The chasm which Sāṅkhya has created by postulating two independent and eternal entities, one the subject and other the object, can never be bridged by it. It must therefore recognize a higher conscious principle which transcends and yet gives meaning to and preserves at a lower level, the subject-object duality.

Moreover, by regarding Pradhāna as a mere agent and Puruṣa as a mere enjoyer, Sāṅkhya opens itself to the charge of vicarious suffering which throws all moral responsibility overboard. Why should the

[1] Shārīraka-Bhāsya, II, 2, 2.

Puruṣa suffer for the actions of Pradhāna? And how can it be possible that Prakṛti knows only to do and not to enjoy?[1]

Brahman alone, therefore, is the cause and it is universally declared to be so by all the Vedānta texts. The words like mahat, avyakta etc. used in certain Upaniṣads, e.g. in the Kaṭha, do not denote the mahat and avyakta of Sāṅkhya. They simply mean the potentiality of names and forms in their cause Brahman. They are not independent of it.[2] Sāṅkhya and Yoga are generally accepted by the wise as conducive to the highest good. But these systems advocate dualism and cannot be supported by the Shruti. The Shruti uses these words only in the sense of knowledge and meditation respectively. Those doctrines of these systems which do not clash with Advaita are accepted by us also.[3] Shaṅkara calls Sāṅkhya as the 'principal opponent' (pradhāna-malla) of the Vedānta and says that its refutation implies the refutation of paramāṇukāraṇa-vāda etc.[4]

Sāṅkhya, therefore, should let its Prakṛti glide into Māyā, its Prakṛti-pariṇāmavāda into Brahma-vivarta-vāda, its satkāryavāda into sat-kāraṇa-vāda, its Puruṣa into jīva, its negative kaivalya into positively blissful mokṣa, and should, instead of maintaining the plurality of Puruṣas representing 'a vast array of sad personalities' and creating an unbridgable chasm between the subject and the object, recognize the non-dual Puruṣa, the Brahman transcending the subject-objcet duality.

III

CRITICISM OF ASAT-KĀRYAVĀDA

SHAṄKARA believes in sat-kāryavāda but his interpretation of it is different from that of Sāṅkhya. By it he really means satkāraṇavāda. His view is known as vivartavāda. The effect, no doubt, must pre-exist in the cause. But ultimately the effect is not something different from the cause. The cause alone is real; the effect is only its appearance.

Shaṅkara agrees with the Shūnyavādins and the Svatantra-Vijñāna-vādins in maintaining, against Sāṅkhya, that if the effect were real and if it really pre-existed in the cause, then it is already an accomplished fact and its production will be a vain repetition. He also agrees with them, against Nyāya-Vaisheṣika, that if the effect were a non-entity, it would be like a hare's horn and its production would be impossible. We have seen that for the Svatantra-Vijñānavādin asatkāryavāda is a misnomer for he does not advocate the production of a non-entity. Reality itself, to him, is efficient causation.[5] Shaṅkara, however, agrees with the Shūnyavādin, against Svatantra-Vijñānavādin, in maintaining

[1] Ibid, II, 2, 3-7: Also Prashna-Bhāṣya, VI, 3. [2] Shārīraka-Bhāṣya, I, 1, 5-10; I, 4, 1-3. [3] Ibid, II, 1, 3. [4] Ibid, I, 4, 28. [5] See Supra, p. 126.

that causation in a real sense is an impossibility. Production cannot be called 'the own essence' of a thing for ultimately there can be neither production nor destruction nor any momentary entity.

The effect, says Shaṅkara, can never exist independently and outside of the cause either before or after its manifestation. Therefore it cannot be said that the effect does not pre-exist in the cause. The effect is only an appearance of the cause. Though the effect and the cause are non-different, yet it is the effect which exists in and depends on the cause and not *vice versa.*

We see that milk produces curd, clay produces pots and gold produces ornaments. Curd cannot be produced from clay nor can pots be produced from milk. But according to asatkaryavāda this should be possible If it is rejoined that the cause has a certain peculiarity (atishaya) according to which only certain effects can be produced from certain causes, we reply that if this peculiarity means 'the antecedent condition of the effect', asatkāryavāda is abandoned; and if it means 'the power of the cause to produce a particular determined effect', then it must be admitted that this power is neither different from the cause nor non-existent because if it were either, production would be impossible.

Again, the relation between the cause and the effect, like that between substance and qualities, must be that of identity (tādātmya). It cannot be of the nature of inherence (samavāya) because inherence will require another relation to relate it to cause and effect and this relation another relation and so on *ad infinitum*; or inherence itself will be impossible for without being related to the two terms it cannot hang in the air.

Again, according to asatkāryavāda, the effect and the cause can have no connexion because connexion is possible only between two existent entities and not between an existent and a non-existent entity or between two non-existent entities. Nobody says that the son of a barren woman was a king. He is a non-entity and never was or is or will be a king.

Again, the theory that when the effect is produced the cause is destroyed is absolutely wrong. The cause can never be destroyed. When milk changes into curd, it is not destroyed. Nor is the seed destroyed when it becomes the sprout. If the cause in the process of change is destroyed, recognition will become impossible.

Hence it is impossible to produce an effect which is different from its cause and which does not pre-exist in it even within a hundred years.[1]

[1] Shārīraka-Bhāṣya, II, 1, 7, 9, 18; Gītā-Bhāṣya, XVIII, 48; Chhāndogya-Bhāṣya, VI, 2, 1-2; Brhadāraṇyaka-Bhāṣya, I, 2, 1.

IV

CRITICISM OF THE PARAMĀṆU-KĀRAṆA-VĀDA OF NYĀYA-VAISHEṢIKA

THIS school maintains that the four substances (earth, water, fire and air) in their subtle (amūrta) form as causes are eternal and atomic. Ākāsha, though itself not atomic, binds the atoms together. The atoms of Democritus are only quantitatively different, are in motion and make up souls also. But the Vaisheṣika atoms are both quantitatively and qualitatively different, are by nature at rest and are distinct from souls. God assisted by the Unseen Power (adṛṣṭa) of the jīvas generates motion in the atoms. This motion (parispanda) joins two atoms together which make a dyad (dvyaṇuka). Three such dyads make a triad (tryaṇuka). Four dyads form a quartrad (chaturaṇuka) and so on till the gross objects of the world are produced. An atom is infinitesimal and spherical (parimaṇḍala); a dyad is minute (aṇu) and short (hrasva); and a triad and others are great (mahat) and long (dīrgha). The things produced are not mere aggregates, but wholes composed of parts, the parts and the whole being related by inherence (samāvāya). The Vaisheṣika says that the cause must transmit its qualities to the effect, e.g., white threads make white cloth, and black threads make black cloth. Therefore conscious Brahman cannot be the cause of the unconscious world. Atoms are its cause.

Shaṅkara in refuting this theory points out that it is not necessary for the cause to transmit all its qualities to the effect. Even on the Vaisheṣika hypothesis an atom which is spherical produces a dyad which is not spherical, but minute and short; and a dyad produces a triad which is neither minute nor short, but great and long. If this is so, why should not the conscious Brahman produce an unconscious world?

Are the atoms essentially active or inactive or both or neither? If active, then creation would become permanent; if inactive, then there would be no creation; if both, the conception would be self-contradictory; and if neither, then their activity must come from outside and this outside agency must be either seen or unseen; if seen, then it should not exist before creation; and if unseen, then it being always present near the atoms, creation would become permanent and if the proximity of the unseen to the atoms is denied, then creation would be impossible. In all cases therefore there can be no creation from atoms.[1]

[1] Shārīraka-Bhāṣya, II, 2, 11-14.

V

CRITICISM OF THE CATEGORIES OF NYĀYA-VAISHEṢIKA

THIS school assumes six categories (padārtha) which, unlike the Aristotelian categories which are mere logical predicates, are metaphysical objects. These categories, says Shaṅkara, are regarded as absolutely different from one another, and still it is maintained that qualities, actions etc. depend upon the substance. If so, then substance alone should exist. If in order to avoid this difficulty it is maintained that substance and qualities are inseparably connected (ayutasiddha), then this inseparable connection must be either in space or in time or in itself, and none of these alternatives can support the Vaisheṣika theory. If it is inseparable in space, then the Vaisheṣika doctrine that 'substances produce other substances and qualities other qualities' will be upset. If it is inseparable in time, then the two horns of a cow would be inseparably connected. If it is inseparable in itself, then no distinction could be made between substance and qualities.[1]

Shaṅkara, like Nāgārjuna, Dharmakīrti and Shāntarakṣita challenges the distinction of parts and whole. The whole can be neither a mere aggregate of parts nor can it be something apart from parts. The whole cannot abide in all the parts taken together, for then it would not be perceived as it is impossible to perceive all the parts. If it is said that the whole abides in all the parts taken together through the help of other parts, then it would lead to infinite regress as we would always be forced to assume further parts. Again, the whole cannot abide in each separate part because if it abides in one part, it cannot abide in another part, just as Devadatta cannot be present at the same time in two different places. Moreover, if the whole were present in separate parts, then they would become so many 'wholes'. But whereas for Dharmakīrti and Shāntarakṣita, the whole is unreal and the parts alone are real, for Nāgārjuna and Shaṅkara, both the whole and the parts are relative and therefore ultimately unreal.[2]

The Vaisheṣika maintains that Ātman is a substance which is unintelligent in itself and becomes intelligent on account of its contact with mind (manas). This, says Shaṅkara, is highly absurd. To say that the unqualified and indeterminate Ātman really comes into contact with something different from itself is to violate the established canon of logic. Again, either the qualities of pleasure, pain etc. will be reduced to the Ātman and then they too will become permanent, or the Ātman will be reduced to the qualities and will become impermanent. By no

[1] Ibid, II, 2, 17. [2] Ibid, II, 1, 18.

stretch of reasoning can it be proved that the Ātman can feel pleasure or pain or that it is made up of parts or that it is changing.[1]

Action or motion (karma) is impossible and with it creation too is impossible because the adṛṣṭa can produce no motion in the atoms. It can inhere neither in the souls nor in the atoms. Hence there can be neither creation nor dissolution.[2]

The universal is also ultimately unreal. We perceive no 'universal cow' in the individual cows. It is only the generic qualities that are present in individual cows. If the 'universal cow', as a 'whole', is present in each cow, then even the horns or the tail of a cow should yield milk.[3]

Inherence too is impossible. Inherence (samavāya) is a category while samyoga or conjunction is a quality, according to Nyāya-Vaisheṣika. Inherence is regarded as an eternal, imperceptible, inseparable and real relation subsisting between parts and whole, qualities and substance, action and agent, universal and particular etc. A dyad is supposed to be related to its two constituent atoms by this samavāya. Shaṅkara, like Chandrakīrti, Dharmakīrti and Shāntarakṣita and like Zeno and Bradley, points out that inherence must lead to infinite regress. Inherence, being different from the two things which it relates, stands in need of another inherence to relate it with them. This second inherence again requires another inherence and so on *ad infinitum*. If it is maintained that samavāya does not inhere in the samavāyin by another samavāya, but is identical with it, then even samyoga should be regarded as identical with the things it conjoins; and as both equally require another relation to relate them to the two terms, no talk of calling samavāya a category and samyoga a quality can remove the difficulty. Shaṅkara's point is that a relation, whatever may be its nature and howsoever intimate it may be regarded, can never be identical with the terms which it relates. If t_1 and t_2 are two terms which are to be related by r, the relation, then the following difficulties are bound to occur:

(1) If r inheres in t_1, it cannot relate it with t_2;
(2) If r inheres in t_2, it cannot relate it with t_1;
(3) The same r cannot inhere in both t_1 and t_2;
(4) If r is absolutely different from t_1 and t_2 and falls outside both, then r itself becomes another term and requires a further relation which can relate it with t_1 and t_2. Thus infinite regress is sure to creep in.[4]

Thus we see that the distinction between samyoga and samavāya is untenable. One and the same thing may be called by different names

[1] Kena-Pada-Bhāṣya, II, 4; Māṇḍūkya-Kārikā-Bhāṣya, III, 5; Bṛhadāraṇyaka Bhāṣya, I. 4, 7. [2] Shārīraka-Bhāṣya, II, 2, 12. [3] Ibid, II, 1, 18. [4] Ibid, II, 2, 13.

according to different considerations. The same Devadatta may be called a Brāhmaṇa, a learned man, a gentleman, a boy, a youth, an old man, a father, a son, a grandson, a brother, a son-in-law etc. etc.

The six categories of the Vaisheṣika, therefore, are nothing but mere assumption and if we proceed with mere assumptions there is nothing to check us if we assume hundreds and thousands of categories instead of six.[1]

VI

CRITICISM OF THE DOCTRINE THAT GOD IS THE EFFICIENT CAUSE ONLY

SOME Yogins and some Vaisheṣikas and others hold that God is the efficient cause only for He is the ruler of Primordial Matter and Souls. This position, say Shaṅkara, is untenable. If God is merely a ruler and makes, according to His sweet will, some persons great, some ordinary and others low, then He will be rightly charged of being actuated by partiality, attachment and hatred and hence He will be one like us and no real God.[2] Nor can the difficulty be removed by supposing that the actions of persons and results given by God form a beginningless series for then that series will be like a line of the blind led by the blind.

Moreover, God cannot be the ruler of Matter and Souls without being connected with them and there can be no such connection. It cannot be conjunction because God, Souls and Matter are regarded as infinite and without parts. It cannot be inherence because it is impossible to decide as to which is the abode and which the abiding thing. For us the difficulty does not arise at all because we maintain the identity (tādātmya) of the cause and the effect. Again, if Prakṛti ceases for the liberated soul, it must be finite and there would be nothing for God to rule. Moreover, these three infinite principles will limit one another and will collapse into a void. The infinite can be only one. Further, if Matter and Souls are infinite, God cannot rule over them and then He will be neither omniscient nor omnipotent.[3]

VII

CRITICISM OF BRAHMA-PARIṆĀMA-VĀDA

SHAṄKARA maintains Brahma-kārana-vāda as he recognizes that Brahman is the cause of the world. But his theory is called Brahma-vivarta-vāda because it takes the world to be only a phenomenal appearance of Brahman. Shaṅkara is opposed to Brahma-pariṇāma-vāda. For him, the world is neither a real creation by Brahman nor

[1] Ibid, II, 2, 17. [2] These objections are urged by Shāntarakṣita also. See Supra, pp. 127-128. [3] Shārīraka-Bhāṣya, II, ii, 37, 38, 41.

a real modification of Brahman. Brahman associated with its power Māyā is the ground on which the phenomenal world is super-imposed. When true knowledge dawns and the essential unity of the jīvātman with the Paramātman is realized, the world is sublated. Modification or change in a realistic manner (satattvato'nyathā prathā), like the change of gold into ornaments or of clay into pots or of milk into curd, is called pariṇāma or vikāra. Unreal change or seeming modification (atattvato'nyathā prathā), like the appearance of water into waves, bubbles, foam etc., is called vivarta. They are not, as Sarvajñātma Muni rightly points out, absolutely opposed; pariṇāmavāda logically leads to vivartavāda which is only a step ahead of it.[1] The world which cannot be called real either in the beginning or in the end, must be unreal in the middle also.

This entire diverse universe of names and forms, of agents and enjoyers, of space, time and causality, says Shaṅkara, proceeds from that omniscient, omnipotent and omnipresent cause, the Brahman which alone is the creator, preserver and destroyer of it.[2] Brahman is the material cause as well as the efficient cause. All the sacred texts which declare Brahman as undergoing modification or change (pariṇāma) do not at all mean a real modification or change as it is illogical. Their real aim is to teach that the world is only a phenomenal appearence of Brahman which is in fact beyond all plurality and phenomena and which is the same as the Real Self. Thus Īshvara or Saguṇa Brahman associated with Māyā is the cause of this world.[3]

Shaṅkara gives some of the objections raised by Shāntarakṣita and others and refutes them. He says that some people object to the simile given in some Upaniṣads that just as a spider produces, maintains and devours a cob-web, similarly Brahman creates, maintains and destroys this world. They say that a spider, on account of its desire to eat small insects, emits saliva which produces the web. What such desire and what external means can Brahman have?[4] To this we reply that creation is not something ultimately real. It is only an appearance, Moreover, Brahman being Consciousness can need no other external means except its own potency, Māyā. Again, it is objected that Īshvara cannot be the creator of this world for then the charges of inequality and cruelty will be levelled against Him. Why should He make some people happy and others miserable? Is He not partial to some and prejudiced against others?[5] We reply that He cannot be so charged. The Shruti and the Smṛti declare that the inequality in the creation is due to the merits and demerits of the creatures. Just as a cloud rains the same water, though different seeds fructify according to their different potentialities,

[1] vivartavādasya hi pūrvabhūmir vedāntavāde pariṇāmavādaḥ. [2] Shārīraka-Bhāṣya I, 1, 2. [3] Ibid, II, 1, 27. [4] Ibid, II, 1, 25; Compare Shāntarakṣita's objections, Supra, pp. 127-128. [5] Ibid, II, 1, 34-35; Compare Shāntarakṣita's objections.

similarly Īshvara is the common cause of creation, though different creatures reap different fruits on account of the difference in their actions. The objection that before creation merits and demerits do not exist is invalid, for creation has no beginning. Actions and inequality, therefore, like seeds and sprouts, are both cause and effect.[1] But it should be remembered that ultimately creation is an impossibility. Shaṅkara agrees with the Shūnyavādins and with Gauḍapāda here. Brahman is the only Reality. It cannot be produced from itself because there can be neither any peculiarity (atishaya) nor any change (vikāra) in the eternal. It cannot be produced from anything other than itself for every other thing except Brahman is non-existent and unreal.[2] Again, why should Brahman really create? It has no desire or ambition to fulfil. If it has, it is not perfect. No desire or ambition of Brahman can be proved either by independent reasoning or by Shruti. (Āptakāmasya kā spṛhā?). Therefore it must be remembered, says Shankara, that whenever we talk of creation, we do not mean real creation; we mean only a phenomenal appearance of Brahman due to Avidyā and this creation-appearance is real only as long as Avidyā lasts.[3] When Avidyā is removed by right knowledge, God, the Ruler, Soul, the Enjoyer, and World, the Enjoyed —all are merged in the Highest Brahman.[4]

VIII

CRITICISM OF JAINISM

THE Jainas believe in the theory of Relativity called the Sapta-bhaṅgī-naya or the Syādvāda: (1) Relatively, it is; (2) Relatively, it is not; (3) Relatively, it both is and is not; (4) Relatively, it is indescribable; (5) Relatively, it is and is indescribable; (6) Relatively, it is not and is indescribable; (7) Relatively, it both is and is not and is also indescribable. They also say that a thing may be one as well as many, eternal as well as momentary.

Shaṅkara, like Dharmakīrti and Shāntarakṣita, bitterly criticizes this theory. He points out that contradictory attributes like existence and non-existence, unity and plurality, eternity and momentariness etc. cannot belong to the same thing, just as light and darkness cannot remain at the same place or just as the same thing cannot be hot and cold at the same time. According to this view, the theory of Syādvāda itself may not be correct. Relativity cannot be sustained without the Absolute which is rejected by the Jainas. The theory looks like the words of a lunatic. Again, the judgments cannot be indescribable, for they are clearly set forth. To describe them and to say that they are indescribable is a contradiction in terms.[5]

[1] Ibid. [2] Ibid, II, 3, 9. [3] Ibid, II, 1, 33. [4] Ibid, III, 2, 13. [5] Ibid, II, 2, 33; Compare with the arguments of Dharmakīrti and Shāntarakṣita, Supra, p. 131.

IX

CRITICISM OF BUDDHISM

(*a*) *Criticism of the Sarvāstivāda School:*—This is the most important School of Hīnayāna. It is divided, according to Shaṅkara, into two major schools—the Vaibhāṣika and the Sautrāntika. The former attaches itself to Vibhāṣa, a Commentary on an Abhidharma work and may be called presentationism or naïve realism as it maintains the independent existence of mind and matter. The latter attaches itself to the Sūtra and may be called representationism or critical realism as it maintains that the existence of external objects is inferred through mental presentations, even as eating of good food is inferred through corpulence or a country is inferred through language. But both these schools are equally realistic and reduce mind to fleeting ideas and matter to fleeting sensations.

Shaṅkara takes both these schools under the name of 'Sarvāstivāda' and says that its followers hold that external reality is either element (bhūta) or elemental (bhautika) and that internal reality is either mind (chitta) or mental (chaitta). Earth, water, fire and air are elements. Colour etc. and the sense-organs like eye etc. are elemental. The internal world consists of the five skandhas—of sensation, idea, feeling, conception and forces.

Shaṅkara objects that these two types of aggregates—external as well as internal—can never be formed at all The unintelligent momentary atoms and the momentary skandhas cannot form any systematic whole. No intelligent principle—enjoyer or ruler—which may unite these aggregates is admitted by the opponents. If it is urged that the momentary vijñāna unites the aggregates, it is untenable, for the vijñāna must come into existence in the first moment and must unite the aggregates in the second moment which would mean that the vijñāna exists at least for two moments and is therefore not momentary. Nor can the aggregates be formed on account of Dependent Causation, for in the Wheel of Causation each preceding link is the immediate efficient cause of the succeeding link only, not of the whole series. The momentary atoms too cannot combine by themselves. When it is impossible even for the permanent atoms of the Vaisheṣika to combine, it is more so with the atoms in Buddhism which are momentary.[1]

Again, the Buddhists maintain that existence arises from non-existence, that a seed must be destroyed before a sprout can spring up or milk must be destroyed before curd can come into being. Shaṅkara replies that an entity can never arise from a nonentity. Had it been so

[1] Ibid, II, 2, 26.

anything would arise from anything. Nothing can originate from the horns of a hare. And even when Buddhists themselves admit that aggregates arise from atoms and mental states from the skandhas, why should they confuse the world with worse than useless contradictions?[1]

(*b*) *Criticism of the Theory of Momentariness* (*kṣaṇabhaṅga-vāda*):— The antecedent link in the causal series, says Shaṅkara, cannot even be regarded as the efficient cause of the subsequent link because, according to the theory of momentariness, the preceding link ceases to exist when the subsequent link arises. If it is urged that the antecedent moment when fully developed (pariniṣpannāvasthaḥ) becomes the cause of the subsequent moment, it is untenable, because the assertion that a fully developed moment has a causal efficiency necessarily presupposes its connection with the second moment and this repudiates the theory of universal momentariness. Again, if it is urged (as is done by the Svatantra-Vijñānavādins) that the mere existence of the preceding moment means its causal efficiency (bhāva evāsya vyāpāraḥ), this too is impossible, because no effect can arise without imbibing the nature of the cause and to admit this is to admit that the cause is permanent as it continues to exist in the effect and thus to throw overboard the doctrine of momentariness.

Again, are production and destruction the nature of a thing (vastunaḥ svarūpameva) or another state of it (avasthāntaram vā) or a different thing (vastvantarameva vā)? All these alternatives are impossible. In the first case, production and destruction would become synonymous with the thing itself. Again, if it is said that production is the beginning, thing is the middle, and destruction is the end, then a thing, being connected with three moments, would not be momentary. And if it be maintained that production and destruction are two absolutely different things like a horse and a buffalo, then the thing, being different from production and destruction would become permanent. Again, if production and destruction are regarded as perception and non-perception, then too, perception and non-perception, being the attributes of the perceiving mind and not of the thing, the thing would become permanent. In all cases therefore the theory of momentariness is entirely untenable.

Again, if the opponent says that things arise without a cause, he violates his own statement that things arise depending on causes and conditions. Then anything may arise out of anything. And if the opponent says that the preceding cause lasts only up to the arising of the succeeding effect, this would imply that the cause and the effect are simultaneous.

Again, there can be neither conscious destruction (pratisaṅkhyānirodha, e.g., of a jar by a stick), nor unconscious destruction (apratisaṅkhyānirodha, e.g., the decay of things), because these can relate themselves neither to the series (santāna-gochara) as in all the series the

[1] Ibid.

members are causally related in an uninterrupted manner, nor to the members of the series (bhāva-gochara) as a momentary thing cannot be completely annihilated because it is recognized in different states as having a connected existence.

Again, if Ignorance is destroyed by Right Knowledge, then the Buddhistic doctrine that universal destruction is going on without any cause is given up; and if it is destroyed by itself, then the Buddhistic teaching pertaining to the 'Path' to help the destruction of Ignorance becomes futile. Moreover, bondage and liberation are also impossible. If the soul is momentary, whose is the bondage and whose is the liberation? Again, there will be vicarious liability in moral life. He who performs an act will lose its fruit and another will have to reap it.

The fact of memory and recognition gives a death-blow to the theory of momentariness. The past is recognized and remembered in the present and this implies the existence of a permanent synthesizing subject without whom knowledge shall always remain an impossibility. Identity cannot mean similarity. Even similarity requires a permanent subject who knows two things to be similar. When the Buddhist himself recognizes all his successive cognitions, till he breathes his last, as belonging to the same Self, should he not tremble in maintaining shamelessly the doctrine of momentariness?[1] Everything may be doubted but the self can never be doubted for the very idea of doubt presupposes the self. Indeed, when philosophers fail to admit a self-evident fact, they may try to uphold their view and refute the view of their opponents, but in doing this, they entangle themselves in mere words and, honestly speaking, they convince neither their opponents nor even themselves.[2]

(*c*) *Criticism of 'Vijñānavāda'* (really of Svatantra-Vijñānavāda):—By the term 'Vijñānavāda', Shaṅkara really means 'Svatantra-Vijñānavāda'. These Buddhists, says Shaṅkara, maintain the existence of momentary ideas only. They say that Buddha taught the reality of the external world to his inferior disciples who cling to this world, while to his superior disciples he gave his real teaching that ultimate reality is the momentary vijñāna only. Shaṅkara, taking his stand mainly on the Ālambanaparīkṣā of Diṅnāga, exposes the Buddhist view as follows:

If external things exist they should be either atoms or aggregates of atoms like posts etc. And both are impossible. Atoms cannot be perceived and their aggregates can be regarded neither as identical with nor as different from the atoms. It is the ideas themselves which appear as different external objects, as a post, a wall, a pot, a cloth etc. The fact that the idea is identical with the external object is proved also by the rule that the internal idea and the external object are always experienced simultaneously—*esse est prescipi* (sahopalambhaniyama). There is also

[1] Ibid, II, 2, 20-25. [2] Ibid, II, 2, 25.

no difference between waking and dreaming states. Just as in states like dreams, magical illusions, mirage, sky-castles, etc. etc., it is the ideas themselves which appear as objects though there are no external objects, similarly in waking state too the ideas themselves appear as external objects. The plurality of the ideas is due the beginningless impressions (anādi vāsanā), and not due to the plurality of the so-called external objects. In the beginningless saṁsāra ideas and impressions succeed each other, like seeds and sprouts, as causes and effects.

Shaṅkara vehemently criticizes this view. According to him it is subjective idealism. And the tragedy is heightened by the fact that ideas are regarded as momentary. Shaṅkara's standpoint here is that of *psychological realism* which is compatible with Absolute Idealism. The external world must exist because we perceive it. If things and ideas are presented together it does not mean they are identical. If objects depend on the mind it does not mean that they are a part of the mind. To be perceived by the mind is not to be a portion of the mind. The arguments of the Buddhist in denying the external world though he is himself experiencing it, are like the words of a person who while he is eating and feeling satisfied, says he is not eating or feeling satisfied. We perceive a black cow and a white cow. Now, the attributes of blackness and whiteness may differ but cowness remains the same. Similarly in 'cognition of a jar' and 'cognition of a cloth', jar and cloth being objects differ while consciousness remains the same. This proves that ideas and objects are distinct.[1]

If the Buddhist replies that he is not denying the *consciousness* of objects but he is only asserting that he perceives no object apart from consciousness, he is only making a purely arbitrary statement which he cannot prove by any sound argument. Nobody is conscious of his perception only, but everybody perceives external objects like post, wall etc. Even the Buddhist while explicitly denying the external object implicitly accepts it. Diṅnāga says that 'internal consciousness itself appears *as if* it is something external'.[2] Now, if there is no external world, how can he say that consciousness appears *as if* it is something external? Indeed, no sane person says that Viṣṇumitra appears like the son of a barren woman. There can be no hypothetical without a categorical basis. Possibility always involves actuality.[3] The possibility or impossibility of things can be determined only through means of right knowledge. Means of right knowledge themselves do not depend on pre-conceived possibility or impossibility. That is possible which can be proved by any valid means of cognition like perception etc. And that is impossible which cannot be so proved. Now, the external objects are apprehended

[1] Ibid, II, 2, 28. tasmād arthajñānayor bhedaḥ. [2] 'yadantarjñeyarūpam tad bahirvad avabhāsate'. Ibid. This is the first-half of the sixth verse of the Ālambana-Parīkṣā of Diṅnāga, quoted by Shaṅkara. [3] Ibid.

by all valid means of cognition. How can their existence be then legitimately denied?[1]

Shaṅkara also quotes a verse from Dharmakīrti to the effect that 'non-dual consciousness itself is wrongly viewed *as if* it appears as the subject-object duality'.[2] Shaṅkara criticizes this view also from the same standpoint from which he criticizes that of Diṅnāga. He objects to the phrase '*as if external*'. He points out that the Buddhists should say that Consciousness appears as the external world, and not that it appears *as if* it is something external.[3] Thus Shaṅkara himself admits that the entire subject-object universe is only an appearance of the Ātman which is Pure Consciousness. His point is simply to reject subjective idealism and to emphasize the phenomenal reality of the external world.

Shaṅkara also emphasizes that the dream state and the waking state cannot be placed on a par. These states are entirely different. Things seen in a dream are sublated in the waking state. Their falsity and illusory character are realized when the dreamer awakes. But the things like posts, walls etc. seen in the waking state are not so contradicted or sublated. Dreams are private; waking life is public. Dreams are remembered; things in waking life are directly perceived. They cannot be treated on the same level on the pretext that both are equally experienced through consciousness. Even the Buddhist himself realizes the acute difference between the two and what is directly experienced cannot be refuted by mere intellectual jugglery.[4]

Again, the Buddhistic assertion that the plurality of ideas is due to the plurality of impressions and not due to the plurality of external objects is also wrong, because if the external objects do not exist then impressions themselves cannot arise. And even if these impressions are held to be beginningless, this position is like a series of the blind, leading to the fallacy of infinte regress and at once negating all practices of this world. Moreover, impressions being mental modifications require a substratum to inhere and in the Buddhistic view there is no such substratum.[5] Ālayavijñāna too which is held to be momentary cannot be, like individual cognitions (pravṛttivijñānas), the substratum of impressions.[6]

Shaṅkara says that his criticism of the theory of momentariness equally applies to this school also.[7] Momentary ideas cannot ideate themselves. There must be a permanent self to synthesize the fleeting ideas and give them a unity and a meaning. The preceding and the succeeding ideas become extinct as soon as they become objects of consciousness. They can neither apprehend nor be apprehended. Hence

[1] Ibid. [2] 'avibhāgo'pi buddhyātmā viparyāsitadarshanaiḥ. grāhyagrāhakasamvittibhedavān iva lakṣyate'. (Pramāṇavārtika, III, 354). Quoted in Upadesha-Sāhasrī, XVIII, 142. [3] bahirevāvabhāsata iti yuktam abhyupagantum na tu bahirvad avabhāsata iti, Shārīraka-Bhāṣya, II, 2, 28. [4] na shakyate vaktum mithyā jāgaritopalabdhir upalabdhitvāt svapnopalabdhivat ityubhayor antaram svayam anubhavatā, Ibid, II, 2, 29. [5] Ibid, II, 2, 30. [6] Ibid, II, 2, 31. [7] Ibid, II, 2, 31.

the various Buddhistic theories like the theory that fleeting ideas succeed one another, the theory of momentariness, the theory of the Unique Particular and the General, the theory that the preceding idea leaves an impression which causes the succeeding idea to arise, the theory of Ignorance, the theory of Existence and Non-Existence of things, the theory of Bondage and Liberation etc. all crumble down.[1]

If the Buddhist replies that the idea is self-conscious and is apprehended by itself like a luminous lamp, he is wrong, for to say that the momentary idea illuminates itself is as absurd as to say that fire burns itself. If he again urges that to say that an idea is apprehended by something else is to involve oneself in infinite regress as this something else would require another thing to apprehend it, and therefore the only way to avoid this infinite regress is to maintain that an idea is self-luminous like a lamp, both these arguments put forth by him are fallacious. In fact it is only the permanent self which apprehends the manifold ideas and synthesizes them into a unity and which may be regarded self-luminous like a lamp needing nothing else for its illumination. But an idea cannot be so regarded. An idea is apprehended by the self. An idea, therefore, is just like an object in relation to the knowing self which is the subject. As the self which apprehends the ideas requires nothing else for its own apprehension, the charge of infinite regress does not arise at all. And so the second objection also becomes ineffective. The self alone is the knowing subject; an idea is only a known object. The witnessing self is a self-evident fact. Its existence is self-proved and can never be denied.[2] Moreover, the view that a momentary idea, like a lamp, manifests itself without being illuminated by the self, means that knowledge is possible without a knowing subject. It is as absurd as to maintain that a thousand lamps manifest themselves inside a deep impenetrable rock.[3] If the Buddhist says that by idea he means consciousness and that we Vedāntins too who accept the ultimate reality of consciousness, accept his view, he is utterly mistaken, because for us an idea is only like an object requiring for its manifestation the self-luminous Self which is the knower. Again, if the Buddhist rejoins that our witnessing Self which is self-luminous and self-proved is only his idea in disguise, he is wrong, because, whereas his ideas are momentary and manifold and are no better than a scattered chaos, originating and dying away, our Self, on the other hand, is non-dual and permanent and is the ultimate knowing subject which synthesizes these scattered ideas into a unity and gives them a meaning.[4] Therefore we see that the difficulty in Buddhism is not removed even if we grant self-consciousness to the vijñānas, for the vijñānas being momentary and manifold will only add to confusion. It is only the Self, the permanent knower and the eternal seer whose

[1] Ibid, II, 2, 28. [2] svayaṁsiddhasya cha sākṣiṇo'pratyākhyeyatvāt, Ibid. [3] Ibid.
[4] vijñānasyotpattipradhvaṁsānekatvādivisheṣavattvābhyupagamāt. Ibid.

sight is never destroyed.[1] Even hundreds of Buddhists cannot disprove the self-proved self nor can they replace it by their momentary idea, just as a dead person cannot be brought back to life again.[2]

These Buddhists believe, says Shaṅkara, that knowledge itself (dhīreva), being self-luminous consciousness (chitsvarūpāvabhāsakatvena), appears in its own form as subject (svākārā) as well as in the form of external objects (viṣayākārā cha), that it is the idea (vijñāna) itself which manifests itself as subject and as object (grāhyagrāhakākārā), and that this transparent (svachchhībhūtam) and momentary (kṣaṇikam) idea (vijñānam) ultimately transcends the subject-object duality (grāhyagrāhaka-vinirmuktam).[3]

All these assumptions, says Shaṅkara, are obstacles to the Vedic path leading to the Highest Good.[4] The illumination of a lamp is not its own; it comes from the self. In this respect there is no difference between a pot and a lamp for both are equally objects. Thus the momentary vijñāna which is only an object to the self which knows it, cannot manifest itself as the subject-object duality. The momentary vijñānas must be known by the self (vijñānasyāpi chaitanyagrāhyatvāt). This self which knows the manifold vijñānas and gives them unity and meaning, is different from them and is the only light or the self-luminous knower.[5] If the ideas alone were real, then they would be synonymous with pots, cloths etc. for they are all objects to the knowing-self.[6] This would lead to the abolition of the distinction between subject and object, means and end, actions and results and would further lead to the annihilation of all phenomenal practices (sarva-samvyavahāralopaprasaṅgaḥ). Bondage and Liberation would be impossible. The sacred texts of the Buddhists would be useless (upadesha-shāstrānarthakyaprasaṅgaḥ) and their authors would have to be regarded as ignorant (tatkarturajñānaprasaṅgah). There would be also vicarious liability (akṛtābhyāgama) and destruction of deeds (kṛtavipraṇāsha). If the self-conscious vijñāna is the only reality and there is no self, then the qualities of momentariness, soullessness etc. would not be imposed on it. Nor can these qualities be regarded as a part of the vijñāna for it is impossible that qualities like suffering etc. which are enjoyed should be a part of the vijñāna which is the enjoyer. Nor can these qualities be natural to vijñāna for if they were so, it would be impossible to remove suffering etc. and then liberation would be impossible. Nor can the annihilation of the vijñāna be regarded as the cessation of suffering etc. for surely if a person who is pierced by a deadly thorn dies, he cannot be said to have been cured of the pain produced by that thorn. Death, certainly, is not the remedy of a disease.[7]

[1] Bṛhadāraṇyaka-Bhāṣya, IV, 3, 30; IV, 4, 25; Muṇḍaka-Bhāṣya, I, 1, 6, Kena-Pada-Bhāṣya, II, 4. [2] Prashna-Bhāṣya, VI, 2. [3] Bṛhadāraṇyaka-Bhāṣya, IV, 3, 7. [4] Ibid. [5] vijñānasya grahītā sa ātmā jyotir antaram vijñānāt. [6] Ibid. [7] Ibid.

Now, it will be easy to see that the view which Shaṅkara exposes and criticizes under the name of 'Vijñānavāda' is in fact Svatantra-Vijñānavāda. We do not find any reference to the doctrines of Laṅkāvatāra, Asaṅga and Vasubandhu. But we find that Shaṅkara has quoted half-a-verse from Diṅnāga, one verse from Dharmakīrti and has often referred to the views of Shāntarakṣita without however mentioning the names of any. We also see that his exposition of 'Vijñānavāda' is in fact a correct and a clear exposition of Svatantra-Vijñānavāda. We should also remember that Svatantra-Vijñānavādins were his immediate predecessors. All these facts support our view that the so-called criticism of 'Vijñānavāda' by Shaṅkara is really the criticism of the Svatantra-Vijñānavāda School; the real Vijñāna-vāda of Asaṅga and Vasubandhu is not refuted by it.

(*d*) *Advance on Vijñānavāda and on Gauḍapāda:*—It may be pointed out however that in regard to those views which Vijñānavāda shares in common with Svatantra-Vijñānavāda, Shaṅkara's criticism applies to Vijñānavāda also. But it is very important to note that here Shaṅkara's criticism loses much of its force. The Ālambana-Parīkṣa of Diṅnāga is not a very original work. Almost all its ideas are based on Vasubandhu's works. We know that Vasubandhu in his Viṁshatikā and in his Bhāṣya on it criticized the atoms of the Vaisheṣikas and of the Vaibhāṣikas. We also know that he declared external objects to be inside consciousness. We also know that he placed dream state and waking state almost on equal footing.[1] We also know that Gauḍapāda too agreed completely with Vasubandhu in many respects.[2] Shaṅkara's criticism, therefore, applies in some respects to Vasubandhu and Gauḍapāda. But we say that this criticism loses much of its force because, firstly, Vasubandhu and Gauḍapāda do not deny the *objectivity* of the external world, as the objects appear as *objects* to the knowing subject, and secondly, because they hold pure Consciousness which is the same as the self-luminous Self to be the *permanent* background of all phenomena. Their view is not subjective idealism. It is absolutism.[3] When it is maintained that pure and permanent Consciousness, which is self-luminous and which transcends the subject-object duality, is the only reality and that the world is only its appearance, the criticism of Shaṅkara falls off the mark because he himself believes in this view.

The difference between Vasubandhu and Gauḍapāda on the one hand, and Shaṅkara on the other, is not the difference of kind but only of degree. The difference is only of emphasis. We know that Vasubandhu and Gauḍapāda distinguish between the illusory (parkalpita) and the relative (paratantra) aspects. They place these two states on a par only in order to emphasize *the ultimate unreality* of the world. Shaṅkara, on the other hand, is keen—and herein his greatness lies—to emphasize

[1] See Supra, pp. 103-104. [2] See Supra, pp. 233-235. [3] See Supra, pp. 110 and 235.

the phenomenal reality of the world. Secondly, he wants to prove the unreality of the external world not by saying that it does not fall outside consciousness but by saying that it is essentially false (mithyā) because it can be described neither as existent nor as non-existent (sadasadanirvachanīya). We have seen that this doctrine was accepted by Gauḍapāda and Shūnyavāda. Thirdly, in Shaṅkara Vasubandhu's Vijñaptimātra gives place to Brahman or Ātman, Ālayavijñāna to Īshvara, Kliṣṭa Manovijñāna to Jiva, Viṣayavijñapti to Jagat, and Pariṇāma to Vivarta. Shaṅkara in fact develops the ideas found in Shūnyavāda, Vijñānavāda and Gauḍapāda almost to perfection and spotless purity.

Shaṅkara's criticism therefore, applies and is intended by him to apply, with full force to Svatantra-Vijñānavāda only which degrades Consciousness merely to momentary and manifold ideas.

(*e*) *Criticism of Shūnyavāda:*—Shaṅkara takes the word 'Shūnya' in the sense of mere negation and says that Shūnyavāda which is pure nihilism is contradicted by all valid means of cognition. It stands self-condemned. The Shūnyavādin, says Shaṅkara, cannot legitimately negate all phenomenal practices unless he finds some higher truth (anyattattva). Shaṅkara therefore summarily dismisses Shūnyavāda taking it to be below criticism.[1] But really Shūnyavāda does admit such higher truth (Tattva)[2] and is absolutism.

(*f*) *General Criticism of Buddhism:*—The more we examine the Buddhistic system, says Shaṅkara, the more it gives way like a well dug in sand. It has no solid foundation. There is no truth in it. It can serve no useful purpose. Buddha by teaching three mutually contradictory systems of Bāhyārthavāda, Vijñānavāda and Shūnyavāda, has proved it beyond doubt that either he was fond of making contradictory statements or his hatred of people made him teach three contradictory doctrines so that people may be utterly confused and deluded by accepting them. Therefore all persons who desire the Good should at once reject Buddhism.[3]

We thus see that Shaṅkara's attitude towards Buddhism is that of hatred and animosity. He uses harsh words for Buddha and for Buddhists. The spirit of Gauḍapāda is gone. As for his criticism of Buddhism we may make the following remarks: Shaṅkara finds it easy to dismiss Shūnyavāda taking the word Shūnya in its popular sense of pure negation or void. When he remarks that Shūnyavāda cannot dismiss the world as pure negation nor even as relative existence unless it finds some higher truth (tattva), he takes it for granted that it has no such higher truth. But our entire treatment of Shūnyavāda bears ample witness to the fact that Shūnyavāda declares the world to be relative

[1] Shūnyavādipakṣastu sarvapramāṇavipratiṣiddha iti tan nirākaraṇāya nādaraḥ kriyate, na hyayam sarvapramāṇaprasiddho lokavyavahāro'nyat-tattvam anadhigamya shakyate'panhotum. Shārīraka-Bhāṣya, II, 2, 31; Bṛhadāraṇyaka-Bhāṣya, IV, 3, 7.
[2] Mādhyamika-Kārikā, XVIII, 9. [3] Shārīraka-Bhāṣya, II, 2, 32.

and therefore ultimately unreal only because it emphatically believes in the reality of the higher truth or Tattva which it calls Paramārtha. Shaṅkara, therefore, only avoids Shūnyavāda. We have also noticed that Shaṅkara does not refute real Vijñānavāda. So far as Bāhyārthavāda or Sarvāstivāda is concerned we know that this school of Hīnayāna was bitterly criticized by the Mahāyānists themselves and Shaṅkara's criticism against it cannot be regarded as altogether new or original, although it is perfectly valid. The full force of Shaṅkara's criticism is therefore directed against the Svatantra-Vijñānavāda school, especially against its theory of momentariness. The criticism is fully justified.

We have noticed Shaṅkara's dialectical criticism of the various schools of philosophy where we have also explained Shaṅkara's own standpoint. We now turn to his exposition of his own philosophy.

X

MĀYĀ AND BRAHMAN

THERE is a famous saying that the entire system of Advaita Vedānta may be summarized in half a verse which runs as follows: Brahman is the only Reality; the world is ultimately false; and the individual soul is non-different from Brahman.[1] Brahman and Ātman or the Supreme Self are synonymous terms. The world is a creation of Māyā. The individual selves on account of their inherent Avidyā imagine themselves as different from Brahman and mistake Brahman as this world of plurality, even as we mistake a rope as a snake. Avidyā vanishes at the dawn of knowledge—the supra-relational direct and intuitive knowledge of the non-dual self which means liberation.

The words Māyā, Avidyā, Ajñāna, Adhyāsa, Adhyāropa, Anirvachanīya, Vivarta, Bhrānti, Bhrama, Nāma-rūpa, Avyakta, Akṣara, Bījashakti, Mūla-prakṛti etc. are recklessly used in Vedānta as very nearly synonymous. Of these Māyā, Avidyā, Adhyāsa and Vivarta are very often used as interchangeable terms. There are two schools among later Advaitins divided on the question whether Māyā and Avidyā are identical or different. The general trend of the Advaitins including Shaṅkara himself has been to treat these two terms as synonymous and to distinguish between the two aspects of Māyā or Avidyā which are called āvaraṇa and vikṣepa, the former being the negative aspect of concealment and the latter the positive aspect of projection. The advocates of the other school who treat Māyā and Avidyā as different say that Māyā is something *positive*, though absolutely dependent on and inseparable from Brahman, which provides a medium for the reflection of Brahman and for the projection of this

[1] brahma satyam jagan mithyā jīvo brahmaiva nāparaḥ.

world, being an essentially indistinguishable power (shakti) of Brahman, while Avidyā is entirely *negative* in character, being pure ignorance or absence of knowledge of Reality. Secondly, Māyā, the cosmic power of projection, conditions Īshvara who is not affected by Avidyā; while Avidyā, the individual ignorance, conditions the Jīva. Brahman reflected in Māyā is the Īshvara and Brahman reflected in Avidyā is the Jīva.[1] Hence, though the individual ignorance is dispelled by knowledge, Māyā, being the inherent nature of Brahman, cannot be so dispelled, Thirdly, Māyā is made mostly of sattva, while Avidyā is made of all the three—sattva, rajas and tamas. But really speaking the two schools are not opposed. Whether Māyā is called the cosmic and positive power of projection and Avidyā the individual and negative ignorance, or Māyā and Avidyā are treated as synonymous and as having two aspects of concealment and projection, the fundamental position remains the same. Further, both the schools agree that Īshvara is ever free from the negative aspect of Ignorance and that in Him sattva preponderates. Hence, whether concealment is called Avidyā or Tūlāvidyā and projection Māyā or Mūlāvidyā, the difference is only in words.

Shaṅkarāchārya brings out the following characteristics of Māyā or Avidyā:

(1) Like the Prakṛti of Sāṅkhya, it is something *material and unconscious* (jaḍā) as opposed to Brahman (Puruṣa in the case of Sāṅkhya) which is Pure Consciousness, though unlike Prakṛti, it is neither real nor independent.

(2) It is the inherent *Power or Potency* (shakti) of Brahman. It is coeval with Him. It is absolutely dependent on and inseparable from Brahman. It is non-different (ananyā) from Him. The relation of Māyā and Brahman is unique and is called tādātmya; it is neither identity nor difference nor both. Māyā is energized and acts as a medium of the projection of this world of plurality on the non-dual ground of Brahman.

(3) It is *beginningless* (anādi).

(4) It is something *positive* (bhāvarūpā), though not real. It is called positive in order to emphasize the fact that it is not merely negative. It has two aspects. In its negative aspect it conceals (āvaraṇa) Reality and acts as a screen to hide it. In its positive aspect it projects (vikṣepa) the world of plurality on the Brahman-Ground. It is non-apprehension as well as misapprehension.

(5) It is *indescribable and indefinable* for it is *neither real nor unreal nor both* (sadasadanirvachanīyā). It is not real, for it has no existence apart from Brahman; it is not unreal, for

[1] kāryopādhir ayam jīvaḥ kāraṇopādhir Īshvaraḥ.

it projects the world of appearance. It is not real, for it vanishes at the dawn of knowledge; it is not unreal, for it is true as long as it lasts. It is not real to constitute a limit to Brahman and yet it is real enough to give rise to the world of appearance. And it is not both real and unreal, for this conception is self-contradictory.

(6) It has a *phenomenal and relative* character (vyāvahārikasattā). It is an *appearance* only (vivarta).

(7) It is of the nature of *superimposition* (adhyāsa). It is an error (bhrānti) like that of a 'rope-snake' or a 'shell-silver'. It is the superimposition upon one thing of the character of another thing. It is wrong cognition or misapprehension.

(8) It is *removable by Right Knowledge* (vijñānanirasyā). When Vidyā dawns Avidyā vanishes. When the rope is known, the 'rope-snake' vanishes.

(9) Its locus (āshraya) as well as object (viṣaya) is Brahman and yet Brahman is really untouched by it, even as a magician is uneffected by his magic or the colourless ākāsha is untouched by the dark colour attributed to it.

It is self-evident, says Shaṅkara, that the subject and the object are absolutely opposed to each other like light and darkness. The subject is Pure Consciousness; the object is Unconsciousness. The one is the ultimate 'I'; the other is the 'non-I'. Neither these two nor their attributes can, therefore, be identified. Yet it is the natural and common practice of people that they wrongly superimpose the object and its attributes upon the subject and *vice versa* the subject and its attributes upon the object. This co-mingling of the subject and the object, this mixing up of truth and error, this coupling of the real and the unreal (satyānṛte mithunīkṛtya) is called superimposition (adhyāsa) or error (bhrama) or illusion (māyā) or ignorance (avidyā). All definitions of error agree in maintaining that error is the superimposition of one thing on another, e.g., the superimposition of silver on shell or the illusion of the moons on a single moon. This superimposition the learned call 'ignorance', and the realization of the true nature of reality by discarding error, they call 'knowledge'. This transcendental Ignorance is the presupposition of all practices of this phenomenal world. Superimposition, therefore, is the notion of a thing in something else (atasmin tadbuddhiḥ). This unreal beginningless cycle of superimposition goes on leading to the false notions of the agent and the enjoyer and to all phenomenal practices. The study of the Vedānta texts is undertaken in order to free oneself from this false notion of superimposition and thereby realize the essential unity of the Self.[1] This superimposition is not secondary or

[1] Shārīraka-Bhāṣya, I, 1, 1, Introduction.

figurative (gauṇa); it is false (mithyā). It is really pitiable that even learned people who distinguish between the subject and the object confuse these terms, like ordinary goatherds and shepherds.[1]

We do not admit any antecedent state of this world as its independent cause. We only admit an antecedent state of this world dependent on Īshvara. This state is called Nescience or Ignorance (avidyā). It is the germinal power or causal potentiality (bīja-shakti). It is unmanifest (avyakta). It depends on Īshvara (Parameshvarāshraya). It is illusion (māyāmayī). It is the universal sleep (mahāsupti) wherein are slumbering the worldly souls forgetting their own real nature. All difference is due to Ignorance. It is not ultimate. Names and forms (nāmarūpe) are only figments of Ignorance. They are neither real nor unreal. Īshvara is limited by His own power of Nescience and appears as many phenomenal selves even as space appears as different 'spaces' limited by the adjuncts of jars etc. The omniscience, omnipresence and omnipotence of Īshvara are all due to the adjuncts of Ignorance; they are not ultimate. Where the essential unity of the Ātman is realized, they all vanish. Creation, therefore, is due to Ignorance. It is not ultimately real.[2]

Māyā is not only absence of knowledge; it is also positive wrong knowledge (mithyāchārarūpā). It is not only non-apprehension, but also misapprehension.[3] It makes the infinite appear as finite. It produces the manifold phenomena when in fact there is only the non-dual Ātman. It makes the unlimited Ātman appear as limited jīvas. It produces the false notions of plurality and difference. But it is not the real characteristic of Ātman or Brahman because it is destroyed by true knowledge, just as rope-snake is sublated by the knowledge of the rope. Brahman, through Avidyā, appears as the manifold world of names and forms, just as pure water appears as dirty foam.[4] The questions like: What is Avidyā? Whose is Avidyā? Where does it appear? etc. are useless (nirarthaka), for if Avidyā is not known they cannot be solved, and if the true nature of Avidyā is realized, the locus and object of Avidyā is also realized. Brahman itself is the locus and object of Avidyā.[5] Avidyā is the darkening power (tāmasa-pratyaya). Its essential nature is to cover or hide the real (āvaraṇātmakatvādavidyā). It operates in three ways: (i) as positive wrong knowledge (viparītagrāhikā), (ii) as doubt (samshayopasthāpikā), and (iii) as absence of knowledge (agrahaṇātmikā).[6] Really it can do no harm to Reality, just as mirage-water cannot make the sandy desert muddy.[7]

The phenomenal world is often condemned by Shaṅkara as unreal exactly in the spirit of Mahāyāna Buddhism and of Gauḍapāda. It is said to be like mirage-water (marīchyambhaḥ) rope-snake (rajju-sarpa), shell silver (shukti-rajata), dusty surface of the sky, (ākasha-tala-

[1] Ibid, I, 1, 4. [2] Ibid, I, 4, 3; I, 4, 10; II, 1, 14. [3] Prashna-Bhāṣya, I, 16. [4] Bṛhadāraṇyaka-Bhāṣya, IV, 3, 20; I, 4, 7. [5] Gītā-Bhāṣya, XIII, 2. [6] Ibid. [7] Ibid.

malinatā), city of Gandharvas (Gandharvanagara), illusion (māyā), plantain-trunk (kadalī-garbha), dream (svapna), bubble (jala-budbuda) foam (phena), moving fire-brand (alāta-chakra), magical elephant (māyānirmita-hastī), hair etc. seen floating in the atmosphere on account of defective vision (keshonḍraka; timiradṛṣṭi), illusion of double-moon (dvichandradarshana), pure magic (Indra-jāla) etc.[1] Like Gauḍapāda, Shaṅkara also uses many words which were commonly used in Mahāyāna. We have already remarked that such words were the heritage of the common language and not the monopoly of Mahāyāna. But they definitely go to prove the influence of that age on Shaṅkara. Many passages are found in Shaṅkara which can be exactly compared with some Buddhistic writings. For example, Shaṅkara observes: Knowing the true nature of all phenomena which represent the cycle of birth-and-death, which are manifest and unmanifest, which are the cause of mutual production like the seed and the sprout, which are beset with innumerable evils, which are unreal like plantain-trunk, illusion, mirage, sky-castle, dream, bubble, foam, which are being destroyed every moment, and which are the result of ignorance, attachment and other defiled actions, and which consist of subject and object, merit and demerit, knowing such phenomena in their reality, a Brāhmaṇa should practice renunciation.[2] The beginningless saṁsāra which is of the nature of suffering and which is rooted in Ignorance, is like a continually flowing stream of water.[3] Just as a person of defective vision sees double-moon or mosquitoes and flies floating in the atmosphere, or just as a dreamer sees many things in a dream, similarly this world of plurality of names and forms, is imagined through Ignorance.[4] From the Absolute is this world-illusion expanded, like the magical illusion from a magician.[5] Ultimately the Absolute is not at all touched by it.[6]

It is very important to remember that the world is not condemned to be utterly unreal even by Mahāyāna and Gauḍapāda, much less by Shaṅkara. Shaṅkara uses such words only to emphasize the ultimate unreality of the world. The metaphors are metaphors and should not be stressed beyond the breaking-point. The world is only an appearance. It is not ultimately real. It becomes sublated when knowledge dawns. But so long as we are in this world, we cannot take it to be unreal. It is a practical reality. It is a workable hypothesis 'absolutely necessary, though in the end most indefensible'. Far from condemning this world, Shaṅkara claims some sort of reality even for error and illusion. 'No appearance is so low that the Absolute does not embrace it.' It is the Real which appears and hence every appearance must have some degree

[1] Kaṭha-Bhāṣya, I, 3, 13; II, 2, 11, II, 3, 1; Bṛhadāraṇyaka-Bhāṣya, IV, 4, 6; Muṇḍaka-Bhāṣya, II, 1, 10; I, 2; Introduction. Prashna-Bhāṣya, VI, 4; Gītā-Bhāṣya, XIII, 26, 27; XV, 3, 4; Shāriraka-Bhāṣya, II, 1, 9, 13, 14. [2] Muṇḍaka-Bhāṣya, I, 2, 12. [3] Ibid, I, 2, Introduction. [4] Prashna-Bhāṣya, VI, 4. [5] Gītā-Bhāṣya, XV, 4. [6] Shārīraka-Bhāṣya, II, 1, 9.

of truth in it, though none can be absolutely true. Objects, seen in a dream are quite real as long as the dream lasts. The water in a dream can quench the thirst in a dream. It is only when we are awake that we can realize the falsity of the dream state. So long as a rope is mistaken for a snake, it is sufficient to frighten the person who mistakes it. It is only when the rope is known that the person may laugh at his folly. Similarly, so long as we are engrossed in Ignorance, the world is quite real for us. It is only when true Knowledge dawns that the world becomes sublated. Just as foam, bubbles, ripples, waves etc. exist separately, though in fact they are not different from water, similarly the subject and the object, the enjoyer and the enjoyed do exist separately, though in fact they are not different from Brahman.[1] The manifold world of experience is the effect; the highest Brahman is the cause. And the effect has no independent existence apart from the cause. Plurality of effects is only a creation of Ignorance.

To the objection that how can unreal Māyā cause the real Brahman to appear as the phenomenal world and how, again, can false personalities through false means reach true end? Shaṅkara's reply is that a person entangled in mud can get out of it through the help of mud alone, that a thorn pricked in the body can be taken out with the help of another thorn, and that there are many instances in this life which show that even unreal things appear to cause real things, e.g., a reflection in a mirror is unreal but it can correctly represent the reflected object; the roaring of a tiger in a dream is unreal but it may make the dreamer tremble with fear and may awaken him.[2] The objection loses its force when it is remembered that the manifold world is taken to be real as long as the essential unity of the Jīva with the Brahman is not realized. As long as this knowledge does not dawn, all secular and religious practices are taken to be real.[3]

The opponent again says that he fails to understand as to how unreal Māyā can cause the real Brahman to appear. If the world is unreal, unreal means like the Vedānta texts cannot lead to real liberation; if the world is real, it cannot be Māyā. The dilemma which the opponent puts forth is: either frankly admit that the world is real or remember that a philosophy which has nothing better to say than that unreal personalities are unreally striving in an unreal world through unreal means to attain an unreal end, is itself unreal. Verily, one bitten by a rope-snake does not die nor can one use mirage-water for drinking or bathing.[4]

Shaṅkara replies that the objection is wrong. If a person imagines

[1] Shārīraka-Bhāṣya, II, 1, 13. [2] Ibid, II, 1, 14; Shatashlokī, 36; Prabodha-sudhākara, 99-102. [3] sarvavyavahārāṇām eva prāg Brahmātmatāvijñānāt satyatvopapatteḥ, svapnavyavahārasyaiva prāk prabodhāt . . . tasmāt upapannaḥ sarvo laukiko vaidikashcha vyavahāraḥ, Shārīraka-Bhāṣya, II, 1, 14. [4] katham tvastyena Vedāntavākyena satyasya Brahmātmatvasya pratipattir upapadyeta? na hi rajjusarpeṇa daṣṭo mriyate, nāpi mṛgatṛṣṇikāmbhasā pānāvagāhanādiprayojanam kriyate, Ibid.

himself to have been bitten by a poisonous snake, and if the imagination is very strong, it may result in heart-failure or in some psychological disaster. Again, the water in a dream can quench the thirst in a dream and a person bitten by a snake in dream may feel himself to be dead in the dream. We have seen that even unreal things can cause real things. The opponent hopelessly confuses the two different standpoints—the empirical and the absolute, even as he is confusing the imaginary with the empirical. The unreality of the effects of the imaginary standpoint (prātibhāsika) can be realized only when the empirical standpoint (vyāvahārika) is attained. Similarly, the unreality of the empirical standpoint can be realized only from the absolute standpoint (pāramārthika). The falsity of the dream-objects is realized when the dreamer gets awake. And even then, though these dream-objects are sublated, the *consciousness* that the dreamer had experienced these objects in the dream is not sublated even in the waking state. Consciousness is, therefore, eternal and real. Right knowledge is not useless because, firstly, it removes ignorance, and secondly, it cannot be sublated. It is only from the absolute standpoint when right knowledge is attained that the Vedānta declares the world to be unreal.[1]

Many critics have failed to understand the real significance of Māyā or Avidyā and have therefore charged Shaṅkara with explaining the world away. But this charge is based on a shifting of the standpoints. Shaṅkara, as we have shown above, has granted some degree of reality even to dreams, illusions and errors. How can he, then, take away the reality of this world? The words 'real' and 'unreal' are taken by Shaṅkara in their absolute sense. Real means *real for all time* and Brahman alone can be real in this sense. Similarly, unreal means absolutely unreal like the hare's horn, which this phenomenal world is not. Hence this world is neither real nor unreal. This shows its self-contradictory and therefore incomprehensible nature. It is relative, phenomenal, finite. But it is not illusory. It is *true for all practical purposes*. What does it matter to us, worldly people, if it is not *absolutely true* in the philosophical sense? When the '*reality*' which is denied to this world means '*reality for all time*', the '*unreality*' which is attributed to it means '*non-eternality*'. Who can stand up and say that the world is not 'unreal' if 'unreal' means 'non-eternal'? Again, the world will be sublated only when knowledge dawns and not before. This should make us humbly strive after true knowledge rather than engage ourselves in futile quarrels. Shaṅkara's intention is perfectly clear—*none can condemn this world as unreal*; he who does it, is *not qualified* to do so and he who is qualified to do so, *will not do so*, for he would have risen above language and finite thought.

[1] yadyapi svapnadarshanāvasthasya sarpadanshanodakasnānādikāryam anṛtam tathāpi tadavagatiḥ satyameva phalam, pratibuddhasyāpyabādhyamānatvāt . . . na cheyam avagatir anarthikā bhrāntir veti shakyam vaktum, avidyānivṛttiphaladarshanāt bādhakajñānāntarābhāvāt cha, Ibid.

XI

ĪSHVARA AND BRAHMAN

BRAHMAN is the only Reality. It is absolutely indeterminate and non-dual. It is beyond speech and mind. It is indescribable because no description of it can be complete. The best description of it is through the negative formula of '*neti neti*' or 'not this, not this'. Yet Brahman is not an abyss of non-entity, because it is the Supreme Self and stands self-revealed as the background of all affirmations and denials. The moment we try to bring this Brahman within the categories of intellect or try to make this ultimate subject an object of our thought, we miss its essential nature. Then it no more remains Unconditioned Consciousness, but becomes conditioned *as it were*. This Brahman, reflected in or conditioned by Māyā, is called Īshvara or God. Īshvara is the personal aspect of the impersonal Brahman. This is the celebrated distinction between God and the Absolute which Shaṅkara, following the Upaniṣads, makes. Īshvara is also known as Apara Brahma or lower Brahman as contrasted with the unconditioned Brahman which is called Para Brahma or Higher Brahman.

The phenomenal character of Īshvara is quite evident. He is the highest appearance which we have. Some critics have missed the significance of Īshvara. They believe that Īshvara in Advaita is unreal and useless. But they are sadly mistaken. Missing the true significance of Māyā is at the root of this mistaken belief. Īshvara becomes 'unreal' only for *him* who has realized his oneness with Brahman by rising above speech and mind. For us Īshvara is all in all. Finite thought can never grasp Brahman. And therefore all talks about Brahman are really talks about Īshvara. Even the words 'unconditioned Brahman' refer really to 'conditioned Īshvara', for the moment we speak of Brahman, He ceases to be Brahman and becomes Īshvara.

Īshvara or God is the Sat-Chit-Ānanda, the Existence-Consciousness-Bliss. He is the Perfect Personality. He is the Lord of Māyā. He is immanent in the whole universe which He controls from within. He is the Soul of souls as well as the Soul of Nature. As the immanent inner ruler, He is called Antaryāmin. He is also transcendental, for in His own nature He transcends the universe. He is the Creator, Sustainer and Destroyer of this universe. He is the Source of everything. He is the final haven of everything. He is the Concrete Universal, the Supreme Individual, the Whole, the Identity-in-difference. He is the object of devotion. He is the inspirer of moral life. He is all in all from the practical standpoint. Thus the description of Brahman which Rāmānuja gave at a much later date is essentially an elaboration of Shaṅkara's Īshvara.

Shaṅkara, like Kant, believes that God cannot be *proved* by our finite thought. All attempts to do so end in failure. They lead to, what Kant has called, the antinomies. The cosmological proof can give only a finite creator of this finite creation and a finite creator is no creator at all. The teleological proof can only point to the fact that a conscious principle is working at the root of creation. The ontological proof can give only an *idea* of God and not God as a *real object*. The Nyāya arguments to prove the existence of God are futile. God is an article of faith. Shruti is the only *proof* for the existence of God. As Kant falls back on faith, so Shaṅkara falls back on Shruti. Shaṅkara agrees with Gauḍapāda's view of Ajāti. There is no *real* creation. God, therefore, is not a '*real*' Creator. God alone is *real*; the creation is only an *appearance* of God.

Īshvara has been a taxing problem for the followers of Shaṅkara. According to some, Īshvara is the reflection of Brahman in Māyā, while jīva is the reflection of Brahman in Avidyā. According to others, Brahman, limited or conditioned by Māyā is Īshvara, while Brahman limited by Avidyā or the internal organ (which is a product of Avidyā is jīva. The former view is called Reflection Theory (pratibimbavāda) and the latter Limitation Theory (avachchhedavāda). Some regard jīva as the reflection of Īshvara. The defect in the Reflection Theory is that Brahman and Māyā both being formless, how can a formless original be reflected in a formless receptacle? To avoid this some have suggested the Identity of the Original and the Reflected Image (bimbapratibimbābhedavāda). But this too cannot be accepted. The defect in the Limitation Theory is as to how can Māyā or Avidyā constitute limitation to Brahman? Those who do not agree with either of these theories have suggested a third, the Appearance Theory, according to which Īshvara and jiva are inexplicable appearances of Brahman (ābhāsavāda). The post-Shaṅkarites have indulged in needless hair-splitting. The problem was not at all taxing to Shaṅkara. He uses the similes of the reflection of the Sun or the Moon in the waves or in the different vessels of water, the simile of the reflection of the red colour of the flower in the crystal, as well as the simile of the limitation of the universal space as the different 'spaces in the jars'. He uses them only as metaphors for their suggestive value. They should not be taken literally and stressed beyond the breaking-point. Shaṅkara himself seems to favour Appearance Theory (ābhāsavāda) because for him Īshvara and jīva are the *inexplicable appearances* of Brahman. They are due to Māyā or Avidyā or Adhyāsa. They are only appearances (vivarta). The 'why' and the 'how' regarding Avidyā are illegitimate questions and therefore an insoluble mystery. God is God only to the jīva who is labouring under Avidyā. God Himself never feels Himself as God; He feels Himself essentially one with Brahman, for Avidyā in its negative aspect of concealment never operates on Him. God is the Lord of Māyā, while jīva is constantly troubled by Māyā. God always enjoys the Bliss of Brahmaṇ while jīva is tortured by the pangs of Avidyā.[1] When Brahman is viewed as saṁsāra, God, Soul and Nature arise simultaneously and when Brahman's own essence is realized, God, Soul and Nature vanish simultaneously.

XII

JĪVA AND BRAHMAN

QUALIFIED Brahman is Īshvara. Phenomenally there is a difference between jīva and Īshvara. The former is the agent and the enjoyer, acquires merit and demerit, experiences pleasure and pain, while the latter is not at all touched by all this. The Muṇḍaka (III, I, 1) declares that 'one bird (jīva) eats the sweet fruit, while the other (Īshvara) merely looks on'. Jīva enjoys (pibati), while Īshvara makes him enjoy (pāyayati). One is the enjoyer, the other is the ruler. The Kaṭha (I, 3, 1; III, 3, 34) only figuratively says that both of these enjoy (chhatrinyāyena). But ultimately there is no difference at all between jīva and Brahman. Only so long as the jīva does not discard Nescience leading to duality and does not realize its own true nature, he remains the individual self. Slumbering in ignorance, when he is awakened by the Shruti, he realizes that he is not the body, senses, or mind, but is the non-dual universal Self—tat tvam asi (that thou art). Realizing his own true nature, he ever dwells in himself shining forth in his own true nature. Jīva through ignorance is regarded as tinged with the false notions of the 'I' and the 'Mine' which arise when mind through senses comes into contact with the fleeting sensations or ideas. It is viewed as something different from the eternal and self-luminous Consciousness which is its immanent inner controller, as the reflection of that Consciousness, as identical with mind and its states, as associated with the seed of ignorance, as the possessor of momentary ideas etc. As long as these false notions about the self persist, the result is the empirical self and the objective world; and when these notions are destroyed by right knowledge, the result is liberation, though ultimately both bondage and liberation are phenomenal, because jīva is really non-different from Brahman.[2] Even the view that he becomes Brahman is only a verbal statement (upachāramātra), for he is always Brahman.[3] Just as a pure transparent white crystal is wrongly imagined to be red on account of a red flower placed near it, or just as the colourless sky is wrongly imagined to be sullied with dirt by the ignorant, or just as a rope is

[1] sa Īsho yad vashe māyā, sa jīvo yastayārditaḥ. [2] Ibid, I, 1, 5; I, 2, 6; I, 2, 20; Kena-Vākya-Bhāṣya, I, 3; III, Introduction; Muṇḍaka-Bhāṣya, III, 1, 1; II, 2, 11. [3] Bṛhadāraṇyaka-Bhāṣya, VI, 4, 6. Compare Vimshatikā, K, 26-27.

wrongly taken to be a snake in the twilight, or just as a shell is mistaken for silver, similarly the non-dual Ātman or Brahman is wrongly imagined to be the empirical self. Just as the Sun or the Moon appears many on account of the reflection in the different waves or vessels of water or just as the same space appears on account of the adjuncts of jars etc. as different 'spaces', similarly the same Self appears as so many phenomenal selves on account of Nescience.[1] Shaṅkara says that he who wants to explain the Scripture as teaching that jīva is not really Brahman, and who thus wants to preserve the ultimate reality of bondage and liberation, is indeed lowest among the learned (paṇḍitāpasada).[2] To refute such and other vain speculations which hinder the realization of the essential unity of the self and to show that there is only one real Self, eternal and unchanging, which is the Luminous Body of Pure Consciousness (Vijñāna-dhātu),[3] and which, through its own power, manifests itself as many, and that except this there is no other Reality, no other Pure Consciousness, is the aim of the Shārīraka-Bhāṣya.[4]

XIII

ĀTMAN AND BRAHMAN

ĀTMAN is the same as Brahman. It is Pure Consciousness. It is the Self which is Self-luminous and which transcends the subject-object duality and the trinity of knower, known and knowledge, and all the categories of the intellect. It is the Unqualified Absolute. It is the only Reality. Brahman is everything and everything is Brahman. There is no duality, no diversity at all. This Self can never be denied, for the very idea of denial presupposes it. It cannot be doubted, for all doubts rest on it. All assertions, all doubts, all denials presuppose it. It is not adventitious or derived (āgantuka). It is self-proved or original (svayamsiddha). All means of cognition (pramāṇas) are founded on it. To refute this Self is impossible, for he who tries to refute it is the Self.[5] The knower knows no change, for eternal existence is his very nature.[6] 'Never is the sight of the seer destroyed' says the Bṛhadāraṇyaka. 'He who knows Brahman becomes Brahman.'[7] He who is the knower is the Self, for he is omnipresent.[8] Everything else is relative and therefore ultimately unreal. The Self alone is not relative. It is, therefore, self-proved.[9] The tragedy of human intellect is that it tries to know everything as an object. But whatever can be presented as

[1] Shārīraka-Bhāṣya, I, 3, 19. [2] Gītā-Bhāṣya, XIII, 2. [3] Compare with Dharmadhātu or Dharmakāya. See Trimshikā, K. 30. [4] Shārīraka-Bhāṣya, I, 3, 19. [5] ya eva hi nirakartā tadeva tasya svarūpam, Ibid, II, 3, 7. [6] na jñātur anyathābhāvo'sti sarvadā vartamānasvabhāvatvāt, Ibid. [7] Brahma veda Brahmaiva bhavati. [8] yo hi jñātā sa eva saḥ, sarvātmakatvāt, Kena-Vākya-Bhāṣya, I, 3. [9] yaddhi anapekṣam tat svata eva siddham, Ibid.

an object is necessarily relative and for that very reason unreal. The knower can never be known as an object. Ultimately there is no distinction between the true knower and pure knowledge. 'How, O dear, can the knower be known?' says the Bṛhadāraṇyaka. Hence all these who rely on the intellect are deluded because they can never truly describe the Self either as existent or as non-existent. It is essentially indescribable, for all descriptions and all categories fail to grasp it fully.[1]

As a matter of fact Brahman ultimately transcends all categories. The best method of describing it, therefore, is by negative terms. But if we want to describe it positively, the best that we can say is that it is Pure Consciousness which is at once Pure Existence and Pure Bliss. True, we cannot say that Brahman is *self-conscious* of its consciousness or that it *enjoys* its own bliss. These determinations of the intellect fail here. The fact is that Brahman itself is Pure Existence, Pure Consciousness and Pure Bliss—all in one. It is its very nature to be such. It cannot be regarded as a substance having these qualities or even as a subject knowing or feeling these qualities. All distinctions of substance and qualities, of subject and object, all determinations of the intellect cease here.[2] Dvaita does not deserve to be taught, for everybody normally assumes it in all phenomenal practices. Therefore taking the normal dualism which people naturally take for granted on account of transcendental ignorance, the Shāstra teaches that though dualism is a practical necessity, yet it is not ultimately real. Brahman is the only reality. It is the End (upeya); and Brahmavidyā or the knowledge of the non-difference of the jīvatman and the Paramātman, is the means (upāya) to realize this end. When the end is realized the Shāstra itself is transcended.[3]

Existence and consciousness are one. 'The Real is the Rational and the Rational is the Real'.[4] But ultimately Brahman is devoid of all characteristics. It cannot be defined as mere Existence and not as Consciousness, for the Shāstra says that it is All-Consciousness (vijñānaghana); nor can it be defined as mere Consciousness and not as Existence, for the Shāstra says: 'it is'; nor can it be defined as both Existence and Consciousness, for to admit that Brahman is characterized by Existence different from Consciousness or by Consciousness different from Existence, is to admit duality in Brahman; nor can it be defined as characterized by Existence non-different from Consciousness for if Existence is Consciousness and Consciousness is Existence why should there be any controversy at all whether Brahman is Existence or Consciousness or both?[5] Again, to say, that Reality exists but is not known is a contradiction in terms, for at least Reality is known as unknowable by intellect. It is like saying that 'coloured objects exist but there is no eye to see

[1] Ibid, II, 1. [2] Bṛhadāraṇyaka-Bhāṣya, III, 9, 28. [3] Ibid, II, 1, 1. [4] sattaiva bodho bodha eva cha sattā, Shārīraka-Bhāṣya, III, 2, 21. [5] Ibid.

them'.[1] Reality, therefore, must exist for us and it is only Pure Consciousness that can ultimately exist. We cannot know it by finite intellect but we can realize it directly through pure intuition. It is non-dual Consciousness where all distinctions, all plurality, all determinations, all qualities, all characteristics, all categories and all concepts are transcended. All determinations of language and intellect are merged in this indeterminate and unqualified Reality. Being and not-being, one and many, qualified and unqualified, knowledge and ignorance, action and inaction, active and inactive, fruitful and fruitless, seedful and seedless, pleasure and pain, middle and not-middle, shūnya and ashūnya, soul and God, unity and plurality etc. etc.—all these determinations do not apply to the Absolute. He who wants to grasp the Absolute by any of these determinations, indeed tries to roll up the sky like a skin or tries to ascend space like a stair-case or wishes to see the footprints of fish in water or of birds in the sky.[2]

The Shāstra, therefore, becomes silent after saying—'not this, not this.' If a man does not understand that he is a man when he is told that he is not a non-man, how can he be able to understand, then, if he is told that he is a man?[3] The two 'no'-es in the formula 'neti neti' are meant for emphasizing the fact that whatever can be presented as an object is ultimately unreal. They cover the entire field of objective existence and point out that it is not real. There is no better way of describing the Absolute than this negative method. But it should be never missed that all these negations pre-suppose and point towards the positive Brahman.[4] The Absolute can be unknowable only for those who are ignorant of the Vedānta tradition, who do not know the means of right kowledge and who desperately cling to the world. True, the Absolute cannot be known as an object by the intellect. But being the only Reality and being always present and so not at all foreign, it is directly realized through spiritual experience (samyagjñāna).[5] The phrase 'neti neti' negates all characteristics of Brahman, but it does not negate Brahman itself. It implies that there is something about which something is denied. Appearances can be negated only with reference to Reality. Effects alone can be negated, for they are unreal. But the cause, the Brahman, cannot be negated, for it is the ultimate ground on which all effects or phenomena are superposed.[6]

Prashna-Bhāṣya, II, 2. [2] Aitareya-Bhāṣya, II, 1, Introduction. [3] Ibid. [4] Bṛhadāraṇyaka-Bhāṣya, II, 3, 6. [5] Gītā-Bhāṣya, XVIII, 50. [6] kiñchiddhi paramārtham ālambyā'paramāthaḥ pratiṣidhyate yathā rajjvādiṣu sarpādayaḥ . . . yuktam cha kāryasya neti netīti pratiṣedhanam na tu Brahmaṇaḥ, sarvakalpanāmūlatvāt. na hi prapañchapratiṣedharūpād ādeshanād anyat paramādeshanam Brahmaṇo'sti, Shārīraka-Bhāṣya, III, 2, 22.

XIV

KNOWLEDGE AND ACTION

SHAṄKARA repeatedly asserts that the Absolute can be realized through knowledge and knowledge alone; karma and upāsanā are subsidiary. They may help us in urging us to know Reality and they may prepare us for that knowledge by purifying our mind (sattvashuddhi), but ultimately it is knowledge alone which, by destroying ignorance, the root-cause of this world, can enable us to be one with the Absolute. The opposition of knowledge and action stands firm like a mountain.[1] They are contradictory (viparīte) and are poles apart (dūramete). Those who talk of combining knowledge with action, says Shaṅkara, have perhaps not read the Bṛhadāraṇyaka nor are they aware of the glaring contradiction repeatedly pointed out by the Shruti and the Smṛti.[2] Knowledge and action are opposed like light and darkness. Actions are prescribed for those who are still in ignorance and not for those who are enlightened. Knowledge only removes ignorance and then Reality shines forth by itself.[3] A liberated sage, however, performs actions without any attachment and works for the uplift of humanity. Shaṅkara's own life bears ample witness to this fact.

XV

KNOWLEDGE AND LIBERATION

ULTIMATE Reality (pāramārthikam vastu) can neither be asserted nor denied by knowledge. Knowledge does nothing else except removing ignorance. Shāstra only generates right knowledge (jñāpakam). It does nothing else (na kārakam).[4]

Knowledge of Brahman, which leads to eternal bliss, does not depend on the performance of any act, for Brahman is already an accomplished fact. Religious acts which lead to prosperity depend on human performance. Religious texts enjoin injunctions or prohibitions. Knowledge merely instructs.[5] Knowledge of Brahman culminates in immediate experience and is already an accomplished fact.[6] Action, whether secular or Vedic, can be done, misdone or left undone. Injunctions, prohibitions, options, rules and exceptions depend on our thinking. But knowledge

[1] Ibid, 2. [2] Bṛhadāraṇyaka-Bhāṣya, II, 4, Introduction. [3] Īsha-Bhāṣya, 2, 7, 8, 9, 18; Kena-Vākya-Bhāṣya, I, Introduction, 1, 2; Kaṭha-Bhāṣya, I, 2, 1; I, 2, 4; Muṇḍaka-Bhāṣya, I, Introduction, III, 1, 4; Taittirīya-Bhāṣya, I, 1, Introduction; Chhāndogya-Bhāṣya, I, 1, Introduction; Bṛhadāraṇyaka-Bhāṣya, I, 4, 7; I, 4, 10; II, 4, Introduction; III, Introduction; Gītā-Bhāṣya, Introduction; II, 10; II, 69; XVIII, 66. [4] Bṛhadāraṇyaka-Bhāṣya, I, 4, 10. [5] Shārīraka-Bhāṣya, I, 1, 1. [6] anubhavāvasānatvād bhūtavastuviṣayatvāt cha brahmajñānasya, Ibid, I,1,2.

leaves no option to us for its being this or that or for its existence or non-existence. It is not in our hands to make, unmake, or change knowledge. Our thinking cannot make a pillar a man. Knowledge of Brahman, therefore, depends on Brahman itself. It is always of the same nature because it depends on the existent thing.[1] True knowledge is produced by Pramāṇas and conforms to its objects. It can neither be produced by hundreds of injunctions nor can it be destroyed by hundreds of prohibitions. Knowledge is not mental activity, because it depends not on mind but on the existent fact.[2] There is also no succession in knowledge. Once it dawns, it dawns for ever and at once removes all ignorance and consequently all bondage. Liberation, therefore, means removal of ignorance by knowledge.[3] That blessed person who has realized Reality is liberated here and now.[4] The Shruti says: 'just as a slough cast off by a snake lies on an ant-hill, similarly does this body lie.' This is Jīvanmukti. Final release (Videhamukti) is obtained after the death of the body. The Shruti says 'the only delay for him is the death of the body'. Just as a potter's wheel goes on revolving for some time even after the push is withdrawn, similarly the body may continue to exist even after knowledge has dawned, though all attachment with the body is cut off.[5] Like an arrow shot from the bow, the body continues to reap the fruits until it expires; but no new actions are accumulated.[6]

XVI

ULTIMATE CRITERION OF TRUTH

WE have to discuss here the claims of Revelation, Reason and Intuition each of which wants to be crowned as the ultimate criterion of truth in Shaṅkara. Shaṅkara attaches supreme importance to the revealed truths of the Vedas which are regarded as the 'breath of God' (yasya nishavsitam Vedāḥ). But it is only jñānakāṇḍa that is stressed, not the karmakāṇḍa. He who condemns Shaṅkara as a mere theologian 'whose faith is pinned to the Vedas', must be either hopelessly ignorant of Shāṅkara-Vedānta or be himself nothing less than a prejudiced dogmatist. Shaṅkara never accepts the Shruti blindly. It is only because he fully knows that the Shruti is the result of the highest realization of the ancient sages, that it is the most valuable pearl that the ocean of human experience can ever boast to yield after having been churned by the rod of the intellect, in short, it is only because Shaṅkara is fully conscious of the fact that the Shruti is the shining pure gold tested at the touch-stone of reason and experience, that he builds his

[1] brahmajñānam vastutantram, Ibid. [2] Ibid, III, 2, 21. [3] mokṣapratibandhanivṛttimātram eva ātmajñānasya phalam, Ibid, I. 1, 4. [4] siddham jīvato'pi viduṣo'sharīratvam. Ibid. [5] Ibid, IV, 1, 15. [6] Chhāndogya-Bhāṣya, VI, 14-22.

many-storeyed magnificent palace of the Advaita on the firm foundation of the Shruti.

Many passages may be quoted from Shaṅkara where he says that Brahman, being supersensuous, can be realized only through Revelation or Shruti.[1] Here too, intellect is not driven out of the palace of philosophy, but kept there as an ancillary to the Revelation-Queen.[2]

Shaṅkara repeatedly asserts that discursive intellect cannot grasp Reality. Brahman cannot become the object of perception as it has no form, and it does not lend itself to inference and other means, as it has no characteristic mark.[3] Partly accepting the position of Bhartṛhari which is criticized by Shāntarakṣita, Shaṅkara remarks that reasoning, because it depends on individuals, has no solid foundation. Arguments held valid by some, may be proved fallacious by others more ingenious.[4] Like Asaṅga, Shaṅkara declares intellect to be insecure and emphasizes the Āgama.[5] But his criticism is directed towards *kutarka*. Shruti, says Shaṅkara, cannot be set aside by mere logical quibbling.[6] A false logician is a quibbler saying whatever he likes.[7] They, whose minds are fouled by logical quibbling, are to be pitied because they do not know the tradition of the Vedānta.[8] What grand feats of reasoning are displayed by such logicans who are bulls without horns and tails! They are princes among liars and among those who violate the tradition of the wise. They cannot enter the Fort of Brahman which is open only to those who are of excellent wisdom, who have the knowledge of the Shāstra and blessings of the teacher.[9] Debators, like carnivorous animals for the sake of bait, fight against one another and fall from Reality. Themselves deluded they also delude innocent people. It is only for the sake that people, who desire liberation which can be obtained by knowledge alone, should reject false views, says Shaṅkara, that he criticizes other doctrines, not for any interest in discussion for its own sake.[10]

It is, therefore, only logical quibbling or kutarka that is condemned by Shaṅkara. Sutarka or refined intellect is admitted as supreme in the phenomenal world where its authority is said to be unquestionable. Only an intellectual, a rational being can understand the meaning of the Shruti. It cannot reveal itself to a beast. As Yāska said that he who only reads or remembers the Veda but does not understand its meaning is only a *coolie* carrying a load of the Veda on his head and is no better than a pillar.[11] Shaṅkara never asks us to accept the Shruti blindly. He is never satisfied with a mere quotation from the scripture on a vital metaphysical issue but always defends it with reason.[12] If we find apparent contradictions in the Shruti, we should interpret other passages of

[1] Shārīraka-Bhāṣya, I, I, 4. [2] Ibid, I, I, I, 2, 4. [3] Ibid, II, I, II. [4] Ibid, II, I, II. [5] Kena-Vākya-Bhāṣya, I, 3. Compare with Mahāyānasūtrālāṅkāra, I, 12. See Supra, p. 99. [6] Chhāndogya-Bhāṣya, VIII, 12, I. [7] Kaṭha-Bhāṣya, I, 2, 9. [8] Br. Bhāṣya, II I, 20. [9] Ibid. [10] Prashna-Bhāṣya, VI, 3. [11] Shārīraka-Bhāṣya, II, 2, I. [12] Māṅḍūkya-Kārikā-Bhāṣya, III, I.

the Shruti in the light of that one central doctrine of the Shruti which appeals to reason. If the Shruti contradicts reason, reason must be our guide for it is nearer our experience.[1] Even if hundred Shrutis declare with one voice that fire is cool and without light or that the Sun does not shine, we cannot accept them.[2] Reason is the sole means of knowing truth and falsity.[3] We cannot question the validity of intellect in the phenomenal world. Here, 'You obey while you rebel'. Even the statement that 'intellect stands condemned' must be made by intellect itself.[4]

Infra-relational intuition is the animal instinct and supra-relational true intuition is the same as Pure Reason. Svānubhava or Svānubhūti or immediate experience or direct self-realization is the same as Pure Consciousness. Here finite intellect casts off its garb of relationality which was put upon it by ignorance and becomes one with the Absolute which is Pure Consciousness. Discursive intellect confesses its impotence only to be rejuvenated with new life and eternal vigour, and what appears to be its suicide is, in fact, its consecration. Shall we not say, then, with deeper meaning, that the ultimate criterion of truth in Shaṅkara is immediate spiritual realization in this truer sense?

[1] Shārīraka-Bhāṣya, II, 4. [2] Gītā-Bhāṣya, XVIII 66. Also Bṛhadāraṇyaka-Bhāṣya, II, 1, 20. [3] Kaṭha-Bhāṣya, VI, 12. [4] etadapi hi tarkāṇām apratiṣṭhitattvam tarkeṇaiva pratiṣṭhāpyate, Shārīraka-Bhāṣya, II, 1, 11.

Chapter Sixteen

POST-SHAṄKARA VEDĀNTA

I

MAṆḌANA-SURESHVARA-EQUATION

BEFORE we deal with the Post-Shaṅkarites, we may briefly refer to this controversy. Tradition identifies Maṇḍana with Sureshvara and the latter with Vishvarūpa. There is no reason to disbelieve that the household name of the Saṁnyāsin Sureshvara, the famous disciple of Shaṅkara, was Vishvarūpa. But the identification of Maṇḍana with Sureshvara is a very controversial matter. Prof. M. Hiriyanna has challenged the traditional view by pointing out important doctrinal divergences between Maṇḍana and Sureshvara.[1] And Prof. S. Kuppuswami Shastri has tried to give a death-blow to this tradition in his long Introduction to the Brahmasiddhi. The following have been pointed out by these scholars as the important doctrinal differences between Maṇḍana and Sureshvara:

(1) Maṇḍana advocates Dṛṣṭisṛṣṭivāda—later on championed by Prakāshānanda—by maintaining that the seat, support or locus (āshraya) of Avidyā is the individual Jīva, while Brahman is only the object (viṣaya) of Avidyā. Neither in itself nor as conditioned by or reflected in Māyā is Brahman the cause of this world. It is only the individual Jīvas who on account of their inherent ignorance (naisargikī avidyā) create the world-appearance which is destroyed by adventitious knowledge (āgantukī vidyā). Individual experiences agree due to similarity and not due to identity. The world-appearance has no objective basis. Sureshvara rejects this distinction maintaining, with Shaṅkara, that Brahman itself is both the locus and the object of Avidyā. The controversy led, later on, to the two important schools of Advaita Vedānta, the Bhāmatī School of Vāchaspati who followed Maṇḍana, and the Vivaraṇa School of Prakāshātman who followed Sureshvara.

(2) Maṇḍana maintains Prasaṅkhyānavāda. The knowledge

[1] J.R.A.S., 1923 and 1924; Introduction to the Naiṣkarmyasiddhi.

arising out of the Upaniṣadic Mahāvākya is only mediate, indirect and relational. Liberation is the direct realization of Brahman. Hence this knowledge in order to lead to liberation must have its mediacy removed by meditation or Upāsanā. Sureshvara rejects this and, following Shaṅkara, strongly upholds the view that knowledge arising out of the Mahāvākya is at once immediate and directly leads to liberation, while Upāsanā, howsoever useful it may be towards liberation, cannot be taken as the cause of liberation. Mahāvākya-jñāna is as direct as the knowledge produced by the statement 'Thou art the tenth' in the parable in which each one of the ten persons, leaving out himself, counted only nine.

(3) Maṇḍana supports Bhāvādvaita on Sadadvaita or Ens-Monism. Brahman is the only positive entity and monism excludes only another positive entity. Dissolution of ignorance (avidyādhvaṁsa or prapañchābhāva) is a negative reality and its existence does not violate monism. But according to Shaṅkara and Sureshvara, negation as a separate entity cannot exist. Dissolution of ignorance is not a negative entity; it is at once positive Brahmanhood.

(4) Maṇḍana favours Jñāna-karma-samuchchayavāda. He has a leaning towards Mīmāṁsā. Performance of Vedic rites is very conducive towards liberation. Ignorance is removed by Ignorance (actions) alone and when it has been thus removed what remains is Pure Knowledge. Sureshvara is a bitter enemy of such combination. Like night and day, action and knowledge can never combine. Action may be useful for purification, but it is knowledge and knowledge alone which leads to liberation.

(5) For Maṇḍana, real liberation is Videha-mukti. He regards Jīvanmuktas as highly advanced Sādhakas only, not Siddhas. For Sureshvara, who follows Shaṅkara, Jivan-mukti is real mukti and Jivanmuktas are Siddhas.

(6) Maṇḍana accepts Viparīta-khyāti while Sureshvara accepts Anirvachanīya-khyāti.

(7) Maṇḍana's attitude towards Shaṅkara is that of a self-confident rival teacher of Advaita and his Brahma-siddhi is based on the Prasthāna-traya of Vedānta, while Suresһara frankly admits that he is a devoted disciple of Shaṅkara and he bases his works on the Shāṅkara-Bhāṣya.

Professors Hiriyanna and Shastri also maintain that in none of the available authoritative works on Advaita is Maṇḍana identified with

Sureshvara, while in some works on Vedānta, they are distinguished as two different persons. The tradition which identifies them is based on works dealing with the life of Shaṅkara which are a hopeless mixture of legend and history.

We readily admit the doctrinal divergences between Maṇḍana and Sureshvara pointed out by these learned scholars. Existing evidence goes in favour of Maṇḍana and Sureshvara being two different persons. But there is one fact which cannot be easily dismissed. There is still room for the hypothesis that Vishvarūpa Mishra whose pet or popular name or title might have been Maṇḍana, and who was probably at the end of a long line of Pre-Shaṅkarite teachers of Advaita who accomodated Mīmāṁsā also, came under the spell of Shaṅkara, modified and changed his views, became a devoted disciple of Shaṅkara, and was then known as the Saṁnyāsin Sureshvara. There is room for the evolution of the ideas of a man and more so when he comes under the spell of a great personality. Moreover, many parallel passages are found in the Brahmasiddhi of Maṇḍana and Bṛhadāraṇyaka-vārtika of Sureshvara.[1] Nothing can be said with absolute certainty and the controversy, therefore, requires further research. Here we shall refer to the author of the Brahmasiddhi as Maṇḍana and to the author of the Naiṣkarmyasiddhi and Vārtika as Sureshvara.

II

AVIDYĀ OR MĀYĀ

AVIDYĀ or Ignorance, says *Maṇḍana*, is called Māyā or illusion and Mithyābhāsa or False Appearance because it is neither the characteristic nature (svabhāva) of Brahman nor an entity different from Brahman (arthāntaram). It is neither real (satī) nor absolutely unreal (atyantamasatī). If it is the characteristic nature of something else, then whether it is identical with or different from it, it is a reality and cannot be called Avidyā. On the other hand, if it is absolutely unreal, then it is like the sky-lotus and can serve no practical purpose which in fact it does. It is therefore indescribable (Anirvachanīyā) as it can be described neither as existent nor as non-existent. And all philosophers in order to be consistent must necessarily accept it as such.[2]

Maṇḍana maintains that the locus of Avidyā is the individual Jīva. Ultimately the Jīvas are identical with the Brahman but phenomenally they are diverse. Diversity is the product of Avidyā. Brahman cannot be diverse because being of the nature of Pure Consciousness it is devoid of Avidyā. This Avidyā should not belong to the Jīvas because the Jīvas themselves are the product of this Avidyā. Thus Avidyā can

[1] Shrī P. P. Subrahmanya Sastri's Foreword to the Brahmasiddhi; p. X-XIII. [2] sarvapravādibhishcha ittham iyam āstheyā, Brahmasiddhi, p. 9.

belong neither to Brahman nor to the Jīvas. But this, says Maṇḍana, should not shock us because Avidyā is itself an inconsistent category and that therefore its relation with the Jīvas should also be inconsistent. If Avidyā becomes a consistent category, it would no more remain Avidyā, but would become real.[1]

Avidyopādānabhedavādins propose another solution which may be accepted. They say that Avidyā depends on the Jīvas and the Jīvas themselves depend on Avidyā and this cycle is beginningless so that, like the seed and the sprout, there is neither an ultimate beginning of Avidyā nor of the Jīvas.[2] If Brahman is tainted with Avidyā then even the liberated soul would remain ignorant; and if Brahman itself is bound and becomes afterwards liberated, then the liberation of one would mean the liberation of all. Thus it is clear that Avidyā cannot belong to Brahman.[3] It belongs to the Jīvas.[4] Through Avidyā the Jīvas become entangled in the cycle of birth and death and through Vidyā they become liberated. Avidyā is inherent in them; Vidyā is not natural to them. This inherent ignorance is destroyed by adventitious knowledge.[5] Hearing of the Vedānta texts, right thinking, meditation etc. help the dawn of true knowledge by which one attains to Brahmanhood. Explaining the eleventh verse of the Īsha (avidyayā mṛtyum tīrtvā vidyayā'mṛtamashnute), Maṇḍana remarks that Ignorance (avidyā) can be destroyed by Ignorance (karma etc.) alone and when it has been thus destroyed, what remains is Pure Knowledge or the Immortal Self shining in its Pure Consciousness.[6]

Maṇḍana accepts two kinds of Avidyā—absence of knowledge (agrahaṇa) and positive wrong knowledge (anyathāgrahaṇa). *Vāchaspati Mishra*, following Maṇḍana remarks that Brahman is associated with two kinds of Ignorance (avidyā-dvitaya-sachiva).[7] One is psychological ignorance. It is, as explained by Amalānanda, 'the preceding series of beginningless false impressions' (pūrvāpūrvabhrama-saṁskāra). The other is an objective entity forming the material cause of the mind as well as of the material world outside. It is positive (bhāvarūpa), beginningless (anādi), objective (jaḍa), and of the nature of power (shakti). It is indescribable (anirvachanīya). It is the material stuff the appearances are made of. Like the Prakṛti of Yoga, it is this Avidyā into which all world-products together with psychological ignorance and false impressions disappear during Mahā-pralaya, where they remain as potential capacities (sūkṣmeṇa shaktirūpeṇa), and out of which they appear again.

The locus of Avidyā, according to Vāchaspati also, is the Jīva. The illusion is psychological for which each individual is himself responsible. Now, a difficulty arises: Avidyā resides in the Jīva, but the Jīva is

[1] anupapadyamānārthaiva hi māyā. upapadyamānārthatve yathārthabhāvān na māyā syāt, Ibid, p. 10. [2] Ibid, p. 10. [3] Ibid, p. 12. [4] jīvānām avidyākaluṣitatvam na brahmaṇaḥ, Ibid, p. 12. [5] jīveṣu . . . avidyaiva hi naisargikī, tasyā āgantukyā vidyayā pravilayaḥ, Ibid, p. 12. [6] Ibid, p. 13. [7] Bhāmatī, Opening verse.

himself a product of Avidyā. Maṇḍana says that Avidyā, being itself inconsistent, its relation with the Jīva is also inconsistent. He also accepts the view of the Avidyopādānabhedavādin that they form a beginningless cycle. Vāchaspati solves the difficulty by maintaining that the Jīva arises due to a false illusion which illusion itself is due to another previous false illusion and so on *ad infinitum*, that psychological ignorance is a beginningless chain of false illusions in which each succeeding illusion is due to its preceding illusion.

An appearance, says Vāchaspati, is an appearance because it is wrongly identified with the self-revealing Consciousness and is thus given a semblance of reality. It is afterwards sublated by right knowledge. Appearances, in order to be appearances, must be confused with Brahman. So Avidyā has Brahman as its object, which it hides and through which it makes its appearances appear. Appearances are neither existent (sat) nor non-existent (asat), neither real nor unreal. They are not existent because they are contradicted afterwards. They are not non-existent like the horns of a hare because they appear, they are expressed, they are experienced as real. They are not real because they are made of Avidyā. They are not unreal because they have Brahman, with which they are confused, as their underlying ground. When Brahman is realized they are set aside because their very existence is due to their being confused with Brahman.

For *Sureshvara*, unlike Maṇḍana and Vāchaspati, Avidyā is based, not on the individual Jīva, but on Brahman itself. Brahman is the locus as well as the object of Avidyā. It is the Pure Self or the Brahman itself which through Avidyā appears as this world. Avidyā is beginningless error (bhrāntishchirantanī). It is the root-cause of saṁsāra and is sublated by knowledge.[1] It is indescribable as it is neither real nor unreal. It is an inconsistent category, a self-contradictory principle. Had it been consistent, it would not have been Avidyā at all. It is based on Brahman and yet at the same time it is a baseless illusion opposed to all reason and cannot stand a logical scrutiny even as darkness cannot stand the Sun.[2] Nothing can surpass the inconsistency and shamelessness of Avidyā; it despises the logical reality as well as the ontological Absolute and yet it exists as the Brahman itself![3]

Padmapāda, Prakāshātmā and Sarvajñātmā also believe that Brahman itself is the locus as well as the object of Avidyā. Avidyā, says *Padmapādā*, is a beginningless (anādi) material (jaḍātmikā) power (shakti). Its function is to obstruct the self-revealing nature of Brahman. It is the canvas on which are painted Ignorance, Actions and Past Impressions —a complex which produces the individual Jīvas.[4] Brahman reflected

[1] Naiṣkarmyasiddhi, II, 103. [2] seyam bhrāntir nirālambā sarvanyāyavirodhinī. sahate na vichāram sā tamo yad vad divākaram, Ibid, III, 66. [3] Ibid, III, 111. [4] Ibid, p. 20.

in Avidyā is the Jīva (pratibimbavāda). The Jīva is a complex (granthi) of Brahman or Ātman and Avidyā, just as a 'red crystal' is a combination of the really white crystal and the reflection in it of the red flower. This ego-complex is the main pillar of this world-theatre.[1]

Avidyā is also called Adhyāsa or superimposition. It is the appearance of 'this' (atadrūpa) as 'that' (tadrūpa). It is the appearance of a thing (this) as that thing (that) which in fact it is not (atadrūpe tadrūpāvabhāsaḥ). This, verily, is false (mithyā). Padmapāda distinguishes between the two meanings of falsehood. It may mean, firstly, simple negation (apahnavavachana), and secondly, something indescribable (anirvachanīyatāvachana).[2] Avidyā is not a simple negation; it is something which cannot be described either as real or as unreal. It is an inconsistent category. There is nothing impossible for Māyā. It is expert in making even the impossible appear as possible.[3]

Prakāshātmā elaborates these ideas and proves that Avidyā is something positive (bhāvarūpā). Padmapāda says that Brahman associated with Māyā is the cause of this world-appearance. Prakāshātmā points out three possible alternatives: (1) Both Brahman and Māyā, like two twisted threads of a rope, are the joint cause of this world; (2) Brahman having Māyā as its power is the cause; and (3) Brahman having Māyā supported on it is the cause. But in all these alternatives it is the Brahman which is the cause since Māyā is regarded as dependent on it.[4]

Sarvajñātma Muni also holds that Brahman is the locus and the object of Avidyā. Avidyā, resting on Brahman and obscuring its real nature, gives rise to threefold appearances; God (Īshvara), Soul (jiva) and Nature (jagat). All the three are ultimately unreal because Avidyā has no independent status. When Brahman is associated with Avidyā, there are two false entities—(1) Avidyā, and (2) Brahman associated with Avidyā. Reality is the Pure Brahman, the true ground (adhiṣṭhāna) which underlies all appearances. Brahman associated with Avidyā is only a false Ādhāra. Sarvajñātma Muni holds that illusion is not psychological but transcendental. Avidyā resides neither in the individual Jīva (which is itself a product of Avidyā) nor in the Pure Brahman (which in fact Avidyā cannot touch), but in Brahman as it reveals itself as the individual Jīvas (pratyak-chit).[5]

Vimuktātmā says that Avidyā or Māyā is neither identical with nor different from nor both identical with and different from Brahman. If it is to be something substantial or real (vastu) it must fall within one of these alternatives. But it falls within neither. Hence it is not real. But it is not absolutely unreal (avastu) too, for it is expressed and experienced in ordinary life. Hence, the only conclusion to which we are drawn is

[1] Ibid, p. 35. [2] mithyāshabdo dvyartho'panhava-vachano'nirvachanīyatāvachanashcha, Ibid, p. 4. [3] na hi māyāyām asambhāvanīyam nāma. asambhāvanīyāvabhāsachaturā hi sā, Ibid, p. 23. [4] Pañchapādikā-Vivaraṇa, p. 212. [5] Saṅkṣepa-Shārīraka, II, 211.

that it is indescribable (anircachanīya). But it is indescribable, stresses Vimuktātmā, only in the sense that it cannot be described either as real or as unreal, and not in the sense that nothing whatsoever can be said about it.[1]

Thus Māyā is regarded by him as ignorance, as positive, as power, as indescribable and as the material cause of all world-appearances.[2] Though indescribable, it can be destroyed by knowledge, since by its very nature it is such that it cannot resist the stroke of knowledge.[3] To stop at the world-appearance is to confess philosophical impotence. Avidyā is not real, for the real is only the Brahman. Avidyā is not unreal, for it is experienced as real. This indescribable nature of Avidyā makes it an inconsistent category. But this Sadasadvilakṣaṇatva or Anirvachanīyatva or Durnirūpatva or Durghaṭatva of Avidyā is not its defect but its glory, for had Avidyā been not such, it would not have been Avidyā at all.[4]

Avidyā, for *Shrīharṣa* also, is ignorance, is positive, is material, and is indescribable as it is neither real nor unreal. It is therefore false.

Avidyā or Ajñāna, says *Chitsukha*, is beginningless and positive and is destroyed by knowledge.[5] Ignorance is in fact neither positive nor negative, yet it is called positive to emphasize the fact that it is not merely negative.[6] An example illustrating the positive character of ignorance is: 'I do not know whether what you say is true'. Here what is said is known but it is not known whether it is true. Another example is when one, after deep sleep, gets up and says: 'I slept happily; I knew nothing.' This is a positive experience of ignorance in deep sleep.[7] The knowers of Vedānta have declared that all things are the objects of the self-revealing Consciousness either as known or as unknown.[8]

An objection is raised by Prabhākara that the false cannot be presented in experience. Experience is always of the true and error is due, not to misapprehension, but to non-apprehension of difference. Refuting this Akhyāti view, Chitsukha remarks that as long as error lasts, the object is not remembered but actually presented to consciousness. The presentation of the false, therefore, is a fact of experience. The presented silver (in the case of shell-silver) cannot be called absolutely non-existent like the hare's horn as that cannot be presented even in illusion or error. Its practical reality is admitted. Nor can it be called existent for it is contradicted afterwards. It is therefore indefinable or indescribable. It is exactly this character of being indescribable either as existent or as non-existent, says Chitsukha, that constitutes the falsity

[1] tena sadasattvābhyām anirvachanīyā, na punar avāchyā, Iṣṭa-siddhi, p. 35. [2] Ibid, p. 69. [3] Ibid, VIII, 4 and 18. [4] durghaṭatvaṃ avidyāyā bhūṣaṇam na tu dūṣaṇam, Ibid, I, 140. [5] anādi bhāvarūpam yad vijñānena vilīyate. tad ajñānam iti prājñā lakṣaṇam samprachakṣate. anāditve sati bhāvarūpam vijñānanirasyam ajñānam, Tattva-pradīpika, p. 57. [6] bhāvābhāvavilakṣaṇasya ajñānasya abhāvavilakṣaṇamātreṇa bhāvatvopachārāt, Ibid. [7] Ibid, pp. 58-59. [8] Ibid, p. 60.

of all world-experiences. Udayana's criticism that 'indefinability' means the inability to define or describe, i.e. the silence of the ignorant (niruktiviraha) misses the mark for the term 'indefinable' or 'indescribable' in Vedānta means that which cannot be described either as real or as unreal.[1]

Similarly *Ānandajñāna* also says that indescribability is not inability to describe; its essence lies in proving that all possible ways in which the opponent wants to describe a thing are untenable.[2]

Avidyā, for *Vidyāraṇya* too, is a beginningless power which is neither real nor unreal. It cannot stand dialectical scrutiny. The essential nature of Avidyā consists in this that it cannot be described in any way by the finite intellect and it is therefore false for it cannot bear logical examination.[3] When true knowledge dawns, Avidyā with all its world-products is realized as something which never was, never is and never shall be *real*.[4] This indefinability is not a defect but a merit of Avidyā.[5] Avidyā is the same as Māyā for both are indefinable.[6]

III

ĀTMAN OR BRAHMAN

ĀTMAN or Brahman is the only reality. It is the locus and the object of Avidyā. It is the ground underlying all world-appearances. Diversity, says *Maṇḍana*, is rooted in unity and not *vice versa*. One sees many reflections of the Moon in many moving ripples of water. But the Moon does not become many on account of its reflections in various waves. It is absurd to believe that so many reflected 'Moons' *appear* as one Moon. Similarly it is far more reasonable to believe that one Brahman on account of its special potency appears as the world of diverse phenomenal objects than to believe that diverse phenomenal objects on account of false notion of similarity appear as if they are one. All difference is, therefore, grounded in the supreme Brahman.[7]

Reality, says *Sureshvara*, is one and so diversity cannot be ultimate. The unqualified non-dual Absolute which transcends human thought is described in innnumerable inadequate ways by different people just as in the famous parable of the 'Blind Men and the Elephant', the same elephant was described in various inadequate ways by the blind men.[8] Everything else may change, everything else may be destroyed, everything else may be momentary except the Self because the very conceptions of change, destruction and momentariness presuppose it.[9]

[1] pratyekam sadasattvābhyām vichārapadavīm na yat. gāhate tad anirvāchyam āhur Vedāntavedinaḥ, Ibid, p. 79. [2] yena yena prakāreṇa paro nirvaktum ichchhati. tena tenātmanā'yogas tad anirvāchyatā matā, Tarka-Saṅgraha, p. 136. [3] Bṛ-Vārtika-sāra, Introduction, Adhikāriparikṣā, 115, 117. [4] Ibid, 114. [5] Vivaraṇaprameyasaṅgraha. p. 175. [6] Ibid, p. 133. [7] Brahmasiddhi, II, 32. [8] Naiṣkarmyasiddhi, II, 93. [9] Ibid, II, 78.

This Self is the judge presupposing whose existence and to whom addressing their case, philosophers, like lawyers, propelled by heated and head-aching arguments, feverishly fight and delude each other.[1]

Reality, according to *Vāchaspati*, is the Pure Self (svaprakāshā chit) which is Pure Consciousness or the self-luminous immediate self-revelation which can never be contradicted. It is the underlying ground of all phenomena. Māyā or Avidyā may be regarded as the pivot of Advaita provided we do not forget that the Reality which underlies the world-appearance is Brahman. The thesis which Vimuktātmā has proved is not māyā, but Brahman as it underlies Māyā.[2]

Padmapāda says that the nature of the self is pure self-revealing Consciousness which, when appearing with and manifesting the objects is called experience or Anubhava, and when shining forth by itself is called the Ātman.[3] *Prakāshātmā* also maintains that Consciousness is self-revealing and that its manifestation is due to no other cause.[4]

Chitsukha gives a full exposition of the Self. He takes many definitions of self-revelation (svaprakāsha) and rejects them after dialectical examination. He then offers his own definition. Self-revelation, says Chitsukha, may be defined as that which is entitled to be called immediate even though it cannot be known as an object of knowledge.[5] Desires, feelings, will, emotions and other subjective states are not cognized in the same way in which external objects are. Though they appear to be called immediate, they have really no right to be called immediate for they are only unreal impositions on the self-revealing Consciousness. External objects, on the other hand, though they are found to be unreal and therefore non-immediate when the self is realized, yet so far as the phenomenal existence is concerned, have every right to be called immediate; but they are known as objects of knowledge. It is only the self which is immediate and yet not an object of knowledge. Our definition, therefore, has the merit, says Chitsukha, of distinguishing self-revelation from the mental states on the one hand and from the external objects on the other.[6]

Moreover, besides being immediate, self-revelation can also be inferred. The inference is as follows:—

> Immediate Experience is Self-revealing, because it is immediate;
> That which is not immediate cannot be self-revealing, as for example, a pot.[7]

The main argument in favour of self-revelation is that if the existence of the ultimate self-revealing Consciousness is not admitted, infinite

[1] Ibid, II, 59. [2] ato māyātmaiko mayeṣṭaḥ siddhaḥ, Iṣṭasiddhi, p. 347. [3] Pañchapādika, 19. [4] Pañchapādikā-Vivaraṇa, p. 52. [5] Tattvapradīpikā, p. 9. [6] Ibid, pp. 9-11. [7] anubhūtiḥ svayaṁprakāshā, anubhūtitvāt, yan naivam tan naivam yathā ghaṭaḥ ityanumānam, Ibid, p. 11.

regress would yawn before us. Again, the fact of experience itself proves that immediate experience is self-revealing because none can doubt his own experience or can stand in need of confirming or corroborating it. Everything else may be doubted, everything else may require proof, but not the self-revealing Consciousness because even the notions of doubt and proof presuppose it.[1]

This self-revealing Consciousness is not the consciousness of consciousness or awareness of awareness like the Anuvyavasāya of the Naiyāyika or the Jñātatā of the Mīmāṁsaka, for this conception is not tenable. When one says: 'I know that I know the pot,' what happens is that the first awareness has already ceased when the second awareness begins and so the former awareness cannot be directly cognized by the subsequent awareness. So when one knows that one knows the pot, it is only the cognized object, the pot, that is known, not the knowledge.[2]

The self-revealing Consciousness is the Self itself for the Self is of the nature of self-revealing Consciousness (ātmā samvidrūpaḥ). Except that of identity there can be no relation between Consciousness and Self.[3] When the Shruti says that the sight of the seer is never destroyed, it only stresses that knowledge is eternal; it does not in fact declare any connection between the sight and the seer or the knowledge and the knower. It says so on account of the convention or usage of language, like the phrase 'the head of Rāhu' even when there is no difference between Rāhu and the head.[4]

IV

DIALECTICAL ARGUMENTS FOR THE ULTIMATE UNREALITY OF DIFFERENCE

BRAHMAN according to *Maṇḍana*, is the only reality and it does not tolerate difference. Absolutism alone can explain all philosophical concepts satisfactorily. Ultimately the subject-object duality must be transcended. If it were real, then the gulf between the two could never be bridged over and the two could never be related. The absolutely pure Self (draṣṭā) which knows no change can never be really related to the changing objects (dṛshya).[5]

Maṇḍana tries to refute difference by means of dialectical arguments. In fact, he says, we do not perceive any 'difference'. Three alternatives are possible regarding perception: (1) perception may manifest a positive object; (2) it may distinguish an object from other objects; and (3) it may manifest a positive object and may also distinguish it from other objects. In the third alternative again there are three possibilities: (a) manifestation of a positive object and its distinction from other

[1] Ibid, p. 16. [2] Ibid, p. 18. [3] jñānātmanoḥ sambandhasyaivābhāvāt, Ibid p. 22. [4] Ibid. [5] chiteḥ shuddhatvāt, apariṇāmāt, apratisaṅkramāt cha, Brahmasiddhi: pp. 7-8.

objects may be simultaneous; (b) first there may be positive manifestation and then negative distinction; and (c) first there may be negative distinction and then positive manifestation.[1]

Now, in the first alternative where only a positive object is manifested, no 'difference' is perceived. The second alternative is untenable because pure negation is an impossibility. Perception always manifests some positive object; it does not negate anything. Hence perception cannot reveal mere difference.[2] Possibilities (a) and (c) of the third alternative are untenable, for positive manifestation and negative distinction can be neither simultaneous nor can there be first negative distinction without positive manifestation. Negation is necessarily rooted in affirmation. Difference or distinction is a relation between two positive objects which it presupposes. Even the negation of a nonentity like the sky-lotus is only a denial of the false relation between two positive entities —the sky and the lotus. Possibility (b) of the third alternative is also untenable, for perception is one unique process and there cannot be two or more moments in it.[3]

There can be four possible conceptions, says Maṇḍana, regarding unity and diversity:

(1) Either we should say like Mīmāṁsaka *Saṁsargavādins* that both unity and diversity are separately real;
(2) Or we should say like Bhartṛprapañcha and the Jaina *Anekāntavādins* that reality is both unity and diversity;
(3) Or we should say like the Buddhist (Svatantra-vijñānavādin) *Ātyantikabhedavādins* that only diversity is real and that unity is an appearance;
(4) Or we should say like the Vedāntin *Abhedavādins* that only unity is real and that diversity is an appearance.[4]

Maṇḍana vehemently criticizes the first three views showing their hollowness and upholds the fourth view.

Against the first view he remarks that things cannot be twofold in their nature, that it is impossible to imagine logically that realities can be two or more.

Against the second view he urges that it is absurd to imagine that the same thing can be both unity as well as diversity. Admitting and negating the same thing in the same breath, the theory of Probability lands in monstrous philosophical contradictions.

The third view is that of the *Svatantra-Vijñānavādins*. They maintain that objects by their very nature are different from one another and that therefore when an object is perceived its difference from other objects is also perceived simultaneously by that very act. Maṇḍana

[1] Ibid, p. 44. [2] Ibid, p. 39, [3] Ibid, pp. 39-45. [4] Ibid, p. 60.

replies that if difference be the very nature of things, then all things would be of the nature of difference and thus there would be no difference among them at all. Again, difference being 'formless', the objects themselves would be 'formless'. Again, difference is of the nature of negation and therefore objects themselves would be of the nature of negation. Again, difference being dual or plural, no object would be regarded as a single object because the same thing cannot be both one and many.[1]

The Buddhist replies that an object is regarded as essentially of the nature of difference only in relation to other objects and not in relation to itself. Maṇḍana rejoins that objects are produced from their own causes and they do not, for their existence, stand in need of a relation to other objects. Relation is a mental operation. It is subjective. It cannot, therefore, be called the essential nature of things which are objective.[2]

The Buddhist tries to prove the difference among objects by his theory of efficient causation. But Maṇḍana points out that he cannot do so. The same fire, for example may 'burn' and at another time may 'cook', and still at another time may simply 'shed light'. The difference between the burning, cooking and illuminating activities of the same fire does not prove that they are really 'three' different fires. It only proves that differences are unreal because they are grounded in the same fire.[3] Similarly the so-called diversity of the phenomenal world is rooted in the supreme Brahman. The Buddhist objects that things are different from one another because they have got different potencies or powers. If there were only unity and no diversity then there would have been simultaneous production and destruction of all things and then milk would have produced oil and oil-seeds curd. Maṇḍana replies that the so-called different potencies or powers are in fact only different qualities of the same thing like the burning, cooking and illuminating qualities of the same fire. Difference in qualities does not imply difference in substance. Just as the same fire has diverse activities of burning, cooking and illuminating, similarly it is the extraordinary potency of the one supreme Brahman, a potency which is beyond human thought, that enables the Brahman to appear as this diverse phenomenal world.[4] Differences, therefore, are purely imaginary.

Maṇḍana supports the fourth view which advocates that unity alone is real while diversity is only an appearance. The moon does not become 'many moons' on account of being reflected in various waves.[5] Difference is an appearance and is grounded in Brahman and not *vice versa*.

Vimuktātmā also observes that difference is unreal and is rooted in

[1] bhedash chet vastunaḥ svabhāvaḥ, naikam kiñchana vastu syāt, Ibid, pp. 47-48.
[2] Ibid, p. 48. [3] Ibid, p. 50. [4] Ibid, pp. 54-55. [5] Ibid, p. 72.

the Brahman. He says that the relation between the perceiver (dṛk) and the perceived (dṛshya) or between the conscious subject and the external objects is indescribable and therefore false. The subject and the object are neither different nor identical nor both.

The self and the world are not different because difference is possible between two perceived entities and the self is never perceived.[1] Again, difference is not of the nature (svarūpa) of the differing entities; for had it been so, difference would not have been dependent on a reference to another. Nor is difference a characteristic (dharma) different from the differing entities; for in that case this difference, in order to be known, would require another difference and the latter yet another and so on *ad infinitum.* Again, the perceiving Self, being self-luminous, is always present and can never be negated. So neither negation nor difference is possible. The perceiving Self is of the nature of perception hence its non-perception is impossible. Negation is of the nature of non-perception. Hence negation is impossible. And difference is of the nature of negation. So difference too is impossible.[2]

The perceiving Self and the perceived world are also *not identical:* for if they were so, the perceiver would be characterized by all the limitations and differences of the perceived world. Simultaneous perception (sahopalambha) cannot prove their identity, for they are perceived as two and not one.[3] Moreover, the perceiver is self-luminous and is never cognized as an object, while the perceived is never self-revealing is always cognized as an object and cannot be experienced independently of the perceiver. Again, if they were identical, all ordinary experiences and practices of this world would come to a standstill. So the Self which is pure Consciousness can never be identified with the perceived world.[4]

And the Self and the world, again, cannot be regarded as *both identical* and *different*; for the Bhedābheda view is self-contradictory. Identity and difference are opposed like light and darkness.

So the manifold world-appearance is neither different from nor identical with nor both different from and identical with the Pure Self.[5] The world therefore is false and with it all its 'difference' is also false.

Shrīharṣa also asserts that neither perception nor inference can contradict the ultimate fact of non-duality as taught in the Upaniṣads. Difference is unreal. It cannot be the essential nature of things that differ (svarūpabheda), because had it been that it would have been identical with the differing things themselves. Again, difference cannot be mutual negation (anyonyābhāva) like that pot is the negation of cloth and cloth is the negation of pot, because if the identity of the pot and the cloth were absolutely unreal, then the negation of such identity would also be absolutely meaningless. Again, difference cannot be

[1] Iṣṭasiddhi, p. 2. [2] Ibid, pp. 3-10. [3] Ibid, pp. 13-14. [4] Ibid, p. 14. [5] na bhinnaḥ, nāpyabhinnaḥ, nāpi bhinnābhinnaḥ anubhūteḥ prapañchaḥ, Ibid, p. 24.

regarded as the possession of opposite characteristics (vaidharmya), because were it so then these opposite characteristics would require further opposite characteristics to distinguish them from one another and so on *ad infinitum*. Difference, therefore, is unreal. It is a product of Avidyā. From the empirical viewpoint it is valid because we perceive it. We do not say, says Shrīharṣa, that difference is absolutely unreal. We deny only its ultimate reality.[1] The empirical validity of difference, however, cannot contradict the ultimate reality of Advaita, for the two are on two different levels. Difference is due to Avidyā and so it is ultimately unreal. To contradict Advaita we require an ultimately real difference and such difference is an impossibility.[2] The reality of Advaita cannot be set aside even by hundreds of arguments.[3] To reject Advaita is to throw away the most precious wish-fulfilling jewel fortunately procured, into the deep sea.[4]

Madhusūdana Sarasvatī in his Advaita-siddhi, which he wrote to prove the truth of non-dualism and to reject the views of the opponents,[5] ruthlessly criticizes the Dvaitins and refutes all their arguments in favour of difference. Vyāsatīrtha, the author of Nyāyāmṛta, is his main target.

V

FURTHER DIALECTICAL EXPOSITION OF THE ULTIMATE UNREALITY OF THE WORLD

Shrīharṣa and *Chitsukha* undertake a thorough inquiry into the nature of the categories and concepts of the intellect and point out their utter dialectical hollowness. Their main polemic is against Nyāya. The Naiyāyikas and the Mīmāṁsakas have given various definitions of right knowledge (pramā), of the means of right knowledge (pramāṇa) such as perception, inference etc., of the various categories of experience (padārtha) such as substance, qualities etc., and of the concepts involved in these categories. Shrīharṣa and Chitsukha take all these definitions one by one, mercilessly criticize them and with their irresistible dialectic tear them into pieces pointing out that they are all 'baseless fabrics of a vision that leaves nothing behind'.

All that is known (prameya) has a defined real existence, says the Naiyāyika. All that is known is indefinable and therefore unreal, rejoin Shrīharṣa and Chitsukha. Reality is Pure Consciousness which can be directly realized but cannot be known by discursive intellect. It is beyond the four categories of understanding. Like the *Chatuṣkoṭivinirmukta* of the Shūnyavādins, Shrīharṣa calls it as 'the Fifth Only', the *Pañchamakoṭimātra*.[6] Intellect which works with its concepts and

[1] Khaṇḍana-Khaṇḍa-Khādya, p. 56. [2] advaitam hi pāramārthikam idam pāramārthikena bhedena bādhyeta, na tu avidyāvidyamānena, Ibid p. 58. [3] Ibid, 59. [4] Ibid, p. 60. [5] Advaitasiddhi, 4. [6] Naiṣadha-Charita, XIII, 36.

categories is necessarily relational. Therefore it can give us only a relative world. The entire world together with all its experiences is necessarily phenomenal. It is a semblance of reality. It is a workable reality. Its reality is based on usage, custom and convention. The moment we examine this so-called real world and its experiences dialectically, they all give way. And intellect too, because it itself arises with this world, gives way. The world is found to be indefinable. It is neither real nor unreal nor both. Hence the inevitable conclusion is that it is indescribable. And because it is indescribable it is false. It is based on Avidyā and is only an appearance. The criticisms offered by Shriharṣa and Chitsukha are mostly destructive. They have undermined not only the particular definitions of Nyāya but also the very concept of definition which has been shown as fraught with inherent contradictions.

Chitsukha who had commented on the Khaṇḍana of Shrīharṣa and who has also written an independent work Tattvapradīpikā, popularly known as Chitsukhī, has fulfilled to a great extent the work left unaccomplished by Shrīharṣa. Shrīharṣa tried to show that all the concepts and the categories of the intellect were indefinable as they were fraught with inherent contradictions. But in practice he mainly criticized and refuted only the particular definitions of the Nyāya writers. Udayana formed the main target of his attack. He did not also develop his interpretations of the concepts of the Advaita Vedānta. Chitsukha gives us an accurate analysis and an elaborate interpretation of the main concepts of the Advaita. Possessing almost the same dialectical genius as that of Shrīharṣa, Chitsukha does not restrict himself to refuting only the definitions of the various categories given by the Naiyāyikas, but often refutes other definitions and also the concepts underlying these definitions. In his refutation of the Nyāya categories, he mostly follows Shrīharṣa, though he sometimes gives new arguments also. Shrīharṣa's main purpose is to show that the categories are indefinable and therefore unreal. Chitsukha's main purpose is to show that though they are mere appearances, they are appearances of the Real.

Shrīharṣa's work is mainly polemical. Like the Shūnyavādins, he has no thesis of his own to prove. He has no definitions to offer. How can he when he says that all definitions are false and that this entire world together with all its experiences is indescribable? Although the criticisms of Shrīharṣa are directed mainly against the particular definitions of the Naiyāyikas and others, they can be used with equal force against all views and against all definitions of all systems. Shrīharṣa himself asks us to apply his criticisms against other definitions and other systems.[1] He goes even to the extent of assuring us that people, by simply mugging up his arguments like a parrot, can conquer all persons in philosophical discussions.[2]

[1] Khaṇḍana, p. 419. [2] Ibid, p. 2.

Shrīharṣa has written a long introduction, called the Bhūmikā to his work Khaṇḍana. This introduction gives us an excellent summary of his philosophy. Formal verbalism which often mars the main body of the work is conspicuous by its absence here. Realization of truth (tattva-nirṇaya) and victory over the opponent (vādi-vijaya), says Shrīharṣa, are the two aims of philosophical discussion (shāstrārtha). In the Bhūmikā the former aim predominates. The main defect which we find in the main body of the work is formal verbalism. Shrīharṣa often criticizes the language of the definitions rather than their thought. There is no doubt that had the main body of the Khaṇḍana been written in the same spirit in which its Bhūmikā is written the work would have been simply matchless. Perhaps Shrīharṣa may be excused if we remember that in his time, challenging discussions (digvijaya) were the fashion of the day. But all the same Dr. S. N. Dasgupta is right in remarking: 'If these criticisms had mainly been directed towards the defects of Nyāya thought, later writers would not have been forced to take the course of developing verbal expressions (in order to avoid the criticisms of Shrīharṣa) at the expense of philosophical profundity and acuteness. Shrīharṣa may therefore be said to be the first great writer who is responsible indirectly for the growth of verbalism in later Nyāya thought'.[1]

Shrīharṣa says that this world with all its manifold phenomena cannot be called existent because dialectical reasoning proves that it is not ultimately real; and it cannot be called non-existent too because then the practical utility of all world-experiences would collapse. The world-appearances therefore are indescribable either as real or as unreal. Hence they are false.

Here the opponent says: If you are unable to describe and define the world you should go to some learned teachers and learn how to describe and define the world-experiences. Shrīharṣa replies: This contemptuous outburst of the opponent would have been valid only if we had said that a particular person or persons was or were unable to define this world. Our point, which the opponent has unfortunately missed, is that we maintain that the world together with all its experiences is by its very nature such that it cannot be described either as existent or as non-existent. Indefinability is the very nature of all world-experiences. All that can be known by the intellect is necessarily indefinable. Our worthy opponent who seems to be proud of his ability to define the world should know that he is grossly mistaken, because even 'description' or 'definition', being a thing which is known, is by its very nature ultimately indescribable and indefinable.[2]

[1] History of Indian Philosophy, Vol. II, p. 146. [2] yadapi nirvaktumasāmarthye gurava upāsyantām yebhyo niruktayaḥ shikṣyanta ityupālambhavachanam tat tadā shobheta yadi meyasvabhāvānugāminīyam anirvachanīyateti na brūyuḥ vaktṛdoṣād iti cha vadeyuh, Khaṇḍana, pp. 31-32.

The main point which Shrīharṣa wants to press is that the world-experiences, being mere appearances, are neither real nor unreal and are therefore false, that our intellect which necessarily functions with the help of its concepts and categories is beset with inherent contradictions and so cannot give us reality, and that reality which is Pure Consciousness is self-luminous and therefore self-proved and is to be directly realized through Pure Experience. Neither the Absolute nor the appearances can be described. The Absolute needs no descriptions because it is self-proved. All the categories of the intellect fail to grasp it in its fulness. To describe it is as useless is to throw the light of a candle over the Sun. Appearances cannot be described because they are neither real nor unreal nor both. And even description itself proceeds from finite thought and is therefore self-contradictory. All arguments as such, says Shrīharṣa agreeing with Chandrakīrti, are self-contradictory. To prove the validity of arguments, says Shrīharṣa like Nāgārjuna and Chandrakīrti, we shall require some Pramāṇas and these Pramāṇas in order to be valid will stand in need of further Pramāṇas and so on *ad infinitum*.

Here the opponent puts a formidable objection to Shrīharṣa. He says that if Shrīharṣa denies the validity of all arguments as such, then he has no right to utter a word. He cannot logically do so because the argument of Shrīharṣa that all arguments are invalid, being itself an argument, is invalid. It is impossible for thought to condemn itself. How can Shrīharṣa logically say that the world is indefinable and that reality is also indescribable when in doing so he is himself *defining* the world and *describing* reality as indefinable and indescribable?[1]

Shrīharṣa, like Chandrakīrti, faces this objection bravely. He replies that he is not denying the validity of logic or intellect from the empirical standpoint. It is simply impossible to do so. In the phenomenal world intellect undoubtedly reigns supreme.[2] None can question its authority here. But intellect itself points to its own limitations and finally merges in immediate experience. The highest philosophy is the philosophy of Silence. Reality can only be realized directly. Ultimately, Pure Consciousness itself shines forth. Description is possible on the phenomenal level only. Even the distinction between the empirical and the ultimate points of view is a distinction made by intellect itself. Shrīharṣa, like Chandrakīrti, frankly admits that the moment we say that Reality is or appearances are indescribable, we have, from the ultimate standpoint, missed the mark because even when we say that Reality or the world is indescribable we are in fact describing it and that therefore even this argument, being an argument, is unreal.[3] The fact is that Advaita cannot ultimately be discussed. It is only to be realized. Intellect has to

[1] tattve dvitrichatuṣkoṭivyudāsena yathāyatham. niruchyamāne nirlajjair anirvāchyatvam uchyate, Nyāyasiddhāñjana, p. 93. [2] vyāvahārikīm pramāṇādisattām ādaya vichārārambhaḥ, Khaṇḍana, p. 10. [3] yo hi sarvam anirvachanīyasadasattvam brūte sa katham anirvachanīyatāsattvavyavasthitau paryanuyujyeta, Ibid pp. 32-33.

be transformed into Spiritual Experience. How can he who has become one with the Absolute take recourse to arguments? How can he who has transcended intellect again descend to its level? Shrīharṣa, therefore, as a Vedāntin, like the Shūnyavādin, ultimately has no thesis to prove, no argument to offer, no contention to support. He is only interested in refuting the arguments of his opponent and that too from the point of view of the opponent himself. Descending on the phenomenal level, on the level of the opponent, on the level where alone arguments are possible, Shrīharṣa shows that (the opponent's) descriptions are hollow, his definitions are defective and his arguments are invalid. It is from this point of view that Shrīharṣa says that the world cannot be described either as existent or as non-existent and that therefore it is false. If the opponent accepts this argument, he is giving up his position and embracing Advaita. If, on the other hand, the opponent challenges this argument, he is challenging the validity of his own logic and is thereby accepting Advaita. In either case therefore Advaita becomes established. Advaita can be refuted only if the opponent is successful in defending his position and this he cannot do. Hence it is proved that the entire phenomenal world is indefinable and therefore false and that Brahman alone which is Pure Consciousness is the ultimate Reality.[1] Having this one Brahman-weapon with him, the Advaitin can never be defeated in the arena of philosophical fight.[2]

Chitsukha also observes that the world, when dialectically examined, is found to be neither real nor unreal. It can be proved neither by itself nor by anything else. Therefore the only conclusion to which we are drawn is that it is superimposed on the self and is ultimately unreal. Thus the falsity of the world is a proved fact.[3]

Another argument is that a whole, in order to be called existent, must exist in its parts which compose it; but it is clear that simply because it is a whole it cannot exist in the parts. And if it does not exist even in the parts, it cannot exist anywhere else. Hence it is false. Chitsukha's point is that a whole is neither a mere aggregate of its parts nor anything outside them. It is therefore false. And if the whole is false, the parts also must naturally be false. Thus the entire world is false.[4]

Another argument for the falsity of the world is that there can be no relation between the self-revealing Consciousness which is the ultimate knower (dṛk) and the object known (dṛshya). Sense-contact does not produce knowledge, because when we perceive illusory silver in a shell there is no actual sense-contact with silver. Subject-object relation

[1] tataḥ parakīyarītyedam uchyate anirvachanīyatvam vishvasya paryavasyatīti. vastutastu vayam sarvaprapañchasattvāsattvavyavasthāpanavinivṛttāḥ svataḥ-siddhe chidātmani Brahmatattve kevale bharam avalambya charitārthāḥ sukham āsmahe, Ibid, pp. 33-34. Compare with this the arguments of Chandrakīrti on pp. 91-92 Supra. [2] Ibid, p. 47. [3] dṛshyaprapañchasya svataḥ paratashchāsiddher dṛgātmanyadhyastatayaiva siddhir iti siddham mithyātvam, Tattvapradīpikā, p. 32. [4] Ibid., pp. 39-40.

cannot be explained. Knowledge or knower cannot produce any change in the object known. Mental states like will, emotion, feeling etc. cannot change the object, for they are internal. Again, the object cannot be contained in knowledge as a *badara* fruit may be contained in a vessel. Again, the subject-object relation cannot be a vague undefined relation because in that case the subject may as well be called object and the object subject. Again, if that is regarded as an object which induces knowledge, then even the senses, light and other accessories which help the rise of knowledge would become objects. Hence the subject-object relation cannot be satisfactorily explained. So the objective world is false and the self-revealing subject alone is real and it ultimately transcends the subject-object duality. Shrīharṣa also remarks that the subject-object relation is indefinable. If we reduce the subject to the object we land in crude materialism. If we reduce the object to the subject we land in crude subjectivism. The subject, whether it is identical with or different from the object, cannot be related to the object. Nor can the object know the subject for it would be absurd to say that the pot knows the consciousness. Hence the subject-object relation is false.[1]

Chitsukha stresses that though the world is false it is not absolutely unreal like the hare's horn. The world is false only when the Absolute is realized. Till then it is true for all practical purposes. Its workable reality cannot be denied. Chitsukha admits the similarity of the Buddhistic *Samvṛti-satya* with the Vedantic *Vyavahāra-satya* and defends the former against the attacks of Kumārila Bhaṭṭa. Kumārila criticizes phenomenal reality (samvṛti) as follows: Samvṛti is not true. How can it then be regarded as a kind of truth? If it is true, it cannot be Samvṛti; if it is false how can it have any truth? Truth is one and it cannot be divided into empirical truth and absolute truth. Chitsukha's reply is that the above distinction is made by the intellect itself. So ultimately this distinction is unreal. Truth undoubtedly is one. And it is the self-luminous Absolute. So Samvṛti is not true. It is ultimately false. But even an appearance, because it is an appearance of the Real, exists. It is not a hare's horn. Samvṛti is falsity which on account of ignorance is mistaken as truth. But as long as we are in ignorance, we cannot question Samvṛti. On the phenomenal plane, therefore, the workable truth of Samvṛti is established.[2]

[1] Khaṇḍana, p. 341. [2] idamapyapāstam yadāhur Bhattāchāryāḥ'samvṛter na tu satyatvam satyabhedaḥ kuto'nvayam. satyā chet samvṛtiḥ keyam mṛṣā chet satyatā katham, iti. vastuto'satyasyaiva yāvad bādham . . . satyatvena svīkārāt, Tattva-pradīpikā, pp. 42-43.

VI

REFUTATION OF THE DEFINITIONS OF PRAMĀ

WE now pass on to the refutation of the various definitions of the Naiyāyikas and others by *Shrīharṣa* and *Chitsukha.*

They criticize the various definitions of *right cognition* (pramā). The definition that right cognition is the direct apprehension of the real nature of things (tattvānubhūtiḥ pramā) is wrong, because if one guesses the right number of shells hidden in another's fist or makes an inference through fallacious data which inference may accidentally be correct (as when one infers fire on a hill from fog looking like smoke and there may accidentally be fire there), the apprehension may be right but it is not right cognition as it is not produced through valid means.

Another definition that right cognition is that which truly corresponds with its object (yathārthānubhavaḥ pramā) is also wrong, because correspondence can neither be said to be the reality of the object itself as the real nature of an object is indeterminable, nor can it be defined as the similarity of the cognition to the object, for qualities which belong to the object do not belong to the cognition, e.g., when we are aware of two white pots, our cognition of the pots is neither 'two' nor 'white'.

Criticizing Udayana's definition of right cognition as 'proper discernment' (samyakparichchhedaḥ pramā) they remark that if the word 'Samyak' means 'entire' then the definition is useless because it is only an Omniscient being who can perceive all qualities and characteristics of a thing, and if it means the discernment of special 'distinguishing features'; then too the definition is faulty for even in the illusory perception of shell as silver we perceive the distinguishing features of silver in the shell. Moreover, it is impossible to perceive all distinguishing features of a thing.

The Buddhists define right cognition as 'an apprehension which is not incompatible with the object known' (avisamvādyanubhavaḥ pramā). If this definition means that right cognition is that cognition which is cognized by another succeeding cognition as being compatible with its object, then even a wrong cognition, until it is contradicted, should be deemed right. Again, the cognition of a shell as white by a person of good eyesight may be contradicted by the cognition of a person suffering from jaundice as yellow. And to say that contradiction must be by a faultless later cognition is to beg the question, for faultless cognition is right cognition in defining which we are facing these difficulties. Moreover, unless right cognition is defined wrong cognition has no meaning.

The definition of right cognition as cognition having causal efficiency (arthakriyā-kāritva) is not satisfactory because even a wrong cognition may have causal efficiency, e.g. even the wrong cognition of a rope as a snake may cause fear. Similarly Dharmakīrti's definition of right cognition as that cognition which enables one to attain the object (artha-prāpakatva) is wrong because it cannot be determined as to which object can be attained and which cannot.

Again, right cognition cannot be defined as uncontradicted cognition (abādhitānubhūtiḥ pramā). Even the cognition of shell as silver, according to this definition, should be right cognition since as long as the error lasts it is not contradicted. If it urged that right cognition is that cognition which cannot be contradicted at any time, then we cannot call any cognition right because it is not possible to assert with certainty that a particular cognition will never be contradicted at any time. Hence it is impossible to define right cognition.

Pramāṇa is generally defined as an instrument of right cognition (pramākaraṇam pramāṇam). But when right cognition itself cannot be defined, it is impossible to define its instrument.

VII

REFUTATION OF THE CATEGORIES OF NYĀYA-VAISHEṢIKA

The categories of Nyāya-Vaisheṣika are also criticized and refuted. *Being* (sattā) cannot be defined as that which exists, for even non-being exists. Again, being cannot be defined as that which is not a negation of anything, for being is a negation of non-being. Pure being is as impossible as pure nothing. Again, being cannot be called a universal in which all particular existent things inhere because each existent thing is a unique individual in itself. Hence being cannot be defined. Similarly non-being too cannot be defined. Both are relative and therefore unreal.

Substance (dravya) cannot be defined as the support (āshraya) of qualities. If 'support' means 'possession', then even some qualities possess other qualities, e.g. we speak of 'two colours', 'three colours', 'white colour', 'black colour' etc. If 'support' means 'subsistence', then qualities subsist in the universal 'quality'. Substance and qualities are both relative. We do not perceive any *substance* over and above *qualities*, and yet qualities themselves cannot be called substance. Both are relative and so unreal. *Relation* too is unreal. Relation cannot relate itself to the two terms, for however well-trained a juggler may be, he cannot dance on his own shoulders.[1] It will require another relation to relate itself and so on *ad infinitum*. *Universals* are also unreal. They are based on convention and convenience. A universal can be neither

[1] Khaṇḍana, p. 330.

perceived nor inferred. We see only individual cows. How can the 'universal cow' subsist in individual cows or jump over a new cow when it is born or pass away from an old cow when it dies? Again, how can the universal and the particular of that class be related? This relation can be neither that of conjunction nor that of inherence nor that of identity. And a fourth relation is impossible.

These criticisms of the Nyāya categories offered by Shrīharṣa and Chitsukha are similar to those given by Dharmakīrti, Shāntarakṣita and Kamalashīla.

Causality also, remark Shrīharṣa and Chitsukha, is not possible. A cause cannot be defined as mere antecedence (pūrvakālabhāvitva), for then even the donkey of a potter on which he brought the clay would become the cause of the pot. And causal operation itself, being the immediate antecedence, will be the cause. And if causal operation is viewed as cause then even the cause of the cause will become the cause. Again, if this antecedence is qualified with the phrase 'invariable' meaning that the cause is invariably present when the effect is present and absent when the effect is absent, the difficulty would not be solved, for the donkey may invariably be present when the potter is making the pot and absent when the potter is not busy with his work. Again, if another qualification 'unconditional' (ananyathāsiddha) is also added, then even the donkey which may be, and space etc. which are, present would have to be regarded as the cause of the pot. Then, symptoms of a disease would also be the cause of the disease because they are unconditionally and invariably present before the disease. Again, the maxim of invariable antecedence is invalidated by plurality of causes. Fire may be produced in different ways. Again, if accessories (sahakāri) are admitted, then either they are identical with the cause, or if they are different, they cannot be related to the cause. Hence the conception of causality is ultimately false.

The main aim of Shrīharṣa and Chitsukha is to show that intellect is essentially discursive or relational and that therefore it is beset with inherent contradictions. The world with all its manifold phenomena is neither real nor unreal nor both. Hence it is indefinable and therefore false. The fault is with the intellect itself. All its concepts and categories are found to be unreal. It must proceed with the subject-object duality and this duality is unreal, for the subject and the object can be neither identical nor different nor both. Reality is Pure Consciousness which is the self-revealing Self. Intellect is only a product of Avidyā. The moment Avidyā is destroyed by right knowledge of non-duality, intellect is transformed into Pure Self. It then becomes one with Pure Consciousness. The Shruti, says Shrīharṣa, represents the highest stage which finite intellect can reach. Here the intellect has shown its own limitation and has pointed towards Reality. When one constantly ponders over the

Mahāvākya declaring the essential unity of the individual with the universal consciousness, then fortunately the finite intellect casts off the garb of discursive relativity put upon it by Avidyā and gets transformed into Pure Experience which is the self-luminous Consciousness shining forth in its pristine purity,[1] and thus embracing the Absolute and becoming one with it, it ever enjoys its eternal bliss.[2] Avidyā is bondage and its destruction which is the calm non-dual Knowledge is liberation.[3]

VIII

POST-SHAṄKARITES AND BUDDHISM

MOST of the Post-Shaṅkarites following Shaṅkara but probably missing his intention, condemn Shūnyavāda as utter nihilism; take Vijñānavāda in the sense of Svatantra-Vijñānavāda only; criticize the momentary Vijñānas; point out the difference between Vijñānavāda and Advaita by mentioning that while the former takes the world to be unreal because it does not fall outside of Pure Consciousness, the latter takes it to be unreal because it is Avidyā or Māyā which is a positive material stuff of ignorance which cannot be described either as existent or as non-existent and which depends on Brahman or Pure Consciousness; and exhibit almost the same spirit of animosity towards Buddhism. Thus, for example, Prakāshātmā says: He who says that Vedānta is similar to the Buddhistic Vijñānavāda talks something which befits an ignorant man and his case is indeed pitiable.[4] Vimuktātmā advises the Buddhist to leave aside his wrong view based on mere logical quibbling and follow the path of the wise, otherwise deluding the dull he will himself be deluded and destroyed.[5] Vidyāraṇya calls him as one who is expert in mere logical hair-splitting (shuṣkatarkapatu) and who is erroneously confused and deluded (bhrānta) and who is correctly criticized by the venerable Shaṅkara.[6] Sadānanda calls him 'dull-headed' (buddhi-shūnya)[7] and Gangādharendra calls him a 'fool' (jaḍa).[8]

But years after Shaṅkara when the struggle died down and when Buddhism was defeated and finally ousted from India, people began to think dispassionately about Buddhism. Thus we find some Post-Shaṅkarites expressing doubt whether Shūnyavāda is really nihilism and whether Vijñānavāda is really subjectivism which advocates the existence of momentary ideas only. And in the same school of Advaita Vedānta we find an eminent person like Shrīharṣa who tries to revive the long-lost spirit of Gauḍapāda and who correctly represents Shūnyavāda and frankly and openly admits the enormous similarities between Shūnyavāda and Advaita.

[1] Khaṇḍana, p. 60. [2] Ibid, p. 60. [3] Brahmasiddhi, III, 106. [4] Pañchapādikā-Vivaraṇa, p. 84. [5] Iṣṭasiddhi, p. 54. [6] Pañchadashī, II, 30. [7] Pratyaktattvachintāmaṇi, I, 68. [8] Svārājya-siddhi, I, 26.

Maṇḍana, like Shaṅkara, criticizes the three schools of Buddhism. The *Bāhyārthavādins*, he says, land in crude materialism. For them even the ephemeral objects, being regarded as real, should be permanent and even the illusory objects like shell-silver should be real. If objects are real, there is no place for illusion and error; if objects are unreal there is no place for the phenomenal world—this is the dilemma they have to face. The *Vijnānamātravādins* land in crude subjectivism. By no stretch of imagination can the unchanging Consciousness transform itself into changing objects. If the objects are real they cannot be made by the individual mind; if the objects are unreal then, like the sky-flower, they cannot be regarded even as an external appearance of the mind. The *Shūnyavādins* land in nihilism. In their system, Avidyā, like the sky-flower, has no practical bearing and fails to explain the phenomenal world which is said to be a mere nonentity.[1] We have already noticed Maṇḍana's criticism of the Svatantra-Vijñānavāda doctrine that difference alone is real and that unity is an appearance.

Padmapāda also criticizes the Svatantra-Vijñānavāda view under the name of Vijñānavāda. He refutes the view that reality is efficient causation and that a permanent entity can never be efficient and therefore real. He rejoins that, on the other hand, a momentary entity can never be a cause. The meaningless, chaotic and momentary Vijñānas must be brought under a unity, like loose threads made into a rope, and must be given some meaning by the permanent Self. Vedānta has proved the existence of such Pure Self through immediate experience and through reasoning. The doctrine of Mahāyāna, therefore, cannot be supported by such flimsy arguments as are advanced in its support by its followers.[2]

Vāchaspati distinguishing Advaita from Vijñānavāda remarks that according to Vijñānavāda the external world is unreal because it is mind-made, while according to Advaita it is unreal because it is indescribable. Objects exist outside and independent of the individual mind. Only they are indescribable and irrational. They are neither real nor unreal nor both. Hence they are false.[3]

Sarvajñātma Muni points out that though both Buddhism and Vedānta admit Avidyā, the fundamental difference between them is that for Vedānta the ultimate reality is Brahman which is Pure Consciousness and this is not admitted by Buddhism.

Criticizing Svatantra-Vijñānavāda under the name of Vijñānavāda, *Vimuktātmā*, like Saṅkara, remarks that though objects known are inseparable from the knower, yet it does not mean that they are identical because while the objects change, the knower always remains the same. Even the expression 'invariable association' (sahopalambha) implies the

[1] Brahmasiddhi, p. 9. [2] Pañchapādikā p. 28. [3] na hi brahmavādino nīlādyākārām vittim abhyupagachchhanti, kintu anirvachanīyam nīlādīti, Bhāmatī, II, 2, 28.

idea that the two are different. Moreover, if the external objects do not exist, the Vijñānavādin has no right to talk that cognitions appear *as if* they are external.[1] The theory of momentariness heightens the absurdity of this subjectivism. If cognitions are momentary, they cannot be called self-revealing. The Vijñānavādin therefore must admit one eternal self-revealing Consciousness.[2]

Again, a momentary thing can never become a cause. If both the preceding and the succeeding things are momentary there should be no distinction between them. Moreover, how can the Buddhist who is himself momentary perceive two moments as causally related? He should therefore stop such babbling and accept the doctrine of the wise, otherwise deluding the dull he will himself be doomed.[3]

Vimuktātmā, like Shaṅkara, takes the word 'shūnya' in the sense of mere negation (asat). If the Mādhyamika, he says, persists in advocating his theory of mere nothing, let him believe that only his doctrine is a mere nothing.[4] To the Vedāntins, on the other hand, māyā is neither sat nor asat. But Vimuktāmā is kind enough to add that if the Shūnyavādin means by his 'asat' not a mere nothing but this māyā, then his position is the same as that of the Vedāntin.[5] And it is needless to add that the Shūnyavādin means exactly this.

Shrīharṣa has done some justice to Shūnyavāda. He points out that according to the Shūnyavādin, shūnya is not mere negation. That negation is necessarily rooted in affirmation is a truism accepted by Shūnyavāda. Even the asat *is*. It has a *svarūpa*.[6] Shūnya means 'unreal, because indescribable as real or unreal'. The equation is as follows: sadasadvilakṣana=anirvachanīya. The whole world is shūnya because it is relative. It is only samvṛti, not paramārtha. This Mādhyamika view of the world with all its experiences, Shrīharṣa boldly confesses, cannot be refuted by the Vedāntin because *so far as the world is concerned*, the Mādhyamika view is exactly the same as that of the Vedāntin himself.[7] Shrīharṣa frankly admits the similarity of Shūnyavāda with Advaita Vedānta by pointing out that both regard the world to be indescribable either as real or as unreal or as both, that both agree in condemning the intellect as essentially relational or discursive and its categories as fraught with inherent contradictions, and that therefore the criticisms of all definitions as such given by both Shūnyavāda and Vedānta are valid against all views of all systems.[8]

Shrīharṣa then points out the fundamental difference between Shūnyavāda and Vedānta. Shūnyavāda, he says, regards everything *including even Consciousness* to be unreal. Buddha has declared in the Laṅkāvatāra (II, 175): All things which can be known by the intellect

[1] Iṣṭasiddhi, p. 13. [2] Ibid, p. 115. [3] Ibid, pp. 114-115. [4] Ibid, p. 118. [5] Ibid, p. 165. [6] Khaṇḍana, p. 21. [7] mādhyamikādivāgvyavahārāṇām svarūpāpalāpo na shakyate. Ibid. [8] yadi shūnyavādānirvachanīyapakṣayor āshrayaṇam tadā tāvad amūṣām nirbādhaiva sārvapathīnatā, Ibid, p. 61.

have no reality of their own. They are therefore said to be indescribable and unreal. But Vedānta makes *an exception* in favour of Consciousness (vijñāna) which it regards self-luminous (svaprakāsha). The Brahmavādins say that everything *except Consciousness* is indescribable as real or unreal or both and is therefore false[1]. So the Vedāntins find it difficult to accept Shūnyavāda as they are dissatisfied with the view that everything, including even Consciousness, is unreal. Consciousness is 'indescribable' *in the sense* that all categories of intellect fail to grasp it fully. But most assuredly it is not unreal, for it is self-luminous and self-proved. Consciousness which is the same thing as the Pure Self is self-revealing and is the only reality.[2] One may doubt everything else but one cannot doubt one's own Self for the very idea of doubt presupposes the Self. Everything else may be denied but not the Self for it is necessarily presupposed even by its denial. Everything else may require proof but not the Self for the very notion of proof rests upon it. Hence the Self-revealing Self-luminous Consciousness stands self-proved.[3]

We may remark here that Shrīharṣa is wrong in saying that Shūnyavāda regards even Absolute Consciousness as unreal. Our exposition of Shūnyavāda has proved that Consciousness is the only Reality (tattva) recognized by Shūnyavāda, though the idea is not so fully developed as it is done in Vijñānavāda and in Advaita.

Shrīharṣa recognizes the genius of Dharmakīrti by saying that one should be very careful in criticizing Dharmakīrti because his arguments appear to be difficult to refute.[4] Shrīharṣa points out that the Vijñānavādins, unlike Shūnyavādins, made an exception in favour of Consciousness and regarded it to be self-luminous. But their sin was to treat this Consciousness as momentary. A momentary vijñāna cannot be called self-luminous. It is itself an object to the Self which knows it. The momentary vijñāna must be unified by the Self. Consciousness therefore must be admitted to be permanent. Only Vedānta which Shrīharṣa calls *Svaprakāsha-Vijñānavāda*[5] or the doctrine which upholds the reality of the self-luminous Consciousness has done this.

Chitsukha too admits the similarity between the Buddhistic samvṛti and the Vedāntic vyavahāra and defends the former against the attacks of Kumārila Bhaṭṭa.

Vidyāraṇya takes the word shūnya in the sense of mere negation and condemns the Shūnyavādins as nihilists who dwell in illusion and who

[1] saugatabrahmavādinor ayam visheṣaḥ yad ādimaḥ sarvam evānirvachanīyam varṇayat i, taduktam Bhagavatā Laṅkāvatāre buddhyā vivichyamānānām svabhāvo nāvadhāryate. ato nirabhilapyās te niḥsvabhāvāshcha deshitāḥ' iti, vijñānavyatiriktam punaridam vishvam sadasadbhyām vilakṣaṇam brahmavādinaḥ saṅgirante, Ibid, p. 31. [2] apare punashchetaso'pi shūnyatāṅgīkāre manaḥpratyayam anāsādayantaḥ . . . manyante vijñānam tāvat svaprakāsham svata eva siddhasvarūpam, Ibid, p. 21. [3] Ibid, pp. 21, 26 31. [4] durābādha iva chāyam Dharmakīrteḥ panthā ityavahitena bhāvyam, Ibid, p. 213. [5] Ibid, pp. 21 and 31.

are expert in mere logical hair-splitting and who are therefore rightly criticized by Shaṅkara.[1] He points out that even negation presupposes the seer (sākṣin).[2] The never-flickering light of Pure Consciousness is self-proved and can never be denied. It cannot be momentary or changing. It is permanent. It neither rises nor sets.[3] This Pure Self is directly realized when the limits of finite thought are transcended. Silence is the highest experience. This experience is not shūnya, for all notions of the intellect including the notion of shūnya are transcended here.[4] Vidyāraṇya adds that if the Shūnyavādin means by 'shūnya' this Reality which appears as the indescribable manifold world of name and form, then may he live long for he is embracing Advaita![5] And we know that Shūnyavāda really means by shūnya this Reality which appears as name and form and which transcends them all for it is essentially non-dual.[6]

Vidyāraṇya also criticizes the Svatantra-Vijñānavādins under the name of Vijñānavādins and distinguishes the eternal Self from the momentary ideas.[7]

Sadānanda also says that if shūnya means not pure nothing but the Reality which is beyond intellect, we have no quarrel with the Shūnyavādin for he has accepted Vedānta.[8] But if shūnya means mere negation then he dare not steal even a glance at us.[9] Sadānanda, distinguishing Advaita from Vijñānavāda, observes that whereas for Vijñānavāda the world exists inside Consciousness and is therefore unreal, for Vedānta, on the other hand, it is māyā or something which can be described neither as real nor as unreal nor as both and is therefore false. This indescribability of the world which baffles intellect is a merit for Vedānta, but not for Vijñānavāda.[10]

Gaṅgādharendra condemns Vijñānavāda as doomed on account of its momentary ideas. The foolish Vijñānavādin, he says, by refuting the self-proved Self wants to commit suicide.[11]

We thus see that the Post-Shaṅkarites say that if shūnya means pure negation, Shūnyavāda is a self-condemned nihilism; but if shūnya means māyā which necessarily points to the self-luminous Reality, they have no quarrel with Shūnyavāda, for Shūnyavāda is then merged into Vedānta. They also say that Vijñānavāda, instead of maintaining that the world is unreal because it does not exist outside of thought, should maintain that it is unreal because it is a positive material stuff of Ignorance called māyā which is neither existent nor non-existent nor both and is therefore indefinable. Again, they do not distinguish between

[1] Pañchadashī, II, 30. [2] shūnyasyāpi hi shūnyatvam tat sākṣiṇi satīkṣyate, Bṛ-Vārtika-Sāra, III, 4, 73. [3] nodeti nāstametyekā samvideṣā svayaṁprabhā, Pañchadashī, I, 7. [4] Ibid, II, 44. [5] Ibid, II, 34. [6] Shatasāhasrikā, pp. 559 and 1676. [7] Bṛ-Vārtika-Sāra, IV, 3, 123-142. [8] shūnyam nāma kiñchit tattvam asti na vā? ādye nāmamātre vivādaḥ vedāntamatapraveshāt, Advaitabrahmasiddhi, p. 104. [10] vedāntasiddhāntasya tvayam saugatamatād bhedaḥ—na jñānākāro'rthaḥ kin tu bāhyānirvachanīyatvān māyāmayaḥ, Advaitabrahmasiddhi, pp. 100 and 104. [11] Svārājyasiddhi, I, 25-26.

Svatantra-Vijñānavāda and Vijñānavāda. They practically omit Vijñānavāda and take Svatantra-Vijñānavāda as real Vijñānavāda. They therefore find it easy to condemn the momentary vijñānas. They themselves maintain that vijñāna is self-luminous, but they say that this vijñāna is the pure permanent Consciousness which is the same as the self-revealing Self, transcending all categories of the intellect and also transcending the trinity of knowledge, knower and known. They accept the criticism of all other systems by the Svatantra-Vijñānavādins, but they point out that the criticisms may be rightly levelled against the Buddhists' own momentary vijñāna. If the Buddhists maintain the permanent self-luminous Consciousness, they have no quarrel with the Buddhists, for then the Buddhists are embracing Vedānta. They agree with Shūnyavādins in maintaining that the world is shūnya or anirvachanīya. They agree with Vijñānavādins in maintaining that Reality is Pure Self-luminous Consciousness which is permanent. Thus by supplementing Shūnyavāda with Vijñānavāda and Vijñānavāda with Shūnyavāda they bring Buddhism nearer Advaita Vedānta.

Chapter Seventeen

BUDDHISM AND VEDĀNTA

I

BUDDHISM and Vedānta should not be viewed as two opposed systems but only as different stages in the development of the same central thought which starts with the Upaniṣads, finds its indirect support in Buddha, its elaboration in Mahāyāna Buddhism, its open revival in Gauḍapāda, which reaches its zenith in Shaṅkara and culminates in the Post-Shaṅkarites.

So far as the similarities between Buddhism and Vedānta are concerned, they are so many and so strong that by no stretch of imagination can they be denied or explained otherwise. So far as the differences are concerned, they are few and mostly they are not vital. Most of them rest on a grave misunderstanding of Buddhism. We have tried to remove it and to clear the way for a correct understanding of Buddhism. However, there are some differences which are real and vital. But they are very few and have been pointed out by us.

II

BUDDHA AND VEDĀNTA

THE fundamental philosophical doctrine which Buddha borrowed from the Upaniṣads is that intellect, being essentially relational, involves itself in insoluble antinomies and in order to be one with Reality, has to get itself transformed into immediate Spiritual Experience (bodhi or prajñā). Intellect, as a matter of fact, is Pure Knowledge itself; it appears to be intellect only on account of Ignorance. Reality is not to be philosophized; it is to be directly realized. The Unborn, Uncreated and Imperishable Reality which is throughout implied by all changing phenomena as their background and which, at the same time, transcends all phenomena, all dualism (ubho ante) of the intellect, as well as the trinty of knower, known and knowledge, is Pure Consciousness and is to be directly realized by the wise. People are surrounded by the darkness of ignorance; they have to look for the lamp of knowledge. And Buddha bequeathes the Lamp of Dharma to them—the Lamp which he borrowed from the Upaniṣads.[1]

III

ASHVAGHOṢA AND VEDĀNTA

ASHVAGHOṢA realized that after Buddha's Nirvāṇa, Buddha's teachings were perverted by the Hīnayānists who reduced mind to fleeting ideas and matter to fleeting sensations, who placed Buddha in place of God and who denied the ultimate existence of mind and matter. Ashvaghoṣa challenged the Hīnyānists and refuted their views. He knew well that Buddha's real philosophy was based on the Upaniṣads and he tried to revive it. The Tathatā of Ashvaghoṣa also called as Bhūta-tathatā, Tathāgatagarbha, Dharmakāya, Dharmadhātu, Ālaya-vijñāna, Bodhi or Prajñā is in fact the same as the Ātman or the Brahman of the Upaniṣads. Relativity (pratītyasamutpāda) is the realm of the intellect which is a product of Avidyā. The Absolute is untouched by it. 'It is wrong to take the work of Ignorance as ultimate and to forget the foundation on which it stands,' says Ashvaghoṣa.[2] The Tathatā of Ashvaghoṣa which is Bodhi or Vijñāna or Pure Consciousness together with its two aspects—the Absolute 'Suchness' and the conditional 'suchness' reminds us of the Ātman or the Brahman of the Upaniṣads with its two aspects—the higher and the lower or the nirguṇa or the para and the saguṇa or the apara. The Tathatā and the Brahman, both are jñānaghana or Pure Consciousness and anirvachanīya or indescribable in the sense that intellect fails to grasp them fully. The 'Ignorance' of Ashvaghoṣa is the avidyā of the Upaniṣads. The phenomenal and the absolute standpoints of Ashvaghoṣa are the vyāvahārika and the pāramārthika standpoints of the Upaniṣads. Ashvaghoṣa uses those very similes commonly used in the Upaniṣads—the similes of waves and water, of pots and clay, of ornaments and gold etc. It is unmistakably clear that the Upaniṣads exercised a great influence on Ashvaghoṣa. Indeed, avoiding all contradictions of Hīnayāna, Ashvaghoṣa has rightly interpreted Buddha in the light of the Upaniṣads and has placed Buddhism on a firm basis.

[1] 'The S'ākyan mission was out "not to destroy, but to fulfil", to enlarge and enhance the accepted faith-in-God of their day, not by asseverating, but by making it more vital. It were Brāhmans who became the leading disciples.'—Mrs. Rhys Davids: A Manual of Buddhism, p. 194. [2] Outlines of Mahāyāna Buddhism: Suzuki, p. 124.

IV

SHŪNYAVĀDA AND VEDĀNTA

OUR exposition of Shūnyavāda will at once make it clear how similar it is to Vedānta. We have clearly proved that shūnya does not mean a mere negation nor does Shūnyavāda mean nihilism. Shūnya is used in a double sense. It means Māyā as well as Brahman. Empirically it means that all dharmas or world-experiences, subjective as well as objective, are svabhāva-shūnya or devoid of ultimate reality. They are pratītya-samutpanna or merely relative. They are ultimately unreal because they can be called neither existent nor non-existent nor both. They are indescribable or māyā. But the mere fact that they are appearances implies that there must be a Reality of which they are mere appearances. This Reality or tattva is prapañchashūnya or beyond all plurality. It is like Brahman. It is Bodhi or Pure Consciousness. It is indescribable or chatuṣkoṭivinirmukta because all categories of the intellect fail to grasp it fully. Samvṛti and paramārtha correspond to vyavahāra and paramārtha of Vedānta. Chandrakīrti divides samvṛti into mithyāsamvṛti and tathya-samvṛti to match parikalpita and paratantra of Vijñānavāda. Mithyā-samvṛti, tathyasamvṛti and paramārtha will now correspond to pratibhāsa, vyavahāra and paramārtha of Vedānta. We know that the two standpoints, empirical and absolute, are found in the Upaniṣads which sometimes use the word 'samvṛti' also.[1]

The Mahāyāna-sūtras, Nāgārjuna and his followers condemn all phenomena to be like illusion, mirage, son of a barren woman, sky-flower etc. etc. which expressions suggest that they are something absolutely unreal. But this is not their intention. They use such expressions only to emphasize the ultimate unreality of phenomena. Their empirical reality is, as we have seen, emphatically maintained. We know that Gauḍapāda and even Shaṅkara use such expressions. They are therefore not condemned to be absolutely unreal.

We have noticed the enormous similarities between Shūnyavādins on the one hand and Gauḍapāda, Shaṅkara and Post-Shaṅkarites on the other. Their dialectical arguments are essentially similar. Their method is also essentially the same. Intellect or logic has got only negative value for them. It has to be transformed into immediate experience so that it may embrace the Absolute. They are interested in pointing out to their opponents that even according to the canons of logic of the opponents the arguments of the opponents can be proved to be false. Ultimate Reality is Silence. It has to be realized directly. It cannot be discussed.

[1] E.g., Bṛhadāraṇyaka, II, 5, 18.

If the opponent accepts it, he is accepting their position. If, on the other hand, he challenges it he is challenging the validity of his own logic. Intellect is essentially discursive or relational. It must work with its concepts and categories. So it gives only the relative world which must be taken to be empirically real. Ultimately it is false because it is neither existent nor non-existent nor both. Rejection of all views is itself not a *view*; it is an attempt to rise above thought.

We have seen that Gauḍapāda frankly approves of the No-origination theory preached by Shūnyavāda. His Kārikās bear striking resemblances with the Kārikās of Nāgārjuna. Shaṅkara knows very well that Shūnyavāda cannot be criticized and so he simply dismisses it by taking the word shūnya in its popular sense of negation and dubbing Shūnyavāda as a self-condemned nihilism. Shaṅkara says that Shūnyavāda has no right to condemn this world as unreal unless it takes recourse to some higher reality (anyat-tattva). We have seen that Shūnyavāda does take recourse to this higher reality. Nāgārjuna uses the very word 'tattva' and defines it as that which is to be directly realized, which is calm and blissful, where all pluraility is merged, where all cries of intellect are satisfied, and which is the non-dual Absolute.[1] The Post-Shaṅkarites, following Shaṅkara, either condemn Shūnyavāda as nihilism or say that if shūnya means the indescribable māyā, as it really does mean, they have no quarrel with Shūnyavāda. Shrīharṣa frankly admits that Shūnyavāda cannot be criticized because it is similar to Vedānta. The only difference which he points out between Shūnyavāda and Vedānta is that while Shūnyavāda declares even Consciousness to be unreal, Vedānta makes an exception in its favour. Shrīharṣa quotes a verse from the Laṅkāvatāra (II, 175): 'All things which can be known by the intellect have no reality of their own. These are therefore said to be indescribable and unreal.'[2] But we know that the Laṅkāvatāra itself repeatedly makes an exception in favour of Consciousness. Shūnyavāda condemns only the individual self to be unreal and not Pure Consciousness. Nāgārjuna's definition of Reality clearly shows that such definition can apply only to Pure Consciousness. Nāgārjuna himself in his Ratnāvalī (I, 45 and 60) identifies Reality with Pure Consciousness or Bodhi or Jñāna. Āryadeva also identifies Reality with the Pure Self or the Chitta.[3] Shāntideva in much-inspired verses praises the only Reality, the Bodhi-Chitta or the True Self which is Pure Consciousness.[4] If the Bodhi of Nāgārjuna, the Chitta of Āryadeva, and the Bodhi-Chitta of Shāntideva are not the self-luminous Self which is Pure Consciousness, what else on earth can they be?

The only difference between Shūnyavāda and Vedānta, therefore, is the difference of emphasis only. This difference is of a double nature.

[1] Mādhyamika-Kārikā, XVIII, 9. [2] Khaṇḍana, p. 31. [3] Chittavishuddhi-prakaraṇa, 27, 28, 74. [4] Bodhicharyāvatāra, I, 8, 10 etc.

Firstly, while Shūnyavāda is more keen to emphasize the ultimate unreality of all phenomena, Shaṅkara and his followers are more keen to emphasize the empirical reality of all phenomena; and secondly while Shūnyavāda is less keen to develop the conception of ultimate Reality, Vedānta is more keen to develop this conception almost to perfection. And this is not unnatural if we remember that Shūnyavāda represents the earlier stage while Vedānta represents the later stage of the development of the same thought.

V

VIJÑĀNAVĀDA AND VEDĀNTA

WE have proved that Vijñānavāda is neither subjective idealism nor does it advocate the reality of momentary ideas only. It is absolute idealism. The theory of momentariness is applied to phenomena only. Reality is declared to be Absolute Consciousness which is the permanent background of all changing phenomena.

This doctrine clearly has its essential roots in the Upaniṣadic philosophy. The parikalpita, paratantra, and pariniṣpanna correspond to the pratibhāsa, vyavahāra and paramārtha of Vedānta. Vijñānavāda and Vedānta both agree in maintaining that Reality is Absolute Consciousness which is the permanent background of all changing phenomena and which ultimately transcends the trinity of knowledge, knower and known. Everything, the subject as well as the object, is its appearance. The Tathāgata-garbha or the Ālaya-vijñāna of the Laṅkāvatāra, the Vishuddhātman or the Mahātman or the Paramātman or the Dharmadhātu of Asaṅga, the Vijñaptimātra or the Dharmakāya of Vasubandhu, and the Ātman or the Brahman of the Vedānta are essentially the same pure and permanent self-luminous Consciousness. The Vijñāptimatra of Vasubandhu corresponds to the Ātman or the Brahman of Vedānta, his Ālayavijñāna to the Vedāntic Īshvara, his kliṣṭa-manovijñāna to the Vedāntic jīva, his viṣaya-vijñapti to the Vedāntic jagat, and his pariṇāma to the Vedāntic vivarta. When the Laṅkāvatāra tries to distinguish its Tathāgatagarbha or Ālayavijñāna from the non-Buddhistic Ātman, the essential difference which it points out is that while the former transcends all categories of intellect (nirvikalpa) and is to be directly realized through Spiritual Experience (nirābhāsaprajñā-gochara), the latter clings to the category of affirmation.[1] But this distinction is superficial and false. The Ātman as much transcends all the categories of intellect (nirguṇa and nirvikalpa), and is as much to be directly realized through immediate experience (jñāna) as is the Tathāgatagarbha. The Ātman does not cling to the category of affirmation. No category can adequately describe it. When it is said that Ātman is Pure Existence what is meant is that though

[1] Laṅkāvatāra, pp. 77-79.

the Ātman cannot be grasped by the category of existence, yet when we describe it from the phenomenal point of view, we must avoid nihilism and say that the Ātman exists by itself and in its own right because it is self-luminous Consciousness.

We have seen that even Shaṅkara admits that Gauḍapāda accepts the arguments of Vijñānavāda to prove that the world is ultimately unreal as it cannot exist independently and outside of Consciousness.[1] Gauḍapāda is profoundly under the influence of Vijñānavāda. We have clearly proved this. The fact stands as it is and cannot be challenged. We have also seen that real Vijñānavāda, like Shūnyavāda, is only avoided by Shaṅkara. The criticism of the so-called 'Vijñānavāda' by Shaṅkara is really the criticism of the 'Svatantra-Vijñānavāda' school. Shaṅkara's criticism of real Vijñānavāda—and this criticism applies to some extent to Gauḍapāda also—loses much of its force because, firstly, Vijñānavāda and Gauḍapāda do not deny the objectivity of the external world as they maintain that the objects appear as objects to the knowing subject, and secondly because they hold self-luminous consciousness to be the permanent background of all phenomena. They distinguish between the parikalpita and the paratantra, and when they place the dream state and the waking state almost on a par, they do so only to emphasize the ultimate unreality of the world.

The main difference, therefore, between Vijñānavada, on the one hand, and Shaṅkara and his followers on the other, is that the latter emphasize the empirical reality of the world and emphatically distinguish the dream state from the waking state, and that they prove the ultimate unreality of the world not by saying that it does not exist outside of thought but by saying, like Shūnyavāda, that it is false because it is relative and can be described neither as existent nor as non-existent nor as both. This view, as we have seen, was already presented by Gauḍapāda. The advance made by Shaṅkara and his followers on Shūnyavāda and Gauḍapāda consists in the development of the view that Avidyā or Māyā is a positive material stuff of Ignorance which baffles all description.

VI

SVATANTRA-VIJÑĀNAVĀDA AND VEDĀNTA

THE only fundamental and most vital difference between this school and Vijñānavāda is that this school degrades the permanent Consciousness of Vijñānavāda to momentary vijñānas. Reality, according to it, is a momentary vijñāna only. It is the unique momentary point-instant of Consciousness. Under the name of Vijñānavāda, Shaṅkara really criticizes this school and we have noticed that Shaṅkara's criticism of

[1] Maṇḍūkya-Kārikā-Bhāṣya, IV, 28.

it is perfectly valid. Post-Shaṅkarites also, following Shaṅkara, criticize this school under the name of Vijñānavāda and mostly repeat Shaṅkara's objections. A momentary idea can be neither self-luminous nor can it ideate itself. The reality of permanent self-luminous Self which is Pure Consciousness must be admitted.

We have pointed out the enormous similarities between the arguments for the refutation of other systems given by Dharmakīrti, Shāntarakṣita and Kamalashīla on the one hand, and the arguments for the refutation of those very systems advanced by Shaṅkara and Post-Shaṅkarites, on the other hand. Vedānta does not reject the criticism of other systems by the Svatantra-Vijñānavādins so far as that criticism does not militate against its own doctrine. Vedānta criticizes only their momentary vijñānas and their view that external world is unreal because it is a projection of momentary consciousness as this view well smacks of subjectivism when consciousness is reduced to momentary ideas. Vedānta points out that the arguments which the Svatantra-Vijñānavādins advance against permanent consciousness are more applicable to their own momentary consciousness. To take an example, if bondage and liberation are impossible when conscious is treated as permanent they are more so when consciousness is taken as momentary. Vedānta accepts that Consciousness is Self-luminous and that it ultimately transcends the subject-object duality and the trinity of knowledge, knower and known and all the categories of the intellect. But from the empirical standpoint, stresses Vedānta, it is far better to describe Reality as Permanent and Pure Consciousness which is at once Pure Existence and Pure Bliss, than to call it momentary for whatever is momentary is miserable and self-contradictory. The momentary vijñāna can be neither self-luminous nor can it ideate itself. It requires the Pure Self which is Pure Consciousness to know it.

Shāntarakṣita and Kamalashīla confess that the view of the followers of the Upaniṣads (i.e. of Gauḍapāda and others) is very much similar to their own view, and that it contains very little error, its only fault is that it declares consciousness to be permanent.[1] Vedānta may well rejoin: The view of the Svatantra-Vijñānavādins is very much similar to Vedānta; it contains very little error, its only fault is that it declares consciousness to be momentary.[2]

VII

NAIRĀTMYAVĀDA

IT is generally said that Nairātmyavāda or the No-Soul theory and Kṣaṇa-bhaṅga-vāda or the theory of Momentariness are the two main

[1] teṣām alpāparādham tu darshanam nityatoktitaḥ, Tattva-Saṅgraha, K. 330. [2] teṣām alpāparādham tu darshanam kṣaṇikoktitaḥ.

and vital theories which distinguish Buddhism from Vedānta. Let us now briefly summarize our views in regard to these two theories.

We maintain that by *Nairātmyavāda* Buddhism does not deny the existence of the true Ātman, the Pure Self which is Pure Consciousness and which is the only reality. Buddhism takes the word 'Ātman' in the sense of the individual ego-complex or the Jīvātman which is a product of beginningless Avidyā, Māyā or Vāsanā and which is associated with the Antaḥkaraṇa or the Buddhi. Thus Buddha and the Mahāyānists have found it easy to repudiate this Ātman (Jīva), while at the same time accepting its empirical reality. It is in fact 'the self of straw' which they have erected simply to demolish it afterwards. The real self is untouched by their criticism. They have, in one sense or the other, either implicitly or explicitly, always accepted its reality. It is called, not generally Ātman, but Bodhi, Prajñā, Chitta, Bodhi-chitta, Tattva, Vijñāna, Chittamātra, Vijñānamātra, Vijñaptimātra, Tathatā, Tathāgatagarbha, Dharmadhātu, Dharma-kāya or Buddhakāya. Ashvaghoṣa calls it Ātman also.[1] Asaṅga calls it Shuddhātman, Mahātman and Paramātman.[2] Even Shāntarakṣita calls it Vishuddhātman.[3]

Thus it is a great irony of fate that the Buddhists and the Vedāntins fought against each other. Nairātmyavāda has been horribly misunderstood both by the Buddhists and by the Vedāntins. And Buddha and the Buddhists themselves were greatly responsible for creating this misunderstanding.

The Upaniṣads have repeatedly used the word Ātman as a synonym of Reality. Buddha admitted this Reality and termed it Bodhi or Prajñā. But instead of frankly identifying his Bodhi with the Ātman, Buddha degraded Ātman to the level of the Jīva and easily condemned it as unreal. There is a famous saying of Yājñavalkya that the husband, the wife, the children, the worldly objects and all things are loved, not for their own sake, but for the sake of the Ātman. Perhaps Buddha wrongly took the Ātman in the sense of the 'I' and the 'mine' which is the cause of attachment and bondage. He therefore condemned it as an unreal thing imagined only by the dull.[4] Love for the Ātman is like the blind passion of a foolish lover for the most beautiful damsel (janapada-kalyāṇī), he is represented to say in the Dīghanikāya, about whose existence, residence, colour, size and age that lover knows nothing.

The Hīnayānists denied the self. Nāgasena tells Milinda that the so-called self is nothing apart from the fleeting ideas. The Mahāyāna-Sūtras, the Shūnyavādins, the Vijñānavādins, and the Svatantra-Vijñānavādins all take the word 'Ātman' in the sense of the notion of the 'I' and the vain-glory of the 'Mine' and condemn it to be ultimately

[1] Saundarananda, XIV, 52. [2] Mahāyānasūtrālaṅkāra, XIV, 37; IX, 23. [3] Tattvasaṅgraha, 3535. [4] kevalo paripūro bāladhammo, Majjhimanikāya, I, 1, 2.

unreal. Dharma-nairātmya means that all objective existents are unreal. Nāgārjuna declares that the self is neither identical nor different from the five skandhas.[1] When the 'I' and the 'mine' cease, the cycle of birth-and-death comes to a standstill.[2] Āryadeva says that in the beginning, evil should be avoided; in the middle, Ātman should be viewed as unreal; and in the end, everything phenomenal should be taken to be unreal.[3] Chandrakīrti declares Ātman to be the cause of all sufferings and demerits and says that a Yogī should deny its ultimate reality.[4] Shāntideva says that just as when one goes on taking off the layers of a plantain trunk or an onion nothing will remain, similarly if one goes on examining the self, ultimately it will be found to be nothing.[5] Asaṅga says that all suffering is due to the ego and the ego itself is due to beginningless ignorance. There is no self as a substance nor even as a subject.[6] Vasubandhu says that Consciousness transcends the duality of the subject and the object, both of which are ultimately unreal.[7] Dharmakīrti regards the self as the root-cause of attachment and misery. As long as one is attached to the Ātman, so long will one revolve in the cycle of birth-and-death.[8] Shāntarakṣita clearly states that Consciousness itself when associated with the notion of the ego is called Ātman. It has only empirical reality. Ultimately it denotes nothing.[9] Thus in Buddhism, right from Buddha himself to Shāntarakṣita, the word Ātman is generally taken in the sense of the empirical ego and its ultimate reality is denied. It is variously called as Ātman, Pudgala, Sattva or Satkāya.

But it is very important to remember that the Pure Self which is Pure Consciousness is always admitted by Buddhism to be the ultimate Reality. Buddha himself identified Reality with Bodhi or Prajñā. The Tathatā of Ashvaghoṣa is Ālayavijñāna or Absolute Consciousness. The Mahāyāna-sūtras identify Reality with Consciousness and call it Prapañcha-Shūnya, Atarkya, Sarvavāgviṣayātīta, Advaya, Achintya, Anakṣara, Anabhilāpya, Atyanta-vishuddha and Pratyātmavedya. It is significant to note that though Reality is not generally called Ātman, it is sometimes described as Brahman. Thus we find in the Aṣṭasāhasrikā[10] that all things are such that they neither come in nor go out, they are neither pure nor impure, they are free from attachment and detachment, they are undefiled, unattached and uncontaminated because they are of the very nature of *Brahman*. The same Sūtra tells that for supreme enlightenment one dwells in *Brahman*.[11] The Shatasāhasrikā[12] and the Lalitavistara[13] describe Reality as Full of Bliss in the beginning, in the middle and in the end, One, Full, Pure and the Abode of *Brahman*. The Saddharmapuṇḍarīka[14] says that one who truly follows the teaching

[1] Mādhyamika-Kārikā, X, 15. [2] Ibid, XVIII, 4. [3] Chatuḥshataka: Verse, 190. [4] Madhyamakāvatāra as quoted in Mādhyamika-Vṛtti, p. 340. [5] Bodhicharyāvatāra, IX, 75. [6] Mahāyānasūtrālaṅkāra, XI, 47; XVIII, 77, 92-103. [7] Viṁshatikā, 9 and 10. [8] Pramāṇavārtika, II, 201, 213, 219. [9] Tattva-Saṅgraha, 204. [10] p. 476. [11] p. 34. [12] p. 1460. [10] p. 3. [14] p. 118.

of the Buddha ever dwells in the *Brahman*, the Absolute, the Pure, the Calm, the Blissful and the Undefiled. Asaṅga[1] also says that by becoming one with Pure Spirit, one realizes the last, the fourth meditation, and then one ever dwells in the blissful *Brahman*.

Nāgārjuna's definition of Reality as the non-dual Absolute, Calm and Blissful and beyond all plurality applies to Pure Consciousness alone. He also openly identified Reality with Pure Consciousness and says that the empirical ego must embrace Pure Consciousness in order to be transformed into Reality.[2] Āryadeva says that the Jewel of Self is absolutely pure and self-luminous and appears to be impure only on account of ignorance just as a white crystal appears coloured on account of a coloured thing placed near it.[3] Shāntideva says that the True Self which is Pure Consciousness or Bodhichitta can transform an impure mortal into a pure Buddha.[4] The Laṅkāvatāra identifies Reality with Tathāgatagarbha or Ālayavijñāna. Asaṅga says that the Chitta or the Pure Self is by its very nature self-luminous (prakṛtiprabhāsvara) and all impurities are adventitious.[5] He calls it Shuddhātman, Mahātman and Paramātman.[6] Vasubandhu says that ultimate Reality is Vijñaptimātrā or Absolute Consciousness which is the permanent background of all changing phenomena. Dharmakīrti says that Reality is Consciousness which is beyond all words, names and concepts.[7] Shāntarakṣita says that Consciousness is self-luminous and free from all impositions. It is one without a second. True knowledge consists in the realization of the Pure Self (vishuddhātma-darshana).[8]

Thus we see that Buddhism generally means by Ātman what Vedānta means by Jīvātman or Buddhi or Chitta or Antaḥkaraṇa. And on the other hand, Buddhism generally means by Chitta or Vijñāna or Vijñapti or Bodhi or Prajñā what Vedānta means by Ātman or Brahman or Samvit or Chit. Thus the Vedāntic Ātman generally becomes the Buddhistic Chitta, and the Vedāntic Chitta generally becomes the Buddhistic Ātman. Had Buddha refrained from committing an error of commission in degrading the Upaniṣadic Ātman to the level of the empirical ego and also an error of omission in not identifying his Bodhi or Prajñā with the Upaniṣadic Ātman or Brahman, the age-old battle regarding the Nairātmyavāda fought without any reasonable ground by the Buddhists and the Vedāntins on the soil of Indian Philosophy would have been surely avoided.

[1] Mahāyānasūtrālaṅkāra, VII, 2-3. [2] Ratnāvalī, I, 45, 60. [3] Chittavishuddhiprakaraṇa, 27-28. [4] Bodhicharyāvatāra, I, 10. [5] Mahāyānasūtrālaṅkāra, XIII, 19. [6] Ibid, pp. 37-38. [7] Pramāṇavārtikā, 88, 93. [8] Tattvasaṅgraha, 3535.

VIII

KṢAṆA-BHAṄGA-VĀDA

THE theory of Momentariness loses all its force and significance in Buddha, Ashvaghoṣa, Shūnyavāda and Vijñānavāda since it is applied to phenomena only. It presents a real problem only in Hīnayāna and in the Svatantra-Vijñānavāda school.

The Upaniṣads recognized the misery and momentariness in this world. Nachiketā kicked away wealth, land, women, sons, grandsons, music, dance and long life by saying that these things simply wear away the senses. And Maitreyi, unlured by wealth, told Yājñavalkya: 'What shall I do with that by which I cannot become immortal?' Buddha also was deeply moved by the misery of old age, illness and death and he declared all world-objects to be momentary. The Hīnayānists in their zeal over-emphasized the dark side of the picture and unreservedly declared everything, without any exception, to be merely momentary. But these people who boasted that the doctrine of momentariness (kṣaṇikāḥ sarvasaṁskārāḥ) is the roaring of the Sugata-lion (Saugata-siṁhanāda) forgot that it was the Sugata (Buddha) himself who proclaimed: The fact that things in this world appear to be born, to be changing, to be made, and to be perishable, logically implies that there is a reality which is Unborn, Immortal, Uncreated and Imperishable.[1] They also forgot that it was the Sugata himself who called his Enlightenment, 'the Middle Path', which transcended both the 'ends' of intellect including momentariness and permanence.

Ashavaghoṣa realized this. He reaffirmed that everything phenomenal is momentary, fleeting and deceptive. But he proclaimed Tathatā to be beyond all categories, to be neither momentary nor permanent, though phenomenally it must be called permanent. Shūnyavāda did the same thing. The 'Madhyamamārga' is a path which at once transcends both the extremes as well as the middle.[2] The Laṅkāvatāra also declares its Ālayavijñāna to be beyond all categories. Asaṅga emphasizes the momentariness of all phenomena, but maintains that Reality is the permanent background of all changing phenomena. Vasubandhu's Vijñaptimātra is openly declared to be permanent, non-dual and blissful. Sthiramati says that whatever is momentary is misery and whatever is permanent is bliss.[3] The theory of Momentariness is applied to phenomena only.

In the Svatantra-Vijñānavāda, the theory is revived and is applied to

[1] yasmā cha kho bhikkhave! atthi ajātam amatam akatam asaṅkhatam tasmā jātassa matassa katassa saṅkhatassa nissareṇam pañāya, Udāna, 73 Sutta. [2] Samādhirāja-sūtra, p. 30. [3] Triṁshikā-Bhāsya, p. 44.

Reality also. Reality is declared to be a unique momentary point-instant of Consciousness. The Criticism of this school by Chandrakīrti and Shaṅkara is fully justified.

IX

A BRIEF HISTORICAL SURVEY OF BUDDHISM AND VEDĀNTA

THE Upaniṣads are the fountainhead of all Indian Philosophy. Buddha did not preach anything absolutely new. He was disgusted with the orthodox Vedic ritual, with the sacrifices in which animals were butchered, with the rigidity of the caste system and with the supremacy of the Brāhmandom. Buddha himself speaks in very high and respectable terms about a true Brāhmaṇa whom he regards an ideal saint who has done away with all sins and ignorance and who shines with the light of pure wisdom.[1]

In the doctrines of Buddha there was nothing which would seriously militate against the Upaniṣadic philosophy. It was in fact based upon it. But after the death of the Buddha, the Hīnayānists misunderstood his teachings. Proclaiming that the No-soul theory and the theory of Universal Momentariness were the corner-stone of Buddhism, they reduced mind to fleeting ideas and matter to fleeting sensations.

This brought a vehement protest from Ashvaghoṣa and from the Mahāyanā-Sūtras. The Sarvāstivādins and others were dubbed as Hīnayānists. They were either Shrāvakas or layman or at best Pratyeka-buddhas or men of inferior intellect, who could not understand the real teaching of the Buddha which was meant for the Mahāyānist Bodhisattvas. Ashvoghoṣa interpreted Buddha in the light of the Upaniṣads and declared Reality to be Pure Existence, Pure Consciousness and Pure Bliss—all in one.

It is to the credit of Nāgārjuna who flourished in the second century that he for the first time synthesized the scattered doctrines of the Mahāyāna-Sūtras. His work was ably carried on by his disciple Ārya-deva. Shūnyavāda brought Buddhism closer to Vedānta.

In the fourth century flourished Asaṅga and Vasubandhu. They agreed with Shūnyavāda in declaring Reality to be devoid of all plurality. They also agreed with it in declaring all phenomena, subjective as well as objective, to be mere appearances. But they developed the view that Reality is Pure Consciousness—the view which was indicated but not fully developed by Shūnyavāda. Vijñānavāda thus brought Buddhism still closer to Vedānta.

In the fifth century flourished Diṅnāga. At that time Brāhmanism

[1] Suttanipāta, 35.

was undergoing a rapid revival and the rivalry between Buddhism and Brāhmanism was increasing. Diṅnāga saw clearly that Vasubandhu had merged Buddhism in Vedānta. He did not like it. In his mistaken zeal to distinguish Buddhism from Vedānta, he turned to Hīnayāna for his inspiration and fell back on the theory of Momentariness. Vasubandhu was so revered and was so famous that he had the unique distinction of being called 'the second Buddha'. Diṅnāga therefore did not think it proper to challenge the authority of Vasubandhu openly. Saying that so far as ultimate reality was concerned he agreed with Vasubandhu, he busied himself with the revival of Buddhistic logic. He wanted to dilute the Absolute Idealism of Vasubandhu with the Critical Realism of the Sautrāntika. He ruthlessly criticized the Naiyāyikas whom he called 'bunglers in logic' and founded the Svatantra-Vijñānavāda school of Buddhistic logic. There was no harm in this. Diṅnāga was perfectly free to do this provided he did not touch ultimate reality. His greatest error lay in declaring Ultimate Reality to be an absolutely dissimilar particular 'thing-in-itself' which was a unique momentary point-instant of Consciousness. He agreed with Vasubandhu in maintaining that Reality was Consciousness. But his error lay in declaring this Consciousness also to be momentary. Thus Diṅnāga, on the one hand, paid lip-homage to Vasubandhu, and on the other, really undermined the very root of Vasubandhu's philosophy. Diṅnāga therefore is the first Buddhist philosopher who is really responsible for the downfall of Buddhism, at least of Buddhistic philosophy. There were also other social, economic, political and religious causes. But the new interpretation of the theory of Momentariness and its application even to the Ultimate Reality created a philosophical chasm between Buddhism and Vedānta. Thus Diṅnāga was the first man who sowed the poisonous seed which grew into a plant in Dharmakīrti and bore fruits in Shāntarakṣita, and led to the doom of Buddhistic philosophy in India. Had Diṅnāga tried to develop or even to explain the philosophy of Vasubandhu this tragedy would have been certainly averted.

In the sixth century came Gauḍapāda who is the first known systematic exponent of Advaita Vedānta. He openly based his philosophy on the Upaniṣads. The influence of Nāgārjuna and Vasubandhu on Gauḍapāda is clear. The phrases and terms used by him were not the monopoly of any particular school. They were the heritage of the common language. Gauḍapāda is charged with being a crypto-Buddhist. If this charge means that Gauḍapāda was really a Buddhist who pretended to be a Vedāntin, it is foolish. If on the other hand, it means that Gauḍapāda was influenced by Buddhism, it is correct. Those who dub Gauḍapāda as a crypto-Buddhist tend to suggest that he had a definite leaning towards Buddhism and only outwardly professed to be a Vedāntin. Their error lies in the mistaken belief that Buddhism and Vedānta are two absolutely opposed systems. Our entire treatment of Buddhism and Vedānta gives a death-blow to such wrong notion. It is a great irony of fate that Buddhism and Vedānta, though they are the offsprings of the same mother, the Upaniṣadic Philosophy, though they are fed by the same ideology, though they are nurtured by the same methodology, though they are brought up in the same ontology, and though they grow up in the same philosophical atmosphere, yet the Buddhist should regard the Vedāntin as a pagan (tīrthika) and the Vedāntin should regard the Buddhist as an alien (bāhya)! The Hinayāna and the Svatantra-Vijñānavāda are philosophically responsible for this grave misunderstanding. Fortunately the Hīnayānists were corrected by the Mahāyānists, but unfortunately no great Buddhist was born to correct the error of Svatantra-Vijñānavāda. If one is really fond of this 'Prachchhanna'-terminology, then instead of dubbing Gauḍapāda as a Prachchhanna-Bauddha, it will be far more appropriate for one to dub the Shūnyavādins and the Vijñānavādins as Prachchhanna-Vedāntins.

We have seen that Gauḍapāda represents the best that is in Nāgārjuna and Vasubandhu. While the Buddhists either kept indifferent or outwardly professed to be, if not exactly the opponents of Vedānta, at least the followers of a faith different from that of Vedānta, it was the mission of Gauḍapāda to convince people including the Buddhists that his philosophy and also the Buddhist philosophy so far as it agreed with his own, were directly rooted in the Upaniṣads. Gauḍapāda's impartial spirit is highly admirable. His attitude towards Buddha and Buddhists is one of love and even of respect. He extended his hand of friendship towards the Buddhists, but unfortunately the Buddhists did not respond.

Bhāvaviveka who flourished in the sixth century and was a junior contemporary of Gauḍapāda, in his Tarkajvālā quotes approvingly from Gauḍapāda. Bhāvaviveka is the first Buddhist to recognize the impartial spirit of Gauḍapāda. But he too, instead of directing his energy towards the bridging over of the chasm created by Diṅnāga, drew his inspiration from Diṅnāga and in his zeal of founding a new school, founded the Svatantra-Mādhyamika school which wanted to support Shūnyavāda by means of independent logical arguments. Against this school, Buddhapālita founded the Prāsaṅgika-Mādhyamika school which rejected all independent arguments.

The seventh century gave rise to the Shūnyavādins like Chandrakīrti and Shāntideva, to the Svatantra-Vijñānavādin Dharmakīrti and to the Mīmāṁsaka Kumārila. At that time Brāhmaṇa religion, culture and philosophy were undergoing a vigorous revival and the antagonism between Buddhism and Brāhmanism had much increased. Buddhistic Tantra degenerating into Vāma-mārga was increasingly prevalent. Due to the changed economic, social and political conditions, Buddhism was loosing the patronage of the wealthy. Under the supervision of perverted monkdom the Buddhist monasteries were rapidly becoming nurseries of corruption. These conditions badly required a Buddhist scholar who could have bridged over the gulf between Buddhism and Vedānta. But unfortunately none rose to the occasion.

Chandrakīrti bitterly criticized the Svatantra-Mādhyamika School of Bhāvaviveka and the Svatantra-Vijñānavāda School of Diṅnāga. But he too failed to imbibe the spirit of Gauḍapāda. Though there were enormous similarities between Gauḍapāda and Nāgārjuna, Chandrakīrti completely ignored Gauḍapāda. Thus he did positively nothing to bridge the chasm between Buddhism and Vedānta.

Shāntideva felt that it was not wise to keep silent on or leave undeveloped the conception of Reality. He therefore fervently extolled the Bodhichitta. But he too failed to remark openly that Buddhism and Vedānta were the offsprings of the same philosophy.

The need of the hour was some staunch Vijñānavādin who could revive and develop the philosophy of Vasubandhu and who could boldly proclaim that it was based on the Upaniṣads. But instead we had Dharmakīrti, the Svatantra-Vijñānavādin, who glorified the error of Diṅnāga and harped on the separatistic tunes. The Naiyāyika and the Mīmāṁsaka were the two major opponents of Buddhism in that time. Dharmakīrti ruthlessly criticized both. To do that was no crime. In fact Shaṅkara and Sureshvara also bitterly criticized Mīmāṁsā. But nothing happened to them. Dharmakīrti ought to have accepted the philosophy of Vasubandhu and openly declared that it was based on the Upaniṣads. Then he could have well busied himself with his logic and with the criticism of Nyāya and Mīmāṁsā and other schools. A genius as he was, he ought to have corrected Diṅnāga's mistake by ousting the theory of momentariness from the realm of Reality and restricting its application to phenomena only. Had he done that Buddhism would not have met the fate it did. But what he actually did was to widen the gulf between Buddhism and Vedānta created by Diṅnāga and thus to hasten the doom of Buddhism in India.

Dharmakīrti's attack on Mīmāṁsā was so damaging that it provoked his contemporary Kumārila to write his voluminous Shloka-Vārtika to refute Buddhism and defend Mīmāṁsā. In fact Kumārila is the first man who dealt effective blows after blows on Buddhism.

The attacks of the Naiyāyikas and of Kumārila, in their turn, gave rise in the eighth century to Shāntarakṣita and Kamalashīla who extensively refuted them and criticized all other schools prevalent in their time. Shāntarakṣita and Kamalashīla also, like Diṅnāga and Dharmakīrti, paid lip-homage to Vasubandhu saying that so far as the ultimate reality was concerned, they were following in the footsteps of Vasubandhu,[1] but they too really undermined Vasubandhu's philosophy and

[1] Tattva-saṅgraha, 2084.

repeated the Himālayan blunder of Diṅnāga. They admit that there are many similarities between Buddhism and Vedānta and that the only error of Vedānta is that it declares Consciousness to be permanent.[1] Vedānta accepts the criticism of other schools by them so far as it does not violate Vedāntic standpoint. Vedānta points out that a momentary vijñāna cannot be called self-luminous or real. Consciousness must be called, at least empirically, permanent, for whatever is momentary is misery and whatever is permanent is bliss. Dialecticians of the first rank as Shāntarakṣita and Kamalashīla undoubtedly were, they could have saved the situation from taking a worse turn.

Perhaps the atmosphere was so much full of hatred and animosity that Shāntarakṣita and Kamalashīla could not even think of bridging the gulf. Shāntarakṣita, of course, remarks that learned Brāhmaṇas have great respect for Buddha,[2] that a true Brāhmaṇa is he who has removed all sins (vāhitapāpatvād brāhmaṇāḥ) and that such Brāhmaṇas are to be found only in the religion of the Enlightened Sage.[3] But such things receded into the background when instead of real arguments dogmatic arguments and repartees often came into the forefront. For example, the Mīmāṁsaka said: Because Buddha taught his doctrine to fools and Shūdras, therefore it is clear that his teaching was false like a counterfeit coin.[4] In fact, just as a herbal medicine which has been touched by the teeth of a mongoose removes, even when playfully used, all poison from a limb bitten by a snake, similarly any argument, whether Vedic or secular, emanating from the mouth of a follower of the Veda removes all poisonous misconceptions of Buddhism.[5] And the Buddhist retorted: Long time has passed and women are fickle by nature. So it is very difficult to ascertain the purity of the Brāhmaṇa race.[6] The feeble and the foolish Brāhmaṇa, at the very sight of the poisonous eyes of a Buddhist-snake, cannot even breathe much less can he think of setting it aside. Even a reasonable argument from the mouth of a follower of the Veda looks ugly like a necklace or a string of beads placed on the feet.[7] Now, the result of all this was that Buddhism could not resist the onslaught of Brāhmanism and was ousted from the land of its birth. Shāntarakṣita himself was forced to retire to Tibet where he called his disciple Kamalashīla too. And with them virtually ended the Buddhistic philosophy in India, though a Buddhist scholar here and a Buddhist scholar there continued even up to a much later date.

Then came the great Shaṅkara in that very eighth century just after Shāntarakṣita. He gave the final death-blow to Buddhistic philosophy. We have seen that Shaṅkara was greatly influenced by Buddhism. But the vital error of the Svatantra-Vijñānavādins together with other things which degraded Buddhism changed the love and respect towards

[1] Ibid, 330. [2] Ibid, 3512. [3] Ibid, 3589. [4] Ibid, 3227. [5] Ibid, 3155-6. [6] Ibid, 3579. [7] Ibid, 3376-7.

Buddhism shown by Gauḍapāda into the outward animosity and hatred exhibited by Shaṅkara. He has nothing but bitter and strong remarks for Buddhism. We have seen that Shaṅkara does not criticize Shūnyavāda and real Vijñānavāda. Svatantra-Vijñānavāda is the only school of Mahāyāna criticized and rightly refuted by Shaṅkara. Why did Shaṅkara not refute Shūnyavāda and Vijñānavāda? There are two hypotheses. It is said that on account of the mutual animosity, hatred and distrust, the Buddhists kept their texts secret from the non-Buddhists. It is also said that Kumārila in order to know the essentials of Buddhism first became a Buddhist and studied in a Buddhist monastery for years. It may be that the Shūnyavāda and the Vijñānavāda texts were not available to Shaṅkara. But there is another hypothesis which seems to be more probable when we remember how faithfully and correctly Shaṅkara has presented Sarvāstivāda and Svatantra-Vijñānavāda. It may be that Shaṅkara fully knew how similar Shūnyavāda and Vijñānavāda were to his own Vedānta and that the differences were more or less a matter of emphasis only. He also knew that the best in them was already preserved in Gauḍapāda's and also in his own philosophy. He also knew that their fundamental teachings could not be refuted because he himself accepted them. Shaṅkara's aim was to oust Buddhism, so he just dismissed Shūnyavāda as nihilism by taking the word Shūnya in its popular sense of negation and avoided Vijñānavāda by taking it in the sense of Svatantra-Vijñānavāda only.

Most of the Post-Shaṅkarites, following Shaṅkara, do the same thing and repeat his arguments. But when Buddhism was ousted and the struggle died down, people began to think dispassionately about Buddhism. Thus we find some post-Shaṅkarites remarking that if Shūnyavāda is not nihilism they have no quarrel with it for then it is merged in Vedānta, and if Vijñānavāda is not subjectivism advocating the reality of momentary vijñānas but is absolute idealism, they have no quarrel with it for then it also embraces Vedānta. We find in the same school an eminent person like Shrīharṣa openly admitting the similarities between Buddhism and Vedānta.[1]

Even in the present time Buddhism is generally misunderstood. We have tried to clear the misunderstandings about it and have pointed out that throughout it is rooted in Vedānta. Mahāyāna Buddhism and Vedānta should now be viewed, not as two opposed systems, but only as different stages in the development of the same Upaniṣadic thought.

[1] Khaṇḍana, p. 21, 31, 61.

Chapter Eighteen

RĀMĀNUJA VEDĀNTA

I

THE VAIṢṆAVA SCHOOLS

RĀMĀNUJĀCHĀRYA attempts a harmonious combination of absolutism with personal theism. The attempt is not new. We find it in the Gītā, in the Mahābhārata, particularly in the section called Nārāyaṇīya, and in the Purāṇas, notably in the Viṣṇu and the Bhāgavata. This tradition was continued by the Āḷvār saints and their interpreters, the Āchāryas to whom Rāmānuja was largely indebted. The attempt to combine personal theism with absolutism took three main lines—Vaiṣṇavism, Shaivism and Shāktism, according as the Personal Divinity was identified with Viṣṇu or Shiva or Shakti. Among the Vaiṣṇavas there are four main sects—Shrīsampradāya (Vishiṣṭādvaita) of Rāmānuja, Brahmasampradāya (Dvaita) of Madhva, also known as Ānandatīrtha, Rudrasampradāya (Shuddhādvaita) of Viṣṇusvāmī and Vallabha, and Sanakasampradāya (Dvaitādvaita) of Nimbārka. Chaitanyasampradāya (Achintyabhedābheda) is treated as a branch of Mādhvism. The Vaiṣṇavas, the Shaivas and the Shāktas all have their different sacred literature called the Āgamas which are placed side by side with the Vedas and sometimes treated as the real Vedas. They are generally divided into four parts—Jñāna or Knowledge, Yoga or concentration, Kriyā or acts connected with the founding of temples and installing of idols, and Charyā or the methods of worship. The Āgamas of Vaiṣṇavism, Shaivism and Shāktism are respectively called the Pañcharātra Samhitā, the Shaiva Āgama and the Tantra. The Shāktas practically allied themselves with the Shaivas. But there was a long struggle between the Vaiṣṇavas and the Shaivas. The cultural history of South India records a triangular fight among the Vaiṣṇavas, the Shaivas and the Jainas and whoever succeeded in winning over a ruler often indulged in persecuting the members of the other two sects in that territory. The eyes of Mahāpūrṇa (Periynāmbi), the maternal uncle and teacher of Rāmānuja were put out by the Chola king, Rājendrachola or Kṛmikanṭha (Koluttuṅga I), who was a Shaiva and Rāmānuja himself was forced to take refuge in the Hoysala province where he converted the Jaina king Biṭṭideva, renamed Viṣṇuvardhanadeva, who constructed a temple at Melukot where Rāmānuja lived for twelve years and returned to Shrīraṅgam only after the death of Koluttuṅga I.

All the Vaiṣṇava schools recognize the authority of the Pañcharātra, but it is most sacred and important for the Shrīvaiṣṇavasampradāya of Rāmānuja. The Puruṣa-sūkta of the Ṛgveda is the foundation of the Vaiṣṇava philosophy. The Shatapatha Brāhmaṇa tells us that Narāyāṇa by performing the Pañcharātra sacrifice became the Great Being—the transcendent as well as the immanent. In the Mahābhārata we find Nara and Narāyāṇa worshipping the changeless Brahman. There are the Vaiṣṇava Upaniṣads also, like the Avyakta, Kṛṣṇa, Narāyāṇa, Gopālatāpinī etc. The Shrīvaiṣṇavas are also called the Pāñcharātras, the Bhāgavatas and the Sātvatas. Yāmunāchārya in his Āgamaprāmāṇya tells us that the Pañcharātra-saṁhitā is as valid as the Veda since both are derived from the same divine source, Narāyāṇa or Vāsudeva. The Viṣṇu, Bhāgavata, Garuḍa, Padma and Varāha Purāṇas favour the Pāñcharātras, while the Kūrma, Vāyu, Āditya, Agni and Liṅga Purāṇas strongly condemn them as absolutely non-Vedic low caste sinners. According to Shaṅkara, Bādarāyaṇa criticizes the Vyūha doctrine of the Pañcharātra in the Tarkapāda of the Brahmasūtra. Among the Pañcharātra literature, the Sātvata-saṁhitā, the Jayākhya-saṁhitā and the Ahirbudhnya-saṁhitā are philosophically the most important. Pāñcharātra was so named because it deals with the five philosophical topics or because it incorporates the essence of the four Vedas and the Sāṅkhya-Yoga or because it was taught by Narāyāṇa to his five disciples during five nights.

II

THE ĀḶVĀR SAINTS

THE Āḷvārs are the most ancient Vaiṣṇava poet-saints of South India who with their Tamil hymns full of intense devotional love for Viṣṇu sang the mystic glory of the Lord. The word 'Āḷvār' means one who has a mystic intuitive knowledge of God and who has merged oneself in the Divine contemplation. Twelve of them have obtained canonical recognition and include a lady, a prince and some Shūdras. The collection of the hymns of these Āḷvārs, consisting of four thousand verses, is called Nāḷāyira-divya-prabandham and is placed side by side with the Veda. It contains as its third part the famous Tiruvāymoḷi of Nāmmāḷvār (Shaṭhakopa or Parāṅkusha) which is called by Veṅkaṭanātha or Vedāntadeshika as Dramiḍopaniṣat and which is popularly known as the Tamil Veda. Among the twelve Āḷvārs, Bhūtatt-āḷvār (Bhūtayogī), Poygaiy-āḷvār (Saroyogī) Pey-āḷvār (Mahāyogī) and Tirumaṛisai-āḷvār (Bhaktisāra) are the earliest. After them come Nāmm-āḷvār, (Shaṭhakopa or Parāṅkusha), Madhura-kavi-aḷvār, Perumāl-āḷvār (Kulashekhara), Periy-āḷvār (Viṣṇuchitta) and his adopted daughter Goḍā or Āṇḍāḷ, Toṇḍar-aḍi-poḍiy-āḷvār (Bhaktāṅghrireṇu), Tiru-pān-āḷvār (Yogivāha) and Tiru-maṅgaiy-āḷvār (Parakāla). These Āḷvārs flourished from the seventh to the ninth century. In the Bhāgavata (VII. 5. 23) complete renunciation to the Lord (ātmanivedana) is described as the highest devotion.[1] The Āḷvārs with their over-flowing devotion to God completely renounced themselves to Him, like a maid offering herself to her lover, and treated themselves as entirely dependent on Him. The entire world is conceived as the Body of God and the real pleasure lies in dedicating oneself to the service of God. The devotee forgets everything else except the Lord and his love for God is beyond space and time. He regards himself as a maid and through the pangs of separation loses himself in the Lord. The devotion of the Āḷvār is compared to the pleasure the ignorant derive from the sense-objects, with this important difference that it is directed to the Eternal and not to the sense-objects, and that it is far more acute in its intensity as it is the purest love for the Lord, the incarnation of Beauty.[2] The Āḷvār, like the Yakṣa of Kālidāsa requesting the cloud, requests the birds to take his message to Kṣṛṇa:[3]

> 'The flying swans and herons I did beg,
> Cringing: "Forget not, ye, who first arrive,
> If ye behold my heart with Kaṇṇan[4] there
> Oh, speak of me and ask it "Sir not yet
> Hast thou returned to her? And is it right?"'
>
> . . . . .
>
> 'Day and night she knows not sleep,
> In floods of tears her eyes do swim.
> Lotus-like eyes! She weeps and reels.'

The foster-mother pities the girl as too young to endure separation and the length of the night:

> 'This child of sinful me, with well-formed teeth,
> Round breasts and rosy mouth, keeps saying,
> "These fair nights eternal are as my desire
> For Tuḷasī!" [5], [6]

[1] shravaṇam kīrtanam Viṣṇoḥ smaraṇam pādasevanam. archanam vandanam dāsyam sakhyam ātmanivedanam. [2] yā prītirasti viṣayeṣvavivekabhājām saivāchyute bhavati bhaktipadābhidheya. [3] J. S. M. Hooper: Hymns of the Āḷvārs, p. 65. [4] Kṛṣṇa. [5] Tuḷasī stands for Kṛṣṇa. [6] Hooper: Hymns of the Āḷvārs.

Āṇḍāl like Mīrā regarded herself as a Gopī longing for Kṛṣṇa. She bursts forth:

> 'Govinda! kinship that we have with thee
> Here in this place can never cease! If through
> Our love we call thee baby names, in grace
> Do not be wroth, for we—like children—we
> Know nought—O Lord!'[1]

The passionate yearning of the Āḷvār should not be confused with ordinary worldly passion:

> 'No kinship with the world have I
> Which takes for true the life that is not true.
> "For Thee alone my passion burns," I cry,
> "Raṅgan, my Lord!" '[2]

The Āḷvārs were succeeded by the theologian-philosophers called the Āḷagiyas or the Āchāryas who provided a philosophical basis for the personal theism of the Āḷvārs and tried to combine their doctrine of bhakti with karma and jñāna. Nāthamuni (tenth century) is the first Āchārya of Vaiṣṇavism and is said to be the disciple of Madhura-kavi-āḷvār, the last of the Āḷvārs and the disciple of Nāmm-āḷvār or Shaṭhakopa. Nāthamuni arranged the hymns of the Āḷvārs in order, restored the Tamil Veda, and set the hymns to music in the Vedic manner which were sung in the temples. Nyāyatattva, the first work of Vishiṣṭādvaita is attributed to him. Tradition says that he entered into the image of the temple at Shrīraṅgam and became one with God. The second great Āchārya is Yāmunāchārya popularly known as Āḷavandār who was the grandson of Nāthamuni. In his Āgama-prāmāṇya he has defended the Āgamas and has placed them side by side with the Vedas and in his Siddhi-traya he has expounded the doctrines of the Vishiṣṭādvaita. His Stotra-ratna expresses the doctrine of Prapatti in beautiful devotional verses[3] and Rāmānuja is said to have become deeply attracted towards Yāmuna after hearing these hymns.

III

HISTORY AND LITERATURE

RĀMĀNUJA was born in 1017 and died in 1137. He thus enjoyed a sufficiently long life of one hundred and twenty years. He studied

[1] Ibid. Compare Gītā XI, 41. [2] Ibid, p. 48. [3] na dharmaniṣṭho'smi na chātmavedī na bhaktimānstvat charaṇāravinde. akiñchano nānyagatiḥ sharaṇya! tvat pādamūlam sharaṇam prapadye, Stotraratna, 22.

Vedānta under Yādavaprakāsha at Conjeevaram. After some time he quarrelled with his teacher regarding the interpretations of certain Upaniṣadic texts and was driven out by Yādava. Under the influence of his maternal uncle Periynāmbi (Mahāpūrṇa), Rāmānuja became deeply attracted towards Yāmunāchārya who also wanted to instal Rāmānuja in the apostolic seat at Shrīraṅgam. But before Rāmānuja could reach Shrīraṅgam, Yāmunāchārya died and tradition says that Rāmānuja found three out of the five fingers of the right hand of the body of Yāmuna folded which signified Yāmuna's three unfulfilled desires, one of them was to write a right commentary on the Brahmasūtra. Rāmānuja fulfilled it by writing his Shrībhāṣya. One day when Rāmānuja was greatly distressed, he heard the voice of God saying: 'I am the Supreme Reality, the illustrious possessor of Shrī, the Divine Power; identity is in and through difference; complete surrender to Me is the way to liberation; individual effort is not so necessary (as the Divine Grace); liberation is bound to follow after death; Mahāpūrṇa is the best of the teachers'. Then Rāmānuja went to Mahāpūrṇa and was initiated by the latter into the Vedānta Order. After some time Rāmānuja renounced the world and was called 'the prince of ascetics' (yatirāja). Besides his *magnum opus*, the Shrī-bhāṣya, he wrote Gītā-bhāṣya, Vedānta-sāra, Vedānta-dīpa, Gadya-traya and Vedārtha-saṅgraha. He established many temples and converted many people to Vaiṣṇavism.

Among the followers of Rāmānuja, Sudarshana Sūri, the author of Shrutaprakāshikā commentary on Shrībhāṣya; Veṅkatanātha or Vedāntadeshika, the greatest scholar of the Rāmānuja school, the author of Tattvaṭīkā commentary on Shrībhāṣya, of Nyāysiddhāñjana, of Shatadūṣaṇī which is a vehement refutation of the Advaita Vedānta of Shaṅkara, and of many other works; Meghanādāri, the author of Nayadyumaṇi, Lokāchārya, the author of Tattvatraya; and Shrīnivāsa, the author of Yatīndramatadīpikā are to be noted.

Two centuries after Rāmānuja, his followers became rigidly divided into two schools. Veṅkaṭanātha is the chief representative of the Vaḍagalai or the Northern school and Lokāchārya that of the Teṅgalai or the Southern school. The Āchāryas were called Ubhaya-Vedāntins because they equally valued the Sanskrit and the Tamil Veda. The Vaḍagalai school carries on their tradition; but the Teṅgalai school regards the Tamil Prabandham as authoritative and is indifferent to the Sanskrit canon. Again, the former school believes that one has to purify oneself in order to receive the Divine Grace, that just as the young monkey clings to the breast of its mother, similarly one has to renounce everything else and has to make individual effort to cling to God in order to receive His Grace, but the latter school seems to accept the dangerous doctrine that God enjoys sin and that no individual effort is necessary for the dawn of Divine Grace, that just as the cat lifts its kitten by its mouth and carries it to a safe place, similarly God bestows His Grace on the sinner and lifts him above.

IV

INFLUENCE OF BHĀSKARA, YĀDAVA AND YĀMUNA

RĀMĀNUJA was greatly indebted to the Āḷvārs, the Āchāryas and to his former teacher Yādavaprakāsha. Rāmānuja tells us that he is carrying on the Vishiṣṭādvaita tradition of the ancient writers like Bodhāyana, Taṅka, Dramiḍa, Guhadeva, Kapardī and Bhāruchi. The Bhedābheda view in Vedānta is quite old and even Bādarāyaṇa refers to Auḍulomi and Āshmarathya as the upholders of this view. Sudarshana Sūri says that Yādava has carried on the Vedāntic tradition of Āshmarathya. Shaṅkara has mentioned and criticized the bhedābheda view of Bhartṛprapañcha. Fortunately the commentary on Brahmasūtra of Bhāskara who preceded Rāmānuja and who upheld bhedābheda view is available. Rāmānuja, in his Vedārthasaṅgraha, has criticized both Bhāskara and Yādava. But their influence on him is undoubtedly very great and he owes much to both of them. Rāmānuja tells us in his Shrībhāṣya that he has closely followed the interpretations of the Sūtras given by Bodhāyana.[1] Unfortunately the works of Bodhāyana and Dramiḍa are not available now. Shaṅkara has referred to Upavarṣa and Veṅkaṭanātha has identified Upavarṣa with Bodhāyana. Rāmānuja owes much to all these Vedāntins—the Āḷvārs, Nāthamuni, Yāmuna, Yādava, Bhāskara, Bodhāyana, Dramiḍa, Bhartṛprapañcha, Āshmarathya and others, though the greatest influence on him is exercized by Yāmuna and Bhāskara and Yādava.

Bhāskara (tenth century) upholds bhedābheda view by regarding both identity and difference as equally real. The same Brahman as cause is one and identical, while as effects, it is many and different. The causal state of Brahman is a unity, while its manifested state is one of multiplicity.[2] As the causal principle, Brahman is non-dual and absolutely formless and pure being and intelligence. The same Brahman as the manifested effects becomes the world of plurality. Bhāskara advocates real modification (pariṇāma) of Brahman. Brahman really evolves as the world. A jīva is Brahman limited by the mind (antaḥkaraṇopādhyavachchhinna). Matter and its limitations are real and they are not due to ignorance. When matter limits Brahman, it becomes the individual soul. Souls are atomic in nature. Māyāvāda is due to the influence of Mahāyāna Buddhism.[3] The jīva is naturally identical with Brahman while its difference is due to material limitations.[4] Brahman, therefore, as the limited souls, really suffers the miseries of the world and obtains

[1] Shrībhāṣya, I, 1, 1, Introduction. [2] Bhāskara-Bhāṣya, I, 1, 4. [3] māhāyānika-bauddhagāthitam māyāvādam, Ibid, I, 4, 25. [4] Ibid, IV, 4, 4.

liberation therefrom through a combination of action and knowledge (jñānakarmasamuchchaya). Rāmānuja criticizes Bhāskara by pointing out that unity and difference cannot be both separately real nor can they be affirmed of the same thing. Pure identity as well as pure difference are mere abstractions and are equally unreal. They cannot be regarded as two real and independent modes of the same Brahman. According to Rāmānuja unity is always qualified by difference. Difference as such has no reality except as it modifies or determines the identical subject to which it refers. Rāmānuja rejects the conception of 'identity *and* difference' and advocates the conception of 'identity *in and through and because of* difference'. Rāmānuja denies the formless and differenceless Brahman. He thinks it stupid to say that Brahman really suffers bondage and enjoys liberation. The essence of Brahman is always pure; it is only His body that undergoes change and this body is constituted by individual souls and matter. The identity of the souls with Brahman is the last word. Their imperfections and finitude etc. are due to ignorance and become false when the souls realize themselves as forming the body of Brahman.

Yādavaprakāsha (eleventh century), one-time teacher of Rāmānuja, agrees with Bhāskara in upholding both identity and difference as separately real and as belonging to everything (bhedābheda), in believing in Brahmapariṇāmavāda or the view that Brahman really changes into this world, and in maintaining Jñāna-karma-samuchchayavāda. But he differs from Bhāskara in leaning more on the advaita side. Yādava, unlike Bhāskara, does not believe in the reality of the limitations (upādhis) and does not maintain that Brahman really suffers bondage and enjoys liberation. Brahman really remains always in pristine purity. According to Yādava, Brahman changes into chit (souls), achit (matter) and Īshvara (God). These three are not different and independent substances; they are simply modes of the same substance. They are the different states (avasthā) of Brahman and are both identical as well as different from Brahman. Our ignorance to mistake them as separately real is the cause of bondage, while the removal of this ignorance through karma and jñāna is the cause of liberation. Rāmānuja criticizes Yādava also in the same manner in which he criticizes Bhāskara so far as both Yādava and Bhāskara agree. Rāmānuja also rejects Yādava's distinction between Brahman and Īshvara as unauthorized. Brahman and Īshvara are one and the same and neither is formless and differenceless. Chit and Achit are not the modes of Brahman; they form His real body.

Yāmunāchārya in his Siddhitraya gives the philosophical basis for the teaching of the Āḷvār saints. He says that there are three real categories—the omniscient and the omnipotent Īshvara, the self-conscious souls and the material world. Yāmuna, agreeing with the Nyāya, tries to prove the existence of God as the cause of the world which is an effect. Rāmānuja improves upon Yāmuna by making the souls and the material world the body of God and by pointing out, like Kant, that God cannot be proved through inference because there are arguments of equal strength for and against, but only through faith, through the scriptures.

V

SOURCES OF KNOWLEDGE

RĀMĀNUJA recognizes three sources of knowledge—perception, inference and verbal testimony, and is indifferent to the rest. He admits the distinction between the indeterminate and the determinate perception, but unlike Nyāya, he holds that both equally involve a complex content. Indeterminate perception is not the bare apprehension of an absolutely undifferentiated object. This a psychological myth. All that is known necessarily involves some differentiation. Discrimination is essential to all knowledge. Whatever is known is known as characterized in some way, as qualified by some specific attribute. Determinate perception is itself primal. The difference between the indeterminate and the determinate perception is that while in the former an object is apprehended for the first time together with its class character, yet the class character is not recognized as such, i.e., as common to the whole class, the determinate perception takes place when the object is apprehended a second or a third time and its class character is recognized as common to the whole class. Determinate perception occurs when the sight of an object revives its former impression and it is apprehended as qualified by the class character. Even in indeterminate perception the object is perceived together with its class character, yet there the class character is not apprehended as such. Recognition or remembrance is regarded as valid knowledge and is granted a separate place. Determinate perception is distinguished from recognition by pointing out that, though in both alike there is a revival of a past impression, yet in determinate perception it is not necessary that the same object should be perceived as it is in the case of recognition. Moreover, recognition refers specially to time and place when and where the same object was previously cognized, while in determinate perception no such specific reference is necessary. Rāmānuja's treatment of inference is almost similar to that of the Nyāya-Vaisheṣika. Regarding verbal testimony, Rāmānuja puts the Pāñcharātra Āgama side by side with the Veda and further holds that the earlier and the later portions of the Veda form a single teaching. He advocates karma-jñāna-samuchchaya. The karma-kāṇḍa and the jñāna-kāṇḍa of the Veda are complementary to each other. He differs from Shaṅkara who subordinates karma-kāṇḍa to jñāna-kāṇḍa and who maintains that the former is desirable only from a lower standpoint to purify the self. Rāmānuja values both equally and believes that the former teaches the modes of worshipping God, while the latter describes the nature of God. Rāmānuja differs from the Mīmāṁsaka also in maintaining that the assertive propositions of the Veda are as important as the injunctive and that the various karmas are to be performed only to secure God's Grace.

VI

SELF, KNOWLEDGE AND ERROR

WE may now note Rāmānuja's views regarding knowledge and error. According to him, as we have pointed above, all knowledge involves discrimination and it is impossible to know an undifferentiated object. Knowledge is always in and through difference. Rāmānuja agrees with the Naiyāyika and the Mīmāṁsaka in maintaining that all knowledge points to a corresponding object existing really and outside of it. Rāmānuja defines a substance as a substratum or support of qualities. A thing may be a substance as well as an attribute. The light is an attribute in relation to the lamp, but it is a substance in relation to its rays. The whole world, as an adjective of God, is an attribute in relation to Him, though it contains many substances like souls and material objects. Similarly, knowledge is both a substance as well as an attribute. It is a substance because it possesses the qualities of contraction and expansion and it is also an attribute because it belongs to a self or to God. Rāmānuja assigns a curious place to knowledge. Substances are generally classified into spiritual (chetana) and material (jaḍa). Rāmānuja regards knowledge as neither and gives a separate intermediate position to it. It is called ajaḍa or immaterial and is distinguished from both matter and spirit. It is unlike unconscious material substances since it can unaided manifest itself as well as other objects. It is unlike self-conscious souls since it is not self-conscious and cannot know itself. Knowledge is never *for itself*, but is always for another, for the self. The self is also self-luminous, but it can only reveal itself and cannot reveal the object. Knowledge can reveal both itself and its object, but it cannot know either itself or its object. Knowledge can show itself as well as its object just as a lamp can show itself as well as a pot, but it cannot know either itself or its object. The self can know itself as well as its object, but it can show only itself and cannot show its object. Rāmānuja distinguishes self-luminosity from self-consciousness. Knowledge is self-luminous, but it is not self-conscious. The self is both self-luminous and self-conscious. Rāmānuja agrees with Prabhākara in maintaining that knowledge is self-luminous and that it reveals its object, that knowledge is a subject-object relation and as such possible only in relation to an object. But he differs from Prabhākara in maintaining that knowledge forms the essence of the self and is not its accidental quality, that the self is not a jaḍa substance, but a self-conscious subject and a self-luminous substance. Rāmānuja agrees with Shaṅkara in maintaining that the self is an eternal self-conscious subject and that knowledge is its essence. But he differs from Shaṅkara in refusing to identify the self with pure consciousness. There is nothing like pure consciousness. Consciousness is always qualified and possesses specific attributes. It always belongs to a subject and points to an object. Nobody says: 'I am consciousness'; everybody says: 'I am conscious'. The self is a self-luminous substance to which belongs and from which proceeds consciousness. The self is a substance, is incapable of contraction and expansion, cannot reveal the object, can reveal itself and can know itself and the object and is atomic in nature, while knowledge is an attribute, is capable of contraction and expansion, can reveal the object as well as itself, cannot know either itself or the object and is all-pervading in nature.[1] Knowledge always belongs to and exists for the self. Hence it is called dharma-bhūta-jñāna or attributive knowledge. It is also substantive and constitutes the essence of the selves and of God. Knowledge is like the light; the self is like the lamp; the dharma-bhūta-jñāna is like the rays. The light constitues the essence of the lamp and cannot be separated from it. The rays belong to and proceed from the light and are subject to contraction and expansion. Knowledge is a unique adjunct of the self and is eternally associated with it.[2] The self is eternal and so is knowledge. It is all-pervasive but its function in earthly existence is obstructed by karma. Here Rāmānuja agrees with Jainism except in that he holds the self to be atomic and to be a part of God and that he regards the presence of the objects as essential for the function of knowledge. In deep sleep also the self remains self-conscious together with the unmanifested dharmabhūta-jñāna for there are no objects then to be revealed by knowledge. In dreams we have knowledge because objects are created there by God in order to make the soul reap the fruits of its karmas, though knowledge is dim and vague because the objects are also dim and vague. In liberation, all karmas cease and so knowledge becomes all-pervasive and the liberated soul acquires omniscience like God.

Coming now to the theory of error according to Rāmānuja to which we have already referred,[3] we may note that error is regarded by him as one of omission only and not of commission. All knowledge is intrinsically valid and can never err. It always corresponds to its object.

[1] svarūpam dharmi saṅkochavikāsānarham svavyatiriktā'prakāshakam svasmai svayaṁprakāshakam aṇu, jñānam dharmaḥ saṅkochavikāsayogyam svavyatiriktaprakāshakam svasmai svā'prakāshakam ātmane prakāshakam vibhu cha, Tattvatraya, p. 35. [2] jñānasvarūpasyaiva tasya jñānāshrayatvam maṇidyumaṇipradīpādivat, Shrībhāṣya, p. 61. [3] Supra, p. 218.

His view is Satkhyāti or Yathārthakhyāti which means that in knowledge it is the existent real alone which is cognized, i.e., there is real object corresponding to its content. According to the doctrine of triplication or quintuplication, some particles of silver are actually present in the shell and so when the shell is mistaken for silver, silver is actually, though partially, presented to consciousness. When a white conch is seen yellow by a jaundiced person, the yellowness of the bile is actually transmitted to the conch through the rays of the eyes. The objects in a dream are actually created by God to make the dreamer reap the fruits of his actions. Hence there is no ideal or subjective element in error, not even in such cases of illusion which are called 'private' like yellow-conch and dream-objects. Error is only partial knowledge and there is no logical distinction between knowledge and error. The distinction is merely practical. Error does not serve the practical interests of life like knowledge; though, unlike the pragmatists, Rāmānuja admits and values the cognitive side of knowledge more than its practical side.

VII

METAPHYSICAL VIEWS

FROM the above account three things become clear and all the three are directly opposed to the Advaitic position of Shaṅkara. First, all knowledge involves distinctions and there is no undifferentiated pure consciousness. Pure identity and pure difference are alike unreal. Rāmānuja here agrees with Hegel. Identity is always qualified by difference. Unity is always in and through and because of diversity. Pure being is pure nothing. Shaṅkara is wrong in saying that Brahman is pure differenceless being. Brahman or Reality cannot be indeterminate, undifferentiated, qualityless substance. It is determinate and qualified (savisheṣa). When the Upaniṣads speak of Brahman as 'devoid of qualities', they only mean that Brahman has no bad qualities and not that it has no qualities whatsoever. It is the abode of all good qualities and is the incarnation of all perfection. Hence Shaṅkara's distinction between Brahman and Īshvara, between higher and lower Brahman, is unwarranted and unjustifiable. Brahman is God and He is not a formless identity, but an Individual, a Person, who is always qualified by matter and souls which form His body. Secondly, the self is distinct from knowledge. It is undoubtedly an eternal self-conscious subject, but it is also a self-luminous substance possessing dharmabhūta-jñāna as its essential attribute. Hence the self is not pure consciousness, but only the eternal substratum of consciousness. All the individual souls are real spiritual substances which are pervaded by God and form His body. They are atomic in nature and in liberation they do not merge in God, but only become similar to Him and serve Him realizing themselves as the body of God. Shaṅkara is wrong in saying that the self is identical with Brahman and absolutely merges in it. Thirdly, knowledge not only belongs to a subject, but also points to an object which exists really and outside of it. All objects are real. Even in error, illusion or dream, it is always the real which is presented to consciousness. Shaṅkara is wrong in saying that whatever becomes an object is false. On the other hand, the truth is that only the real is given in knowledge. Shaṅkara is also wrong in saying that the pure subject or pure knowledge never becomes an object, because it is not necessary that an object should, by that very fact, be a material (jaḍa) object. Even God, souls and knowledge are presented as objects—the first two are spiritual (chetana) and the last is non-material (ajaḍa). Shaṅkara's distinction between the higher and the lower standpoints is also unwarranted and wrong. All objects, spiritual as well as material, are absolutely real. Avidyā or Māyā as interpreted by Shaṅkara is sheer nonsense.

VIII

VISHIṢṬĀDVAITA OR IDENTITY-IN-DIFFERENCE

RĀMĀNUJA'S view is vishiṣṭādvaita or non-dualism qualified by difference. The Absolute is an organic unity, an identity which is qualified by diversity. It is a concrete whole (vishiṣṭa) which consists of the inter-related and inter-dependent subordinate elements which are called 'visheṣaṇas' and the immanent and controlling spirit which is called 'visheṣya'. Unity means realization of being a vital member of this organic whole.[1] God or the Absolute is this whole. He is the immanent inner controller, the Supreme Real who holds together in unity the dependent matter and individual souls as His body. Rāmānuja recognizes three things as ultimate and real (tattva-traya). These are matter (achit), souls (chit) and God (Īshvara). Though all are equally real, the first two are absolutely dependent on God. Though they are substances in themselves, yet in relation to God, they become His attributes. They are the body of God who is their soul. God is the soul of nature. God is also the soul of souls. Our souls are souls in relation to our bodies, but in relation to God, they become His body and He is their soul. The relation between the soul and the body is that of inner inseparability (apṛthaksiddhi). This is also the relation between substance and attribute. The Nyāya inherence (samavāya) is an external relation which is rejected by Rāmānuja because it involves infinite regress. Apṛthak-siddhi is the relation between the body and the soul, between a substance and its attributes, between parts and whole, and may be between one substance

[1] vishiṣṭāntarbhāva eva aikyam.

and another. It is an inner, inseparable, vital and organic relation. God is qualified by matter and souls.[1] They form His body and are inseparable from and utterly dependent on Him.[2] Rāmānuja defines a body as that which is controlled, supported and utilized for its purposes by a soul.[3] Matter and souls are called attributes (prakāra) of God; they are the controlled (niyāmya), the supported (dhārya), the parts (aṁsha) and the accessory means (sheṣa,) while God is their substance (prakārī), controller (niyantā), support (ādhāra), the whole (aṁshī) and the principal end (sheṣī). They are eternal with God, but are not external to him. God is free from all external differences—homogeneous (sajātīya) as well as heterogeneous (vijātīya), since there is nothing either similar or dissimilar which is external to or other than Him. But He possesses internal differences (svagata bheda) as His organic body is made of real and diverse elements like matter and souls. His relation with them is natural (svābhāvika) and eternal (sanātana). God is both the material and the instrumental cause of the world. He is the immanent as well as the transcendent ground of the world. He is immanent in the whole world as its inner controller (antaryāmī) and yet in His essence He transcends the world. His is a perfect personality. He is full of all good qualities—Existence, Knowledge and Bliss; Truth, Goodness and Beauty; Lustre, Love and Power.

Rāmānuja finds justification for his doctrine of the Absolute as a Triune Unity in such following Upaniṣadic passages. The Shvetāshvatara[4] says: There are three ultimate existences—the eternal and all-knowing and all-powerful God, the eternal powerless soul and the eternal matter, and these three constitute the Absolute. The same Upaniṣad further tells us: This alone need be known and there is nothing else to be known—that there are three entities, the enjoyer (bhoktā), the enjoyed (bhogya) and the mover (preritā), which constitute the Absolute. If a man knows these three he knows Brahman.[5] The same Upaniṣad goes on: The One God who runs through all beings, who is all-pervasive and who is the immanent inner controller of all beings is the Supreme Reality. There is nothing greater than He, there is nothing external to Him, He fills the whole universe. The Taittirīya tells us that all beings arise from, live in and return to this Brahman.[6] God is the soul of Nature and also the soul of souls. He is immanent and yet He is transcendent also. The Bṛhadāraṇyaka describes Him as the running thread (sūtra) which binds together all the worlds and all the souls. He is the immanent inner controller (antaryāmī) of all. He is present in matter and yet He is different from matter; matter does not know Him; matter forms His body; He controls matter from within; He is the Supreme Soul, the

[1] chidachidvishiṣṭa Īshvaraḥ. [2] sarvam paramapuruṣeṇa sarvātmanā svārthe niyāmyam dhāryam tachchheṣataikasvarūpam iti sarvam chetanāchetanam tasya sharīram, Shrī-Bhāṣya, II, 1, 9. [3] Shrī-Bhāṣya, II, 1, 9. [4] I, 9. [5] I, 12. [6] III, 1.

Antaryāmī, the Immortal.[1] Just as the spokes are bound together within the wheel, so also all the elements and all the souls are bound together within this Ātman.[2] He is like fire; they are like sparks. They are real; He is their reality. They are true; He is their truth. Hence He is called the Truest of the true.[3]

IX

GOD

IN Rāmānuja's account of God, we may notice three points of importance. First, God is identified with the Absolute. He is Brahman and Brahman must be a savisheṣa or a qualified unity. God stands for the whole universe and matter and souls form His body, He being their soul. As the Absolute, the ultimate unity-in-and-through-trinity, the concrete Whole, God may be viewed through two stages—as cause and as effect. During the state of dissolution (pralaya), God remains as the cause with subtle matter and unembodied souls forming His body. The whole universe lies latent in Him. During the state of creation (sṛṣṭi), the subtle matter becomes gross and the unembodied souls (except the nitya and mukta souls) become embodied according to their karmas. In this effect-state the universe becomes manifest. The former state is called the causal state (kāraṇāvasthā) of Brahman, while the latter state is the effect-state (kāryāvasthā) of Brahman.[4] Secondly, God is considered as the immanent inner controller (antaryāmī), the qualified substance (visheṣya or prakārī) who is in Himself changeless and is the unmoved Mover of this world-process. In His essence He does not suffer change which is said to fall to the lot of His attributes or modes only. Rāmānuja makes no distinction between an attribute and a mode. Matter and souls may be called either attributes or modes (prakāra). They are absolutely dependent on God and are inseparable from Him. They are His body and He is their soul. Just as in the case of an ordinary individual only the body undergoes change while the soul is changeless, similarly it is only the body of God, i.e., the matter and the individual souls, that undergo changes and not God himself who is their soul. Hence God is the unchanging controller of all change and the limitations of matter as well as the miseries and the imperfections of the finite souls do not affect the essence of God. Thirdly, God is also transcendent. He is the perfect personality. He has a Divine body (aprākṛtadehavishiṣṭa). Embodiment is not the cause of bondage. It is karma which is the cause of bondage. Hence God, though embodied, is not bound, for He is the Lord of Karma. The first two points about God are derived from the

[1] yaḥ pṛthivyām tiṣṭhan pṛthivyā antaro, yam pṛthivī na veda, yasya pṛthivī sharīram, yaḥ pṛthivīm antaro yamayati eṣa te ātmā antaryāmi amṛtaḥ, III, 7. [2] II, 5, 15. [3] tasya upaniṣat satyasya satyam iti, II, 1, 20. [4] Shrībhāṣya, p. 82.

interpretation of the Upaniṣads, while this point which is theistic in character is the result of the Bhāgavata influence on Rāmānuja. Rāmānuja tries to fuse the immanent Upaniṣadic Absolute with the transcendent God of the Pāñcharātra or Bhāgavata theism. God, as the perfect personality, is devoid of all demerits and possesses all merits. He has infinite knowledge and bliss. He has a Divine body and is the creator, preserver and destroyer of this universe. He has His consort Lakṣmī, the symbol of power and mercy. He is called Nārāyaṇa or Vāsudeva. He lives in His citadel Vaikuṇṭha which is made of Pure Sattva (shuddha sattva) or Nityavibhūti. His qualities like knowledge, power and mercy etc. are eternal, infinite, numberless, unlimited, undefiled and matchless. He is knowledge to the ignorant, power to the powerless, mercy to the guilty, grace to the afflicted, parental affection to the impure, perennial attachment to those who fear separation, nearness to those who pine to see Him, and kindness to all.[1] Though One in Himself, He manifests Himself in five forms in order to help His devotees. As the immanent soul of the universe, He is Antaryāmī (first form). As the transcendent personal Lord, Nārāyaṇa or Vāsudeva, He is Para or Supreme (second form). As the creator, preserver and destroyer, He reveals Himself through four-fold Vyūha (third form). His manifestation as the Lord is called Vāsudeva (this should be distinguished from the Para Vāsudeva of whom this is the first manifestation). His manifestation as the ruler of the cognitive aspect of the souls (buddhitattva or jīvatattva) and as the destroyer of this universe is called Saṅkarṣaṇa. His manifestation as the ruler of the emotional aspect of the souls (manastattva) and as the creator of this universe is called Pradyumna. His manifestation as the ruler of the volitional aspect of the souls (ahaṅkāratattva) and as the preserver of this universe is called Aniruddha. All these four manifestations are called Vyūha and they are the partial and incomplete manifestations of the Supreme Lord (Para). When God descends down on this earth in the human or the animal form, He is called Vibhava or Avatāra (incarnation) (fourth form). He does so in order to protect the good, punish the wicked and restore the dharma, the Law.[2] Vibhava is of two kinds—primary (mukhya) when the Lord Himself descends, like Kṛṣṇa, and secondary (gauṇa) when the souls are inspired by the Lord, like Shiva, Buddha etc. Of these only the former are to be worshipped by the seekers for liberation. The fifth and the last form of God is when out of His extreme mercy He takes the form of the holy idols (archāvatāra) enshrined in the recognized temples like Shrīraṅgam so that His devotees might get opportunities to serve Him physically.

[1] Tattva-traya, p. 95. [2] Gītā, IV, 8.

X

SELF

WE now consider Rāmānuja's conception of chit or the individual soul. Though the individual soul is an attribute or mode (prakāra) of God and forms part of His body, yet it is also a spiritual substance in itself and is absolutely real. It is an eternal point of spiritual light. It is beyond creation and destruction. In the state of creation, it is embodied according to its karmas, while in the state of dissolution and in the state of liberation, it remains in itself. But in the state of dissolution (pralaya), it is tinged with karmas so that in the next cycle of creation, it has to descend to the mundane life and to become embodied in order to reap the fruits of its karmas. The relation of the soul and karma is said to be beginningless. But in liberation, the soul shines in its pristine purity untouched by karma and therefore can never descend to the mundane existence any more. Though it is eternal, real, unique, uncreated and imperishable, yet it is finite and individual, being only a part or a mode of God. Hence it is regarded as atomic (aṇu) in size. As an atomic point of spiritual light, it is imperceptible, eternal and changeless. Though it is really subjected to earthly existence and to the various imperfections, defects and miseries which the wordly life implies, yet these do not affect its essence. In its essence it is changeless and perfect. Through all its births and deaths—which do not touch its essence—it maintains its identity and essential nature. The soul is different from its body, sense-organs, mind, vital breaths and even cognition. In saṁsāra, it wrongly identifies itself with these due to ignorance and karma. There are innumerable individual souls. They are essentially alike, like the monads of Leibnitz or the jīvas of the Jainas, and they differ only in number. Rāmānuja advocates qualitative monism and quantitative pluralism of souls. The soul is conceived as a real knower (jñātā), a real agent (kartā) and a real enjoyer (bhoktā). Action and enjoyment are regarded as merely different states of knowledge which is said to be the essence of the soul. The soul is a self-luminous substance as well as a self-conscious subject. It manifests itself without the aid of knowledge and it is also self-conscious. It is the substance of its dharma-bhūta-jñāna which is capable of contraction and expansion. It knows the objects through its knowledge which reveals itself as well as the objects to be known by the self. Knowledge exists for the self and though knowledge shows itself and the object, it can know neither. The self alone can know itself as well as its object, though it can reveal only itself and not its object which is revealed for it by knowledge. Knowledge or consciousness is not an accidental property of the self. It is its very essence. The self is of the nature of knowledge. It is the substance of knowledge which is its essential and inseparable attribute. Knowledge always belongs to the self and persists even in deep sleep and in liberation. Knowledge does not manifest itself in deep sleep for there are then no objects to be revealed. Knowledge is essentially infinite and all-pervasive. While the self is in bondage its knowledge is obscured by its karmas and therefore functions in a restricted manner. When the self obtains liberation, all the karmas are destroyed and there remains no impediment in the way of knowledge with the result that it becomes all-comprehensive. The liberated soul becomes omniscient because its dharmabhūta-jñāna is restored to its original status and in the absence of karmic obstructions comprehends all objects. Thus the soul, though atomic in size, in infinite in knowledge. Bliss also constitutes the essence of the soul. In its essence, it is ānandarūpa or ever blissful. The imperfections and miseries of saṁsāra, as has been pointed out above, do not touch its essence. In liberation, it enjoys infinite knowledge and everlasting bliss. It is the self-conscious 'I', the pure Ego and should be distinguished from the empirical ego (ahaṅkāra) which is the result of the false identification of the soul with the not-soul, like body, senses, mind, vital breaths etc. Though the individual soul is absolutely real, yet it is not independent. It is utterly dependent on God. It is an attribute or a mode of God Who is its substance. It is the body of God Who is its soul. It is supported by God, controlled by God and utilized by God. It is the supported (dhārya) and God is its support (dhartā). It is the controlled (niyāmya) and God is its controller (niyantā). It is the means (sheṣa) and God is its end (sheṣī). It is a mode (prakāra) and God is its substance (prakārī). It is a part (aṁsha) and God is the Whole (aṁshī). It is the body (sharīra) and God is its soul (sharīrī). And yet it is a real agent and performs and reaps the fruits of its actions. Its defects and imperfections and miseries do not affect God. Rāmānuja tries to reconcile human freedom with Divine sovereignty. God is the master of the Law of Karma. He is the inner controller of the soul. Yet the soul has got freedom of will and God, as a self-determined Whole, does not interfere with it.

Rāmānuja describes three classes of souls. To the first belong the ever-free (nitya-mukta) souls which were never bound. They are ever free from karma and prakṛti and live in Vaikuṇṭha in constant service of the Lord. They are Sheṣa, Garuḍa, Viṣvaksena etc. To the second belong the Released or Liberated (mukta) souls who were once bound but who obtained liberation through their action, knowledge and devotion. To the third belong the Bound (baddha) souls who are wandering in saṁsāra on account of ignorance and bad karmas. These are further divided into four classes: superhuman, human, animal and immobile.

XI

BONDAGE AND LIBERATION

THE souls are bound on account of their ignorance and karma. How does the pure soul come to be at all tinged with karma? This question is explained away by Rāmānuja, like the Jainas. The relation is beginningless. The cosmic process is beginningless. Due to its karmas, the soul becomes associated with particular body, senses, mind and life. This has to be taken as true. For obtaining release from saṁsāra, therefore, the soul has to remove its karmic obstacles, it has to purify itself from the dross and dust of karma that has somehow surrounded it. And this can be done by a harmonious combination of action and knowledge (jñānakarmasamuchchaya). Rāmānuja, as has been pointed out before, regards the Pūrva and the Uttara Mīmāṁsās as one science. The study of the Pūrva-Mīmāṁsā is a pre-requisite for the study of the Vedānta. The duties enjoined by the Veda, if rightly performed, help the soul in removing its karmic dross. But Rāmānuja insists that the karmas should be performed in an absolutely disinterested manner simply to please God. When the soul performs these actions, it will realize that only this performance cannot lead to liberation. Hence it will turn towards the study of the jñānakāṇḍa, the Vedānta, which teaches the nature of God, soul and matter. The soul will now realize that matter and souls qualify God who is their inner ruler, that they form the body of God who is the real soul. Rāmānuja admits that knowledge is the immediate cause of liberation, but this knowledge is real knowledge and not the ordinary verbal knowledge. Otherwise all those who studied Vedānta would obtain liberation. The real knowledge is identified by Rāmānuja with the highest bhakti or devotion which is obtained by prapatti or self-surrender and by constant remembrance of God as the only object of devotion (dhruvā smṛtiḥ) which remembrance is also called pure meditation (upāsanā) or dhyāna or nididhyāsana (concentrated contemplation). It is very important to note that constant meditation itself is not the highest bhakti (which is the same thing as real jñāna), but only a means to realize it. Enjoined actions (karma) and ordinary knowledge (jñāna) are means to realize ordinary bhakti which may be identified with prapatti or flinging oneself on the absolute mercy of God and with constant remembrance and contemplation of God called smṛti, upāsanā or nididhyāsana. This ordinary bhakti which means prapatti and upāsanā is itself a means to realize the highest bhakti which is pure jñāna or the immediate intuitive knowledge of God which is the direct cause of liberation and which dawns only by the grace (prasāda) of God. The Āḷvārs and the Āchāryas emphasized prapatti as the easiest and the surest means of liberation. God is pleased by the utter self-surrender of the devotee and takes care of him. Prapatti is open to all without any distinction of caste or creed. Among the Āḷvārs themselves there were some Shūdras and one woman. God is pleased by purest devotion, says the Bhāgavata, and everything else is only a mockery. Prapatti is also called sharaṇāgati or flinging oneself on the mercy of God and is said to consist of six steps: (1) to so think, will and act as would please God, (2) not to so think, will and act as would displease God, (3) faith that God would protect, (4) appeal to God for protection, (5) absolute self-surrender to God, and (6) feeling of absolute dependence on God.[1] The Āḷvārs and the Āchāryas regard prapatti itself as real bhakti and take it in the sense of extreme and supernormal emotional love and passion for God. They do not hold contemplation as necessary (nāvashyakī cha smṛtiḥ). They believe that God Himself takes care of the devotee when the latter has surrendered himself to God. Rāmānuja has modified these views. He distinguishes between prapatti and bhakti and identifies highest bhakti not with emotional *love* of God but with the immediate intuitive *knowledge* of God and ordinary bhakti with constant contemplation on God. Both prapatti and contemplation are means to realize highest bhakti. But contemplation or ordinary bhakti is reserved by Rāmānuja, out of deference to orthodox tradition, for the three upper castes, as it presupposes knowledge of both the Mīmāṁsās to which the Shūdras are not entitled, while prapatti is said to be open to all including the Shūdras. Liberation, according to Rāmānuja, is not the merging of the individual soul into the Absolute, but only the direct intuitive realization by the individual soul of its own essential nature as a mode of God. This realization presupposes two things—firstly, the utter destruction of the karmas by which the soul acquires its innate purity, and secondly, the dawning of the Divine Grace which transforms constant meditation into the immediate intuition of God. Hence for Rāmānuja there is no jīvanmukti for as long as the soul remains associated with the body, the karmas persist and as long as the karmas persist, the soul cannot acquire its innate purity. And there is no liberation without God's grace for unless the Divine grace dawns, the constant meditation cannot mature into real bhakti or jñāna which means the immediate intuitive knowledge of God and unless this real knowledge dawns, liberation cannot take place. The removal of all karmas and the dawning of immediate knowledge of God take place simultaneously and not successively and both are produced at once by the Divine grace which itself dawns on account of prapatti and upāsanā. The liberated soul does not become *identical* with Brahman, but only *similar* to Brahman (Brahmaprakāra). It realizes itself as the body of Brahman and ever

[1] ānukūlyasya saṅkalpaḥ prātikūlyasya varjanam. rakṣiṣyatīti vishvāso goptṛtve varaṇaṁ tathā. ātmanikṣepakārpaṇye ṣaḍvidhā sharaṇāgatiḥ.

dwells in direct communion with God, enjoying like God, infinite consciousness and infinite bliss. But it retains its individuality for otherwise enjoyment of bliss in communion with God is not possible.[1] Egoity and not individuality is the cause of bondage. Though the liberated soul in essence becomes similar to God, it differs from Him in two important respects. It is atomic and finite, while God is infinite. It is a mode qualifying God. It is the body of God who is its soul. And secondly, it does not share with God His immanent controlling power and his transcendent power of being the creator, preserver and destroyer of this universe.

XII

SELF AND GOD

THE relation of the individual soul with God should be very carefully understood. Rāmānuja has used many seemingly contradictory expressions which have baffled most of his interpreters. He vehemently criticizes the views of identity (abheda), of difference (bheda) and what is most puzzling, of identity-and-difference (bhedābheda) also. Some people, like Mādhavāchārya, therefore, believe that Rāmānuja in a sense advocates all these relations. The soul essentially is identical with God and shares omniscience and bliss with Him. Yet it is also different from God for it is an atomic mode of God. And because it is identical with as well as different from God, the relation between them is also that of identity-and-difference. But others, who are puzzled by Rāmānuja's wholesale and vigorous attack on the conception of bhedābheda which he condemns as self-contradictory, have opined that he believes in a fourth type of relation which he has called 'apṛthaksiddhi' and which may be translated as 'inseparable dependence'. This means that the relation between the individual soul and God is a unique relation which signifies their inseparability and the soul's absolute dependence on God. But if so, even the Advaitin's 'relation of non-difference' (tādātmya sambandha) which turns out in the last analysis to be 'identity' will not be different from 'apṛthaksiddhi' which will then be reduced to identity. Added to this is the difficulty of Rāmānuja's using so many different similes to signify the relation of the soul with God. Sometimes he calls the soul as a part of God, sometimes the body of God, sometimes a mode of God, sometimes an attribute or qualification of God and sometimes as absolutely dependent on, and controlled, supported and utilized by God. In our opinion this difficulty is mainly due to the loose translation of 'bhedābheda' as 'identity-in-difference'. The view of 'bhedābheda' has been advocated by different Indian philosophers in different senses.

[1] nāpi nirastāvidyasya svarūpaikyasambhavaḥ, Shribhāṣya, I, 1, 1.

When Rāmānuja criticizes this view he has in mind certain interpretations of this view by certain philosophers, notably Bhāskara and Yādava, from whose interpretations he differs. This criticism is not the criticism of all forms of bhedābheda. Rāmānuja's own view is a specific form of bhedābheda. But because this word was used in certain senses from which Rāmānuja differed he preferred to call his view vishiṣṭadvaita rather than bhedābheda which he vehemently criticized. If bhedābheda is translated into English as 'identity-in-difference' and if it is interpreted in the Hegelian sense, then neither Bhāskara nor Yādava nor Nimbārka is a real bhedābhedavādin, while Rāmānuja who is apparently opposed to this view becomes a real bhedābhedavādin. It is therefore wrong, according to us, to translate the word 'bhedābheda' as 'identity-*in*-difference'. It should be translated as 'identity-*and*-difference', and interpreted in this sense, Bhāskara, Yādava and Nimbārka are bhedābhedavādins, while Rāmānuja is not. It is for this reason that Rāmānuja calls his view vishiṣṭadvaita and neither bhedābheda nor dvaitādvaita. For Bhāskara, Yādava and Nimbārka, identity and difference are both separately and equally real, they co-exist and belong to everything and are of equal value, while for Rāmānuja both identity and difference cannot be separately and equally real nor can they have equal importance. For him, to affirm identity and difference in the same thing or to maintain their co-existence is self-contradictory. Pure identity and pure difference are mere abstractions and are equally unreal. For Rāmānuja identity is the principal thing and it is always qualified by difference which has no separate existence except as it determines the identical subject to which it belongs as an attribute. Rāmānuja rejects the conception of bhedābheda or identity-and-difference and advocates the view of vishiṣṭādvaita or identity-*in-and-through-and-because-of*-difference or identity-*as-qualified-by*-difference. The individual souls are organically related to the Absolute. They form the body of God and have no independent existence apart from Him. Yet they have their own individuality and merely qualify God. As essence, they are one with God; as modes, they are different from Him. They become similar to God and share His glory and greatness. They enjoy, like God, infinite consciousness and infinite bliss which is the essence of God and through Him their own.

According to Rāmānuja every judgment is a synthesis of distincts. Subject and predicate are *different* meanings referred to the *same* substance. If S and P are absolutely distinct, the judgment 'S is P' would be impossible; if S and P are absolutely identical, the judgment 'S is P' would be mere tautology. Pure identity and pure difference are alike abstractions. S and P are the two forms of the same substance. They have different meanings but refer to the same substance. They have two different meanings, but they fall within the same complex whole.

When we say, for example, 'the cloth is white' the quality of whiteness points towards a white substance which is a complex whole, similarly the cloth also is a complex whole which has the quality of cloth-ness. The judgment 'the cloth is white' points to the identity of these two complexes. Again, when we say—'*this* is *that* Devadatta', the judgment asserts the identity of two complexes—the 'this', i.e., Devadatta seen at present and the 'that,' i.e., Devadatta seen in the past. The person seen at present and the person seen in the past differ in their meanings because the person occupies different positions at different times, yet both refer to the same person, Devadatta. Similarly the Upaniṣadic saying 'tat tvam asi'—'that thou art'—means that the two complexes 'that' and 'thou' are identical, that though they have distinct meanings yet they refer to the same substance. 'That' signifies God as the cause of this universe and 'thou' signifies God as the inner self of the jīva and both refer to the same substance. The identity is asserted between the two forms of the same substance. Identity is never bare; it is always qualified by some difference. The individual soul is a mode of God Who is its inner self. God constitutes the 'I' of the soul. 'I live, yet not I, but God liveth in me'. Tat tvam asi, therefore, does not teach absolute identity (which is a mere abstraction) between soul and God as Shaṅkara imagines, but a qualified identity which means that God as the inner self of the soul and God as the cause of the universe are one and the same.

XIII

ACHIT OR MATTER

LET us now proceed to describe Rāmānuja's conception of Achit or unconscious substance. It is of three kinds: Prakṛti or Mishrasattva, Nitya-vibhūti or Shuddhasattva, and Kāla or Sattvashūnya. Of these Prakṛti is ordinary matter which makes saṁsāra. It is an object of enjoyment (bhogya) and suffers change (vikārāspada). It has three qualities of sattva, rajas and tamas. It forms the body of God and is more completely dependent on God than souls who have freedom of will. At the time of creation, the process of world-evolution starts from Prakṛti. The order of evolution is the same as that in Sāṅkhya and need not be repeated here. The important points of difference between the Sāṅkhya conception of Prakṛti and Rāmānuja's conception of it might be noted. Sattva, rajas and tamas are the constitutive elements of Prakṛti in Sāṅkhya, but here they are merely qualities of Prakṛti. In Sāṅkhya, these three elements can never remain separate; but here Nityavibhūti is made up of pure sattva. In Sāṅkhya, Prakṛti is infinite, but here Prakṛti is limited from above by Nityavibhūti. In Sāṅkhya Prakṛti is independent, but here Prakṛti is absolutely dependent on God and is inseparable from Him. It is His mode or His body. It is also called His Līlāvibhūti because creation is His sport.

Nityavibhūti or Shuddhasattva is made up of pure sattva and is called ajaḍa or immaterial like dharmabhūtajñāna. The ideal world and the bodies of God and of eternal and liberated souls are made of this stuff. 'It is "matter without its mutability" and has been described as a fit means to the fulfilment of divine experience.' Vaikuṇṭha, the city of God, is made up of this. Also Holy Idols in sacred places like Shrīraṅgam are said to be made of this stuff.

Kāla or time is another unconscious substance and is given a separate status. Space is identified with ākāsha which is an evolute of Prakṛti.

Thus Rāmānuja admits six substances of which two—Prakṛti and Kāla—are unconscious (jaḍa), two—Chit and Īshvara—are conscious (chetana) and two—Dharmabhūtajñāna and Nityavibhūti—are immaterial (ajaḍa).

XIV

CREATION IS REAL

CREATION, according to Rāmānuja, is absolutely real. The world and souls are as real as God Himself. They are neither created nor are they destroyed. Rāmānuja believes in satkāryavāda, the theory that the effect necessarily pre-exists in its material cause. Creation, therefore, like that in Sāṅkhya, means only explicit manifestation of the effect which was already implicitly contained in its material cause, and destruction means only the return of the effect in the bosom of its material cause. Rāmānuja believes in the pariṇāmavāda form of satkāryavāda which means that the material cause really changes itself in the form of its effect. The effect is a real transformation of its material cause, just as curd is a real transformation of milk or a gold ornament is of gold or an earthen pot is of earth. Change is not apparent but real. His view is known as Brahmapariṇāmavāda because according to it the entire universe including the material world and the individual souls is a real modification of Brahman. Though Rāmānuja, like Sāṅkhya, believes in Prakṛti, yet, unlike it, he makes Prakṛti absolutely dependent on God and controlled by God from within just as the body is controlled from within by the soul. The world of matter and the souls, as stated above, are as real as God. Independence, according to Rāmānuja, does not constitute the essence of reality. A thing in order to be real need not be independent. The material world and the souls are absolutely real though they are absolutely dependent on God. Though substances in themselves, in relation to God they are merely His attributes or modes. They always qualify God and form His body and He is their soul. They are organically related to Him and are not external to Him. God is

All-inclusive and includes matter and souls within Himself as His body controlling them both from within. Matter and souls are different from each other and also different from God, the controller, though they are not external to Him. They are co-eternal with Him. God neither creates them nor destroys them. Creation means that the subtle matter called Prakṛti evolves into gross elements and the immaterialized souls become housed in gross bodies according to their karmas. The process of creation starts in order to enable the souls to reap the fruits of their past deeds and this process is said to be beginningless so that there ever remains the possibility of past deeds. The law of Karma, therefore, necessitates creation. And yet Rāmānuja says that creation and dissolution of the world are due to the sweet will of God; they are His līlā or sport. The contradiction has to be reconciled by supposing that the Law of Karma represents the will of God. God is self-determined and Karma is the expression of His self-determined will. The charges of tyranny, cruelty and partiality are thus ruled out.

XV

REFUTATION OF MĀYĀ AND ITS EVALUATION

MANY passages in the Upaniṣads which emphatically assert the unity of the Absolute and strongly condemn multiplicity in unambiguous terms are simply explained away by Rāmānuja by pointing out that these passages deny only the *independent existence* of the world of plurality outside Brahman and not its *reality*. Rāmānuja strongly attacks the Shaṅkarite doctrine of Māyā or Avidyā. By the term Māyā, he understands the real power of God by which He creates this wonderful world. By Avidyā he means the ignorance of the jīva by which he identifies himself wrongly with the material objects like the body, the senses, the mind etc. which are evolutes of Prakṛti. He too, like Shaṅkara, admits that ignorance is the cause of bondage and that the immediate intuitive knowledge of God is the cause of liberation. But the explanations of ignorance and knowledge and of bondage and liberation that he gives are radically different from those given by Shaṅkara.

Rāmānuja levels seven important charges (anupapatti) against the theory of Māyā:

(1) *Āshrayānupapatti:* What is the locus or support of Māyā? Where does Avidyā reside? If there is any such thing as Māyā or Avidyā, we are justified in asking for its seat or abode. Verily, it cannot exist in Brahman, for then the unqualified monism of Brahman would break down. Moreover, Brahman is said to be pure self-luminous Consciousness or Knowledge and Avidyā means Ignorance. Then how can

Ignorance exist in Knowledge? Again, Avidyā cannot reside in the individual self, for the individuality of the self is said to be the creation of Avidyā. How can the cause depend on its effect? Hence Avidyā cannot exist either in Brahman or in Jīva. It is an illusory concept, a figment of the Advaitin's imagination. If it resides anywhere, it resides only in the mind of the Advaitin who has imagined this wonderful pseudo-concept, this logical myth.

(2) *Tirodhānānupapatti:* How can Avidyā conceal Brahman? If it does, then Brahman is not self-conscious and self-luminous subject. If Brahman is of the nature of self-luminosity and self-proved pure knowledge, Ignorance cannot cover or veil its essence. It is as absurd as to say that darkness can hide light or that night can act as a veil on day.

(3) *Svarūpānupapatti:* What is the nature of Avidyā? Is it positive or negative or both or neither? If it is positive then how can it be Avidyā? Avidyā means Ignorance and Ignorance means absence of knowledge. To regard Ignorance as positive is to accept self-contradiction. Moreover, if Ignorance is positive how can it be ever destroyed? No positive entity can be destroyed. As the Advaitin admits that Ignorance is removed by knowledge, Ignorance can never be positive. And if Avidyā is negative, then how can it project this world-illusion on Brahman? To say that Avidyā is both positive and negative is to embrace self-contradiction. And to say that it is neither positive nor negative is to give up all logic.

(4) *Anirvachanīyatvānupapatti:* Avidyā is defined by the Advaitin as Indefinable; it is described as Indescribable. This is a clear self-contradiction. To avoid this the Advaitin says that Avidyā is not absolutely indescribable, that to call it 'indescribable' means that it cannot be 'described either as real or as unreal'. Indescribability is equated with being neither real nor unreal. But this is absurd. This shows that the Advaitin is giving up all logic. How can a thing be neither real nor unreal? This is merely verbal jugglery. Reality and unreality are both exhaustive and exclusive. They are contradictories not contraries. Between themselves they exhaust all possibliities of predication. A thing must be either real or unreal. There is no third alternative. All our cognitions relate to either entities or non-entities. To refute this is to refuse to think. To maintain a third alternative is to reject the well-established canons of logic—the Law of Contradiction and the Law of Excluded Middle.

(5) *Pramāṇānupapatti:* By what pramāṇa or means of valid cognition is Avidyā cognized? Avidyā cannot be perceived, for perception can give us either an entity or a non-entity. It cannot be inferred for inference proceeds through a valid mark or middle term which Avidyā lacks. Nor can it be maintained on the authority of the scriptures for they declare Māyā to be a real wonderful power of creating this wonderful world which really belongs to God.

(6) *Nivartakānupapatti:* There is no remover of Avidyā. The Advaitin believes that knowledge of the unqualified attributeless Brahman removes Avidyā. But such knowledge is impossible. Discrimination and determination are absolutely essential to knowledge. Pure identity is a mere abstraction. Identity is always qualified by difference and distinction. Hence there can be no knowledge of an undifferentiated attributeless thing. And in the absence of such knowledge nothing can remove Avidyā.

(7) *Nivṛtyanupapatti:* In the last point we were told that there is no remover of Avidyā. This point tells us that there is no removal of Avidyā. Avidyā is said to be positive (bhāvarūpa) by the Advaitin. How, then, can a positive thing be removed? A thing which positively exists cannot be removed from existence by knowledge. The bondage of the soul is due to Karma which is a concrete reality and cannot be removed by abstract knowledge. It can be removed by Karma, Jñāna, Bhakti and Prasāda. The ignorance of the soul is destroyed when the karmas are destroyed and when the soul flings itself on the absolute mercy of the Lord Who, pleased by the soul's constant devotion, extends His grace to it.

All these charges of Rāmānuja against Avidyā or Māyā are based on the misunderstanding of the meaning of this term. It is called 'indescribable either as real or as unreal' due to the genuine difficulty of our finite intellect to reach Reality. It is a self-contradictory notion. Rāmānuja takes it in the sense of something 'real' and demands a seat and a pramāṇa for it. However, we may say that Brahman is the seat of Avidyā. Avidyā being not real, the monism of Brahman is not destroyed. Brahman is not really affected by it. The rope is not really affected if it is mistaken as a snake. The shell does not become silver if it is mistaken as that. Mirage cannot make the sandy desert muddy. The power of the magician does not affect his knowledge. And we may also say with Vāchaspati Mishra that the individual self and Avidyā go on determining each other in a beginningless cycle. Rāmānuja himself, when he fails to explain the cause of bondage of the pure soul, falls back upon the notion that the relation of Karma and ignorance with the soul is beginningless. Again, Avidyā does not really conceal Brahman even as a cloud does not really conceal the sun. Again, Avidyā is called positive only to emphasize the fact that it is not merely negative. In fact, it is neither positive nor negative. There is no point in saying that indescribability of Avidyā is a self-contradictory notion when the Advaitin himself admits it. But its self-contradictory nature is realized only when one rises above it and not before. As long as error or dream or illusion lasts it is *quite real*. Real means 'absolutely real' and unreal means 'absolutely unreal' and Avidyā is neither. These two terms are not contradictories and hence the Laws of Contradiction and Excluded Middle are not overthrown. The Law of Contradiction is fully maintained since all that which can be contradicted is said to be false. The Law of Excluded Middle is not overthrown since 'absolutely real' and 'absolutely unreal' are not exhaustive. Again, since Avidyā is not 'real' but only a superimposition, it vanishes when the ground-reality is known. The rope-snake vanishes when the rope is known. It is only the direct and intuitive knowledge of Reality which is the cause of liberation. Even Rāmānuja admits it though he calls it highest bhakti which dawns by the grace of God.

XVI

REFUTATION OF ADVAITA BY VEṄKAṬA AND ITS EVALUATION

VEṄKAṬANĀTHA, also known as Vedāntadeshika, a great follower of Rāmānuja has made a vigorous attack on the Advaita in his 'Shatadūṣaṇī' ('Century of Refutations') where he levels sixty-six charges on the Advaita.[1] The crux of these charges is already contained in the 'Seven Refutations' of Rāmānuja given above. Most of these charges are either repetitions with minor variations or deal with minor points of detail or are of theological and sectarian interest carrying little philosophical or truly religious value. We may, however, note some of the most important charges levelled against Advaita by Veṅkaṭanātha and try to answer them:

(1) If Brahman is a qualityless homogeneous entity, the word 'Brahman' cannot denote it either in a primary sense or in an implied sense (lakṣaṇā) and hence it becomes useless.

Veṅkaṭanātha forgets that words, according to Shaṅkara himself, can never denote the Absolute which can be realized

[1] Either this work as available now is incomplete or the word 'Shata' here is taken in its general sense of 'many' and not in its specific sense of 'hundred'. For a summary of these charges the interested reader is referred to Dr. S. N. Dasgupta's History of Indian Philosophy, Vol. III, pp. 304-346.

only by direct spiritual vision. Language and thought would become insignificant only when they are transcended, not before. As long as we are in the phenomenal sphere, they are the only instruments available to us and we have to work with them however defective they may be.

(2) There can be no inquiry into the nature of Brahman, for all inquiries are possible about qualified objects only. No knowledge, whether general or specific, is possible about an unqualified Brahman. If it is said that this knowledge about Brahman is ultimately false, then no purpose would be served by such false knowledge.

Veṅkaṭa forgets that real Brahman-knowledge is not verbal knowledge, otherwise all those scholars who know Vedānta-texts should have obtained liberation. Real Brahman-knowledge is the direct spiritual realization of Brahman. Veṅkaṭa also forgets the distinction between the relative and the absolute standpoints so much emphasized by Shaṅkara. He forgets that it is only through the relative that we can go to the absolute. He forgets the detailed classical exposition by Shaṅkara of the view that even 'unreal' (only ultimately) means like the Vedānta-texts lead to real knowledge, just as 'unreal' (only from the waking standpoint) dream-experiences lead to real physiological reactions and that the 'unreality' of the Vedānta-texts can be realized only after Brahman-realization, not before. (S.B.II, 1, 14.)

(3) Liberation can be obtained only by devotion and worship and not by mere knowledge. Even all illusions do not vanish by a mere knowledge of them, e.g., the illusion of 'yellowness' in the case of a jaundiced person does not vanish by the mere knowledge of its falsity, but by taking medicine which removes the excessive bile. If mere knowledge of the Unity-texts leads to liberation, then Shaṅkara himself would have obtained it and then he would have been merged in Brahman and would not have explained his teachings to his disciples.

Veṅkaṭa should know that illusions can be destroyed only by knowledge and by nothing else. Let there be no illusion about this. If a dreamer knows he is dreaming, he is not a dreamer but a pretender. If a jaundiced person knows that he is suffering from jaundice and that the 'yellowness' is only an illusion, then certainly he is not labouring under an illusion, though suffering he might be from a disease. Again, how can Veṅkaṭa know that Shaṅkara has not obtained liberation? Veṅkaṭa feels as if liberation is to be obtained in the same manner in which he can obtain a handful of rice.

He forgets the fact that bondage and liberation are equally unreal ultimately, that ignorance means bondage and knowledge means liberation. This knowledge is not verbal or intellectual knowledge but direct spiritual vision. He forgets that the great Āchāryas kindly descend on the phenomenal plane to preach their doctrine for the benefit and uplift of mankind. If we do not take advantage of their teaching, it is our fault, not theirs.

(4) Even though the final knowledge of unity be attained, the world-appearance may still continue due to vāsanā until the body is destroyed. How can it happen?

Veṅkaṭa forgets that the world-appearance may continue due to the force of vāsanā, just as a potter's wheel may continue to revolve for some time even though the potter has withdrawn his hand from it. The jīvanmukta who is liberated *here* and *now* has no attachment with the body, just as a snake has no attachment with the slough it has cast off on an ant-hill. If liberation cannot be attained in this life, it is futile to talk of it as happening after death. Shaṅkara believes in jīvanmukti;[1] it is Veṅkaṭa who rejects it.

(5) If the world is false because it is knowable, then Brahman too, being knowable, would be equally false. Again, if the world is false, there is no sense in saying that it is negated by right knowledge.

The world is false because it cannot be described either as real or as unreal. All objects of the intellect are false in this sense. But Brahman is not an object of the intellect and hence it is not 'knowable' in the empirical sense. It is the transcendental background of all empirical knowledge and stands self-luminous and self-proved. To *know* Brahman is to *be* Brahman. Again, the world becomes false from the higher standpoint and not from its own standpoint.

(6) Difference cannot be denied. The so-called 'absence of difference' is itself *different* from 'difference' and therefore establishes the reality of difference. If there is no difference, there would be no identity also, because these terms are relative. We have, therefore, to admit both.

It is true that difference and identity are relative and one cannot remain without the other. We have, therefore, either to admit both or reject both. It is further true that bare identity and bare difference are mere abstractions. Identity, in the empirical world, is always qualified by difference. But this does not mean that that which is the highest truth for

[1] S. B. I, 1, 4.

the intellect must be the highest truth for Reality also. There is a higher 'unity' which is above the notion of 'unity-in-difference'. This 'unity' or 'identity' is not abstract identity which alone is relative and opposed to difference. Shaṅkara's system called 'Advaita' is not bare identity, but the highest identity which transcends the intellectual notions of identity, difference and even identity-in-difference. The best description of the Absolute is through negative terms (neti neti), though the Absolute itself thereby does not become negative. Hence the term 'non-dualism' (advaita) is preferred to 'monism' (aikya), 'absence of difference' (abheda) to 'identity' (ekatva) and 'without a second' (advitīya) to 'one' (eka).

(7) The falsity of the world is proved by logical proofs which are themselves false. The distinction between the two supposed standpoints is a distinction within thought itself and therefore, by its own logic, false. Again, Māyā is *described* as indescribable. Again, if 'indescribability' means 'falsity', then Brahman too, being indescribable, would be equally false.

These charges are based on a confusion between the two standpoints. Though this distinction is not ultimately true, yet it is very vital and absolutely essential for the phenomenal world which would otherwise lose even its phenomenality and merge into nihilism. The intellect reigns supreme in the empirical world. But it has to realize its own limitation and point to the Absolute, even though it cannot lead us to it. Māyā is indescribable because it is 'neither real nor unreal'. Brahman is indescribable because it, being the self-proved Real, cannot be fully described by the intellect.

XVII

RĀMĀNUJA AND SHAṄKARA

LET us now give a general estimate of Rāmānuja's philosophy. There are many people who believe that Shaṅkara's Absolute is a bare intellectual and abstract identity without any shade of difference. It has been called 'rigid and motionless, staring at us with frozen eyes', 'a bloodless Absolute dark with the excess of light' and Shaṅkara's philosophy has been said to be 'a finished example of learned error'.[1] It has been compared to God of Spinoza and the Neutrum of Schelling. Like the former it is said to be 'a lion's den' where we see the footprints of animals going inside but of none coming outside and like the latter it has been called

[1] Indian Philosophy, Vol. II, p. 659, by Dr. S. Radhakrishnan.

a 'dark night where all cows are black'. Rāmānuja shares this view about Shaṅkara. On the other hand, Rāmānuja's Absolute has been called a concrete individual, an identity-in-and-through-difference and has been compared to the Hegelian Absolute. But it is much more. It is also a personal God like that of Pringle-Pattison. Rāmānuja is accredited with reconciling the demands of philosophical thinking with those of religious feeling. These people do justice to Rāmānuja but grave injustice to Shaṅkara. They forget the important fact that neither Shaṅkara overlooked the demands of religious feeling nor could Rāmānuja satisfactorily harmonize religious feeling with logical thinking. To dub Shaṅkara's Absolute as a bare identity is to betray ignorance even of the significant name his philosophy bears—'Advaita'—which means not 'bare identity' but 'denial of ultimate difference'. He who imagines that Shaṅkara's position means complete denial of this world, of the souls, of action, of philosophy, of religion and even of God, may know anything but Shāṅkara Vedānta. The veteran idealist of England, T. H. Green has rightly remarked: 'the fact that there is a real external world —is one which no philosophy disputes'.[1] Again, to say that Shaṅkara has no place for religious feeling is, to say the least, to make a mischievous arbitrary statement. It is to miss the depth of his philosophical writings and to betray ignorance of his soul-inspiring hymns—a great and a rich contribution to Sanskrit poetry—in which the words almost burst forth due to the pressure of intense emotional devotion with which they are packed. One need only go to any admirer of Shaṅkara and hear the following verse to see the heart of Shaṅkara: 'Although there is not the slightest difference between Thee and me, O Lord, yet it is I who belong to Thee, Thou dost not belong to me, just as the wave belongs to the sea, the sea does not belong to the wave'. For all *practical* purposes therefore, the distinctions remain real. They become false only for him who has realized the unity of Brahman. This 'unity', like the 'unity of apperception' in Kant, is not a category of unity, it is not bare identity; it is the unity of the fundamental consciousness which is the foundation of all categories. And yet, unlike Kant's 'unity of apperception', it is not formal. Shaṅkara's conception of the 'unity' of Brahman is not an intellectual conception. It is the unity which for want of any better word is called 'non-difference' and this suggests that the intellect cannot positively grasp it but only point to it. Self-realization alone which means immediate intuitive knowledge can reveal this unity of Brahman which is not bare identity but foundational unity which is necessarily presupposed by and which in itself transcends all the categories of identity, difference and identity-in-difference. Only for those who are qualified to tread the 'razor-like' path and to be one with Brahman—and they are hardly one in a million—are the distinctions

[1] Works, Vol. I, p. 376.

sublated. For others Shaṅkara has strongly recommended the path of action and devotion and followed it himself in his practical life. Let no man stand up and say that Shaṅkara's philosophy is the philosophy of bare identity or that it lacks religious fervour. One has only to turn to the practical life of Shaṅkara which has always been a paradox to those who have misunderstood or half-understood the teachings of the great Āchārya. Shaṅkara would gladly say with Bradley that 'the man who demands a reality more solid than that of the religious consciousness knows not what he seeks'. Bosanquet, a great idealist, has said in connection with realism-idealism controversy: 'Certainly for myself if an idealist were to tell me that a chair is really not what we commonly take it to be, but something altogether different, I should be tempted to reply in language below the dignity of controversy.'[1] A follower of Shaṅkara might be tempted to reply similarly to one who tells him that Shaṅkara's philosophy advocates bare identity or that it is devoid of religious fervour or that it denies the world outright. Or perhaps he would not. He would simply smile remembering the words of Gauḍapāda: It is only the dualists who in order to establish their respective views fight with one another; Advaitin fights with none.[2]

Let us try to do justice to both Shaṅkara and Rāmānuja. It has been already pointed out that Rāmānuja was much influenced by the Āḷvārs and the Āchāryas and by the bhedābhedavādins who preceded him. Indeed his main task was to combine the Pāñcharātra theism with the Upaniṣadic Absolutism. He wanted to find philosophical justification for the Vaiṣṇava theism in the Prasthāna-traya of the Vedānta and thus tried to harmonize the demands of religious feeling with logical thinking. But he confined himself to justify Pāñcharātra theism by means of Upaniṣadic Absolutism. It is one thing to combine Philosophy with Religion, but quite another thing to combine one particular philosophical doctrine with a particular religious creed. Shaṅkara has attempted the former, while Rāmānuja has attempted the latter. For Shaṅkara, the only scriptures were the Vedāntic texts and he interpreted them so as to harmonize logical thinking with religious feeling. For Rāmānuja, the scriptures included besides the Vedāntic texts, the Vaiṣṇava Purāṇas, the Pāñcharātra-Āgama and the Tamil Prabandham, and his main task was to prove that the doctrines of the Vaiṣṇava theism are in conformity with the Vedāntic tradition. There are some doctrines of the Vaiṣṇava theism which can be harmonized with the Vedāntic Absolutism, but not all. And if, therefore, Rāmānuja failed, his failure is due not to his personal incapacity but due to the very nature of the difficult task he undertook to perform. It must be admitted without any reservation and in all fairness to Rāmānuja that no one else could have done it better. He has given us the best type of monotheism pregnant with

[1] Contemporary Philosophy, p. 5. [2] Kārikā, III, 17.

immanentism. He has emphasized the religious side but not at the cost of the philosophical. His intense religious fervour and his bold logic undoubtedly make him one of the immortals in Indian Philosophy. His task became more difficult on account of Shaṅkara's exposition of the Vedānta and Rāmānuja therefore had to refute Shaṅkara almost on all important points. And yet there is much truth in the remark that Rāmānuja's position is essentially similar to the position of Shaṅkara viewed from the practical or phenomenal (vyavahāra) standpoint. For all *practical* purposes Shaṅkara too maintains the reality of all secular and Vedic acts. From this standpoint the entire universe including the material world and the individual souls is as *real* as it can be. And though the highest reality is the indeterminate Brahman, yet the highest conception open to us, finite intellectual beings, is Īshvara and Īshvara alone. Though the universe is only a *vivarta* or an appearance of Brahman, yet as long as it lasts it is as good as real. Sarvajñātma-Muni is right in holding that Pariṇāmavāda (the position of Rāmānuja) is an earlier stage of Vivartavāda (the position of Shaṅkara) and that the two are not opposed.

XVIII

CRITICAL ESTIMATE

LET us now turn to the dialectical unfolding of the inherent contradictions in the philosophy of Rāmānuja. Rāmānuja has failed to express the relation between the universe and God. According to him matter, souls and God are the three realities and all the three make up the Absolute. And yet he identifies the Absolute with God who is only one of the three realities. God is the underlying substratum of matter and souls which are said to be His attributes. But if they are His attributes or modes, how can they be as real as God? The criticism which Spinoza levelled against Descartes that matter and souls cannot be called 'substances' if they are dependent on God can be very well levelled against Rāmānuja also. Rāmānuja abolishes the distinction between attributes and modes and though he explicitly maintains the distinction between attributes and substance, yet he implicitly undermines this distinction also. According to him a thing can be a substance as well as an attribute. The distinction is relative. Though matter and souls are substances in themselves yet in relation to God they are merely His attributes. The very definition of 'substance' is that it has an independent existence. Rāmānuja undermines this definition when he says that independence does not constitute the essence of substance, that a thing may be dependent and yet be a substance. This is logically most unsatisfactory. If matter and souls are absolutely dependent on God, how can they be as real as God? Shaṅkara defines the real as that which has independent existence for all times and tells us that Brahman alone is real. But he does not deny the existence of matter and souls. The dilemma before Rāmānuja is this—either maintain the relative existence of matter and souls or abolish your Absolutism. And Rāmānuja is prepared to do neither. Loyalty to the Upaniṣads makes him cling to Absolutism while sympathy for Vaiṣṇavism makes him recognize ultimate distinctions. Thus Vishiṣṭādvaita is a house divided against itself. But Absolutism precludes divided loyalites. One cannot run with the hare and hunt with the hound. Rāmānuja, therefore, has been unable to solve the problem of the relation between the universe and the Absolute. He has stated that the universe is organically related to the Absolute, that it is the body of God, that though it has a right to exist separately it is not external to God who is All-inclusive, that identity is always qualified by difference. But he fails to explain his position further. The relation between the universe and God is not pure identity, for the very notion is a pseudo-concept, a bare abstraction. This relation is not that of difference for pure difference also is equally an abstraction. Difference belongs to and cannot remain separate from identity. This relation is not that of identity-and-difference (bhedābheda) for it is self-contradictory. Both identity and difference, like light and darkness, cannot belong to the same thing in the same sense. Then what is this relation? Rāmānuja calls it vishiṣṭādvaita or qualified identity, i.e., identity qualified by difference or identity-in-and-through-and-because-of-difference which he also calls apṛthaksiddhi or dependent existence, i.e., dependence of the attributes or modes on the substance, of the body on the soul. It is an inner relation and is intended to replace the Nyāya-Vaisheṣika relation of samavāya which is rejected as external by Rāmānuja. While samavāya unites the different, apṛthaksiddhi separates the identical. But the difficulty is that Rāmānuja cannot maintain the relation of identity-in-difference on account of his sympathy with pluralism. Absolutism and pluralism cannot go together. Rāmānuja is keen to preserve the differences between the attributes themselves and between the attributes and the substance. The simile of the body and the soul also does not solve the problem. The body exists for the soul and perishes when the soul departs and so cannot claim independent and absolute existence. The simile of the parts and the whole also is of no avail for the parts can have no separate existence from the whole and even within the whole they cannot claim as much reality as the whole.

Rāmānuja reduces all the distinct material objects to their subtle cause—the Prakṛti. But when he comes to the souls he maintains the separate individuality of each. The souls are essentially alike, but numerically different. But quantitave pluralism is no real pluralism. The difference which makes no difference is no difference. There is no meaning in saying that the souls are diverse atomic points of consciousness. Monadology is a figment of the imagination. Rāmānuja, on the one hand, identifies the soul with the individual jīva, the 'I'-consciousness (aham), the object of introspection, the substratum of knowledge, the empirical ego, the finite subject of empirical knowledge whose individuality he is anxious to preserve but whose individuality nobody denies, and yet, on the other hand, he identifies the soul with the self-luminous and self-conscious subject which preserves its identity through all its births and deaths and is essentially changeless. This also is a grave inconsistency. If the soul is essentially changeless and is not affected by births and deaths, then the body, the senses, the mind, the birth, the death and all the facts of experience in the mundane existence are not fundamental to the self. Such a self is the transcendental Self. It is really, as Rāmānuja says, self-luminous and self-conscious and eternal and changeless. It is the pure subject, the transcendental background of all empirical knowledge. It can never become the object of experience and cannot be called finite and individual. How can then it be identified with the empirical 'I'? How can it be dragged to the level of a finite object? How can it be a real agent and a real enjoyer? How can its plurality be proclaimed?

Rāmānuja says that matter and souls form the body of God. But the distinction between the body of God and the soul of God is not clearly brought out. In order to avoid the difficulty which is present in the Nyāya-Vaisheṣika that if matter and souls are co-eternal with God, God cannot be the real Creator nor can He be unlimited and infinite because so many souls and atoms of matter which are all co-eternal and external to God constitute a limit to Him, Rāmānuja makes matter and souls form the body of God. Matter and souls are not external to God but are organically related to Him. He is both the material cause and the efficient cause of the universe. God's body is the material cause while His soul is the efficient cause of this universe. But even here the difficulties are not solved. Neither matter nor souls are really created by God. The soul does not create the body. They exist eternally within Him and creation means only the manifestation of the subtle matter as gross and of the immaterialized souls as embodied. But the distinction between the body and the soul of God is not logical. If the entire universe consisting of matter and souls is the real body of God, then God must suffer all the changes and miseries and pains and defects and imperfections of matter and souls, just as the individual suffers the pain in his body. How can then God be perfect and changeless and infinite? Rāmānuja says that God is not affected by the change of the universe and the imperfections and pains of the souls, even as a soul is not affected by the change and the pains of the body. But if a soul is not affected by the change and the pains of the body, it cannot be identified (as Rāmānuja does) with the empirical ego and the plurality of the souls cannot be maintained. Then, the soul becomes the Universal Ātman, the Absolute itself. Moreover, on this assertion the body becomes an accident to the soul. Is the body of God, then, an accident to His soul? If so, God becomes like an ordinary soul suffering bondage and the sooner He shakes off His body the better it is. Rāmānuja answers that it is ignorance and not embodiment which is the cause of bondage. But then why does he not admit jīvanmukti? Why does he regard the shaking off of the body as absolutely essential for obtaining liberation? Verily, then, Rāmānuja's Absolute is Shaṅkara's Brahman bound to this world, while Shaṅkara's Absolute ls Rāmānuja's Īshvara liberated from this world. Rāmānuja cannot sustain the distinction between God's body and soul. One cannot, as Shaṅkara says, keep half a hen for cooking and reserve another half for laying eggs.[1] It cannot be logically maintained that the soul of God is changeless and perfect while His body suffers change and imperfections.

Again, Rāmānuja tries to combine the Upaniṣadic Absolutism with the personal Theism of the Pāñcharātras. Here also he fails. If God is the immanent soul of the universe, how can He at the same time be a transcendent Person living in Vaikuṇṭha with His consort Lakṣmī and attended upon by the nitya and the mukta souls? As Dr. Radhakrishnan says: 'Rāmānuja's beautiful stories of the other world, which he narrates with the confidence of one who had personally assisted at the origination of the world, carry no conviction. . . . The followers of Rāmānuja move with as much Olympian assurance through the chambers of the Divine Mind as Milton through the halls of heaven'.[2] The distinction between Prakṛti or Līlāvibhūti and Shuddhasattva or Nityavibhūti is arbitrary. If the body of God is made up of Prakṛti and souls, what is the necessity of assuming Nityavibhūti as the stuff where God dwells and which constitutes the body of God? Is Prakṛti the apparent and Nityavibhūti the real body of God? Moreover, when sattva, rajas and tamas are the guṇas of Prakṛti and as such inseparable from it how can sattva be abstracted and made to form Nityavibhūti which limits Prakṛti from above?

The distinction between the nitya and the mukta souls is also arbitrary. Souls may be either bound or liberated. What is the necessity of maintaining the third variety?

The relation between the soul and its dharmabhūta-jñāna is also untenable. If the essence of the soul is consciousness, then how can consciousness be its quailty which is liable to contraction and expansion? To say that jñāna can reveal itself as well as its object but can know neither, is as absurd as the Sāṅkhya saying that Prakṛti can prepare beautiful dishes but cannot enjoy them. Revelation and knowledge are one and the same. Though Rāmānuja admits the self as the self-conscious

[1] Māṇḍūkya-Kārikā-Bhāṣya, IV, 12. [2] Indian Philosophy, Vol. II p. 720.

subject, yet he is unable to shake off the Nyāya-Vaisheṣika influence that the self is a substance possessing the quality of consciousness.

Again, Rāmānuja, like the Jainas, cannot explain the cause of bondage. If the soul is essentially pure and changeless and self-conscious subject, why should it get associated with Karma and be bound? If the soul can be tinged with Karma it is already bound. Rāmānuja explains this difficulty by the conception of a beginningless saṁsāra. But if you have to fall back on something beginningless why not admit the beginningless Avidyā?

Again, the distinction between prapatti and bhakti and between lower and higher bhakti is arbitrary. If lower bhakti means dhyāna and dhyāna means smṛti or upāsanā and this upāsanā leads, through Divine grace, to the dawn of higher bhakti which means intuitive knowledge of God which is the direct cause of liberation, then why, instead of putting the whole thing in a complicated manner, not frankly say that direct intuitive Knowledge or Self-realization alone is the cause of liberation?

Chapter Nineteen

OTHER SCHOOLS OF VEDĀNTA

I

MADHVA-VEDĀNTA

As Hegel is said to be a born foe of mysticism, so Madhvāchārya may be said to be a born foe of Shaṅkarāchārya. He was born in A.D. 1197 and lived for seventy-nine years. He is also known as Ānandatīrtha or Pūrṇaprajña. He is regarded as an incarnation of Vāyu and was the disciple of Achyutaprekṣa whom he converted to his views later on. He has written thirty-seven works, most important of which are—Commentary on the Brahmasūtra called Madhva-bhāṣya, Anuvyākhyāna, Gītā-bhāṣya, Bhāgavata-tātparya-nirṇaya, Mahābhāratatātparya-nirṇaya, Viṣṇu-tattva-nirṇaya and Tattvoddyota. Jayatīrtha, the author of the Tattvaprakāshikā Commentary on the Madhva-bhāṣya and Nyāyasudhā on the Anuvyākhyāna, and of Pramāṇapaddhati; and Vyāsatīrtha, the author of Tātparya-chandrikā Commentary on the Tattvaprakāshikā, and of Nyāyāmṛta and Tarka-tāṇḍava; and Rāmāchārya, the author of the Taranginī Commentary on the Nyāyāmṛta—are some of the most eminent followers of Madhva.

Madhva is the champion of unqualified dualism (dvaita) and accuses Shaṅkara of teaching the false doctrines of Shūnyavāda Buddhism under the cloak of Vedānta.[1] His hatred of Advaita is so great that he calls Advaitins 'deceitful demons' who play in the darkness of Ignorance and who must run away now that the omniscient Lord (the Sun of Dualism) is coming to destroy their darkness of arguments and false interpretations of the scriptures.[2] Madhva advocates the reality of five-fold differences—between soul and God, between soul and soul, between soul and matter, between God and matter, and between matter and matter.[3] His bias for difference is so great that he advocates difference of degrees in the possession of knowledge and in the enjoyment of bliss even in the case of liberated souls—a doctrine found in no other system of Indian philosophy.

Madhva, like Rāmānuja, accepts the three sources of knowledge—perception, inference and testimony, and like him holds that God who

[1] yachchhūnyavādinaḥ shūnyam tadeva brahma māyinaḥ. [2] Tattvoddyota, p. 245.
[3] jagatpravāhaḥ satyo'yam pañchabhedasamanvitaḥ. jīveshayor bhidā chaiva jīvabhedaḥ parasparam. jaḍeshayor jaḍānāñcha jaḍajīvabhidā tathā, Mahābhārata-tātparya-nirṇaya, I, 69-70.

is Hari, Viṣṇu, Nārāyaṇa or Vāsudeva can be known only by the scriptures. Like Rāmānuja, Madhva also regards the Pūrva and the Uttara Mīmāṁsā as forming a single science. Like the Mīmāṁsaka, Madhva upholds the authorlessness of the Veda. Madhva, unlike Nyāya which regards God as the author of the Veda, regards God as the great teacher (mahopādhyāya) of the Veda. Like the Mīmāṁsaka, Madhva believes that knowledge reveals the knower and the known as independently real and upholds the intrinsic validity of knowledge. The world is real and so are the differences that constitute it. Difference is the very nature of things. To perceive things is to perceive their uniqueness which constitutes difference. Distinctions of things account for the distinctions of ideas.

Madhva, like Rāmānuja, believes in God and souls and matter as the three entities which are eternal and absolutely real, though souls and matter are absolutely dependent on God. God alone is independent. He possesses infinitely good qualities. Existence, knowledge and bliss constitute His essence. He is the creator, preserver and destroyer of this universe. He has a divine body and is transcendent. But He is also immanent as the inner ruler of all souls. He damns some and redeems others. His is a perfect personality. He is the Lord of Karma. He is pleased only by bhakti. He manifests Himself in the various Vyūhas and in incarnations and is present in sacred images. Lakṣmī is His consort. She is all-pervading and eternal like Him, but her qualities are a little less than those of her Lord. She is ever-liberated (nityamukta) and possesses a divine body. She is the Power of God. The individual souls are numberless and are atomic in size. The soul is by nature conscious and blissful. It becomes subject to pains and imperfections on account of its connection with the material body, sense-organs, mind etc. which connection is due to its past karmas. The souls are eternal and are of three kinds—eternally free (nityamukta), freed (mukta) and bound (baddha). Though God controls the soul from within, yet it is a real agent and a real enjoyer and is responsible for its acts. Bhakti is the only means of liberation. It is defined as the Eternal Love for God with a full sense of His Greatness.[1] Prakṛti is primal Matter. Under the influence of God when He wants to create the world, it evolves itself into the various material products which return to it again at the time of dissolution. Creation means manifestation of subtle matter as gross and the embodiment of the souls in order to reap the fruits of their acts. So far Madhva agrees with Rāmānuja whose philosophy and religious approach have exercised a very great influence on Madhva. But there are certain important points of difference between them which may be noted: Madhva is a rank dualist and does not believe in qualified absolutism. According to Rāmānuja differences have no separate

[1] jñānapūrvaparasneho nityo bhaktir itīryate, Ibid, I, 107.

existence and belong to identity which they qualify. Identity, therefore, is the last word. But for Madhva differences have separate existence and constitute the unique nature of things. They are not mere qualifications of identity. Secondly, Madhva rejects the relation of inseparability (apṛthaksiddhi) and the distinction between substance (dravya) and non-substance (adravya). He explains the relation of identity and difference by means of unique particulars (visheṣa) in the attributes of a substance. The attributes are also absolutely real. Hence, Madhva does not regard the universe of matter and souls as the body of God. Matter and souls are different from each other and from God. They do not qualify God because they have substantive existence themselves. Though God is the immanent ruler of the souls and though the souls as well as matter depend on God, yet they are absolutely different from God and cannot form His body. Thirdly, Rāmānuja advocates qualitative monism and quantitative pluralism of the souls, believing as he does that all souls are essentially alike. But Madhva advocates both quantitative and qualitative pluralism of souls. No two souls are alike. Each has, besides its individuality, its peculiarity also. Fourthly, Madhva, therefore, believes that even in liberation the souls differ in degrees regarding their possession of knowledge and enjoyment of bliss (ānandatāratamya). Rāmānuja rejects this. Fifthly, Madhva, unlike Rāmānuja, does not make any distinction between the body and soul of God. Hence, he regards God as only the efficient cause of the world and not its material cause which is Prakṛti. God creates the world out of the stuff of Prakṛti. Rāmānuja regards God as both the efficient and the material cause of the world. Sixthly, while Rāmānuja makes the liberated soul similar to God in all respects except in some special respects like the possession of the power of creation, preservation and dissolution of this world, and the power of being the inner ruler of the universe, Madhva emphasizes the difference of the liberated soul from God. The soul becomes similar to God in some respects when it is liberated, yet even in these respects it is much inferior to God. It does not enjoy the full bliss of God. The bliss enjoyed by the redeemed souls is fourfold: sālokya or residence in the same place with God; sāmīpya or nearness to God; sārūpya or having the external form like that of God; and sāyujya or entering into the body of God and partially sharing His bliss with Him. Thus, though according to Rāmānuja the liberated soul enjoys the full bliss of the realization of Brahman which is homogeneous, ubiquitous and supreme, according to Madhva even the most qualified soul which is entitled to sāyujya form of liberation can share only partial bliss of Brahman and cannot become similar to Brahman (Brahma-prakāra) in the strict sense of the term.[1] Seventhly, Madhva

[1] muktāḥ prāpya param Viṣṇum taddeham saṁshritā api. tāratamyena tiṣṭhanti guṇair ānandapūrvakaiḥ, Madhva's Gītā-Bhāṣya.

believes that certain souls like demons, ghosts and some men are eternally doomed and damned. They can never hope to get liberation. Rāmānuja rejects this. The doctrine of eternal damnation is peculiar to Madhva and Jainism in the whole field of Indian philosophy.

Madhva and his followers Jayatīrtha and Vyāsatīrtha who are among the greatest dialecticians of India vigorously attack the Māyāvāda of Shaṅkara. Most of the objections in essence are the same which Rāmānuja has urged and may be replied to similarly. There has been a famous controversy between Vyāsatīrtha, the author of Nyāyamṛta and Madhusūdana, the author of Advaitasiddhi. Shrīharṣa and Chitsukha had directly attacked the very notion of difference and all possible ways of conceiving it. The Madhvites try to answer them and are further replied to and attacked by Madhusūdana. The defence of difference as compared with its refutation by the Advaitins, appears to be very weak and the dualists do not face the attacks squarely. Even Dr. S. N. Dasgupta, who is all admiration for the Madhvites and in whose opinion 'Jayatīrtha and Vyāsatīrtha present the highest dialectical skill . . . almost unrivalled in the whole field of Indian thought',[1] has to admit that 'This defence of difference appears, however, to be weak when compared with the refutations of difference by Chitsukha in his Tattva-pradīpikā, Nṛsimhāshrama Muni in his Bheda-dhikkāra, and others. . . . Vyāsatīrtha does not make any attempt squarely to meet these arguments'.[2]

II

NIMBĀRKA-VEDĀNTA

ĀCHĀRYA Nimbārka, Nimbāditya or Niyamānanda, a Telegu Brāhmaṇa whose philosophy is called Dvaitādvaita or Bhedā-bheda or Sanakasampradāya of Vaiṣṇavism is very much indebted to Rāmānuja. He revives the philosophy of the bhedābhedavādins like Āshmarathya, Bhartṛprapañcha, Bhāskara and Yādava, modifying it according to his notions. His philosophy bears a very close resemblance to that of Rāmānuja and it appears that he has borrowed the whole thing from his illustrious predecessor adding his own important amendments and modifications here and there. His date is uncertain. Some people believe that he flourished after Rāmānuja and before Madhva. Some think that he lived even after Vallabha. There is no doubt that he flourished after Rāmānuja. Nimbārka refers to the Shrī and the Brahma Sampradāya of Rāmānuja and Madhva respectively. A work, Madhva-mukha-mardana, which is yet in manuscript is attributed to him. Mādhavāchārya who belongs to the fourteenth century and who in his Sarva-darshana-saṅgraha where he deals with all the then-existing important systems of philosophy does

[1] A History of Indian Philosophy, Vol. IV, Preface, viii [2] Ibid, p. 179-180.

not refer to Nimbārka. On account of these reasons we shall not be wrong if we place Nimbārka somewhere in the middle or the later half of the fourteenth century. He has written a short commentary called Vedānta-pārijātasaurabha on the Brahmasūtra, Dashashlokī, Shrīkṛṣṇastavarāja and Madhvamukhamardana. Shrīnivasa has commented on his Bhāṣya in his Vedāntakaustubha on which Keshava Kāshmīrī has written his Kaustubhaprabhā. Puruṣottama has commented on the Dashashlokī in his Vedāntaratnamañjūṣā and on the Stavarāja in his Shrutyantasura-druma. Mādhava Mukunda has written his Para-pakṣa-giri-vajra or Hārdasañchaya to refute the absolutism of Shaṅkara.

Nimbārka, like Rāmānuja, admits three realities—God, souls and matter, the last two being dependent on God. The individual soul is essentially of the nature of knowledge (jñānasvarūpa). But it is also the substratum of knowledge. The relation between the substantive and the attributive knowledge is that between the qualified and the qualification (dharmi-dharma-bhāva). It is one of identity as well as of difference. The Sun, for example, is of the nature of light and yet it is also the substratum of light which is its attribute. The soul is a real knower, agent and enjoyer. It is dependent on God, is supported by God, pervaded by God and controlled from within by God. The souls are atomic in size and many in number. A soul is eternal and yet it suffers births and deaths on account of its embodiment which is due to karma and avidyā.[1] Liberation is due to knowledge which is brought about by God's grace which itself is due to devotion.

The inanimate is of three kinds: (1) Aprākṛta which is immutable super-matter of which the divine body is made and which is like the Shuddhasattva or Nityavibhūti of Rāmānuja; (2) Prākṛta which is derived from Prakṛti with its three guṇas; and (3) Kāla or time.[2]

God, who is the highest Brahman and who by His very nature is free from all defects and is the abode of all good qualities, who manifests Himself in the four Vyūhas and in incarnations, who is the ruler of this universe, is identified with Kṛṣṇa.[3] Rādhā is His consort. Souls and matter are His parts in the sense that they are His powers.[4] He is both the efficient and the material cause of this universe. He is the efficient cause because as the Lord of Karma and as the inner ruler of the souls, He brings about creation in order to enable the souls to reap the fruits of their Karma. And He is also the material cause because creation means manifestation of His powers of chit and achit; it is a real transformation (pariṇāma) of His powers. The relation between the universe and God is one of identity-and-difference which is quite natural. If the universe is absolutely identical with God, then God will

[1] jñānasvarūpam cha Harer adhīnam sharīrasaṁyogaviyogayogyam. aṇum hi jīvam pratidehabhinnam jñātṛtvavantam yadanantam āhuḥ, Dasha-shlokī, 1. [2] Ibid, 3.
[3] svabhāvato'pāstasamastadoṣam asheṣakalyāṇaguṇaikarāshim, Ibid, 4. [4] aṁsho hi shaktirūpo grāhyaḥ.

suffer all its imperfections, miseries and pains and would lose His pure nature. On the other hand, if the universe is absolutely different from God, then it would constitute a limit to God and He would not be its all-pervading inner ruler and controller. The souls and matter have no independent existence (svatantrasattābhāvaḥ) and therefore are not different from God. And yet because they have dependent existence (paratantrasattābhāvaḥ) and are limited, therefore they are different from God who is independent and unlimited ruler. In the formula 'tat tvam asi', 'tat' means the eternal all-pervading Brahman; 'tvam' means the dependent soul; and 'asi' means the relation of difference-cum-non-difference between them. The rays and the Sun, the sparks and the fire, the coils of a snake and the snake are both distinct and non-distinct.

The main differences between Nimbārka and Rāmānuja are these: First, while Rāmānuja believes in identity-in-and-through-difference or identity-qualified by-difference, Nimbārka believes in identity-and-difference. For Rāmānuja difference cannot exist separately from identity which it qualifies and to which it belongs. Thus identity is primary for Rāmānuja. But for Nimbārka both identity and difference are separately and equally real. Secondly, Nimbārka rejects the view that matter and souls are the attributes of God. The function of qualities is either to distinguish the object from other objects or to make that object better known. For example, when we say 'Rāma, the son of Dasharatha', the attribute here distinguishes Rāma from Balarāma and Parashurāma who are also known by the name 'Rāma', and it also throws light on Rāma for we know now his father also. But matter and souls as the attributes of God serve no such purpose. As there is nothing outside God, they cannot distinguish Him from anything else. Nor can they throw any light on God for they do not constitute His essence. Thirdly, Nimbārka also rejects the distinction between the body and the soul of God and the view that matter and souls form the body of God. If matter and souls are the body of God, then God must be subjected to all the pains, miseries, defects and imperfections of the universe. One portion of God cannot be reserved for change and imperfection and the other for eternity and perfection. Nimbārka, therefore, calls matter and souls as the 'parts' or 'powers' of God.

III

VALLABHA–VEDĀNTA

ĀCHĀRYA VALLABHA, a Telegu Brāhmaṇa, was born in 1479. Tradition says that he developed the views of Viṣṇusvāmī. His view is known as Shuddhādvaita or Pure Non-dualism undefiled by Māyā.[1] He has

[1] māyāsambandharahitam shuddham ityuchyate budhaiḥ, Shuddhādvaitamārtaṇḍa.

written a Commentary on the Brahmasūtra called Aṇubhāṣya, and on the Bhāgavata called Subodhinī. His son Viṭṭhalanātha wrote Vidvanmaṇḍana. Puruṣottama has commented on Aṇubhāṣya in his Bhāṣyaprakāsha on which Gopeshvara has commented in his Rashmi, and on the Subodhini and also on Vidvanmaṇḍana in his Suvarṇasūtra. The Shuddhādvaitamārtaṇḍa of Giridhara and the Prameyaratnārṇava of Bālakṛṣṇabhaṭṭa are some other famous works of this school. It is also known as Rudrasampradāya and as Puṣṭimārga. Puṣṭi means the grace of God[1] which dawns through devotion and is the cause of liberation.

Brahman is the independent reality and is identified with Shrīkṛṣṇa. His essence is Existence (sat,) Knowledge (chit) and Bliss (ānanda). Souls and matter are His real manifestations. They are His parts. He is the abode of all good qualities and includes even the seemingly contradictory qualities. He is smaller than the smallest and greater than the greatest. He is one as well as many. It is by His will that He manifests Himself as matter and as souls revealing His tripartite nature of Existence, Knowledge and Bliss in different proportions. Māyā or Avidyā is His power through which He manifests Himself as many. But this manifestation is neither an error nor an illusion. It is a real manifestation. Vallabha's view is neither Vivarta nor Pariṇāma. It is something in between the two and is called Avikṛtapariṇāmavāda. The universe is not a Vivarta for it is a real manifestation and not an unreal appearance. But it is also not a pariṇāma for this manifestation does not involve any change or transformation. The universe is a natural emanation from God which does not involve any notion of change and is, therefore, called avikṛtapariṇāma.

Vallabha rejects the relation of samavāya and explains it as tādātmya or identity. The substance and its attributes, the cause and its effects are identical. The substance really appears as its attributes and the cause really appears as its effects. In place of 'upādānakāraṇa' Vallabha prefers to use the expression 'samavāyikāraṇa' to denote the notion of the material cause. Thus material cause really means inherent cause which expression suggests that the material cause is identical with its effect and does not involve, so far as Brahman is concerned, any notion of change. Brahman is the material or inherent cause (samavāyi-kāraṇa) of this universe in the above sense and He is also its efficient cause. Brahman really manifests Himself as this universe without undergoing any change. It is universally and unconditionally pervaded by Brahman. Creation means manifestation of God as this universe in diverse forms without undergoing change, in which manifestation God reveals His tripartite nature of Existence, Knowledge and Bliss in different proportions. Dissolution means withdrawal of this manifestation by God within Himself. The universe springs forth from Brahman as sparks spring

[1] poṣaṇam tadanugrahaḥ.

forth from fire or as lustre emanates from a jewel or rays shoot forth from a lamp. Just as cotton spreads itself as threads so does God spread Himself as this universe. From His nature as Existence spring forth life (prāṇa), senses and bodies etc. which act as the elements of bondage for the souls. From His nature as Knowledge spring forth the atomic souls which are the subjects of bondage. And from His nature as Bliss spring forth the antaryāmins who are the presiding deities of the souls and are as many in number as the latter.[1] God is the one supreme Antaryāmin, the inner ruler of the universe. In the material world only the Existence-aspect of God is manifested, while His aspects of Knowledge and Bliss remain obscured. In the individual souls the aspects of Existence and Knowledge are manifested while the aspect of Bliss remains obscured. In the antaryāmins all the aspects are manifested. All these three forms—jagat, jīva and antaryāmī—are essentially identical with God. Jagat is dissimilar to Him (vijātīya); jīvas are similar to Him (sajātīya); and antaryāmins are inside Him (svagata). He runs through all the three forms which are non-different from Him. There is no difference either homogeneous or heterogeneous or internal in God.[2]

Vallabha distinguishes between jagat or prapañcha and saṁsāra. Jagat is the real manifestation of God, while saṁsāra or the cycle of births and deaths is imagined by the soul on account of ignorance which is fivefold—(1) ignorance of the real nature of the soul, (2) false identification with the body, (3) with the senses, (4) with the vital breaths, and (5) with the internal organ. When knowledge dawns ignorance vanishes and with it vanishes the saṁsāra. But the world, the jagat, continues because it is the real manifestation of God.

For Rāmānuja, the soul, though different from God, is essentially identical with Him as forming His body. For Madhva, the soul, though a dependent part of God, is essentially different from Him. For Nimbārka, the soul as limited and dependent is different from God, though as the power of God it is identical with Him. For Bhāskara, the soul is naturally identical with God and through limiting conditions appears as different from Him. For Vallabha, the soul as a part of God is identical with Him and appears as different on account of the limited manifestation of some divine aspects and obscuration of others.

Bhakti which is defined as a firm and all-surpassing affection (sneha) for God with a full sense of His Greatness is the only means of salvation.[3] It is the 'loving service' of God. It means attachment to God which presupposes detachment from all other things. It is neither worship nor knowledge. Affection or prema is its dominant phase (sthāyībhavā). The

[1] Bhāṣya-Prakāsha, p. 161-162. [2] Tattvadīpaprakāsha, p. 106. [3] māhātmyajñāna-pūrvasṭu sudṛḍhaḥ sarvato'dhikaḥ. sneho bhaktir iti proktas tayā muktir na chānyathā, Tattvadipa, p. 65.

feeling of oneness with God is not its culmination. It is gained through the grace of God which is won by the purity of heart. The Maryādā-mārga is the Vedic path in which bhakti is attained by karma and jñāna and upāsanā when through individual efforts sins are destroyed. But in Puṣṭi-mārga bhakti is attained without any individual effort simply by the grace of God which destroys sins forthwith. God, pleased by devotion, takes the devotee within Himself. Or, when He is highly pleased keeps him near Himself to enjoy the sweetness of service.

IV

MAHĀPRABHU CHAITANYA AND HIS FOLLOWERS

THE school of Bengal Vaiṣṇavism of Chitanya (1485-1533) is known as Achintyabhedābheda or Identity-in-difference the nature of which is essentially indescribable and unthinkable due to the unthinkable power of God. Historically the school is associated with Mādhvism and is also called Mādhva-Gauḍīya school. But on account of certain fundamental philosophical differences with Mādhvism, it should be regarded as an independent school. Chaitanya Māhaprabhu wrote no works. His disciple Shrī Rūpa Gosvāmī has written Ujjvalanīlamaṇi and Bhakti-rasāmṛta-sindhu. Shrī Jīva Gosvāmī has commented on both these works and has written his great work Ṣaṭsandarbha together with its running commentary, Sarvasamvādinī. Baladeva Vidyābhūṣaṇa has written a commentary on the Brahmasūtra called Govindabhāṣya, the introduction of which is known as Siddhāntaratna. Rūpa and Jīva and Baladeva have furnished philosophical basis for the teachings of Chaitanya which are mainly based on the Bhāgavata.

Brahman or Shrī Kṛṣṇa is essentially Sachchidānanda and is the auspicious abode of infinite good qualities and powers. The attributes are identical with the substance, though they also appear differently. The concept of Visheṣa is borrowed from Madhva to explain the unity which appears as different. The concept of Unthinkability is accepted to reconcile the apparent contradictions in the nature of Brahman. God is free from all differences—homogeneous, heterogeneous and internal, and yet He really manifests Himself as the world and the souls through His powers which are identical and yet different from Him. In Himself, He is the efficient cause of the universe, while in association with His powers, He is the material cause.

His inner power which forms His essence is called Antaraṅga Svarūpa Shakti and manifests itself as threefold power—as Sandhinī which is Sat or Existence, as Samvit which is Chit or knowledge, and as Hlādinī which is Ānanda or Bliss. The power through which He manifests Himself in the form of the atomic souls is called Taṭastha Shakti or

Jīva Shakti. The power through which He manifests Himself as the material world is called Māyā Shakti and is said to be His external power (Bahiraṅga Shakti). God as Bliss is the qualified, while all His powers are His qualifications or manifestations. The atomic souls are innumerable and remain distinct even in liberation. They emanate from Him, like rays from the Sun, and are absolutely dependent on Him. The world is the manifestation of His external power and is not false. The impurities and defects of the world do not affect Him at all. In liberation, the wrong notions and the ignorance of the soul vanish, though the world as the power of God remains.

Bhakti is the sole means of liberation. It is of two kinds—Vidhibhakti which is according to the Vedas and the Shāstras, and Ruchibhakti or affection. Bhakti is the affectionate service of God for His sake alone.[1] Ruchi or Rāgānugā Bhakti is the end. It consists in the intense spiritual love for God like that of the Gopīs and culminates in the love of Rādhā. To love God as one's lover and to regard oneself as the beloved of God and to brook no separation from Him is the highest Bhakti. Liberation consists in the eternal enjoyment of this blissful love for Kṛṣṇa in His Nityavṛindāvanadhāma.

V

S'RI AUROBINDO

THE justification for including S'ri Aurobindo's philosophy under 'the Schools of Vedānta', if any justification were required, is that almost every page of 'The Life Divine' is inspired by the creative vision of the seers of the Vedas and the sages of the Upaniṣads. As a free commentator on Vedānta, S'ri Aurobindo comes after the great Āchāryas of Vedānta, like Shaṅkara, Rāmānuja, Madhva, Vallabha and Nimbārka. 'The Life Divine' is a challenge to the false notion that philosophy in India died after the sixteenth century.

The Supreme Reality, according to S'ri Aurobindo, is Brahman, the Divine. It is eternal, absolute and infinite. In itself it is absolutely indeterminate, indefinable and free. It cannot be completely described either positively or negatively. Though it is indescribable in itself, yet it is not absolutely unknowable to us, for the Spiritual Being in us is in essence nothing but the Divine itself. For us the highest positive expression of Brahman is the Sachchidānanda or Existence-Consciousness-Bliss, all in one. It manifests itself as indeterminate as well as determinate, as nirguṇa as well as saguṇa, as one as well as many, as being as well as becoming, and yet it transcends them all.

The Existence (Sat) of Brahman appears to us as Ātman, Īshvara and

[1] anyābhilāṣitāshūnyam jñānakarmādyanāvṛtam. ānukūlyena Kṛṣṇā'nusevanam bhaktir uttamā, Bhaktirasāmṛtasindhu, I, 1, 9.

Puruṣa. The Consciounsess (chit) of Brahman which is always a Force (shakti) manifests itself as Māyā, Shakti and Prakṛti. Consciousness-Force, the own-Nature of the Divine, 'measures the Immeasurable, informs the Formless and embodies the Spirit.' The Bliss (ānanda) of Brahman underlies all these manifestations and it is out of sheer bliss that the Divine manifests Himself as this world. These three aspects and these powers embrace all reality and when taken as a whole, reconcile all apparent contradictions.

The Sachchidānanda through his Consciousness-Force manifests Himself as this world out of sheer bliss. Bliss gives us the 'why' of creation. 'Out of bliss all things arise,' says the Taittirīya Upaniṣad. 'World-existence,' says S'ri Aurobindo, 'is the ecstatic dance of Shiva which multiplies the body of the God numberlessly to the view; it leaves that white existence precisely where and what it was, ever is and ever will be; its sole absolute object is the joy of the dancing.'[1] The Supreme in itself is the 'timeless and spaceless pure Existence, one and stable, to which measure and measurelessness are inapplicable,' and yet it manifests itself as the 'measureless movement in time and space'.[2]

The self-consciousness of Brahman which is at the same time the power of self-manifestation is called by S'ri Aurobindo 'the Supermind'. The Supermind is a 'Real-Idea', a 'Truth-Consciousness'. 'It is,' says S'ri Aurobindo, 'conscious Reality throwing itself into mutable forms of its own imperishable and immutable substance.'[3] It is the Divine alone who can know himself in all his aspects and the Supermind is the Divine's own knowledge of himself which is at once his own innate power of self-manifestation. The Supermind is absolute knowledge and power. It is through the Supermind that the Divine manifests himself as this world. It is with the Supermind that the process of self-limitation and self-individualization starts in Brahman.

The unitary Sachchidānanda, out of sheer joy, puts himself under self-limitation and self-individualization and manifests himself as innumerable real Selves of Bliss who are always conscious of their essential unity with the Sachchidānanda. The eternal Selves are Divine and are untouched by the cosmic process, by the space-time matrix. The true Self is the Unborn and Immutable Spirit of man who always lives in the divine plane. He is not involved in the world of Ignorance, but sends down a ray, a spark of Divinity, as it were, into this world. S'ri Aurobindo calls this spark of Divinity which is the soul by the name of 'psyche'. The psyche, though it does not change its essential spiritual nature, yet is subject to evolution. The psychic element is inherent even in matter and evolves towards a fuller existence in life. In man this psyche takes the form of the Psychic Being. The Psychic Being is in direct touch with its reality, the Divine Self, but man normally is not

[1] The Life Divine, V. I, p. 119. [2] Ibid. [3] Ibid, p. 177.

aware of his own soul. Mind, life and matter are the instruments available to the soul and however defective they may ultimately be, the soul has to work in and through them for its knowledge and activity. Hence, in spite of being spiritual and blissful, the soul is actually subject to mentality, vitality and physicality. Because of this the intuitions of the soul, in spite of giving immediate awareness of Reality, are not complete and comprehensive. Also, like its knowledge its power is limited. To have absolute knowledge and absolute power, the soul must attain to Supermind which is the source of mind, life and matter. 'To merge the consciousness in the Divine,' writes S'ri Aurobindo, 'and to keep the psychic being controlling and changing all the nature and keeping it turned to the Divine till the whole being can live in the Divine is the transformation we seek.'[1]

The Sachchidānanda, through the Supermind, descends into mind, life and matter. The descent of the Divine is called 'involution' and is the result of the self-concealment of the Divine. The Supermind is absolute knowledge and power. It is Vidyā. It is the knowledge of Reality and also of the world-to-be. It never misses the essential unity with the Sachchidānanda. But in mind the knowledge of unity is lost which means that ignorance starts from here. Mind is Avidyā which is the immediate manifestor of the world in which we live. Next stage in the descent is life where the tendency towards multiplicity or fragmentation becomes prominent. The last stage in descent is matter where each atom is separate from the others so that fragmentation is complete and unity is completely lost. It should be noted that ignorance is not the total denial of knowledge, but knowledge hiding itself and thereby appearing as something else. Hence, there is always some element of knowledge even in ignorance which element is a very dim sentience in the field of matter. S'ri Aurobindo conceives of a stage where even this sentience is absent and calls it Inconscience. This is the complete loss of Spirit. All this process of involution takes place behind the screen as it were. It is an *ideal* process.

Involution or descent is not the end of the process. The next phase is evolution or ascent which S'ri Aurobindo calls 'the spirit's return to itself'. It is defined by him thus: 'All evolution is in essence a heightening of the force of consciousness in the manifest being so that it may be raised into the greater intensity of that which is still unmanifest, from matter into life, from life into mind, from the mind into the spirit.'[2] Evolution according to S'ri Aurobindo, as Dr. S. K. Maitra explains, 'is a widening, a heightening and an integration.' 'Evolution is an ascent from a less manifest condition of the Consciousness-Force to a more manifest condition. It is also an integration of the higher with the lower

[1] Letters of S'ri Aurobindo, Second Series, pp. 46-47. [2] The Life Divine, V. II p. 659.

states. This means that when a higher principle emerges, it descends into the lower ones and causes a transformation of them.'[1] As matter, where spirit is sleeping or apparently lost, is the last term of involution, it is the first to become manifest in the space-time world and to evolve into a higher term. The dormant spirit in matter feels an urge to rise to life. There is a call from below and a response from above. And then life emerges in this world. With the emergence of life, matter undergoes a considerable change. Then, the dormant spirit in life feels an urge for mind and with the response from above, mind emerges in this world. The evolution of mind introduces a very great change in life and matter. The evolution until now has been up to the mental plane and has been through Ignorance. But Consciousness in mind itself is feeling an urge to evolve into Supermind. The supra-mental descent, therefore, is a logical necessity. After the descent of the Supermind, evolution will proceed through knowledge. The supra-mental being is called Gnostic Being. With the descent of the Supermind, mind, life and matter will be radically transformed. Their defects and mutability will vanish. The race of the Gnostic Beings will be above quarrels, diseases and death. The entire personality will be revolutionized and direct communion with the Sachchidānanda would be established.

Mind can know the Supreme in one or more of its aspects, but it can never know it completely and as a whole. Only the Supermind can do that. Great sages, according to S'ri Aurobindo, have achieved salvation. But it has been individual salvation. They have freed themselves from the cycle of birth and death. Some of them have realized Brahman. But their realization, though highest, has yet been incomplete and partial, for their approach to the Supreme has been through the mind or the Over-mind. Mind by its very nature breaks the indivisible Reality into bits as it were. It must divide and exclude. It cannot function without the subject-object duality. 'Mind,' says S'ri Aurobindo, 'cannot possess the Infinite, it can only suffer or be possessed by it; it can only lie blissfully helpless under the luminous shadow of the Real cast down on it from planes of existence beyond its reach.'[2] Some of the great sages through their intuitions did have the glimpses of the Supreme, but their intuitions—even the highest intuitions—could not be free from the mental coating. 'Intuition,' says S'ri Aurobindo, 'brings to man those brilliant messages from the Unknown which are the beginning of this higher knowledge. . . . (But) its action is largely hidden by the interventions of our normal intelligence; for what we call by the name is usually a point of direct knowledge which is immediately caught and coated over with mental stuff, so that it serves only as an invisible or a very tiny nucleus of a crystallization which is in its mass intellectual

[1] Studies in Sri Aurobindo's Philosophy: Dr. S. K. Maitra, p. 30. [2] The Life Divine, V. I. p. 248.

or otherwise mental in character.'[1] Integral spiritual experience is the sole privilege of the Supermind.

For S'ri Aurobindo the descent of the Supermind is the great logical necessity which heralds the dawn of a new era for mankind hitherto before unknown. It will lead to cosmic salvation here and now—'ihaiva' and 'adhunaiva' as the Upaniṣads put it—by transforming the human life into the Life Divine. Our mind cannot give its complete description, for, as S'ri Aurobindo says, 'what is magic to our finite reason is the logic of the Infinite'. 'The supramental change,' he says, 'is a thing decreed and inevitable in the evolution of the earth-consciousness; for its upward ascent is not ended and mind is not its last summit. But that the change may arrive, take form and endure there is needed the call from below with a will to recognize and not deny the light when it comes, and there is needed the sanction of the Supreme from above.'[2] The integral Yoga of S'ri Aurobindo aims at ascending to the Supermind and also at bringing about the descent of the Supermind. 'By this Yoga,' he says, 'we not only seek the Infinite, but we call upon the Infinite to unfold himself in human life.'[3] The supramental descent will 'make earth a heaven and life beatitude's kiss'. Mind cannot describe this state through its categories. It can give only a vague and a general description. S'ri Aurobindo himself attempts this description thus: 'As if honey could taste itself and all its drops together and all its drops could taste each other and each the whole honey-comb as itself, so should the end be with God and the soul of man and the universe.'[4] The aim of S'ri Aurobindo's life-long sādhanā has been to bring down the Supermind to the world of mind, life and matter. Whether he has succeeded or not, time alone will answer. But one thing is certain that throughout his life he has undauntedly and with confidence marched ahead, singing:

> 'And how shall the end be vain when God is guide?
> The more the goal recedes, the more it lures;
> However his mind and flesh resist or fail,
> A will prevails cancelling his conscious choice.
>
> . . . . .
>
> There is a Light that leads, a Power that aids;
> Unmarked, unfelt it sees for him and acts:
> Ignorant, he forms the All-Conscient in his depths,
> Human, looks up to superhuman peaks:
> A borrower of Supernature's gold,
> He paves his road to Immortality.'[5]

[1] Ibid, p. 120 and 418. [2] The Mother, pp. 83-84. [3] The Synthesis of Yoga, p. 6. [4] Thoughts and Glimpses, pp. 18-19. [5] Sāvitrī: A Legend and a Symbol, Book 3, Canto IV.

Chapter Twenty

SHAIVA AND SHĀKTA SCHOOLS

I

SHAIVA SIDDHĀNTA

THE worship of Shiva or Rudra goes back to the Vedas. In the Yajurveda we have the Shatarudrīya. The Taittirīya Āraṇyaka tells us that the whole universe is the manifestation of Rudra. Some of the Upaniṣads, the Mahābhārata and some Purāṇas glorify Shiva or Rudra. The sacred literature of the Shaivas is called Shaivāgama. Shrīkaṇṭha places it side by side with the Vedas. Mādhavāchārya refers to the four schools of Shaivism—Nakulīsha-pāshupata, Shaiva, Pratyabhijñā and Raseshvara. Besides these we find mention of two more sects, Kāpālika and Kālāmukha, in Yāmuna's Āgamaprāmāṇya. Shaivism of the 'Shaiva' type is further divided into Vīra Shaivism[1] or Shakti-vishiṣṭādvaita and Shaiva Siddhānta. The former is also known as Liṅgāyata or Ṣatsthala. We may select here Shaiva Siddhānta as the representative of the Southern Shaivism and Pratyabhijñā or Kāshmīra Shaivism as the representative of the Northern Shaivism and briefly deal with these two.

Shaiva Siddhānta recognizes eighteen Āgamas. From the fifth to the ninth centuries many great Shaiva saints like Sambandar, Appar and Sundarar flourished in South India whose hymns constitute a magnificently rich devotional literature. The collection of these hymns is called Tirumurai. Māṇikkavāsagar (seventh century) has written his famous Tiruvāsagam. Meykaṇḍar, the author of the Shivajñānabodham, who belongs to the thirteenth century, is regarded as the first systematic expounder of the Siddhānta philosophy. His disciple Arulnandi Shivāchārya is the author of the famous work Shivajñānasiddhiyar. Shrīkaṇṭha Shivāchārya (fourteenth century) has written a commentary on the Brahmasūtra, which is commented upon by Appaya Dīkṣita in his Shivārkamaṇidīpikā, in the light of Shaivism in general, though not strictly according to the Siddhānta philosophy.

Shaiva Siddhānta calls itself 'Shuddhādvaita', the name which Vallabha's school bears. But whereas Vallabha means by the word

[1] According to Shrīpati Paṇḍita, Vīra Shaivism is Visheṣādvaita and not Shakti-Vishiṣṭādvaita.

'Shuddha' 'that which is free from the impurity of Māyā' (māyāsambandharahita) and by the word 'Advaita' 'the Non-dual Brahman', Shaiva Siddhānta takes the word 'Shuddha' in the sense of 'unqualified' and the word 'Advaita' in the sense of 'Dvaita devoid of *duality*' which means that difference is real in existence but inseparable from identity in consciousness. This means that though matter and souls are real yet they are not opposed to Shiva but are inseparably united with Him who is the supreme reality. This suggests the influence of Apṛthaksiddhi of Rāmānuja. But whereas Rāmānuja makes matter and souls only the attributes of God, Shaiva Siddhānta agrees with Madhva in giving them substantive existence.

Shiva is the supreme reality and is called Pati or the Lord who possesses the eight attributes of 'self-existence, essential purity, intuitive wisdom, infinite intelligence, freedom from all bonds, infinite grace or love, omnipotence, and infinite bliss'. Just as the potter is the first cause, his staff and wheel is the instrumental cause and clay is the material cause of a pot, similarly Shiva is the first cause, his Shakti is the instrumental cause and Māyā is the material cause of this world. The relation of Shiva and Shakti is that of identity (tādātmya), though it is the power of the Lord. This Shakti is conscious, unchanging and eternal energy and is known as Svarūpa Shakti. Like the shuddhasattva and the prakṛti of Rāmānuja, Shaiva Siddhānta also believes in pure matter (shuddha or sāttvika jagat) and defiled matter (ashuddha or prākṛta jagat). The material cause of pure creation is called Mahāmāyā or Bindu or Vidyā, while that of defiled creation is called Māyā or Ashuddha Bindu. Mahāmāyā and Māyā both are the material (jaḍa) powers of the Lord and are called Parigraha Shakti which is different from the Svarūpa Shakti which forms the essence of the Lord. The Lord is omnipresent, omnipotent and omniscient and performs the five functions of creation, preservation and destruction of the universe and obscuration (tirodhāna) and liberation (anugraha) of the souls.

The individual souls are called Pashu for like cattle they are bound by the rope of avidyā to this world. The soul is really an all-pervading, eternal and conscious agent and enjoyer (ichchā-jñāna-kṛiyāyukta). It has consciousness the essence of which is in the act of seeing. It is different from the gross and the subtle body and the sense-organs, etc. The bound souls mistake themselves as finite and limited in will, thought and action and in liberation are restored to their original nature.

The fetters which bind the souls are called Pāsha and are threefold —Avidyā, Karma and Māyā. Avidyā is one in all beings and is beginningless. It is also called Āṇavamala or the impurity which consists in the false notion of the soul to regard itself finite or atomic and confined to the body and limited in knowledge and power. It is avidyā because it makes the soul ignorant of its inherent glory and greatness. It is Āṇava because it makes the soul mistake itself as atomic and finite. It is the bondage (pashutva) of the beast (pashu). Karma is produced by the deeds of the souls and is subtle and unseen (adṛṣṭa) and is the cause of the union of the conscious with the unconscious. Māyā is the material cause of this impure world. The souls are of three kinds according as they are tainted with one or two or three of these impurities. The highest souls are tainted with the Āṇavamala only; the next with the Kārmaṇamala also; and the last with all the three—Āṇava, Kārmaṇa and Māyīya. They are called respectively Vijñānakala, Pralayakala and sakala. In order to obtain release the soul has to get rid of these three impurities. And for this God's grace is absolutely essential. The Divine Grace is there for us all without the asking for it for the Lord desires that all the souls should know Him; it is only for us to avail of it or not.

After the removal of the Pāsha, the soul becomes one with Shiva. It becomes co-pervasive with Him and shares His glory and greatness. It is not conscious of its individuality (which is there) on account of the experience of Bliss. Meykaṇḍar says that just as salt dissolves into water and becomes co-pervasive with it, similarly the liberated soul merges in God and becomes co-pervasive with Him. It attains the status of Shiva, though the five functions of creation etc. are reserved for the latter alone. The essential quality or svarūpalakṣaṇa of the soul is to identify itself with its object and become co-pervasive with it (taddharmadharmī), its essence (svarūpa) is its co-pervasiveness with the infinite Shiva. Thus the bound soul identifies itself with matter and the liberated soul with Shiva and realizes its own pure nature.

The binding aspect of Āṇava-mala when it is called Pāsha is accidental (taṭastha) and therefore can be removed, but Āṇava-mala itself is eternal. Āṇava-mala, in the case of the liberated, keeps the world away and thereby indirectly helps them in their Shivānubhava. Sāyujya is the real liberation. Jīvanmukti is admitted. The ethical virtues are emphasized as the preparation for receiving God's grace. Siddhiyar says: 'They have no love for God who have no love for all mankind.'

II

KĀSHMĪRA SHAIVISM

THIS school is also known as Pratyabhijñā or Trika or Spanda system. Shiva-sūtra (said to have been revealed to Vasugupta), Vasugupta's (eighth century) Spandakārikā, Somānanda's Shivadṛṣṭi (ninth century), Utpala's Pratyabhijñāsūtra (tenth century) Abhinavagupta's Paramārthasāra, Pratyabhijñāvimarshinī and Tantrāloka, and Kṣemarāja's

Shivasūtravimarshinī and Spandasandoha—are some of the most important works of this system. The system claims to be based on the Shaiva Āgamas.

Kāshmīra Shaivism admits thirty-six tattvas or principles of cosmic manifestation. Through the five important aspects of Shakti known as chit, ānanda, ichchā, jñāna and kriyā arise Shiva, Shakti, Sadāshiva, Īshvara and Shuddhavidyā, the five transcendental tattvas. That aspect of Shakti which makes the Infinite appear as finite is the sixth Māyā tattva. It gives rise to the five kañchukas—power (kalā), knowledge (vidyā), attachment (rāga), time (kāla) and space (niyati). Through these Māyā makes the Infinite Shiva appear as finite Puruṣa which is the twelfth tattva. The rest of the twenty-four tattvas are the same as Prakṛti and its twenty-three evolutes recognized in the Sāṅkhya system.

Shiva is the only reality, the one without a second. He is infinite Consciousness and absolute independence. (Svātantrya). He creates everything by the mere force of His will. He is the subject as well as the object. He is the foundation of all knowledge and all proof and disproof equally presuppose His existence. 'He makes the world appear in Himself as if it were distinct from Himself, though not really so; even as objects appear in a mirror. . . . By His own wonderful power (Shakti) inherent in Him, God appears in the form of souls and constitutes objects for their experiences. The only reality is the unlimited pure self, the one and only substratum of the universe, whose activity or vibration (spanda) is the cause of all distinctions.' The changing manifestations of Shiva do not stain His purity and unchanging nature since He transcends His own manifestations (ābhāsa). Shiva is the transcendental eternal background of this universe. In this transcendental aspect He is Vishvottīrṇa. In the immanent aspect He is called Vishvātmaka. The immanent aspect is Svātantrya or Shakti which is conceived as a Power of Self-consciousness by which Shiva manifests Himself as this universe on His own transcendental background. His Shakti has infinite aspects, most important of which are chit, ānanda, ichchhā, jñāna and kriyā. Māyā is neither the material cause of the universe nor the principle of illusion. It is that aspect of the power (shakti) of Shiva through which He manifests Himself as many. The individual soul is pure consciousness and as such identical with Shiva. It is the ultimate reality under conditions of self-limitation. Plurality of souls is not final. Apart from Shiva, the world is not; different from Shiva, the soul is not.

Recognition (pratyabhijñā) of this reality is essential for obtaining liberation. A love-sick woman cannot get any consolation and joy even though her lover may be present near her unless she *recognizes* him. The moment recognition dawns she becomes all joy. This is also the meaning of the famous formula 'tat tvam asi'. Recognition at once overcomes bondage. The liberated soul becomes one with Shiva and ever enjoys the mystic bliss of oneness with the Lord. Jīvanmukti is admitted.

III

SHĀKTA SCHOOLS

THE worship of Shakti also dates back to the Ṛgveda where she is praised as 'the supporter of the earth living in heaven'. 'Umā of golden hue' of the Kena is the 'Great Mother of the Universe'. The Shaivas made her the consort of Shiva. The various Purāṇas describe her greatness. She is known as Shakti, Devī, Chaṇḍī, Chāmuṇḍā, Durgā, Umā and Mahāmāyā. Shakti is the power of Existence, Knowledge and Bliss of Brahman and is inseparable from it. Shakti may be taken as male, female or neutral. Shiva is the pure indeterminate Brahman, while Shakti, the power of Māyā, makes him determinate, endowed with the attributes of knowledge, will and action. Saundaryalaharī says: 'Shiva, when he is united with Shakti, is able to create; otherwise he is unable even to move.'[1] Shiva, without Shakti, is a Shava, a corpse. Shakti is the life of Shiva as she is his wife. The whole world of matter and souls exists potentially in Shakti who is the inseparable power of Shiva. Māyā or Prakṛti, the matrix of the world, lies within Shakti. The souls mistake themselves as finite and many due to the influence of Māyā. Liberation is due to the knowledge that the so-called soul is non-different from Brahman. Knowledge of Shakti leads to this knowledge. Liberation means 'dissolution in the blissful effulgence of the Supreme'. Jīvanmukti is admitted. The mystic side of Yoga is emphasized. Mantra and Tantra are sacred, secret and divine. Awakening of the Kuṇḍalinī and piercing of the six Chakras is practiced. Nādayoga is glorified.

The Shakti Tantra is divided into three schools—Kaula, Samaya and Mishra. Bhāskararāya, the author of Saubhāgyabhāskara, the commentary on Lalitāsahasranāma, and Lakṣmīdhara, the commentator on the Saundaryalaharī are the eminent Shākta writers. Some Kaulas are called Vāma-mārgī and are generally believed to be indulging in abominable and ghastly practices. Though most of the Kaulas must have indulged in such practices on account of their ignorance, yet the real significance of these practices like the five Mudrās lies in their spiritual interpretation. Kula means Shakti or Kuṇḍalinī and Akula means Shiva. He alone is therefore a Kaula who succeeds in uniting Shakti with Shiva. He is a Jīvanmukta, a Sthitaprajña for whom mud and sandalpaste, enemy

[1] Shivaḥ Shaktyā yukto yadi bhavati shaktaḥ prabhavitum. na chedevam devo na khalu kushalaḥ spanditum api, Saundaryalaharī.

and son, wood and gold, life and death are the same. External marks are useless. Kulārṇava Tantra says: 'If the mere rubbing of the body with mud and ashes gains liberation, then the village dogs who roll in them have attained it'. The highest is the union with Brahman; the middle is the meditation on Brahman; the lower is the praise of the Lord and the recitation of hymns; and the lowest is the external worship'.[1]

[1] uttamo Brahmasadbhāvo dhyānabhāvastu madhyamaḥ. stutir japo'dhamo bhāvo bahiḥpūjā'dhamā'dhamā, Mahānirvāṇatantra, XIV, 122.

GLOSSARY

The glossary includes only important terms not immediately defined in the text and terms which have widely varying meanings. In general, the more literal meaning is given first. The following abbreviations are used:

(B)	Buddhism	(J)	Jainism	(N)	Nyāya-Vaisheṣika
(SB)	Shūnyavāda Buddhism	(S)	Sāṅkhya	(PM)	Pūrva Mīmāṁsā
(VB)	Vijñānavāda Buddhism	(Y)	Yoga	(V)	Vedānta

abhūtaparikalpa (VB). That which gives rise to the "illusion or construction of the non-existent," viz., the *ālayavijñāna* as manifesting itself in phenomenal reality as (ultimately) illusory objects; relative reality; the stream of ideas.

abhūtārtha. That which has not happened; false; (VB) an object as an illusory construction.

āchārya. A teacher.

achintya. Unthinkable, inconceivable.

ādhāra. Support, substratum.

adharma. Non-merit, non-virtue; (J) principle of non-motion or rest (cf. *dharma*).

adhyāropa. (V). Superimposition (see *adhyāsa*).

adhyāsa (V). Superimposition, the erroneous perception of the unreal as the real (e.g., the veiling of *Brahman* by *māyā* and the projection of world-appearance on it).

advaita. Non-dual; absolute.

advaitin. A non-dualist; an absolutist.

advaya. Non-duality, not two; without a second.

āgama. That which is handed down and fixed by tradition, a traditional doctrine or collection of doctrines.

ahaṅkāra. The ego, the principle of individuation.

ahiṁsā. Non-injury.

aja. Unborn; eternal.

ajara. Not subject to age, undecaying.

ajñāna. Ignorance.

akartā. Not an agent.

ākāsha. Space, the ether.

akhyāti (PM). Non-perception; the doctrine of Prabhākara school of Mīmāṁsā that an error is imperfect knowledge and is due to omission only.

akṣara. Imperishable (a synonym for reality); the syllable *auṁ*.

ālayavijñāna (VB). The repository consciousness containing potentially all empirical manifestations of consciousness; the residium of all ideas and actions.

amara. Undying, immortal, imperishable.

amātra. Without measure, boundless.

anātman. Non-self, devoid of self.

anabhilāpya. Ungraspable; unutterable.

anakṣara. Unutterable; inexpressible.

anekāntavāda (J). The doctrine of the manifoldness of reality; pluralism; realistic relativism.

anirvachanīya. Unutterable, not to be spoken of or described.

anirvachanīya-khyāti (V). The doctrine of Advaita Vedānta that perception or error can be called neither absolutely real or valid nor unreal or invalid.

anirvachanīyatva. Indescribability, inexpressableness.

anityaparamāṇuvāda (B). The doctrine of non-eternal atoms (cf. *kṣaṇabhaṅgavāda*).

antaḥkaraṇa. The internal organ, the seat of thought and feeling. In the *Vedānta* and *Yoga* this includes *buddhi*, *ahaṅkāra*, and *manas*.

aṇu. An atom.

anumāna. Inference. In the *Sāṅkhya*, a synonym for *prakṛti*, which is only "inferred" from its evolutes or products.

apara. Lower or inferior (cf. *para*).

aparā vidyā. Lower or empirical knowledge.

aparokṣānubhūti (V). Real perception; immediate spiritual experience.

apavarga. Emancipation (see *mokṣa*).

ārambhavāda (N). The doctrine of causation which holds that production is a new beginning, a fresh creation, i.e. that the effect is new and not preexistent in the cause.

artha. Wealth, property; object; end; reality.

āryajñāna (B). Aryan knowledge, viz., noble or excellent knowledge.

asaṅga. Unattached.

asat. Not existing, non-existent; non-being.

asatkāryavāda (N). The doctrine of causation which holds that the effect does not pre-exist in the cause.

ashūnya. Not empty.

asmitā. "I-am-ness," viz., egoism.

atarkya. Incomprehensible, surpassing reasoning or thought.

ātman. The self, the soul; the self as the ultimate reality (see Index).

atyantavishuddha. Completely pure or purified.

auṁkāra. The syllable *auṁ*; pronouncing the syllable *auṁ*.

avaktavya. Not to be spoken of, indescribable.

avidyā. Ignorance.

avyakta. Unmanifested, unapparent, undeveloped (a synonym for *prakṛti*).

avyaya. Undiminishing, unchanging, imperishable.

baddha. Bound, fettered.

bāhyārthavāda (B). The doctrine that external objects have a real existence.

bhakti. Devotion, worship.

bhava-chakra (B). The wheel of becoming, of birth and death (a synonym for *saṁsāra*).

bhedābheda (V). Difference and identity, identity plus difference.

bhikṣu. A religious mendicant.

bhikṣutā. Monkhood; holy nature.

bhoktā. The enjoyer, the experient or subject of experience.

bhoga. Enjoyment, experience.

bhrama. Confusion, error, mistake.

bhūmi. Stages or degrees of perfection.

bhūtādi (S). The tāmasa ahaṅkāra which produces the five subtle elements.

bhūtārtha. That which is existent, a fact; a reality.

bhūtatathatā (B). True or real suchness, the ultimate reality.

bījashakti. The "seed-power," the original force or creative potency (synonym for *prakṛti* in Sāṅkhya and *māyā* in Vedānta).

bodhi (B). Enlightenment, perfect wisdom.

bodhisattva (B). One whose essence is enlightenment (*bodhi*), one who is on the way to the attainment of Buddhahood.

brahmakāraṇavāda (V). The doctrine of causation which holds that the cause of all effects is *brahman*.

brahman (V). Prayer, holy word; the ultimate principle underlying the world, ultimate reality (see Index).

brāhmaṇas. The prose ritual texts of the *Veda* (see Index).

brahmapariṇāmavāda. The doctrine of causation in Rāmānuja Vedānta which holds that all effects are actual modifications or transformations of *brahman*.

brahmavivartavada. The doctrine of causation in Shaṅkara Vedānta which holds that all effects are an erroneous or illusory appearance of *brahman*.

buddhakāya (B). The body of the Buddha (see *dharmakāya*); the ultimate reality.

buddhi. Intellect, intelligence; (S) the material principle which directly reflects the pure consciousness of the *puruṣa*.

chakra. A wheel; one of the psychic centers in the body.

chāritra (J). Good conduct.

chatuṣkoṭi. The four alternative categories of thought, viz., affirmation, negation, conjunction, and disjunction ("A," "not-A," "both A and not-A," "neither A nor not-A").

chatuṣkoṭivinirmukta. Freed from the four categories of understanding.

chit. Thinking; pure consciousness, spirit.

chitta. Thought, intelligence, mind; the mental organ or *antaḥkaraṇa*.

chittamātra (VB). Thought or consciousness alone, pure consciousness.

darshana. Perception; vision of truth; philosophy.

deva. Divine, a god.

dharma. Social and moral order, law, duty, right, virtue, merit. (B) The Law or body of doctrine attributed to the Buddha; a phenomenal fact or object, a thing as a particular, an element of existence. (J) Principle of motion.

dharmadhātu (B). The realm of the Law; the Reality of dharmas or world-objects, the ultimate ground of phenomena.

dharmakāya (B). The body of the Law; the Cosmic Body of the Buddha; the ultimate reality, the essence of all things.

dharmanairātmya (B). The doctrine that things (*dharmas*) "have no self," i.e., that ultimately there is no such "thing" as a "thing," that all objects of thought are ultimately unreal.

dhruva. Fixed, immovable, permanent.

dhyāna. Meditation.

dravya. A substance.

drasta. One who sees, the seer, the true self.

duḥkha. Suffering, misery, pain.

durghaṭatva. Difficulty in accomplishing or carrying out (a definition or explanation); self-contradictory nature.

durnirūpatva. Difficulty in defining or pointing out.

dvaita. Dualistic, dualism, diversity.

dvaitin. A dualist.

dveṣa. Aversion, hatred.

guṇa. Quality, attribute; (S) the three material constituents or attributes of *prakṛti*, viz., *sattva*, *rajas*, and *tamas*.

hīnayāna. The lesser vehicle, the earlier systems of Buddhist doctrine (see *mahāyāna*).

ichchhā. Wish, desire.

indriya. A sense faculty or organ.

īshāna. Reigning; the ruler, the master.

jaḍa. Unintelligent, inanimate, unconscious; a synonym for *prakṛti*, viz., the objective or material as opposed to the subjective or spiritual.

jagat. The world.

janma-maraṇa-chakra (B). The wheel of birth and death (a synonym for *saṁsāra*).

jīva. The individual living soul or spirit; the soul as embodied; the empirical ego.

jīvanmukti. Emancipation or release while still alive.

jīvātman. The living self, the personal or embodied self (cf. *paramātman*).

jñāna. Consciousness; knowledge.

jñānakāṇḍa. The portion of the *Veda* dealing with knowledge, esp. the *Upaniṣads*.

jñāna-karma-samuchchayavāda. The doctrine that *jñāna* (knowledge) and *karma* (action) should be combined.

jñātā. One who knows, the knower, the self, the subject.

jñeya. That which can be known, a cognizable object.

jñeyāvaraṇa (VB). The screen or covering of cognition, the veiling of reality caused by false cognition; the wrong belief in the reality of the object.

kaivalya. Isolation, detachment of the soul from matter, illusion, or transmigration; the pure shining nature of the soul.

kāla. Time.

kāma. Sensual pleasure, love, desire.

karma. Action; religious act or rite, sacrificial action; past actions as producing good or evil results.

karmakāṇḍa. The portion of the *Veda* dealing with sacrificial action, viz., the *mantras* or hymns and the *brāhmaṇas*.

kartā. One who acts, the agent.

kārya. That which is to be done; effect, result.

kevala. Alone, isolated; pure.

kevalajñāna (J). Pure or absolute knowledge.

kleshāvaraṇa (VB). The screen or covering of afflictions, the veiling of reality caused by the afflictions or passions; moral defilement.

kliṣṭa manovijñāna (VB). Afflicted consciousness, the intermediate form of consciousness between the *ālayavijñāna* or universal consciousness, and the *manovijñāna* or empirical consciousness.

kriyā. Activity, acting.

kṣaṇa. An instant, a moment.

kṣaṇa-bhaṅga-vāda (B). The doctrine of the "instant perishing" of things, momentary existence, momentariness.

kṣaṇika. Instantaneous, momentary; existing for only an instant.

kuṇḍalinī. In esoteric *Yoga*, the "serpent" power which sleeps at the base of the spine until awakened through yogic meditation.

kūṭastha. Standing at the top; immovable, unchangeable; highest reality.

laya. Rest, repose, mental inactivity.

lokāyata. Materialism, a materialist.

madhyamamārga (B). The middle path or road.

madhyastha. Standing in the middle, neutral, indifferent.

mahābhūtas (S). The gross elements, viz., ether, air, fire, water, earth.

mahāpralaya. The great dissolution or devolution of the cosmos back into the *mūlaprakṛti* (see *pralaya*).

mahātman. The great self; a great sage.

mahāvākya. A sacred utterance, esp. the formulas of the *Upaniṣhads*.

mahāyāna. The great vehicle, the later systems of Buddhist doctrine (see *hīnayāna*).

manana. Thinking, active intelligence; critical reflection.

manas. Mind, esp. as the central sense-organ, the coordinator of sense-organs and of motor-organs.

mantra. A prayer or song of praise, a hymn or sacrificial formula addressed to a deity.

maryādāmārga. The path of propriety and customary rules (cf. *puṣṭimārga*).

māyā. Illusion; the Vedāntic doctrine of relativity of thought.

mithyā-saṁvṛti (SB). False empirical (knowledge); opposed to *tathya-saṁvṛti* or true empirical (knowledge).

mishrasattva. Mixed *sattva*.

mlechchha. A foreigner, barbarian.

mokṣa. Emancipation, liberation, release from *saṁsāra*.

mūlaprakṛti. Root or original nature (see *prakṛti*).

mūlāvidyā. Original ignorance; transcendental ignorance, the cause of this world.

nairātmyavāda (B). The doctrine of non-self; the ultimate unreality of the empirical ego.

nāma-rūpa (B). Name and form or matter; empirical or material reality as the combination of these two.

nāstika. A denier or nihilist; a heretic, one who denies the authority of the *Vedas*.

nibbāna (B). The Pali form of Sanskrit *nirvāṇa*.

nirguṇa. Without qualities, devoid of attributes; the transcendental Absolute.

nirvāṇa (B). Blowing out, extinction (specifically of the "flame" of clinging desire); emancipation from *saṁsāra*.

nirvisheṣa. Indeterminate.

niṣprapañcha. Free from phenomenality, diversity, or manifoldness; absolute.

nissvabhāvatā (SB). Devoid of independent existence. (See *svabhāvashūnyatā*).

nistraiguṇya. Free of the three *guṇas*.

nitya. Eternal.

nityaparamāṇukāraṇavāda (N). The doctrine that eternal material atoms are the ultimate causes.

nityavibhūti. Eternally pervading, abundant, powerful.

nivṛtti. Inactivity; the contemplative life (cf. *pravṛtti*).

para. Higher or superior (cf. *apara*).

paramārtha. Ultimate, absolute; ultimate or absolute reality.

paramārthika. Relating to ultimate reality.

paramātman. The highest or ultimate self (cf. *jīvātman*).

paratantra (VB). Phenomenal, dependent, or relative reality.

parā vidyā. Higher or absolute knowledge.

parigraha-shakti. In *Shaiva*, the creative energy in its acquired, assumed, or manifested material form.

parikalpita (VB). Imagined, constructed; illusory or imagined reality.

pariṇāma. Change, transformation, modification.

pariniṣpanna (VB). Perfect, real; ultimate reality.

paryāya (J). A mode or modality (of a *dravya*).

prabhu. Mighty, powerful; lord, king.

prachchhanna. Hidden, concealed, secret.

pradhāna (S). The original source of the material universe, primary or unevolved matter or nature (see *prakṛti*).

prajñā. Knowledge, intuition, wisdom; (B) true or transcendental wisdom, spiritual intuition.

prakṛti (S). The original substance, nature as the material first-cause.

prakṛtipariṇāmavāda (S). The doctrine of causation which holds that the effect is a modification or transformation of *prakṛti*, or material nature.

pralaya (S). The state of dissolution or devolution of the world, its reabsorption into the original *prakṛti*.

pramāṇa. A measure or standard; a means of acquiring valid knowledge; valid knowledge.

prameya. An object or cognition, a knowable object.

prāṇa. Breath, the vital breath.

praṇava. The sacred syllable *auṁ*.

prapañchashūnya. Devoid or empty of phenomenality, diversity, or manifoldness; non-dual, absolute.

prārabdha karma. The actions done in the past which have started yielding fruits.

prasāda. Kindness, grace.

pratibhāsa. Appearance, illusion.

pratītya-samutpāda (B). Dependent origination; the doctrine of causal relativity.

pratītyasamutpanna (B). Dependently originated; relative, conditioned.

pratyakṣa. Direct perception, apprehension by the senses.

pratyātmavedya. To be known in one's own self; to be realized through intuition.

pratyekabuddha (B). One who becomes enlightened by himself, but does not concern himself with the enlightenment of others.

pravāhanitya (VB). Eternal in the sense of continuously flowing.

pravṛtti. Activity; the active life (cf. *nivṛtti*).

preyas. Dearer, that which is more pleasurable (cf. *shreyas*).

pudgala (B). The person, the individual, the soul; (J) matter.

pudgala-nairātmya (B). The doctrine that the person or soul "has no self," i.e., that ultimately there is no such "thing" as a "person" or "soul."

puruṣa. A man, person; soul, spirit.

puruṣārtha. The goal or object of human pursuit, esp. *mokṣa*.

puṣṭimārga. The path of devotion seeking Divine Grace; the Vallabha school of Vedanta (cf. *maryādāmārga*).

rajas. Impurity, dust (S) The principle of motion, pain, restless activity as one of the three *guṇas* or material constituents of *prakṛti*.

sachchidānanda (*sat-chit-ānanda*). Existence-knowledge-bliss, in reference to ultimate reality.

sadāprakāshasvarūpa. Always shining or eternally self-luminous.

sadasadvilakṣaṇatva. Characterized as neither existent nor non-existent.

sadasatkāryavāda. The doctrine of causation which holds that the effect is both pre-existent in and different from the cause.

sādhaka. One who is in the process of perfecting himself.

sādhanā. A spiritual discipline, an effective practice in meditation or a method of meditation.

saguṇa. Having qualities or attributes.

sākṣī. The witness, the subject or seer.

samādhi. Intense concentration, trance.

samatva. Sameness, indifference, equanimity, balance of mind.

saṁnyāsa. Renunciation.

saṁsāra. Transmigration, the cycle of death and rebirth; mundane existence; phenomenal reality.

saṁvit (V). Consciousness.

saṁvṛti. Covering, relative, empirical.

saṁvṛti satya (B). Empirical or relative truth.

saṁvyavahāra (J). Usual, common, conventional (knowledge).

samyagjñāna. Complete or true knowledge.

saṅghātavāda (B). The doctrine that a "thing" is simply a (momentary) collocation or aggregation of discrete elements. Specifically, the doctrine that the soul is simply an aggregate of the five *skandhas*.

santānavāda (B). The doctrine of continuity, flux, or ceaseless flow.

santatinitya (VB). Eternal in the sense of cintinuous or uninterrupted.

sarvāstivāda (B). The doctrine of the *hīnayāna* which maintains that all things, physical as well as mental, actually exist, albeit momentarily; the Vaibhāsika.

sarvavāgviṣayātīta. Surpassing all words and objects; inexpressible.

sat. Being, existing; existence, the real.

satkāraṇavāda (V). The doctrine of causation which holds that only the cause (i.e., *brahman*) is real.

satkāryavāda. The doctrine of causation which holds that the effect pre-exists in the cause.

satkāya (B). The empirical ego; a synonym for *pudgala*.

satkhyāti. Perception of the existing, the view of Rāmānuja that in erroneous perception the existent or real alone is cognized.

sattva. Real-ness, existing-ness; the principle of goodness, light, bliss as one of the three *guṇas* or material constituents of *prakṛti;* (B) the existing or living being, the person (a synonym for *pudgala*).

sattvashūnya. Devoid of *sattva*.

satya. Real, actual, true; truth.

savisheṣa. Having specific qualities or attributes, discriminate.

sāyujya. Identification with, absorption into (viz., the divinity).

shabda. Sound; a word; verbal authority.

shakti. Force, potency, energy; (S) the active power of *prakṛti*.

shāshvata. Eternal.

shāstra. An authoritative composition or treatise, esp. a religious or scientific treatise.

shrāvaka (B). A hearer or disciple not yet enlightened.

shreyas. Better, that which is more excellent or preferable; the good (cf. *preyas*).

shruti. That which has been heard, sacred knowledge orally handed down; specifically, the Vedic literature, including the *Upaniṣads* (cf. *smṛti*).

shuddha-naya (J). The pure point of view, true knowledge.

shuddha-sattva. Pure *sattva.*

shūnya. Empty, void; (B) causally dependent, relative, phenomenal; also the non-dual Real.

shūnyatā. Emptiness, vacuity; (B) dependent causation, relativity of thought; also the non-dual Reality.

shūnyatāvivartavāda (SB). The doctrine of causation which holds that the effect is ultimately an erroneous or illusory appearance of *shūnyatā* (non-dual Absolute).

shūnyavāda (SB). The doctrine of relativity of thought; phenomena are devoid of self-existence and that Reality is the non-dual Absolute.

siddha. One who has become perfected; one who has realized the Real.

skandhas (B). The five groups or aggregates which make up the person: *rūpa,* form or matter; *vedanā,* feeling; *saṁjñā,* conception; *saṁskāra,* innate predispositions (or will); and *vijñāna,* consciousness.

smṛti. Memory, remembrance; the body of sacred tradition as remembered, thus the religious and philosophical literature exclusive of the Vedic literature including *Upaniṣads* (cf. *shruti*).

svarga. Heaven.

svabhāvashūnyatā (SB). "Emptiness of own-being," the doctrine that things have no nature of their own, that they are devoid of ultimate reality; relative, phenomenal.

svabhāvavāda. In materialism, the doctrine of "own-nature" that the nature of a thing is only what it is perceived to be, but not what is inferable from perception, such as a causal relation to another thing; that everything is self-caused.

svalakṣaṇa. That which has its own specific characteristics which cannot be described, viz., a particular; unique and momentary; an existent, ultimate moment cognized in pure intuition.

svarūpa. Something's own nature or character; essence.

svarūpa-shakti. In *Shaiva,* the creative energy in its own, eternal, form (cf. *parigraha-shakti*).

syādvāda (J). The doctrine of relative or limited knowledge; realistic and pluralistic relativism.

tādātmya. Identity, having the same nature.

taijasa. Consisting of energy, ardor, vital power.

tamas. Darkness; the principle of inertia, ignorance, passivity as one of the three *guṇas* or material constituents of *prakṛti.*

tanmātras (S). The five subtle essences from which the gross elements, *mahābhūtas,* arise, viz., sound, touch, sight, taste, smell.

tantra. A class of esoteric literature usually of the *Shaiva* and *Shākta* schools and certain Mahāyāna Buddhist schools; generally, esoteric teachings based on that literature.

tathāgata (B). He who is "thus gone," i.e., "gone into the Real," who has realized nirvāna, the Buddha; the Perfect Being.

tathāgatagarbha (B). The "womb" or source of the *tathāgatas.*

tathatā (B). Suchness; ultimate reality; the pure "that" or pure being.

tathya-saṁvṛti (SB). True empirical (knowledge); opposed to *mithyā-saṁvṛti* or false empirical (knowledge).

tattva. Reality; as a *mahāvākya* or sacred utterance it is considered to be a combination of *tat* (that) and *tvam* (thou), *tattvam* thus meaning "thou are that."

tripuṭīpratyakṣavāda (PM). The doctrine that the three-fold elements of perception, viz., the knower, the known, and the knowledge, are simultaneously revealed in every knowledge-situation.
udāsīnā. Sitting apart, indifferent, uninvolved.
upāsanā. Worship, meditation.
vaikārika. Subject to modification.
vairāgya. Freedom from desire, dispassion, detachment.
vaishāradya. Infallibility, clearness of knowledge.
vāmamārga. The "left-hand way," doctrines of Buddhist or Shākta *tantra* usually of a highly unconventional or sexual character.
vāsanā (B). The impression of anything remaining unconsciously in the mind; force or disposition of *karma*.
videhamukti. Emancipation after release from the body through death.
vihāra. A way of life; a dwelling; Buddhist Church; meditation.
vijñāna. Consciousness, cognition; pure awareness without content.
vijñānamātravāda (VB). The doctrine that ultimate reality is pure consciousness.
vigñānavāda (VB). The doctrine that reality is pure consciousness.
vijñānavivartavāda (VB). The doctrine of causation which holds that the effect is an erroneous or illusory appearance of absolute consciousness.
vijñapti (VB). Cognition, consciousness.
vijñaptimātra (VB). Consciousness only; the doctrine that ultimate reality is pure absolute consciousness.
vikalpa (SB). Discrimination, discriminative imagination, relative knowledge; verbal or imaginary knowledge; conceptual construction; a category of thought.
vikṣepa. Distraction, perplexity; projection; the projecting power of māyā.
vipāka (VB). The "ripening" place or repository consciousness (*ālayavijñāna*).
viparīta-khyāti (PM). Contrary or incorrect perception; the doctrine of Kumārila that an error derives from an improper combination of an actual perception and a memory image; that error is misperception of a thing as something else.
viṣayavijñapti (VB). Consciousness as manifested in apparently external objects.
vishuddhātman. The completely pure self.
vivarta. Appearance; illusion.
vivekajñāna (Y). Knowledge arising from discrimination (viz., between *puruṣa* and *prakṛti*, spirit and matter).
vyāpti. Inseparable association, invariable concomitance.
vyavahāra. Common, customary; relative, phenomenal.
vyavaharaṇa (J). Conventional, usual, customary (knowledge).
vyavahārasatya. Relative truth.
vyāvahārika. Relating to relative truth.
vyūha. Form, manifestation.
yathārthakhyāti. The synonym for *satkhyāti*, the view of Rāmānuja that in error it is the real which is perceived, that error is only partial truth.

BIBLIOGRAPHY

The first part of this bibliography is a brief, selective list of basic and introductory books which are relatively easily available in American bookstores and/or libraries. (More complete bibliographies can be found in the works cited and especially in Farquhar, *An Outline of the Religious Literature of India.*) The second part of this bibliography consists of sources to which the footnotes throughout the manuscript refer.

H.O.S. refers to "Harvard Oriental Series." S.B.E. refers to "Sacred Books of the East."

PART I

GENERAL

Dasgupta, Surendranath. *A History of Indian Philosophy*. 5 vs. Cambridge, 1922-1955.

Farquhar, J. N. *An Outline of the Religious Literature of India*. Oxford, 1920.

Hastings, James (ed.). *Encyclopaedia of Religion and Ethics*. 13 vs. New York, 1928. (See the articles on the particular topics; e.g., "Jainism," "Sāṅkhya," "Yoga," "Vedic Religion," "Mīmāṁsā," "Nyāya," "Vaisheṣika," "Vedānta," etc.)

Hiriyanna, M. *Outlines of Indian Philosophy*. London, New York, 1932.

Muller, F. Max. *Six Systems of Indian Philosophy*. New York, 1899.

Radhakrishnan, S. *Indian Philosophy*. 2nd ed. 2 vs. London, 1929.

Radhakrishnan, S. and Moore, Charles A. *A Source Book in Indian Philosophy*. Princeton, 1957.

De Bary, William Theodore, *et al.* (compilers). *Sources of Indian Tradition*. New York, 1958.

Zimmer, Heinrich R. *Philosophies of India*. New York, 1956.

VEDAS AND UPANIṢADS

Bloomfield, Maurice. *The Religion of the Veda*. New York, 1908.

Deussen, Paul. *Philosophy of the Upanishads*. (Trans. by Rev. A. S. Geden.) Edinburgh, 1906.

Hume, Robert Ernest. *The Thirteen Principal Upanishads*. Oxford, 1931.

Keith, Arthur Berriedale. *The Religion and Philosophy of the Veda and Upanishads*. (H.O.S., vs. 31, 32) Cambridge, Mass., 1925.

MacNicol, Nicol (ed.). *Hindu Scriptures*. London, New York, 1938.

BHAGAVAD GĪTA

Edgerton, Franklin (trans.). *The Bhagavad Gītā: Translated and Interpreted*. (H.O.S.) Cambridge, Mass., 1944.

JAINISM

Jacobi, Hermann (trans.). *Jaina Sūtras*. S.B.E., vs. 22, 45) Oxford, 1884, 1895.

Jaini, Jagmanderlal. *Outlines of Jainism*. Cambridge, 1940.

Stevenson, Mrs. S. *The Heart of Jainism*. Oxford, 1915.

BUDDHISM

Conze, Edward (ed.). *Buddhist Texts Through the Ages*. Oxford, 1954.

Conze, Edward (trans.). *Buddhist Wisdom Books*. London, 1958.

Davids, T. W. Rhys (trans.). *The Questions of King Milinda*. S.B.E., vs. 35, 36) Oxford, 1890, 1894.

Keith, Arthur Berriedale. *Buddhist Philosophy in India and Ceylon*, Oxford, 1923.

Murti, T. R. V. *The Central Philosophy of Buddhism: A Study of the Madhyamika System*. London, 1955.

Stcherbatsky, Theodore. *Buddhist Logic.* 2 vs. Photographic reprint, 's-Gravenhage, 1958.
Suzuki, D. T. (trans.). *The Laṅkāvatāra Sūtra.* London, 1932.
Thomas, Edward J. *The History of Buddhist Thought.* London, 1933.
Warren, Henry Clarke (trans.). *Buddhism in Translations.* (H.O.S., v. 3) Cambridge, Mass., 1922.

SĀṄKHYA AND YOGA

Keith, Arthur Berriedale. *The Sāṁkhya System.* Oxford, 1918.
Eliade, Mircea. *Yoga: Immortality and Freedom.* New York, 1958.
Woods, James Houghton (trans.). *The Yoga-System of Patañjali.* (H.O.S., v. 17) Cambridge, Mass., 1927.

NYĀYA AND VAISHEṢIKA

Ingalls, Daniel H. H. *Materials for the Study of Navya-nyāya Logic.* (H.O.S., v. 40) Cambridge, Mass., 1951.
Keith, Arthur Berriedale. *Indian Logic and Atomism.* Oxford, 1921.

MĪMĀṀSĀ

Keith, Arthur Berriedale. *The Karma-Mīmāṁsā.* Oxford, 1921.

VEDĀNTA

Deussen, Paul. *The System of the Vedānta.* (Trans. by Charles Johnston). Chicago, 1912.
Thibaut, G. (trans.). *The Vedānta Sūtra with Śankara's Commentary.* (S.B.E., vs. 34, 38) Oxford, 1890, 1896.
Thibaut, G. (trans.). *The Vedānta Sūtra with Rāmānuja's Commentary.* (S.B.E., v. 48) Oxford, 1904.
Sri Aurobindo. *The Life Divine.* 2 vs. Calcutta, 1939.

SHAIVA-SHAKTA

Woodroffe, Sir John. *Shakti and Shākta.* Madras, 1929.
Woodroffe, Sir John. *The Serpent Power.* Madras, 1924.

PART II

THE VEDAS AND THE UPANIṢADS

Max Müller and Oldenberg. The Vedic Hymns. (S.B.E., vs. 32, 46.)
Max Müller. Six Systems of Indian Philosophy.
Bloomfield. The Religion of the Veda.
B. M. Barua. Pre-Buddhistic Indian Philosophy.
Max Müller. The Upaniṣads. (S.B.E., vs. 1, 15.)
Deussen. The Philosophy of the Upaniṣads.
Hume. The Thirteen Principal Upaniṣads.
Gītā Press, Gorakhpur. The Eleven Principal Upaniṣads (with the Commentaries of Shaṅkarāchārya).
R. D. Ranade. A Constructive Survey of Upaniṣadic Philosophy.

BHAGAVADGĪTA

Gītā Press, Gorakhpur. Shrīmadbhagavadgīta (with the Commentary of Shaṅkarāchārya).
Tilak. Gītārahasya.
S'ri Aurobindo. Essays on the Gītā.

MATERIALISM

Mādhavāchārya. Sarva-darshana-saṅgraha.
Haribhadra. Ṣaḍ-darshana-samuchchaya.
Vātsyāyana. Kāma-sūtra.
Kṛṣṇapati Mishra. Prabodha-chandrodaya, Act ii.
Dakshinaranjan Shāstri. A Short History of Indian Materialism.

JAINISM

Kundakunda. Samayasāra (Nirṇayasāgar edition, 1919). Pravachanasāra (Ed. by A. N. Upadhye, Bombay, 1935). Pañchāstikāyasāra (Ed. by A.Chakravartinayanar, Arrah, 1920). Ṣaṭprābhṛta (Ed. by Pannalal Soni, Bombay).
Amṛtachandra Sūri. Ātmakhyāti Commentary on Samayasāra (Nirṇayasāgar Ed.). Tattvapradīpikā Commentary on Pravachanasāra (Upadhye's Ed.).
Umāsvāmī. Tattvārthādhigamasūtra.
Samantabhadra. Āptamīmāmsā or Devāgamastotra.
Pūjyapāda Devanandī. Sarvārthasiddhi (Commentary on Tattvārthasūtra).
Akalaṅka. Rājavārtika (Commentary on Tattvārthasūtra). Aṣṭashatī (Commentary on Āptamīmāṁsā).
Vidyānanda. Shlokavārtika (Commentary on Tattvārthasūtra). Aṣṭasāhasrī (Commentary on Aṣṭashatī).
Siddhasena Divākara. Dvātrimshikā. Sanmatitarka. Nyāyāvatāra.
Hemachandra. Pramāṇamīmāṁsā. Ayogavyavachchedikā-dvātrimshikā. Anyayogavyavachchedikā-dvātrimshikā.
Malliṣeṇa. Syādvādamañjarī (Commentary on Anyayoga; Prof. A. B. Dhruva's Ed.).
Vādideva Sūri. Pramāṇanayatattvālokālaṅkāra and its Commentary Syādvādaratnākara (Ed. by Motilal Ladhaji, Poona).
Haribhadra. Ṣaḍdarshanasamuchchaya. Anekāntajayapatākā.
Nemichandra. Dravyasaṅgraha.
Vimaladāsa. Saptabhaṅgītaraṅgiṇī.
Yashovijaya. Adhyātmasāra.
Hermann Jacobi. The Jaina Sūtra (S.B.E.).
Mrs. S. Stevenson. The Heart of Jainism.
J. Jaini. Outlines of Jainism.
S. Mukerji. The Philosophy of Non-absolutism.

BUDDHISM

The Pāli Tipitaka. Edited by the Pali Text Society, London.
Dhammapada and Suttanipāta. (S.B.E., v. 10.)
Saddharmapuṇḍarīkasūtra. Edited by Profs. N. Kern and B. Nanjio, Bibliotheca Buddhica X, St. Petersbourg, 1908.
Laṅkāvatārasūtra. Edited by B. Nanjio, Kyoto, 1923.
Lalitavistara. Edited by Dr. S. Lefmann, Halle, 1902.
Shatasāhasrikāprajñāpāramitā. Edited by P. Ghosa, Asiatic Society of Bengal, Calcutta, 1902.
Aṣṭasāhasrikāprajñāpāramita. A.S.B., Calcutta.
Vajrachchhedikāprajñāpāramitā. Edited by Max Müller, Oxford, 1881.
Suvarṇaprabhāsa sūtra. 'Buddhist Texts'.
Samādhirājasūtra (Incomplete). 'Buddhist Texts'.
Dashabhūmikasūtra. Edited by Dr. J. Rahder, Paris, 1926.
Sukhāvatīvyūha. Edited by Max Müller and Nanjio, Oxford, 1883.
Nairātmyaparipṛchchhā. Edited by Prof. S. Levi in the Journal Asiatique, Oct.-Dec., 1928, pp. 207-211.
Rāṣṭrapālaparipṛchchhā. Edited by L. Finot, Bibliotheca Buddhica, 1901.

Minor Tibetan Texts. Bibliotheca Indica, Calcutta, 1919.

Ashvaghoṣa. Saundarananda (Ed. by Mm. Haraprasāda Shastri, Bibliotheca Indica, Calcutta, 1910). Buddhacharita (Ed. by E. B. Cowell, Oxford, 1893).

Nāgārjuna. Mūlamadhyamaka Kārikā (Ed. by Poussin, Bib. Bud. IV, St. Petersbourg, 1903). Mahāyānaviṁshaka (Ed. by Pt. V. Bhattacharya, Calcutta, 1931). Ratnāvalī (Ed. by G. Tucci, Journal of the Royal Asiatic Society, April, 1934, and April, 1936). Vigrahavyāvarttanī with the author's own Commentary (Ed. by Pt. Rāhul Sānkrityāyana, as Appendix to the Journal of Bihar and Orissa Research Society, Patna, Vol. XXIII, 1937). Bhavasaṅkrāntisūtra (Restored to Sanskrit from Tibetan and Chinese by Pt. N. Aiyaswami Shastri, Adyar Library, 1938).

Āryadeva. Chatuḥshataka (Chapters VIII to XVI; Ed., with the lost Karikas reconstructed into Sanskrit, by Prof. P. L. Vaidya, Paris, 1923). Chatuḥshataka (Chapters VIII to XVI; Ed., with the lost Karikas and Chapter VII reconstructed into Sanskrit, by Pt. V. Bhattacharya). Fragments from Chatuḥshataka (Ed. by Pt. H. Shastri, Memoirs of the Asiatic Society of Bengal, Vol. III No. 8, 1914). Chittavīshuddhīprakaraṇa (Ed. by Pt. H. Shastri in the Journal of the Asiatic Society of Bengal, 1898). Hastabālaprakaraṇa (Ed. by F. W. Thomas and H. Ui in the J.R.A.S. 1918).

Chandrakīrti. Prasannapadā, the Madhyamakavṛtti (Ed., by Poussin, Bib. Bud. IV, St. Petersbourg, 1903). Fragments from the Commentary on Chatuḥshataka (Reconstructed by Pt. V. Bhattacharya in his edition of the Chatuḥshataka). Madhyamakāvatāra Ch. VI, J.O.R. Madras, 1929-33.

Shāntideva. Bodhicharyāvatāra (Ed. by Poussin, Bib. Ind., 1902). Shikṣā Samuchchaya (Ed. by Bendall, Bib. Bud. I).

Prajñākaramati. Bodhicharyāvatāra-Pañjikā (Ed. by Poussin, Bib. Ind., 1902).

Asaṅga. Mahāyānasūtrālaṅkāra (Ed. by S. Levi, Paris, 1907). Bodhisattvabhūmi (given as an Appendix to the Dashabhūmikasutra, edited by J. Rahder, Paris, 1926).

Vasubandhu. Vijñaptimātratāsiddhi: Vimshatikā with the author's own Commentary (Ed. by S. Levi, Paris, 1925). Vijñaptimātratāsiddhi: Trimshikā with Sthiramati's Commentary (Ed. by S. Levi, Paris, 1925). Abhidharmakosha (Ed. and Restored into Sanskrit by Pt. Rāhulji, Benares, 1931). Abhidharmakoshakārikā (Ed. by G. V. Gokhale, J.R.A.S., Bombay, Vol. 22, 1946). Abhidharmakoshavyākhyā of Yashomitra (Ed. by Wogihara, Tokio). Trisvabhāvanirdesha (Reconstructed by S. Mukhopadhyaya, Vishvabhāratī, 1939).

Sthiramati. Madhyāntavibhāga-Sūtra-Bhāṣya-Ṭīkā (Ed. by S. Yamaguchi, Nagoya, 1934).

Diṅnāga. Fragments from Diṅnāga (Ed. by H. N. Randle, Royal Asiatic Society, London, 1926).

Diṅnāga. Pramāṇasamuchchaya Chapter I (Reconstructed by H. R. Rangaswamy Iyenger, Mysore University, 1930). Ālambanaparīkṣā (Reconstructed by N. Aiyaswami Shastri, Adyar Library, 1941).

Dharmakīrti. Nyāyabindu (Ed. by P. Peterson, Calcutta, 1889). Pramāṇavārtika (Ed. by Pt. Rāhul Sānkrityāyana in the Journal of Bihar and Orissa Research Society, Patna, Vol. XXIV, 1938). Pramāṇavārtika-Svavṛtti (Ed. by Pt. Rāhul Sankrityāyana, Kitab Mahal, Allahabad, 1943). Vādanyāya with the Commentary of Shāntarakṣita (Ed. by Pt. Rāhul Sānkrityāyana, J.B.O.R.S., Vol. XXI, 1935 and Vol. XXII, 1936).

Manorathanandin. Pramāṇavārtikavṛtti (Ed. by Pt. Rāhulji, J.B.O.R.S., Vols. XXIV-XXVI, 1938-1940).

Dharmottara. Nyāyabinduṭīkā (Ed. by P. Peterson, Calcutta, 1889).

Shāntarakṣita. Tattvasaṅgraha (Ed. by Pt. K. Krishnamacharya, Gaekward Oriental Series, Baroda, 1926).

Kamalashīla. Tattvasaṅgrahapañjikā (do).

T. Suzuki. 'The Awakening of Faith in the Mahāyāna' (Mahāyānashraddhotpādashāstra of Ashvaghoṣa; translated from the Chinese tr. of Paramārtha, Chicago, 1900).

T. Richard. Ibid, Shanghai, 1907.

The Questions of King Milinda. (S.B.E., vs. 35, 36.)

Th. Stcherbatsky. Buddhist Logic, Vol. I and II. The Conception of Buddhist Nirvāṇa. The Central Conception of Buddhism and the Meaning of the word 'Dharma'.
Yamakami Sogen. Systems of Buddhistic Thought.
D. T. Suzuki. Outlines of Mahāyāna Buddhism. Studies in the Laṅkāvatāra-sūtra.
Rhys Davids. Buddhism: Its History and Literature.
B. C. Law (Ed.). Buddhistic Studies.
B. C. Law Volume (Part I). The Indian Research Institute, Calcutta, 1945.
Paul Dahlke. Buddhism.
Bhattacharya. The Basic Conception of Buddhism.
Oldenberg. Buddha.
B. M. Barua. Prolegomena to a History of Buddhistic Philosophy.
McGovern. Manual of Buddhism.
Mrs. Rhys Davids. A Manual of Buddhism.
Poussin. The Way to Nirvāṇa.
Coomaraswamy. Buddha and the Gospel of Buddhism.
S. Mukherji. Buddhist Philosophy of Universal Flux.
M. Winternitz. History of Indian Literature, V. II.

SĀṄKYA-YOGA

Īshvarakṛṣna. Sāṅkya-kārikā (Madras Ed.).
Gauḍapāda. Sāṅkya-kārikā-bhāṣya.
Vāchaspati Mishra. Sāṅkya-tattva-kaumudī (Calcutta Ed.).
Vijñānabhikṣu. Sāṅkya-pravachana-bhāṣya (Chowkhamba, Banaras).
Garbe. Philosophy of Ancient India.
A. B. Keith. The Sāṅkhya System.
Nandalal Sinha. The Sāṅkhya Philosophy.
S. C. Banerjee. The Sāṅkhya Philosophy.
A. K. Majumdar. The Sāṅkhya Conception of Personality.
Patañjali. Yoga-sūtra.
Vyāsa. Yoga-sūtra-bhāṣya (Ed. P. Vedānta Cuñcu, Calcutta).
Vāchaspati. Tattva-vaishāradi (Com. on Vyāsa-bhāṣya).
Bhojarāja. Yoga-sūtra-vṛtti (Ed. by K. Vedāntavāgīsha, Calcutta).
Hariharānanda Āraṇya. Pātañjala Yoga Darshana.
N. K. Brahma. The Philosophy of Hindu Sādhanā.
S. N. Dasgupta. Yoga as Philosophy and Religion.

NYĀYA-VAISHEṢIKA

Gotama. Nyāya-sūtra.
Vātsyāyana. Nyāya-sūtra-bhāṣya (with Vishvanātha's Vṛtti, Ed. by Jivananda Vidyāsāgara, Calcutta).
Gangānātha Jha. Nyāyasūtra with Vātsyātana's Bhāsya and Uddyotakara's Vārtika, Eng. Tran., Indian Thought, Allahabad).
Uddyotakara. Nyāyabhāṣyavārtika.
Vāchaspati Mishra. Nyāyavārtikatātparyatīkā.
Udayana. Nyāyakusumāñjali Tātparyaṭīkā-parishuddhi.
Jayanta Bhaṭṭa. Nyāyamañjarī.
Vishvanātha. Kārikāvalī with the Com. Siddhāntamuktāvalī (with Dinakarī and Rāmarudrī Commentaries; Nirṇaya Sagar Press, Bombay).
Annam Bhaṭṭa. Tarkasaṅgraha with Dīpikā (Athalye's Ed.).
Gaṅgesha Upādhyāya. Tattvachintāmaṇi (with the Com. Dīdhiti, Gādādharī and Jāgadīshī).
Kaṇāda. Vaisheṣika-sūtra.

Prashastapāda. Padārtha-dharma-saṅgraha.
Shrīdhara. Nyāyakandalī (Com. on Padārtha-dharma-Sangraha) Eng. Tr. by Gangānatha Jha.
Udayana. Kiraṇāvalī (Com. on Padārtha-dharma-sangraha).
Shivādityā. Sapta-padārthī.
Laugākṣī Bhāskara. Tarka-kaumudī.
A. B. Keith. Indian Logic and Atomism.
J. C. Chatterji. The Hindu Realism.

PŪRVA-MĪMĀMSĀ

Jaimini. Mīmāṁsā-sūtra (Eng. Tr. by G. N. Jha).
Shabara. Shabara-bhṣāya.
Kumārila Bhaṭṭa. Shloka-Vārtika (Eng. Tr. by G. N. Jha).
Gangānātha Jha. Prabhākara School of Pūrva-Mīmāmsā.
Pārthasārathi. Shāstradīpikā, Tarkapāda (Nirṇaya Sagar Ed.).
Shālikanātha. Prakaraṇa-pañchikā (Chowkhamba, Banaras).
Pashupatinath Shastrī. Introduction to the Pūrva-Mīmāṁsā.

VEDĀNTA

Eleven Principle Upaniṣads. Gita Press, Gorakhpur.
Bhagavadgītā. Gita Press, Gorakhpur.
Gauḍapādāchārya. Māṇḍūkya-Kārikā (Gita Press, Gorakhpur). The Agamashāstra of Gauḍapāda (Ed. by Mm. Pt. V. Bhattacharya, Calcutta University, 1943).
Shaṅkarāchārya. Shārīraka-Bhāṣya (Ed. by N. L. Shastri, Nirṇaya Sagar Press, Bombay, 1927). Īsha-Bhāṣya (Gita Press, Gorakhpur). Prashna-Bhāṣya (do). Kena-Bhāṣya (do). Kaṭha-Bhāṣya (do). Muṇḍaka-Bhāṣya (do). Māṇḍūkya-Kārikā-Bhāṣya (do). Taittirīya-Bhāṣya (do). Aitareya-Bhāṣya (do). Chhāndogya-Bhāṣya (do). Brhadāraṇyaka-Bhāṣya (do). Shvetāshvatara-Bhāṣya (do). Minor Works of Shaṅkarāchārya Vol. I. and II. (Ashtekar and Co., Poona).
Maṇḍana Mishra. Brahmasiddhi (Ed. by Mm. Prof. S. Kuppuswami Shastri, Madras, 1937).
Sureshvarāchārya. Naiṣkarmyasiddhi (Ed. by Prof. M. Hiriyanna, Bombay, 1925). Bṛhadāraṇyaka-Bhāṣya-Vārtika.
Padmapādāchārya. Pañchapādikā (Ed. by Rāma Shāstri, Vizianagram Series, Banaras, 1891).
Prakāshātman. Pañchapādikāvivaraṇa (Ed. by Rāma Shāstri, Vizianagram Series, Banaras, 1892).
Vimuktātman. Iṣtasiddhi (Ed. by Prof. M. Hiriyanna, Baroda, 1933).
Shrīharṣa. Khaṇḍanakhaṇḍakhādya (Ed. by Pt. Chandiprasad Shukla, Achyuta Karyalaya, Banaras). Naiṣadhacharita (Nirnayasagar Press, Bombay).
Chitsukhāchārya. Commentary on the Khaṇḍana (Banaras Ed.). Tattvapradīpikā or Chitsukhī (Nirnayasagar Press, Bombay, 1931).
Madhusūdana Sarasvatī. Advaitasiddhi (Bombay Ed.).
Vāchaspati Mishra. Bhāmatī (Nirnayasagar Press, Bombay).
Amalānanda. Kalpataru (do).
Appaya Dīkṣita. Parimala (do). Sidhāntaleshasaṅgraha (Achyuta Karyalaya, Banaras).
Sarvajñātmamuni. Saṅkṣepa-Shārīraka.
Vidyāraṇya. Pañchadashī. Bṛhadāraṇyakavārtikasāra (Achyuta Karyalaya, Banaras). Vivaraṇaprameyasaṅgraha (do).
Ānandajñāna. Tarkasaṅgraha (Ed. by Mr. Tripathi).
Prakāshānanda. Vedāntasiddhāntamuktāvalī (Achyuta Karyalaya, Banaras).
Sadānanda Yati. Advaitabrahmasiddhi (Calcutta, 1890).
Gangādharendra Sarasvati. Svārājyasiddhi.

Sadānanda. Pratyaktattvachintāmaṇi (Achyuta Karyalaya, Banaras).
Narahari Svāmī. Bodhasāra.
G. Thibaut. The Vedāntasūtras with the commentaries of Shaṅkara and Rāmānuja (Eng. Tr.; S.B.E.).
Sūryanārāyaṇa Shāstri. Bhāmatī (Sūtras 1-4) Eng. Tr.
Gangānātha Jha. Shāṅkara Vedānta.
Kokileshvar Shastri. The Introduction to Advaita Philosophy.
T. Madadevan. The Philosophy of Advaita.
M. N. Sirkar. The System of Vedāntic Thought and Culture.
B. L. Atreya. The Philosophy of Yogavāsiṣṭha.
S. K. Das. A Study of the Vedānta.
A. C. Mukerji. The Nature of Self.
V. S. Urquhart. The Vedānta and Modern Thought.
Belvelkar. Vedānta Philosophy.
V. S. Ghate. The Vedānta (A Comparative account of Shaṅkara, Rāmānuja, Nimbārka, Madhva and Vallabha).
Veda-Vyāsa. Shrīmadbhāgavatapurāṇa (Nirṇayasagar, Bombay).
Bhāskara. Brahmasūtra-bhāṣya.
Nāthamuni. Nyāyatattva.
Yāmunāchārya. Āgamaprāmāṇya. Siddhitraya. Ālavandār Stotra.
Rāmānuja. Shrībhāṣya (Nirṇayasagar Ed.). Gītābhāṣya. Vedāntasara. Vedāntadīpa. Gadyatraya. Vedārthasaṅgraha.
Sudarshana Sūri. Shrutaprakāshikā (Com. on Shrībhāṣya; Nirṇayasagar Ed.).
Venkaṭanātha or Vedāntadeshika. Tattvaṭīkā (Com. on Shrībhāṣya). Nyāyasiddhāñjana. Shatadūṣanī (Ed. by Anantāchārya, Conjeeveram).
Lokāchārya. Tattvatraya.
Shrīnivāsa. Yatīndramatadīpikā.
Shrīnivāsāchāri. The Philosophy of Vishiṣṭādvaita.
Madhva. Brahmasūtrabhāṣya. Gītābhāṣya. Mahabhāratatātparyanirṇaya. Anuvyākhyāna. Tattvasaṅkhyāna. Tattvodyota. Viṣṇutattvanirṇaya.
Jayatīrtha. Pramāṇapadd-hati. Nyāyasudhā. Tattvaprakāshikā (Com. on Madhvabhāṣya).
Vyāsatīrtha. Tātparyachandrikā (Com. on Tattvaprakāshikā). Tarka-tāṇḍava. Nyāyāmṛta.
Rāmāchārya. Taranginī (Com. on Nyāyāmṛta).
Nāgarāja Sarmā. The Philosophy of Madhva. The Reign of Realism in Indian Philosophy.
Krishnasvami Aiyar. Shrī Madhva and Madhvism.
Padmanābhāchārya. Life and Teachings of Shrī Madhva.
Nimbārka. Vedānta-pārijāta-saurabha (Com. on Brahmasūtra). Dashsahlokī. Shrīkṛṣṇastavarajā.
Shrīnivāsāchārya. Vedāntakaustubha (Com. on Pārijātasaurabha).
Keshava Kāshmīrī. Kaustubhaprabhā (Com. on Kaustubha).
Puruṣottama. Vedāntaratnamañjūṣā (Com. on Dashasholkī). Shrutyanatasuradruma (Com. on Shrikṛṣṇastavarāja).
Mādhava Mukunda. Parapakṣagirivajra or Hārdasañchaya.
Umesha Mishra. Nimbārka Philosophy.
Vallabha. Aṇubhāṣya (Com. on Brahmasūtra). Subodhinī (Com. on Bhāgavata, I, II, III and X skandhas). Tattvadīpanibandha.
Viṭṭhalanātha. Vidvanmaṇḍana.
Puruṣottama. Bhāṣyaprakāsha (Com. on Aṇubhāṣya). Subodhinīprakāsha. Suvarṇasūtra (Com. on Vidvanmaṇḍana).
Gopeshvara. Rashmi (Com. on Bhāṣyaprakāsha).
Giridhara. Shuddhādvaitamārtaṇḍa.
Telivala. Philosophy of Vallabhāchārya.

Rūpa Gosvāmi. Ujjvalanīlamaṇi. Bhaktiṛasāmṛtasindhu.
Jīva Gosvāmī. Ṣaṭsandarbha with the Com. Sarvasamvādinī.
Baladeva Vidyābhūṣaṇa. Govindabhāṣya (on Brahmasūtra).
H. D. Bhattacharya. Foundations of Living Faiths.
R. G. Bhandārkar. Vaiṣṇavism, Shaivism and Minor Religious Sects.
Rai Choudhary. Early History of the Vaiṣṇava Sect.
B. K. Gosvāmī. Bhakti Cult in Ancient India.
Gopināth Rao. History of Shrīvaiṣṇavas.
G. N. Mallick. Philosophy of Vaiṣṇava Religion.
Kenedy. Chaitanya Movement.
Shrīkantha Shivāchārya. Brahmasūtrabhāṣya.
Appaya Dīkṣita. Shivārkamaṇidīpikā (Com. on Shrikaṇṭhabhāṣya).
Vasugupta. Spandakārikā.
Abhinavagupta. Īshavarapratyabhijñāvimarshinī.
Kṣemarāja. Shivasūtravimarshinī.
Shaṅkarāchārya. Saundaryalaharī.
Bhāskararāya. Saubhāgyabhāskara (Com. on Lalitāsahasranāma).
Nallasvāmi Pillai. Studies in Shaiva Siddhānta.
S. S. Sastri. Shivādvaita of Shrī Kaṇṭha.
J. C. Chatterjee. Kāshmīra Shaivism.
K. C. Pande. Abhinavagupta—A Study.
Woodroffe. Shakti and Shākta.
Woodroffe and Mukhopādhyāya. World as Power Series.
S'ri Aurobindo. The Life Divine. The Synthesis of Yoga. Essays on the Gītā. The Mother. Letters of S'ri Aurobindo. Collected Poems and Plays. Thoughts and Glimpses. Sāvitrī: A Legend and a Symbol.
S. K. Maitra. Introduction to the Philosophy of S'ri Aurobindo. Studies in S'ri Aurobindo's Philosophy.

GENERAL

S. N. Dasgupta. A History of Indian Philosophy, vs. I, V.
M. Hiriyanna. Outlines of Indian Philosophy.
S. Radhakrishnan. Indian Philosophy, vs. I, II.
Chatterji and Datta. Introduction to Indian Philosophy.
J. Sinha. Introduction to Indian Philosophy.

INDEX

Intellect—
and Pure Knowledge, 306
opposed to Reality, 99
Isha, 5
Ishvara, 14
and Brahman, 268–270
Ishvarakṛṣna, 138
Iyengar, H. R. Rangaswamy, 113